THE SOCIAL AND
ECONOMIC HISTORY
OF THE
ROMAN EMPIRE

Oxford University Press, Amen House, London E.C.4

GLASGOW   NEW YORK   TORONTO   MELBOURNE   WELLINGTON
BOMBAY   CALCUTTA   MADRAS   KARACHI   LAHORE   DACCA
CAPE TOWN   SALISBURY   NAIROBI   IBADAN   ACCRA
KUALA LUMPUR   HONG KONG

I. BUST OF A STATUE OF C. JULIUS CAESAR

(Rome, Palazzo dei Conservatori)

THE SOCIAL AND ECONOMIC HISTORY
OF THE
ROMAN EMPIRE

BY

M. ROSTOVTZEFF

SECOND EDITION
Revised by
P. M. FRASER

VOLUME I

OXFORD
AT THE CLARENDON PRESS

FIRST EDITION 1926

SECOND EDITION 1957

REPRINTED LITHOGRAPHICALLY IN GREAT BRITAIN
AT THE UNIVERSITY PRESS, OXFORD
FROM CORRECTED SHEETS OF THE SECOND EDITION
1963

TO MY FRIEND

J. G. C. ANDERSON

IN GRATITUDE FOR HIS

CO-OPERATION

PREFACE TO SECOND EDITION

THE appearance of a new edition of Rostovtzeff's *Social and Economic History of the Roman Empire* requires a few words of explanation. The first edition (1926) went out of print in 1940, and rapidly became a rarity. It had, however, been replaced as an instrument of study first by the German edition (1931) and then by the Italian edition (1933). The preparation of a second English edition was recognized as desirable, even before the outbreak of the Second World War. Rostovtzeff's preoccupation with other studies, followed by the breakdown of his health, meant, however, that the work would have to be undertaken by someone other than the author.

With a good deal of misgiving I finally undertook the work at the request of the Delegates of the Clarendon Press in 1952. After discussion, it was decided that no new material should be added, and that the new English edition should simply incorporate all the material found in the text and notes of the Italian edition, the last to which Rostovtzeff made additions. And it was along these lines that I undertook the task.

I do not think this plan needs justification. It is an obvious fact that no single person could hope to bring Rostovtzeff's material up to date in every field, and the employment of several hands would inevitably lead to postponement. A more important consideration, however, is that Rostovtzeff's work has become a classic, if not necessarily a wholly correct, account of the subject with which it deals, and therefore revision on a large scale could hardly be justified in the way that it could be in a new edition of a handbook. On the other hand, no justification is needed for providing his latest views on the subject as presented in the Italian edition. There seems little doubt that this book substantially represents Rostovtzeff's final considered views on the social and economic history of the Roman Empire. The activities of the last phase of his life were in different fields: the excavation of Dura and the preparation of his great work on the social and economic history of the Hellenistic world.

The present edition, then, basically reproduces the text and notes of the original edition with the additions and modifications present in the Italian edition, as translated by myself. There are, however, many differences from the Italian edition, and this work should be regarded as superseding all previous editions. The main differences, apart from minor changes in the text, derive from corrections and additions in the notes, and alterations in the arrangement of the plates.

(1) Corrections. I have checked to the best of my ability a large number of the references given in the notes. This laborious and unattractive occupation has led to the correction of numerous errors which, committed originally in the English edition, passed unnoticed into the German and Italian editions. Numerous mistakes in quotations of Greek authors, and, to a less extent, inscriptions and papyri, have also been corrected. I have no doubt that errors still lurk in the notes, particularly in the references to periodicals, but their number has been considerably diminished.

(2) I have added, wherever I was able, references to subsequent and more accessible publications of material (particularly inscriptions and papyri) which was still unpublished, or else had only been published in a periodical or similar publication, when Rostovtzeff referred to it. I have also attempted to introduce order and system into Rostovtzeff's confused and confusing method of referring to documents.

(3) The position and consequent numeration of some of the plates have been altered both to place them in a closer relation to the text which they illustrate, and to ensure them a more advantageous position in binding.

The reader should be warned that in a few places in the text I have been compelled to exercise my own judgement as to what Rostovtzeff really meant, since there are occasional discrepancies between the various versions which seem rather to be errors in translation than to reflect changes in Rostovtzeff's views. These passages are few and unimportant and I have not felt it necessary to indicate them.

Almost all additions introduced by myself into the references are in square brackets. I have not normally indicated, in reference to a later edition of a papyrus or inscription, whether the later edition represents an improvement on that used by Rostovtzeff, though in a few exceptional cases I have called attention to the improvement by the use of the symbol ‡ preceding the new reference.

The Indexes of Inscriptions and Papyri have been compiled by myself. I have, at the same time, added an Index of Passages quoted from ancient authors.

The Index of Names and Subjects has been compiled by Mr. H. C. Oakley, M.A., of the City of London School. I must express my deep gratitude to him for relieving me, at short notice, of an additional burden.

P. M. FRASER

All Souls College, Oxford

PREFACE TO FIRST EDITION

My aim in writing this book has not been to add another History of the Roman Empire to those which already exist. My purpose is more modest and much more limited. We possess very good surveys of the foreign policy of the Roman emperors, of the constitutional history of the Roman Empire, of the system of administration, both civil and military, and of the organization of the army. Valuable work has been done in describing the municipal life of Italy and of some of the provinces, and attempts have been made to present complete pictures of the historical development of some of the provincial areas under Roman rule. We have not, however, a single book or monograph treating of the social and economic life of the Roman Empire as a whole and tracing the main lines of its evolution. There are valuable contributions dealing with one or another partial problem or with some special period. Most of these contributions, however (for example, the excellent work of L. Friedländer), have been written from the antiquarian, not from the historical, point of view; and no one has endeavoured to connect the social and economic evolution of the Empire with its constitutional and administrative development or with the home and foreign policy of the emperors. The present volume is the first attempt of the kind. I am very well aware that it is far from satisfactory. The task has been arduous and complicated. The material is scanty and scattered. No statistics are available. The interpretation of the few data which we have is open to dispute, and most of the conclusions drawn by modern scholars are hypothetical and often arbitrary. Yet, with all its difficulty, the task is attractive in itself. I am convinced that, without a thorough investigation of the social and economic conditions, no attempt to write a general history of the Roman Empire can be successful.

To illustrate my point of view and my method, I may briefly summarize the main results to which a careful study of the social and economic aspect of Imperial history has led me. Such a sketch may help the reader to find his way through the chapters of the book.

An alliance between the Italian *bourgeoisie* and the Italian proletariate, headed by ambitious politicians and military leaders, resulted in the collapse of the hegemony of the two privileged orders of Rome, the senatorial and the equestrian, which together had formed a class of large half-feudal landowners and business men who owed their material prosperity to the exploitation of the resources of the state and their political power to their wealth. The activity of Augustus gave expression to this victory of the middle and lower classes of Roman citizens, and represented a compromise between the opposing forces. The Julii and Claudii resumed the struggle: their policy was to build up a state based on the city *bourgeoisie* of the Empire as a whole, and by a ruthless and cruel terrorism they dealt the final blow to the influence and the aspirations of the magnates of the late Republic. The remnants of this class as well as the temporary substitutes for it—the favourites of the Emperors—were eliminated by the Flavians, when a fresh outbreak of civil war had proved the stability of the new form of government, which was supported by the middle class in all the cities of the Empire. This strong middle class formed the economic backbone of the state, and it was consciously developed by the emperors, who pursued a consistent policy of fostering city-life, alike in the western and in the eastern provinces; but, through the medium of the body which represented it in the capital—the new imperial senate of the Flavians—and through the municipal aristocracy of the provinces, it showed its unwillingness to lend support to the system of government into which the Augustan principate had degenerated under the Julio-Claudians—that personal military tyranny which, after Vespasian's attempt to restore the Augustan principate, was revived in the autocratic régime of Domitian. The result was the establishment of the constitutional monarchy of the Antonines, which rested on the urban middle class throughout the Empire and on the self-government of the cities. Despite his autocratic power, the monarch was regarded as the chief magistrate of the Roman people. At his side, as an advisory council, stood the senate which represented the municipal *bourgeoisie*. The imperial bureaucracy and the army were co-ordinated with the self-governing bodies in Italy and the provinces.

This adaptation of the constitution of the Empire to the leading social forces had one weak point. The foundation of the Empire, the urban middle class, was not strong enough to support the fabric of the world-state. Resting as it did on the toil of the lower classes—the peasants of the country and the proletariate of the cities—the municipal *bourgeoisie*, like the imperial aristocracy and bureaucracy, was unwilling to open its ranks to the lower orders. All three groups became more and more exclusive, and the society of the Empire became more and more divided into two classes or castes—the *bourgeoisie* and the masses, the *honestiores* and the *humiliores*. A sharp antagonism arose and gradually took the form of an antagonism between the country and the cities. The emperors sought to remove this hostility by promoting urbanization and by supporting the peasants in the country and the workmen in the cities. The effort was vain. It was this antagonism which was the ultimate cause of the crisis of the third century, when the aspirations of the lower classes were expressed by the army and countenanced by the emperors. After the failure of the endeavours of the Severi to establish a *modus vivendi* between the two classes, the struggle degenerated into the civil and social war and the political anarchy of the second half of the third century. The *bourgeoisie* and the upper classes of society were destroyed, and there arose a new form of government which was more or less suited to the conditions—the Oriental despotism of the fourth and fifth centuries, based on the army, on a strong bureaucracy, and on the mass of the peasants.

There is no need to emphasize the close connexion between the social evolution and the gradual, though slow, development of economic life. Far be it from me to overestimate the historical significance of the economic facts; yet I cannot but think that a picture of social life, without a companion picture of the economic conditions underlying it, would be both incomplete and misleading. Side by side with my study of the social history of the Roman Empire, I have, therefore, endeavoured to present a corresponding picture of the general lines on which its economic life developed. Here again I have had no predecessors. The economic conditions of the Empire have been the subject of repeated study. Much valuable work has been done in various special fields. But no one has attempted to trace the main lines of the economic development of the Empire as a whole, no one has tried to show how and why its material aspect gradually changed, and how and why the brilliant life of the early Empire so completely degenerated into the primitive and half-barbarous life of the later period.

The results to which my investigation has led me are briefly these. To the first stage in the social evolution—the end of the domination of the class of great landlords and business men—corresponded, in the economic field, the ruin of that typical form of feudal capitalism which had been characteristic of the late Republic and had handicapped the sound economic development of the ancient world. With the collapse of the immense fortunes of the imperial aristocracy and with the concentration of their wealth in the hands of the emperors, the forms of the Hellenistic city-capitalism, based on commerce, industry, and scientific agriculture, revived again and developed rapidly under the benign influence of the peace and quiet re-established by Augustus. The representatives of this form of capitalism were the city *bourgeoisie*, which steadily increased in numbers and in social and political importance. The urbanization of the Empire was at once the chief factor in this process and its plainest manifestation. The result was an unprecedentedly rapid and striking development of commerce, industry, and agriculture; and the constant growth of the capital accumulated in the cities gave a fresh impetus to the brilliant efflorescence of city life throughout the Empire.

This city-capitalism, however, gradually degenerated. The prevailing outlook of the municipal *bourgeoisie* was that of the *rentier*: the chief object of economic activity was to secure for the individual or for the family a placid and inactive life on a safe, if moderate, income. The creative forces which in the early Imperial period produced a rapid growth of industrial activity in every quarter of the Empire, and promoted a high standard of technical improvement alike in commerce, in industry, and in agriculture, suffered a gradual atrophy, which resulted in an increasing stagnation of economic life. The activity of the urban middle class degenerated into a systematic exploitation of the toiling lower classes. Its accumulated wealth was mostly invested in land. Commerce and industry became decentralized, and they came to be pursued as a means of adding to an income derived mainly from agriculture. The exclusiveness of the *bourgeoisie* and the system of economic exploitation prevented the lower classes from raising themselves to a higher level and improving their material welfare. On the other hand, the State required more money and labour to maintain internal peace and security. Confining itself, as it did, to the problems of State life and being indifferent to economic progress, the government did nothing to promote and foster the latter. Rather, it helped to accelerate the process of stagnation by protecting the city *bourgeoisie* and taking very little thought for the prosperity of the masses. Thus the burden of supporting the life of the State lay entirely on the working classes and caused a rapid decline of their material welfare. As they were the chief consumers of the industrial goods produced by the cities, their diminished purchasing power reacted adversely on the development of commerce and industry and greatly aggravated the torpor which had come over them. The decay had definitely set in as early as the beginning of the second century. The wars of that century demonstrated the hopeless economic weakness of the Empire and awakened the interest of the emperors in economic problems. But, even when they realized the danger, they were helpless to cure the disease. Their constructive measures were puerile and brought no relief. To save the state they resorted to the old practice of the ancient world—the policy of force and compulsion. Force and compulsion were applied both to the city *bourgeoisie* and to the lower classes, and they embittered each against the other. The result was the collapse of city-capitalism and the acute economic crisis of the third century, which brought about the rapid decline of business activity in general, the resuscitation of primitive forms of economy, and the growth of state-capitalism. These were the salient features of life in the fourth and following centuries.

I regret that I have been unable in this volume to deal with the third aspect of the same development—the spiritual, intellectual, and artistic life of the Empire. Without a thorough treatment of those sides of life the picture must clearly be one-sided and incomplete. But to have included them would not only have meant doubling the size of the book but would have involved a constant shifting from one aspect of the subject to another without a proper investigation of any one of them. Such an exposition must find a place in a work which aims at presenting a complete picture of the Roman Empire—which, as I have said, is not the purpose of this book. The fact is that the spiritual, intellectual, and artistic life of the Empire developed along the same lines as its economic and social life. The late Republic and the early Empire created a refined, delicate, highly aristocratic civilization, foreign alike to the urban middle class and to the masses. The same is true of the lofty philosophic religion of the higher classes. As time passed, this high civilization was gradually absorbed by the growing middle class and adapted to their standards and requirements. In becoming so widely diffused, the delicate creation of the first century was bound to become more and more simplified, more and more elementary, more and more materialistic. Even this civilization, however, remained foreign to the lower classes, and it was finally destroyed by them in their onslaught on the cities and the city *bourgeoisie*. The new culture of the late Empire was, on the one hand, a very thin decoction of the ancient one, spread among the masses by the Christian Church, and, on the other hand, an exotic and highly refined but empty and archaistic culture of the upper classes, pagan and Christian alike.

A few words on the distribution of the matter of the book and on the treatment of it may be useful to the reader. The first chapter, dealing with the late Republic, is a mere sketch. A more comprehensive examination would require a whole volume, and I hope soon to provide it, in connexion with a study of the social and economic life of the Hellenistic period in general. The next two chapters, on Augustus and on the military tyranny of the Julii and Claudii, are not so detailed as those on the second and third centuries, the reason being that for the most essential points in my narrative I am able to refer the reader to modern books where the subject is thoroughly treated and the sources are quoted in full. The core of my book is the portion (Chaps. IV–XI) dealing with the second and third centuries, which are the most neglected periods in the history of the Roman Empire. The last chapter is again a sketch, designed to illustrate in a very general way the difference between the social and economic structure of the early and of the late Roman Empire.

The volume is divided into two parts, the text and the notes. In the text I have endeavoured to give a readable general picture of the social and economic development of the Empire, intelligible to everybody who is interested in the subject. The notes fall into two classes. Where I am able to refer for all the details to a good modern book or article, and where my own

judgement is based on the work of others, I have generally given
to the notes a purely bibliographical character. I am aware that
the bibliography is far from complete. The book is not a text-
book nor a handbook. As a rule, I have abstained from piling
up references to antiquated books and articles. The books and
articles cited are those which I have carefully read and on which
my own information is based; those which did not help me are
not quoted, as being unlikely to help my readers. I have refrained,
in general, from criticizing modern works in the notes. I have
done so only when I have quoted as the leading work on the
subject a book which reaches conclusions different from those
which I myself have drawn from the same evidence. Most of the
notes, however, are not of a bibliographical character. In those
sections where I have found no modern books to help me and
where I have had to collect and elucidate the evidence myself,
I have generally inserted some notes which are really short
articles on various special points and of the nature of excursuses
or appendices. Some of these notes are long and overburdened
with quotations; only specialists are likely to read them in full.
The illustrations which I have added to the text are not intended
to amuse or to please the reader. They are an essential part of
the book, as essential, in fact, as the notes and the quotations
from literary or documentary sources. They are drawn from the
large store of archaeological evidence, which for a student of
social and economic life is as important and as indispensable as
the written evidence. Some of my inferences and conclusions are
largely based on archaeological material. I regret that I have
been unable to give a larger number of illustrations and that I
have been forced to confine myself to reproducing specimens of
the realistic art of the Empire, to the exclusion of products
of industrial activity, such as pots, lamps, glass-ware, remains of
textiles, jewels, metal work, and so forth. As it was impossible
to give an adequate set of plates of this type, I have preferred to
dispense with this kind of illustration altogether.

At the end of his preface an author usually permits himself the
pleasure and the privilege of mentioning those who were kind
enough to help him in his work. My list is a long one. It shows
how earnestly I have laboured to make my information as complete as possible, and how little the disasters of war and revolution have impaired the international solidarity of scholars. The

only melancholy exception is the existing Russian government, which makes it impossible, at least for me, to use for scientific purposes the treasures stored in Russia.

The volume is dedicated to my dear friend, J. G. C. Anderson, as an expression (feeble though it is) of my high appreciation of his collaboration and my deep gratitude for it. Mr. Anderson not only revised my manuscript and made my English readable —*magni sudoris opus*; he also read all the proofs, introduced a reasonable system of quotations, and verified a good many of them. Last, but not least, he made me give a definite statement in many cases where I was inclined to remain vague: evidently the English mind, in this respect unlike the Slavonic, dislikes a lack of precision in thought or expression. Very often, too, he prevented me from formulating over-hasty, and therefore erroneous, conclusions. Finally, in many instances he helped me by his great knowledge and his sound suggestions to elucidate points which had remained dark to me. My only desire is that, after having finished his labours on my book, he may say: *Forsan et haec meminisse iuvabit.* Throughout the proof-stage Mr. Anderson has enjoyed the assistance, generously offered and freely rendered, of Dr. George Macdonald. To that distinguished scholar I tender my warmest thanks.

In the next place I have to express my gratitude to the Clarendon Press. It is a real privilege and pleasure to have a book published by that institution: the broad-minded and scientific spirit of its representatives is known to all the world. I was pleasantly surprised to find my modest volume set up in such beautiful type and with such a wealth of illustrations.

In writing the chapters on the Roman provinces, and in collecting the material for the illustration of the volume, I have enjoyed the most liberal help of a large number of my colleagues. In England Sir Frederic Kenyon, H. I. Bell, O. M. Dalton, H. R. Hall, G. F. Hill, H. Mattingly, and A. H. Smith of the British Museum, D. G. Hogarth, E. Thurlow Leeds, Miss M. V. Taylor, and B. Ashmole of the Ashmolean Museum at Oxford, A. E. Cowley and the staff of the Bodleian Library; in France, the late E. Babelon, R. Cagnat, J. Carcopino, R. Dussaud, E. Espérandieu, P. Jouguet, A. Merlin, E. Michon, P. Perdrizet, L. Poinssot, E. Pottier, M. Prou; in Germany, G. Rodenwaldt, K. Schumacher, and R. Zahn; in Italy, W. Amelung,

S. Aurigemma, G. Brusin, G. Calza, M. Della Corte, A. Minto, R. Paribeni, A. Spano, P. Sticotti; in Austria, R. Egger, J. Keil, and E. Reisch; in Poland, the late P. Bienkowski; in Serbia, N. Vulič; in Bulgaria, B. Filow and G. Kazarow; in Romania, V. Pârvan; in Belgium, F. Cumont and F. Mayence, and in the United States E. Robinson and Miss G. F. Richter of the Metropolitan Museum, the Field Museum of Natural History at Chicago and the Wisconsin University and Library—all have done their best to make my work on the volume less tedious and difficult. I ask them to accept my most sincere thanks.

Finally, I am indebted to my wife, Mrs. S. Rostovtzeff, for undertaking the task of compiling the Indexes.

[In the Introduction to the German edition (1931) Rostovtzeff further expressed his thanks to Professor A. Maiuri, Professor M. Abramic, Professor A. E. R. Boak and the University of Michigan Excavations Committee, Mr. H. Jayne and Mr. Fiske Kimbell, the Directors of the Museums of Cairo and Alexandria, and, finally, M. A. Merlin and Professor R. Paribeni.

In the Introduction to the Italian edition (1933) he added thanks to Professor A. Maiuri, Professor G. Calza, and Professor G. Guidi.]

CONTENTS

VOLUME I

Contents

VOLUME II

LIST OF ILLUSTRATIONS

ABBREVIATIONS
OF TITLES OF PERIODICALS, ETC., USED IN
THE DESCRIPTIONS OF THE PLATES
AND IN THE NOTES

Abh. Berl. Akad.	*Abhandlungen der preußischen Akademie der Wissenschaften.*
Abh. d. sächs. Ges.	*Abhandlungen der k. sächsischen Gesellschaft der Wissenschaften.*
AJP	*American Journal of Philology.*
Amer. Hist. Rev.	*American Historical Review.*
Amer. Journ. Arch.	*American Journal of Archaeology.*
Anal. Acad. Rom.	*Analele Academiei Române* (Annals of the Romanian Academy, in Romanian with French summaries).
Annali d. Ist.	*Annali dell' Istituto di corrispondenza archeologica di Roma.*
Ann. d. R. Sc. arch. di Atene	*Annali della Reale Scuola archeologica di Atene.*
Ann. ép.	R. Cagnat et M. Besnier, *Année épigraphique*, in *Revue archéologique* and separately.
Arch. Anz.	*Archäologischer Anzeiger*, in *Jahrbuch des deutschen archäologischen Instituts.*
Arch. d. miss. scient.	*Archives des missions scientifiques.*
Arch.-ep. Mitth. aus Oest.	*Archäologisch-epigraphische Mittheilungen aus Oesterreich.*
Arch. Értesítő	*Archeologiai Értesítő* (in Hungarian).
Arch. f. Papyr.	*Archiv für Papyrusforschung.*
Arch. f. Rel.	*Archiv für Religionswissenschaft.*
Arch. Journ.	*Archaeological Journal.*
Arch. Zeit.	*Archäologische Zeitung.*
Ath. Mitth.	*Mittheilungen des deutschen archäologischen Instituts, Athenische Abtheilung.*
Atti e Mem. della Soc. Istriana.	*Atti e Memorie della Società Istriana di archeologia e storia patria.*
BCH	*Bulletin de correspondance hellénique.*
Berl. phil. Woch.	*Berliner philologische Wochenschrift.*
Bibl. des Éc.	*Bibliothèque des Écoles françaises d'Athènes et de Rome.*
Boll. di fil. cl.	*Bollettino di filologia classica.*
Bonn. Jahrb.	*Jahrbücher des Vereins der Altertumsfreunde im Rheinlande.*
BSA	*Annual of the British School of Archaeology at Atheus.*
Bull. arch. du Com. des trav. hist.	*Bulletin archéologique du Comité des travaux historiques.*

Bull. Comm. arch. com.	*Bullettino della Commissione archeologica comunale di Roma.*
Bull. de la Comm. arch. de Russie	*Bulletin de la Commission archéologique de Russie* (in Russian, with French sub-title).
Bull. d. Ist. di dir. rom.	*Bullettino dell' Istituto di diritto Romano.*
Bull. Soc. arch. Alex.	*Bulletin de la Société archéologique d'Alexandrie.*
Bull. Soc. Ant. de France	*Bulletin de la Société nationale des Antiquaires de France.*
Byz.-Griech. Jahrb.	*Byzantinisch-griechische Jahrbücher.*
Byzant. Zeitschr.	*Byzantinische Zeitschrift.*
Class. Phil.	*Classical Philology.*
Class. Rev.	*Classical Review.*
Class. Weekly	*Classical Weekly.*
C. R. Acad. Inscr.	*Comptes-rendus de l'Académie des Inscriptions et Belles-Lettres.*
Denkschr. Wien. Akad.	*Denkschriften der österreichischen Akademie der Wissenschaften.*
E. Espérandieu, *Rec. gén.*	E. Espérandieu, *Recueil général des bas-reliefs de la Gaule romaine*, i–ix, 1907–1925.
Gaz. arch.	*Gazette archéologique.*
Gött. gel. Anz.	*Göttingische gelehrte Anzeigen.*
Gött. gel. Nachr.	*Nachrichten der Gesellschaft der Wissenschaften zu Göttingen.*
Hist. Zeitschr.	*Historische Zeitschrift.*
Jahrb. f. Altertumsk.	*Jahrbuch für Altertumskunde.*
JDAI	*Jahrbuch des deutschen archäologischen Instituts.*
JEA	*Journal of Egyptian Archaeology.*
JHS	*Journal of Hellenic Studies.*
Journ. Sav.	*Journal des Savants.*
JRAS	*Journal of the Royal Asiatic Society.*
JRS	*Journal of Roman Studies.*
Korr.-Blatt der Westd. Zeitschr.	*Korrespondenzblatt der westdeutschen Zeitschrift für Geschichte und Kunst.*
Lit. Zentralbl.	*Literarisches Zentralblatt.*
Mél. de l'Éc. fr. de Rome	*Mélanges de l'École française de Rome.*
Mém. de l'Ac. d. Inscr.	*Mémoires de l'Académie des Inscriptions et Belles-Lettres.*
Mém. prés. à l'Acad.	*Mémoires présentés par divers savants à l'Académie des Inscriptions et Belles-Lettres.*
Mem. d. Acc. di Napoli	*Memorie della Reale Accademia di archeologia di Napoli.*
Mon. Ant. *or* Mon. dei Lincei	*Monumenti antichi pubblicati per cura della R. Accademia dei Lincei.*
Mon. Piot	*Monuments et Mémoires E. Piot.*
Mus. belge	*Musée belge.*
Nachr. d. gött. Ges.	See *Gött. gel. Nachr.*
Neue Heid. Jahrb.	*Neue Heidelberger Jahrbücher.*
Neue Jahrb. (kl. Alt.)	*Neue Jahrbücher für das klassische Altertum.*
Not. d. Scavi	*Notizie degli Scavi di Antichità.*
Nouv. Arch. d. miss. scient.	*Nouvelles Archives des missions scientifiques.*

Nouv. Rev. hist. du droit fr. et étr.	*Nouvelle Revue historique du droit français et étranger.*
Num. Chr.	*Numismatic Chronicle.*
Numism. Zeitschr.	*Numismatische Zeitschrift.*
Oest. Jahresh.	*Jahreshefte des österreichischen archäologischen Instituts.*
Pauly–Wissowa	Pauly–Wissowa–Kroll, *Realencyclopädie der klassischen Altertumswissenschaft.*
Philol.	*Philologus.*
Phil. Woch.	See *Berl. phil. Woch.*
Preuss. Jahrb.	*Preußische Jahrbücher.*
S. Reinach, *Rép. d. peint.*	S. Reinach, *Répertoire des peintures grecques et romaines* (1922).
S. Reinach, *Rép. d. rel.*	S. Reinach, *Répertoire des reliefs grecs et romains*, i–iii (1909–1912).
Rend. (Acc.) Lincei	*Rendiconti della Reale Accademia dei Lincei.*
Rev. arch.	*Revue archéologique.*
Rev. bibl(ique)	*Revue biblique internationale.*
Rev. ét. anc.	*Revue des études anciennes.*
Rev. de phil.	*Revue de philologie.*
Rev. ét. gr.	*Revue des études grecques.*
Rev. d. quest. hist.	*Revue des questions historiques.*
Rev. hist.	*Revue historique.*
Rev. num.	*Revue numismatique.*
Rh. Mus.	*Rheinisches Museum für Philologie.*
Riv. fil.	*Rivista di filologia.*
Riv. di st. ant.	*Rivista di storia antica.*
Röm. Mitt.	*Mittheilungen des deutschen archäologischen Instituts, Römische Abtheilung.*
Schmollers Jahrb.	*Schmollers Jahrbuch für Gesetzgebung, Verwaltung und Volkswirtschaft im deutschen Reich.*
Sitzb. Bayr. (*or* Münch.) Akad.	*Sitzungsberichte der bayrischen Akademie der Wissenschaften.*
Sitzb. Berl. Akad.	*Sitzungsberichte der preußischen Akademie der Wissenschaften.*
Sitzb. Heid. Akad.	*Sitzungsberichte der Heidelberger Akademie der Wissenschaften.*
Sitzb. Wien. Akad.	*Sitzungsberichte der Akademie der Wissenschaften in Wien.*
Sonderschr. d. öst. Inst.	*Sonderschriften des österreichischen archäologischen Instituts.*
Studien Gesch. Kol. *or* Studien	*Studien zur Geschichte des römischen Kolonates*, von M. Rostowzew. 1910 (*Arch. f. Papyr.*, Beiheft I).
TAPA	*Transactions of the American Philological Association.*
Westd. Zeitschr.	*Westdeutsche Zeitschrift für Geschichte und Kunst.*
Wiss. Mitt. (aus Bosnien)	*Wissenschaftliche Mittheilungen aus Bosnien und Herzegowina.*
Woch. kl. Phil.	*Wochenschrift für klassische Philologie.*
Zeitschr. d. Sav.-St.	*Zeitschrift der Savigny-Stiftung für Rechtsgeschichte.*
Zeitschr. f. äg. Spr.	*Zeitschrift für ägyptische Sprache und Altertumskunde.*
Zeitschr. f. ges. Staatsw.	*Zeitschrift für gesammte Staatswissenschaften.*

Zeitschr. f. Neutest. Wissenschaft	*Zeitschrift für die Neutestamentliche Wissenschaft.*
Zeitschr. f. Num.	*Zeitschrift für Numismatik.*
Zeitschr. f. öst. Gymn.	*Zeitschrift für österreichische Gymnasien.*
Zeitschr. f. vergl. Rechtswiss.	*Zeitschrift für vergleichende Rechtswissenschaft.*

I

ITALY AND THE CIVIL WAR

THE Roman Empire as established by Augustus was the outcome of the troubled and confused period of civil war which
lasted, both in Italy and in the Roman provinces, for more than
eighty years, with some longer or shorter lulls. The civil wars, in
their turn, owed their origin to two main causes, which also determined their course: on the one hand, the dominating position
in the affairs of the civilized world occupied by Rome and Italy
in the third and second centuries B.C., which led to the establishment of the Roman world-state, and, on the other hand, the
gradual development of class antagonism and class war in Rome
and Italy, a development which was closely connected with the
growth of the Roman world-state.

A description of the social and economic evolution of the
Roman Empire must therefore start with a brief sketch sum-
marizing the causes which brought about the subjection of the
rest of the civilized world to Italy and subsequently led to the
civil wars in Rome, in Italy, and in the provinces.

Before the outbreak of the civil wars in Rome and Italy the
aspect of the ancient world may be thus described. During the
so-called Hellenistic period the centre of civilized life gradually
shifted from the West to the East. Athens was replaced as the
leader in civilization by Alexandria on the Nile, Antioch on
the Orontes, and Pergamon on the Caicus. Greece and especially
Athens, which in the fifth and fourth centuries B.C. had developed, from the economic point of view, a flourishing state of
commercial capitalism,[1] began gradually to lose their importance. The primary cause of the steady decline of economic life
in Greece proper was the constant, almost uninterrupted, succession of wars in which the cities were involved in the fourth
and third centuries B.C. These wars, in spite of many efforts to
minimize their ruinous effects and to subject them to some inter-
state regulation, became ever more bitter, more cruel, and more
disastrous for all the participants, whether victors or vanquished.
The practice of devastating the enemy's land, of destroying his

B

crops, his vineyards and olive-groves, of burning down farm-houses, of carrying off and selling men and cattle as war booty, of feeding the troops from the resources of the invaded lands, became increasingly common. Some states, for instance the Aetolian league and the Cretan cities, specialized in conducting wars of robbery on land and sea, and the other states, not excepting the great Hellenistic monarchies, followed them on this fatal path.[2]

Concurrently with the external wars there raged within the Greek cities, alike in Greece proper and in most of the islands, an unceasing class-warfare, which originated in the steady growth of a well-to-do *bourgeois* class and the corresponding impoverishment of the masses. This class-war made the growth and development of a sound capitalistic system very difficult. Indeed, it made a healthy economic life within the city-states almost impossible. The strife in the Greek cities assumed more and more the character of an almost purely social and economic struggle. The main aim of the struggle was, not the increase of production by the betterment of labour conditions and the improvement and regulation of the relations between labour and capital, but the redistribution of property, which was generally achieved by violent revolutionary means. The war-cry was the immemorial one of γῆς ἀναδασμὸς καὶ χρεῶν ἀποκοπή, redistribution of land and abolition of debts. This cry was so freely used as early as the end of the Peloponnesian war that the Athenians introduced into the oath of the Heliasts in 401 a clause which forbade the putting of such an issue to the vote. In the fourth century the fear of a social revolution was constantly present to the minds of Aristotle and Isocrates, and in 338 the League of Corinth formed a sort of association for protection against it. It is significant of conditions in Greece during the third century and later that a clause forbidding the redistribution of land and the cancellation of debts was introduced into the oath of the citizens of Itanos in Crete.[3]

The revolutions which aimed at such a redistribution of property were utterly disastrous for Greece. Revolution and reaction followed each other with brief delays, and were marked by the wholesale slaughter or expulsion of the best citizens. The exiles, as a matter of fact, either tried to return and to take revenge on their enemies or emigrated to the Eastern monarchies as mercenary soldiers, as colonists of the new cities which were created all over the East by the Hellenistic kings, as civil officials of the Hellenistic states, or as merchants and business men. A few cities like Athens were more or less unaffected by these periodical crises and so remained comparatively prosperous.[4]

What was lost by the Greek cities of the European mainland and most of the islands was gained by the Hellenistic monarchies and more especially by the Greek cities of the East.[5] Most of these cities stood under the direct or indirect control of the Hellenistic kings and enjoyed no political freedom. The result was that every attempt at a social revolution within their gates was stopped by the strong hand of the Hellenistic monarchs, and that the cities were very rarely involved in external warfare. Thus the accumulation of capital and the introduction of improved methods in trade and industry proceeded more freely and successfully in the East than in the cities of Greece proper. Hence the commercial capitalism of the Greek cities of the fourth century attained an ever higher development, which brought the Hellenistic states very near to the stage of industrial capitalism that characterizes the economic history of Europe in the nineteenth and twentieth centuries. The Hellenistic cities of the East had at their disposal a large internal market. They carried on an important and steadily growing external trade in competition with each other. They gradually improved the technique of agricultural and of industrial production with the aid of pure and applied science, which advanced with rapid strides in all the Hellenistic kingdoms; and they employed both in agriculture (including cattle-breeding) and in industry the methods of pure capitalistic economy based on slave-labour. They introduced for the first time a mass production of goods for an indefinite market. They developed banking and credit and succeeded in creating not only general rules for maritime commerce (the so-called Rhodian maritime law) but also a kind of common civil law, which was valid all over the Hellenistic world. The same tendency towards unification may be noticed in the attempts to stabilize the currency, or at least to establish stable relations between the coins of the various independent trading states. The leading part which was played by the Hellenistic monarchs in the commercial and industrial life of their countries, and the enormous importance of commercial considerations in shaping their foreign policy, make it tempting to compare the economic conditions of these monarchies with those of the mercantile period in the history of modern Europe.

Very soon, however, the sound economic development described above was first stunted and then gradually atrophied by many and various causes. As in the fourth century B.C., one of the main causes was the constant warfare which raged almost without interruption all over the Hellenistic world. I cannot dwell on this subject here. The fact and the reasons for it are well known. From the economic point of view these endless wars gradually became a real calamity for the Greek world. It was not only that large tracts of land were devastated, cities pillaged, and their residents sold into slavery. Much more important was the fact that the wars forced the Hellenistic states, both great and small, to concentrate their efforts on military preparations, on building up the largest possible armies and navies, on inventing new devices in military engineering, and thus wasting enormous sums of money—as, for instance, in the case of the siege of Rhodes by Demetrius Poliorcetes. Almost all the income of the states was devoted to military preparations. This led at first to sound and wholesome efforts on the part of the Hellenistic kings to increase, in mutual rivalry, the productivity of their lands by a rational and scientific exploitation of their natural resources. Gradually, however, such healthy and progressive methods of increasing the income of the states gave place to a series of easier and more immediately profitable measures. The most important of them was the nationalization (*étatisation*) of both production and exchange, which was carried out in some at least of the Hellenistic monarchies, especially in Egypt. By nationalization I mean the concentration of the management of the most essential branches of economic activity in the hands of the state, that is to say, of the king and his officials. Profitable at first for the state, this system gradually led to dishonesty and lawlessness on the part of the officials and to the almost complete elimination of competition and of the free play of individual energy on the part of the population.

Hand in hand with this tendency towards state control went the minute elaboration of a highly refined system of taxation, which affected every side of economic life. It was based on the experience of the Oriental monarchies, but it went much farther both in inventing new taxable objects and in improving the mode of collecting the taxes. The burden of taxation lay heavily on the population of the Hellenistic world. For the native element of this population the burden was aggravated by the constant use of the age-old system of compulsory work, of *corvées*. This system, like the system of taxation, was highly elaborated by the logical and constructive mind of the Greeks, and the *corvée* gradually became transformed into a regular additional item in the long list of obligations which bound the subjects of the Hellenistic monarchies to the state and to the king.

The main sufferers from the policy of nationalization and from the refined fiscal system of the Hellenistic kings were not the new settlers in the Oriental lands, the immigrants, who were mostly Greeks. They knew how to evade those burdens or to shift them on to the shoulders of the native population; and in fact the majority of the immigrant population were employed by the kings as instruments for the oppression of the native element— as tax-farmers, as superintendents of the *corvées*, as concessionaires of the state in commerce and industry, as managers of large estates, and so forth.

The disastrous economic system of the Hellenistic monarchies produced ever-growing discontent among the masses of the natives. From the end of the third century onwards the native population of Egypt, for example, rose repeatedly against its foreign oppressors. The leaders of these revolts were generally the native priests. Their ultimate aim was the expulsion of the foreigners, including the kings—the same aim which had been pursued, often with success, by the Egyptians under the Assyrian and Persian dominations. The revolts forced the kings to enlarge their mercenary armies, to grant new privileges to the foreign oppressors, and to increase still further the burdens of taxation and of compulsory work. The opposite system of granting concessions to the native population, which was from time to time tried by the Ptolemies, aggravated the evil by encouraging the belief that the government was too weak to enforce its demands. These developments prevented the transformation of the Hellenistic monarchies into national states. They remained, with few exceptions, what they had been from the beginning—military tyrannies ruling over an enslaved population and resting in the last resort on mercenary armies.[6]

Hence the civilization of the Hellenistic period never became

a Greco-Oriental civilization. It remained almost purely Greek,
with a very slight admixture of Oriental elements. The chief
novel feature of Greek civilization in the Hellenistic age was not
its Greco-Oriental, but its cosmopolitan character. This made it
acceptable to the various new national states, which arose both
in the East and in the West. In the East, however, none of the
new states—Parthia, Bactria, India, Armenia, and the rest—
adopted Greek culture thoroughly. Greek forms and Greek ideas
remained a thin veneer over a local, purely Oriental substratum.
Moreover, Greek influence in the East was confined to the cities
and to the upper classes of the population, and never affected the
masses. Deeper was its penetration into the life of the Western
nations—the Italians, the Celts, the Iberians, and the Thracians.
But here also Greek civilization remained true to its origin and
to its real character. It had been, and remained, a civilization of
cities and of city residents. Thus the Hellenistic civilization was
simply a new phase in the development of the civilization of the
Greek city. Even in the Hellenistic monarchies—in Asia Minor,
in Syria, in Egypt, on the shores of the Black Sea—the masses of
the country people were never affected by Greek culture and
retained persistently their old customs and habits and their traditional religious beliefs.

The desultory intervention of Rome in the affairs of the civilized world during and after the Punic wars brought no relief.[7]
Rather it greatly complicated the situation and effectively aided
the destructive forces. The aim of the growing Roman Republic
was to prevent any strong political formation in the East which
might be dangerous to the Roman state. The more troubles
there, the better. The greater the number of independent states,
the more advantageous was it for Rome. And the more embro-
glios in the domestic affairs of every state, the greater the hope
of Rome's becoming the controlling, that is, the ruling power in
the East. The freedom which was proclaimed for the Greek cities
after the first (sometimes called the second) Macedonian war,
and which was extended to the Greek cities of Asia before, during,
and after the war against Antiochus III, made the internal conditions of those cities almost desperate. The Greek cities in Asia
Minor were suffering the same economic decay which was constantly growing in Greece proper. On the other hand, the Roman
danger increased the tendency of the greater Hellenistic monar-

chies to continue the development of their military forces to the
detriment of the healthy economic progress of the most prosperous lands of the Near East. With the exception of Macedonia,
however, the accumulated resources of the Hellenistic monarchies
were used, not for a struggle against Rome, but for constant internecine wars with each other, in which the lesser states were protected and aided by Rome in their efforts to reduce the strength
of the greater, particularly Macedonia, Syria, and Egypt.

Roman intervention in the affairs of the East passed through
many stages of development. The first phase, that of the first (or
second) Macedonian war and of the war against Antiochus III,
was (as has been said) the phase of preventive wars, carried on
with the main object of defending Rome and Italy against the
supposed imperialistic tendencies of Macedonia and Syria. The
second, following the first crushing blows dealt to Macedonia
and Syria, was the phase of a regular protectorate over the Greek
cities and over some minor Hellenistic monarchies, designed to
prevent a revival of the two humbled powers. The second (or
third) Macedonian war was the most outstanding event of this
period. Macedonia, endeavouring to free herself from the heavy
pressure of Roman interference, was completely beaten and disappeared as the leading political power of the Hellenistic world.
As a result of this disappearance, the protectorate of Rome was
practically transformed into a mild form of domination. This
was the third phase of Roman intervention. The Greek cities
and the Hellenistic monarchies were alike treated by Rome as
vassals who had to obey her orders.

Exasperated by the ruthless way in which Rome used her
power, Macedonia and Greece both attempted to liberate themselves from her domination and regain their political independence. Rome regarded their attempt as rebellion and crushed it
with terrible cruelty. Her treatment of these two countries created
chaotic conditions which were very dangerous for herself as well
as for them. Hatred against Rome was now the dominant feeling
among the Greek population throughout the East. Further, the
national forces of Greece and Macedonia were no longer sufficient to defend their northern frontiers against the barbarians—
the Celts, the Thracians, and the Illyrians. The same conditions
were gradually developing in Asia Minor. Finally, the internal
life of the Greek cities grew more and more complicated and

troubled. Class-warfare raged all over Greece and Asia Minor. It assumed the form of a bitter struggle between the aristocracy, which was protected by Rome, and the rest of the population, which was opposed both to the local aristocracy and to Roman domination.

These conditions led to the fourth stage in the development of the relations between Rome and the Greco-Oriental world, the phase of complete subjection. Rome now introduced into the East the system of provinces which she had already adopted for the government of the former Carthaginian dominions (Sicily, Sardinia, Corsica, and Spain) as well as of the territory of Carthage (the province of Africa), and which took the form of a permanent military occupation under the direction of one of her annual magistrates. Macedonia became the first Roman province in the Greek East. Some years later Attalus III, the last king of Pergamon, on his death-bed deemed it prudent to subject his kingdom to the same régime. He was probably convinced that a vassal, an enslaved king, was not strong enough to protect the land against the growing anarchy in Asia Minor. He therefore bequeathed his kingdom to the senate and people of Rome. His death was followed by a bloody social revolution, after the suppression of which Rome transformed the Pergamene kingdom into the province of Asia. It is significant that, as we learn from an inscription of Cyrene,* Ptolemy Euergetes II, a contemporary of Attalus, followed the same policy, at least in as far as Cyrene was concerned.

The reduction of one portion of the Greco-Oriental world into Roman provinces, together with the strict control exercised by Rome over the remaining, still legally independent, Hellenistic states, brought a temporary relief to the Greek East. External wars and internal class-struggles were stopped once and for all by the iron hand of Rome, and the economic life of Greece and the Hellenized East began to revive at the end of the second century B.C. But the rule of Rome and her administration of the provinces soon proved to be very far from efficient. She took little thought for the prosperity of her new dominions. Witness the constant growth of piracy in the Aegean and the Black Sea, which was a heavy handicap to the development of sound economic conditions in the Greek world. Moreover, her rule became

* *SEG* ix. 7.

increasingly selfish. Roman governors and capitalists were given almost a free hand in exploiting the provinces and they usually did so, in the most selfish spirit, for their own profit. Their behaviour led to a growing discontent among the Greeks and to the whole-hearted, though short-lived, support which was given to Mithradates, the famous king of Pontus, who came forward as a champion of Greek liberty against Roman oppression.

The Mithradatic war coincided with the beginning of the bitter civil wars in Italy. In these wars, of which we shall speak later, the rival leaders of the contending political parties at Rome regarded the East merely as a field of exploitation, as a source whence they could provide themselves with money. As the civil wars were largely fought on Greek soil, Greece and Asia Minor suffered severely. Requisitions of food for the men and horses of the opposing armies, requisitions of labour, of means of transport, and of quarters for soldiers and officers, and, above all, the heavy contributions imposed on the cities which were forced to support a leader who happened to have been defeated, brought almost complete ruin on the Greek cities of the Balkan peninsula and of Asia Minor. The ruin was aggravated by the Roman capitalists, always ready to advance money to the cities, provided that they were willing to pay excessive interest. At the end of the civil wars the Greek East lay ruined and prostrate beneath the feet of Roman capitalists and profiteers.

While this gradual economic decay was going on in the East, Italy became the richest country of the ancient world.[8] We are ill-informed on the economic conditions prevailing in Italy before the Eastern conquests of Rome and before the appearance of the first general survey of Roman economics (more particularly Roman agriculture) given by Cato in his treatise *De re rustica*. But even from the scanty evidence which is available we may infer that Italy in the early period of her history was not a poor country. South Italy, Sardinia, and Sicily were for a long time the richest grain markets of the world. The Greek cities of the peninsula exported large quantities of grain to Greece, while the Carthaginian dominions (Sardinia and part of Sicily) and Etruria fed with their corn the Punic cities of Africa, which devoted themselves to commerce and to the production of wine, olive-oil, and fruit for the Western market, including Etruria herself.

Apart from corn, certain regions of Italy, particularly Apulia, and parts of Sicily produced from time immemorial some of the finest kinds of wool. Campania and Etruria possessed, along with a flourishing agriculture, a highly developed industry, famous for its metal wares and its pottery. It is probable also that at a very early date the Greek cities of Southern Italy and of Sicily took up the culture of the vine and olive on an extensive scale in competition with their motherlands and with the Punic cities of Africa. Moreover, these Greek cities, as well as the Punic cities of Africa and of the Punic dominions abroad, shared in the economic evolution of Greece and gradually became centres of the Hellenistic—that is to say, the capitalistic—system. The economic organization of Sicily under Hiero II, as revealed by the speeches of Cicero against Verres, in which the fundamental fiscal law of Hiero II is constantly quoted, did not differ very greatly from that of other contemporary Hellenistic states. We know, too, how flourishing was the territory of Carthage and other Punic cities, how intense was the concentration of their agriculture on the higher forms of production, and how jealously they watched their subjects, vassals, and allies, to prevent them from introducing those higher forms of cultivation and to limit them to the production of corn, which was imported into the Punic cities. This policy of Carthage is clearly attested by the measures which she took both in Sardinia and Sicily to promote corn-growing, and by the character of Mago's treatise on agriculture, which was a Punic adaptation of Greek scientific treatises on the subject to the conditions of Northern Africa.

In Central and Northern Italy the situation was different. So far as we are able to judge, the Celtic peoples of Northern Italy lived the primitive life of shepherds and peasants, with pasture predominating over agriculture. The breeding of pigs and sheep was one of their main occupations. We have no data to show that the Celts of Northern Italy shared in the gradual progress which was achieved in Gaul by the other Celtic tribes. Before they could make a start, they were conquered by the Romans, and, to a large extent, driven out of the most fertile districts. The economic organization of Etruria was similar to that of some Greek cities of Asia Minor in the archaic period. So far as the evidence goes, the cities of Etruria were residences of the Etruscan aristocracy, which consisted of large landowners, owners of shops and factories, and merchants on a great scale. Their prosperity was based on the work of the enslaved population—serfs who tilled their estates for them and pastured their herds, slaves and serfs who toiled in their workshops. I greatly doubt whether the higher types of cultivation were introduced into Etruria outside the suburban gardens of the aristocracy. There is no evidence to show that the archaic conditions, which were created probably at the time of the conquest, underwent any serious change in the six centuries of the existence of the Etruscan federation of cities. The frescoes of the Etruscan graves, which depict some of the features of Etruscan life, remained, so far as the subjects are concerned, almost unchanged for at least three centuries (from the fifth to the third century B.C.) and portray the same life of leisure throughout that period.

Our information on the early economic life of the Latins, of the city of Rome, and of the Umbro-Sabellian and Samnite stock is very scanty indeed. It is well known, too, that the chief questions concerning the agricultural life of the early Roman community are matters of warm dispute. No reader will expect a full discussion of those questions in a volume devoted to the Roman Empire. Suffice it to give a short sketch of the conditions which, in my opinion, probably prevailed in Latium and the other parts of Central Italy. Whatever the early beginnings of economic life in Latium may have been, there is no doubt that the Etruscan domination was decisive for its further development. The Etruscans, together with some families of the Roman aristocracy, formed the upper class of large landowners and merchants in Rome. The masses of the native population were forced to toil and sweat for their new masters. The overthrow of the Etruscan dynasty by the aristocracy of Rome did not alter the prevailing economic conditions. Much more important for Rome was the need of maintaining and developing a strong military organization able to defend her from attacks coming from the North and from the rivalry of the other Latin cities.

It was during this darkest period in the history of Rome that the foundations of the Roman peasant state were laid. How and when those who had once probably been serfs of the aristocracy became free peasants, owners of small plots of land and members of the plebeian class, we do not know. It is probable that there was no radical reform like that of Alexander II in Russia, but a gradual evolution bringing with it both an emancipation of

Description of Plate II

1. BRONZE HANDLE OF A LID OF A PRAENESTINE *CISTA*. Found at Palestrina in the 'terreno Franciosi'. Exhibited first in the Museo delle Terme, now in the Museo della Villa Giulia (Rome). Probably unpublished. Mentioned in W. Helbig–W. Amelung, *Führer*, ii, no. 1519, p. 220. Similar handles are comparatively frequent on the Praenestine *cistae*, R. Schöne in *Ann. d. Inst.* 1866, pp. 151 ff., and 1868, pp. 413 ff., nos. 21 and 42, cf. no. 58; *Mon. d. Inst.*, suppl. 13, 14; A. Mau in Pauly–Wissowa, iii, pp. 2593 ff.; Helbig–Amelung, *Führer*, ii, no. 1768, p. 318; G. Matthies, *Die praenestinischen Spiegel* (1912), p. 71.

The handle of the *cista* (a cylindrical bronze box for keeping articles used for the bath, in the palaestra, and for toilet purposes, generally adorned with engraved designs, commonly found in Praenestine graves of the 4th–3rd cent. B.C.) represents two bearded warriors wearing helmets and complete armour, including greaves, and leaning on heavy spears. They are carrying the dead body of a comrade, unbearded, clad in the same kind of armour except for the helmet and the spear. The general appearance of the figures is archaic, but they certainly belong to the same time as the engravings on the lid, which cannot be earlier than the 4th cent. B.C. The motive of two warriors carrying a dead comrade is well known in archaic Greek art. The most famous example is the Spartan black-figured *kylix* of the Berlin Museum showing a procession of Spartans carrying the bodies of comrades killed in battle, see E. Pernice in *JDAI* 16, 1901, pp. 189 ff., pl. III; E. Buschor, *Greek Vase-painting* (1921), p. 92, pl. XLV. The Praenestine *cistae* certainly reproduce similar originals with some modifications. I am convinced, however, that the heavy style of the figures, their peculiar archaistic aspect, and some peculiarities in their armour (e.g. the helmet) assure the Latin origin of the statuettes, which were probably made at Praeneste by Latin or Latinized artists. I feel certain, too, that the owners of the *cistae* regarded these figures of soldiers as representing members of their own armed forces, and that we may safely assume that the appearance of the Roman soldiers of the 4th cent. was not very different from that of the figures on the Praenestine *cistae*. The group is very impressive and may serve as an excellent symbol of Roman and Latin life in the 4th cent., when the Roman state was based on military strength and on the self-sacrifice of its members. Compare the similar figures on bone-plaques which originally adorned a wooden box also found at Palestrina (E. Fernique, *Étude sur Préneste* (1880), pp. 208 ff., pls. III–IV; Helbig–Amelung, *Führer*, ii, no. 1768, W., pp. 323 ff.) and some of the engraved gems of Italian workmanship of a slightly later date (A. Furtwängler, *Die antiken Gemmen*, pls. XXII, 46, and XXIII, 24–29; cf. iii, pp. 232 f., 235 f., and 268). On the general character of the Latin art of the 4th cent. see G. Matthies, op. cit., pp. 123 ff.

2. GROUP OF ETRUSCAN VOTIVE BRONZE FIGURINES. Found near Arezzo in Etruria. Formerly in the Museo Kircheriano, now in the Museo della Villa Giulia. Helbig–Amelung, *Führer*, ii, no. 1723, p. 297, with bibliography. 6th cent. B.C.

The group (apart from the figure of Minerva behind the peasant, which is a modern addition, and not part of the original) represents an Etruscan peasant ploughing his own or his master's field. He wears a hat, a *chiton*, and a hide, perhaps also boots. The plough consists of a wooden share-beam of one piece of wood (*buris*), a metal-share (*vomer*), and a wooden handle (*stiva*). A similar plough (4th–3rd cent. B.C.) has been found near Telamone (*Not. d. Scavi*, 1877, p. 245; A. Milani, *Studi e Mater. di Archeol. e Numism.* i (1899), p. 127). Though Etruscan and archaic, the group may be safely used to illustrate the rural peasant life of Latium in the Republican period. Most of the Etruscan peasants were not of Etruscan but of Italic origin. The same plough is still used by the peasants in many remote corners of Italy.

1. LATIN WARRIORS

2. ETRUSCAN PEASANT PLOUGHING

II. REPUBLICAN ROME

former serfs and an increase in the numbers of free plebeian landowners, who had never disappeared from Roman economic life,
even in the times of the Etruscan domination. Both developments
are probably to be explained by the military needs of the Roman
community, especially at critical moments in its life, like the war
against Veii, the invasions of the Gauls, the struggle with the
Latin cities and with the Volscians and Aequians, and, finally,
the Latin and Samnite wars of the end of the fourth century.
The Servian reform, which in the shape in which it is known to
us belongs to the fourth century B.C., was the formulation and
consecration of the results of an economic and social process
which took place in the dark fifth century.

However it came about, Rome in the fourth century, and especially the second half of that century, was a city of peasants. I
can see no reason to doubt that the Licinian laws (367–366 B.C.)
contributed to the growth of this peasant state by limiting the
possibility of increasing indefinitely the size of plots owned or
rented by one family. The exact number of *iugera* prescribed by
the Licinian law for the largest plots may be an antedating of the
prescriptions of a later agrarian law of the second century, but
earlier legislation in the same spirit is very probable. The existence of such laws explains both the character of the so-called
Servian constitution and the fact that fresh increases of the territory of the Roman state in the fourth century resulted in an increase of peasant plots corresponding with the increase of the
peasant population of Rome. There does not seem to be the
slightest ground for disbelieving the statements of some of our
sources which depict certain aristocratic families of Rome as
families of rich peasants living the same life as the rest of the
Roman citizens.

Thus the basis of the economic life of Rome in the fourth century was peasant husbandry, a primitive agricultural system of
life in which all the members of a family worked hard in the
fields, employing in exceptional cases the help of some slaves, and
of clients who from time immemorial were attached to aristocratic families by religious ties. Peasant husbandry and concentration on corn-growing were the main features of the economic
life of Latium in general as well as of all the new territories of the
new tribes (*tribus*) and of the new colonies, Roman and Latin,
which were gradually included in the *ager Romanus*. Every new

Roman settlement was a peasant settlement, every new centre of urban life, every new colony was a fortified village of peasants.

The little we know of the conditions in the uplands between Latium and Campania, in the Sabine mountains, in Umbria, Picenum, and Samnium indicates a close resemblance to those which prevailed in Latium, with a preponderance perhaps of tribal grazing over individual landownership and agriculture. The development of town life in these lands was slow, and it was confined mostly to the districts bordering on the territories of the Greek cities and the Hellenized cities of Campania. Even in Campania such a city as Pompeii, with its early houses of the atrium-and-garden type, was more a city of well-to-do peasants than of rich merchants and great landowners.

The greater the growth of the influence of Rome, the more extensive her conquests, and the more numerous her colonies, the more widely did peasant husbandry spread over Italy. At the same time the isolated centres of capitalistic husbandry decayed. The history of the Greek cities of Southern Italy need not be repeated. One after another, with few exceptions, they fell victims to their Samnite neighbours. Some of them perished; some—all the cities of Campania, except Naples and a few others—entered on a new life of Samnitic cities, that is to say, of cities of peasants like Pompeii; few kept their purely Greek character. The fate of the Etruscan cities after the Roman conquest is unknown. Most of them were colonized by Latin settlers; some probably lived their old life, the life of landowners and serfs.

The Punic wars on the one hand accelerated the decay of the few centres of progressive economic life in Italy and in the Carthaginian dominions (as well as in the Greek part of Sicily) and on the other enlarged the range of Roman colonization. Roman and Latin colonists spread to the former Celtic lands in the north of Italy; some went to settle in the devastated regions of Central and Southern Italy. The new provinces of Rome—Sicily and Sardinia, and probably also Spain—did not immediately attract large numbers of Roman colonists. They preserved the features of economic life that had prevailed before the Roman conquest. The former kingdom of Hiero was ruled in his spirit and by his methods. The Punic parts of Sicily, Sardinia, and Spain remained for the Roman state what they had been for Carthage—granaries and storehouses of various metals. In fact, as is shown by the picture given by Cicero, even the Greek part of Sicily was reduced by the Romans to the position of a corn granary for Rome. Notwithstanding the annexation of the first dominions of the *Senatus Populusque Romanus*, the Roman state remained for a while a state of peasants. It was the peasant armies of Rome that vanquished the Phoenicians and it was the same peasants who conquered the East. The story of the Eastern conquests has already been told.

What were the economic results of Rome's victories over Carthage and the Eastern states? We must bear in mind that these victories were victories at once of the Roman state, that is, the peasant population, and of the military and political leaders of the state, who were members of the ruling hereditary aristocracy of Rome, the Roman senate. Being an achievement of the state, the victories meant for the state as such an enormous and steady increase in wealth. Besides acquiring immense sums of coined money and masses of precious objects in gold and silver, Rome became a large landowner. Vast tracts of arable and pasture land, forests, fisheries on lakes and rivers, mines, and quarries, both in Italy and in the former dominions of Carthage which were now Roman provinces, became the property of the state. The arable land, which accumulated gradually, was mostly divided among Roman citizens, who were planted out in new peasant settlements. Nevertheless, the increase in the number of Roman and Latin citizens did not keep pace with the increase of the *ager Romanus*, even in Italy, especially after the Gallic and the Punic wars. The foundation of new colonies was dictated more by political than by economic considerations. It is not surprising that most of the colonies were sent out to the north of Italy to protect the peninsula against dangerous invasions from the North: Rome never forgot the story of her capture by the Gauls, nor did she forget that the Gauls furnished Hannibal with his best soldiers. The south of Italy, devastated and decaying as it was, was less exposed to danger and, of course, less attractive to Roman and Latin settlers, except for Campania which, however, was only partially settled with Roman colonists and retained as a whole its Samnite aspect. We must assume that most of the cities of Campania remained faithful to the Romans during the Punic wars.

Large tracts of land, even arable land, thus became the property of the Roman state, not of individual Roman peasants.

But it was not only the state that was enriched by the Punic and the Oriental wars. The citizens of Rome shared in the enrichment. The lion's share fell to the leaders of the Roman army, members of the senatorial class. From time immemorial they were the richest among the Roman peasants, like the corresponding class in the Latin and the allied cities. During the wars of conquest they increased their wealth. Large numbers of men and cattle fell into their hands.[9] When cities were looted, they had the larger share of the booty. They returned to Italy with their 'belts' (or, as we should say, pockets) full of money, and, if they did not dispose of them at once, with gangs of slaves and herds of cattle. Further, it was men of the senatorial class that were sent by the senate to administer the new provinces, the former dominions of Carthage. We have seen that these dominions and the Greek part of Sicily, the kingdom of Hiero II, retained their ancient status or, in other words, were regarded by the Roman people as part of their property, as their estates (*praedia populi Romani*). As conquered lands, they were ruled by military officers, magistrates of the Roman people, with almost unlimited power. The same system, as already stated, was applied to the annexed territories of the East. The government of the provinces thus became a new source of wealth for the senatorial class. Finally, by force of circumstances, by the fact of their growing wealth, this class was led to take part both in the credit operations which, as we have seen, were the natural consequence of the Eastern conquests and, despite a strict prohibition, in the commercial activity which followed from the concentration of capital in the hands of Roman and Italian citizens.[10]

Apart from the senatorial class of Rome and a corresponding class in the allied cities of Italy, large numbers of Roman and Italian citizens shared in the profits which were derived from the dominating position of Rome in the civilized world. A large and influential class of business men grew up both in Rome and in Italy. Its members started on their career of economic prosperity by helping the state, including the allied cities, to exploit the extensive real estate which it owned—arable land, mines, forests, fisheries, houses, shops, &c. During the period of the wars of conquest they supplied the armies with food, clothing, and arms; they bought up war booty from the state and from the generals, the officers, and the common soldiers; they sold various goods to the soldiers during campaigns, and so forth. When the wars were over, they used the money acquired by these activities to lend to the allies and vassals of Rome, whether kings or cities; they farmed the collecting of taxes and other state revenues in the provinces; they also settled down in ever-increasing numbers in the provinces, taking an active part in the highly developed business life of the East, as money-lenders, merchants, owners of land and herds, and proprietors of houses and shops in the cities.[11]

Some of these business men never left Italy. Some went to the East, remained there for a long time, and gradually became absorbed in the local population.[12] But perhaps most of those shrewd and energetic fortune-hunters, after having made their money in the East, returned to Italy and invested their capital there. When Sicily, Sardinia, and parts of Spain, Gaul, and Africa became Roman provinces, the Roman business men extended their activity to these provinces as well. The richest members of this new body of capitalists, the equestrian class, lived mostly in Rome itself and aspired to the honour of admission into the senatorial order by being elected to one of the magistracies. But the majority remained in their native cities, whether Roman and Latin colonies in Italy or Italian cities allied to Rome. There they ranked next to the municipal senatorial class, if indeed they did not form part of it, and, along with it, formed the upper section of the population.

The influx of money, slaves, goods of different kinds, and cattle from the provinces stimulated the economic life of Italy. The capital which was now concentrated in the hands of Roman citizens and of residents in Italian cities remained partly in the provinces, but mostly came to Italy. The majority of the new rich acquired their fortunes through speculation. Naturally, after gaining wealth, they wanted to find for it the safest possible investment, which would guarantee them a quiet and pleasant life in familiar surroundings. The safest investment which would secure an idle and pleasant life in the cities was landed property, the next best was money-lending and investment in Italian industry. This tendency on the part of the large capitalists was welcome to the state. We have seen that it now owned an enormous amount of real estate both in Italy and in the provinces. Unless these large resources were to lie idle—which of course was not in the public interest, when money was needed for public buildings, for aqueducts, for the construction of military roads, and for the public worship of the gods, including the games—they had to be exploited in one way or another. The only way was to attract private capital and to interest it in their exploitation. It is not surprising, therefore, that the state encouraged the new capitalists to invest their money, above all, in the large areas of arable and pasture land which lay waste, especially in North and South Italy, after the horrors of the Gallic and Punic wars. There was no other means of bringing these lands under cultivation again. The number of Roman and Italian citizens resident in Italy and engaged in agriculture was reduced not only by losses during the wars but also by a steadily increasing emigration first to the East, and later to the West as well. There were no peasants available for settlement on the waste lands. On the other hand, there were large masses of slaves and there was a group of men willing to use them for the cultivation of the land. It is no wonder that the Roman senate gave these men every facility to restore the shattered economic life of Italy either by letting to them large tracts of land in the regular way through the censors, who had charge of such matters, or by allowing them to occupy the land informally with the obligation to pay to the state part of the produce of the land thus reclaimed.

That was the reason why in the second century B.C. a rapid concentration of landed property was steadily taking place. The landowners were either members of the senatorial and equestrian classes in Rome or the most energetic, shrewd, and thrifty of the residents in the Italian towns, whether allied cities or Roman and Latin colonies. These men never intended to take up residence on the farms and work the land with their own hands. From the very beginning they were landowners, not farmers, and therefore they swelled the numbers of landed proprietors in the cities to the detriment of the peasants, who lived in the country and were genuine farmers. The same class of men, on the other hand, by investing their money in industrial concerns and creating new shops and factories, which were run by means of slave-labour, revived the old-established industries of Campania and Etruria, at the expense of the small free artisans.[13]

The members of the old and of the new aristocracy of Rome and Italy, most of whom had acquired their wealth in the East and had become acquainted with the capitalistic system which prevailed there, introduced this system into Italian agriculture and industry. They were aided in their efforts by the Greek manuals of scientific and capitalistic agriculture, which were translated into Latin from Punic and from Greek and thus were made accessible to everybody in Italy. We may safely presume that similar manuals existed for industry, manuals at least which aimed at making generally accessible the developments of Greek technique in that particular field. In the Hellenistic East capitalistic activity in the sphere of agriculture was concentrated almost wholly on the production of wine and olive-oil, the chief articles exported by Hellenistic landowners; good returns were expected also from scientific cattle-breeding; corn-production was left almost wholly in the hands of the peasants, who were either small landowners or the tenants and serfs of great landlords. It need not surprise us that this system was taken over by the pupils and heirs of the Hellenistic landowners, the aristocracy and the *bourgeoisie* of Rome and the Italian cities. These men applied the capitalistic system of management to industrial concerns also, especially in Rome, Etruria, and Campania.

For many parts of Italy the capitalistic tendencies of the second century B.C. and the introduction of Hellenistic methods into Italian husbandry were, as we have seen before, not novelties but revivals of ancient forms of economy. The development of the capitalistic system was facilitated by many factors besides the existence of an ancient tradition and the fact that the rich natural resources of Italy made it a good field for the purpose. One of the most important was the abundance and the cheapness of labour. Enormous masses of slaves, mostly from Greece and Asia Minor, poured into Italy—they were partly skilled artisans, partly men who used to work on the scientifically managed estates of the Hellenistic kings and the Hellenistic *bourgeoisie*— and the stream never ceased to flow all through the second and first centuries.

On the other hand, there were now splendid opportunities for selling the goods which were produced in Italy, particularly olive-oil and wine, metal plate and pottery. The chief markets of Italy were the Western parts of the ancient world: Gaul, Spain, Africa on the one hand, and the North and the Danube provinces on the other. After the second Punic war Carthage was no longer the leading commercial power in the West. Her activity was

Description of Plate III

1. FUNERARY STELE FROM BOLOGNA. Museo Civico di Bologna. Gaetano dall' Olio, *Iscrizioni sepolcrali romane scoperte nell' alveo del Reno presso Bologna* (1922), pp. 121 ff., no. 59, fig. 27; *Not. d. Scavi*, 1898, pp. 479 ff., no. 15, fig. 3.

The inscription on the stele is a metrical warning to the reader not to profane the tomb: it does not contain the name of the deceased. The figure represents a *suarius* (swineherd) in a belted tunic, leaning on a stick; in front of him is a herd of seven pigs. It is to be noted that Northern Italy was famous for its swine from the prehistoric to the Roman period; Polyb. ii. 15. 3 says that the pork produced in the Po valley was enough to feed not only the population of Italy, but also the army; Strab. v. 1. 12 (218 c) adds that large quantities of pork were imported to Rome from this region. Cf. the funerary stele of a *mercator frumentarius*, Dall' Olio, op. cit., p. 118, no. 58, fig. 26, of the early 1st cent. A.D.

2–4. GROUP OF BRONZE FIGURINES. Found presumably at Città Castellana. The Metropolitan Museum of Art, New York. G. M. Richter, *Bull. Metr. Mus.* 1910, April, pp. 95 ff., fig. 1; *Catalogue of Bronzes of the Metr. Mus.*, nos. 712–725; Helen McClees, *The Daily Life of the Greeks and Romans* (1924), pp. 109 ff.; M. Rostovtzeff, 'Ein spätetruskischer Meierhof', *Antike Plastik (Festschrift W. Amelung)*, pp. 213 ff., pl. 17. The date is uncertain (see further below).

This group consists of figurines of two bulls, two cows, a pig and a sow, a ram, and a ewe, a goat and a she-goat. There are also two double yokes, a plough and a cart. The arrangement of figs. 2–4 is that adopted by the Metropolitan Museum. The two bulls certainly go with the plough and one of the double yokes, the two cows with the cart and the other yoke, or vice versa. The ensemble gives a complete picture of the stock and implements of a farmstead. The plough resembles that on pl. II. 2. It was made of wood, the joints of the wooden original being carefully reproduced. The pole is attached to the share-beam by pegs, and the share-beam to the share by thongs or ropes. The cart is 'merely a platform with a front-board and tail-board, mounted on solid wheels'. The whole is purely realistic, and the style does not permit of a date earlier than the Hellenistic period; the workmanship, however, is Italian, not Greek. By a curious coincidence, similar groups of domestic animals are represented on the archaic ships frequently found in early Etruscan, Italian, and Sardinian graves. The best example is that from the Tomba del Duce at Vetulonia. On the gunwale of the ship found in this grave are tied a dog, a pair of oxen united by a yoke (with remains of an iron plough), pigs, goats, and sheep; almost all are provided with baskets out of which they feed. Inside the barge is stowed chaff or ears of corn. If we are right in ascribing the figurines of Città Castellana to the Hellenistic period, we must assume an amazing persistence of traditions, which lasted almost unchanged for centuries. See Falchi, *Not. d. Scavi*, 1887, p. 503 and pl. XVII; id. *Vetulonia*, pp. 109 ff.; Montelius, *La Civilisation prim. en Italie*, pls. 184–188; D. Randall MacIver, *Villanovans and Early Etruscans* (1924), p. 118, pl. XXII, 1.

5. PART OF A FUNERARY MONUMENT. Sulmona. Museo Civic. M. Besnier, *Mem. Soc. Ant. de France*, viième sér. 1, 1906, pp. 242 ff.; M. Rostovtzeff in *Antike Plastik* (cf. under 2–4, above), p. 215, fig. 1. Late 1st cent. B.C., or early 1st cent. A.D.

The fragment shows scenes of peasant life. On the left a peasant, leaning on a stick or a plough, watches his sheep (and pigs?). To his right another peasant holds a pair of horses or of mules, harnessed to a loaded cart. Further to the right is a woman, probably the wife of the preceding. The relief perhaps represents the yearly migration from mountain to plain (or the reverse). The damaged inscription reads: 'I warn men; do not distrust yourselves': that is, 'work willingly, and you will be rich and happy'.

2. OXEN AND PLOUGH

3. COWS AND CART

1. SWINEHERD

4. PIGS, SHEEP, AND GOATS

5. PEASANT LIFE

III. LIFE IN ITALY IN THE LATE REPUBLICAN PERIOD

confined to the improvement of her agriculture, especially to extensive gardening and the culture of the vine and olive.[14] The heritage of Carthage passed to her ancient rivals, the Greeks of Sicily and of South Italy, now the faithful allies of Rome. The Eastern part of the Greek world, which was then suffering gradual economic decay, had no share in it. The destruction of Carthage completely and finally eliminated the Punic city as a commercial and economic power. Probably it was the Italian capitalists and landowners, led by Cato, who insisted on the destruction of the city. They were now large producers of wine and olive-oil, and they had every reason for endeavouring to get rid of a dangerous rival and to transform her territory from a land of gardens, vineyards, and olive-groves into one of vast cornfields.[15]

We must not underestimate the importance of the Western and of the Northern markets and their purchasing power. Gaul was a rich country, very eager to buy wine and olive-oil and manufactured goods, which the Greek cities of Gaul and (in the last quarter of the second century) that part of the country which was occupied by the Romans did not produce in sufficient quantities. In Spain and Britain the conditions of life were almost the same as in Gaul. The ruling class in Britain and in part of Spain belonged to the same Celtic stock. The Iberian portion of the Spanish peninsula had been accustomed for centuries to Greek and Phoenician imports. Even Germany and the Danube lands became gradually acquainted with the products of Greco-Italian economic activity.[16]

The developments we have described, which took place in Italy in the second century B.C., had far-reaching consequences for the political, social, and economic life of the country. Rome ceased to be a peasant-state ruled by an aristocracy of landowners, who were mostly richer peasants. There arose now all over Italy not only an influential class of business men, but a really well-to-do city *bourgeoisie*. In fact it was in the second century that Italy became for the first time urbanized, in the Greek sense of the word. Many ancient cities, partly Greek or Etruscan, enjoyed an unexpected revival of prosperity. Many towns, villages, market-places and hamlets not only received a city-constitution but also assumed the social and economic aspect of real cities. This was due to the growing importance of the already mentioned class of municipal shopowners and landed proprietors, who during their stay in the Hellenistic East had become habituated to the comfort of city life and had assimilated the ideals of the *bourgeois* class, and returned to promote city life and *bourgeois* ideals in Italy.

This new city *bourgeoisie* took no active part in the political life of the state. The leading position was still held by the Roman aristocracy. The *bourgeoisie* was too busy in organizing its economic life, and in building up the cities (such as Pompeii, with its beautiful houses of the Tufa period, adorned with artistic fronts and gorgeous wall paintings and mosaics) to aspire to any share in the public life of the capital. Moreover, this class was perfectly satisfied with the policy of the leaders of the Roman state. Their material interests and their political ideals mostly coincided with those of the Roman aristocracy. Like the members of that class, they generally invested their money in Italian lands, which were chiefly cultivated as vineyards and olive-groves or used as pasture lands. Hence the tacit support which they gave to the ruthless policy of Rome towards Carthage and to such measures of the senate as the prohibition of vine-planting in the newly acquired western provinces of Rome.[17] Like the senators and the Roman knights, they also invested their money in vine and olive land in Greece and Asia Minor.[18] Hence they supported the policy of the senate in the East, and had a large share in the financial and economic exploitation of the provinces in general. They were therefore staunch supporters of the government when it took the first steps on the path of imperialism.

The growing enrichment of the two upper classes of Roman citizens and of the Italian *bourgeoisie* had a profound influence on the political, social, and economic life of the Roman state. The investment of large capital in vine and olive land increased the value of land in many regions of Italy and induced many a peasant to sell his holding and either to settle in the cities or emigrate to the East. The peasant population in the districts which were suitable for planting with vines and olive-trees, or for cattle-breeding on capitalistic lines, gradually decreased. The never-ending wars which were carried on by the Roman senate after the defeat of Hannibal weakened the economic strength of the Italian peasants. This was one main reason why capital got hold of large tracts of land not only in Southern but also in Central Italy, the stronghold of the Italian peasantry, and why a large part of the peasant population of Central Italy was transformed from landowners into tenants, tilling the estates of Roman and municipal capitalists. In Etruria the evil was widely spread as early as the first half of the second century. This special case may be explained by the peculiar conditions which prevailed there. From remote antiquity Etruria had been a land of large estates and of huge masses of serfs.[19]

All these important developments caused, as is well known, an acute crisis in Italy. With the decrease of the peasant population and the increase of the numbers of slaves and of tenants, and with the accumulation of capital, particularly in the city of Rome, the Roman commonwealth was threatened by grave dangers. The traditional Roman aristocratic régime, based on a peasant army, gradually degenerated into an oligarchy of opulent noble families, while the military strength of Italy, based on the Italian peasantry, dwindled. We have to remember that only landowners were obliged to serve in the Roman army—another reason, by the way, why peasants who were overburdened with military service should sell their lands to large proprietors and remain on them in the capacity of tenants.

The first act of the political and social drama, which now began to be enacted in Italy, was the attempt at a radical political, economic, and social reform initiated by Tiberius Gracchus, and carried on after his death by his brother Gaius. Both Tiberius and Gaius were supported by the rural population of Italy and by the landless proletariate of the Italian cities. Their chief aim was similar to that of many revolutionary leaders in the Greek cities. Redistribution of land and the consequent restoration of the peasantry and of the army formed at once the starting-point and the goal of their reforms, while the introduction of a popular government under the leadership of one man was the necessary sequel of such a revolutionary movement. It is no wonder that the tenants and the landless proletarians gave the Gracchi wholehearted support.[20] This is not the place to describe the internal troubles which followed the first attempt at a political and social revolution. It will be enough to indicate, in a few words, the underlying forces which gave the movement its peculiar and complicated aspect.

The great crisis of the Roman state was not surmounted by the Gracchi. Their activity did not even produce a redistribution of land on a large scale, much less a complete change in the political structure of the Roman state or a regeneration of the Roman peasantry. The Roman peasant-state could not be restored: it was dead for ever. Some new peasant plots were of course created, some landless proletarians were provided with holdings, some large estates were confiscated. But soon the process was first arrested and then finally stopped by the stubborn resistance of the ruling oligarchy. The only result of the Gracchan revolution was that it stirred up large masses of the Italian population and, for the first time in the history of Rome, drew a sharp line of cleavage between rich and poor, 'oppressors' and 'oppressed'. The struggle between those two classes once begun could not be ended.

The main issue of the struggle—the land question—was, however, somewhat obscured in the next stage of the development of civil troubles in Italy. Instead of, or along with, the land question another purely political question occupied for a time the foreground. This was the question of the political rights of the Roman allies, especially the *bourgeois* class in the Italian cities. Their hopes of becoming members of the Roman commonwealth, with the same rights as the citizens of Rome, had been aroused by the promises of the Gracchi and were, as it seemed, hopelessly dashed by the oligarchic reaction. But the allies did not yield. A bitter and bloody war ensued, a war which brought ruin and devastation on Central Italy and particularly on the flourishing lands occupied by the North-Samnite tribes. It ended in a compromise. The allies gave up their scheme of a new Italian federal state, the Romans granted the franchise practically to all the citizens of the allied cities. The claims of the allies could not be disregarded, lest the Italo-Roman state should cease to exist.[21]

After this episode the main struggle was resumed on a larger scale. The incorporation of the Italians in the Roman citizen body swelled the numbers of the discontented, among whom the landless proletariate bulked largely; almost all of them were ready to take an active part in the contest. On the other side, the municipal *bourgeoisie* strengthened the ranks of the supporters of the existing order. Not only was the struggle enlarged and complicated by the new participants, but its aspect changed almost completely. When the dangerous invasion of some Celto-Germanic tribes into Italy, shortly before the 'Social' War, and the 'Social' War itself had shown the impossibility of adhering to the principle of enrolling in the army only a part of the population, consisting primarily of landowners, the character of the Roman army and its social composition gradually underwent a radical alteration. After the reform initiated by Marius it was no longer a militia of Italian peasants but a more or less professional long-service army of proletarians and poor peasants. On the other hand, the popular assembly of Rome, which consisted after the 'Social' War of a ridiculously small minority of the Roman citizens, ceased to be a true representative of the aspirations of the Roman citizens and became a tool in the hands of clever politicians. Far more important as expressing the wishes of a large body of Romans, and far more efficient as an instrument in the hands of ambitious leaders, was the new army.

The new army owed its origin not merely to barbarian danger and the civil war but mainly, like the civil war itself, to the Roman Empire, the *Imperium Romanum*, the Roman world-state. Without such an army the world-state could not continue to exist; it was bound to fall to pieces. This was shown by every war that had been conducted by Rome between the conclusion of the great Oriental wars and the reform of Marius. Such minor wars as that against Jugurtha in Africa and that against the Celto-Iberians in Spain cost the Roman state enormous losses in men and money, and added nothing to the glory of the Roman arms. A serious complication, the invasion of Italy by Celtic and German tribes, demonstrated finally both the weakness of the Roman militia and the incapacity of the non-professional generals to transform this militia into a real fighting force. Two improvements, closely connected with each other, were therefore needed: the creation of an armed force having more or less the character of a standing army, and new professional generals who should devote their whole life and activity to military problems.

As the army in its new shape was the greatest organized force in Rome, its chiefs were bound not only to represent the military strength of the state but also to become its political leaders, and so gradually to depose both the senatorial class and the popular assembly of Rome, the *Senatus Populusque Romanus*, from the position which they had hitherto occupied. The main task which confronted these new leaders was the adaptation of the city-state system to the needs of a world-state, its transformation into a new form of polity capable of governing the vast territories which now formed the Roman Empire. Thus the struggle which had been begun by the Gracchi as a fight for the restoration of the old peasant-state, and had been supported by the masses of land-less proletarians and poor peasants who fought under the old war-cry of 'redistribution of land', became a struggle for the complete remodelling of the state and for the remoulding of its machinery into an instrument better adapted to the needs of a world-empire.

The first to realize the new aspect of the struggle, and to use the new factor in the political life of Rome to carry out his policy, was L. Cornelius Sulla, one of the Roman generals in the 'Social' War. The main political idea which animated him in a bitter revolutionary fight against the supporters of the Gracchan pro-gramme—'all power to the political assembly of Rome led by the elected magistrates of the city proletariate, and restoration of the old peasant-state'—was the adaptation of the rule of the senatorial minority to the needs of the Empire. His own role in the new state was that of a helper and moderator, whose influ-ence on public affairs was based on his personal popularity both with the army and with the great body of Roman citizens, espe-cially the upper classes. It may appear strange that in a struggle of such a character he was supported by an army which con sisted of proletarians and poor peasants, and which would seem bound to be on the side of his adversaries. But we have to remem-ber that the new army always had in view its personal interests only; and Sulla promised his troops greater and more tangible advantages than did his foes—war booty in his campaigns against Mithradates, land and money after their return to Italy, and (not least attractive) a higher social standing in their native cities for the rest of their lives. We must bear in mind also that the army of Sulla still consisted of the old stock of Roman citizens, who were afraid of the new mass of citizens enfranchised by the 'Social' war. The latter were supported in their claims by Marius and his partisans and successors.

After the death of Sulla the civil war was immediately re-sumed and became essentially a struggle for power, a struggle between the most capable and most ambitious members of the senatorial aristocracy for the controlling voice in the govern-ment of the state. The combatants stood for no definite political programme, no radical social or economic reform. The fight was a fight of personal influence and of personal ambitions alike in the capital and in the field. An extraordinary military command, which was the only way out of the serious entanglements that periodically arose from the complicated political and military life of the world-empire, gave to the best men of the Roman aristocracy the chance of getting into closer contact with the army and of attaching it to themselves personally by strong ties of gifts and promises; and this in its turn made the army-leader master of the state, so long as he kept his popularity with the soldiers. His rivals used the same methods and the same means. Thus the civil war became practically a war between well-organized and well-trained armies led by ambitious politicians. The majority of the Roman citizens and, naturally, the provincial population took no active part in that war. All that they wanted was peace and order. The combatants were the professional soldiers of the Roman Empire. They fought because they expected a rich compensation at the close of hostilities in the shape of land and money.[22]

That is the reason why the next act in the tragedy of the civil wars, the contest between Caesar and Pompey, was so confused and so little clear in its main issues. The war was won by Caesar because he was a better organizer, a military genius, and a man of immense personal influence with his soldiers. Pompey's public career had differed but slightly from Caesar's, and the difference, of course, was beyond the understanding of the soldiers of either army. The support given by Pompey to the senatorial régime was never taken seriously even by the senators. They chose as their leader the man who seemed to them less dangerous than Caesar, and they expected to find in him a milder master in the event of victory. The mass of the Roman citizens took no part on either side, unless they were obliged to.

Caesar perished at the hands of a group of conspirators before his civil work had wellnigh begun. We have no means of judging what would have happened if he had had time to reorganize the state. There are some indications that he had a definite programme of reforms in his mind, but it is beyond our power to reconstruct it in detail. Some historians in antiquity and the majority of modern scholars maintain that Caesar intended to create a real monarchy, based not only upon the Roman citizen-body, but also upon the Roman Empire as a whole. Pompey, on the other hand, it is claimed, was the representative of an idea which enjoyed great sympathy among the upper classes of the population of Rome, namely, the possibility of a 'principate', or the rule of the best among the good, that is among the members of the senatorial order.[23]

The ensuing conflicts between the murderers of Caesar on the one side, and the generals and the adopted sons of Caesar on the other, show the usual chaotic character of a struggle for power. The veterans of Caesar supported Antony and Octavius because they expected from them, and from them only, the fulfilment of Caesar's promises of lands and money. Some enthusiasts, mostly intellectuals, who believed in the tyranny of Caesar and the blessings of liberty, as represented by the senate and the murderers of Caesar, fought on the side of Brutus and Cassius. The rest who fought on either side fought because they were mobilized, because they were promised land and money, and because they believed that they were fighting for the restoration of peace and order.

The victory of Octavius and Antony over the murderers did not clear up the situation. Meanwhile Octavius—after his adoption by Caesar sometimes called Octavianus, and later named Augustus—endeavoured gradually to create among the Italian population the impression, already used as a means of propaganda by the murderers, that Caesar's intention had been to establish a pure monarchy and that Antony was endeavouring to achieve the same aim. As Octavian spent almost all his time in Italy, and Antony almost all his time abroad, residing in the East, the propaganda was fairly successful. The mistakes committed by Antony, his liaison and later his marriage with Cleopatra, made the rumours spread by Octavian that Antony was intending to make Italy a province of Egypt—which was of course nonsense—the more credible to the masses of the Roman citizens in Italy.

The Roman citizens, however, were alarmed by the prospect of losing their privileges and of being submerged by the population of the provinces. Accordingly, in the contest between Octavian and Antony the citizens of Rome, especially the powerful city *bourgeoisie* all over Italy and even the majority of the higher classes, the senators and knights, were ready to support Octavian against Antony, and that not merely for the sake of getting land

and money. The battle of Actium was the first battle in the civil wars which was won, not by the armed proletariate fighting for its own material profit, but by the mass of the Italian citizens, inspired by the idea that they were struggling for the existence of the Roman state and liberty against Oriental barbarism and slavery. Octavian fought his last battle in the civil war, not as a revolutionary leader fighting for personal power, but as a champion of Roman ideas, a champion of the Roman past and the Roman future. He fought for them against the spectre of an Oriental kingship. If the power of Octavian, won by the battle of Actium, was to endure, it was essential for him never to forget how and why he had been victorious at Actium.

The period of the civil wars was a period of great suffering for almost every member of the Roman state, not only in Italy but in the provinces. In Italy many perished in battle or in the privations of the campaigns. Many prominent leaders were killed during the renewed periods of political terrorism, many, both rich and poor, were deprived of their possessions, which were sold by the leaders to fill their empty treasuries or divided among the victorious soldiers, the veterans of the revolutionary armies. Economic conditions were thoroughly unstable. Nobody knew precisely what would happen to him tomorrow. Psychologically, Italy was completely unbalanced and wanted one thing and one thing only—peace.

The strength of this craving for peace is shown, for instance, by the early poems of Horace and Virgil. It is very instructive to follow, as has often been done, the psychological development of Horace in the dark years after the battle of Philippi. Like millions of the inhabitants of the Roman Empire, and especially those who were Roman citizens, he ultimately, after a period of sheer despair, fixed his hopes on the final victory of Augustus, who promised to put an end to civil war. Augustus was well acquainted with the prevailing mood of the population of the Empire. Peace was the universal cry. Everybody was ready to accept Augustus and his rule, provided that he would restore peace and tranquillity. Restoration of peace was therefore imposed on Augustus; it was, so to say, an indispensable condition of the permanence of his power. We shall see in the next chapter that Augustus recognized and understood the feelings of the people, and acted accordingly.[24]

However complete may have been the change in the mood of the population, even as compared with the times before and after the death of Caesar, it is clear that from the economic and social point of view the situation in Italy did not alter very much during the civil wars. Italy remained the centre of the economic life of the ancient world, almost as flourishing and prosperous as before. Varro, in the second half of the period of civil war, depicted Italy as the most flourishing country in the world as regards natural resources and cultivation.[25] He was perfectly right. The civil wars did not undermine the foundations of the social and economic life of the past. The same gorgeous villas with their marble porticoes, surrounded by shady parks, gleamed on the hills and on the sea-shore, in Latium, in Etruria, in Campania. The same model farms, run on capitalistic lines and organized on Hellenistic patterns with a dense slave-population, in which the cultivation of vineyards, olive-groves, gardens, fields and meadows was effected under the supervision of overseers (themselves slaves), were spread all over South and Central Italy. The owners of these *villae rusticae* were the big capitalists of Rome and the rich municipal *bourgeoisie*. Remains of such villas have been excavated since the eighteenth century in the neighbourhood of Pompeii, Stabiae, and Herculaneum, and some of them probably date from the first century B.C.[26] Pasture lands on which grazed hundreds of thousands of sheep and goats, oxen and cows, tended by groups of armed slave-shepherds, were the distinctive features of the economic life of Apulia, Samnium, some parts of Latium, and a large portion of Sicily, Sardinia, and Corsica.[27] On the other hand, villages and scattered farms of small landowners were still characteristic of part of Etruria, of Umbria, Picenum, and the Po valley. In villages and farms of the same type lived the tenants of the large landed proprietors, producing corn for themselves and for the markets of the neighbouring cities. In these parts of Italy men like Domitius Ahenobarbus, the contemporary of Caesar and Pompey, possessed such large tracts of land that they were able to promise to thousands of their landless soldiers plots of ground which would provide them with adequate means of subsistence. He and Pompey were able to form large regular armies from the ranks of their tenants (*coloni*) and slaves. Pompey was not exaggerating when he said that he had only to stamp his foot on the ground to get thousands of soldiers. Without doubt he meant chiefly those veterans who were his clients and the people on his own estates.[28]

The cities of Italy were inhabited by a well-to-do, sometimes even rich *bourgeoisie*. Most of them were landowners; some were owners of houses, let at rent, and of various shops; some carried on money-lending and banking operations. The largest and the richest city was Rome. Rome grew feverishly during the second and the first century B.C. The best sites were occupied by the beautiful palaces of the powerful magnates of Rome, senators and knights. Business was daily transacted at the exchange, near the temple of Castor in the large public *place* of Rome, the Forum. Here crowds of men bought and sold shares and bonds of tax-farming companies, various goods for cash and on credit, farms and estates in Italy and in the provinces, houses and shops in Rome and elsewhere, ships and storehouses, slaves and cattle. In the shops of the Forum and of the adjacent streets thousands of free artisans and shopowners and thousands of slaves, agents, and workmen of rich capitalists produced goods and sold them to customers. In the less central parts of Rome masses of unemployed or half-idle proletarians lived in large tenement houses willing, for a living, to sell their votes and their fists to anybody who had money enough to pay for them.[29]

One wave of terrorism, one spasm of civil war, after another, came and went. They carried away some of the members of the groups mentioned above. But the groups as such remained intact and unchanged, the missing being replaced by their heirs and by new-comers. A group of landowners, residing in one of the cities of Italy, became deprived of their paternal lands, and veterans of the revolutionary armies—themselves born in Italy—farmers, peasants, and landowners, took over their country houses, their fields, sometimes their city residences. The deprived landowners were, of course, ruined. They emigrated to the large cities or to the provinces, increased the numbers of workless proletarians, entered the ranks of the revolutionary armies, and so on. But the change was hardly felt by Italy in general. The veterans were all Roman citizens. All, or almost all, of them were born in the fields and in the mountains of Italy. Generations of city proletarians hardly existed even in Rome. The proletarian of today was a landowner of yesterday, a soldier or a business agent, an artisan or a menial workman of tomorrow. Islands of such new

Description of Plate IV

THE FUNERAL MONUMENT OF M. VERGILIUS EURYSACES. Rome, Via Casilina, near the Porta Maggiore. Canina–O. Jahn in *Ann. d. Inst. di Corr. Arch.* 1838, pp. 219 ff. (the monument) and 240 ff. (the bas-reliefs); cf. *Mon. Ined. dell' Inst.* ii, tab. 58; H. Blümner, *Technologie und Terminologie*, i² (1912), pp. 40 ff., figs. 13–15 (from photographs). Late Republican or early Augustan period.

The monument has a peculiar form, not easy to explain. The intention of Eurysaces was to remind the spectator of his trade both by the form of the monument and by its inscriptions and bas-reliefs. The same inscription is repeated on all the sides of the monument: *Est hoc monimentum Marcei Vergilei Eurysacis, pistoris, redemptoris; apparet* (with slight variations). See *CIL* i. 1013–15; vi. 1958; Dessau, *ILS* 7460 *a–c*, cf. the funeral inscription of his wife, *CIL* i. 1016; vi. 1958; Dessau, *ILS* 7460 *d*, and of one of his friends, *CIL* i. 1017; vi. 9812. The inscription means: 'This is the monument of Marcus Vergilius Eurysaces, baker and contractor; he was also an *apparitor* (attendant of a magistrate).' The bas-reliefs, which are reproduced here from the drawings of the *Mon. Ined.*, represent various operations of the bakery trade: the first is that of sieving and washing grain, the second grinding, the third kneading, the fourth rolling and baking (1 and 2), while the last shows the delivery of the bread to the magistrates for whom Eurysaces worked as a contractor (3). It is a typical picture of a big business concern of the late Republican or early Imperial period, in which scores and perhaps hundreds of working-men, both slave and free, were engaged. On (2) the baking is represented as preceding the mixing.

1

2

3

Bas-reliefs of the monument of Eurysaces

IV. TOMB OF EURYSACES

settlers in a densely populated land were readily absorbed both in the country and in the cities. How easy the absorption was, is shown by the example of Pompeii, where a colony of Sullan veterans gradually amalgamated with the original population of the city.

We must not, indeed, minimize the importance of the periodical redistribution of landed property during the civil wars. According to careful calculations, not less than half a million men received holdings in Italy during the last fifty years of that troubled period.[30] After the great changes of the 'Social' war these redistributions were perhaps the most potent factor in the history of the Romanization and Latinization of Italy: witness Pompeii, where the Oscan language was almost completely replaced by Latin in the first century B.C. On the other hand, we must not exaggerate the importance of this change of ownership from the strictly economic point of view. Even if we admit that most of the veterans became regular peasant farmers who worked the land with their own hands—which, of course, was true only of a portion of them—the creation of such new peasant properties could hardly change the economic trend, which moved towards the formation of estates owned by men who never resided on them but regarded them merely as one of their sources of income. In any case it is certain that as the civil wars proceeded, even the grants of land to veterans tended more and more to create, not new peasant holdings, but new landed estates for city residents. This is shown by the constantly increasing size of the holdings which were given to the veterans. For the most part, therefore, the veterans increased the numbers not of the peasants but of the city residents, not of the working but of the *bourgeois* class in Italy.[31] Nor did the redistribution of land affect the growth of large estates. Some of the large estates which were confiscated by the military leaders in the civil wars may have been parcelled out among small landowners. As a rule, however, either such estates were kept by the temporary rulers of the state and formed the basis of their personal influence, which rested on the number of clients dependent on them, or the land was sold for cash to fill their continually depleted treasuries.

Much more important were the changes in the provinces. Though the provinces, apart from the Roman citizens residing in them, took no active part in the civil wars, they were the real sufferers. They had to bear the enormous expense of these wars. The heaviest burden fell on the provinces of the East, which have already been dealt with. Let us glance for a moment at the situation in the West.

For the first time in the history of Rome the Western provinces underwent a systematic colonization from Italy. The attempts of C. Gracchus and of some of his successors to carry out such a colonization in the West, particularly in Africa, had proved futile. Nothing of importance was achieved. But during the civil wars one wave of Roman emigrants after another flowed to Gaul, Spain, and Africa. The most notable settlements were the new Roman colonies organized by the leaders of the revolutionary movement, especially those of Marius in Africa* and of Caesar, Antony, and Augustus in Gaul, Spain, and Africa, and even in some parts of the East, particularly Asia Minor. These organized settlements, however, were not the only ones that appeared in the provinces during the civil wars. Important bodies of Italians settled there on their own account. As traders, money-lenders, agents of the tax-farming companies, they associated themselves with the Roman colonists and the native population of the cities in Gaul, Spain, Africa, and Numidia. The story of many a city in Africa and Numidia shows how important an element such bodies of Roman citizens were in the civic life of these countries. We may take as examples the city of Thugga in Africa and the city of Cirta, the capital of the Numidian kings, in Numidia. Neither of these settlements was originally a military colony (Cirta received a Roman colony only in 44 B.C.), but in both the population of Roman citizens played a leading part in economic and social life. There cannot be the slightest doubt that there were similar emigrations to the Greek and half-Hellenized native cities of Southern Spain and of the earliest Gallic province of Rome. And, although no direct evidence is available, we may suppose that some of the Italian emigrants, the poorer *coloni* of the large estates of Italy, readily listened to the suggestions of their masters that they should emigrate to the happy lands of Africa, and there rent better and larger plots of land from the rich landowners of the province.

The flow of Roman citizens which in the earlier times set mostly towards the East was thus diverted in the first century B.C.

* See below, Chap. VII, p. 318.

to the West. The conditions in the East were so bad, the dangers which threatened the Roman settlers (as had been shown by the massacre of Mithradates) were so real, the opportunities so reduced by Roman misgovernment, that the large mass of emigrants preferred to go to the new lands of the West and to try their fortune there. If Gaul, Spain, and Africa became more or less Romanized, this result was due to the intense colonization of these lands during the civil wars. New capital, new energy, new habits of life reached the Western provinces from Italy, and after the Italians came Greeks and Orientals. How many of these new settlers went to the provinces as manual workers and peasants we do not know. The majority were certainly not common peasants, tenants, and artisans; most were landowners, traders, and business men who settled down, not in the country, but in the cities.[32]

If we seek for a general formula to express the political, economic, and social conditions of the Roman state in the first century B.C., we can hardly find one that is short and comprehensive. From the political point of view, the Roman state was an Empire ruled *de jure* by the mass of Roman citizens, who as a matter of fact were represented by a governing body of rich and noble citizens, members of the senate. The provinces were regarded as estates of this ruling community. Within the community the structure of the city-state was maintained almost intact, with only some slight modifications. From the social point of view, the community consisted of a rather small ruling class, residing in the city of Rome and mostly large landowners in Italy and in the provinces. A numerous and influential class of business men and landowners formed, along with the senatorial class, the upper section of the population both in the capital and in the cities of Italy. Some of these business men were immensely rich, some less opulent. The majority of them lived the life of *rentiers*. The real working-class consisted of retail-traders and artisans in the cities, of slaves in the offices and shops of the *bourgeoisie*, of free peasant landowners in the country, and of a huge and ever-growing multitude of slaves and tenants on the estates of the landed *bourgeoisie*. The same distribution in groups was reproduced among the bodies of Roman citizens in the provinces.

From the economic point of view, we have almost the same type of capitalism which had existed in the East before and during the Hellenistic period. Goods were freely exchanged inside the Roman state and with its neighbours. The most important branch of trade was, not that which dealt in luxuries, but the exchange of articles of prime necessity—corn, fish, oil, wine, flax, hemp, wool, lumber, metals, and manufactured products. Foodstuffs and raw materials came from the outlying parts of the Greco-Roman world; oil, wine, and manufactured goods from the Greek cities and from Italy. Money business and banking affairs became almost the exclusive privilege of Italy and above all of Rome, as most of the coined money was concentrated in the hands of Roman capitalists. Political conditions contributed very largely not only to make this business a monopoly of Rome, and especially of the bankers of the capital itself, but also to give it the character of usury, which hampered very seriously the sound development of a normally growing capitalistic system. Another handicap was the rather slow growth of industry, an arrest both of the development of industrial technique and of the transition from the workshop to the true factory. The workshop persisted in being the leading method of production, and even the fact that many shops of the same kind belonged to one man did not transform them into a factory in the modern sense of the word. We must, however, bear in mind that the work in the workshops was highly differentiated, and that most of them, especially in large industrial centres, produced their goods not to special order but for an indefinite market. Among the large industrial centres of the ancient world some Italian cities began to play a prominent part, such as Capua and Cales for metal wares and pottery, Tarentum for woollen stuffs and silver-plate, and Arretium for a special kind of red varnished pottery. Italy, however, never became the leader in industrial development. This role was reserved for the cities of the Greek East.[33]

V. STATUE OF AUGUSTUS FROM PRIMA PORTA
(Rome, Vatican)

II

AUGUSTUS AND THE POLICY OF RESTORATION AND RECONSTRUCTION

THERE is a wide divergence of opinion among modern scholars about the character and the significance of the activity of Augustus. Beyond doubt he was a great man, and the constitution which he gave to the Roman state went on developing for at least two centuries on the lines which he had originally laid down. Beyond doubt, also, with him there begins a new era in the history of the ancient world, an era which we are wont to call the age of the Roman Empire. On these points all modern scholars are in complete agreement. But as soon as we endeavour to define more closely the character of what we call the reforms of Augustus, the divergences begin, and they seem to be irreconcilable. Some scholars insist on the point that the work of Augustus was a work of restoration and of restoration only, that his main object was to bring back the ancient Roman state. Others claim for Augustus the title of a revolutionary reformer, who succeeded in creating under the cover of certain ancient formulae a brand-new constitution, a purely monarchical rule by the chief of the Roman army. Others again take up an intermediate position.[1]

I do not propose to discuss these theories in all their variations, but only to adduce some facts and to put forward my own explanation of them, concentrating attention on the social and economic aspects of the question. It has been shown in the last chapter that the termination of the civil wars was imposed by the almost unanimous will of the population of the Roman Empire, especially its more active and influential portion, the large masses of Roman citizens in Italy and in the provinces. All classes of this citizen-population insisted on one main point, the termination of civil war and the restoration of peace. If Augustus desired to consolidate his power, he had first of all to make the restoration of peace possible. Everybody was wearied and disgusted, and confidently expected the battle of Actium to be the last battle of the civil wars.

Yet the leading part of the population of the Empire was not ready to accept any and every solution of the problem. The citizens of Rome had fought for the restoration of the *Roman* state, not for the creation of an Oriental monarchy, even under a disguise. They wanted peace, but peace for the *Roman* state. This meant that they were ready to support Augustus so long as he was willing and able, in restoring peace, to maintain all the privileges which the Roman citizens of all classes enjoyed in the state. By his appeal to the patriotism of the Roman citizens in his struggle with Antony, Augustus had pledged himself to keep the promise tacitly made to them not to diminish the rights and the privileges of Roman citizens, but rather to increase them, or in any case to define them better and consolidate them. Only under these conditions were the citizens of Rome ready and willing to recognize Augustus as their leader and as the constitutional chief of the Roman community, of the *Senatus Populusque Romanus*.

Thus far the task of Augustus was clear and comparatively easy, and it was, in the main, a work of restoration. No far-reaching reforms were needed or expected. Most of the reforms which were necessary to adapt the Roman constitution, the constitution of a city-state, to the requirements of a world-state had already been introduced by the predecessors of Augustus, the military leaders of the Roman state during the civil wars— Marius, Sulla, Pompey, Caesar, Antony, and Augustus himself. All that was required was to put the machinery of the Roman state in motion again and to direct its working.

But with restoration alone a lasting revival of the Roman state could not be regarded as secured. The civil war had created two new elements in the state machinery which could not be disregarded and discarded in a work of pure restoration, since they were the chief moving forces in that machinery. These elements were the now permanent army and its commander-in-chief the Emperor Augustus, *Imperator Caesar divi filius Augustus*. The army was there. It could not be disbanded, as it was urgently needed to guard external and internal peace. No tranquillity and order, no peace and prosperity were possible without a strong, well-disciplined, well-paid army. And the army, or at any rate the nucleus of it, had to be an army of Roman citizens, if the Roman citizens were to keep their position of masters and rulers in the Empire.

The civil war had shown, on the other hand, that a permanent well-disciplined army was efficient only if commanded by one man, a man whom the army recognized as its chief, not one who was imposed on it by the Roman people and the Roman senate, but one who was loved and trusted, if not formally chosen, by the soldiers and officers. Herein lay the great antinomy of the new conditions in the Roman Empire. The new state was to be a restoration of the old one, a restoration of the constitutional state of the Republican period, but at the same time it had to keep the main instruments of the revolutionary period, the revolutionary army and its revolutionary leader. Many solutions of this problem had been proposed by the predecessors of Augustus. One, the solution of Sulla and perhaps of Pompey, was that the army should be given back to the senate and that the chief of the army should rule in the capacity of an ordinary magistrate of the Roman state. The other, which seems to have been the solution planned by Caesar, was to keep the army under the command of the supreme magistrate of the Roman people, completely debarring the senate from all relations with it. Augustus chose, in the main, the second solution.

It was out of the question to give the army back to the senate. To have done so would have involved a renewal of the civil wars, as the army was not willing to accept such an arrangement. The only possibility for Augustus was to remain head of the army, its commander-in-chief, and not to allow any one to have an equal share in the command. Practically this meant the creation of a military tyranny along with the restored constitutional state, the maintenance of a revolutionary institution side by side with the normal administration of the state. And—what was of no little moment—it meant also that it was in theory fully open to the army to replace its commander by another, if that commander ceased to be loved and trusted by it or did not fulfil his obligations towards it.

The political work of Augustus was, therefore, not a restoration of what existed *before* the civil wars but a consolidation and readjustment of what was created *by* the civil wars. Some measures were taken to make the army as inoffensive as possible from the political point of view. The legions were stationed not in Italy but on the frontiers of the Roman state. In Italy there was only a small body of troops, the praetorian guard of the emperor.

The legions and the guard consisted of Roman citizens only, and were commanded by officers who belonged exclusively to the two upper classes of Roman citizens, the senatorial and equestrian classes. The auxiliary forces, which were supplied by the provinces, were regarded as irregular troops, troops of the 'allies', and were commanded by Roman officers. The fleet, which was stationed in Italy, was manned by Roman citizens of the lowest class, the freedmen, and by provincials. The freedmen served also in the seven regiments of the city firemen. Alongside of the urban cohorts they acted as the policemen of Rome. All these measures, however, were futile. As a matter of fact, the army was the master of the state, and in the restored Roman Republic the emperor ruled wholly through the army and for so long as the army was willing to keep him and to obey. An army of professionals, who served for sixteen, twenty, or twenty-five years (according as they belonged to the praetorian or legionary or auxiliary branch of the service), an army of actual or prospective Roman citizens, actual or future members of the sovereign Roman people, could not be easily eliminated from the political life of the state, and if it was not eliminated, it was bound to be practically (though not constitutionally) the decisive political force.

There was no other solution of the problem. If the Roman citizens who had won the war for Augustus were to remain the ruling class in the Empire, they had to fulfil their first duty, the duty of defending the state from enemies and of protecting their own power within the Empire. The army had to be permanent, and had to be an army of professionals: no militia could defend the frontiers of the Roman state. The military technique of that age was too complicated to be learned in a short time. A short-service army in the Roman Empire was an impossibility, as an efficient fighting force required many years of assiduous training. If the army was to be a long-service army of professionals, it could not, as a rule, be levied compulsorily. It had to be recruited more or less from volunteers, so long as there were enough men willing to enlist. Men levied compulsorily would never make good professional soldiers, ready to devote their lives to the service. This being so, the army must be adequately paid, and the service must be as attractive as possible. Thus the expense of the army was a very heavy burden on the finances of the state.

In fact, however, the army remained quiet all through the long period of the rule of Augustus, even towards the end of his rule when the serious complications on the Danube and on the Rhine—the 'revolt' of the Pannonians and of the Dalmatians and the 'united front' of the German tribes—made military service very dangerous and rendered the task of completing and increasing the legions, cohorts, and *alae* very difficult. Yet, even in these difficult times, when recourse was had to compulsory levies, the army was almost completely quiet and did not attempt to take any part in political life. The explanation of this fact is to be found in the character of its composition in the time of Augustus.

The army of Augustus was no longer an army of proletarians. Military service, especially in the first years of Augustus' reign, was comparatively remunerative and not very perilous. Meritorious service meant advancement, and advancement did not stop after the service came to its normal end. Good subaltern and non-commissioned officers either remained in the army on higher pay or entered the ranks of civil officials, personal agents of the emperor. Common soldiers were sure to receive at the close of their service a parcel of land or a good bounty sufficient to build up a home and family or to raise one which had in fact, if not in a legal form, been started in the period of military service. Many people, therefore, even people of higher social standing, were now willing to join the ranks. Moreover, the army did not now consist exclusively of Italian-born men. After the civil wars Italy by itself was no longer able to supply the army with recruits. So the Romanized provinces, and even some parts of the East, came to the rescue and furnished good and trustworthy soldiers, few of whom probably were proletarians. Not all of them were Roman citizens, but Augustus was ready, in case of need, to grant the franchise to every recruit who promised to be a good soldier and who was Romanized enough to understand written and spoken Latin, or civilized enough to learn it quickly and efficiently. These provincial soldiers were perhaps even more loyal and more reliable than the Italians, since for many of them service in the army meant an enormous advance in social status. Equally reliable were the auxiliary troops, who consisted of provincials, slightly Romanized or even almost untouched by Greek or Roman civilization. For them enrolment in the army meant

Roman citizenship after the end of their service, and that was a high privilege. Little wonder if for them political questions and political aspirations practically did not exist.[2]

The most important point, however, was that the army was drawn from the population of the Empire in general, and represented all classes of the population—the senatorial and equestrian orders, the Roman citizens of Italy and the provinces, the Romanized and Hellenized residents in the Eastern provinces (whether they lived in town or country), the countless tribes and peoples which did not yet share in the ancient civilization of the city. As such, the army reflected the mood of the population. Moreover, Roman citizens had learned from time immemorial to obey the state. The state was now embodied in the person of Augustus who was its legal head, recognized as such by the senate and the Roman people. To obey him was, therefore, the duty of every loyal citizen of Rome and still more of every ally and provincial. There cannot be any doubt that with the masses of the people throughout the Empire Augustus was exceedingly popular, if we may use this modern word to describe the half-religious awe which the Romans felt towards the new ruler. For them he was really a superman, a higher being, the saviour, the restorer, the bringer of peace and prosperity. We may explain the termination of the civil wars as we will. We may say that war ceased because the population of the Roman Empire was tired and disgusted and unwilling to fight any more. But we must recognize that the personality of Augustus had played a very important part in making the renewal of civil war impossible. And, even if we believe (as I do not) that Augustus' share was confined to gathering in the harvest which had ripened under his predecessors, we must not forget that the mass of the population of the Empire connected the restoration of peace and prosperity with the person of Augustus.

To my mind there is not a shadow of doubt that the term 'bureau of propaganda', used by some modern scholars to characterize the activity of the Augustan poets, is utterly wrong. But if we allow that Virgil and Horace were working in concert with Maecenas and Augustus and setting themselves to spread the ideas of these two men and to advocate their schemes—which seems to me too narrow a view—we must say that their propaganda was entirely successful. Their enormous popularity all through the Roman world is eloquent testimony. No propaganda can be successful unless it grasps the prevailing mood of the masses, unless it appeals to them. We may, therefore, be quite sure that the leading ideas of Virgil and Horace were the ideas of thousands and thousands in the Roman Empire, who believed with Horace (for whom personally it might, no doubt, have been a poetic flight only) that Augustus was one of the mightier gods, Mercury or Apollo or Hercules, who appeared among men (ἐπιφανής), that he was the Messiah and the Saviour of the mighty and holy Roman Empire.

Another 'propaganda bureau' was provided by the beautiful monuments of art which were erected by the senate, the Roman people, and some private citizens of Rome in honour of Augustus. These monuments impressed the population, not because they were beautiful, but because in their picturesque language they said the same things as the poets expressed, things which everybody felt to be perfectly true. As one example out of many may be taken the altar of the *Gens Augusta* which was found in a private sanctuary built by a Roman citizen at Carthage. It is probable that it reproduced a similar monument in the city of Rome. One of the sculptures on the altar shows the mighty goddess Roma, seated on a pile of arms. Her left arm leans on a shield; in her outstretched right hand she holds a pillar with a round *clipeus*, the shield which was consecrated to Augustus by the senate and people and which adorned his house on the Palatine. The shield has just been brought down by Victory descending from heaven and placed in the hand of Roma. Before the goddess is seen an altar on which rests a large *cornucopiae* with a *caduceus* and in front of them the globe—the *orbis terrarum*.

Is not this a beautiful and perfectly true symbol of Augustan Rome, of the mighty world-Empire consolidated by Augustus? The majestic figure of Roma is resting. War is over, Rome is victorious, there is no need of arms and weapons any more. They may serve now as the main base of the Roman power. Peace is restored. Rome looks proudly at the symbols of her world-Empire: the basis is piety, the foundation is religion, which is indicated by the altar; it supports the prosperity of the world as symbolized by the *cornucopiae*, the *caduceus*, and the globe.

The same ideas recur in the classical sculptures, breathing the

Description of Plate VI

1. ONE SIDE OF A MARBLE ALTAR FOUND AT CARTHAGE. Carthage, in the house of Ch. Saumagne near the hill of St. Louis. A. Merlin in *Bull. arch. du Comité des travaux historiques*, 1919, pp. clxxxvi ff. and ccxxxiv, note 1; M. Rostovtzeff, 'Augustus', *Univ. of Wisconsin Studies in Language and Literature*, 15, pl. 1; id. *Röm. Mitt.* 38/39, 1923/4, pp. 281 ff.; G. Gastinel, *Rev. arch.* 1926 (1), pp. 40 ff.; S. Gsell, *Rev. hist.* 156, 1926, pp. 12 ff.; L. Poinssot, *Gouv. Tunis. Notes et Documents*, 10, 1929, *L'Autel de la Gens Augusta*; J. Sieveking, *Gnomon*, 7, 1931, pp. 16 ff. (review of Poinssot, op. cit.).

The inscription on the temple to which the altar belonged reads: *Genti Augustae P. Perelius Hedulus sac(erdos) perp(etuus) templum solo privato primus sua pecunia fecit.* 'To the Gens Augusta P. Perelius Hedulus, priest for life, built this temple at his own expense on his own ground, being the first to do so.' For a description of the bas-relief, see p. 43.

2. A SCULPTURED MARBLE SLAB NOW IN THE RESTORED MONUMENT OF THE ARA PACIS [see G. Moretti, *Ara Pacis* (1948), pp. 232 ff.]. Found in Rome in 1568. Generally regarded as one of the bas-reliefs which adorned one of the entrances into the sacred precinct of the *Ara Pacis* of Augustus in the Campus Martius at Rome. A good bibliography and an excellent description of the bas-relief in Mrs. Strong's *La Scultura Romana da Augusto a Costantino* (1923), p. 38 and pl. VI [see G. Moretti, *Ara Pacis*, tav. xvii].

The bas-relief is a beautiful illustration of the most cherished ideas of Augustus. In the centre is *Terra Mater*, with fruit in her lap and two children on her knees, seated on a rock surrounded by flowers and ears of corn. She is the *Tellus* of the *Carmen Saeculare* of Horace (29 ff.):

> Fertilis frugum pecorisque Tellus
> Spicea donet Cererem corona;
> Nutriant fetus et aquae salubres
> Et Iovis aurae.

The two animals at the feet of *Terra Mater* represent agriculture (the bull) and grazing (the sheep). The two figures to left and right seated, the one on a swan and the other on a sea-dragon, are personifications of the rivers and the sea, or the air and the water, or perhaps the *Aurae* of whom Horace speaks. I take them to be a combination of the first and the last: the beautiful *Aurae* gently blowing over the sea and the rivers. Cf. the similar figures on the armour of the statue of Augustus (pl. V) and on the *patera* of Aquileia (pl. XIII, 1).

ALTAR OF CARTHAGE

ONE OF THE SLABS OF THE ARA PACIS

VI. THE LEADING IDEAS OF AUGUSTUS

best Roman spirit, of the *Ara Pacis* at Rome, the Altar of Peace built on the Field of Mars, especially in the idyllic scenes with the figure of Terra Mater surrounded by the elements and symbolizing the creative forces of nature as restored and protected by Augustus.[3]

What has been said of the mood of the population of the Roman Empire in general is not intended to imply that everybody was of the same opinion. There were, to be sure, exceptions, and the most striking was the majority of the senatorial class. Nobody would expect those Stoics and Epicureans to look upon Augustus as a divine being, son of the equally divine Julius. They regarded him as one of their own class, one who was more successful than themselves. Some of them hated Augustus because he had practically put an end to the exclusive domination of the senate; some had personal reasons, some were actuated by jealousy and regarded themselves as having the same right as Augustus to be leaders of the state, *principes*. Hence the not infrequent plots and conspiracies against the life of Augustus. The attitude of the senatorial class, however, was of no importance. Besides, the majority of the senate and of the senatorial class, glad to have peace restored again, indulged not so much in displays of republican spirit as in demonstrations of contemptible servility.

From time to time agitations also broke out in the provinces, which showed how Augustus never felt completely secure and how both he and the provincial governors considered it opportune to take adequate measures. One such agitation—certainly of slight importance—occurred in, or shortly before, 7/6 B.C.[4]

Nevertheless, the anxieties of Augustus and of the provincial governors were undoubtedly excessive. The quiet temper of the army, which reflected that of the people in general, made it possible for Augustus, despite the latent contradiction in the political system of the Roman state, to carry out the work of restoration undisturbed by new outbursts of civil strife. The fulfilment of his promise to the Roman citizens meant not merely the maintenance of their political privileges, but, above all, the avoidance of encroachment on their social and economic position, and indeed the increase of their opportunities in comparison with the other classes of the population of the Empire. Here again what was demanded of Augustus was not a work of antiquarian restoration but a consolidation of what he found firmly established in the economic and social life of the Roman state and what, to a great extent, was a creation of the civil wars.

During these wars the differences between the classes of Roman citizens had not been wiped out. The senatorial class remained as exclusive as it had been before. The knights realized their great importance for the state and regarded those who had not the same standing and the same means as far inferior beings. The same classes existed in the Italian cities. The senatorial aristocracy, members of the municipal councils, some of them Roman knights, formed the upper order. Alongside of them, but inferior to them, was the mass of the well-to-do *bourgeoisie*, in part not even freeborn men and women. The distinction between the different groups of these higher classes, alike in the city of Rome and in the Italian *municipia*, was very sharp. Among the senators only those who were members of the patrician order and those who numbered a consul among their ancestors counted as belonging to the *nobilitas*. In the eyes of these *nobiles* all the others were more or less *parvenus*. The Roman knights who succeeded in breaching the wall that surrounded the senatorial aristocracy were regarded as intruders, as new men. The senators and knights of the capital smiled at the boorishness of the municipal *gransignori*. The latter in their turn despised the rich freedmen and others. And separated from them all stood the lower classes of the free-born population, the mass of free peasants, free artisans, half-free farmers, and manual workers. Among the lower classes, again, those resident in the city looked with a kind of contempt on the peasants, the *pagani* or *rustici*. In the background there was the enormous mass of slaves—servants, artisans, agriculturists, miners, sailors, and so forth. We are speaking here, not of the provinces, but of the social divisions among the Roman citizens in Italy.

Augustus never dreamt of altering these conditions; he took them for granted. What he did was to sharpen the edges, to deepen the gulf between the classes and to assign to each its part in the life of the state. If the Roman citizens were to be the masters and rulers, each group of them must have its special task in the difficult business of ruling the world-empire. The work of Augustus in this respect is well known and hardly requires detailed description. The senatorial class furnished the state with the members of the supreme council of the Empire—the senate—

with the magistrates of the city of Rome, with the governors of the provinces (whether appointed by the senate or representing the emperor in the provinces which were governed by him), with generals, and with a large part of the officers of the citizen army. The equestrian class supplied the jurors of the Roman courts, one part of the provincial governors, the commanders of the fleet and of the troops stationed in Rome, the officers of the auxiliary troops and, to some extent, those of the legions, and finally the ever-growing mass of civil officials in the personal service of the emperors. The cities of Italy, except for the higher aristocracy, which mostly belonged to the equestrian class, had to provide the state with good soldiers for the praetorian guard and the legions, and with non-commissioned officers for the guard, the legions, and the auxiliary troops. The freedmen furnished sailors for the navy and firemen for the capital. Lastly, a higher class of slaves and freedmen—those of the emperor—served in the bureaux and offices of the Imperial household, branches of which were spread all over the Empire.

This discrimination between the various classes was not new. It was taken over from the established habits and customs of the later Republic. The distinguishing features were of a purely materialistic character. To a certain extent birth played a part in drawing the lines of distinction. But the main point was material welfare, a larger or smaller fortune, a *census* of definite dimensions. Nobody, of course, asked for a particular standard of education. That was taken for granted, as one of the distinguishing features of the higher classes in general. The only educational training required by the state from the aristocratic and freeborn youth of the capital and of the Italian cities was some degree of physical and military training. As the promotion from one class to another depended practically on the emperor, loyalty towards the emperor was required as one of the most important conditions.[5]

Such was the situation in Italy. It was a stabilization and consecration of conditions which had prevailed during the period of the civil wars. The same policy was pursued by Augustus in regard to the provinces. Nothing of importance was done to give them a share in the management of the state. The provinces remained what they had been before, estates of the Roman people. It was as difficult as before for the provincials to attain the franchise. In this respect the policy of Augustus was a reaction as compared with that of Pompey, Caesar, and Antony. Very little, too, was done to promote the provincial cities to the higher stages of municipal dignity, that is to say, to assimilate their rights to those of the Italian cities and of such provincial cities as had already received Italian rights. The only noticeable exception was the treatment of the oldest province of the Roman Empire— Sicily, which practically formed a part of Italy, like the valley of the river Po. Progress in this direction was rather slow in the time of Augustus after the end of the civil wars. What he did was done mostly during the turmoil of the civil wars and immediately after their close.[6]

Nevertheless the provinces, and especially the provinces of the East, were the first to experience the blessings of the new régime. Without making any change in the system of provincial administration, Augustus succeeded in improving enormously the practice of government. The provinces continued to be ruled by members of the senatorial class. They governed either in the name of the emperor or under his steady control. But the rule of the senatorial class as such came to an end, and simultaneously the methods of government became much fairer and much more humane. With the establishment of peace came the end of requisitions and contributions. With it, too, came the end of the domination of Roman usurers. Direct taxation became gradually stabilized and, being stabilized, ceased to offer an attractive field for the companies of Roman tax-collectors. These companies began to die out and were gradually replaced (for instance, in the case of the new taxes paid by Roman citizens only, which were introduced by Augustus) by agents of the government who dealt directly with the taxpayers. The taxes were not reduced. For some sections of the population they were even increased. But a better system of collection meant a good deal for the provinces.[7] Moreover, the provincials were now well aware that if they complained to the emperor or the senate, through the representatives of the cities who gathered every year to celebrate the festivals of the imperial cult, they would get a more sympathetic hearing and obtain greater satisfaction than they had received before.[8] In case of conflict with the governor the provincial councils could always approach the emperor himself. And, what was not of least importance, provincials knew perfectly well that everything which went on in the provinces was known to the emperor through his personal agents, the procurators, who managed his private financial business in the senatorial provinces and collected the taxes in the others.[9]

In their internal affairs the cities of the Eastern provinces (with the exception of Egypt) remained as independent as before, and perhaps became more independent than they had ever been. No attempt was made by Augustus to effect any change in the social conditions which prevailed in these provinces, most of which were aggregates of Greek and Hellenized cities. The city administration with its magistrates and its council (βουλή) was such a good medium for reaching the masses of the population that a change in the system would have been a foolish attempt to divert the course of natural evolution.

In the time of Augustus the cities of the Greek East never dreamed of the possibility of regaining the ancient liberty of the city-state. They acquiesced in the fact that their political liberty was gone for ever. They were glad to retain their local self-government. The Roman government on its side desired quiet and order to prevail in the cities. The age of social and political revolutions was past. The best guarantee for the stability of internal conditions in the cities was the rule of the wealthiest citizens. The protection of this social class had been the traditional policy of the Romans ever since they had appeared in the East, and it was the policy of Augustus also.

The only new feature, if new it was, discernible in Augustus' policy towards the Eastern provinces was the fresh impetus given to the movement initiated by some of the Hellenistic rulers, which aimed at the rapid transformation of city-less territories into regular city-states. All over the East Augustus faithfully followed the policy of Pompey, Caesar, and Antony as against that of the senate, creating new city-states out of villages, hamlets, and temple territories. The Roman Empire was to become a commonwealth of self-governing cities.[10] Exception was made only in the case of Egypt, with its immemorial organization, so different and so far removed from the system of a Greek city-state.[11]

A splendid confirmation of my remarks on the work of Augustus in the East is to be found in two of the five edicts issued by him (namely, the first and the fourth; compare also the third), found in Cyrene (cf. notes 6 and 8 to this chapter). These deal with various problems in the life of the city, particularly the difficult question of relations between the Roman citizens resident there and the Greeks who, as a whole, were not necessarily citizens either of the city of Cyrene or of the cities of the Pentapolis. The privileges of the few Roman citizens domiciled in Cyrene and who were in part of Greek blood—for the most part not very wealthy—remained what they had been before, but some slight reforms assured the Greeks of not insignificant improvements, particularly in regard to the organization of the tribunals, and to the liturgies and municipal taxes. The question of the privileges granted to the new Roman citizens of Greek origin was of importance: probably these were those who had received citizenship *en masse* from Pompey, Caesar, Antony, and Augustus himself. The emperor decided to consider them as a special class of Roman citizens possessing restricted rights. They remained members of the Greek community in respect of taxes and liturgies, with the exception of those who had received a personal grant of *immunitas*; and even this last privilege was valid only for estate already in possession and not for subsequent acquisitions (see note 6).

The same principle of policy was applied by Augustus to the West—to Gaul, Spain, and Africa. Not satisfied with creating new colonies of Roman citizens, he endeavoured to introduce city life into the tribal system of the Celtic peoples in Gaul and Spain, and to revive it in the former Carthaginian state of Africa. It would be out of place to deal fully with this topic here. The importance for the future of the Western provinces of the policy of urbanizing their social and economic life will be plain to every reader. In the new cities the leading class was, of course, the wealthy citizens, who were staunch supporters of the Roman régime.[12]

Mainly as the result of this policy, the external aspect of many countries began to change almost completely. In Asia Minor and Syria the difference was less marked, for here (as we have said) the process of transforming tribes, villages, and temple-lands into city territories had begun with Alexander the Great and perhaps earlier. But in the Western provinces it was very striking. The Celtic towns on the tops of hills and mountains, fortified refuges and market-places, died out. The ruling aristocracy of the Celtic tribes settled in the plains near the great rivers of France and of Spain. Here they built houses and erected the usual public buildings. The new centres of life attracted merchants, artisans, and sailors. A real city was thus formed. In Africa the great city of Carthage was rebuilt and began to be prosperous again. The old Phoenician communities on the coast started a new life. The mixed Punic and Berber communes of the fertile plains of Africa and Numidia, some of which sheltered a community of Roman emigrants, recovered from the shattering effects of the civil wars and resumed their economic activity. New agglomerations of houses were formed in the South, East, and West, under the protection of Roman soldiers, soon to assume the shape of regular cities. In Africa, as elsewhere—on the Rhine, on the Danube, and in Spain—large settlements consisting of shops and houses, called *canabae*, grew up around the forts of the legions and auxiliary troops and on the roads leading to them, to form the nucleus of future cities. Discharged soldiers increased the population of these settlements or received, as a group, land on which to settle and build a city.

Thus the Roman Empire was gradually transformed by the conscious efforts of its ruler into an aggregate of city-states. Augustus stood out as the leader not only of the Roman citizens in Rome, Italy, and the provinces, but also of all the urban, that is to say, the civilized elements of the Empire, as a leader who was assured of their support. This fact was emphatically expressed in the composition of the Roman imperial guard and of the Roman imperial legions. They were representative both of the Roman citizens and of the urban population of the Empire, though the former element was, of course, the more dominant. To the non-urban elements, the tribes and villages which were attached to the cities, was assigned a secondary role in the life of the Empire. They had to work and to obey, they were not free in the ancient sense of the word.

We turn now to the economic policy of Augustus. His main endeavour was to fulfil his promise to restore peace and prosperity. In this task he succeeded admirably. But we must not forget that behind Augustus stood the traditions of the Roman past, the glorious records of brilliant conquests and the longing of the majority of the Roman citizens for peace. They wanted peace, but a peace with dignity. For Romans this meant a further advance on the path of conquest and annexation. We must remember, too, that Augustus himself was a Roman aristocrat and that for him, as for all the leading men of Rome, military glory and military laurels, victories and triumphs were the most desirable achievements of human life. Moreover, the fabric of the Roman Empire was far from completed. Augustus was the adopted son of Caesar, and everybody knew that Caesar had had two main tasks in mind: the consolidation of the Roman power in the North and in the North-east, and the redeeming of Roman honour, so badly tarnished in the East and South-east by the defeat of Crassus and the half-successes of Antony.

On the foreign policy of Augustus a few words must suffice. The rule of Augustus was not a time of rest. Peace for the Roman Empire was secured, not by a policy of passive resistance, but by a policy of unflagging and strenuous military efforts. The chief problem was to find and to establish for the Empire such frontiers as would assure both stability and safety, and so make a lasting peace possible.[13] By the efforts of Augustus himself, of his friend and companion Agrippa, and of his stepsons Tiberius and Drusus, a complete pacification of the mountainous Alpine districts, of Gaul, and of Spain was achieved. The conquest of Britain was for the moment postponed. The more serious was the effort made to solve the difficult problem of consolidating the Empire in the North and in the North-east, on the Rhine and on the Danube. One part only of this task was carried through, the pacification of the lands south of the Danube, and that after a long and bloody fight against the Pannonians and the Dalmatians. The second part of the task, the advance of the Roman frontier to the Elbe, was not successfully accomplished. The defeat of Varus in Germany, a disastrous but not fatal reverse, drove Augustus to abandon the idea of adding Germany to the Romanized provinces. We must bear in mind that the disaster happened in the second half of his reign, when he was already old. The decisive step in the relations between Rome and Germany was taken not by Augustus but by his stepson and successor Tiberius.

In the East no important military effort was made to redeem the shame of Crassus' defeat by the Parthians. To satisfy public opinion, the Parthians were threatened with the prospect of a serious war and agreed to restore to Rome the captured standards. The same aim was pursued in the expedition of Augustus' grandson, Gaius Caesar, against Armenia. The principal factors in the extension and consolidation of Roman influence in the East were diplomacy and trade. But they were supported by strong military forces and by a strenuous military activity. An identical policy was followed in Egypt and Arabia and in Northern Africa. The Arabian expedition of Aelius Gallus was not a complete success, but at any rate it secured good harbours for Roman traders on their way from Egypt to the ports of India.[14]

By these means a lasting peace was secured for the Roman Empire. The splendid altar built to the 'Augustan Peace' (*Pax Augusta*) on the Field of Mars (*Campus Martius*) was a symbol of the fact that peace had overcome war and was now the prominent feature of Augustus' rule. The same idea was symbolized by the repeated closing of the doors of the Temple of Janus and by the games celebrating the 'new Golden Age' which had dawned with Augustus for the civilized world. The goddess Roma might now rest on the arms that protected peace and prosperity, based on Piety.

It is needless to insist upon the fact that the establishment of peaceful conditions on land and sea was of the utmost importance for the economic life of the Empire. For the first time after centuries of unceasing wars the civilized world enjoyed a real peace. The dream of the leading spirits of the ancient world for century after century was at last realized. Small wonder that economic life showed a brilliant revival throughout the length and breadth of the Empire. The best times of the Hellenistic age returned, with the sole difference that instead of many rivals in the field, represented by many independent states, which used their economic resources for political purposes, the whole civilized world was now one huge state comprising all the kingdoms of the Hellenistic period. The competing states had disappeared, competition was now a purely economic rivalry between business men and went on unhampered by political considerations.

With this competition neither the Roman state nor the emperor interfered. They left economic life to its own development. The only handicap to trade within the Empire was the customs-duties levied on the borders of each province, and these duties were not very high. We do not know how heavy was the burden of taxation imposed by the state on industry and agriculture. But the amount of the taxes paid by Roman citizens on inheritances, for instance, and on the manumission of slaves (both 5 per cent.)—the former introduced, the latter reorganized by Augustus—cannot be called exorbitant. We must, of course, take into account that besides state-taxation there was a municipal taxation of various kinds, of which we know very little. But the growing prosperity of the cities, both in Italy and in the provinces, shows that this taxation was not heavy enough to be a real handicap to the development of private enterprise and of economic activity. Apart from taxation, we can hardly discover any measure of an economic character taken by the government. The period of Augustus and of his immediate successors was a time of almost complete freedom for trade and of splendid opportunities for private initiative. Neither as a republic nor under the guidance of Augustus and his successors did Rome adopt the policy pursued by some Hellenistic states, particularly Egypt, of nationalizing trade and industry, of making them more or less a monopoly of the state as represented by the king. Everything was left to private management. Even in Egypt, the classical land of *étatisation*, with its complicated system of interference by the state in all branches of economic life—a land retained by Augustus as a province under his personal management after his victory over Cleopatra and Antony—some changes were introduced with the primary purpose of reducing the pressure of state-control. Thus, for example, he protected the development of private landed property in Egypt, which was guaranteed by the state in the same way as in other provinces. Many flourishing estates, large and small, belonging to private owners, especially Roman veterans, made their appearance in Egypt.[15]

In the economic life of the Empire the great capitalists of Republican times seem to have remained dominant; some of them were of senatorial rank, some of equestrian, but a large number were former slaves, freedmen. One of these capitalists, and the largest of all, was the emperor. Unlike the Hellenistic monarchs who identified their own fortune with that of the state, claiming for themselves the right of property over all its land and all its resources, Augustus, like other financial magnates of the time, managed his enormous private fortune by means of his slaves and freedmen. But, despite his own wish, he could not definitely separate his private fortune from those moneys which he possessed as the highest magistrate of the Roman Republic, as governor of many provinces, and as ruler of Egypt in direct succession to the Ptolemies. His family, or household, purse (*arca*) very soon became hopelessly mixed up with his magisterial purse (*fiscus*), and it was attractive and easy to manage both of them in the same way and by the same men. Thus the slaves of the emperor's household, his private secretaries and in particular his 'chief accountant' (*a rationibus*), held in their hands the control of the finance alike of the imperial household and of Egypt and other provinces.

For the senate the easiest way to get rid of the obligations involved in the financial management of the imperial provinces, where the main body of the Roman army was quartered, was to transfer the management to the emperor and leave him free to collect the taxes and to dispose of the proceeds as he pleased. If, as may be presumed, such provinces as Gaul with the Rhine frontier, the Danube provinces with the Danube frontier, and Syria with the Euphrates frontier, cost much more than they paid, their financial management, including the pay of the troops, entailed a regular deficit which was met from the private purse of the emperor.

Thus by the force of circumstances, by the weight of the enormous personal wealth accumulated in the hands of the emperor during the civil wars, conditions were created in the Roman Empire which bore a strong resemblance to those of the Hellenistic monarchies. The more the emperor disbursed for public purposes—for feeding and amusing the Roman proletariate, for transforming Rome into the capital of the world, for regulating the course of the Tiber, for building new military roads all over the empire—the more difficult it became to draw a line between his private resources and the income of the state. Not that this implied the absorption of the emperor's fortune by the state. It implied rather the right of the emperor to dispose of the resources of the state in the same manner as he disposed of his own private resources. This condition of things was inherited by Tiberius and his successors, who gradually became accustomed to regard the revenues of the state as their own personal income and to use them for any purpose they pleased.[16]

The emperor was not the sole possessor of an enormous private fortune. We do not know how many of the old aristocratic families retained their wealth after the turmoil of the civil wars.

Description of Plate VII

1. ONE OF THE GOBLETS OF THE TREASURE OF BOSCOREALE. Found in the ruins of a villa near the village of Boscoreale (Pompeii). Louvre Museum (Paris). A. Héron de Villefosse, *Mon. Piot*, 5, 1899, pl. VIII, 2.

The goblet here reproduced is one of a pair, adorned with human skeletons, some of which represent famous writers and philosophers of Greece. The scene shown in the photograph is the best expression of the spirit which inspired the decoration of these goblets. The left side is occupied by an altar, on which are placed two skulls; behind it a column supports a statuette of one of the Fates (with the inscription Κλωθώ). Above the left skull is a purse, with the legend Σοφία ('Wisdom'), to which corresponds a roll of papyrus placed above the other skull with the inscription Δόξαι ('Opinions'). The field is filled by three large skeletons. The one nearest the column holds in its right hand a large purse full of money, and in its left a butterfly (typifying the soul), which it presents to the second skeleton. Near the purse is engraved Φθόνοι ('Envy'). The second skeleton is engaged in placing a wreath of flowers on its head. Between the two is a small skeleton playing the lyre, with the inscription Τέρψις ('Joy'). The third examines a skull held in its right hand, while its left grasps a flower, inscribed Ἄνθος ('Flower'). Between the second and the third skeleton another small skeleton is represented clapping its hands. Above it runs an inscription which summarizes the artist's main idea: Ζῶν μετάλαβε, τὸ γὰρ αὔριον ἄδηλόν ἐστι —'Enjoy life while you are alive, for tomorrow is uncertain'.

2. A CLAY GOBLET WITH A GREENISH VARNISH. Museum of Berlin. R. Zahn, Κτῶ Χρῶ, 81st Winckelmann's Programm, Berlin, 1921, pls. I–III.

A human skeleton surrounded by a wreath, a ham, a pipe, a flute, and an amphora of wine. On right and left two dancing pygmies, one of them holding a purse. To the left and right of the skeleton's head is engraved: κτῶ, χρῶ ('Acquire and use'). Cf. *IG* xii. 9. 1240 (Aidepsos; Preuner, *JDAI* 40, 1920, pp. 39 ff.): an old shipowner, in command of a ship at the moment of his death, gives to those who survive him the counsel contained in his funerary inscription: κτῶ χρῶ.

These two goblets are only two specimens of a large series of objects which express the ideas of life current in the late Hellenistic, and still more in the early Roman, period. Allusion need hardly be made to well-known examples which have often been collected and illustrated, such as the little silver skeleton which adorned the banquet table of the rich parvenu Trimalchio in the novel of Petronius (*Cena*, 34. 8). The two goblets are reproduced here because they admirably illustrate the prevailing mood of the people during the early Roman Empire, especially the well-to-do *bourgeoisie* of the cities. A superficial materialism and a sort of trivial epicureanism were the natural result of the age of peace and prosperity which followed the turmoil of the civil wars from the time of Augustus onwards. 'Enjoy life so long as you are alive' is the motto. 'The best things in the world are a full purse and what it can buy: meat and drink, music and dance'. These are the real facts, and the speculations of the philosophers and poets, mortal men yourself, are mere opinions (δόξαι); or in the words of Trimalchio, 'eheu nos miseros, quam totus homuncio nil est. sic erimus cuncti, postquam nos auferet Orcus. ergo vivamus, dum licet esse bene' (*Cena*, 34. 10). It is interesting to compare this philosophy of life with the mildly epicurean metrical precepts, reminding us of Ovid, which are written on the walls of the recently discovered *triclinium* of the house of Epidius Hymenaeus, M. Della Corte in *Riv. Indo-Greco-Italica*, 8, 1924, p. 121.

1. CUP FROM BOSCOREALE

2. CUP IN THE BERLIN MUSEUM

VII. CONCEPTION OF LIFE IN THE AUGUSTAN AGE

The fact that Augustus came frequently to the rescue of impoverished aristocratic houses shows that many of these families were utterly ruined and depended entirely on imperial charity. We know, however, that the richest men among the aristocrats of Rome were those who were closely connected with Augustus —members of his own family and personal friends like Agrippa and Maecenas. We may safely assume that scores of minor men, who lent their support and aid to Augustus, possessed large and ever-increasing fortunes which they owed to their close relations with him.[17]

But although these men were a remarkable phenomenon, they nevertheless did not represent the leading type of men who figured in the economic life of the time of Augustus. The emperor's favourites were not very numerous and probably lived mostly on their income or, if they increased their fortune, they did so in the same way as the more energetic and more productive class of business men, who were the first to profit by the restoration of peace and order. These business men were not confined to the city of Rome. Most of them lived in fact not in Rome but in the Italian cities and in the provinces. They were the city *bourgeoisie* spoken of in the first chapter, the class which gradually grew up in the second and the first century B.C. in Italy and in the West, and which was not shattered by the civil wars to such an extent as the higher aristocracy of Rome—the senatorial class and the upper section of the equestrian. As soon as peace and order were restored, these men resumed their business activity on a large scale, and most of them were no doubt successful.

A typical representative of this class is the wealthy retired business man of one of the South Italian cities, the freedman Trimalchio, whose portrait is so vividly drawn by Petronius. The active part of his life fell certainly in the time of Augustus. Petronius depicted him when he was already old and when his life-work was already accomplished. He had started as a slave, the favourite of his master, had inherited a large fortune from him and invested it in commercial enterprises, especially in the wholesale trade in wine. At the end of his life he lived in his beautiful house in a Campanian city on the income of his large estates and on the interest of his money, which he lent on good security.[18] Trimalchio is one type of this age. He lived, characteristically, in Campania and not in Rome: we shall see that

Campania was at this time a much better place than Rome to build up a large fortune. Characteristically, too, his main occupation was first commerce and only in a second stage agriculture and banking, and possibly he was typical in being a freedman, though I am inclined to think that Petronius chose the freedman type to have the opportunity of making the *nouveau riche* as vulgar as possible. I have no doubt that many a resident in Campanian cities like Pompeii, freeborn and probably not uneducated, had the same business career as Trimalchio. They were the owners of the large and beautiful houses and villas of the Augustan period in Pompeii, Stabiae, and Herculaneum, the period when the most refined, the most vigorous, and the most artistic styles of decorative painting flourished; the men whose houses were adorned by the paintings of the second and the third styles had certainly had a good education and were at the same time prosperous in business. We have a fair knowledge of the composition of the leading class of Pompeii in the Augustan period. Most of them were descendants of the Sullan veterans, some of them were members of the old Samnitic aristocracy of Pompeii, very few of them freedmen.[19] The same is true of the larger cities, such as Puteoli, and of the Hellenistic East.[20] I feel confident that the pulse of economic life beat very briskly in the Augustan age both in Italy and in the provinces. The *bourgeoisie* of this period was not idle, and the ideal of a *rentier*-life was no more widespread among its members than it is among men of the same class in our own days.

The best proof of this can be deduced from a general survey of the ruins of the Italian cities. They were not badly off in the first century B.C., though some of them suffered heavily during the civil wars. But the time of real prosperity for Italy was the age of Augustus. Even a very superficial glance at the ruins of all the Italian cities, especially those of Central and Northern Italy, shows that most of them assumed their definitive shape at that time, and that the most beautiful and the most useful buildings were erected then. I do not refer to cities like Turin and Susa and others in Northern Italy, which were created by Augustus, nor even to Aquileia. But if we take the cities of Umbria, centres of agricultural life with almost no commerce and industry— Perusia, Asisium, Hispellum, Aquinum, &c.—or some of the cities in Picenum and in Etruria, and read a description of their still existing ruins, we shall see that most of the best buildings were a creation of the Augustan period. Not, however, a creation of Augustus himself. He contributed his share towards building up the magnificent system of Italian roads, but the cities were created by the city *bourgeoisie*, both the ancient municipal families and the new settlers, veterans of the civil wars. Later in the first century certain new buildings were added. Some cities were still prosperous in the second century, but, as has been said, the really flourishing age of the cities and of their *bourgeois* creators (who still consisted mostly of freeborn elements) was the period of Augustus, the time between 30 B.C. and A.D. 14.[21]

Another proof is the rapid development of economic life in the Augustan age. This will be made clear by a brief survey of it as it appears in contemporary sources. Our information is, indeed, almost exclusively limited to Italy and to the economic conditions which prevailed there. Is that a mere accident? Or does it not rather show that Italy was the leading land both in politics and in economics? The East was slow in repairing its shattered forces, the Western provinces were too young to develop at once a brilliant economic life. However, as we shall find later, the East recovered more quickly in the field of industry and commerce than in that of agriculture.

We have seen that the civil wars had not affected the development of agriculture in Italy. After their conclusion the conditions of agricultural life remained as they were, except that they became more stable. In its main features the agrarian situation underwent no important change. Large estates were constantly growing at the expense, chiefly, of peasant plots. Alongside of the large estates, medium-sized and small holdings increased somewhat in importance: a process which owed much to the division of confiscated land among veterans. Both large and middle-sized properties had this in common, that they were managed on a scientific and capitalistic basis and were owned by men who resided not on the land but in the cities. To this class belonged almost all the veterans who had received their land from Sulla, Pompey, Caesar, and Augustus.

The management of properties of intermediate size is well illustrated by Horace's description of his Sabine estate. He had received his *Sabinum* as a gift from Maecenas, and he belonged therefore to the same category of landowners as the veterans of

Description of Plate VIII

1. PART OF THE MURAL DECORATION OF THE *TABLINUM* OF THE HOUSE OF LUCRETIUS FRONTO AT POMPEII. Pompeii. My article in *JDAI* 19, 1904, pp. 103 ff., pl. v, 1. A detailed description is given on pp. 104 ff. Time of Augustus.

Front of a rich villa, consisting of beautiful porticoes (two storeys) and of the entrance to the central apartment (*atrium*). Before the entrance is seen a round temple-pavilion with a cupola. Behind the villa, a beautiful park with various buildings scattered all over it. Between the wings of the porticoes, a lawn in the English style with flower-beds.

2. THE SAME AS NO. 1. My article, loc. cit., pl. vi, 2.

Front of another villa of the same type, formed by a long portico. Behind the portico are the villa buildings dotted about a splendid park extending over the slopes of two hills which rise behind the villa. The portico of the front follows the line of the shore of a little bay or an inland lake. The shore has been transformed into a quay, which is adorned with Herms. Close to the shore are two small temples. In the sea (or the lake) lies a pleasure-boat.

3. PART OF THE MURAL DECORATION OF A HOUSE IN STABIAE. Naples, National Museum. My article in *Röm. Mitt.* 26, 1911, p. 75, pl. vii, 1.

A large palace-like villa on a promontory surrounded by the sea. The front portico has two storeys; behind are the high tower of the *atrium* and tall pine-trees. Two moles or breakwaters protect the quay.

4. AS NO. 3. My article, ibid., p. 76, pl. vii, 2.

A huge summer-palace in the form of a *basilica* of three storeys built on a promontory or an island. Behind the villa is a park of pine-trees.

Scores of similar landscapes among the wall-decorations of the Imperial period furnish splendid illustrations of the descriptions of Horace and his contemporaries, and show that in attacking the luxury of the Augustan age, he and public opinion in general were not exaggerating. To those who travelled by land and by sea, along the shores of Campania, Latium, Etruria, and the lakes of North Italy, large and beautiful villas were undoubtedly the outstanding feature of the landscape. The owners of these villas were certainly not exclusively members of the Imperial house and of the highest aristocracy, but in many cases rich freedmen.

I. MAIN BUILDING OF A CAMPANIAN VILLA

2. CAMPANIAN VILLA

3-4. ROMAN VILLAS BY THE SEA

VIII. ROMAN VILLAS

the revolutionary leaders. The careful investigation of Horace's scattered remarks on his estate by I. Greaves[22] has shown that it was a plot of land large enough to provide its owner with a decent income. The poet paid much attention to his property and transformed part of it into a model farm run on scientific lines. But he never spent much time on it. The work of management was done not by himself personally but by his steward (*vilicus*), a slave. The estate, from the economic point of view, consisted of two parts—a model farm run by the owner by means of eight slaves, and five plots leased to five families of *coloni*, who may formerly have been proprietors, possibly of the same plots which they cultivated for Horace as his tenants. On the model farm one part of the land was cultivated as a vineyard, another as a fruit and vegetable garden, the largest part as cornfields. The meadows and woods which were owned by Horace were used for feeding a large number of oxen, sheep, goats, and pigs.

There is no doubt that estates of similar size and character, belonging to men who lived in the cities, were a characteristic feature of Central Italy. These medium-sized estates were probably more dangerous rivals of the peasant holdings than even the *latifundia* of great landowners. Somewhat different were the farms in South Italy. We know some of them in the territory of Pompeii, Stabiae, and Herculaneum. Their ruins have been excavated more or less fully and scientifically. It is beyond doubt that most of these villas did not form part of a *latifundium*. Farms which belonged to big landowners who never lived on them would not have had sets of comfortable, sometimes luxurious, rooms destined to be used by the owners as living quarters. It may be inferred, therefore, that most of the owners of these farms were from the very beginning citizens and residents of Pompeii, Stabiae, and Herculaneum, not senators and knights who resided in Rome. So far as we can infer from a close study of the remains of these villas, the Campanian farms were more or less similar to the estate of Horace, and included the meadows and woods on the slopes of Vesuvius. They must have been of comparatively large size, as is shown by the spacious store-rooms for wine and oil. Their chief products were wine and olive-oil, which undoubtedly were intended for sale. As the plan and the distribution of rooms in the farms agree closely with the descriptions

Description of Plate IX

1. PART OF THE MURAL DECORATION OF A HOUSE IN STABIAE. Naples, National Museum. See my article, 'Die hellenistisch-römische Architekturlandschaft', in *Röm. Mitt.* 26, 1911, p. 75, pl. VIII, 2.

A gorgeous villa built on the shore of the sea, probably in Campania. A quay on arcades projects into the sea. Near it in the harbour is a boat. On the quay some figures are strolling, while a fisherman runs busily about with his fishing implements. The villa, with beautiful porticoes in front, follows the sinuous line of the shore. Behind are other buildings and a park.

2. PART OF THE MURAL DECORATION OF THE *TABLINUM* OF THE HOUSE OF LUCRETIUS FRONTO AT POMPEII. Pompeii. My article in *JDAI* 19, 1904, pp. 103 ff., pl. VI, 1.

Another villa near the sea. The porticoes and the quay, which seems here to be treated like a lawn, are of the same type. Behind the porticoes is seen a series of separate buildings, scattered among the old trees of a fine park. The background is occupied by pleasant hills of no great height.

1. CAMPANIAN VILLA ON THE SEA

2. GROUP OF BUILDINGS OF A CAMPANIAN VILLA

IX. ROMAN VILLAS

of both Varro and Columella, it is clear that they were managed according to the scientific manuals on agriculture and that the labour employed was the labour of slaves. There was hardly room on them for the peasant plots of the *coloni* of Horace. The Campanian farms were entirely capitalistic, with no survivals of the peasant economy of the past.[23]

It is not open to doubt that those portions of the large estates which produced wine and oil consisted of rather small farms of the same type as those excavated near Pompeii. The *latifundium* of Campania was certainly a combination of several *fundi* and several *villae*. In Apulia, Calabria, Etruria, Sardinia, and Africa the *latifundia* were evidently of a different type, to judge from the allusions to large estates in these regions by Horace, Tibullus, and Propertius. For the poets the outstanding features of such estates were the thousands of slaves, oxen, and ploughs employed in tilling the soil. We must suppose, therefore, a large villa as the centre of the estate and around it a village populated by slaves and hired workmen.[24]

The gradual disappearance of the peasants and the transformation of most of them into *coloni* of landowners was a phenomenon which was well known to the contemporaries of Augustus. Ancient Italy was disappearing. For romantic spirits like Virgil, Horace, Propertius, and Tibullus this was a matter of regret. But it was not only the romantic spirits that were alarmed. The gradual change in the social aspect of Italy, the increasing mass of slaves and freedmen even in the fields of Northern and Central Italy—former strongholds of the Italian peasants—the transformation of peasants into *coloni* were phenomena not entirely new, but very disturbing; they were signs of a new stage in the history of the country. To judge by some poems of Horace, which echoed, no doubt, the talk at the tables of Maecenas and Augustus, the subject of the disappearance of the peasants was a common topic of discussion among the leading men of the Augustan period.[25] Public opinion voiced by patriotic and loyal Romans appealed to Augustus to save the peasants. But in fact we hear nothing of any interference on his part with the conditions of land-tenure in Italy. The attacks of the poets on the morality of contemporary society, on the luxury of the rich, are in keeping with certain laws of Augustus. But after the end of the civil wars we hear nothing of any agrarian law. An agrarian law had been

Description of Plate X

1. PART OF THE MURAL DECORATION OF THE HOUSE OF THE 'FONTANA PICCOLA'. Pompeii: Casa della Fontana Piccola. My article, 'Die hellenistisch-römische Architekturlandschaft', *Röm. Mitt.* 26, 1911, p. 95, pl. XI, 1.

A tower-shaped rustic house inside a walled court with a wide entrance-gate. In the court are seen palms and other trees, a shed attached to one of the walls of the house for protection against the sun's rays, and a high building like a pavilion, which perhaps represents the super-structure of a well. On one side of the entrance-gate is a plough, on the other are three women seated on a bench, talking. The aspect of this building does not favour the view that it belongs to the same type as the villas which have been excavated round Pompeii. It suggests rather the house of an Egyptian peasant, but I am less confident than I was that that is the true identification. The picture may represent a Campanian peasant's house of a type different from that of the villas near Pompeii and Stabiae; cf. pl. XXXIII, 1.

2. IRON STOCKS FOUND IN A *VILLA RUSTICA* NEAR GRAGNANO. M. Della Corte in *Not. d. Scavi*, 1923, p. 277, fig. 4.

These iron stocks for the imprisoned slaves of a *villa rustica* were found in the *ergastulum* (prison) of a villa recently excavated in the 'fondo Marchetti' (com. di Gragnano). This villa is a typical example of the *villae rusticae* near Pompeii, which are spoken of in the text (cf. p. 30), and especially of the business part of them. I reproduce here the plan of the villa as published in the *Not. d. Scavi*.

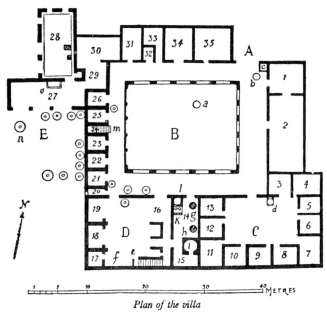

Plan of the villa

DESCRIPTION OF THE PLAN. The living-rooms for the owner, or the manager, of the villa have not been excavated. *A.* Main entrance. *B.* The large central court, within which are (1) the porter's lodge and (2) the stable (*stabulum*) where skeletons of horses and cows, or oxen, were found together with two terracotta mangers (*a* and *b*), and a water-basin of masonry (*c*). *C*, *D*. Lateral courts with bedrooms for the slaves, storehouses of different kinds, and other rooms. One of the rooms in *D* was a prison (*ergastulum*), one of those in *C* probably a small cheese-factory. Rooms 14 and 15, between the two courts, were used as a bakery, which was well furnished. *E.* The store-court (*cella vinaria* and *olearia*), with big jars (*dolia*) in which wine, olive-oil, and grain were stored. Room 28 was a wine-press (*torcular*). In room 27 there was a shed, under which a large amount of lumber was kept. Some of the beams found in this place are now in the Museum of Pompeii. The general arrangement of the villa is an excellent testimony to the accuracy of Varro's description of a *villa rustica*. It was a big agricultural concern of the factory type, run by slave-labour, self-supporting as far as possible, and forming a little world in itself.

I

2

X. 1. VILLA RUSTICA, POMPEII: 2. IRON STOCKS FOR SLAVES,
POMPEII

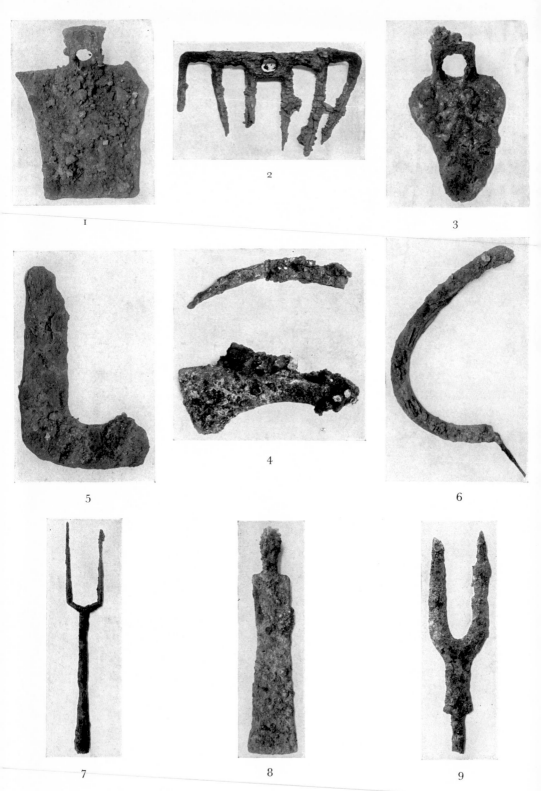

1

2

3

5

4

6

7

8

9

XI. AGRICULTURAL IMPLEMENTS, POMPEII

Description of Plate XI

1–9. IRON AGRICULTURAL IMPLEMENTS FROM POMPEII. Found in the large villa of L. Herennius Florus (usually called that of P. Fannius Synistor, but see M. Della Corte in *Neapolis*, 2, 1915, p. 172) near Boscoreale. Field Museum of Natural History at Chicago. H. F. Cou, *Antiquities from Boscoreale in the Field Museum of Natural History* (Field Museum Public., 152, Anthr. Ser. 7. 4), 1912, pp. 210 ff., and pls. CLXIII–CLXVI; cf. the similar implements found in the famous villa of Boscoreale, *Mon. Ant.* 1897, pp. 436–40. Large quantities of such implements are to be seen in the Museum of Naples.

(1) Hoe of the usual Roman shape.
(2) Rake with six prongs.
(3) Pointed hoe.
(4) Bill, probably a pruning instrument.
(5) Pick and hatchet.
(6) Sickle.
(7 and 9) Forks.
(8) Spud.

Most of these are typical instruments used in the vineyards. Some of them still retain their old shape both in Italy and in France. I have seen many of them, for example, in Burgundy. A shop full of such instruments is one of the newest discoveries at Pompeii. The owner was a certain Jucundianus. In his shop were found *falces stramentariae, serae, compedes, falces vinitariae*, chains, and other implements not for agricultural but for domestic use (M. Della Corte, *Riv. Indo-Greco-Italica*, 7, 1923, p. 113). Close by was the shop of another *faber ferrarius* (M. Della Corte, ibid., p. 115).

too marked a feature of the period of the civil wars to permit of recourse to it, even if it were urgent.

Apart from agriculture, the chief factor in the economic life of the early Roman Empire was certainly commerce. Wide opportunities were opened to the commercial activity of the people of the Empire after the end of the civil wars. The unification of the civilized world; its transformation practically into one world-state; peace within and without; complete safety on the seas, protected by the Roman navy, now a standing force; the increasing numbers of well-paved roads, built for military purposes, but used also for commercial intercourse; the absence of state interference with the commercial activity of individuals; the gradual opening up of new and safe markets in Gaul, Spain, and the Danube provinces; the pacification of the Alpine zone; the restoration of Carthage and Corinth, and so forth—all these factors combined to produce a brilliant revival and a notable increase of commercial activity in the Empire.

Commerce with neighbours and with far distant lands, like China and India, played no very important part in the economic life of the early Empire. This type of commerce struck the imagination of contemporaries as it strikes that of some modern scholars, and both of them have exaggerated its importance. Even tin came chiefly from Spain and not from Britain. Moreover, bronze, for the manufacture of which tin was used, had no longer such importance in the life of the Roman Empire as it had had in the Hellenistic period. From Germany came amber, some furs, and slaves. South Russia still supplied Greece with corn and exported a certain amount of hemp, furs, wax, and perhaps honey. Some gold may have come from the Ural mountains. The Bedouins of the Sahara may have exported dates and large numbers of negro slaves. More important was the trade of Egypt with Central Africa: ivory, certain kinds of precious wood, gold, aromatic substances, condiments of different kinds, were the chief articles. The same type of trade developed with Arabia. A special military expedition was sent thither by Augustus to secure for Rome some of the most important harbours in the south of the peninsula. The chief exports here were aromatic goods, condiments, precious stones, and camels. A similar trade in luxuries went on between India and Egypt and between India and China (silk) and Syria.

The articles bought in foreign lands were paid for in the North almost entirely by the export of oil and wine and manufactured goods. The goods of the East were paid for, without doubt, partly with silver and gold coins, as Pliny says, but mostly by goods produced in the Empire, especially in Alexandria. Taken all together, the foreign trade was almost wholly a trade in luxuries and had no real importance for the economic life of the Empire.[26]

Of far greater moment was the internal trade of the Empire, the trade of Italy with the provinces and of the provinces with each other.[27] As in the Hellenistic period, it was mostly a trade in products of prime necessity. Corn was imported and exported in large masses. Italy was unable to live on the corn which she produced. The same is certainly true of Greece and the Greek islands, not of Sicily, though Sicily seems to have become to a large extent a land of pastures and vineyards, of olive groves and orchards.[28] Many commercial and industrial cities of the coast preferred to receive their corn by sea rather than pay the heavy cost of transportation by land. Lumber was undoubtedly exported and imported in great quantities for shipbuilding. The famous boat of Catullus was built of the timber of Mount Ida in Asia Minor. Wax, hemp, pitch, and tar could not be produced in large quantities everywhere, and they were required by all the shipbuilding provinces for sea-going and river ships. Metals, which were needed by Italy for coinage and by all large and small centres of metallic industry, were not produced in sufficient amounts either in Italy or in the neighbourhood of most of the cities which were famous for their work in metal (for example, Capua and Tarentum in South Italy, Alexandria in Egypt, perhaps some cities in Asia Minor and in Greece, and some places in Gaul). Metals were chiefly mined in Spain, in Gaul, and in the Danubian provinces; the mines of the East seem to have been of less importance in the imperial period. Sulphur was obtained almost exclusively from Sicilian mines; it was indispensable to all vine-growing countries.

Commerce in olive-oil and wine played, as before, a leading part in the economic life of Italy, Greece, and Asia Minor. One of the largest consumers was no doubt the Roman army. Greece and Asia Minor supplied with oil and wine the eastern provinces of Rome and the shores, especially the Northern shores, of the Black Sea. Italy was the chief source of supply for the Danubian

Description of Plate XII

1. PART OF THE MURAL DECORATION OF ONE OF THE HOUSES OF STABIAE. Found at Gragnano. Naples, National Museum. *Pitture di Ercolano*, ii. pl. LVI, o (from which the illustration is reproduced). Cf. K. Lehmann-Hartleben, 'Die antiken Hafenanlagen des Mittelmeeres', *Klio*, Beiheft 14 (1923), pp. 224 ff., and G. Spano, 'La "Ripa Puteolana"', *Atti di R. Acc. Arte ed Archaeol. di Napoli*, 8, 1930, pp. 295 ff., esp. pp. 323 ff., and, on the harbour of Pompeii, L. Jacono, *Neapolis*, 1, 1913, pp. 353 ff.

A typical Campanian harbour with moles, various buildings, a small rocky island, 'triumphal' arches, and columns with statues. It cannot be certainly identified with any of the harbours of Campania (e.g. Puteoli), but it is safe to assume that the general aspect of Puteoli was not unlike our picture, though everything was undoubtedly on a larger scale.

2. PART OF A FUNERAL STELE OF CAPUA. Museum of Capua. H. Gummerus, *Klio*, 12, 1912, pp. 500 ff.; cf. a bas-relief of Arlon published by B. Laum, *Germania*, 2, 1918, p. 108. Late Republican or early Augustan period.

The upper part of the stele is occupied by two standing male figures, the Satur and Stepanus of the inscription engraved beneath them: *M. Publius M. l. Satur de suo sibi et liberto M. Publilio Stepano. Arbitratu M. Publili M. l. Cadiae praeconis et M. Publili M. l. Timotis* (*CIL* x. 8222). The lower part of the stone shows the bas-reliefs here reproduced. A nude man is represented standing on a stone base. On his left a man moves quickly towards him, probably talking and pointing at him; he wears the Greek *chiton* and *chlamys*. On his other side another man, clad in a *toga*, quietly extends his right hand towards him. The scene no doubt represents the slave trade. The nude man is the slave, the man in the Greek dress is the seller, and the *togatus* the buyer. There can be little doubt that the two executors of the will of Publilius Satur intended to represent an episode of his early life—his purchase by his master and later *patronus*—in order to show the modest beginnings of one who became a great man in Capua and whose personality and history were probably known to everybody there. Similar was Trimalchio's idea in adorning the peristyle of his house with pictures which portrayed various episodes of his own life, beginning with the 'venalicium cum titulis pictum' (Petron. *Cena*, 29. 3).

3. FRAGMENT OF A BAS-RELIEF OF THE COLLECTION WAROCQUÉ. Mariemont (Belgium). F. Cumont, *Collection Warocqué*, no. 70; Daremberg–Saglio, *Dict. d. ant.* iii, p. 1585, fig. 4827 (Ch. Lécrivain); E. Cuq, 'Une Scène d'affranchissement par vindicte au premier siècle de notre ère', *C. R. Acad. Inscr.* 1915, pp. 537 ff.; S. Reinach, *Rép. d. rel.* ii, p. 164, 3 [= *Musée de Mariemont* (1952), p. 138, no. R.14, and pl. 49]. 1st cent. A.D. (?).

Fragment of a bas-relief representing the *manumissio vindicta*. One of the manumitted slaves is kneeling before the magistrate, who touches him with the manumission-rod (*vindicta*). He wears the *pileus*, the symbol of liberty. The other, already manumitted, is shaking hands with the magistrate or his former master (symbolizing the *fides* established between him and his *patronus*). I see no reason for regarding this fragment as a modern forgery.

1. CAMPANIAN HARBOUR

2. TRADE IN SLAVES

3. MANUMISSION

XII. BUSINESS LIFE IN ITALY IN THE AUGUSTAN AGE

provinces, Germany, Britain, and Africa. It is probable that even Gaul and Spain still, to some extent, imported these products from Italy.

The exchange of manufactured goods, articles not of luxury but of everyday use, was exceedingly active. Egypt remained the only centre of production for linen garments and papyrus. Large masses of woollen stuffs were exported from Asia Minor, Italy, and Gaul. Italian red-glazed pottery dominated all the markets. The metal plate of Capua and of Alexandria had no rivals. Glass was produced in Syria, in Alexandria, and in large masses in South Italy. Clay lamps were one of the main specialities of Italy. Toilet articles in amber were made exclusively in Aquileia, which imported the raw material from Germany and made it into fine small mirrors, boxes, flagons, &c., for export. We cannot enumerate here all the minor places in the Roman Empire which were famous for special articles and exported them in large quantities to other parts of the Empire.

In comparison with this exchange of goods of prime necessity, the commerce in luxuries appears, as has already been said, to have been less important, although some of our sources, for instance, the poets of the Augustan age, in dealing with the topic of Roman luxury, concentrate their attention on those particular articles. But it is significant of the highly developed conditions of exchange that the gourmets of Italy obtained without difficulty all the *primeurs* of every season and special *delicatessen* from places far remote. Nor had they to order them expressly. Large special shops kept stocks of such articles.

In the commercial life of the Empire in the Augustan period Italy played a prominent part, more prominent than even in the first century B.C. This was not merely a result of the growing importance of Rome as one of the largest consumers in the world. Italy as a whole, with its numerous cities, was a gigantic and rich market for the rest of the civilized world. It would be well worth while to investigate from this point of view the many thousands of objects which have been found in Pompeii, with the aim of defining what was local production and what import, and in the latter case whether it was import from other Italian cities or from the transmarine provinces. It is, however, hardly correct to affirm that Rome and Italy paid for the imported goods with the tribute which Rome received from the provinces. We have no statistics; but what can be gathered about the industrial productivity of Italy shows that the largest part of the import was covered by a corresponding export.

The largest item in this export was Italian wine and oil. We cannot account for the aspect of Campania, which was one enormous vineyard, and for the rapid development of viticulture in Northern Italy, unless we assume that Italian wine and oil were exported in large amounts to the Western and Northern provinces of the Empire and even to the East. Puteoli, as the chief harbour of South Italy, and the other harbours of Campania dealt to a very large extent in wine and oil, and so did Aquileia in the North. We must bear in mind that Trimalchio acquired his fortune by exporting wine and that he was in relations with Africa.[29] Along with wine and oil Italy exported to the West manufactured goods in great quantities. We have already pointed out that the Arretine pottery and the early *terra sigillata* dominated for a while the world-market as far as Britain in the North and the shores of the Black Sea in the East. Great masses of Capuan metal plate are found as far away as the Caucasus and the river Kama.[30] The peculiar Aucissa safety-pins, a speciality of the Augustan period, found their way to all the provinces of the West and even to the shores of the Black Sea.[31] The lamps of the factory of Fortis in the neighbourhood of Mutina were genuine products (not local counterfeits) and were turned out in vast numbers in the Augustan period. They are found in every part of the Roman Empire. The Campanian imitations of the Syrian blown glass, very fine specimens indeed, have been found in large quantities, together with the Syrian models, in many a grave of South Russia belonging to the Augustan age.[32] Can we say, in view of these facts, that Italian production was far too small to cover the cost of imports? If Rome and the Roman government paid for part of the imported corn, for the wild beasts which were killed in the amphitheatres, and for the luxuries and extravagances of the emperors with the gold and silver which came from Egypt, Syria, Gaul, and Spain, the *bourgeoisie* of Italy covered the balance by production, and most of the ships which imported goods from the provinces sailed back with a valuable return cargo.

Although wine, olive-oil, corn, and raw materials like lumber, metals, &c., played a large part in the commercial interpro-

vincial exchange of the Empire, the products of industry (as we
have seen) must not be disregarded in appreciating the commerce of the Augustan age. The most thriving part of the Roman
Empire, so far as industry was concerned, was certainly Italy
and, in Italy, Campania and Etruria. The evidence on this point
has been collected by Professor Tenney Frank, and I need not
repeat the pages devoted to this subject in his two recent books.
He has pointed out the ever-growing importance of the red-
glazed pottery which was produced in Etruria in large quantities
for mass-consumption and mass-export. Well known, too, are
the fame and the fine quality of the bronze and silver plate made
in Capua.[33] We have just alluded to the factory of lamps which
flourished in North Italy. It may be added that in the Augustan
age the Campanian cities, in imitation of, and in competition
with, Alexandria, developed many new branches of industry
hardly noticeable in Campania in the earlier period, above all the
beautiful glass ware, especially the coloured sorts and the vessels
adorned with reliefs. In this branch of trade Campania beat
both Syria and Alexandria almost completely, as is shown by
finds in South Russia. At the same time the cities of Campania
undoubtedly began to use their abundance of fine oil for the
preparation of perfumes, and to revive the ancient industry of
jewellery, which had flourished in Etruria in the Hellenistic
period and now passed to Campania. To this subject we shall
return in the next chapter. Still more important was the rapid
development of the manufacture of woollen garments, the fine
South Italian brands of wool being used for this purpose.[34]

Campania and Etruria were not alone in developing Italian
industry in the Augustan age. At that time a second Puteoli
arose in Aquileia, which became a flourishing centre of both
commercial and industrial life in the North. We have already
spoken of the commercial importance of this city and of her
trade in wine with the Danube regions and with the Western
shores of the Adriatic Sea. A colony of Roman veterans—active
and progressive landowners, who rapidly transformed the territory of their city into a flourishing vineyard and acquired large
fortunes by exporting the wine to the Danubian lands—Aquileia
quickly realized the opportunities which her wonderful situation
afforded for the further development of her commerce. The pacification of Noricum gave her citizens access to the iron mines of

that country. The export of wine attracted large masses of amber to the city. The excellent qualities of the Aquileian sand and clay opened up wide possibilities of exporting home-made (not imported) glass and clay ware to customers in the Danube region. The ancient bronze industry of North-western Italy and the abundance of copper and silver in the neighbouring mines of Noricum, Raetia, and Dalmatia spurred the activity of bronze- and silversmiths. Agricultural implements and iron weapons were manufactured: the mention of an *aciarius* in one inscription from the city is significant. The discovery of gold near Virunum gave good opportunities to jewellers, who used also the semi-precious stones found in this region. Thus Aquileia gradually became not only a city of vine-growers and merchants but also one of the most important centres of industry. In visiting the Museum of the town, one is struck by the abundance of refined and original glass products, especially of imitated engraved stones and cameos and vases of different shapes, by the masses of amber articles, by the large quantities of iron implements, by some valuable products of bronze and silver toreutic art, which belong in part to the Augustan age, and by the great number of gold jewels. And in every case the oldest specimens belong to the Augustan age. Beyond doubt Aquileia became the Puteoli of North Italy as early as the time of Augustus, thanks probably to the efforts of Augustus himself and of some members of his family who often resided in the city. Such men as the Barbii and Statii were certainly pioneers not only of Aquileian commerce but also of Aquileian industry.[35]

Another important phenomenon in the development of industry in Italy is the gradual industrialization of life not merely in large cities like Puteoli and Aquileia, which were great export harbours and centres of important trade routes, but also in smaller local centres and ports. A good example is Pompeii. There is no doubt that Pompeii, which had always been the centre of a flourishing agricultural region and a harbour of some importance for the group of inland cities that lay near, gradually became a centre of local industry which sold goods produced in her workshops to customers not only in the city but also in neighbouring cities and in the homesteads of the country round. As early as the time of Cato some agricultural implements were manufactured there. In the period after Sulla and especially under Augustus other branches of industry were started and developed. A clear sign of the industrialization of the town is the development of a new type of dwelling-house surrounded by shops. These shops were partly owned and managed by the owners of the houses, partly rented to artisans and retail traders. It seems as if from the very beginning one of the specialities of Pompeii was the production of various woollen stuffs and clothes which in part were dyed in the city itself. We shall see later how this trade developed, and how the city became more and more industrialized. It is enough to note here that the beginning of the process dates from the reign of Augustus. To the same time probably belongs the growth or the revival of another speciality of Pompeii—a famous fish-sauce, the Pompeian *garum*.

The organization of Pompeian industry as described by Frank, a combination of a small factory and a retail shop, may have been typical of a small local centre of commerce and industry, as the Pompeian *atrium* and peristyle house was typical of a country town of a rather archaic type. The excavations at Ostia reveal the development as early as the first century A.D. of a more modern type of house and shop, which indicates different conditions, more like those of our own days. We cannot form a judgement about the economic life of Europe or of the United States of America by merely studying the shops of Foligno or Urbino in Italy or of Madison in the United States.[36]

Unfortunately our evidence about the life of the larger cities in the Augustan age, whether in Italy or in the provinces, is very scanty. None of the larger commercial and industrial cities has been excavated; many could not be. Ostia is just beginning to reveal to us the earlier periods of her life; at Puteoli, Naples, and Brindisi no excavations on a large scale are possible; in Aquileia the opportunities are good, but the work has only just begun. The same is true of the provinces, where in many centres industrial life awoke to renewed prosperity. At Alexandria industry, in fact, never ceased to produce masses of goods for home-consumption, for sale in Egypt, and for export to foreign lands. But we know almost nothing of the industrial organization of this city, and it must be confessed that, so long as we know so little, our information about ancient industry in general will be hopelessly defective. My own studies of the archaeological material found in South Russia showed that industrial life in Alexandria

was never so prosperous as after the civil wars. Alexandria produced for the whole of the civilized world papyrus, some brands
of linen, perfumes, some glass articles (especially beads), ivory
articles, a special type of jewellery, a large part of the silver plate
which was in circulation in the ancient world, and other things.
The attempts of Campania to introduce some of these branches
of industry into her cities have already been described.[37]

Alexandria did not stand alone in the Greek East in developing her industrial life. Syria invented and perfected the blowing
of glass, which was soon imitated by the most active industrial
centres in Italy. Syrian jewels and linen competed with the
Alexandrian products. In Asia Minor the ancient woollen industry began to flourish once more. It was not only rugs that
were exported thence. The speciality of the country was the
fabrication of dyed stuffs and clothes, and in this speciality her
only rival was Syria. Italy, of course, produced some good
brands of woollen stuffs of natural colours which, in part, were
also dyed on the spot (we recall the *infectores* of Pompeii); in the
other parts of the Roman Empire, as in Italy, house industry
could provide families with plain everyday clothes of one colour,
though I am inclined to think that even such clothes were
bought on the market and in the shops, and that the shops in the
towns offered cheap coloured material and dresses. But there was
no competition with Egypt, Asia Minor, and Syria in the production of coloured woollen and linen stuffs. One has only to
remember how large was the export of coloured stuffs made in
Moscow to Central Asia and even to India, where house industry still flourishes, to realize how important was the manufacture of dyed stuffs in Asia Minor and in Syria.[38]

The economic situation in the Augustan age is marked by two
features on which special stress must be laid. We have spoken of
the non-interference of the government in the economic life of
the Empire. Augustus, it must be repeated, had no special economic policy. The labour question did not exist for him at all.
If he took certain protective or restrictive measures, he did so for
reasons of a political or moral character. Such were the restrictive laws on luxury (*leges sumptuariae*) or the projected measures
for the protection of Italian agriculturists—the small landowners
of Italy—measures which were claimed for him by Horace in
some of his Odes but were never carried out. The policy of

laissez-faire prevailed. The second point which must be emphasized is the importance of Italy in the economic life of the Empire. Italy remained the richest land of the Empire, and had as yet no rival. She was the greatest centre of agriculture, of commerce, and of industry in the West. The time might seem to be approaching when her economic supremacy would be challenged, as she herself had challenged the supremacy of Greece, Alexandria, and Asia Minor. But we hardly perceive yet the very slightest signs of the beginning of this new period. The production of the most valuable articles of agriculture and industry was still, as in the Greek and Hellenistic periods, concentrated in a few places, particularly in Asia Minor, Alexandria, Syria and Phoenicia, and in Italy; the rest of the Empire produced mostly raw material. But even in the Western provinces economic life in general was becoming ever more complex, and the day of their emancipation was nearing.

In refraining from regulating the economic life of the Roman Empire Augustus followed the same policy which he deemed best for its political and social life. There he accepted the existing conditions, and only modified them slightly, when absolutely necessary. In the economic sphere also his policy was a policy of restoration and reconstruction, and that was in fact a policy of adaptation to existing conditions.

Description of Plate XIII

1. SILVER *PATERA* FOUND AT AQUILEIA. Museum of Vienna. The *patera* has often been published; see the bibliography in S. Reinach, *Rép. d. rel.* ii, p. 146, 1; cf. E. Loewy, 'Ein römisches Kunstwerk', *Studien zur Geschichte des Ostens (Festschrift J. Strzygowski*, 1923), pp. 182 ff., and pl. xx.

The composition (in bas-relief) is a Roman imitation, or a slightly modified copy, of the famous Hellenistic-Egyptian 'Tazza Farnese', treated in the new-Attic style. A Roman heroized emperor is represented as a new Triptolemos, bringing fertility and prosperity to the Earth, figured as a reclining, half-naked woman, near whom is a cow resting (cf. pl. VI. 2). The emperor has just alighted from his chariot, drawn by serpents, and is performing a sacrifice to Demeter, who is throned in the background, seated on a rock under an old olive or fig tree. In the heaven above is a bust of Zeus. The emperor is surrounded by the four seasons (*Horae*), two of whom feed and caress the serpents. Two boys and a girl act as the *camilli*. The boys hold two *paterae*, the girl brings a basket laden with fruit and ears of corn; another basket stands behind her. It is not easy to identify the emperor. I should suggest Caligula or Nero rather than Claudius. I do not think that the children are those of Claudius; they symbolize the fertility and prosperity of the Golden Age in general. The *patera* admirably illustrates the way in which the emperors of the 1st cent. adhered to the ideas of Augustus and laid stress on being, like him, divine bringers of peace and prosperity, the great protectors and restorers of agriculture.

2. SILVER CUP FROM THE TREASURE OF BOSCOREALE. Found at Boscoreale near Pompeii. Collection of the Baron E. de Rothschild, Paris. A. Héron de Villefosse, *Mon. Piot*, 5, 1899, pp. 31 and 134 ff., pl. XXXII. 1 and 2; S. Reinach, *Rép. d. rel.* i, pp. 92 ff.; M. Rostovtzeff, *Mém. prés. à l'Acad.* 14, 1924; cf. id. 'L'Empereur Tibère et le culte impérial', *Rev. hist.* 163, 1930, pp. 1 ff.

The cup, one side of which is reproduced in the plate, and both sides in the upper drawing on this page (from *Atene e Roma*, 6, 1903, pp. 111 ff.), may be called the Augustus–Tiberius cup. Augustus is here glorified by Tiberius as the great military hero, the great restorer of the glory of the Roman arms, and the foremost member of the divine family of the Julii. Along with him appear the deified mother of Tiberius and Tiberius himself, as the emperor's most faithful and most successful assistant, and as his only heir. On one side of the cup Augustus is seen seated on a *sella curulis*, holding a globe and a roll (as master of the *orbis terrarum* and its law-giver). He looks towards a group of divinities on his right: Venus Genetrix (with the features of Livia?), who presents him with a Victory, the Honos, and the Virtus of the Roman people. On his left Mars, the divine forefather of the Julii, leads a group of seven conquered peoples. On the other side of the cup Augustus receives the submission of the Sugambri in the presence of their conqueror Tiberius. The cup is a striking witness to the efforts of Tiberius and his successors to link themselves to the glorious memory of Augustus (cf. the inscription of Gythion, discussed in the article in *Rev. hist.*). The bas-reliefs of a second cup, figured in the lower drawing, give a representation of the triumph of Tiberius over the Sugambri (?).

1. PATERA OF AQUILEIA

2. CUP FROM BOSCOREALE

XIII. TIBERIUS AND CLAUDIUS

III

THE SUCCESSORS OF AUGUSTUS: THE JULII AND CLAUDII

At the death of Augustus his power passed to his stepson Tiberius, whom he had adopted in the last years of his rule. Tiberius was succeeded by Caligula, one of the sons of his nephew Germanicus, Caligula by his uncle Claudius, Claudius by Nero, the son of his second wife Agrippina, one of the sisters of Caligula. Thus power remained in the hands of the family of Augustus for about a century. We cannot, however, speak of the principate being then a hereditary monarchy. In truth the transmission of power from one member of the family of Augustus to another was based wholly on the popularity of Augustus with the soldiers of the Roman army. Nearly all the emperors of the first century were appointed by the army, and more especially by the Praetorian Guard. The only exception was Tiberius, to whom, however, the army took the oath of allegiance without delay. Legally and constitutionally, the emperors received their power from the hands of the senate and people of Rome. In actual fact, the principate of the successors of Augustus depended on the good-will of the army.

This was understood and recognized by every one in the Roman Empire and above all by the emperors themselves. They knew perfectly well that their rule was based wholly on their relationship to Augustus and on the support given them by the army. They knew also that every member of the senatorial class had theoretically the same right to the office of supreme magistrate of the Empire. They knew it, and they acted accordingly. Hence the arbitrary, ruthless, and cruel character of their rule in the capital, their constant fear of falling victims to a conspiracy, and their systematic extermination of all the members of the family of Augustus and of all the leading members of the imperial aristocracy, those sanguinary persecutions so dramatically described by Tacitus. Hence, too, their almost servile attitude towards the praetorian guard and the population of the city of Rome. Hence also their dissipated and immoral private life; they realized that they were 'caliphs for an hour'.

All the emperors of the Augustan dynasty felt keenly the need of stabilizing their power, of giving it more than a merely legal basis. The legal sanction was of course given to the imperial power by the act of the senate in bestowing on the new *princeps* all the powers which had been held by Augustus and which had made him the first magistrate of the city of Rome and of the Roman Empire. What the emperors needed was a higher and more solid sanction, independent of the will of the senate and inherent not only in the institution of the principate but also in the person of the emperor. That was why the successors of Augustus, especially Caligula and Nero, made renewed efforts to develop the imperial cult and transform it into a state institution. Hence also the endeavours made to bind the religious feelings of the population of the Empire to the person of the living emperor by bestowing on him divine names and attributes and by identifying him with some of the gods of the Greco-Roman Pantheon, especially with Apollo and Hercules, who were both of them promoters of civilized life and protectors of mankind against the forces of darkness. Tiberius and Claudius were highly educated men, trained in philosophic thought. They thoroughly understood the absurdity of such claims and resisted both adulation and expressions of genuine religious feeling coming, particularly, from the Eastern provinces. The attitude of Tiberius is attested by the inscription found at Gythion in Laconia, which contains a short letter of the emperor. The city had sent a special embassy to offer him and his mother divine honours. In his reply Tiberius announces very briefly the maxim which is developed at length in his famous speech to the Senate, as recorded by Tacitus.* Tiberius made this speech in reply to a request made by the province of Hispania Ulterior, asking for permission to build a temple to the emperor and his mother. The underlying idea, both in the discourse and in the letter is this: 'I am a mortal, and divine honours belong only to Augustus, the real saviour of mankind.' It was probably a series of similar requests, coming from the East, which induced Tiberius to issue the edict referred to by Suetonius.† That Claudius had a similar point of view from the same motives is

---

* Tac. *Ann.* iv. 37, 38. † Suet. *Tiber.* 26.

strikingly shown by a papyrus found in Philadelphia, containing a letter addressed by him to the Alexandrians in which he flatly refused to accept any divine honour. But even Tiberius and Claudius were forced by political considerations to accept a certain amount of divine worship, especially in the Eastern provinces and in the newly annexed provinces of the West.[1]

The bloody and cruel aspect of the rule of the Julii and Claudii was, however, only one aspect of the life of the Roman Empire after the death of Augustus. Behind the screen the slow process of remodelling the structure of the Empire begun by Augustus went on undisturbed by the sanguinary struggle in the city of Rome. The most significant features of this process were the gradual development of bureaucracy, the elimination of the senate from the work of administration and the concentration of it in the hands of the emperors. The most important side of the work was the management by the emperor of all the resources of the Roman state, the exclusive right to dispose of the income of the Roman Empire, and to organize the expenditure. The assessment of taxes both direct and indirect, the collection of the indirect taxes, the management of the domains of the Roman state, were all gradually concentrated in the hands of the imperial administration. The senate finally retained the management only of those sums which were paid to the treasury of the Roman people by the cities of the senatorial provinces.

In this respect the reign of Tiberius and still more the notable government of Claudius were of the highest importance. It is not necessary to repeat here what O. Hirschfeld and many other scholars have shown to be the achievement of the latter emperor. In many directions he took the decisive steps and created precedents on which the further development of imperial bureaucracy, especially under the Flavians and the Antonines, was based. The attention which he paid to the minutest details of the administrative organization of the whole Empire is shown, for example, by the great number of extant inscriptions and papyri which reproduce his edicts and letters and by the numerous mentions of such documents in our literary sources. Of these the most striking are perhaps the fragments of an edict on the organization of the imperial postal service (*cursus publicus*), found at Tegea, and the letter to the Alexandrians which has been mentioned above. In dealing, in the latter document, with the complicated problem of the municipal organization of Alexandria (the question of the βουλή) and with the delicate matter of the relations between the Jews and the Greeks in Alexandria, Claudius shows an astonishing amount of knowledge, a perfect understanding of the actual conditions, viewed from the practical and not the theoretical standpoint, and a fine tact. It is hard to understand how such a man could have been at the same time a slave in the hands of his wives and freedmen. All the documents which are signed by him were certainly either written or carefully revised by him personally, for they all show not only the same peculiar style but also the same peculiar logic and the same individual mode of reasoning. But the truth is, as Mr. Anderson suggests, that it was only in his later years, when his mental powers were steadily declining, that he was dominated by the will-power of those who stood nearest to him; and it may be that even then the actual facts have been somewhat exaggerated by Tacitus and other writers of the senatorial class.[2] ·

The senate never protested against these encroachments of the imperial power on its rights. The reason was the same as in the time of Augustus, fear of assuming the responsibility for the enormous expenditure necessary for the state. The senate had now still smaller revenues to cover this expenditure than at the beginning of the principate. The emperors, on the contrary, who emerged from the civil wars as the richest men in the Empire, who inherited from Antony and Cleopatra the resources of Egypt, who were constantly increasing their fortune by confiscations and by inheritances, were willing and ready to aid the state out of their own income by taking over the heavy cost of rebuilding and maintaining the capital, of feeding and amusing the population of Rome, of distributing gifts to the soldiers and creating a special fund for the pensions payable at the end of their service, of building roads in Italy and in the provinces, and other charges. In all this they followed in the footsteps of Augustus. In thus helping the state the emperors undertook a very serious responsibility and had the right to claim the control of the management of the state finances. The assumption of responsibility, which led to a gradual improvement of the system of administration, especially in the provinces, made the new régime increasingly popular among the masses of the population and correspondingly weakened the authority of the senate. In this way the principate became firmly established as a permanent institution.

To illustrate this essential feature of the history of the Empire, I shall select two points and dwell on them for a moment. They are familiar, but they may profitably be emphasized.

The administration of the city of Rome was a heavy burden on the Roman state. Besides the necessity of making Rome a beautiful city, worthy of its position as the capital of the world, besides the obligation to secure for her growing population the elementary needs of life such as water supply, drainage, sanitary arrangements, safety from fires and floods, good paved streets, bridges over the Tiber, a sufficient police force—things which all the more important cities of the Greek world already possessed in the Hellenistic period—there was the enormous expense of feeding and amusing the population of Rome. The hundreds of thousands of Roman citizens who lived in Rome cared little for political rights. They readily acquiesced in the gradual reduction of the popular assembly under Augustus to a pure formality, they offered no protest when Tiberius suppressed even this formality, but they insisted on their right, acquired during the civil war, to be fed and amused by the government. None of the emperors, not even Caesar or Augustus, dared to encroach on this sacred right of the Roman proletariate. They limited themselves to reducing and fixing the numbers of the participants in the distribution of corn and to organizing an efficient system of distribution. They fixed also the number of days on which the population of Rome was entitled to a good spectacle in the theatres, circuses, and amphitheatres. But they never attacked the institution itself. Not that they were afraid of the Roman rabble; they had at hand their praetorian guard to quell any rebellion that might arise. But they preferred to keep the population of Rome in good humour. By having among the Roman citizens a large group of privileged pensioners of the state numbering about 200,000 men, members of the ancient Roman tribes, the emperors secured for themselves an enthusiastic reception on the days when they appeared among the crowd celebrating a triumph, performing sacrifices, presiding over the circus races or over the gladiatorial games. From time to time, however, it was necessary to have a specially enthusiastic reception, and for this purpose they organized extraordinary shows, supplementary largesses of corn and money, banquets for hundreds of thousands, and distributions of various articles. By such devices the population was kept in good temper and the 'public opinion' of the city of Rome was 'organized'. The expense of organizing public opinion, added to that of maintaining the city of Rome in good condition, was no doubt enormous. The senate, whose financial means were, as we know, reduced to the direct taxes from the senatorial provinces, was unable to meet this expense, and the emperors were ready to take the responsibility, provided that the senate left the whole business entirely in their hands. This, like the management of the army, was one of the *arcana imperii* of the early Empire.[3]

Along with the concentration of the management of state income and expenditure in the hands of the emperor went an increased imperial supervision of the senatorial provincial administration. From the very beginning the emperors had in the senatorial provinces—those of which the governors were appointed by the senate—their procurators or personal agents who managed their private estates. From the outset these procurators were the 'eyes and ears' of the emperor in those provinces. They kept him informed of everything that went on there, so as to enable him in case of necessity to raise in the senate the question of maladministration; and the senate, under the pressure of public opinion, was naturally unwilling to cover up with its authority the misconduct of its governors. The larger the number of the imperial agents in the provinces became, as the result of the increase of the imperial domains and of the transfer to them of the collection of indirect taxes, the more effective was the control of the emperors over the senatorial governors. On the other hand, the larger the part taken by the emperors in the appointment of new senators and in the elimination of old ones, by means of the recommendation of candidates and by periodical revisions of the list of members, the more decisive was their voice in the matter of selecting senators for the government of the provinces. In fact, as early as the first century A.D. the provincial governors were all practically appointed by the emperor, directly for his own provinces, indirectly for those of the senate.[4] In this way the imperial administration became more and more bureaucratic and a new social class of imperial officials was created—most of them slaves and freedmen of the emperors—

a class which existed only in germ under Augustus but increased rapidly in numbers and influence under his successors, especially under Claudius.

No less important was the work of the emperors in urbanizing the Empire, that is to say, the Roman provinces of East and West. Many volumes have been written on the municipal organization of the Empire, but none of them has dealt with this problem of urbanization, by which is meant the development of new cities out of former tribes, villages, temples, and so forth. We urgently need a complete list of cities in the various provinces, arranged according to the chronological order of their existence as cities. Among them, no doubt, would be found in every province scores which began their urban life after the end of the civil wars. Most of them were creations of the age of Augustus, some were added under his successors, particularly under Claudius, who in this matter was no less consistently active than in the work of developing imperial bureaucracy. This is shown, for instance, by his foundation of new colonies. The incorporation of the tribe of the Anauni in the municipium of Tridentum and the grant of the *ius Latii* to the Octodurenses and the Centrones of the Vallis Poenina, which amounted, in each case, to their urbanization—the urban centres were Forum Claudii Vallensium and Forum Claudii Centronum—agree perfectly with the efforts which the emperor made to urbanize the various parts of the Roman Empire, particularly the West. In the same spirit after a local war Claudius attributed a certain number of native Mauretanian tribes to Volubilis in Mauretania, and incorporated them in the city with the status of *incolae*. By this measure he aimed not only at rewarding Volubilis for its loyalty to the Roman cause, but also at creating Roman bastions in countries the population of which still maintained in many ways the forms of tribal life. There is no doubt that the urbanizing of the provinces which had been begun by Augustus advanced rapidly under Claudius. A good example is afforded by Spain, of which we shall speak later, when we come to discuss the general problem of the city and the country in the Roman Empire.

In dealing with the problem of the urbanization of the Empire under the successors of Augustus, we must take into account the fact that it was both a natural process of development in the

provinces—the provincials being attracted by the higher standards of civilized life which were connected with city organization—and a conscious policy of the emperors, who were eager
to forward the process and to give an official stamp to it in order
to enlarge the basis on which their power rested, since it was on
the civilized portion of the Empire, the city residents, that this
power depended. The easiest course was to proceed along the
path which had been traced by the 'Social' war and had been
followed by almost all the revolutionary leaders, Sulla, Pompey,
and especially Caesar, and to confer Roman citizenship on all
the urbanized elements of the Empire. But we must remember
that the victory of Augustus was due mainly to the support of the
Roman citizens of Italy, and that these citizens were very jealous
of their privileges and of the dominant position which they occupied in the Roman state. Hence the slowness and the moderation of both Augustus and Tiberius in granting the franchise to
provincials and the strong opposition to Claudius which forced
him, probably against his conviction, to adhere, to some extent,
to the traditions of Augustus and to be rather cautious in granting the privilege of the Roman franchise. Here again the creators
of the principate, the Roman citizens, imposed their will on their
nominees and succeeded in making the process of political
levelling, which was inherent in the principate, as slow as possible.

Greater freedom was enjoyed by the emperors in promoting
the development of city life within the Empire, since this policy
found no opposition among the higher classes or among the
Roman citizens in general. This is the reason why Augustus and
even Tiberius and, above all, Claudius were so ready to create
new cities. In default of large numbers of new Roman citizens
they created ever-increasing numbers of city residents. They
were conscious that, once initiated into civilized life, the latter
would be the best supporters of a régime which opened up to
them important and wide opportunities. We must bear in mind
that along with the Roman citizens it was the mass of the city
residents, especially the provincial *bourgeoisie*, which had supported Augustus and was ready to support his successors, provided that they would guarantee them, together with peace and
order, their privileged position among the masses of the provincial rural population. For the time being, however, those cities

which were not Roman or Latin colonies were largely forced to be satisfied with a citizenship of the second class, with the position of 'allied' or subject cities; but the day was drawing near when under the Flavians a more consistent policy would be applied at once to the ancient and to the new cities of the Empire.[5]

The result of this movement was that the structure of the Roman Empire came more and more to resemble that of the Hellenistic monarchies. But there remained many fundamental differences. The power of the Roman emperor was based, like that of the Hellenistic monarchs, on the army. But he was not a foreigner, and his power did not rest on foreigners and mercenary soldiers. He was a Roman, a member of the ruling nation of the Empire, the first citizen among Roman citizens. His army was an army of Roman citizens and served, not the emperor personally, but the Roman state and the Roman gods. The emperor was indeed a god himself, but his cult had a less personal character than that of the Hellenistic monarchs. He was a god so long as he governed the state and because he governed the state. The sanctity of the state was embodied in his person. After his death he might be added to the number of the gods in heaven, but equally he might not; all depended on how he had governed the state.

The rule of the family of Augustus, the Julii and Claudii, came to an end with the suicide of Nero, which was caused by a military revolution and resulted in a civil war lasting for about a year, the 'Year of the Four Emperors'. The causes of this new crisis in the life of the Roman state are not obscure. The power of Tiberius, Caligula, Claudius, and Nero was in practice based on the Roman army. By force of circumstances the leading part in the nomination of a new emperor became a right, not of the army as a whole, but of the praetorian guard which was stationed in Rome and took an active part in political life. The choice of the praetorians was generally accepted without demur by the provincial armies. This practice, however, gradually degenerated into a kind of dictatorship of the praetorians. Their support was granted to those who were willing to pay for it. When that fact became patent to every one, an atmosphere of envy, suspicion, and disgust towards them and their nominees was created throughout the Empire, and particularly among the soldiers stationed in the provinces. Moreover, the last emperors of the Augustan dynasty neglected their relations with the army and hardly ever appeared among the troops. They became emperors of the city of Rome, almost unknown to the mass of the soldiers and of the civil population of Italy and the provinces. Furthermore, to enable them to collect the money necessary for their personal expenses and for the extravagances with which they tried to ensure for themselves the favour of the garrison and of the populace of Rome, they undoubtedly overburdened the provinces; while, at the same time, they were less zealous than Augustus and Tiberius in the supervision of their provincial officials and governors. Finally, the scandalous private life of the rulers, their dreadful crimes, and their cynical behaviour, did not accord with the conception which the Romans, and the soldiers of the provincial armies in particular, had of the first citizen and leader of the Roman state. Above all, Nero, the murderer of his own mother and his brother, the artist and charioteer, the emperor who never visited the armies and spent his life among the city rabble and the Greeks, entirely destroyed the prestige of the Augustan dynasty.

The revolutionary military movement of the year 69–70 was thus a protest of the provincial armies and of the population of the Empire in general against the degenerate military tyranny of the successors of Augustus. It began as a revolt of the Celts against Nero's domination, but it soon assumed the form of a military revolt of the armies of Spain and Germany against the emperor. The Spanish soldiers proclaimed Galba emperor of Rome. At first recognized by the army and the senate, he was soon put to death by the praetorians who sold the purple to Otho, an intimate friend of Nero. Simultaneously the legions of Germany proclaimed Vitellius emperor; and he succeeded in vanquishing Otho and the praetorians. But he showed himself utterly unable to rule the state and had to face a new pronunciamento, this time in the East. The Oriental troops gave the imperial power to Vespasian, who was recognized by the army of the Danube: some officers operating in his name crushed the forces of Vitellius.

I am well aware that this conception of the civil war of A.D. 69 does not coincide with current opinion. Most of the scholars who have dealt with the year of the four emperors are inclined to assume, as the ultimate cause of the bloody revolution, a kind of separatist movement on the part of the provinces and of the provincial armies, which expressed the feelings of the provincials. I do not see the slightest trace of the supposed separatist tendencies of the Roman soldiers. Certainly the Gauls used the revolution for their very vague national aspirations, but the first act of the Roman army was precisely to crush, against the will of its leaders, the local revolt of the Gauls. Moreover the main core of the Roman forces was still the legions, and they consisted to a large extent of men of Italian origin, mostly even born and educated in Italy. It is difficult to believe that these men had so easily forgotten their past, that they had lost the feeling of being masters of the provinces and thought of imposing the will of the provinces upon the Roman state.

What really happened was, as has been said, that the Roman army expressed its discontent with the form which the principate had assumed in the hands of the last Julio-Claudian rulers. The soldiers showed that they were masters of the situation, and that nothing bound them to the one Julio-Claudian house. They desired the best Roman of the senatorial class to be *princeps*, to be the first man of the Empire and commander of the Roman army. In this point they were in full agreement with the public opinion of the large body of Roman citizens. Like the latter, they never thought of eliminating the principate; and they opposed with energy and resolution the disintegration of the Roman Empire, as promoted first by the Celts of Gaul and afterwards by some auxiliaries, mostly Germans of the Rhine army. In itself the movement was a healthy reaction against the degenerate military tyranny of Nero, the scandalous private life of an Oriental despot which he led, his neglect of all military and civil duties, and his undisguised sympathy for everything which was not Roman—in which he was the true, although unconscious, follower of Caligula. The struggle against Nero was gradually transformed into a regular civil war because of the political ambitions of the leaders and the bitter rivalry and competition between the different sections of the Roman army.[6]

But this civil war came to a speedy conclusion under the pressure, we may presume, of public opinion, especially in Italy, which was the battle-field of the opposing armies and the homeland of large numbers of the soldiers. We must remember that the majority of the troops were still Romans, trained and educated on the same lines as the Italian burgesses and peasants, that they still spoke the same good Latin as was spoken in Italy, and that they met in Italy many veterans with the traditions of the army of Augustus. Of the disgust which civil war created among them and among the people of Italy in general two illustrations may be quoted. They are drawn from the wonderful picture of the civil war given by the greatest psychologist among the historians. In his *Histories* (iii. 25) Tacitus says: 'A Spaniard named Julius Mansuetus who had been enrolled in the legion called "Rapax" had left a young son at home. The boy grew up and was enlisted by Galba as a soldier in the seventh legion. He met his father on the field of battle and struck him down. While he was rifling the dying man, the two recognized each other. Flinging his arms round the bleeding body, in a voice choked with tears he implored his father's spirit to be appeased and not to loathe him as a parricide. The deed, he cried, is the deed of all: a single soldier is but a drop in the ocean of civil strife! With these words he lifted the body, dug a grave, and paid the last duties to his father. This was noticed by those who were nearest, and then by others, till there ran through the whole army astonishment and horror and curses against this cruel war.' 'Nevertheless,' adds Tacitus, 'they did not slacken in their zeal to slay and despoil kinsmen, relatives, and brothers.' Tacitus was right in saying that the soldiers, in spite of their feeling of disgust, did not cease fighting; but the feeling was no doubt growing, and the soldiers were reminded of their responsibility for the war, and of the futility of continuing it, by the attitude of their fellow-citizens in Italy towards them and their deeds. The second illustration is also from Tacitus. After a pitched battle and a short siege, Cremona was taken by the partisans of Vespasian. Scenes of horror followed—wholesale pillaging, murder, and violation. The feelings of Italy in regard to this crime ran high. 'Antonius,' says Tacitus, 'ashamed of the atrocity and aware of the growing reprobation of the public, issued a proclamation that no citizen of Cremona should be kept as a prisoner of war; and indeed such booty had already been rendered valueless to the soldiers by a general agreement throughout Italy not to buy such slaves. The soldiers then began to massacre their captives and, when this became known, their kinsmen and relatives began secretly to redeem them' (*Hist.* iii. 34).

It is clear, then, that the civil war of 69–70 was in its very essence a political movement. It was, however, complicated by other motives which made it very perilous for the future of the Empire. The bitterness and the cruelty of the struggle, the tragedy of the sack of Cremona, the wholesale slaughter of rich men by the soldiers, whether victors or vanquished, in Italy and in Rome,[7] show that even among the legionary soldiers, to say nothing of the auxiliaries, there was a growing enmity towards the ruling classes of Italy and their supporters, the praetorians, who represented the city population, and especially the city *bourgeoisie*, of Italy. We must not forget that one of the first measures taken by Vespasian after the end of the civil war was gradually to reduce the number of legionaries recruited in Italy, including Northern Italy. Recruitment never wholly stopped in Italy, even under Hadrian; but the Roman legions of the Flavians and of Trajan no longer represented the Roman citizens of Italy: for the most part the soldiers were still Roman citizens, but of the Romanized provinces.[8] Was this a privilege granted to Italy for failing to support Vespasian in his struggle for power? Was it a recognition of the incapacity of Italy to furnish a sufficient number of soldiers for the legions? I am disposed rather to believe that the cause is to be sought in another direction.

As we have seen, the Roman legions, as a rule, were not recruited compulsorily but consisted of volunteers. Already the predecessors of Vespasian had preferred Northern Italy to Central and Southern Italy for purposes of recruitment. The fact that Vespasian, contrary to the prevailing practice, excluded Italian volunteers from the legions, leaving open to them the praetorian cohorts only, shows that his measure was not a privilege granted to Italy. How is it to be explained? I incline to the view that Vespasian, who must have thoroughly understood the history and the causes of the civil war, became afraid of the aspirations and the political mood of the Italian volunteers. He must have wished not to have Italian-born soldiers in the legions, because these soldiers would be drawn from the unruly, discontented, and highly inflammable elements of the population, the city and rural proletariate of Italy. There was a danger that the army might again become an army of proletarian citizens of Rome, as under the later Republic, and renew the age of the civil wars. It seems as if the better elements of Italy succeeded in securing for themselves the higher posts in the army, access to which was given by service in the praetorian cohorts, and that only the poorer part of the Italian population served in the legions. While reducing the numbers of the Italian volunteers, Vespasian left the constitution of the corps of officers and of the praetorian guard as it had been before, but in large measure provincialized the legions. We shall see later that this view is in complete accord with the activity of Vespasian in the Western provinces generally. The soldiers drawn from the romanized provincial cities represented not the proletariate but the higher classes of the population.

The question, however, arises, how are we to account for the existence of comparatively large numbers of proletarians in Italy? To answer it, we must investigate the changes in Italian life which had resulted from the economic development of the Empire under the emperors of the Julio-Claudian dynasty.

It is no easy task to compare the economic conditions which prevailed under Augustus with those which were peculiar to the period of the Julii and Claudii. It is still more difficult to draw a line between the latter period and that of the Flavians. Yet such a distinction is necessary, and without it we shall fail to understand the evolution of economic life in the Roman Empire. We should reflect that more than half a century had elapsed between the death of Augustus and the accession of Vespasian, and that half a century is a long time, especially in a period so full of events and of new phenomena as was the first century of our era. The difficulty of investigating the economic conditions of the Julio-Claudian age arises from the character of our sources and the meagreness of their evidence. The historians were not interested in the economic life of the Empire. Our second source of information—the moralists and the scientific writers—contains more valuable material: for the former the economic conditions of the first century provided a good illustration of the moral perversity of their contemporaries, while the latter were either directly concerned with economic problems or were forced to mention economic facts in dealing with various scientific problems. Thus while Tacitus, Suetonius, and Cassius Dio give us but little information on the economic situation of the Empire between A.D. 14 and 70, important evidence is supplied by such writers as the two Senecas, Persius, even Lucan, and above all Petronius on the one hand, and Pliny the Elder and Columella on the other. But unfortunately no one has endeavoured to collect and interpret this material, except in the case of Petronius and Columella.[9] The student of the economic history of the period might derive assistance from a careful investigation of the inscriptions and of the archaeological material, especially as furnished by Pompeii. It is impossible in this short book to undertake such a complete investigation. I must limit myself to giving the impression which I have obtained after re-reading all the above-mentioned sources.

It seems at the first glance as if there were no difference between the economic conditions of the Augustan period and those of the Julio-Claudian epoch. In depicting the latter period we are involuntarily inclined to use promiscuously Virgil, Horace, Tibullus, Propertius, and Ovid on the one hand, and Persius, Petronius, Seneca, Pliny, and Columella on the other, as well as the writers of the Flavian period, both Latin and Greek. And it is true that the main phenomena remained identical. The difference consists in the degree of their development and in the emergence of some new factors. The attitude of the emperors towards economic life, their economic policy, or their lack of one, remained the same as in the days of Augustus. A policy of _laissez-faire_ prevailed. In time of great catastrophes the state felt obliged to help the victims, as for example after the great earthquake in Asia Minor under Tiberius. Some measures were taken which might have had an influence on economic life in general, for instance, measures for the improvement of tax-collection, measures introducing new taxes, measures relating to the conditions of transport, and so forth. But such measures were always taken from the purely fiscal point of view; they aimed at the improvement of the state finances, not at the betterment or readjustment of economic conditions. Economic development went on almost undisturbed by any interference on the part of the state. Its main features were those which characterized the Augustan period, but with the free play of natural forces they became more strongly marked.

The most important of these features was the gradual resurrection of economic life in the provinces. The revival is very noticeable in the East. Even a superficial glance at the ruins of the

Description of Plate XIV

1–4. FOUR PICTURES ON THE STRIP BELOW THE PANELS OF THE BLACK ROOM OF THE HOUSE OF THE VETTII AT POMPEII. Pompeii, House of the Vettii. A. Mau, *Pompeji in Leben und Kunst*² (1908), pp. 350 ff.; id. *Röm. Mitt.* 11, 1896, pp. 1 ff.; A. Sogliano in *Mon. Ant.* 8, 1898, pp. 233 ff.; M. Rostovtzeff in *Mem. of the Arch. Soc. of St. Petersburg*, 1899 (in Russian); P. Herrmann, *Denkmäler der Malerei des Altertums* (Bruckmann, München, 1904–31), pp. 29 ff., pls. xx ff.

1. TRIUMPHAL PROCESSION OF BACCHUS AND ARIADNE followed and preceded by Cupids, Psyches, and a Pan.

2. VINTAGE AND WINE-MAKING. The left portion is occupied by Cupids gathering grapes from vines attached to trees, the right (of which only a part is reproduced here) by Cupids turning the windlass of a wine-press by means of long levers. (A press was recently reconstructed in the *Villa dei Misteri* by L. Jacono: see A. Maiuri, *La Villa dei Misteri* (1931), pp. 89 ff.). Cf. S. Reinach, *Rép. d. peint.*, p. 85, 3.

3. WINE-DEALERS. In a cellar where a large number of wine-jars is stored the buyer, a rustic fellow with a cane in his left hand, is tasting a sample which is given to him by an elegant city man, the dealer, assisted by his slaves, who are filling another cup with another sample of wine.

4. FLOWER-DEALERS. Flowers are carried from the garden on the back of a goat. Cupids are making garlands. The garlands are exhibited for sale on a special stand, from which a fine lady-buyer is taking one. A Cupid holds up two fingers to indicate the price (two *asses*). Cf. S. Reinach, *Rép. d. peint.*, p. 86, 8; p. 92, 1 and 2.

I have no doubt that the prominent place which is given in the ornamentation of the room to scenes dealing with wine and flowers indicates that the Vettii owned many farms in the neighbourhood of Pompeii and were large dealers in these products. I formed this idea long before I read the careful discussion of the House of the Vettii by M. Della Corte, 'Le case ed abitanti di Pompei', *Neapolis*, 2, 1915, pp. 311 ff. Della Corte has shown that the Vettii owned many wine-farms in the territory of that city and of Stabiae, and carried on a large and important business in wine. They produced various brands, which are mentioned in the inscriptions on the wine-jars found in large quantities in their house. Of these inscriptions the most characteristic are: (1) 'XV Kal(endas) Ian(uarias) de Arriano dol. XV', *CIL* iv. 5572; (2) 'Idibus Ian(uariis) de Asiniano racemat(o) dol. I', *CIL* iv. 5573; (3) 'Idibus . . . de Formiano dolio XXV', *CIL* iv. 5577. I agree with Mau that the wine in the jars was brought from the various farms of the brothers Vettii, which were planted with vines of different sorts, and that the *dolia* (jars) of each kind were numbered. *Diffusio* of wine, which is mentioned in our inscriptions, is represented on the bas-relief of Ince Blundell Hall, pl. xxxiii, 2. Note also the manifest symbolism of the familiar picture in the *vestibulum* of the house (Priapus with purse and fruit) and the frequency, in the decoration of the house, of figures of Cupids and Psyches picking flowers. Similar symbolism recurs in many other houses of Pompeii, e.g. that of Meleager, which was owned by L. Cornelius Primogenes, with its well-known figures of Ceres or Demeter seated and Mercury placing a well-filled purse in her lap (M. Della Corte, *Neapolis*, 2, 1915, p. 189). I think that the Vettii who were owners of this house were freedmen of the noble house of the Vettii.

1. BACCHUS AND ARIADNE

2. VINTAGE

3. WINE-DEALER

4. FLOWER-SELLER

XIV. PICTURES FROM THE HOUSE OF THE VETTII, POMPEII

cities and a rapid survey of the epigraphy of Asia Minor and
Syria and of the papyri of Egypt show how rapid was the economic progress of the East under Augustus and still more under his
successors.[10] The Western provinces, too, especially Gaul, Spain,
and Africa, resumed their economic activity, which had been
arrested first by the wars of conquest and afterwards by the civil
wars. One of the signs of their revival was the rapid growth of
town life, which was fostered by the emperors but was based
mainly on the natural development of these lands. In Spain and
Africa, at least, urbanization was the continuation of an evolu-
tionary process which had begun long before the Romans. Spain
had always been a land of cities, like Italy and Greece. In
Africa urbanization had been already carried out, to a great
extent, by the Carthaginians and by the natives who lived
under Carthaginian rule and under the kings of Numidia and
Mauretania.[11]

From the economic point of view urbanization meant the formation of a city *bourgeoisie*, of a class of landowners, traders, and
industrialists, who resided in the city and who developed an
energetic business activity on capitalistic lines. Urbanization
meant, therefore, the re-introduction into Africa and the introduction into large parts of Spain and Gaul of a capitalistic husbandry, similar to that which prevailed in Italy and in the East.
In agriculture this involved a transition from peasant economy
to that of landowners who ran their estates on capitalistic and
scientific lines. It involved also the tendency to replace the culture of cereals by more profitable forms of cultivation, especially
vines and olive-trees. There was nothing new in this so far as
large parts of Spain and Africa, as well as the Greek cities of
Gaul, were concerned. But their natural development in that
direction had been stunted first by the selfish policy of the agrarian magnates of the second century B.C., and then by the civil
wars of the first century. Under Augustus and his successors,
viticulture and the planting of olive-trees developed rapidly, the
former mostly in Gaul, the latter in Spain first and afterwards in
Africa. The rate of progress was accelerated by the emigration
of Italians into the Western provinces, which has been described
in the first chapter.[12]

Another phenomenon of the same type was the gradual migration of industry to the provinces. From the earliest times Gaul

showed an unusual capacity for developing industry. Under Roman rule she continued to do so on a very large scale and soon appeared as a serious rival of Italy in the production of articles which were most characteristically Italian, such as relief clay vases and metal ware. The wonderful system of the French rivers and the age-long connexion of Gaul with Britain and Germany made a rapid development of Gallic industry easy and profitable, as the discoveries made at Graufesenque in Southern Gaul indicate in no uncertain manner. Italian products began to disappear from the Celtic and German markets.[13]

The development of commerce also gradually assumed new and unexpected aspects, especially in the East. We have seen how the trade with Arabia and India, which had dealt almost exclusively in luxuries, began to play a certain part in the commercial relations of the Roman Empire in the time of Augustus, and how the expedition of Aelius Gallus was partly dictated by the necessity of protecting this growing trade. Its growth proceeded steadily throughout the time of the Julii and Claudii. The main current of Indian and central Asiatic trade passed from India to Egypt either directly or via Arabia, and concentrated in Alexandria. In the Hellenistic and Roman periods Petra was the great centre of commerce in Northern Arabia. In the earlier Hellenistic age Indian and Arabian merchandize went from Petra to Egypt via Leuke Kome, Aila, or Gaza. Later, when Syria and Phoenicia passed into the hands of the Seleucids, these rulers attempted to divert the commerce of Arabia towards the ports of Palestine, Phoenicia, and Syria, and thus oust their Egyptian rivals. With this aim in view they favoured the old military colonies of the early Hellenistic period in Transjordan, in particular Philadelphia in the land of the Ammonites (Rabbath–Ammon), Antioch in the territory of Gerasa, Berenice, Gadara, and Dion, and attempted to transform them into regular caravan-cities, which would protect the caravans coming from Petra on their route to Damascus and the Syrian ports. The Seleucids never entirely succeeded: Petra remained loyal to the Ptolemies. With the beginning of Roman suzerainty the position changed. Under the protection of Pompey, the Greek cities of Transjordan, the greater part of which had been destroyed by the fanatic Alexander Jannaeus (102–76 B.C.), began to revive, although they did not really flourish again until the end of the first century A.D. The peace and security established by the Empire enabled them to attract in lasting fashion towards the Syrian and Phoenician ports a good part of the trade of Petra, without at the same time impairing seriously the position of Alexandria.[14]

From earliest times Indian and central Asiatic trade discharged itself through another route, that through the valleys of the Tigris and the Euphrates. At the end of the Hellenistic period the hostility between the Parthians and Seleucids, and then between the Parthians and Romans, combined with the anarchy prevailing on the Euphrates, resulted in the abandonment of this ancient route by transports from the Persian Gulf and from Persia, which took instead the route across the desert to Petra. In the first century A.D. after the Romans had found a *modus vivendi* with the Parthians, things changed. The route via the Euphrates was re-opened. The little village of Palmyra, inhabited by an Avamaean tribe, realized the great advantage of its position, half-way between the Euphrates and Damascus, in the immediate neighbourhood of one of the few springs in the desert. Palmyra was thus enabled—certainly with the approval and protection of the Romans and the Parthians—to unify the tribes of the surrounding desert and create conditions which would guarantee to the caravans coming from Seleucia–Ctesiphon the security lacking farther to the North, on the upper reaches of the Euphrates. At the time when Strabo's source was writing, Palmyra in fact did not exist; already under Augustus and Tiberius she built one of the most beautiful temples in Syria, and became, under the dual protection of the Parthians and the Romans, a large and wealthy caravan-city with fine streets and squares and notable public buildings.[15]

However the field of oriental commerce was so great that the opening of the route Petra–Transjordan–Damascus, and the re-opening of the Palmyra route was not ruinous to Alexandria. The maritime traffic of Egypt with Arabia and thence with India preserved its ancient importance. The rapid development of the latter is illustrated by the interesting handbook of an Alexandrian merchant, the *Periplus Maris Erythraei*, which was written in the time of Domitian, and by the evidence furnished by Pliny the Elder.[16] On the other hand, large finds of Roman

Description of Plate XV

1–4. FOUR PICTURES ON THE STRIP BELOW THE PANELS OF THE BLACK ROOM OF THE HOUSE OF THE VETTII. Pompeii, House of the Vettii. Bibliography as for pl. XIV.

1. MAKERS AND SELLERS OF PERFUMES OR PERFUMED OIL (*UNGUEN-TARII*). A special brand of fine olive-oil is being prepared on a special type of oil-press (at the right). The oil is boiled. The boiling oil is mixed with special essences (probably extracts of flowers). Next comes the desk of the manager and accountant. Near him is a cupboard with bottles of various sizes and forms containing the various essences (?). The rest of the picture shows the sale of perfumed oil to a lady customer, who has come in with her slave-maid. See A. Mau, *Röm. Mitt.* 15, 1900, pp. 301 ff. Cf. S. Reinach, *Rép. d. peint.*, p. 86, 4; p. 91, 2.

2. FULLERS (*FULLONES*). Treading the clothes in vats, carding, inspecting the clothing, and folding the finished garments.

3. GOLDSMITHS (*AURIFICES*). A large furnace on the right. Behind the furnace a Cupid is intensely occupied in chiselling a large metal bowl, probably a bronze bowl which is being prepared for inlaying with silver. (A bronze bowl inlaid with silver has been found in a shop of a *negotiator aerarius*, M. Della Corte, *Riv. Indo-Greco-Italica*, 6, 1922, p. 104.) Another Cupid is busy keeping the furnace going by means of a blow-pipe, and heating a piece of metal which he holds with a pair of tongs. A third is hammering a small piece of metal on an anvil. Near him stands a counter with three open drawers and a large and a smaller pair of scales. A lady customer discusses with the proprietor the weight of a jewel. Beyond them two Cupids are hammering a large piece of metal on an anvil. There is no doubt that these scenes illustrate the jeweller's trade (A. Blanchet, *Procès verb. de la Soc. fr. de Numism.* 1899, pp. xvi ff. and xlviii ff.; cf. *Études de Num.* 2, 1901, pp. 195 ff. and 224 ff.; A. Mau, *Röm. Mitt.* 16, 1901, pp. 109 ff.). It is strange that prominent scholars could seriously discuss the view that they represent, not a jewellery shop, but a mint (*Röm. Mitt.* 22, 1907, pp. 198 ff.; *Num. Chron.* 1922, pp. 28 ff.; P. Herrmann, *Denkm. der Malerei*, p. 37). What could a lady customer have to do with a mint? There is, I think, every reason to believe that some of the silver-plate found at Pompeii was made in Pompeian shops, such as that of Laelius Erastus, the owner of a large house in the town (*CIL* x. 8071. 10, 11, and Della Corte, *Neapolis*, 2, 1915, p. 184). Cf. the shop of Pinarius Cerialis, *caelator*, recently discovered at Pompeii, M. Della Corte, *Riv. Indo-Greco-Italica*, 8, 1924, p. 121.

4. THE FEAST OF THE VESTALIA. Cupids and Psyches at a banquet. Behind are seen asses, the sacred animals of Vesta. Are the banqueters the bakers (*pistores*)? Cf. another fresco with the same subject, S. Reinach, *Rép. d. peint.*, p. 88, 3.

The gradual industrialization of economic life in Pompeii has been described in Chap. I, note 25, and Chap. II, notes 25 and 36. It is very probable (as already stated) that the Vettii, who owned this beautiful house, selected the special trades which are portrayed on the walls of its best room because they had a personal interest in them; and those were in fact the chief trades of Campania in general. It is plain, too, that the rich Pompeians took pride in exhibiting to their friends pictures illustrating—in a slightly romantic manner (Cupids being substituted for men)—the modest occupations which contributed to their wealth and influence. The *bourgeoisie* of the cities was not ashamed of its prosaic callings: witness, for example, the candour with which the typical representative of the class, Trimalchio, tells the whole story of his life in conversation, in the pictures which adorned his house, and on his funeral monument; witness also the pride with which his Pompeian prototype Fabius Eupor, a rich business man, in an electoral programme adds to his name 'princeps libertinorum' (*CIL* iv. 117).

1. PERFUMERY

2. FULLERS

3. JEWELLERS

4. THE VESTALIA

XV. PICTURES FROM THE HOUSE OF THE VETTII, POMPEII

coins in India enable us to verify the data of the literary sources.[17]
It seems as if the commerce was concentrated in the Arabian
harbours until the time of Claudius and Nero. The Arabian
merchants served as intermediaries between the Egyptian
traders and those of India. It was, as has been said, to a great
extent a commerce dealing in luxuries. For these luxuries the
Romans paid mostly in gold and silver. This kind of exchange
was inevitable in a trade which was carried on chiefly through
intermediaries.

The discovery of the monsoons by Hippalus of Alexandria
in the late Ptolemaic or early Roman period, as well as the natural
tendency of a growing trade to become more than a trade in
luxuries and a merely passive trade on one side, led to the establishment of a direct route by sea between Egypt and India.
The main centre of traffic was now Alexandria. The Arabian
harbours lost their importance; some of them (Adana and perhaps Socotra) were occupied by the Romans and served as
watering stations and refuges for the sailors. Like the military
and naval stations in the Crimea, they served also to protect the
merchants against pirates. This advance was due to the efforts
of the Egyptian merchants of the imperial period, who secured
the active aid of the Roman government, first under Augustus
and later under Claudius and Nero. The new route was fully
established at the date of the *Periplus*, that is, under Domitian.
The trade with India gradually developed into a regular exchange of goods of different kinds between Egypt on the one
side and Arabia and India on the other. One of the most important articles which came from India was cotton, another probably was silk. Both of these products were worked up in the
factories of Alexandria—the considerably later *Expositio totius
mundi et gentium*, § 22, seems to show that the silk was mainly
worked up in the Phoenician cities—which sent in exchange
glass, metal ware, and probably linen.[18]

Roman trade also made important progress towards the North.
From scattered literary references and from archaeological discoveries made in Eastern Germany, Scandinavia (Sweden and
Norway), and Russia, we know that in fact in the age of Claudius
and Nero Roman merchants maintained large-scale traffic with
Eastern Germany, Norway, and Sweden. The oldest route they
followed to reach Denmark, the Scandinavian countries. and

Eastern Germany was the sea-route from the ports of Northern Gaul towards the East. At about the same time Roman goods, transported from the mouth of the Danube and from the Greek cities of the Black Sea Coast, by way of the Dnieper, began to reach the Baltic and the Scandinavian countries. At the same time the territory of the Dnieper came gradually to be occupied by the Germans. But the safest route was that which led to Eastern Germany, and thence to Scandinavia, from Aquileia through Carnuntum and the kingdom of Maroboduus. The main articles of this trade were bronze and glass, both, no doubt, products of Campania.[19]

Italy did not at first feel the results of this slow economic emancipation of the provinces. As before, her landowners produced large quantities of wine and olive-oil on their capitalistic farms. As before, the workshops of Campania and Northern Italy displayed an important activity.[20] But a certain uneasiness began to show itself. Columella and Pliny still advocate the cultivation of the vine on the largest possible scale. They both feel, however, that it is necessary to stimulate the activity of the Italian landowners, who were not much inclined to invest money in the upkeep of existing vineyards and in the plantation of new ones. Pliny tells marvellous stories about the fabulous success of some wine-growers in Italy.[21] Yet the landowners were not enthusiastic about following the advice given. They were more inclined to let their land to tenants (*coloni*), thus gradually reverting to peasant husbandry and to the production of cereals.[22] How are we to explain this tendency? The ordinary view is that they did not want to supervise the management of their farms personally. They are accused of laziness and indolence. I can hardly believe that this was the main reason. Nor can I believe that shortage of labour was the chief cause of the decline of scientific agriculture. There was still plenty of slave labour. Slaves were employed in large numbers in households, in industrial shops, in commerce, in banking, and in the imperial administration. There was no lack of slaves for agriculture either. If the import of slaves from the usual places became more difficult, it became more common to make the contracting of marriages and the raising of children attractive for the slaves.[23]

The real reason, which was well understood by the landowners, though it was disregarded by Pliny and Columella, was that the conditions of the market grew worse and worse every day with the economic development of the Western provinces. Central Italy and Campania were the principal sufferers. For Northern Italy the Danubian market was still open and was daily increasing in importance, and therefore Northern Italy did not feel the changed conditions as much as did the centre and the south of the peninsula. Over-production of wine began to make itself felt from time to time, a phenomenon well known to modern Italy and even to France. The situation was not disastrous as yet, but it was grave. We shall see in the sixth chapter how these conditions led to a serious crisis under Domitian.[24]

Hand in hand with this change went the growing concentration of landed property in the hands of a few rich owners. This concentration was going on both in Italy and in the provinces, especially in Africa. There may perhaps be a certain amount of exaggeration in the well-known statement of Pliny that in Nero's time six landowners possessed half of the territory of Africa,* but the fact remains that large estates were the outstanding feature of the agrarian conditions in that province. The growth of large estates was characteristic of Egypt also. Enormous οὐσίαι were formed in Egypt under Augustus, and still more under Claudius and Nero. Most of them were gifts of the emperors to their favourites, women as well as men. We must not, however, exaggerate the importance of these facts, nor generalize from the conditions which prevailed in Africa and gradually developed in Egypt. From time immemorial Africa was the Promised Land of large estates, a land of a peculiar type of plantations, exploited by Roman magnates in the first century B.C. In Egypt the large estates were a creation of the emperors, who granted and sold large tracts of land to the members of their family and to their favourites. We hear very little of corresponding phenomena in Gaul and Spain. And in Italy the process seems to have been rather slow. Yet there is no doubt that in Italy also the large estates grew larger and gradually absorbed the medium-sized farms and the peasant plots. Seneca is quite explicit on this point, and he ought to know, as he was one of the richest men, if not the richest man, in Italy under Claudius and Nero, and was himself an owner of large properties. The explanation lies again in

* *NH* xviii. 35.

Description of Plate XVI

1–2. TWO FRESCOES ON THE ENTRANCE PILASTERS OF A SHOP IN THE STRADA DELL' ABBONDANZA, POMPEII (REG. IX, INS. X, NO. 7). M. Della Corte, *Not. d. Scavi*, 1912, pp. 176 ff., figs. 2 and 3, and *Riv. Indo-Greco-Italica*, 7, 1923, pp. 110 ff. (with bibliography).

The upper part of the right pilaster is occupied by a small temple on a *podium*, with a *pronaos* of two columns. From the *cella* of the temple Mercury emerges in full dress: *petasos*, winged shoes, *chiton* and *chlamys*, *caduceus* and purse, ready to start probably for a visit to the shop of Verecundus. On the square beneath the temple is painted a comfortable shop, in the centre of which a lady is solemnly seated talking to a customer and holding in her hands two coloured slippers. The customer, sitting on a fine couch, is arguing with her. In front of the shopkeeper stands a table covered with the articles which are sold in the shop—coloured rugs or garments and slippers—while in the street, in front of the shop, is placed a wooden stand for drying the goods (*Dig.* 43. 10. 1. 4). The space above the temple and the picture of the shop are covered with electoral posters, but not the picture of the temple and the god.

On the upper part of the left pilaster is painted in bright colours Venus Pompeiana, the protectress of Pompeii, wearing a mural crown, as Tyche of the city. To right and left fly Cupids; her son—himself a Cupid—offers her the mirror. She rides in a boat drawn by four African elephants. On the right Fortuna stands on a globe, and on the left the Genius with *patera* and *cornucopiae*. The lower part of the area depicts the little factory, as it seems to be, where the goods sold by the lady were manufactured. In the centre four workmen are engaged in heating wool which is to be made into felt. Two other workmen to the left, and one to the right, are seen seated behind low benches in the typical attitude of shoemakers. In the right corner the shop-owner (whose name Verecundus is written beneath his figure and is repeated twice as a graffito) triumphantly displays a piece of finished cloth—a heavy rug. The picture of the shop is covered with an electoral notice which reads 'Vettium Firmum aed(ilem) quactiliar(i) rog(ant)' (*Not. d. Scavi*, 1912, p. 188, no. 29 [= *L'An. Ép.* 1913, 94]). It is hardly possible that such an outrage could have been perpetrated on the shop-sign by anybody but the owner and the workmen of the shop themselves. The notice, it should be observed, does not encroach on the space occupied by the figure of the goddess. It shows that Verecundus was a *coactiliarius* or *lanarius coactiliarius* (*CIL* vi. 9494), a manufacturer of felt (cf. *Not. d. Scavi*, 1912, p. 136, no. 2 [= *L'An. Ép.* 1913, 85]). He may also have been a tailor; cf. *CIL* iv. 3130: 'M. Vecilius Verecundus vestiar(ius)', and a graffito which reads 'tunica lintea aur(ata)', both quoted by Della Corte. On signs of shops in general, see A. Mau in Pauly–Wissowa, ii, cols. 2558 ff., and cf. Kubitschek, ibid., Zw. R. ii, cols. 2452 ff., 2565 f. The pictures express the spirit of the age—'Business under the aegis of religion'. Mercury was the chief god; and along with him the patron-goddess of Pompeii, who protected the trade and commerce of the town and assured its prosperity, the victorious and successful Venus Pompeiana, was worshipped and adored by every citizen. She was the queen and, as such, she was drawn in her triumphal procession by the royal animals, the elephants, like the Hellenistic kings and the Roman emperors. The importance of the textile industry at Pompeii is described in Chap. III, note 20. It may be added that in the part of the Strada dell' Abbondanza recently excavated there have been discovered, besides the shop to which this plate refers, another shop of *coactiliarii* (Della Corte, *Riv. Indo-Greco-Italica*, 7, 1923, p. 113), one of *infectores* (ibid., p. 112)—with which may be compared the shop of the *offectores* (Della Corte, ibid. 4, 1920, pp. 117 ff.)—and many *fullonicae*, two of which are of very large dimensions (Della Corte, ibid. 7, 1923, pp. 114 and 123).

1

2

XVI. POMPEIAN SHOP-SIGNS

the conditions of agriculture which have been described in the preceding pages. The middle-sized estates were gradually undermined by the conditions of the market and were readily sold to big capitalists. These latter naturally sought to simplify the management of their properties and, being content to receive a safe though low rent, they preferred to let their land to tenants and to produce chiefly corn.[25]

Italy was therefore gradually becoming a corn-land again. This conclusion does not accord with accepted views. How, it is asked, could Italy regard the production of corn as more profitable than that of wine? Was not cheap provincial corn always available, and was it possible for Italy to compete with it? I very greatly doubt whether after the reforms of Augustus and Tiberius many provinces still paid their tribute in corn.[26] Corn came to Italy and especially to Rome from the imperial domains in Egypt and in Africa. It formed the main revenue of the emperors and was used by them for purposes which they deemed indispensable for the maintenance of their power—the provisioning of the army and the feeding of the rabble in Rome. The rest they sold in the same way as other landowners. The prices were fixed by the conditions of the market, and these conditions were favourable to the corn-dealers. There was no overproduction of corn in the Roman Empire. One of the most important branches of administration in all cities, particularly in the East, was that which dealt with the supply of corn for the needs of the population ($\epsilon\vartheta\eta\nu\iota\alpha$). And yet famines were quite a common occurrence in the city life of the Empire.[27] The emperors were aware of this, and they encouraged corn-production and restricted the freedom of the corn trade, especially in Egypt. Under such conditions the production of corn was certainly profitable in Italy, perhaps more profitable, or at least safer, than the production of wine.

Concurrent with the growth of large estates in Italy and in the provinces was the rapid concentration of many of them in the hands of the emperors. The bitter fight between the emperors and the senatorial aristocracy ended under Nero in an almost complete extermination of the richest and oldest senatorial families. Few of them, and those the least influential, were left. Many families disappeared also because of the aversion of the aristocracy to form families and beget children. The result of those two factors was the concentration of vast properties in the hands of the emperors through confiscation and inheritance. Though the lands confiscated from those who were condemned for *lèse-majesté* went legally to the state, in practice they were taken by the emperors, this practice being a sort of heritage from the times of the civil wars. Most rich men, especially bachelors, left a large part of their fortunes to the emperors in order to secure the rest for their natural or chosen heirs. These facts are too well known to be insisted on. Confiscated and inherited property consisted mostly of real estate. It was impossible to conceal a house or a parcel of land and comparatively easy to dispose of money. Thus the emperors became the greatest landowners of the Roman Empire. That fact is important not merely from the political point of view: it has a significance for economic history. Though large estates remained one of the chief features of the economic life of the Empire, the personnel of the landowning class changed. The ancient magnates disappeared; they were replaced by the emperors, and partly by their favourites, though the latter disappeared in their turn. Alongside of them there were the new wealthy landowners, who belonged to the ranks of the municipal aristocracy. At the head of the whole class stood the emperor. The management of the imperial estates was a serious problem for the emperors. How were they to obtain a secure rent from these enormous tracts of land? How were they to solve the question of labour? All these matters will come up for discussion later. The time of the Julii and Claudii was a time of confiscation and concentration, not of organization.[28]

I have repeatedly spoken of the increasing prosperity which the provinces, especially those of the East, enjoyed under the Julio-Claudian emperors. There are, however, some signs that this process was not unbroken, even though the period as a whole formed one of continual progress. We have not much relevant material; but if we confront the panegyric given by Philo of the prosperity brought to Egypt by Roman rule in the time of Tiberius with the sketch of Egypt in the time of Caligula and Claudius* given by the same author, the comparison shows that the rule of the successors of Tiberius was not a blessing to that country. This impression is reinforced by numerous

* Philo, *Leg. ad G.* 8 ff., cf. 47 ff., 141 ff. (Tiberius); cf. *in Flaccum*, 5 (behaviour of the soldiers), 150 (confiscation of estates), 93 (search for arms).

documents from the Fayyûm, from which we learn that once flourishing villages were abandoned under Nero, probably through fiscal pressure and neglect of the system of irrigation. This latter trouble may be explained by the increase of large estates in Egypt, and by the preference shown by the government to the Roman magnates at the expense of the peasants and small landowners. The famous edict of Ti. Julius Alexander* shows that he found the country in a bad condition, and much in need of reform. Nevertheless the decline of Egypt in the last part of the first century A.D. may have been an exception, resulting from the heedless exploitation of the country as a private estate of the emperor and as corn-reservoir of the Roman Empire. I incline, furthermore, to the belief that the reckless extravagance of Nero's last years contributed not a little to the partial ruin of Italy.[29]

It is easy to understand how such conditions were bringing about an important change in the social aspect of the Empire. The old aristocracy of the city of Rome disappeared. New men came to replace them: some from the municipal nobility of Italy, some from the more or less romanized provinces, some from the ranks of adventurers and favourites of the emperors. Statistics, incomplete as they may be, show the gradual development of the process. The equestrian nobility both in Italy and in the provinces grew enormously in numbers. The majority of the knights lived in Italy and in the provinces; they were partly well-to-do landowners, partly officers in the army and officials employed by the emperors.[30]

The growing prosperity of Italy, the renascence of the Oriental provinces, and the urbanization of the Western and of some of the Eastern provinces created a strong and numerous city-*bourgeoisie* all over the Roman Empire. It was the leading force in the Empire. The older men were members of the city councils and of the colleges of magistrates and priests. The younger generation served in the army and in the praetorian guard, as officers, as non-commissioned officers, as soldiers. For this task they were prepared by a careful training in their municipal clubs, the *collegia iuvenum*, which were never stronger and never better organized than in the time of the Julio-Claudian dynasty.

* Dittenberger, *OGIS* 669 [= ‡Evelyn White–Oliver, *Temple of Hibis* (1939), ii, pp. 25 ff., nos. 3–4].

On this *bourgeoisie*, along with the army, rested in the last resort the power of the emperors.[31]

In Rome, Italy, and the provinces there grew up along with this freeborn *bourgeoisie* a class of thrifty and energetic men, that of the freedmen. Their importance in the life of the Empire cannot be over-estimated. In administration they played, along with the imperial slaves, a very important part as assistants and agents of the emperor. The emperors still looked upon themselves as living the life of a Roman magnate, and organized their 'household' (*domus*) on the same lines as the other Roman nobles, that is to say, with the help of their private slaves and freedmen. But in fact their household, though not identical with the state, like that of the Hellenistic monarchs, was at least as important as, and perhaps more important than, the machinery of the state, and thus their slaves and freedmen—the *Caesaris servi* and the *liberti Augusti*—formed a kind of new aristocracy as rich as the freeborn senatorial, equestrian, and municipal *bourgeoisie*, and certainly not less influential in the management of state affairs.

These imperial slaves and freedmen formed, however, but a small part of the slaves and freedmen in the Roman world. The slaves were the backbone of the economic life of the Empire, especially in commerce and industry, where they supplied the labour employed by the owners of the various workshops. Indeed, the owners of these shops themselves were, to a great extent, former slaves who succeeded in receiving or buying their liberty and in acquiring a considerable fortune. The municipal freedmen formed the lower section of the municipal aristocracy or plutocracy, just as the imperial freedmen formed the lower section of the imperial aristocracy. As an influential class they were given a place in municipal society by the institution of *magistri* and *ministri* (the last being sometimes even slaves) in various municipal cults and especially by the institution of the *Augustales* in the cult of the emperors. Their part was to furnish money for the upkeep of the cult. As a reward they received the title of 'Augustalis' and certain privileges in municipal life.[32]

The incipient disturbance in the economic life of Italy and the growth of large estates and of the numbers of tenants created or increased the urban and rural proletariate—unemployed men in the cities, tenants and hired labourers in the country. Most of them—like a section of the *bourgeoisie* and of the proletariate in the city of Rome, and like many residents in the Italian and provincial cities—did not belong to the Italian or native provincial stock. They were chiefly Orientals imported as slaves and retaining their non-Roman characteristics for many generations.[33] It is no wonder that many of them were willing to take up service in the army. Nor is it surprising that many of them proved untrustworthy from the military as well as from the political point of view. It was only natural that Vespasian should be glad to get rid of them.

IV

THE RULE OF THE FLAVIANS AND THE ENLIGHTENED MONARCHY OF THE ANTONINES

WITH the victory of Vespasian over Vitellius the orgy of civil war ended, apparently under the pressure of public opinion in Italy and because the soldiers were confident that they had finally achieved their aim. They had shown that the emperor ought to be, not a nominee of the praetorians, but the best man in the Empire, recognized as such alike by the army and by the senate and people of Rome, regardless of his relation to the family of Augustus. The 'Year of the Four Emperors' was therefore an episode, but an episode which had important consequences for the future of the Empire and led to a new phase in the history of the principate.

This new phase began with the rule of restoration under Vespasian and his son Titus. In its essential features their government resembled that of Augustus and that of Tiberius in the earlier years of his reign. The chief problem was the restoration of peace. It is not an accident but a significant indication of the ideas which guided Vespasian that one of his first acts was the closing of the Janus temple, that his most splendid building was the *forum Pacis*, a counterpart to the *ara Pacis* of Augustus, and that the figure of *Pax Augusta* reappeared on his coins.[1]

The essential condition of peace was the tranquillity and obedience of the army. The task of restoring quiet and discipline in the ranks both of the praetorians and of the provincial armies was not an easy one. It was facilitated to some extent by the depressed mood of the army after the terrors of the year of the four emperors, and by public opinion in Italy and in the provinces. But there was no certainty that the influence of these two factors would last for long. Hence the military reforms of Vespasian. By these reforms I do not mean his redistribution of troops, his disbandment of some legions, and his creation of new ones. Important as they were, these changes could not guarantee the maintenance of peace and quiet in the army for the future. The main point was to remodel the constitution of the army from the social point of view.[2] I have already explained what seems to have been the guiding principle of Vespasian in this matter: the elimination of the Italian proletariate from the ranks of the army. The army, save for a portion of the praetorians, was to be an army of provincials; not, however, of provincials taken from all parts of the Roman world without regard to their origin and their social standing. We have, it is true, very little evidence even about the provenance of the soldiers in the Flavian period, not to speak of the social class to which they belonged. But the facts that in stating their place of origin they generally name a city and that Vespasian, like Augustus and Claudius, consistently promoted the urbanization of the Empire and favoured the largest possible extension of Roman and Latin citizenship to the urbanized areas, especially in the West,[3] show that his policy of provincializing the army did not mean barbarizing it. We have every reason to suppose that the grant of a city constitution to rural and tribal communities and the grant of Roman or Latin franchise to existing cities involved not only privileges but also duties, and pre-supposed a fair degree either of romanization or of hellenization. The first duty of the newly constituted cities was to send their youth to the legions. It is noteworthy that under the Flavians the institution of the *collegia iuvenum*, the seminaries of future soldiers in Italy, was revived and spread all over the Western provinces.[4]

Thus the Roman legionary army of the Flavian period was, in the main, an army recruited from the higher, that is, the most civilized and best educated, classes of the urbanized parts of the Empire. It was an army of '*bourgeois*', to use a modern word much abused by the socialists, an army drawn from the propertied classes of the provincial cities, the landowners and farmers— whether they lived in the cities or continued to reside on their farms and in their country houses—not from the city or the rural proletariate. In most of the provincial cities both old and new, as we shall see later, the proletariate did not belong to the body of citizens. It was easier therefore in the provinces than it was in Italy to exclude this class from the ranks of the army.

Another reform of Vespasian, carried out in the same spirit, was the new system of recruiting the auxiliary troops. It is very

Description of Plate XVII

1. ONE OF THE BAS-RELIEFS ON THE FUNERAL MONUMENT OF TRAJAN, THE COLUMN IN THE FORUM TRAIANI AT ROME. C. Cichorius, *Die Reliefs der Trajanssäule*, pl. LXXVII, text III, p. 169; K. Lehmann-Hartleben, *Die Trajanssäule*, pl. 49, no. 104.

Trajan with his staff on a *podium*, delivering one of his speeches (*allocutiones*) to the soldiers of his expeditionary army. The first row is composed of the bearers of the invincible standards (*signiferi*), behind whom are the legionary soldiers and the horsemen. Like the other sculptures of the column, this scene portrays Trajan as the great leader of the Romans, the first Roman, the *princeps*, who toils for the welfare and glory of the Roman Empire.

2. ANOTHER BAS-RELIEF OF THE COLUMN OF TRAJAN. Cichorius, op. cit., pl. LXXIII, nos. 262–4, text III, pp. 142 ff.; K. Lehmann-Hartleben, op. cit., pl. 46, no. 100.

Trajan surrounded by his staff, all in civil dress, receiving an embassy which consists of at least eight groups of enemy chieftains—Germans, Sarmatians, Thracians, and perhaps the forefathers of the Slavs. In the background is seen a fortified city with an amphitheatre and a house outside the walls. The sculpture is a real masterpiece of the great artist who decorated the column. It is not only an artistically beautiful group but also a triumph of psychological intuition. Two worlds face each other—the proud world of the Romans, the civilized dwellers in cities, the *togati* (represented by the emperor, his staff, and the Roman soldiers), and the new world, the world of the Germans, the Balkan peoples, and the Slavs, the barbarians who were ready to take up the heritage of the Roman Empire and start a new life on the ruins of the ancient cities. They have come to greet the great Roman not as slaves or subjects but as equals, no less proud and self-confident than he. The duel between the two worlds has just begun, and its deep significance was well understood by the artist of genius who created this scene. No doubt its momentous importance was fully realized by the great emperors of the second century.

3. ONE OF THE BAS-RELIEFS OF THE COLUMN OF MARCUS AURELIUS AT ROME. Rome, Piazza Colonna. E. Petersen, A. von Domaszewski, G. Calderini, *Die Marcussäule auf der Piazza Colonna in Rome* (1896), pl. 119A, §§ cx–cxi.

The Roman army on the march. The emperor M. Aurelius, bare-headed, without arms, walking as a soldier between two of his generals in similar dress and two *vexilla* (standards). His horse is led by a soldier. Behind him are shown the herds which were taken from the people to feed the army, and before him heavy cars loaded with arms and drawn by oxen and horses requisitioned in the land of the enemy and in the neighbouring Roman provinces. From the purely technical and artistic point of view the sculpture is far inferior to the sculptures of the column of Trajan. But it is full of life and movement, and the figure of the emperor, conspicuous among the others, is a striking testimony to the manner in which M. Aurelius carried out in practice his lofty ideas of duty. What but the consciousness of duty could induce the aged philosopher to march hour after hour among the forests and swamps of the almost uncivilized Danubian lands?

1. TRAJAN ON CAMPAIGN. ALLOCUTIO

2. TRAJAN AND THE BARBARIAN CHIEFS

3. M. AURELIUS ON CAMPAIGN

XVII. WARS OF THE ROMAN EMPIRE

probable that he abandoned the policy of raising these troops almost exclusively from the peoples and ·tribes who had no city life at all and therefore formed the least civilized element of the provincial population. From his time the essential difference between the legionary and auxiliary troops gradually disappeared: both classes were recruited in the provinces, in both we find some soldiers who were Roman citizens by birth, both contained a comparatively large number of men (greater in the legions, smaller in the auxiliary troops) who by birth and education belonged to the urbanized section of the population. Moreover, despite their ethnical names, the auxiliary troops did not consist exclusively of men who belonged to one tribe or one locality. In a *cohors Thracum*, for instance, there were not only Thracians but men of other origin. This policy of mixing up nations and tribes in the military corps is one which was followed for many years in Tsarist Russia and is a wise policy for a state composed of many nationalities. From Vespasian's time, too, the locally recruited auxiliary regiments never formed the majority of the auxiliary troops of a province. The local *cohortes, alae,* and *numeri* of Egypt or Africa were always less numerous than those which bore other than Egyptian or African names and which consisted of soldiers of whom few, if any, were born in Egypt or in Africa.

The same system was applied to the troops permanently stationed in Rome. The necessity of recruiting them from among Roman citizens resident in Italy had had the result that their selection had not been very rigorous. Now, on the other hand, we find, alongside the Italians in the garrison of Rome, a certain number of provincials of urbanized regions, especially of South Gaul, Spain, Noricum, Macedonia, and, in addition, men from the Alpine regions, from Lusitania, from Dalmatia, and from Pannonia.

The measures of Vespasian for neutralizing the army (from the political point of view) were not less effective than those which had been taken many years before by Augustus with the same object. Here again Vespasian was a good pupil and a faithful follower of the policy of Augustus. The restored discipline and fighting power of the Roman army were tested in the difficult wars of Domitian and during the crisis which followed his murder. The army, apart from the praetorians, took no active part in the political events of this troubled period and silently recognized the *fait accompli* when Nerva was chosen by the senate and Trajan was adopted by Nerva. A vivid illustration of the conditions of this time is afforded by the well-known experience of Dio Chrysostom in the fortress of one of the Moesian legions. It is hard to believe that his brilliant speech (was it delivered in Greek or in Latin?) quelled the incipient revolution there. It is more likely that the disturbances were of a purely superficial character.[5]

Like Augustus, Vespasian was not merely a restorer. He carried on valiantly the work which had been begun by Augustus and Claudius in the two most essential branches of imperial administration—in the sphere of finance, where he continued the development of bureaucracy, and in the promotion of town-life in the provinces. Into these two subjects we cannot enter in detail. As regards the former, the essential points have been well set forth by Hirschfeld in his indispensable book and need not be repeated here.[6] There is only one detail that should be emphasized because of its immense importance for the economic history of the second century, and that is the attention paid by Vespasian to the imperial and public lands. The far-reaching confiscations of Nero on the one hand and the chaos of the year of the four emperors on the other, when many rich senators and municipal burgesses were killed off by the wild soldiery and by their imperial masters, created conditions more or less similar to those inherited by Augustus from the civil wars.[7] The task of Vespasian was far from easy. Nevertheless he succeeded in satisfactorily organizing the vast estates belonging both to the emperors and to the state and in practically merging these two branches of administration into one, a fusion which resulted in an enormous increase in the financial resources of the emperors. In Italy and in the provinces the state still owned large tracts of arable land, as well as mines, quarries, fisheries, forests, and so forth; and the concentration of these in the hands of the emperors called for a well-defined policy of exploitation. The system of management which the greatest landowner in the Empire should decide to adopt, far from being a matter of indifference, was in reality of supreme importance for the economic life of the Roman world as a whole. We shall discuss this problem in the sixth and seventh chapters, and describe the main lines of the policy of the Flavians and its importance for the further development of the economic life of the Empire in general. We can, however, already note now that the reorganization of the economic and social life in the large estates of the state and of the emperor, begun by Vespasian, was effected according to what Schönbauer calls the 'normative' Hellenistic system, rather than according to the 'liberal' system of Roman civil law. The conditions which continued to prevail in the Hellenistic East, under the Romans, and particularly in Egypt, probably served as models.[8]

Vespasian displayed equal vigour in carrying out his policy of fostering the growth of city life in the provinces. We shall treat this subject also in greater detail in the sixth and seventh chapters. His purpose, it is plain, was primarily to enlarge the basis on which in the last resort the power of the emperors rested. The events of the bloody year of the four emperors showed how weak and unreliable was the support afforded by the Roman citizens, particularly those resident in Italy. A principate based on them alone was bound to relapse into the anarchy of the period of the civil wars. We have seen that Vespasian was fully aware of the situation, and that his military reforms were dictated by his appreciation of the facts. But he understood well enough that, as things were, it was impossible to depart from the constitutional principle established by Augustus, that the masters and rulers of the Empire were the Roman citizens or those who legally belonged to the Italic stock. It was impossible to equalize the whole of the inhabitants of the Empire and to extend the franchise to all alike. On the other hand, it was unsafe to maintain the restrictive policy of the Julii and Claudii as regards the bestowal of Roman and Latin citizenship. Vespasian, as we shall see, chose the middle course. He accelerated the urbanization of the more or less romanized provinces, especially those which were the main recruiting areas, those where large bodies of Roman soldiers were stationed—Spain, Germany, and the Danubian provinces. In creating new *municipia* in the territory of half-civilized tribes and clans he promoted the formation of a romanized aristocracy, consisting mostly of former soldiers, who had become romanized during their service, and he gave to these nuclei of Roman civilization rights and privileges, both economic and social, which made them the rulers of the rest of the population. The urbanization of Spain, Germany, Illyricum, and to a lesser extent of Africa, Gaul, and Britain meant, therefore, the concentration of certain elements in cities, which made it easier for the government to control those elements and, through them, the mass of the provincial population. In the more romanized provinces the rights of Roman or Latin citizenship were granted to the new urban centres. In the less romanized just as in the hellenized parts of the Empire this grant was withheld, at least for the time being. Everywhere urbanization was hastily pushed forward, to the very limits of what was practically possible.

A fresh basis was thus created for the principate, and in particular for the power of the Flavian house. As the new elements owed their social promotion to Vespasian and his sons personally, and as they also furnished recruits for the legions and to some extent for the auxiliary troops, the Flavian principate seemed to rest on sound and sure foundations. The new colonies and cities were destined to play the part which the colonies of Caesar and Augustus had played after the civil wars. Vespasian's policy was a challenge to the old Italian cities and to the ancient centres of city life in the provinces, a challenge, too, to the old body of Roman citizens which failed to support the principate as established by Augustus, and a direct appeal to the provinces against Italy in acknowledgement of the support which they had given to the principate as such, as well as to Vespasian personally, during the year of the four emperors. After the reform the principate still represented the body of Roman citizens, but that body was no longer confined to the limits of Italy.

Of great importance for the social development of the Empire was the policy of Vespasian and Titus towards the senate. We are concerned here, not with the constitutional aspect of this question, which has often been studied and illustrated by eminent scholars and which has but little bearing on the problems dealt with in this volume, but with Vespasian's restoration of the senate, with his activity as censor in removing certain members of that body and filling up the vacancies with new men. It was stated in the last chapter that this question has been carefully investigated.[9] The results of the investigation show that the senate as constituted by Vespasian was very different from the senate of the Julio-Claudians. It did not represent the ancient aristocracy of Republican Rome, nor the families which were ennobled and introduced into the senate by Augustus and which, like the old nobility, belonged mostly to the city of Rome itself. The persecutions of the emperors of the Julio-Claudian house and the 'race suicide' committed by the senatorial families eliminated the old stock almost completely. The new men who took their place were of varied and sometimes of doubtful origin. But the main trend of policy all along was towards replacing the old aristocracy by members of the municipal aristocracy of Italy and the Western provinces. These formed the majority of the equestrian class and their military and civil career had shown them to be faithful servants and staunch supporters of the principate. This process was brought to completion by Vespasian. Under him the senate was drawn almost wholly from the upper strata of the municipal *bourgeoisie*. The provincial element was mostly Latin-speaking. Orientals, including Greeks, were not, as a rule, admitted. If not Roman and Italian in the narrow sense of the word, the attitude of the Flavians was still, like that of Augustus, at any rate certainly Latin. They emphasized the importance and the dominant position of the Latin-speaking elements in the Empire.[10]

The position of the new emperor, as emperor, was much more difficult than that of Augustus. The civil war had lasted for one year only, the East had not been affected by it, nor had even Gaul, Spain, and Africa been seriously involved in the troubles. The real sufferer had been Italy and especially the richer parts of Italy, the northern and central areas. Vespasian therefore did not have in the eyes of the majority of the population of the Empire the halo of Augustus, his personal quasi-divine charm; he was not *the Saviour*. There is no doubt that even Augustus had met with opposition from some senators who were hostile to him personally, and that from time to time he had had to compromise with them. This was still more the case with Vespasian. We know from Tacitus, Suetonius, and Cassius Dio that he found many bold and resolute opponents among the senators and that he was forced, almost against his will, to deal harshly with these men and to inflict on a few of them the death penalty.

Our information on the reign of Vespasian is so scanty and meagre that it is hard to judge what were the aims of the senatorial opposition to him. It was not, as under the Julio-

Claudians, an opposition of a personal character. We know that as early as Nero's time the personal opposition had been replaced by one of a philosophic type, of which Thrasea Paetus was one of the prominent leaders. Based on theoretical philosophic reasoning, this new form of opposition was certainly stronger and more consistent than that with which the predecessors of Nero were faced. Of the same kind was the opposition against Vespasian led by Helvidius Priscus. Our sources may tempt us to think, with modern historians in general, that the senatorial opponents of Vespasian desired the re-establishment of the Republic, that they 'talked more or less open Republicanism'.[11] It is difficult to believe that a serious opposition could have been based on such Utopian ideas. It is still more difficult to think that the Roman senate, which certainly could not, in view of its social constitution, share the aspirations of the ancient Republican senate, had learnt nothing from the year of the four emperors. Even the philosophical character of the senatorial opposition does not favour the view that 'Republicanism' was its main political ideal. The two most popular creeds of philosophic thought at this time, Stoicism and Cynicism, were fundamentally non-republican.[12]

There is one man of this age who is better known to us than the rest, better known even than those whose portraits are given by Tacitus. Dio, later called Chrysostom, a citizen of Prusa, came as a young but already famous sophist to Rome in the reign of Vespasian. A rich man and a member of the aristocracy of his city, he had the opportunity of forming friendly relations with many leading men in the capital and even with members of the imperial family. At the very beginning of his stay in Rome he does not appear to have been opposed to Vespasian. Rather he seems to have supported him, even in the measures which he took against the philosophers and in his conflict with the famous Musonius, one of the leaders of the philosophic opposition.[13] Yet Dio came gradually into touch with the leaders of the senatorial opposition. It is evident that he gradually adopted their views. The political views of Dio are well known to us. In none of his writings is there the slightest hint of republican sympathies. His Rhodian speech, which belongs probably to the time before his exile and thus to the period of his closest relations with the senatorial opponents of the Flavian rule, contains no praise of democracy as such. It is, therefore, impossible to believe that the senatorial opposition talked pure republicanism and sought to bring back the golden age of senatorial rule. It is clear that they talked something else.

The senatorial opposition was not alone in fighting Vespasian. A curious feature of his rule is that he was obliged to expel from the city the so-called philosophers. In a well-known speech (to the Alexandrians, no. xxxii) Dio Chrysostom subdivides the philosophers of his time into four classes: first, the philosophers who do not teach at all; second, those who are real professors, that is, who teach a definite group of students; third, those who act as public orators, travelling from place to place and giving public lectures; and fourth, the most interesting class, which he describes as follows:* 'Of the so-called Cynics there is a large number in the city. . . . At the cross-roads, in the by-streets, at the entrance-gates of the sanctuaries these men gather together and deceive slaves and sailors and people of that sort, stringing together jests and a variety of gossip and vulgar retorts. Thus they do no good, but the very greatest evil.' This last class of philosophers is familiar to every student of the Roman Empire. They were the most conspicuous feature of the cities of the Roman East in the first and second centuries of our era. It was only natural that many of them should go to Rome, where they found a number of people who could understand Greek and who were interested in their teaching. Of this teaching we know very little, but it was certainly in the spirit of Cynic doctrine in general, which attacked the conventionalities of life and preached a return to nature.[14] Yet, if that was the sum and substance of their teaching, why did they appear a serious nuisance to Vespasian, and why were they expelled from Rome with the philosophers in general, those philosophers who were the teachers and inspirers of the senators who were opposed to the rule of Vespasian? It seems impossible to find any other explanation than that all the philosophers, higher and lower alike, carried on both a political and a social propaganda which appeared decidedly dangerous to Vespasian.[15.]

What in particular did they preach? The social aspect of their sermons was objectionable enough, as it aroused the bad feelings of the proletariate. This social aspect is not, however, in itself

* *Or.* xxxii. 10.

sufficient to explain the action of Vespasian; and, moreover, it was peculiar to the street philosophers. There must have been something political in the propaganda of the street Cynics. The only common subject of Cynic and Stoic teaching, so far as political questions were concerned—a subject which might have appeared really dangerous to Vespasian—was the theme of the tyrant as opposed to the king, a theme which was often treated both by the Cynics and by the Stoics and which was later developed by Dio Chrysostom in his famous speeches on tyranny and kingship. One of the main points of contrast between the king and the tyrant was that the king receives his power from God, that he is chosen by God as the best man, and that this power cannot therefore be hereditary. If this was the point of connexion between the philosophic opposition of the senators and the street sermons of the Cynics, we can understand the persecution which involved both the senators and the street philosophers, and also the remark made by Vespasian in the senate, after certain conspiracies against him had been discovered, that either his sons should succeed him or no one. This remark, we may say incidentally, does not seem to contain the slightest hint of the presumed republican tendencies of the senate. It is merely a harsh answer to those who preached the doctrine that the best man ought to be king—the doctrine of adoption.[16]

Along with the strong current of public opinion which denounced the rule of Vespasian as a tyranny because of his desire to see his sons succeed him, there flowed another current, less dangerous but very characteristic of the social conditions of the period. We know from Suetonius* that some of the Greek provinces and free cities as well as some of the vassal kingdoms were subject to disturbances during this reign (*tumultuosius inter se agebant*) and were punished by the loss of their 'freedom'. Suetonius names Achaea, Lycia, Rhodes, Byzantium, and Samos, all prosperous places, some of them commercial and industrial cities of great importance. At the same time the Alexandrians showed their ill humour towards Vespasian.†[17] How is such behaviour on the part of the Greek East to be explained? It should be noted that this bad temper was not peculiar to the era of the Flavians. It persisted under Trajan and even after Hadrian, especially in Alexandria. From the speeches which Dio Chrysostom delivered

* *Vesp.* viii. 2.　　　　　　† Suet. *Vesp.* xix. 2; cf. Strabo, xvii. 796.

in certain Oriental cities under Trajan, and from the treatise of
Plutarch on 'How to govern the state', which belongs probably
to the same period, we know more or less what was going on in
the Greek cities. Apart from the perpetual rivalry and competition between them (an inheritance from the times of political
liberty) there were two marked features of civic life which
troubled both the city authorities and the Roman government—
a continuous social struggle between the rich and the poor, and a
strong opposition on the part of the whole population, rich and
poor alike, to the administrative methods of the Roman governors. Thus the social movement in the cities, especially among
the proletarians, necessarily assumed an anti-Roman aspect,
since the Romans as a rule supported the governing classes, the
manifest oppressors of the proletariate.[18]

I am convinced that those two political and social factors
were the chief causes of the periodical disturbances which took
place in Alexandria. About these troubles we have fairly full information both from literary sources and from certain documents
of fragments of a political pamphlet, the so-called 'Acts of the
Heathen Martyrs', a curious collection which had a large vogue
among the Greek and hellenized population of Egypt. The disturbances assumed the form of Jewish 'pogroms', but were certainly directed against the Roman government and had an
almost purely political character. There is, moreover, no doubt
that, as in the cities of Asia Minor, the Cynic street philosophers
had a powerful influence on the unruly elements of the population of Alexandria, especially the proletariate. This influence is
shown by the Cynic themes which frequently appear in the so-
called 'Acts of the Martyrs' of Alexandria, such as 'king and
tyrant', 'freedom and slavery', and so forth.[19]

How did this state of things arise? In Alexandria the disturbances begin as early as the reign of Caligula. The rest of the
East, however, shows no signs of discontent at any date earlier
than that of the Flavians. In explanation of this phenomenon I
would remind the reader of what has been said in the last chapter about the marvellous economic renaissance which began in
the East after the end of the civil wars.[20] The economic revival
was followed by a cultural renascence against which the West
had not very much to set. Greek civilization, art, and literature
were again regarded even by the Romans as *the* civilization, *the*

art, *the* literature. Nero was the first to proclaim *urbi et orbi* the new gospel and to act on it. The self-esteem of the Greek cities and especially of the better classes there, the intellectuals, rose high, higher indeed than was reasonable. Under Vespasian came the reaction. The East, which was the first to recognize Vespasian, expected all sorts of privileges from him, a new golden age: liberty, the Roman franchise, seats in the senate, and what not. The disillusionment was bitter indeed. Vespasian, as we have seen, was far from following the path which had been taken by Nero. He was not a cosmopolitan, nor a Greek. Of Italian birth, he had all the prejudices of the Italians and did not believe in the supremacy of the Greeks. Moreover, he knew that without the support of the West he was lost, and that the opposition of the East was a *Fronde*, not a real danger. He carried his policy perhaps too far, and added to the numbers of his enemies even in Rome. The Rhodian speech of Dio shows that Dio and other men of his type (he was not the only Greek of reputation and standing at Rome) shared the belief in the renascence of the Greek world and claimed more respect for it. Men like Dio never, indeed, preached revolt or disturbances, but their moderation was counterbalanced by the activities of the street philosophers, who used every means of becoming popular with the masses— another reason why Vespasian should make life in Rome as unpleasant as possible for them. It is characteristic, however, of their persistence that despite their banishment they succeeded in making their way into Rome again and resuming their preaching in public places.[21]

The rule of Titus was a brief episode in the history of the relations between the emperors and the population of the Empire. His concessions to the senate and his policy of mild tolerance did not stop the spread of discontent, particularly in the East. It is worthy of note that in his time (probably in A.D. 80) a 'false' Nero appeared in Asia Minor and gathered a large crowd of followers.[22] The crisis came when Domitian succeeded Titus. It is needless to repeat well-known facts about his rule. For the opponents of the military tyranny, of the personal and selfish character of the principate of the Julii and Claudii, and for the enemies of the dynastic monarchy, now, as it seemed, firmly established in Rome, the rule of Domitian was an undisguised tyranny or despotism in the Stoic and Cynic sense of the word.

Domitian never concealed his ideas about the imperial power. He was perfectly frank and sincere. He would never accept the Stoic teaching of an ideal 'king'. He wanted to be obeyed and to have full autocratic power as master and god. This did not necessarily mean an alteration of the outward aspect of the principate as created by Augustus and his successors. It is possible that Domitian was forced to show his colours by renewed attacks of the enemies of the existing régime. The harshness and cruelty of his measures against the opposition are notorious. The worst times of Tiberius, Caligula, and Nero returned. It is fairly certain that the upper classes throughout the Empire were unanimous in condemning his policy and in advocating an understanding between the imperial power and the claims of its opponents. It seems, too, that the army, in spite of the favours bestowed on it by Domitian, was not entirely on the side of the emperor. It is, therefore, very probable that the court plot which ended his life was not an accident, but had wide ramifications in the provinces and among the troops. If so, the curious stories of the prophecy of a certain Larginus (?) Proclus (perhaps a soldier) in Germany, and of the vision of Apollonius of Tyana in Ephesus, which are accepted as facts by Dio Cassius, may be satisfactorily explained.[23]

Thus under Domitian the opposition renewed its attacks on the imperial power in general and on the emperor personally.[24] The struggle was not confined to the city of Rome. We know that Dio Chrysostom, who was exiled from Rome and was forbidden to stay in his native country of Bithynia, led a nomadic life, living in disguise, probably under assumed names, and preaching everywhere the new Stoico-Cynic gospel which now became his creed. He devoted himself almost entirely to disseminating his new ideas, and it is noteworthy that his propaganda was in fact directed against Domitian and his system of government. It is typical of the conditions which prevailed in the Orient that Dio was not allowed to live in Bithynia: his influence in his native land might be dangerous for the ruler.

What was the nature of his propaganda? His speeches and the evidence about the activity of the philosophers in Rome show that it was primarily an attack on the tyranny which was identified with the rule of Domitian. This was the negative side. Had the opponents of Domitian something else, something positive, to oppose to the tyranny? Later, under Trajan, Dio tells the emperor and us what he thinks about the ideal constitution of the Roman Empire and the ideal state in general. Against the tyranny he sets the Stoic and Cynic kingship (βασιλεία), and depicts it in colours which seem to be derived, partly at least, from the practice of the principate of Trajan.[25] The current opinion is that Dio and the opposition, in drawing such a picture, were forced to submit to necessity, to accept the monarchy and *faire bonne mine au mauvais jeu* by identifying the monarchy of Trajan with the Stoic βασιλεία; it was only with reluctance that they gave up their republican ideals. I see no reason whatever to accept this view. It seems to me that from the very beginning the opposition, with perhaps some exceptions (if it be true that Helvidius Priscus was a genuine republican), accepted the principate but, taking the point of view of Antisthenes, the younger Cynics, and the Stoics, demanded that it should be fashioned on the model of the Stoic and Cynic βασιλεία.[26] The programme of the Stoic and Cynic kingship, as drawn up by Dio,* is familiar and need not be detailed here. The main points are these: the emperor is selected by divine providence and acts in full agreement with the supreme god; during life he is not himself a god; he regards his power, not as a personal privilege, but as a duty; his life is toil (πόνος), not pleasure (ἡδονή); he is the father and the benefactor (πατὴρ καὶ εὐεργέτης) of his subjects, not their master (δεσπότης); his subjects are free men, not slaves; his subjects must love him, and he must be both φιλοπολίτης and φιλοστρατιώτης; he must be πολεμικός, but also εἰρηνικός in the sense that nobody worth fighting is left; finally, he must be surrounded by friends (an allusion to the senate) who ought to have a share in the management of all the affairs of the state, being free (ἐλεύθεροι) and noble (γενναῖοι) men. No doubt, in this programme as specified by Dio there are many points which are not theoretical but correspond to the character and activity of Trajan.[27] But a mere glance at Pliny's consular speech in honour of Trajan, and a comparison of it with Dio's first and third speeches on kingship, show to what an extent these latter were not only a registration of existing facts but, first and foremost, an exposition of eternal norms which must be accepted or rejected by Trajan.[28]

* Περὶ βασιλείας, i and iii.

I believe therefore that the majority of those who were opposed to the rule of the Flavians were not opposed to the principate as such, but that their attitude towards it was rather that of Tacitus. They accepted it; but they wanted it to approach as nearly as possible to the Stoic βασιλεία and to be as dissimilar as possible to the Stoic tyranny, which was identified with the military tyranny of the Julio-Claudians in general and of Nero in particular, and with that of Domitian. With Nerva and Trajan peace was concluded between the mass of the population of the Empire, especially the educated classes of the city *bourgeoisie*, and the imperial power. The speeches of Dio on kingship, delivered in the presence of Trajan and often repeated by their author in the most important cities of the East, probably at Trajan's wish, formulated the points of Stoic doctrine which the principate accepted and those in which that doctrine accommodated itself to the requirements of practical life.

The fact that this peace was accepted by the army, which remained quiet and obedient for about a century, shows that the soldiers were not on the side of the military tyranny but were ready to accept the solution suggested by the public opinion of the educated classes throughout the Empire. The principate of the second century of our era, the enlightened monarchy of the Antonines, was a victory of the educated classes, just as the principate of Augustus had been a victory of the *cives Romani*. The spectre of an Oriental monarchy grafted on a military tyranny was laid once more, but, as we shall presently see, it was laid for the last time.

There was no document showing the terms on which the compromise between the educated classes and the emperors had been concluded. The constitution of the Roman Empire remained unwritten, as it had been from the very beginning of Roman history. What had taken place was a new adaptation of the imperial power to existing conditions. The power of the Roman emperors was not reduced. On the contrary it was increased. The rule of one man had now been recognized by all classes of the population as a fact and as a necessity. Without a single will the Roman Empire was bound to fall to pieces. The development of imperial bureaucracy went on unhampered. But the main principle of the Augustan principate was emphasized afresh. The emperor was not a monarch of the Oriental type; he was the supreme magistrate of the Roman Empire, both of Roman citizens and of provincials. He was not elected by any constituent body, but the power was not transmitted from father to son merely in virtue of blood relationship. The emperor adopted the best man among the best men, that is, among the members of the senatorial class, the peers of the emperors, the seminary of emperors. The senatorial class as such was well prepared for the task, as all its members devoted their lives to the service of the state. The imperial power also was regarded not as a personal privilege but as a burden, a service imposed by God and by the senate on the bearer of power. The emperor personified, so to say, the Empire, and so his power and his person were sacred and he himself was an object of worship. The majesty of the Empire was embodied in him. He was not the master of the state but its first servant; service to the state was his duty. When he was with the army, he had to bear all the hardships of the military life like a common soldier. When in the capital, he had to attend to his duties as ruler of the state, to work hard day and night for the safety and prosperity of the Empire. Therefore his life must be the life of a head of the state, not that of a common mortal, and yet it should be as modest and as unextravagant as possible. His private fortune was merged in the fortune of the state. What was imperial was public, what was public was imperial. Only from this point of view can we understand the saying of Antoninus Pius. Arguing with his wife after his adoption by Hadrian, he said:* 'Foolish one, now that we have passed over to empire, we have lost even what we had before.' The saying may be an invention, but it emphasizes the common opinion of the time on the matter. In his family life the emperor had to disregard his love for his own children; he had to look for the best man among his peers and raise him to the throne by adoption.

Such was the policy of all the Roman emperors of the second century down to Commodus. One can scarcely believe that this unanimity of outlook was accidental, for example that the introduction of the system of adoption was due simply to the fact that none of the emperors before M. Aurelius had sons, and that their policy was determined by their personal characters, which differed greatly. Trajan, the great warrior and conqueror;

* *Scrip. Hist. Aug. M. Anton. Pii* c. 4.

Hadrian, the intellectual, the man of refined artistic tastes, the last great citizen of Athens, the romantic on the throne; Antoninus Pius, the good Italian *bourgeois* of the senatorial class, who had no intellectual tendencies but a sound common sense and a gift of humour; M. Aurelius, the stern philosopher, who lived in his books and for his books, for whom abstract meditation was the greatest joy in life—all of them, despite their striking difference in character, followed the same course of imperial activity. The facts are well known. The picture given in the preceding pages is drawn not from the speeches of Dio or from the treatise of M. Aurelius, but from the life of the emperors, as emperors. Their line of conduct was imposed on them by public opinion. The long years of imperial rule, long hours of meditation, the process of natural selection in the new senatorial class—which had nothing, except the name, in common with the old senatorial aristocracy of the time of Augustus and his successors, but consisted of well-trained officers, generals, and governors of provinces—created a mood which found expression in the public life of the emperors, who all belonged to this class.

Stern discipline, duty, service to the state were the watch-words of the leading classes of the Roman people at this period. If the emperors endeavoured to conform to these principles, they required at least the ruling classes and the army to live up to the same standards. Discipline and obedience were demanded from the senate, from the equestrian class, from the officers of the state, whether military or civil, and from the soldiers. It was no accident that the cult of 'Discipline' was first introduced into the Roman army by Hadrian; and it is to be observed that discipline and obedience were not only required by the emperors, but were recognized even by the army as a duty. Never before was the army so well trained and so well disciplined, never before did it work so hard and so contentedly as in the time of the enlight-ened monarchy. The history of the expeditions of Trajan, or of the difficult wars under M. Aurelius, shows the army equal to the severest possible demands, although it suffered great losses and experienced grave disasters. The same must be said of the administration of the Empire, which never before was so fair, so humane, so efficient as under the strong rule of the Antonines. The only explanation which I can see of all these facts is that the mood of the population of the Empire had changed, that a reaction had taken place against the frivolity and materialism of the first century and had secured for the ancient world some further scores of years of peace and tranquillity.[29]

One of the most important features of this time is the policy of the emperors towards the provinces. Most of the emperors of the second century were themselves of provincial birth. Trajan and Hadrian were Roman citizens from Spain, Antoninus Pius and M. Aurelius descended from Roman citizens settled in Gaul.[30] They belonged to the senatorial class, and they maintained the privileges of that class as well as the privileges of the second class in the Empire, the equestrian. They did not encroach on the right of these two classes to be the highest servants of the state after the emperor. But the composition of both classes was now completely changed. Neither was any longer confined to Italy. All their members alike were required to have their domicile and to hold some property in Italy, but few of them had been born there. Sprung from the municipal aristocracy of the provinces, they kept up their connexion with their old homes both in the East and in the West. Thus the higher classes of Roman society, now enormously increased in numbers, represented, not the aristocracy of Rome or of Italy, but the aristocracy of the Empire, the wealthiest and the best educated sections of the city population throughout the Roman world. This fact probably accounts for the moral change of which we have just spoken. The new nobility was a nobility selected by the emperors for the service of the state from the more highly educated men all over the Empire. The Roman state was indeed still ruled by an aristocratic and plutocratic class, but the selection of its members was based not so much on birth and wealth as on personal merits, efficiency, and intellectual gifts.[31]

This new aristocracy, almost wholly of provincial origin, naturally understood better the needs of the provinces and had a fuller appreciation of their right to be regarded and ruled, not as estates of the Roman people, but as constituent parts of the Roman state. The change began as early as the Flavians. Some measures in the same direction had already been taken by Augustus and certain of his successors, especially Tiberius and Claudius. The climax was reached under the Antonines. It is to be noted that none of the early successors of Augustus, except Tiberius, ever ruled a province before he became emperor; none of the early successors of Tiberius knew anything of the needs and aspirations of the provincials by personal experience; the visits of Caligula and Claudius had been made for military purposes only. All the emperors before the Flavians, with the exception of Galba, Vitellius, and Otho, whose elevation was merely a reaction of the provinces against the prevailing practice, were Romans who lived in Rome and for whom Rome was the centre of the universe. From the Flavians onwards there was a complete change. Vespasian spent most of his life in commanding armies and in governing provinces, and so did Titus. Domitian, no doubt, represented once more the old stock of city-emperors. But after him every emperor down to Commodus spent his life before his accession, and some, like Hadrian, even after their accession, almost entirely in the provinces.

Under such conditions it was only natural that the old theory and practice of provincial government should completely disappear, and that the emperors of the second century should feel themselves, not emperors of the city of Rome or of the Roman citizens only, but emperors of the whole Empire. This is shown both by the rapid spread of the rights of Roman citizenship all over the Empire and by the growing practice of conferring on provincial towns the rights of a Roman *municipium* or of a Roman or Latin colony. What was even more important, the provinces now felt themselves to be individualities, local unities, 'nations' if we care to use the term. The Roman Empire now consisted of the union of such nations. This thought is brilliantly expressed in the well-known series of coins of Hadrian, the provincial series. The changed financial, economic, and social policy of the emperors of this century testifies to the same fact, but of this we shall speak later, after we have given a survey of the Empire in the second century from the economic and social point of view.

It is to be observed that, concurrently with the change in the attitude of the Roman government toward them, the provinces as a whole and particularly the upper classes became more and more reconciled to Roman rule. Of the Western provinces our knowledge is very limited. But the enormous mass of inscriptions erected in the cities of the West in honour of the emperors of the second century shows how well satisfied their upper classes were with the existing conditions. Even in the Eastern provinces the attitude of the population began gradually to change. The activity of Dio and Plutarch, the speeches of Aelius Aristides, even the diatribes of Lucian, all show that the leading classes in the Greek-speaking portions of the Empire gradually acquiesced in the existing state of things, that they abandoned their dreams of liberty, and worked for the consolidation of Roman power in the East.[32] The most obstinate were the Alexandrians. They persisted in fighting the Roman government and in speaking of tyranny instead of kingship as the characteristic of the imperial power. But it must be noted that this contention is found in a document which belongs to the time of Commodus and that in this document Commodus is contrasted with his father.[33]

Another fact which should not be overlooked is that the emperors of the second century did not persecute the philosophers, not even the Cynics. The task of fighting and of ridiculing them was undertaken by the loyal philosophers and sophists. In this literary strife the government did not interfere, but it must be remembered that it favoured the spread of culture in the cities of the East no less than of the West, and that it subsidized both individual teachers and rhetoricians and also certain educational establishments.[34]

It cannot, however, be affirmed that there were no discontented elements in the Roman Empire during the second century. Even in the East the upper classes were more or less reconciled to the Empire. But this is not true of the lower classes. The example of Bithynia and the disturbances in Alexandria under Trajan show that the social antagonism of which we have spoken never subsided in Asia Minor or in Egypt, and that it was not easy for the Roman government and the magistrates of the cities to deal with the lower classes of the city population.[35] To this subject we shall return in the next chapter.

A few words may be added on the social constitution of the Roman army under the Antonines. It has frequently been stated in this chapter that the Roman army was the decisive factor not only in the political but also in the social and economic life of the Empire. The question arises, Did the army remain just the same under M. Aurelius and Commodus as it had been under the Flavians and Trajan? Was it still, in the main, an army of actual or prospective Roman citizens, commanded by Roman citizens born in Rome and in Italy? This question is of great importance for the true comprehension of the events of the second and third centuries. How far can we answer it? It is clear that from the constitutional point of view the composition of the army had not changed. All through the second century the officers were taken from the ranks of the senatorial and equestrian classes, the non-commissioned officers were Roman citizens born and educated in Italy or in the romanized parts of the western provinces. The soldiers of the praetorian guard were Italians or natives of the romanized provinces of Spain and Noricum or of the province of Macedonia. The legionary soldiers were all *de iure* Roman citizens. The soldiers of the auxiliary regiments were supposed to understand Latin and they received the Roman citizenship at the end of their term of service. There is no doubt, however, that, despite this political qualification, almost all the soldiers were provincials, the Italians serving only in the imperial guard, which also formed a nursery of non-commissioned officers for the rest of the army. After Hadrian each province had to supply its own soldiers.

These facts have been thoroughly investigated by modern scholars and are well known. Much less known is the composition of the army from the social point of view. To what class or classes of the population did the soldiers belong? Which part of the Empire was more fully represented in the army—the city or the country? Were the majority of the soldiers city residents or peasants? The fact that, in giving their full official name, they almost always mention a city as their place of origin does not solve the problem. The soldier may have belonged to the territory of the city and may have been a peasant or a *colonus*, a tenant. Without doubt the auxiliary troops were mostly recruited from peasants and shepherds. But what of the legionaries? The common opinion is that even the legionary soldiers were now mostly peasants, the city dwellers having no inclination to serve in the army and not being very highly rated by the military officers. In my view this opinion is correct. The emperors of the second century tried, of course, to enrol in the army as many romanized young men as possible, and such were mostly to be found in the cities. They approved and promoted the formation of provincial associations of young men, who if necessary acted as a local militia. But in fact even these associations of young men, the prospective soldiers of the Roman legions, gradually lost their civic character, especially in the frontier provinces. It is interesting to follow the development of the *collegia iuvenum* in the Rhine provinces in the post-Flavian period. The associations of the youth of these provinces were not confined to the few regular cities of the two Germanies. We find them also in the *civitates*, the *pagi*, and the *vici*, communities which were closely connected with the German and Celtic tribes and clans. The associations themselves were unlike the 'colleges' of the Italian cities. In the Celto-German frontier provinces these Italian organizations were grafted on to national half-religious institutions, which were common to the Indo-Europeans in general and existed also in Italy in pre-Roman times. The *iuvenes* of Germany may have originally represented only the better class of the inhabitants of the German provinces, the class of well-to-do farmers and landowners, whether of foreign or of local origin, but there is no doubt that they gradually came to include the whole of the local youth suitable for military service.

Thus in the second century the Roman army gradually lost its connexion with the cities and became what it had been in the ancient period of Roman history, an army of landowners and peasants, of country people, who had not yet severed their connexion with the country and with agricultural life. We shall see in the sixth and seventh chapters that this rural element formed the majority of the population of the Empire. The best soldiers, of course, were furnished by the lands where city life developed slowly and did not absorb a large part of the country population, as it did for instance in Greece, Italy, and to a certain extent even in Gaul.

It is possible that the composition of the army accounts for the quiet and law-abiding disposition which it showed all through the second century. It was easier to discipline and to keep in control an army of peasants, who had never taken any part in political affairs, than an army composed of city proletarians, more highly developed intellectually and more habituated to political life in general. The hypothesis that the army of the second century, and more especially of the second half of the century (under the rule of M. Aurelius and Commodus), was composed mostly of the rural inhabitants of the Empire is corroborated by the fact that it was no longer an army of volunteers. In the time of M. Aurelius when the emperor was engaged in a severe struggle on the Southern and the Northern frontiers, when the Germans were on the. point of invading Italy, when plague ravaged the East and Italy, it was not possible to rely upon voluntary enlistment any longer. It is well known that under the pressure of circumstances M. Aurelius conscribed slaves, gladiators, municipal policemen, and even Germans and robber tribesmen of Dalmatia and Dardania. This may have been an exceptional measure, but it indicates that even in less critical times M. Aurelius could hardly have refrained from filling up his army by conscription. We must bear in mind that military service was at all times the duty both of Roman citizens and of provincials, and that conscription was the regular method of recruiting for the auxiliary troops. As the greater part of the population of the Empire consisted of country people, and as the city residents, particularly in these hard times, tried to escape military service in one way or another, it is clear that the army of M. Aurelius consisted in the main of peasants, and especially peasants of the less civilized provinces of the Roman Empire, which furnished the sturdiest soldiers.[36]

A good idea of the composition of the provincial armies as compared with the praetorian guard is given by the picture drawn by Cassius Dio in speaking of the reform of Septimius Severus, who dismissed the old praetorian guard and replaced it by picked soldiers of the provincial armies, mostly Danubians. 'Thereby', says Dio, 'he completely ruined the youth of Italy, which turned to robbery and to the gladiatorial profession in place of military service, and filled the capital with a motley crowd of soldiers savage in aspect, terrible to hear'—it is evident that most of them did not speak Latin—'and rough in their manners.'* There is no doubt, then, that the Roman army of the end of the second century, though still consisting of Romans, in the sense of inhabitants of the Roman Empire, became more and more barbarized and less and less representative of the civilized population. Apart from the officers and the non-commissioned officers, the spirit of the army was the spirit, not of the urban, but almost wholly of the rural, classes.

* lxxiv. 2.

V

THE ROMAN EMPIRE UNDER THE FLAVIANS AND THE ANTONINES

The Cities. Commerce and Industry

THE best general picture of the Roman Empire in the second century, the most detailed and the most complete that we have, may be found in the speech Εἰς ʿΡώμην, which was delivered at Rome in A.D. 154 by the 'sophist' Aelius Aristides. It is not only an expression of sincere admiration for the greatness of the Roman Empire but also a masterpiece of thoughtful and sound political analysis. It has become usual to speak of this 'encomium' of Aristides as a rhetorical production poor in original thought, as a repertory of commonplaces which were familiar to everybody. The arguments in favour of such a view are drawn from an analysis of the sources of Aristides. Isocrates, it is said, was his main source for the historical parallels; Plutarch, Dionysius of Halicarnassus, and Polybius suggested most of his leading ideas; the structure of the speech was based on the theoretical precepts of the handbook of rhetoric written by Menander.[1] The accuracy of all these statements may be admitted. How many of the most brilliant modern political speeches would stand the test of such an analysis? But the analysis of the sources of Aristides' speech fails to prove the most essential point, that his ideas are empty and flat, and that the speech in general is a mere collection of commonplaces. Some of the ideas may reproduce the current opinion of the time. That does not necessarily mean that they are empty and flat. Undoubtedly, commonplaces may be found. But the critics may be challenged to quote any other literary work of the second century A.D. which gives as full and precise a picture of the structure of the Roman Empire as that of Aristides. Can they cite any other work so rich in brilliant and vivid pictures illustrating the various aspects of the Empire, political and social and economic? Moreover, there are some ideas in the speech of Aristides which cannot be found, at least so clearly and so fully expressed, in any other work. Such are the

favourite views of the second century on the character of the enlightened monarchy and on the relations between the monarchy
and the different classes of the population of the Empire; the
characterization of the Empire as a coherent aggregate of free,
self-governing city-states; and—not the least important of all—
the masterly sketch of the part played in the Roman state by the
army. The speech of Aristides is to me one of the most important
sources of information not only on the general structure of the
Roman Empire as viewed by contemporaries but also on the
mentality of the age of the Antonines, on the political ideas
current at the time. In an 'encomium' no one would expect to
find a criticism of the Empire. The speaker's task was to seize
and to point out the positive aspects, and to do it without exaggeration and without undue flattery. In this task Aristides succeeded fairly well.

The speech 'To Rome' must be compared with the speeches
of Dio on kingship ($\beta\alpha\sigma\iota\lambda\epsilon\iota\alpha$). These speeches expounded a programme on which the emperors and the intellectual leaders of
Roman imperial society were agreed. The speech of Aristides
shows how the programme was carried out, and how far the
actual conditions of the period of the Antonines, and more particularly of the time of Antoninus Pius, corresponded to the
aspirations of the best men in the Empire. There is no doubt
that, in his high praise of the achievements of the enlightened
monarchy, Aristides was in complete accord with the leading
spirits of his time and with the mass of the urban population, the
city *bourgeoisie*, throughout the Empire. Witness the thousands
of inscriptions set up all over the Roman world in praise of the
emperors of the second century, and above all in praise of
Antoninus Pius and the eternal Roman State.

It is natural, therefore, that this chapter, which deals with the
cities of the Empire, should begin by quoting some of the ideas
expressed in the speech of Aristides. To Aristides the Roman
Empire is a world-state and Rome the centre of the world. By
'world' Aristides means, of course, the civilized world ($o\imath\kappa o\upsilon\mu\epsilon\nu\eta$),
the Mediterranean lands. The Roman Empire succeeded in
building up and achieving the unity of the civilized world, a
task in which both the Oriental monarchies and the Greek cities
had failed. This unity was not based on slavery, as it had been
in the Oriental monarchies and even in the monarchies of

Description of Plate XVIII

1. SILVER DISH, partly gilt and inlaid with gold, partly treated in the niello-technique or enamelled. Found at Lampsacus. Istanbul Museum. *Gaz. arch.* 3, pl. XIX; H. Graeven, *JDAI* 15, 1903, p. 203, fig. 6; S. Reinach, *Rép. d. rel.* ii, p. 174, 1; E. H. Warmington, *The Commerce between the Roman Empire and India* (1928), p. 143. Graeven ascribes the dish to the early Byzantine period. I see no reason to assign to it such a late date. 2nd or 3rd cent. A.D.? Greco-Indian or Alexandrian workmanship?

Personification of India seated on a peculiar Indian chair, the legs of which are formed by elephant tusks. Her right hand is lifted in the gesture of prayer, in her left she holds a bow. Around her are grouped Indian animals—a parrot, a guinea-hen, and two pet monkeys with necklaces. Under her feet are two Indians leading a pet tiger and a pet panther, ready to fight, and making the gesture of adoration. The dish furnishes a valuable proof of the excellent knowledge which the Romans possessed about India and of the interest which they took in that country. On the animals of India as reflected in Greco-Roman tradition, see Wecker in Pauly–Wissowa, ix, cols.. 1301 ff.

2. LAMP OF THE COLLECTION BARONE. Found in Campania. A. Héron de Villefosse in *Mon. Piot*, 5, 1899, pp. 180 ff., fig. 44.

A Victory with large wings representing Rome as the goddess of prosperity: she holds the *cornucopiae* and pours a libation on an altar or a *cista* enlaced by a snake (the *cista mystica* of the Eleusinian mysteries?). Symbols of all the gods of prosperity and civilization are grouped around her: under her seat, the eagle of Jupiter; behind it, the dolphin of Neptune; between her wings, the hawk of Horus; on the left side, the club of Hercules, the *sistrum* of Isis, the lyre of Apollo, the tongs of Vulcan, the *caduceus* of Mercury, and the *thyrsus* of Bacchus; between the altar and the goddess, the torch of Demeter. The central position, however, is occupied by the symbols of the great gods of Asia Minor and Syria: the corn-ears, the pomegranate, the cymbal, and the raven of the Great Mother of Asia Minor, and a standard which consists of the full face of the Sun and the crescent of the Moon fastened to a sphere—the symbols of the Solar gods of Asia Minor and Syria. The lamp is a beautiful emblem of the mighty Roman Empire which brought peace, prosperity, and civilization to the East and the West alike.

3. RESTORATION OF THE *AGORA* (MARKET-PLACE) OF ASSOS IN ASIA MINOR. F. H. Bacon, *Investigations at Assos* (Expedition of the Arch. Inst. of America) (1902–21), p. 27; cf. p. 21 (Plan of Assos) and p. 33, fig. 4 (Plan of the Agora at Assos).

The two ends of the Agora are occupied by a temple (on the left) and by the *Bouleuterion,* or Hall of the municipal Council, on the right. Near the *Bouleuterion* and the temple are two monumental entrance-gates. The long left side of the Agora is occupied by a large Stoa (portico), similar to the Basilicae of the Roman Forum, the right side by an interesting 'Bazaar' with shops, store-rooms, &c. Near the Bazaar is a small Heröon. In the Imperial period Assos was a typical city of the smaller size, a modest but comfortable town, with a splendid past represented by the beautiful archaic temple of the Acropolis.

1. INDIA

2. ROMA PANTHEA

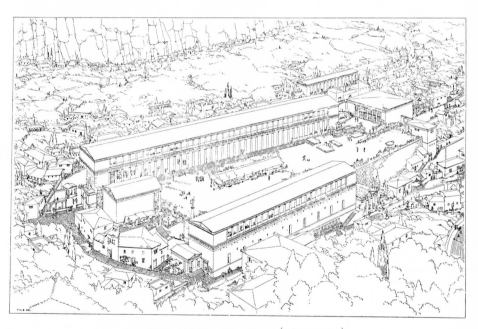

3. THE AGORA OF ASSOS (RESTORED)

XVIII. PROSPERITY OF THE EARLY ROMAN EMPIRE

Alexander and his successors. The head of this united world is not a master (δεσπότης) but a ruler (ἄρχων) or leader (ἡγεμών). He rules over free men, not over slaves, and he rules because he is willingly recognized by his subjects. They feel that cohesion is their salvation: the world has become one city-state (μία πόλις πᾶσα ἡ οἰκουμένη). In this state there are no Greeks and barbarians, natives and foreigners: all, we may say (though Aristides does not), are men. Before the state all are equal—great and small, rich and poor. Yet there is a distinction: there are the best men, and there are the masses. The best are the rulers, who are the Roman citizens; the masses must obey them. The rulers, however, are not necessarily natives of Rome or of Italy. They are the best men of all parts of the Roman Empire. The fact that they are the best makes them Roman citizens and therefore rulers; they rule over the constituent parts of the Empire, the cities; and it is the duty of the masses to obey. If they do not, if they begin rioting, if they attempt an upheaval of the existing order, there is force to compel obedience.

To the united world peace is secured both by a masterly administration of the Empire—a wonderful centralized system of bureaucracy—and by a strong permanent army, which consists of professional soldiers who are at the same time Roman citizens. Like the governing class in general, the Roman army represents the whole Empire, not one tribe or one nation or any combination of tribes and nations; and, like the governing class, the members of the army are all members of the ruling portion of the population: they are Roman citizens. Thanks to the officials and to the army, peace and prosperity reign all over the world, a peace and prosperity without precedent. General peace makes cities prosper and develop, and it has made the Empire an aggregate of cities that are most flourishing and beautiful, notably in Greece, Ionia (Asia Minor), and Egypt.

We have given a very bald sketch of Aristides' main ideas as expressed in his speech. But even this sketch shows the close connexion between his ideas and those of Dio. In addressing his audience at Rome, Aristides was well aware that he was speaking in the spirit of the enlightened monarchy and that his words might easily have been spoken by the emperor Antoninus himself. These words, too, were eagerly caught up by his audience. They desired to hear the praise of Rome—a genuine praise, not mere flattery—praise of the modern conditions that would be convincing and would drive away the gloomy feeling of coming decay, spoken of quite openly by many people, like the historian Annaeus Florus, for whom the period of the Roman Empire represented the old age (*senectus*) of human civilization.

Side by side with the picture of Aristides let us set a picture of the Roman Empire drawn according to our modern conceptions and related not only to its past but also to its future history, which is the only advantage we have over Aristides.

Aristides was perfectly right in emphasizing the fact that the Roman Empire was an aggregate of cities, Greek, Italian, and provincial, the last inhabited by more or less hellenized and romanized natives of the particular province concerned. Every city had assigned to it a smaller or larger tract of land which we usually call its 'territory'. This territory was either that of an ancient Greek or Italian city-state, or the land assigned by the Romans in Italy or the provinces to a new or old city, whether a Roman or Latin colony or a native town. We have already dealt with the gradual development of city life in the Empire, which was promoted more or less consistently by all the emperors of the first century, especially by Augustus and Claudius. This development did not cease under the Flavians and the Antonines. Mention has also been made of the activity of Vespasian in creating new cities or granting city rights to native towns throughout the Empire and particularly in Northern Italy, Spain, and Dalmatia. The same policy was pursued by the new 'dynasty' of the Antonines, especially Trajan and Hadrian. Since the fall of the Hellenistic monarchies the number of towns with dynastic names, particularly in the East, was never so imposing as in the time of these two emperors. Along with cities named Iuliopolis and Flaviopolis many bearing the title of Trajanopolis, Plotinopolis, Marcianopolis, and Hadrianopolis (or other compounds with Hadrian's name) arose in the Greek and the half-Greek East. It seems as though Trajan and Hadrian aimed at surpassing the Seleucids, Attalids, and Ptolemies. The activity displayed by Trajan in Dacia, Moesia Superior and Inferior, and Thrace was particularly important. The strong impression which he made on the indigenous population of these vast territories, comparable to the impact of Alexander's personality in the East, is reflected in several material remains, in

geographical names and in legends born in an age when the
Empire itself was no more than a legend. If Trajan could exercise such influence, it was due not only to his military victories,
but also, in great part, to the fact that he was the first to undertake the urbanization of modern Romania and Bulgaria, and
opened these countries to Greek and Roman civilization. What
Caesar and the emperors of the first century, including the
Flavians, had done for Northern Italy, for Gaul, for the regions
of the Rhine, for Britain, for Spain, and for Dalmatia, Trajan
and his successors, particularly Hadrian, did for the eastern
parts of the Danubian lands. Less important was the work of
urbanization undertaken by Trajan in Transjordan and Arabia,
where much of the work had already been done by the Flavians.
In Africa urbanization had proceeded without cessation since
the time of Augustus. Even in Egypt Hadrian created the first
and last Greek city since the foundation of Ptolemais, giving it
the name of Antinoupolis.

The new cities with dynastic or native names were partly
former villages and small towns, inhabited mostly by natives,
partly colonies of Roman veterans, especially in Africa, on the
Rhine, and on the Danube. Even some centres of the large
ex-territorial estates of the Roman emperors (which are dealt
with in the next chapter) were recognized as cities, and the imperial estate, or part of it, became their territory. None of these
new cities was an artificial creation. All were the development
of a natural tendency of the provinces towards urban life. But
this rapid urbanization of the provinces would not have been
possible if the emperors had not assisted it both by the formulation of a precise and methodical plan and by the investment of
large sums of money in the projects. It is to be noted that this
aspect of imperial activity did not last throughout the period
of the Antonines. After Hadrian the creation of cities becomes
more and more rare, though the process never stopped completely.[2]

Thus the Empire in the second century presented more than
ever the appearance of a vast federation of city-states. Each city
had its local self-government, its local 'political' life (in the
ancient sense of that adjective), and its own economic and social
problems to solve. Over the cities stood a strong central government which managed affairs of state—foreign relations, military

Description of Plate XIX

1–2. RUINS OF THE CITY OF GERASA IN TRANSJORDAN.

1. MAIN STREET WITH COLONNADE, FROM THE NORTHERN GATE.
It has been recently cleared by G. Horsfield, Director of the Department of Antiquities
in Transjordan. To the right, on the height, the imposing ruins of the large 'haram' of
the town, the temple of Artemis.

2. TEMPLE OF ARTEMIS. This has never been completely excavated, and its
history is still a problem.

We reproduce the plan of the city, from M. Rostovtzeff, *Caravan-Cities*, 1932, p. 54.

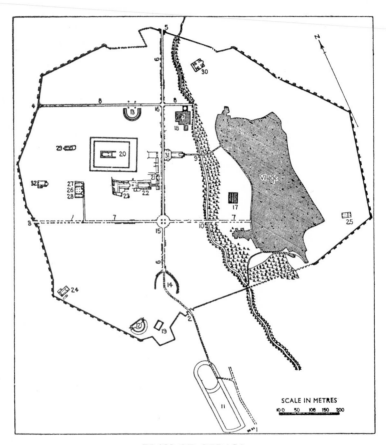

PLAN OF GERASA

GATES: 1. Arch, 2. Philadelphia, 3. Pella, 4. Gadara, 5. Damascus. STREETS, ETC.:
6. Antonine, 7. Pella, 8. Gadara, 14. Forum, 15. South Tetrapylon, 16. North
Tetrapylon, 9. Artemis Bridge, 10. Pella Bridge. THEATRES: 11. Hippodrome,
12. South, 13. North. CIVIC BUILDINGS: 17. East Bath, 18. West Bath,
21. Nymphaeum. TEMPLES: 19. Zeus, 20. Artemis. CHURCHES: 22. Cathedral,
23. St. Theodore, 24. St. Peter and St. Paul, 25. Bishop Paul, 26. St. John the
Baptist, 27. Damianos, 28. St. George, 29. Church over Synagogue, 30. Prophets,
Apostles, and Martyrs, 31. Propylaea, 32, Genesius.

1. MAIN STREET OF GERASA WITH COLONNADE

2. TEMPLE OF ARTEMIS AT GERASA

XIX. GERASA: CARAVAN CITY OF TRANSJORDAN

XX. HERCULANEUM: THE SOUTHERN QUARTER OF THE CITY, IN COURSE OF
EXCAVATION

XXI. HERCULANEUM: INTERIOR OF A HOUSE

Description of Plate XIX (cont.)

Gerasa is a typical caravan city. The main route of the caravans, transformed into a beautiful colonnaded street, runs almost due north to south on the line of the river. Outside the southern gate are the remains of a fine 'triumphal' arch connected with a large stadium (usually called 'Naumachia'). At the southern corner of the town is its most ancient building: a beautiful theatre which probably belongs to the Hellenistic age and was restored more than once (recently excavated by Horsfield), and, close to it, a temple. Near the southern gate is a remarkable oval *piazza*, probably a resting-place and market for the caravans (not yet completely excavated). The main street is adorned with two *tetrapyla* and a *nymphaeum*, the latter of which has been excavated and partially restored by Horsfield. Near the *nymphaeum* imposing *propylaea* give access to the steps which lead straight to the chief temple. The propylaea have now been completely excavated by Horsfield and are in process of reconstruction (see G. Horsfield, *Government of Transjordan, Antiquities Bulletin*, i, 1926, plates I–IV (*nymphaeum and propylaea*)). Near the temple are the remains of another theatre. Most interesting ruins of Christian churches have been excavated by a joint expedition of Yale University and the British School of Jerusalem (and the American School of Jerusalem): see the preliminary reports by J. W. Crowfoot, in *Palestine Exploration Fund, Quarterly Statement*, and by the directors of the American School in the *Bulletin of the American School of Oriental Research*, of Jerusalem [see *Gerasa, City of the Decapolis*, ed. C. H. Kraelling (1938)]. The inscriptions discovered have been published by A. H. M. Jones, *JRS* 18, 1928, pp. 144 ff., and ibid. 20, 1930, pp. 43 ff. [C. B. Welles, in *Gerasa*, pp. 355–494].

Description of Plate XXI

NEW EXCAVATIONS AT HERCULANEUM. Museo Nazionale, Naples. The interior of a house of Samnite type with decoration and restoration of the Roman period. Between the Atrium and the Tablinum there is a large wooden partition, with three doors, two of which are preserved. Cf. A. Maiuri, *Ercolano*[2] (1937).

affairs, state finances. The head of this central government was the emperor, the first ἄρχων, the *princeps*, the ἡγεμών. In his name his agents, both civil and military, acted. The senate was still regarded as the source of imperial power in so far as it, in theory, bestowed this power on the emperor; but it played in fact only a secondary part in state life, as the High Court and the Council of the Empire. *De jure* the central government was still the government of the senate and people of Rome, *de facto* it was an absolute monarchy modified by some privileges granted to the higher classes of the Roman citizens and by the self-government of the cities. In truth the self-government of the cities was almost complete. The imperial bureaucracy very seldom interfered with local city affairs. It dealt almost exclusively with the collection of taxes (mostly through the cities), with the administration of the imperial and state domains, and with one part of jurisdiction.

The difference between the Roman Empire and modern states of the same type lies in the fact that the central government of the Roman Empire was neither elected nor controlled by the constituent parts of the Empire. It was there to control and direct the self-government of the cities, not to be controlled or directed by them. It existed as an independent thing, a heritage from the time when the central government was the government of a single city, now the mistress of the world. The Roman Empire of the second century was thus a curious mixture of a federation of self-governing cities and of an almost absolute monarchy superimposed on this federation, the monarch being legally the chief magistrate of the ruling city of Rome.

It is not surprising, therefore, that the literary evidence about the Roman Empire bears almost wholly on the city of Rome and on the activity of the central government. Occasionally, however, we hear of the life of other cities in the Empire. It is sufficient to mention the works of such writers as Statius, Martial, Juvenal, and Pliny the Younger for the cities of Italy and of the Western half of the Empire, and the writings of the same Pliny, Dio Chrysostom, Lucian, Flavius Josephus, Philo, and Aristides for the cities of Greece and the Greek East. Moreover, the cities themselves are very loquacious. Through the medium of scores of thousands of inscriptions and papyri, both Greek and Latin, they have told us so many important and unimportant details of their life that it is comparatively easy to restore its essential features. Further, modern archaeological excavations naturally attacked the ruins of the cities first. Some of these ruins, especially in the countries which lay waste after the end of the Roman domination—Asia Minor, Syria, and Africa—are exceptionally interesting and in a beautiful state of preservation. Finally, hundreds of thousands of coins, which were still to a large extent struck by the cities of the Empire, supply us with first-class information on some important points in their political, religious, and economic life. These sources have revealed to us not only the external appearance of many ancient cities but also the main features of every aspect of their life—their walls, gates, streets, public places, public and private buildings on the one hand, and on the other their municipal organization, their income and expenditure, their wealth and their sources of wealth, both public and private, their religious beliefs, their amusements, and their intellectual interests.

The first impression derived from the study of these sources is overwhelming. Never before had so considerable a part of Europe, Asia, and Africa presented an aspect so civilized, so modern, one may say, in its essential features. Some of the cities were large, some were small, some were rich and luxurious, some poor and modest. But all of them had this in common, that they exerted themselves to the utmost to make city life as easy and as comfortable as possible.

Rome, the huge and beautiful capital of the world, was of course the most admired and flattered of all the cities of the Empire. And she deserved the admiration of contemporaries as she fully deserves ours: so beautiful is Rome even in her ruins, so impressive her public monuments—her temples, the palaces of her emperors with their 'gardens' in the city and their villas in the suburbs, her palaces for the people (baths, basilicas, porticoes), and her public places and public gardens. With the city of Rome vied the capitals of the richest and most prosperous provinces: Alexandria in Egypt, Antioch in Syria, Ephesus in Asia Minor, Carthage in Africa, and Lyons in Gaul.[3] Behind them came hundreds of large and beautiful cities both in the East and in the West. We may enumerate a few of them: Pompeii, Puteoli, Ostia, Verona, and Aquileia in Italy; Tauromenium, Syracuse, and Panormus in Sicily; Massilia, Narbo,

THE RUINS OF PART OF THE CITY OF THAMUGADI (TIMGAD) IN NUMIDIA.
P. Boeswilwald, A. Ballu, and R. Cagnat, *Timgad, une cité africaine* (1901–5); A. Ballu, *Guide illustré de Timgad (antique Thamugadi)*, 2nd ed. (1904).

View taken from the Theatre (no. 18 on the plan). The square near the centre is the Forum with its buildings (no. 13 on the plan). The building with the two columns seen in the photograph is the temple of Victory; in front of it was a platform which was used by the magistrates as a tribune for delivering speeches and making official announcements to the citizens. Near the temple was the well-known public lavatory (*latrinae*, no. 12 on the plan). The Forum was surrounded by porticoes. Behind the Forum runs one of the main streets, the *decumanus maximus* (no. 6 on the plan). Where the *decumanus* cuts the fortifications of the original city (a military colony of Trajan), a fine Arch was built in honour of Trajan. Its imposing ruins are seen in the photograph (no. 41 on the plan). The other ruins are mostly the remains of private houses, public baths, markets, and Christian churches (e.g. nos. 44 and 46 on the plan are Christian churches, while nos. 45 and 62 are private houses). No. 5 on the plan is the famous Public Library of Timgad.

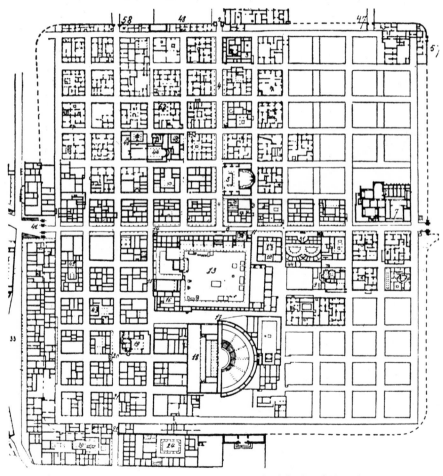

Plan of the central part (the original colony) of the city of Timgad

XXII. A ROMAN PROVINCIAL CITY. TIMGAD (THAMUGADI)

Arelate, Nemausus, Arausio, Augusta Treverorum, Colonia Agrippinensis, Bonna, Moguntiacum, and Argentorate in Gaul and Germany; Londinium and Eboracum in England; Tarraco, Corduba, Hispalis, Italica, Emerita, and Asturica in Spain; Hadrumetum, Cirta, Hippo Regius, and Caesarea in Africa, Numidia, and Mauretania; Cyrene in Cyrenaica; Tergeste and Pola in Histria; Salona in Dalmatia; Emona and Poetovio in Pannonia; Thessalonica in Macedonia; Athens, Corinth, and Rhodes in Greece; Smyrna, Pergamon, Sardis, and Miletus in Asia; Ancyra and Antiochia Pisidiae in Galatia; Pessinus and Aezani in Phrygia; Tarsus in Cilicia; Nicaea and Nicomedia in Bithynia; Cyzicus and Byzantium on the Sea of Marmora and the neighbouring straits; Sinope on the Black Sea, Tomi and Istrus on its western coast; Panticapaeum (a vassal city) and Chersonesus in the Crimea; Tyre, Sidon, and Aradus in Phoenicia; Heliopolis, Palmyra, Damascus, Philadelphia (Amman) and Gerasa in Syria; Seleuceia-on-Tigris in Mesopotamia; Petra and Bostra in Arabia; Jerusalem in Palestine.[4]

These are but a few cities selected from thousands, partly because they are glorified in our literary sources and partly because they are famous for their well-preserved ruins. The list could be greatly extended. In addition, archaeological excavations have revealed to us many cities almost unknown to our literary sources, but nevertheless beautiful and prosperous centres of life. Such are, for instance, Thugga, Thuburbo Majus, Thubursicu Numidarum, Bulla Regia, Sufetula, Althiburos, Gigthis, Tripolis (Oea, Sabratha, Lepcis), Theveste, Lambaesis, Thamugadi, Madaurus, Cuicul, and Volubilis in Africa, Numidia, and Mauretania; Carnuntum, Aquincum, and Nicopolis ad Istrum on the Danube; Vindonissa and Augusta Raurica in modern Switzerland; Castra Regina (Regensburg), and Cambodunum in Raetia; Virunum in Noricum; Doclea in Dalmatia; Calleva Atrebatum (Silchester), Venta Silurum (Caerwent), and Aquae Sulis (Bath) in England; Assos in Asia Minor; some large villages and small cities in Egypt, and so on.[5]

The cities of the Roman Empire were of course not all of the same type. They varied in accordance with their historical evolution and with local conditions. First come the large and rich commercial and industrial towns, mostly centres of an extensive sea or river traffic, some—like Palmyra, Petra, and Bostra—

important meeting-places of merchants engaged in a lively caravan trade. To this class belong most of the cities which have been
enumerated above as the most beautiful and the richest cities
of the Empire. Behind these leaders of civilized life follow many
large and well-built towns—centres of extensive and fertile agricultural districts, capitals of provinces or of subdivisions of provinces. Most of them were at the same time important centres
of a local, provincial commerce, being situated at the crossing-
points of important trade routes or on a navigable river. Of
practically the same type are the smaller cities which gradually
developed out of villages in more or less rich agricultural districts, such as almost all the African cities mentioned above,
scores of cities in Britain, Spain, Gaul, Germany, in the Alpine
and the Danubian provinces, in Thrace, Macedonia, Greece,
Asia Minor, Syria, and Egypt. In Egypt such cities were legally
not cities at all but villages, though they were the administrative
centres of large and rich territories. By natural development they
had assumed the aspect of regular well-kept Greco-Oriental towns.

Despite differences in size, in number of population, in wealth,
in political and social importance, all the cities of the Empire
presented some common features. They all aimed, as has been
said, at the largest possible degree of comfort for their inhabitants; they all looked like some of our modern Western cities
rather than like the cities and villages of the East at the present
day. I have no doubt that some, or most, modern Italian cities
differ very little from their Roman ancestors. Almost all the
cities of the Empire, especially in the Hellenistic East, had a
good scientific system of drainage, an abundant water supply
even in the upper storeys of the houses, provided by most skil-
fully built aqueducts, well-paved streets and squares, covered
porticoes lining the streets and destined to protect pedestrians from
sun and rain, hygienic and spacious markets—particularly fish and
meat markets with a copious supply of water—large and beautiful
baths in various parts of the city enabling every citizen to have his
daily bath for little or nothing, extensive and well-arranged
buildings for sport and exercise—gymnasia and palaestrae. For
religious purposes there were splendid temples and altars, sacred
woods and long rows of beautiful funeral monuments bordering
the public roads outside the gates. Large and imposing public
buildings appear in all the cities: *curiae* (the meeting-places of the

local senates), offices of the magistrates, halls for the official *collegia* and for the voters in public elections, *basilicae* for the judges, prisons, and so forth. Others were destined for public recreation and education: theatres, circuses, stadia, amphitheatres, public libraries, *auditoria* for declamations and public lectures, and picture galleries. The private houses were mostly of good size and equipped with modern conveniences, for example, private baths, running water, good stone stairs to the upper storeys, &c.[6]

These are all familiar facts. We may say that as regards comfort, beauty, and hygiene, the cities of the Roman Empire, worthy successors of their Hellenistic parents, were not inferior to many a modern European and American town. It is no wonder that so many of their inhabitants had such a deep and sincere love for them. Of this affection illustrations may be found in the description of Smyrna by Aristides—and he was not a native of the city, but only an adopted citizen—or in the description of Rhodes by Dio who was not connected with it, or in the many descriptions of Athens. They show the pride taken by the people of the Roman Empire in their best creations, their cities and their urban civilization. The splendour of the cities was almost entirely due to the munificence of the higher and wealthier classes of their population. Their current expenditure was, of course, covered by their regular income, which was collected in the form of various taxes from the residents, both citizens and sojourners or 'by-dwellers' (κάτοικοι, πάροικοι, &c., in the Greek East; *incolae, inquilini, populi attributi* in the West). The system of taxation was elaborated by centuries of experience, gained especially in the Hellenistic period. Taxes were paid for the land in the territory of the city, for real estate in the city, for import and export (municipal customs-duties), for the exercise of a trade, for contracts and business transactions, for the use of the market-places (rent of the shops which belonged to the city) and of other municipal real estate, and so on.[7]

The income of the cities, particularly the large and rich cities, was therefore in some cases very considerable. But we must not forget that the current expenditure of a city was very great, greater indeed to all appearance than that of modern cities. They did not, of course, pay salaries to their magistrates. Service performed for the city by civil or religious officials was regarded either as an honour or as a burden; in either case it meant that

1. RUINS OF THE HOUSE OF DIANA AT OSTIA. G. Calza, 'Le origini latine dell' abitazione moderna', *Architettura ed Arti Decorative*, 3, 1923, fig. 8.

Typical ruin of a large house, divided into flats, belonging to the 2nd cent. A.D. The appended plan shows the arrangement of the apartments in the two storeys around the central court.

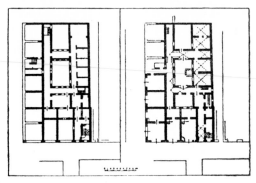

Plan of the house of Diana

2. RESTORATION (BY THE ARCHITECT I. GISMONDI) OF THE CORNER HOUSE IN THE VIA DELLA FORTUNA. G. Calza, ibid., fig. 22.

A four-storeyed apartment-house. The first floor was occupied by shops (one of which is a bar-restaurant, *thermopolium*), the upper floors by private apartments, some of them of large size (for well-to-do people). Note the fine verandah and the balconies.

3. RESTORATION (BY THE ARCHITECT I. GISMONDI) OF THE INNER FRONT OF THE 'CASA DEI DIPINTI' AT OSTIA. G. Calza, ibid., fig. 28.

The view shows the inner court of the large house with plants, trees, basins, &c. The appended plan, restored by the architect Lawrence, shows the distribution of the apartments on the ground floor and first floor.

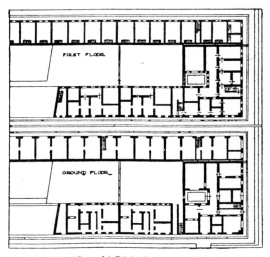

Plan of the 'Casa dei Dipinti' as restored by Lawrence

I

2

3

XXIII. HOUSES AT OSTIA

the service was gratuitous. But the cities paid their minor officials, who were either public slaves (δημόσιοι, *servi publici*) and
had to be provided with quarters, clothing, and food, or free
salaried men.[8] The payment of these officials was a considerable
expense. Still greater was the expense for the repair and maintenance of the various public buildings.

One of the most complicated tasks of the cities and the city
magistrates was to secure 'abundance' (*abundantia*) of foodstuffs,
especially of corn (*annona*, εὐθηνία), for public consumption. In
Rome the emperor undertook this task. In the other cities it was
one of the main duties of the city council and the city magistrates. The conditions under which a plentiful supply of food
had to be secured were not very favourable. In many cases the
city territories were not large enough to provide a sufficient
supply. Moreover, the variability of crops was an outstanding
feature of economic life in the ancient world, even in such lands
as Egypt. Thus all the cities depended more or less on a regular
or emergency import of foodstuffs. None of them was permanently self-sufficient. The organization of the market and
especially of the transportation of large masses of foodstuffs was,
therefore, a question of prime importance for the cities of the
Empire. The problem of regulating the market was not tackled
by the central government. On the contrary many serious
obstacles were placed in the way of the free development of
trade concerned with the necessities of life. The state and the
requirements of the state were paramount for the emperors and
their agents. Even more urgent for the emperors was the safeguarding of their power. Thus they monopolized for themselves
large masses of corn which they used to supply the city of Rome
and the army: export of corn from Egypt was permitted only to
those who secured special imperial authorization. The large
domains of the emperor all over the Empire, which produced
enormous amounts of corn, were used for the same purpose.
Corn produced on these domains very rarely appeared on the
open market. Moreover, as we shall see later, the means of transport were everywhere under the direct control of the state, and
the owners of ships and draught animals were not free to devote
all their activity to the solution of the problem of satisfying the
needs of the population. The needs of the state and of the emperor had to be satisfied first. Still more important and more

complicated was the problem of transportation. Though the sea
was now safe and piracy had disappeared, though a wonderful
system of land-roads was created by the emperors, the question
remained as serious and as difficult as before. New cities grew
up in large numbers in all the provinces, some of them far away
from the sea, far from the great water-ways and even from the
main roads. The cities endeavoured to build district roads and
to connect their territories with the main roads, the rivers, and
the sea. But this was a slow process and the building and repairing of roads cost vast sums of money. The burden of the construction and maintenance of these district roads lay entirely on the
cities. Even the construction of good roads, however, did not
solve the problem. Land transport was exceedingly expensive,
as compared with transport by sea and river. To move large
masses of foodstuffs by the land-roads was, therefore, beyond the
resources of smaller and poorer cities.

That is the reason why almost all the cities of the Empire, even
those situated in the most fertile regions, and still more those
lying in the mountainous districts of Italy and the provinces, had
from time to time very bad periods of dearth and high prices.
Often we actually find years of real famine. Such times were
generally marked by grave social disturbances, the magistrates
and the senates being accused of carelessness and the great landowners and corn-merchants of profiteering. In these circumstances riots and demonstrations were common. To prevent such
disasters was far from easy, and even in normal times it cost the
city enormous sums of money. The office of σιτώνης (buyer of
corn) was, therefore, one of the most difficult and perilous in the
career of a municipal magistrate. The task of the *agoranomoi*, who
corresponded to the *aediles* of the West, was scarcely less difficult.
It was their responsibility to see that bread was cheap and that
the prices of other commodities were kept within moderate
bounds. The life of these pathetic victims of municipal ambition
and local patriotism is well characterized by certain speeches
about the *aediles* and their activity; for instance, the well-known
observations made at the banquet of Trimalchio on the question
of the price of fish or those made in the fish-market of a Thes-
salian town by the no less famous friend of Lucius, whom Apu-
leius immortalized. It is therefore not surprising that when a city
was enabled to keep the price of corn low, it recorded this meri-

torious act in the inscribed list of its magistrates by the side of
their names, as was done for some of the *agoranomoi* of Ephesus.
The office of σιτώνης appears more frequently in the East than
the corresponding office of *curator annonae* or the like in the West.
The explanation is simple: the Greek cities, even in some parts of
Asia Minor, never produced sufficient corn for their population,
and the crops were more variable in Greece and Asia Minor,
owing to the hot climate and the scarcity and irregularity of rains,
than in the lands of Central Europe and even in Italy, Spain, and
Africa. On this we shall have more to say in the next chapter.⁹

Another large item in the budget of a city was the expense of
public education and the physical training of young and old,
especially in the completely hellenized cities of the East. To
have gone through a course of instruction in a palaestra and in
a gymnasium was the distinguishing mark of an educated man,
as opposed to one of low breeding. In Egypt, for example, those
who were educated in the gymnasia formed a special class of the
population, which enjoyed certain rights and privileges (οἱ ἀπὸ
τοῦ γυμνασίου): thus, freeborn youths of Alexandria who had
received such an education were considered by the Emperor
Claudius qualified for the important privilege of Alexandrian
citizenship. Many inscriptions show that the cities of the Greek
East had not forgotten the glorious traditions of their past and
were as eager as before, and perhaps more eager, to secure a
good education on Greek lines for the city youth, so far at least
as they belonged to the privileged classes. This, however, was expensive. Huge sums of money were required to pay the teachers,
to provide and keep in good repair the schools and athletic
grounds, and to distribute oil to those who were unable to buy
it. To secure for the city a sufficient supply of oil was almost as
important as to have abundant corn at reasonable prices. Buyers
of olive-oil (ἐλαιῶναι) were consequently almost as common in
the Greek cities as buyers of corn (σιτῶναι). The office was both
important and burdensome.¹⁰

Besides public education, religion demanded attention and
expenditure. Every city had many temples, which had to be
maintained in good condition. Some of them had funds of their
own, but many had not. Some revenue was derived from the
lease of the priestly offices, to which was attached the right to
certain allowances in kind. But the money received in this way

amounted to very little compared with the expense of the maintenance of a well-organized religious life—the expense of sacrifices to the gods and heroes, processions, religious feasts, contests (ἀγῶνες) and games in honour of various gods, and so forth.
No wonder that some cities had a special finance department for
public worship, special treasurers, and special treasuries. Closely
connected with the cult of the gods were the various games which
gradually became as important in the life of the cities as the food
supply. Most of these games were given by the magistrates and
by rich citizens at their own expense. But sometimes the city was
obliged to give them in order to prevent bad feeling and even
riots among the masses of the proletariate.[11]

It is not surprising that under such conditions the city expected
her rich citizens to help by undertaking part of the expense. This
was to a certain extent obligatory on them. For the honour of
being elected a magistrate of the city a certain sum (*summa
honoraria*) had to be paid. A certain amount of expense was connected with many honorary posts, such as that of gymnasiarch.
Some priests were supposed to bear part of the expenditure
necessary for the cult of their god or for the city cults in general.
In some cases patrons and presidents of religious associations
were expected to finance the worship of the gods who protected
these associations. In difficult times a loan was raised by the city
and, though the participation of the citizens was supposed to be
voluntary, practically every rich citizen was forced to subscribe
a certain amount of money if he wished to escape discredit in the
eyes of the public and even to avoid becoming a target of not
very friendly demonstrations. In case of necessity the city recurred also to the ancient practice of liturgies, that is, of compulsory contributions by rich citizens to aid in the execution of
some important public work.

It must be noted, however, that compulsion was very seldom
required in the first century, and still less in the first half of the
second, either to fill up the offices of magistrates, priests, gym-
nasiarchs, and the rest, or to obtain effective assistance in embel-
lishing the city, in creating or maintaining social or religious
institutions, and even in meeting current expenditure. The rich
citizens were ready to help and gave money freely for everything
that was needed by the city: we may say that most of the beautiful public buildings in the cities of East and West were their gifts.

In time of famine the same men liberally furnished money to feed the starving population. In normal times they spent large sums in enhancing the splendour of municipal games or in giving games and contests on their own account. Very often, too, they gave doles to the people, both rich and poor, in the form of money or food and wine. Public banquets for large numbers of citizens were a common feature of municipal life. Some of these gifts took the form of foundations, large sums of money being provided to be invested, or land and other real estate to be rented, for the creation and upkeep of one or other of the religious or social institutions of the city.[12]

It is amazing to see what enormous sums were given by wealthy citizens, especially in the Greek East. We know of hundreds of such donors all over Greece and Asia Minor, and we must suppose that there was an exceedingly large number of opulent men who were moved by public opinion and by their own patriotism to spend freely on their native cities. The tradition of liberality, which arose in the free Greek cities and developed vigorously in the Hellenistic period, especially in the third and second centuries B.C., was revived and maintained in the Roman Empire, notably in the first two centuries A.D. From the East the habit spread to Italy along with the other traits of Greek municipal life, and from Italy to the Western provinces. It was a revelation to scholars when Austrian explorers discovered in a small city of Lycia the funeral monument of a man called Opramoas, a native of Rhodiapolis, who had spent millions for the needs of his own city, of other Lycian cities, and of the common council (κοινόν) of the Lycian cities. Nor was he the only Lycian to do so. Men of the same type appear in all parts of the Greek East; among the most famous of them are Julius Eurycles of Sparta and his descendants, and Herodes Atticus of Athens who are celebrated alike in our literary and in our epigraphic sources. And it is worthy of note that the leaders of this movement were the best-educated men, the intellectuals of the time, rich 'sophists' such as Polemon, Damianus, and Herodes Atticus. The same spirit was shown by the new aristocracy of Rome, the Italian and provincial senators and knights (everyone knows of the gifts and foundations of the younger Pliny which are mentioned in his letters), and by the new provincial city aristocracy, the rich merchants, landowners, and industrial employers of the cities of Gaul, Spain, Africa, and other provinces. When we observe that these gifts and foundations had a general tendency to increase both in number and in size all through the first century, and still more in the first half of the second, that most of them were given not under compulsion but freely, and that there were plenty of men of wealth ready to take up the duties of magistrates, priests, presidents and patrons of various associations, officials and priests of the provincial councils (κοινά), it becomes plain not only that the municipal spirit was at its height in the first half of the second century, but also that the wealth which was concentrated in the hands of the city *bourgeoisie* both in East and West steadily increased.[13]

What were the sources of the growing wealth of the city *bourgeoisie*, of those thousands and thousands of men who lived in the various parts of the Empire and accumulated for themselves large tracts of land, huge sums of money, houses and shops in the cities, ships and transport animals on the rivers and roads? The first point to emphasize in this connexion is the increasing number of rich men throughout the Empire. Wealth was no longer concentrated in a few hands and a few places, as in the time of the domination of the Athenian Republic or the Roman senate. As in the Hellenistic period, we witness a decentralization of wealth, if we may use the expression. Some of the Roman senators were still very rich, but they were no longer the 'nabobs' of the first century B.C. or the multi-millionaires of the period of the Julii and Claudii. Among the senators of the second century A.D. (chiefly of Italian or provincial cities) wealthy men were not exceptional, but as a rule they were of the type of Pliny the Younger—moderately rich men, mostly landowners. It is to be observed that in the second century there is no mention of senators whose wealth equalled that of the favourites of the early Empire—Maecenas, Agrippa, Seneca, Acte (the mistress of Nero), Narcissus, Pallas, and the rest. The era of favourites was past. Juvenal, to be sure, still uses the commonplaces about millionaires playing the leading role among the city aristocracy, but they are merely commonplaces. We have no names to corroborate his statement, but we have scores of them for the period that preceded.[14]

Very rich men are now to be found partly in Rome (mostly not among senators but among freedmen), chiefly in the pro-

vinces, not in Italy: Trimalchio exists no more, or he lives now not
in Campania but somewhere in the provinces. The wealth which
was accumulated in the hands of individual citizens of provincial
cities was sometimes very large. We have quoted the examples of
Opramoas in Lycia, Eurycles in Sparta, and Herodes Atticus in
Athens. The treasure which Herodes' father found in his house in
Athens was (we may parenthetically remark) not a treasure but probably money hidden by Herodes' grandfather, Hipparchus, in the
troublous times of Domitian's persecutions (of which Hipparchus
was himself a victim). In the absence of statistics we cannot esti-
mate the size of the fortunes of Opramoas and other men of his
type, nor can we compare them with those of the rich men of the
first century A.D. or with the large fortunes of modern times. Of
greater importance is the fact that rich men are now to be found
everywhere in the most unexpected places, like Rhodiapolis in
Lycia or one of the small cities of Africa, Gaul, Spain, or even
Thrace. In proof, if proof be needed, we have not only the gifts
and foundations of the second century, which require to be more
carefully collected and classified, but also the beauty and the
luxury of the funeral monuments. Is it not characteristic of the
conditions of this period that the most beautiful monuments are
now to be found, not in Rome or in Italy, but in the provinces?
Such are the monuments near the modest city of Assos, excavated and restored by the American expedition; the beautiful
funeral temples and massive sarcophagi all over Asia Minor,
especially in Lycia; the mighty tumuli near Olbia and Panticapaeum, and the painted rock-tombs of the latter city; the
'Mausolea' of Africa and Syria, real shrines for the cult of the
deceased; and in Syria particularly the funerary towers of
Palmyra and district, and the five monuments of the mountainous territory, now deserted, between Aleppo and Antioch;
the sculptured tombs all over Gaul, especially near Trèves,
in Luxembourg, and near Arlon. Even in the new Danube
lands we meet with large and expensive tombs; for example,
the painted tomb adorned with statues of a rich landowner
near Viminacium. Men who could bear the expense of
such buildings, and could bequeath money enough for the
upkeep of the monuments and of the gardens which were
connected with them, were people who had accumulated large
fortunes.[15]

Description of Plate XXIV

1. THE LOWER PANEL OF THE FUNERAL STELE OF 'IUCUNDUS M. TERENTI L(IBERTUS) PECUARIUS'. Mainz, Central-Museum. *CIL* xiii. 7070; E. Espérandieu, *Rec. gén.* vii, no. 5824; *Germania Romana, ein Bilder-Atlas*, pl. xxxix, 6.

The shepherd Jucundus, freedman of a certain M. Terentius, is represented leading a flock of sheep to pasture in a forest. The metrical inscription on the stele, which was erected in his memory by his *patronus*, says that Jucundus was killed at the age of thirty by a slave, who then drowned himself in the river Main. Terentius was no doubt a rich landowner and Jucundus his chief shepherd, who had many slaves under him as assistants.

2. ONE OF THE BAS-RELIEFS OF THE FUNERAL MONUMENT OF A RICH MERCHANT OF MOGUNTIACUM (MAINZ). Found at Mainz in the city wall. Mainz, Central-Museum. E. Espérandieu, *Rec. gén.* vii, no. 5833; *Germania Romana*, pl. xlii, 6; S. Reinach, *Rép. d. rel.* ii. 71, 5.

One man is seen sifting grain, another carrying away a basket of grain already sifted.

3. FRAGMENTS OF A SCULPTURAL FRIEZE OF A FUNERAL MONUMENT OF AGEDINCUM (SENS). Sens, in the Museum. G. Julliot, *Musée Gallo-Romain de Sens*, p. 97 and pl. vii; E. Espérandieu, *Rec. gén.* iv, nos. 2852, 2853.

Various implements used for making wine or cider: four empty baskets, two baskets full of fruit, a wooden box, four mortars (two of them with their pestles), a fork, and three heaps of a substance in which Julliot recognizes *le marc de raisin*.

4. ONE OF THE BAS-RELIEFS OF NEUMAGEN (TRÈVES), PART OF A FUNERAL MONUMENT. Museum of Trèves. Hettner, *Illustrierter Führer durch das Provinzialmuseum in Trier* (1903), p. 16, 13; E. Espérandieu, *Rec. gén.* vi, no. 5148; *Germania Romana*, pl. xli, 3; S. Reinach, *Rép. d. rel.* ii. 91, 3.

A banker or a landowner and his two assistants, all clean-shaven and in Roman dress, receiving payments from four bearded peasants in typical rustic half-Celtic dress.

5. ONE OF THE BAS-RELIEFS OF THE FUNERAL MONUMENT OF THE SECUNDINII AT IGEL (NEAR TRÈVES). Dragendorff und Krüger, *Das Grabmal von Igel* (1924), pl. x, 1, and Abb. 47, p. 77; E. Espérandieu, *Rec. gén.* vi, no. 5268, p. 443; Drexel in *Röm. Mitt.* 35, 1920, pp. 83–142.

Trade in clothes. Two men are inspecting a piece of cloth. Four other men form one group with the two inspectors. One of them registers the piece in his book. A seventh man is entering the room.

This set of pictures is intended to illustrate the brisk business life which went on in the Western provinces in every field of economic activity.

I. SHEPHERD

2. SIFTING GRAIN

3. IMPLEMENTS FOR MAKING WINE OR CIDER

4. BANKING

5. TRADE IN CLOTHES

XXIV. BUSINESS LIFE IN THE WESTERN PROVINCES

Thus the first thing to be emphasized is that the second century was an age of rich or well-to-do men distributed all over the Empire, not modest landowners like the municipal *bourgeoisie* of Italy in the Republican and the early Imperial periods, but big men, capitalists on the large scale who very often dominated the social life of their cities and were known to every one not only in the city, but throughout the district or even throughout the whole province.

The question whence their wealth was derived is one of great interest. Wealthy men cannot be created by the will of emperors. The policy of the emperors was naturally to give these men the largest possible influence in city affairs. Unfortunately, we have no learned work dealing with this problem. No scholar has endeavoured to collect the evidence about the rich men of the second century, about the sources of their income, and about the character of their economic activity. A careful investigation of this subject promises good results. Our information is fairly abundant. As far as I can judge from the evidence I have got together, the main source of large fortunes, now as before, was commerce. Money acquired by commerce was increased by lending it out mostly on mortgage, and it was invested in land. Along with commerce and with the closely connected business of transportation, industry played a part, but it was a subsidiary part, though some fortunes were undoubtedly made in this way.[16] The development of commerce and of transport business in the second century is full of interest. We recognize some of the old phenomena, of which we have treated in the preceding chapters, but along with them we find new features which were almost unknown to the first century.

As before, and to a greater extent than before, this commerce was a world commerce. The Roman Empire was linked by commercial relations with all its neighbours and with peoples who were not in territorial touch with it. A lively commerce went on between Gaul and the Danube lands and Germany. The products of Roman industry reached even the Scandinavian lands and the shores of the Baltic Sea, and in comparatively large quantities. From the Danube Roman commerce spread to the region of the river Dnieper and reached a high importance which it maintained all through the second century,[17] as is shown by the finds of Roman coins and by the frequent occurrence in the tombs of that region of Roman pottery and glass-ware belonging to the first two centuries. The Greek cities on the shores of the Black Sea, especially Olbia, Chersonesus, Panticapaeum, and Tanais, flourished again throughout the second century. Olbia and Panticapaeum were connected both with the Southern and with the Western shores of the Black Sea. The Bosporan kingdom still exported large masses of corn and of other raw materials (especially hides, fish, and hemp). This export was directed partly to the cities of Greece, but mostly through the cities of the Southern and Western coasts of the Black Sea to the permanent quarters of the Roman armies on the Danube and in Cappadocia. Its volume naturally increased when the emperors had to move large numbers of soldiers from East to West and from West to East, as in the time of Vespasian, Domitian, Trajan, and M. Aurelius. The importance of South Russia for the Roman Empire is shown by the fact that Olbia and the cities in the Crimea, particularly the free city of Chersonesus, which became the main centre of Roman influence in South Russia, were protected by Roman troops against the incursions of the inhabitants of the steppes. How large a part was played by the Bosporan and Olbian merchants in forwarding wares from Central Russia (furs and wax) and Asia to the Roman Empire, we do not know. But such a traffic certainly existed and enriched the Sarmatian tribes which were now dominant in the steppes of South Russia and in the Caucasus and linked South Russia with the great Chinese silk-route. The commerce of South Russia was concentrated partly in the hands of the Bosporan kings and of Bosporan and Olbian merchants, partly in those of merchants of Sinope, Amisos, Tomi, and Istros.[18]

As regards the commerce of the South and the South-East, the African trade with the tribes of the Sahara was of no real importance. Some slaves were brought to the provinces of Africa, Numidia, and Mauretania, and perhaps some ivory; in addition large numbers of wild beasts, destined to be shown to the public and killed in the amphitheatres now being built everywhere. Also the wood of the African cedar was famous for tables. More important was the Southern trade of Egypt with the kingdom of Meroë and with Abyssinia (Axum) and, through these half-civilized states, with Central Africa. The finds in Meroë show that for the wares exported from Central Africa the Roman

Empire paid with the products of Egyptian industry. But most important of all was the trade of Egypt, and particularly of Alexandria, with Arabia and—partly through Arabia, partly directly—with India and through India with China. This subject has been dealt with in the preceding chapter, but it should be added that the commerce of the Roman Empire now reached not only the region of the Indus but also Indo-China and Sumatra, and that the trade with India and with China steadily developed and became quite regular. Moreover, it was no longer a trade merely in luxuries. Some of the imports were no doubt of this sort, but the largest part consisted of articles like cotton and condiments. The same is true of the wares exported from the Roman Empire to the East. These were partly raw materials and foodstuffs (for instance, iron and corn), partly and chiefly products of Alexandrian industry. The active agents in the exchange of goods between the Roman Empire and India and China were the Alexandrian merchants. Without them the commerce with India would probably not have existed.[19]

Documents discovered in recent years have made us realize that trade with the Somaliland coast, with Arabia, and with India, already flourishing in the Ptolemaic period, was even better organized under the Romans. A tariff of duties payable for escort, compiled about A.D. 90 and found at Coptos, attests a lively traffic on the desert-route between Coptos and Berenice. The travellers are mostly sea captains, officers of the escort-troops, skilled craftsmen, naval carpenters and sailors of the commercial fleet of the Red Sea (the first-named are expressly called 'captains of the Red Sea'). Masts and sail-yards were also transported. The mention of wives of soldiers proves that troops were stationed at Berenike. The soldiers probably belonged in part to the personnel of the war-fleet which protected this commerce. A road had been built in the desert between Coptos and Berenike, wells dug, military posts established: all this service was controlled by the *Arabarches* and by the Prefect of the mountains of Berenice. Each caravan was escorted by armed troops in the Roman service, among whom the Arabs, used to the desert since childhood, played an important role. Similar measures safeguarded the traffic between the Western oases and the Fayyûm and between the Fayyûm and Egypt. A well-organized river-police force supervised navigation on the Nile

Description of Plate XXV

1. CHINESE CLAY STATUETTE. Chicago Natural History Museum. Acquired by B. Laufer in 1908 at Si-anfu; found in a tomb near Si-anfu, capital of the province of Scen-si. Unpublished. Period of the T'ang dynasty, 7th–8th cent. A.D. Published by kind permission of the Director of the Chicago Natural History Museum. I owe the description of the statuette to Dr. B. Laufer.

Loaded camel kneeling. A central Asiatic, probably a Turk, dressed in goat fur and cloak, sits astride between the humps, and goads the beast to get up. The camel, loaded with two heavy bales, tries to get up, sniffing. The tension of the muscles is well portrayed.

2. CHINESE CLAY STATUETTE. Pennsylvania Museum. Unpublished. Period of the T'ang dynasty. I owe the photographs and the descriptions of figs. 2 and 4 to the kindness of Horace H. F. Jayne, Curator of Oriental Art in Pennsylvania Museum.

Pedlar with parcel of samples of material under his left arm and probably a trumpet to call attention in his right hand; pedlars still announce their arrival by these trumpets. The type of the head, with heavy beard and moustaches, denotes western Asia; the man is probably a Persian. He is wearing a tall, pointed hat, a dress with short sleeves and a V-opening at the neck, a long belt of soft material, high gaiters and soft shoes. Figures of this sort are very common. Cf., for example, *The Eumorphopoulos Collection, Pottery and Porcelain*, i, no. 195, pl. 28; no. 297, pl. 44; no. 298, pl. 44. C. Hentze interprets the figures as musicians, playing the trumpet held under their left arm (C. Hentze, *Chinese Tomb Figures*, 1928).

3. CHINESE TERRACOTTA STATUETTE. London, British Museum, Collection George Eumorphopoulos. H. L. Hobson and A. L. Hetherington, *The Art of the Chinese Potter* (1923), pl. 17; *The Eumorphopoulos Collection, Pottery and Porcelain*, i, no. 196, pl. 35. Cf. C. Hentze, op. cit., pl. 17B. Period of the T'ang dynasty.

Pedlar or slave with package firmly fixed on his shoulders, and a jug in his left hand. He wears a Western hat, with top *à la basclyk*, a dress with V-opening and pleats, belt and gaiters; he has semitic features and is bearded. I reproduce here, with some modifications, the description given by Hobson in the catalogue of the Eumorphopoulos collection.

4. CHINESE TERRACOTTA STATUETTE. Pennsylvania Museum. Unpublished. Period of the T'ang dynasty.

Similar to fig. 2. Same dress. The head is different: its type closely resembles that of the famous terracotta figurines of the Eumorphopoulos collection (belonging to the period of the 'Six Dynasties'), in which some have wished to see an Indian. See *The Eumorphopoulos Collection, Pottery and Porcelain*, i, no. 171, pl. 25; cf. Seligman, *Man*, August 1924. Our man, however, may be a Turk. A similar figure in C. Hentze, *Chinese Tomb Figures* (1928), pl. 74B.

All the terracotta statuettes described above are items of sepulchral furniture. They represent men, women, and animals, which must provide the dead man with all he needs in the other world; or they are sacrificial animals. This latter opinion has been well maintained by C. Hentze in his admirable *Chinese Tomb Figures* (1928, original ed. in French). The camels were buried with the corpse because they were able to provide the dead with those articles which were imported into China by caravan. The presence of the pedlars (if such they are) can probably be explained in the same way. The musicians, dancers, actors, servants, and various kinds of women need no explanation. It is to be noticed that nearly all the companions of the dead man are foreigners, mostly of Central Asia, India, and Western Asia. See C. Hentze, op. cit., pp. 51 ff. I have reproduced here these Chinese statuettes, although they are considerably later than the first period of the Roman Empire, to illustrate the commerce of Central Asia in general. These same camels and drivers, and doubtless these same itinerant merchants, visited also the Western shores of Asia, Parthia on the South and South Russia on the North. It is not impossible that under the Han and T'ang dynasties the camel caravans imported wares from the West to China, e.g. textiles on a large scale; cf. the new objects of the early 1st cent. A.D. found by Colonel Kozlov in Mongolia (see M. Rostovtzeff, *Inlaid Bronzes of the Han Dynasty* (1927), pp. 54 ff.; id. *The Animal Style in S. Russia and China*, pls. XXIV and XXIVA, p. 110; cf. *Chinesische Kunst. Ausst. chinesischer Kunst, 12 Jan. bis 2 Apr. 1929*, pp. 438 ff., nos. 1216–1272).

1. CAMEL DRIVER AND CAMEL

3. ITINERANT SEMITIC
MERCHANT IN CHINA

2. ITINERANT PERSIAN MERCHANT
OR MUSICIAN IN CHINA

4. FOREIGN MERCHANT IN CHINA

XXV. CARAVAN COMMERCE IN THE FAR EAST

and the canals. This whole system still survived in the fifth century A.D. Other documents have also shed light on the agents for oi ental and African trade; an inscription of Medamut shows that the Ptolemaic associations of shipowners and merchants still existed in the third century A.D. The same inscription, together with some others, long known, prove that a war-fleet was stationed in the Red Sea at this time; it is, however, uncertain when it was established. Pliny (*NH* vi. 101, 105) seems to know nothing of it: he speaks in fact of archers given as escort for groups of ships bound for India.

The development of the foreign trade of Alexandria did not kill the caravan trade of Arabia and Syria. The ruins of Petra in Arabia show that the period after its annexation to the Roman Empire (A.D. 106) was in no way one of decay. As is well known, Trajan built a magnificent road from Syria to the Red Sea. The second century was also the period of the greatest prosperity of Palmyra in Syria; and the brilliant development of the Parthian capital, Ctesiphon on the Tigris, affords another proof. The best sculptures of Palmyra, the most beautiful buildings, the richest tombs, as well as the majority of the inscriptions—including the famous tariff—testify to a large commercial activity, which extends far beyond the reigns of Hadrian and Antoninus Pius. This is not surprising, since the victorious expeditions of Trajan against the Parthians, and the peaceful policy of Hadrian and Antoninus, secured for the Palmyrene trade long years of secure development. Both in Palmyra and in Petra trade was entirely in the hands of the native merchants, who accumulated large fortunes. The beautiful ruins of both cities and their gorgeous funeral monuments, like those of Bostra, Philadelphia (Amman), Gerasa, and Dura, which were connected with the same trade, show how opulent their merchants were. Through them wealth came to Antioch and to the coastal cities of Syria, Phoenicia, Palestine, and Asia Minor.[20]

But, however important foreign commerce was for the Roman Empire, it was not to this that the wealth of the provinces was due. Even for Egypt and Syria the inter-provincial exchange of goods formed at least as important a source of income as did trade with foreign lands. Commerce in corn, in linen, in paper, in glass, and in those products of Alexandrian industry which were partly made of raw stuffs imported from outside (ivory and

ebony articles, perfumes, jewellery) was as important for Egypt
as the transit trade in articles imported from India and China.
The same is true of Syria with her glass-ware, her linen and
woollen stuffs dyed with the true Tyrian purple. Inter-provincial
commerce was the main source from which the wealth of the
large maritime and river cities all over the Empire was derived,
and it was almost entirely a commerce in articles of prime necessity. From the second century we have hundreds of inscriptions
which mention the profession of men of the time. Many of these
give us the names of merchants (*mercatores, negotiatores*) and even
tell us their special line of business. If we eliminate from the
mass those which refer to retail-traders in the various cities and
take into account the wholesale merchants only—the importers
and the exporters—we see that the majority of them dealt in
foodstuffs, especially corn, wine, and oil, in metals, lumber,
clothes, and pottery. Corn was exported by many provinces,
notably by Egypt, Africa, Sardinia, Sicily, and to a large extent
also by Gaul and Spain. Greece was fed by Asia Minor and South
Russia. The largest quantities of the finest olive-oil were now
produced by Spain and exported to Gaul, Britain, Italy, and
other countries. African olive-oil was not of so good a quality as
that of Spain, but it was undoubtedly cheaper and was therefore
used for lamps and for toilet purposes. The lands which produced
the best wine were now Italy, Greece, Asia Minor, and Gaul.
It would be easy to enumerate all the articles of provincial export and import, but the main fact which would emerge from
the enumeration would be that articles of luxury played almost
no part in the big wholesale trade, which dealt almost exclusively
with the necessities of life.[21]

Who were the consumers of all these articles? For whom were
such quantities of corn, meat, oil, and wine moved from one
place to another? It must be admitted that a careful investigation of the sources shows that the largest consumer was the imperial *annona* and that most of the merchants, who frequently
were at the same time shipowners and owners of storehouses,
worked on behalf of the emperor, that is to say, on behalf of the
population of the city of Rome and the army. Such an impression is conveyed, above all, by the study of the inscriptions which
speak of the *collegia* of merchants and of shipowners, the *navicularii*
of the sea, and the *nautae* of the lakes and rivers. Most of these

collegia were recognized and even favoured by the state, because they were useful or rather indispensable to it. No doubt men of the same profession felt a natural desire to associate, to meet together and promote their professional interests; but there is equally little doubt that the imperial government would never have recognized, not to say protected, these associations had it not been for their utility to the state. It is a notable fact that the first *collegia* to be not merely recognized but also granted protection and privileges were those of merchants and shipowners. Already in the Hellenistic period, at least in Egypt, such associations were in the service of the state. The Romans inherited these relations in Alexandria. It was natural that they should extend them to the associations which existed at Rome, Ostia, Puteoli, Aquileia, and to those which were developing in Gaul, Spain, and Africa. It was easier to deal with an organized body, of which the members were known, than with a loose mass of unknown men; and without their help the imperial administration would never have solved the extremely difficult problem of transporting large and bulky masses of goods. That as early as Claudius the work of organizing the merchants and shipowners was far advanced is seen from certain privileges which this emperor granted to individual members of the corporations of shipowners and corn-merchants. Moreover, it is very likely that the great portico of Ostia behind the theatre, in which the corporations connected with *annona urbis* had their offices, was assigned to this use in the reign of Claudius: in its present form it belongs to the reign of Septimius Severus.[22] From time to time the emperors were naturally forced to requisition corn on behalf of the *annona urbis* and the army, and probably also to exert strong pressure on the corporations of merchants and shipowners. However, according to Pliny the Younger (*Paneg.* 29), the enlightened monarchy did not as a rule confiscate corn, but bought it, and availed itself of the services of the corporations only in a liberal way.[23]

We must, however, be careful not to lay undue stress on this aspect of the case. It is true that the imperial *annona* was the chief moving force in the inter-provincial trade, buying and transporting large masses of corn, oil, wine, meat, fish, lumber, hides, metals, and clothes for the needs of the armies on the Rhine, Danube, and Euphrates, and some of these articles for the needs

Description of Plate XXVI

1. BAS-RELIEF IN THE COLLECTION TORLONIA AT ROME. Museo Torlonia, Rome. C. L. Visconti, *I monumenti del Museo Torlonia*, no. 430, tav. 110; Th. Schreiber in *JDAI* 11, 1896, p. 99, fig. 6; S. Reinach, *Rép. d. rel.* iii, p. 344, 4. On the paintings and bas-reliefs which reproduce harbours of Italy and of the provinces in general, see K. Lehmann-Hartleben, 'Die antiken Hafenanlagen des Mittelmeeres', *Klio*, Beiheft 14, 1923, pp. 233 and 235 ff. On the merchant ships of the Greek and Roman periods, A. Köster, *Das antike Seewesen* (1923), pp. 151 ff., esp. p. 175, fig. 42.

The bas-relief represents the arrival of a big merchant ship in a harbour where a smaller one, probably belonging to the same owner, is unloading her cargo of wine-jars. Between the two ships stands the god Neptune. On the shore are seen a gigantic lighthouse, with the statue of a heroized emperor on the top of the fourth storey, and a large triumphal arch crowned by an elephant-*quadriga* bearing an emperor with a palm branch in his hand. On the roof of the cabin of the big ship the owner, his wife, and the captain (?) are performing a sacrifice of thanksgiving. Between the buildings are shown certain divine figures—the Tyche of a harbour city with a lighthouse on her head (Alexandria?), the Roman eagle on a wreath, the Genius of Rome (?), and the god Liber (Bacchus). Beneath the sail of the smaller ship is seen a large eye (a charm against the evil eye, cf. pl. XLVI, 1). The relief does not give an exact picture of one of the Italian ports. It is a typical harbour. But all the details suggest that the harbour which is meant is that of Ostia or the Portus Trajani. Note the Roman eagle, the figures of the she-wolf and the twins on the sail of the large ship, the figures of Venus (and Mars?) and Amor on the stern, and the Nymph of the river beneath Liber. The relief is either a votive one or the signboard of a wine merchant. Note the figure of Liber, which also appears on the prow of the large ship, the bust of the same god on the prow of the smaller one, and the two letters *V(otum) L(ibero)* on the sail of the large ship. A detailed description of the bas-relief and of the two ships may be found in the books and articles quoted above. A similar bas-relief has recently been discovered at Ostia (G. Calza, *La Necropoli del Porto di Roma nell' Isola Sacra* (1940), p. 203, fig. 7): it portrays a ship entering a harbour, and the proprietor and the captain in the inn after their safe arrival.

2. FRESCO OF A FUNERAL MONUMENT OF OSTIA. Vatican, Rome. Restored. The left part of the fresco is lost. Published soon after its discovery in *Annali d. Inst.* 1866, pl. 1; B. Nogara, *Le Nozze Aldobrandine*, &c., Milan (1907), pl. XLVI; S. Reinach, *Rép. d. peint.*, p. 273, 1.

The left part of the picture was occupied by a large figure of Mercury with his usual attributes. The extant portion shows us a small merchant-ship being loaded with sacks of corn. Near the stern is written its name, *Isis Geminiana*. On the stern stands the captain, with his name inscribed, *Farnaces magister*. A porter is pouring grain out of a smaller sack (inscribed *res*) into a larger one in the presence of two men, one of whom has his name, *Abascantus*, written above his head. Another porter, waiting on the bow, lifts his right hand and says *Feci*, while two others carry sacks from the shore to the ship. The ship was probably in the service of the *annona*. Probably also Abascantus (the *navicularius*) was the owner of the ship and of the tomb. By his side is the *mensor frumentarius*, an agent of the state.

1. ITALIAN HARBOUR

2. ISIS GEMINIANA

XXVI. TRADE OF THE EARLY ROMAN EMPIRE

XXVII. COMMERCE IN THE EARLY IMPERIAL PERIOD: ROMAN SARCOPHAGUS

Description of Plate XXVII

BAS-RELIEF OF A ROMAN MATRIMONIAL SARCOPHAGUS. Rome, Museo delle Terme. R. Paribeni, *Boll. d'arte*, 1909, pp. 291 ff.; id., *Le Terme Diocleziane e il Museo nazionale Romano*, p. 142, no. 287; *CIL* vi. 29809. 3rd cent. A.D.

Wedding. The central group consists of husband, wife, Juno Pronuba, and a bearded man with a roll. By the husband's feet a bundle of rolls (his account-books). The central group is surrounded by symbolic figures. In the left corner stands the personification of the great port of Rome, Portus (above the figure is the inscription *Portus*); she holds the famous lighthouse in her right hand. Beside her is another personification, a woman with diadem, facing to the right, in the act of showing her companion a small tablet; in her left hand she holds a remarkable object shaped like an oar. I am inclined to regard her as *Liberalitas* (or *Frumentatio*), although the traditional representation of *Liberalitas* on imperial coinage (on which *Frumentatio* never appears) does not have the attributes shown here. These may perhaps be identified as the *tessera frumentaria* and the little rod (*rutellum*) with which the *mensores frumentarii* levelled the corn in the *modii*. The *modius* with *rutellum* is often represented on monuments of the Roman period, particularly on funerary stelae. The best example has been found at Bologna; Brizio, *Not. d. Scavi*, 1898, p. 477, no. 14; G. Dall' Olio, *Iscrizione sepolcrali romane* (1922), p. 118, no. 58, fig. 26, the sepulchral monument of a *mercator frumentarius*. Brizio and Dall' Olio have collected all the monuments on which the *modius* and the *rutellum* appear; cf. the mosaic of the *porticus annonaria* at Ostia (Paschetto, *Ostia*, p. 332; G. Calza, *Bull. Com.* 43, 1915, p. 187, no. 5, and Cagnat in Daremberg–Saglio, iii. 2, p. 1727). The symbolic figures on the right of the central group are Annona with *cornucopiae* and oar, and fruits and ears of corn in her lap, and by her side a *modius* full of ears, and Africa (as in the inscription) with ears of corn in her right hand, and on her head, as commonly, the skin of an elephant-head; close beside her another *modius* with ears of corn. Figures of this sort are common on imperial coins. The man is probably a *mercator frumentarius Afrarius* (*CIL* vi. 1620), or an employee of the *annona*.

of the capital. But the *annona* did not stand alone in requiring the good offices of the great merchants and the rich transporters. Many large cities especially in the East would have starved if they had been deprived of imported foodstuffs; and many products of industry could not be produced in every city. The frequent mention of σιτῶναι in the Greek cities shows that the corn-dealers did not deal with the *annona* only, but that they had other no less important customers.

Commerce between the provinces existed, of course, in the first century, but it assumed much larger proportions in the second. Almost wholly new was the internal commerce which was now developing in almost every province of the Empire. It was not indeed entirely new. Egypt, Greece, Asia Minor, and Syria had always had a good system of land and river roads; and an active exchange of goods within the frontiers of these lands, now Roman provinces, had gone on for centuries. In Gaul, too, with her wonderful system of rivers and a corresponding network of well-kept natural roads, internal trade already existed. But for the largest part of the West including Africa, and for many regions of the East, internal commerce became possible only under the Empire. The almost complete security of travel by road and river, the absence of high customs-duties, and above all the splendid system of Roman roads[24] produced an efflorescence of provincial commerce never seen before. This development in its turn gave a powerful impulse to the growth of trade within the cities, as is shown by the number of inscriptions which mention retail-traders and shopowners, and by the ruins of their shops, in most provincial towns.

The growth of commerce between provinces and within provinces is an indication of the tendency of commerce to become decentralized. The tendency was strongly marked. Italy was losing the dominant position in commercial life which she had inherited from the Greek East and had held, not without success, for about two centuries, during which she developed her agriculture and industry side by side with trade. True, Italian merchants still held the Danubian market, they still exported some Italian products, they still formed a large and rich class in Rome, but they were unable to prevent a growth of commerce and of a commercial class in the provinces, and even the conquest of Italy by it. The decay of Italian, and especially of South Italian, commerce is shown most strikingly by the gradual decline of Puteoli, the greatest harbour of the Republican period, especially for Italy's Oriental commerce, the successor of Delos and the rival of Alexandria in both trade and industry. It is usual to attribute this decline to the construction of an artificial harbour at Ostia by the Emperor Claudius, a harbour which was enlarged by Nero and rebuilt by Trajan. But that fact alone is not enough to account for the decay of the city. In the early Empire Ostia was not a neglected spot, as G. Calza has shown. She was the greatest harbour of Italy for the foodstuffs (*annona*) which the state imported into Italy and Rome, mostly from the Western provinces. Ships from Spain, Gaul, Sardinia, and Africa found good accommodation in the port of Ostia, as is proved by the 'corporation-hall' and by the immense storehouses of the early imperial period. The importance of the city is attested by its constant growth in the first century B.C. and the first century A.D. Nevertheless in the first century of our era Ostia was unable to compete with Puteoli and failed to attract to her harbour private merchants from West or East or even the supply fleet of Alexandria. The reason was that Puteoli was a better place for the merchants and the shipowners, not that it was a better harbour. It was a better place because the Campanian market was more valuable for the merchants than the Roman, and because a return cargo was easily found there, whereas none was available at Ostia, since Rome never was an industrial centre of importance.

The fact that Puteoli declined and that Ostia grew at her expense shows that these conditions had changed. The best testimony to the decay of the Campanian port is furnished by the well-known inscription relating to the Tyrian *statio* in the city. This once prosperous *statio* now recognizes the supremacy of its former Ostian and Roman branch and humbly appeals for money. Without doubt the main stream of commerce had left Puteoli for Ostia. The only explanation of the change is that Puteoli had lost her old advantage over Ostia, the ability to provide return cargoes. The goods of Campania—wine, oil, and manufactured goods—were apparently no longer in such demand as to attract large numbers of merchants to the port, and the reason can only have been that the typical Campanian goods were produced better and more cheaply in places nearer

Description of Plate XXVIII

1. FRAGMENT OF A LARGE FUNERAL MONUMENT. Found at Til-Chatel, near Dijon. Museum of Dijon. E. Espérandieu, *Rec. gén.* iv, no. 3608; S. Reinach, *Rép. d. rel.* ii, p. 221, 3.

Two retail shops. The one on the left (completely preserved) is a wine shop. The merchant sits behind his counter, on which are three receptacles whence the liquid is conveyed by pipes to the customers. A customer is buying wine, which the merchant pours into one of the receptacles, and the client receives into a bottle which he has brought with him. On the wall behind the merchant are hung measures of varying capacity. The wine is probably taken from a barrel behind the counter. The second shop deals in *charcuterie*. Behind the counter, where a boy is seated, are hung three bundles of sausages, three pigs' heads, and three quarters of bacon. Before the counter stands a large wooden bucket (containing lard?). Note that Dijon is the capital of Burgundy, a famous wine-producing region and a great centre of the wine trade at the present day.

2. ONE OF THE BAS-RELIEFS OF THE FUNERAL MONUMENT OF A MERCHANT. Lillebonne (Juliobona, Caleti). Museum of Rouen. E. Espérandieu, *Rec. gén.* iv, no. 3097; S. Reinach, *Rép. d. rel.* ii, p. 303, 4.

The monument is adorned with sculptures on both sides. On one face are the figures of the husband and the wife. On the left half of the other face the husband is shown in his shop, behind his counter. He deals in goods (perfumes and toilet articles), which are kept in boxes of various sizes and in bottles of various forms. On the right half is portrayed his wife, holding a pet dog in her arms.

3. BAS-RELIEF ON ONE SIDE OF A PENTAGONAL BLOCK. Langres (Lingones). Museum of Langres. E. Espérandieu, *Rec. gén.* iv, no. 3232; Daremberg–Saglio, *Dict. d. ant.* iv, p. 1561.

A pair of mules dragging a heavy four-wheeled cart, elaborately and cleverly built, which is loaded with a large barrel. The driver, dressed in a heavy Gallic cloak with the typical hood, sits on the box, holding the reins and a long whip. On another side of the same block the same two mules are being driven to their stable by a man who holds a chain (with a hook at the end) to which the mules are attached. The deceased was apparently the happy owner of a pair of mules which played an important part in his business life. Cf. C. Jullian, *Hist. de la Gaule*, v, pp. 154 ff.

4. BAS-RELIEF OF A FUNERAL STELE. Rheims (Durocortorum, Remi). Hôtel-Dieu at Rheims. E. Espérandieu, *Rec. gén.* v, no. 3685; S. Reinach, *Rép. d. rel.* ii, p. 302, 3.

A cobbler in his shop, seated astride a bench, is making a (wooden?) shoe (sabot). His instruments are partly hung up on the wall, partly kept in a basket beneath the bench.

5. VOTIVE STELE. Grand. Museum of Épinal. E. Espérandieu, *Rec. gén.* vi, no. 4892; S. Reinach, *Rép. d. rel.* ii, p. 222, 1.

A woman (goddess?) with a *patera* and tablets seated in a niche. To her right is a furnace and on the furnace a boiler, on which is placed a wooden basin, with a plank under it. From the basin projects a spoon. In a shelf on the wall there are two large spherical objects. To the left of the goddess four wooden basins are piled one above the other. In the right-hand corner a girl is beating the contents of a wooden tub fixed to the wall. Perhaps a factory of Gallic soap (*sapo*), with the goddess Juno Saponaria? See C. Jullian, *Rev. ét. anc.* 19, 1917, pp. 199 ff.; *Hist. de la Gaule*, v, p. 263, note 1, and cf. Pauly–Wissowa, ii A, cols. 1112 ff. Or perhaps a pharmacy? The Gallic *sapo* was used mainly for dyeing hair. Professor J. Pijoan suggests, in a letter, that a cheese-factory is represented (of the type of 'caciocavalla' factories).

1. RETAIL TRADE IN WINE AND IN PORK   2. A RETAIL MERCHANT

3. TRANSPORT OF WINE

4. A COBBLER   5. A PHARMACY OR A SOAP-SHOP

XXVIII. INDUSTRY AND COMMERCE IN GAUL

to the consumers—not that Rome and Ostia began to produce them, which notoriously was not the case. Ostia remained what she had been, the largest import harbour for the food-supply and for other goods needed by the city of Rome.[25]

While Ostia grew at the expense of Puteoli, the provincial commerce developed at the expense of the commerce of Italy in general and even of Ostia. It was much easier for the imperial department of the *annona* to give orders for the corn, wine, oil, lumber, hides, ropes, metals, clothing, shoes, arms, &c., required for the army and the navy, to Gallic merchants and transporters, who were well acquainted with the conditions of the local market and had at their disposal large numbers of river and sea-going ships and other means of transportation, than to have recourse to Italian dealers. Most of the articles needed by the soldiers were ready to hand in Gaul, Britain, Spain, and in the Alpine regions (lumber, pitch, metals, hides), and in a land with such splendid natural resources as Gaul it was very easy to develop new branches of industrial and agricultural production, such as vine-planting, bee-keeping, the manufacture of cloth, shoes, and soap, and so forth. The system of river-ways, which has been frequently mentioned, and the good sea-harbours on the Southern, Western, and Northern shores of Gaul made it easy for the Gallic merchants—much easier than for the Italians—to collect the products not only of Gaul but of the neighbouring provinces partly in Lyons and Trèves, partly in the cities of the lower Rhine (where the products of Britain were also assembled), and to distribute them among the military posts on the Rhine. We have to remember, too, that the lake of Constance (*Brigantinus*) and the connexion between Switzerland and the Danube regions, as well as the predominantly Celtic character of the population of Noricum, made access to the Danube regions easy for the merchants of Gaul and enabled them to compete, at least in the case of less bulky articles, with the Italian merchants and with the harbour of Aquileia and the Dalmatian cities.

Thus, in the second century, the commerce of Gaul and with it agriculture and industry reached an unprecedented state of prosperity. To realize the brilliant development of commerce and industry in Gaul, it is sufficient to read the inscriptions in the twelfth and thirteenth volumes of the *Corpus* and to study the admirable collection of sculptures and bas-reliefs found in the country and published by Espérandieu. The inscriptions of Lyons, for instance, whether engraved on stone monuments or on various articles of common use ('*instrumenta domestica*'), and particularly those which mention the different trade associations, reveal the great importance of the part played by the city in the economic life of Gaul and of the Roman Empire as a whole. Lyons was not only the great clearing-house for the commerce in corn, wine, oil, and lumber; she was also one of the largest centres in the Empire for the manufacture and the distribution of most of the articles consumed by Gaul, Germany, and Britain.[26]

No less important than Lyons was Trèves, the beautiful city on the Moselle. Trèves was in the first place a commercial city, and secondly an industrial centre. Her merchants, like those of Lyons and of Arelate (Arles), were mostly agents of the imperial government; they bought various goods in Gaul, shipped them on the Moselle, and transported them to the cities of the Rhine and the forts of the *Limes*. Their chief speciality was clothes and wine. The particular part played by the city in the economic life of Gaul and Germany is depicted on the highly interesting funeral monuments, derived from the pillar type, which were a distinctive feature of the Moselle lands. These monuments are practically covered with sculptures, partly representing mythological scenes but mostly illustrating in detail the business and private life of their builders, whose main occupation was clearly wholesale trade, not industry. The well-known monument at Igel, erected on the grave of the family of the Secundinii in the early third century A.D., depicts in minute detail the wholesale trade in clothes and the means of transportation it employed. A series of panels displays the great office of the Secundinii trading-house with the samples, the shop, the packing of the goods, their transportation by land in big carts and by river in ships towed by haulers. While the Secundinii were big clothes-merchants, the owners of the luxurious monuments discovered in fragments at Neumagen were dealers in wine. On these monuments the same series of scenes is represented as on the Igel monument, but the wares consist of large wooden barrels of wine. The rich merchants of Trèves, as appears from various scenes sculptured on their funeral monuments, invested their money, like Trimalchio and the other wealthy men of the first century, partly in land, partly in banking or money-lending. We shall return to this subject in the next chapter.[27]

Two other great commercial cities of Gaul were Arelate and Narbo. They, however, were mostly concerned not with supplying the army of the Rhine, like Lyons and Trèves, but with the export of Gallic products, especially wine, to Rome and other cities of Italy and even to the Oriental provinces. We know of many of their citizens who acquired large fortunes by combining the business of wholesale merchants with that of transporters.[28]

Once started, the business life of Gaul was bound to develop. Enriched by the growth of commerce, agriculture, and industry, the country became an important consumer of local and foreign goods, which easily reached the remotest corners of Britain. Nor was there any reason why the activity of the Gallic merchants should stop at the frontiers of Roman provinces. They resumed again the commercial relations which had existed from time immemorial with Germany. The products of the industry of Gaul, cheap and solid as they were, though not very elegant, were welcomed all over the Empire; and with these products and her wine and corn Gaul paid for her imports from Italy and the East.

In comparison with Gaul, the commercial life of Spain, Africa, and Britain did not attain a high development. The market for the products of these lands was not very large, and their trade, apart from exports to Rome and Italy, was chiefly internal and in local products. The only commercial rivals of Gaul in the western part of the Empire were the Adriatic harbours and particularly Aquileia. The fertility of Northern Italy and the favourable situation of Aquileia, whence natural roads led to the main rivers of the Danube region, gave the city and the district in general such an advantage that Gaul was not able to become sole mistress of the Danube market. This fact explains why Northern Italy and Dalmatia grew in prosperity, while Central and Southern Italy gradually decayed. Aquileia was a clearing-house for the army of the Danube in the same way as were Lyons and Trèves for the army of the Rhine. The cities at the mouth of the Danube could hardly compete with her, as they had no developed industry or scientific agriculture.[29]

The same process of emancipation from Italy, or rather a

Description of Plate XXIX

MOSAIC OF MEDEINA (ALTHIBUROS) IN AFRICA PROCONSULARIS. Musée Alaoui, Tunis. *Inventaire des mosaïques de la Gaule et de l'Afrique*, ii (1910), no. 576; S. Reinach, *Rép. d. peint.*, p. 274, 3. Cf. the bibliography given in note 35 to this chapter, and for the inscriptions *CIL* viii. 27790.

This mosaic covered the floor of the *frigidarium* of a bath in a rich man's house at Althiburos. The two ends of the mosaic show (1) the head of the Ocean surrounded by fishes, other sea animals, and Cupids riding on dolphins, and (2) the figure of a river-god surrounded by reeds, with a branch of a tree in his left hand. The space between them represents the water on which various sea-going and river ships float. Most of the ships are designated by their special names, which are sometimes accompanied by quotations from Latin poets. Some of the names are given both in Latin and in Greek. The best-preserved inscriptions—the others may be found in the works quoted above and in note 35—are the following. (1) $\Sigma\chi\epsilon\delta\iota\alpha$, *ratis sive ratiaria*. (2) *Celetes*, $\kappa\epsilon\lambda\eta\tau\epsilon\varsigma$: 'hypereticosque celetas' (Lucilius?). (3) *Celoces*: 'labitur uncta carina per aequora cana celocis' (Ennius). (4) *Corbita*: 'quam malus navi e corbita maximus ulla'st' (Lucilius). (5) *Hippago*, $\iota\pi\pi\alpha\gamma\omega\gamma\delta\varsigma$ (laden with three horses—Ferox, Icarus, and Cupido). (6) *Catascopiscus*. (7) *Actuaria* (the captain is indicating the proper time to the oarsmen by means of a wooden hammer, *portisculus*). (8) *Tesserariae*. (9) *Paro*: '[tunc se fluctigero tradit mand]atq[ue] paroni' (Cicero). (10) *Myoparo*. (11) *Musculus*, $\mu\upsilon\delta\iota\upsilon$.

The mosaic shows the great variety of ships used by the ancient world for different purposes. A similar variety of names and forms existed in modern times until the creation of steamers destroyed the picturesque and the individual elements in sea and river life. On the different forms of ships mentioned in the inscriptions of the mosaic and depicted on it, see the relevant articles in Daremberg–Saglio, *Dict. d. ant.*

RIVER AND SEA-GOING SHIPS
(Mosaic of Althiburos)

XXIX. TRADE OF THE ROMAN EMPIRE

revival of the conditions which had existed before the Roman domination, was going on in the East. Here again the state contributed greatly to the resumption of a lively economic activity by the Oriental provinces of the Empire. The armies of the middle and upper Euphrates were good customers for the inhabitants of Syria and Asia Minor. Another valuable market for the East was Rome itself, which absorbed large quantities of articles produced there or imported thither from Central Asia, China, and India. The same was true of Egypt. The army of Egypt, of course, was not large enough for its consumption to form a considerable item in the trade-balance of so rich a country; but an important market was provided by the city of Rome, which Egypt supplied with corn, linen, papyrus, glass, hemp, and goods manufactured in Alexandria from raw materials imported from India and China. The state, the army, and the city of Rome were not, however, the largest consumers of Oriental goods. The growing prosperity of the cities of the Empire increased the demand for articles of finer quality, which were not exclusively luxuries but mostly things ministering to the comfort of civilized men, such as the better brands of coloured woollen and linen stuffs and of leather ware, more or less artistic furniture, fine silver plate, perfumes and paints, artistic toilet articles, spices and the like. These things became more and more necessities of life for the city population throughout the Empire, and it is not surprising that they were imported in ever-increasing quantities from the few places where they were made to the cities of the East and the West. The number of Alexandrian articles, for instance, found in the half-Greek cities of South Russia is astonishing, and yet these cities were not exceptional. The trade of the East with the cities of the Empire was the main source of wealth for the eastern provinces and for Egypt.[30]

This Oriental trade was no longer concentrated in the hands of Roman and Italian merchants. During the first century A.D. the Italian merchants gradually disappeared from the East. The causes of their disappearance have already been stated. Discouraged by the bad conditions prevailing in the East in the second half of the first century B.C. and attracted by the new markets in the West, the Italians gradually moved from East to West. When peace came and the East began to revive, the Italians who remained behind were unable to compete with the shrewd Orientals who had never abandoned to the Western immigrants the key positions of the Oriental trade, Alexandria and the Syro-Phoenician harbours. From here in the second and first centuries B.C. the Syrian and Egyptian merchants had sent out their agents to Delos and afterwards to Puteoli, and they had maintained their depots (*stationes*, comparable to the later 'fonduks') all through the difficult times of the civil wars. On the restoration of peace these *stationes* became the natural intermediaries between East and West. The East had no longer any attractions for the Italians, as they had no hope of overcoming their rivals. The result was that the Italians disappeared from those parts as they disappeared from the West, and the Orientals not only monopolized trade in the East but appeared in steadily growing numbers in the harbours of Italy and the Western provinces.[31]

Of the organization of commercial activity in the Roman Empire we know but little. There was no change in the attitude of the central government towards commerce. Its policy was the policy of free trade both in the first and in the second century. As has been pointed out above, the emperors retained the moderate customs-duties which were levied on the frontiers of all provinces, and encouraged those merchants and shipowners who were necessary to the state by granting them privileges and so allowing them to develop their business and their professional organizations. Thus in the sphere both of foreign trade and of internal commerce, whether between or within provinces, the policy of the government remained a policy of *laissez-faire*.

In Egypt under the Ptolemies commerce had been more or less nationalized, but the Roman emperors did not maintain this system intact, much less develop it. The method of granting concessions was not entirely abandoned, but was employed more sparingly, and the state agents of the Hellenistic epoch now became in part free retail-traders, and their obligations towards the state were reduced to the payment of certain taxes.[32]

The existence of great numbers of associations both of wholesale and retail merchants, and of shipowners and transporters, may seem to indicate that the commerce of the first and second centuries began to lose its individualistic character and gradually to assume the form of modern capitalistic commerce, based on large and wealthy trade-companies. The facts, however, do not support this view. Business life throughout the history of the Greco-Roman world remained wholly individualistic. The only exception was the companies of tax-collectors with their quasi-modern organization, but they were a temporary phenomenon. They grew up with the approval and under the protection of a state which was neither willing nor able to deal with the complicated problem of tax-collection, and they began to die out as soon as the state withdrew its protection and began to control their activity more strictly. The tax-farming companies left practically no traces in the legislation of the Roman Empire concerning trade-companies and trade-corporations. The trade associations of the Imperial period were in no sense the offspring of the tax-collecting companies. They developed as professional associations and were recognized as such by the state because, as has been said, it was easier for the state to deal with groups than with single persons. I do not affirm that they were mere clubs and religious groups, but I am convinced that, in so far as they had an economic importance, this was limited to the regulation of the relations between them and the state, relations which had more of a social and juridical than of an economic character. In normal times the state dealt with the single members of an association. It dealt with the group as such only when it granted a privilege to all the members or imposed a burden on all. To pass from individualism directly to compulsion and to nationalization was the normal way for a Greco-Roman community. The individualistic character of commercial life in the Imperial period is shown by the peculiarities of Roman legislation on the companies (*societates*). Roman law never mentions the type of companies that is so familiar in modern times, clearly because such companies did not exist. The Roman *societates* were mere groups of individuals who were but slightly limited in their individual activity by the existence of the company.[33]

It is worthy of note that the only exception to this rule was the companies of merchants at Palmyra. They had their own ἀρχέμποροι or presidents, who certainly cannot be identified with the συνοδιάρχαι or chiefs of caravans. Both of these were probably elected for a single caravan-journey; but while the συνοδιάρχαι were the conductors of the caravan, the ἀρχέμποροι were the presidents of the bands of merchants who formed part of the caravan. The scantiness of our evidence on the Palmyrene merchants prevents us from forming a definitive judgement on their organization. It seems, however, that the parallels to these companies must be sought not in the Roman Empire but in Babylonian traditions and among the Babylonian trade associations.[34]

Our survey of the evolution of commerce in the Roman Empire in the first two centuries A.D. establishes the fact that commerce, and especially foreign and inter-provincial maritime commerce, provided the main sources of wealth in the Roman Empire. Most of the *nouveaux riches* owed their money to it. Industry, land, and money-lending were regarded as more or less safe investments for wealth gained by commercial enterprise. The richest cities of the Empire (I would emphasize the fact at the risk of repetition), the cities in which the most opulent men in the Roman world resided, were those that had the most developed commerce and lay near the sea on great trade-routes or were centres of a lively river traffic.[35]

Another source of wealth was industry. Goods which were produced by local industries, especially such as could not be reproduced and imitated elsewhere, were widely distributed over the Empire. The East, and particularly Asia Minor and Phoenicia, remained famous for the production of fine coloured clothes and carpets. Asia Minor was the chief centre for woollen garments, Syria and Egypt for linen. The best leather goods were also a speciality of the Near East—of Syria, Babylonia, Asia Minor, and Egypt. The papyrus of Egypt had no rival except the parchment of Asia Minor and Syria. Syrian and Egyptian glass was still prized throughout the Roman world. Fine jewellery, too, was mostly of Oriental origin. One fact is striking: industry forsook the mainland of Greece for ever. Only one or two articles of importance are named in our sources as being produced by Greece itself.[36]

The most important feature in the development of industry is its rapid decentralization. The East still plays an important part in industrial life, but it does not stand alone. The West begins to develop a brilliant industry. Of Italy we have already spoken. The fate of Italian industry was to a certain extent similar to that of the industry of Greece proper. With the extension of civilization and city-life to the Western provinces Italy lost her leading position as the centre of industrial activity in the West. The woollen clothes of South Italy, especially Tarentum, and those of North Italy were still appreciated and bought. But the dominant part which had been played by Italy in the production of glass, pottery, lamps, and even metal vessels, was gone for ever. So far as these goods were still produced there, they were destined almost wholly for the local market. The most dangerous rival of Italy was Gaul. Her wealth in metals and her splendid clay, her large forests and meadows, her wonderful system of river communications, made it easy for the spirited business men of the country to beat Italy and drive her almost entirely from the North-western markets. The red-glazed pottery of Gaul and Germany killed out the Italian product which was its prototype; glass made on the Rhine was cheaper and better than that of Campania; woollen cloaks for everyday use, a speciality of Gaul and later of Britain, found their way not only to Italy but also to the East; bronze safety-pins, enamelled in the *champlevé* style, and bronze vessels from Gallic shops flooded Italy, Spain, Britain, Germany, and reached even the steppes of South Russia. In short, Gaul now became what Italy had been in the first century B.C., the greatest industrial land of the West. The Danube provinces, Spain, and Africa could not rival the Gallic shops.[37]

But the decentralization of industry was not limited to the industrialization of Gaul. Every province of the Empire and every provincial district endeavoured as far as possible to compete with the imported goods by replacing them with cheap local imitations. It is well known that the factory (or the shops) of Fortis in North Italy, which at first almost monopolized the production of clay lamps, lost its world-wide market in the second century, its products being replaced in the various provinces by local lamps of the same shape, which sometimes even reproduced the Fortis trademark. Specially instructive is the history of lamp manufacture in Africa. The Italian lamps were first replaced by lamps made in Carthage, which swept the local African markets. But gradually the Carthaginian ware was ousted from some of the markets by lamps of local make. Another instructive example is the factory of clay vases, with *appliqué* figures, owned by a certain Navigius near El-Auja. These vases were reproductions of types which originally came from the East to Italy, and they succeeded in obtaining a wide market (cf. pl. LX).[38]

The central government did nothing to protect Italian industry. There was no legislation in the Imperial period comparable to modern legislation concerning patents. Everybody was free to imitate, and even to counterfeit, the products of a rival. Was this due to lack of initiative or to a definite policy on the part of the government? In any case it shows that industrialists as such had no political influence whatever. The great landowners could induce the government to protect the wine production of Italy (as will be explained in the next chapter), the rich merchants succeeded in getting important privileges for commerce, but apparently no influential men were interested in industry. The inference is that industry remained in the hands of comparatively small shopkeepers and never took the form of great industrial concerns in which large capital was invested. This was a distinct decline, even by comparison with the organization of industry as it probably developed in the Hellenistic states, and certainly by comparison with the gradual industrialization of life which we have observed in Italy in the first century A.D., especially at Pompeii. Decentralization of industry stopped the growth of industrial capitalism in Italy, and it was now stunting the growth of large industrial concerns in the provinces. We cannot indeed deny that the process of industrialization which had begun in Italy spread over most of the provinces, and that in many small provincial towns we may follow the same evolution as took place at Pompeii. Most of the cities in the provinces which had been originally centres of agricultural life and headquarters of the administration of a larger or smaller agricultural territory developed an important local industry. Every larger territory, too, every province, had its own commercial and industrial centres, which produced goods not merely for the local, or even the provincial, market. The reader will recollect what has been said of the growing industrial production of Gaul, and the part played in it by Lyons, and of the big commercial and industrial centres of the East. In these large cities we must assume the same development towards capitalistic mass production which we noticed both in the East and in Italy. Yet even in these greater centres the big capitalistic concerns never became larger and more efficiently organized than they had been in the Hellenistic period. Local shops of petty artisans competed successfully in many fields with larger capitalistic organizations.

The small artisans were not wiped out by the great industrial firms as they have been wiped out in Europe and America in the nineteenth and twentieth centuries. Even such products as glass and pottery were successfully manufactured by local workshops, and the competition of these local products did not allow the large businesses to develop indefinitely. The local shops, as for example in Timgad, kept the old form of artisan shops which both produced and sold a special article.[39]

Another interesting feature of economic life in the provinces was the competition with the city shops and factories of large industrial establishments which had developed on some of the great agricultural estates. Some of these properties belonging to wealthy owners began in the second century to organize workshops which produced goods, not for consumption on the estate, but for sale. A big woollen factory has been discovered in a villa in South France near Toulouse, another in a villa in Britain. Pottery kilns have been found in a villa in Belgium, and it is well known that a factory of enamelled bronze articles formed part of the famous villa of Anthée in Belgium. The capitalistic character of such concerns is evident. But their development meant a further decentralization of industry.[40]

At the same time as industrial activity was becoming decentralized, the goods produced were gradually simplified and standardized, whether they were produced in large factories or in small shops. The sense of beauty which had been dominant in the industry of the Hellenistic period, and still prevailed in the first century A.D., gradually died out in the second. No new forms were created, no new ornamental principles introduced. The same sterility reigned in the domain of technique. Save for some new devices in the glass industry, we are unable to detect any new invention in industrial technique after the first century. It is very instructive to compare the early Arretine pottery with the early *sigillata* of Italy and Gaul, and the latter with the products of the second century of our era. The beautiful Arretine bowls and jugs are full of charm, the *terra sigillata* of the first century is a marvel of technical skill and is still pretty, while the similar pottery of the second century is flat and dull and repeats the same motives and the same combinations of motives, though still remaining a good and solid ware for practical use. The same observation applies to jewellery, products of toreutic art,

Description of Plate XXX

1. BAS-RELIEF. Galleria degli Uffizi, Florence. W. Amelung, *Führer durch die Antiken in Florenz*, no. 168; S. Reinach, *Rép. d. rel.* iii, p. 44, 3.

Interior of a shop. On the wall are hung pillows (or rugs?), belts, and a large piece of cloth (or a rug?). Two shop-assistants, in the presence of the shopowner (?), open a box with a pillow inside it, which is inspected by two customers, a man and a woman, seated on a bench. Behind them stand two slaves.

2. AS NO. 1. W. Amelung, l.l., No. 167; S. Reinach, l.l., p. 44, 2.

Two customers (or the owners of the factory), attended by two slaves, inspect a large piece of cloth which is displayed before them by two men.

J. Sieveking, in *Oest. Jahresh.* 13, 1910, p. 97 and figs. 56, 57, assigns these two reliefs to the second half of the 1st cent. B.C., and this date is accepted by Mrs. A. Strong, *Scult. rom.*, chap. I. The style, as Amelung points out, is similar to that of the Augustan (so-called Hellenistic) bas-reliefs; the composition recalls the shop-signs and mural decorations of Pompeii (see pls. xiv–xvi). I am inclined to think that the bas-reliefs belong rather to the 1st cent. A.D.

3. PART OF A FUNERAL STELE. Ravenna. In the Museum. S. Reinach, *Rép. d. rel.* iii, p. 128, 3.

The upper part of the stele contains two busts in a niche. Above and below the niche runs the inscription: 'P. Longidienus P. f. Cam. faber navalis, se vivo constituit et Longidienae P. l. Stactini. P. Longidienus P. l. Rufio, P. Longidienus P. l. Piladespotus impensam patrono dederunt' (*CIL* xi, 139 = Dessau, *ILS* 7725). The lower part of the stele shows Longidienus working hard at building a ship; near it is a plaque with the legend 'P. Longidienus P. f. ad onus properat' ('Longidienus pushes on with his work').

4. FRAGMENT OF A FUNERAL STELE. Aquileia. In the Museum. E. Maionica, *Guida dell' I.R. Museo dello Stato in Aquileia* (1911), p. 56, no. 36; G. Brusin, *Aquileia, Guida storica e artistica* (1929), p. 118, no. 18, fig. 71.

A blacksmith, seated on a chair, is hammering on an anvil a piece of iron which he holds with a pair of tongs. Behind him a boy or a slave blows the fire in the furnace with a pair of bellows, fixed to a shield to protect him from the blaze. On the right are displayed some products of the smith's work—tongs, a hammer, a spear-head, and a lock. Of the inscription only the end is preserved, 'et l(ibertis) l(ibertabus)que'; cf. pl. xxxii, 1.

I. SALE OF BELTS AND PILLOWS

2. EXHIBITION OF A SAMPLE OF CLOTH

3. SHIPBUILDING

4. A BLACKSMITH

XXX. INDUSTRY IN ITALY

engraved gems, furniture, domestic utensils, arms and weapons, and so forth.[41]

How are we to explain the concurrence of industrial decentralization and of decay in artistic taste and technical skill? We shall discuss this question in the last chapter, and we content ourselves here with a few considerations. It is evident that industrial products spread quickly all over the civilized world and were successfully ousting home production even in the remotest corners of the Empire. Witness the statistics of finds, for instance, in the villages of Egypt. Hardly a single piece found in these villages was produced at home: everything was bought in the village shops and on the market. The same is true of the graves of the poorer inhabitants whether of the cities or of the country, throughout the Empire. The general demand, therefore, alike in the cities and in the country was not for the better products of industry. The demand for these was confined to the circles of the richer town *bourgeoisie*. The mass of the population asked for cheap things, the cheaper the better. We shall see later that the purchasing power of the country population and the lower classes of the city residents was very small. But their numbers were large. The existence of such conditions was bound to give rise to mass production and factory work. Another factor which must not be left out of account was the state of transport. The seaports were provided with an abundant supply of cheap articles, sea transport being comparatively cheap. But the risk was somewhat high. Thus even in cities situated near the sea an article produced on the spot was much cheaper than one imported from a distant place. These conditions produced the first stage of industrial decentralization. In Egypt and Gaul the rivers facilitated the transport of goods to the remotest parts of the country: hence the important development of industry both in Alexandria and in the large Gallic cities. The conditions were different in some parts of Spain, in Africa, in many regions of the Danube lands, in Asia Minor, and in Syria. The more Greco-Roman civilization advanced into lands remote from the sea and lost its strictly Mediterranean character, the more difficult it was to forward the various products of industry to regions which lay far from the sea and from the rivers. This accounts for the second stage of decentralization. Every inland city tried to become self-sufficient and to produce on the spot the goods needed by the population, using the improved methods of technique and imitating the current types.

As the demand was for cheap, that is to say, standardized goods, the artisans of the small cities, unlike those of the Greek cities of the archaic period, did not produce original articles, which would have been too expensive to compete with imported wares. They simply reproduced the standardized articles by the methods they had learned in the large factories. As machines were unknown and no protection was given against counterfeiting, the business of the artisans in the small cities flourished and they were able to compete with the larger concerns in almost all fields of industry. This forced the large shops to lower the quality of their products: they made them still cheaper and naturally still more standardized and lifeless.

The labour employed both in small workshops and in large concerns of the factory type was chiefly, though not exclusively, slave labour. This explains why no labour question existed and why no organization of labour was attempted. The associations of men of the same profession were probably mostly associations of large merchants and of shipowners, of shopkeepers, and of artisans. If, however, a trade was connected directly with the imperial administration, the government protected not only the associations of merchants and shipowners, but also those of workmen, and for the same reason—in order to have organized bodies and not a loose mass of individuals to deal with. The slaves and free wage-earners of the industries in which the state had no interest could join the so-called *collegia tenuiorum*, which pursued no economic aims.[42]

An exception to the above rule is to be found in the industrial *collegia* of the East, especially Asia Minor. In all the large industrial cities of Asia Minor we meet with numerous and influential associations of men engaged in a given industry, mostly in some branches of the textile industry. Who were the members of these associations? Were they shopowners or workmen, or a combination of both? I am inclined to think that they included none but shopowners. They were guilds or corporations of men whose hereditary occupation was a special trade, successors perhaps of certain families of priests who knew the trade-secrets of one or other branch of industry. The situation of labour in Asia Minor seems to have been peculiar. Dio speaks of the linen-workers (λινουργοί) of Tarsus as if they formed an inferior class of the city population, which did not enjoy the full city franchise. It is very likely that these linen-workers were descendants of serfs who originally had been attached to the temple-factories.[43] Similar conditions prevailed in Egypt. Here also the temple-monopoly of industry had been destroyed by the earliest Ptolemies. A period of almost complete nationalization followed, the work-men being attached to a special branch of industry producing on behalf of the state. Finally, in the Roman period the ties of the state-monopoly were relaxed; the shopowners began to work (at least partly) for themselves, using the labour of members of their families, of apprentices, and of hired men or slaves. To what extent nationalization survived, and how far the practical en-slavement of the workmen to the state went, it is as yet impossible to say.[44]

It is typical of the conditions prevailing in Asia Minor, where the workmen had ceased to be serfs but had not become citizens of the cities, that it is the only country where we hear of strikes, real professional strikes, not flights (ἀναχωρήσεις) to the temples to seek the protection of gods or to the swamps and the desert, as in Egypt. It is in Asia Minor, too, that we frequently hear of the city mob, which certainly consisted of workmen employed in shops and factories, organizing genuine attempts at social revo-lution. Such were the disturbances in the Bithynian cities of which Dio often speaks, the tumults of the Tarsian linen-workers related by the same author, and the riots which occurred from time to time in other Greek cities of Asia Minor, the Balkan peninsula, and Palestine.[45]

Besides commerce, industry, and agriculture (which will be dealt with in the next chapter, together with mines, quarries, &c.), an important branch of business life was the profession of bankers and private money-lenders. Credit and credit operations were fully developed in the cities of the Empire. The growth of trade and industry and the increasing number of landowners residing in the cities required ever larger amounts of currency which could be used in developing and improving any given concern. On the other hand, quantities of cash accumulated in the hands of many capitalists. It is no wonder that money-lending was a profitable occupation both for rich men who were not professionals in the business and for regular bankers.

Real banks, private and municipal, developed throughout the Empire.

The complicated nature of the business transacted by the many banks (τράπεζαι) of Egypt is highly instructive. In the Ptolemaic period the banks, like commerce and industry, had been monopolized by the state and had not developed any very considerable activity. The Roman government set free the banking business, and scores of private banks sprang up in the various cities of Egypt. Our information is indeed limited to some small provincial towns, and we cannot therefore form any conception of the business life of bankers in such a great centre of commerce and industry as Alexandria. But even the local banks form a most interesting subject of study. It is certain that they accepted money on deposit and paid interest on some of these deposits. It is also clear that they effected payments by mere transfer from one account to another. Even transfers of money from one city to another were occasionally carried out through the medium of local banks. Another important feature of banking operations was the buying and selling of foreign coins and the testing of genuine and of false or adulterated coins. The extent to which the Egyptian banks were engaged in credit operations is unknown. It is evident that the money which they accumulated did not lie idle; but, so far as our information goes, their main occupation was to help their customers in transacting business, in paying taxes, and so forth.

The same range of business is attested by the evidence which we have for the banks of Rome, Italy, and the provinces. The banking system came to the West from Greece and the Greek East, and the banks of Italy and the Western provinces were managed mostly by men of Greek origin. Among the main reasons for the successful development of banking operations were the existence of different types of currency, even in the imperial period, and the scarcity of coined money which made the introduction of a system of credit-transfer both for money and for natural products highly desirable and even indispensable. We should be glad to know more of the credit operations carried out by the banks, but what we do know indicates that they acted in a manner not very different from that of private money-lenders. We have to remember that the banks, like all other branches of business, were individual enterprises, and that no large joint-stock banking companies existed in the ancient world, although some of the banks, of course, were managed by partners.[46]

We have said that the development of banking operations was to some extent due to the conditions prevailing in regard to the circulation of coined money. A discussion of this difficult and complicated problem would be out of place here. Suffice it to say that the monetary chaos which reigned in the Greek cities and the Hellenistic monarchies before the period of Roman domination in the East was greatly reduced by the introduction of the paramount currency of the Roman state. The local coinage gradually decreased and slowly disappeared. In the first two centuries of our era, save for the issues of the vassal kingdom of Bosporus, gold and silver were coined solely by the Roman state; although silver was coined temporarily also in some cities of the East, e.g. in Tyre. A provincial silver coinage was maintained by the state in Alexandria and temporarily in Antioch, the two commercial capitals of the East, while copper money was struck by the senate at Rome and by very many cities, especially in the East. The city coinage is explained by the fact that the Roman mint was unable to meet the increasing demand of the Empire for small coins, and it was therefore natural to decentralize the coinage by allowing certain Oriental cities to keep their currency and to strike copper coins which were indispensable for the development of local trade. The evil effects of the existence of various types of coins were lessened by the establishment of definite rates of exchange. Gold and silver coinage, on the other hand, with the exception noted above, was monopolized by the state. Though the amount of currency was not sufficient even in these metals, the evil was lessened by the activity of the banks. As agents or concessionaires of the cities, the banks also took an active part in the issue and distribution of local currency, which often led to speculation and profiteering and provoked acute crises. We know of two cases (at Pergamon and at Mylasa) where the disappearance of small currency from the market caused disturbances and even riots.[47]

The dearth of coined money of small denominations produced some interesting results which testify to a powerful development of economic life, the claims of which were but slowly and incompletely met by the state. In the reigns of Claudius and Nero, after the suppression of local Gallic and Spanish coinages, numerous imitations of the copper coins minted at Rome appeared in the Western provinces, including the Rhine lands and Britain, and these imitations were tolerated by the government. Moreover, in almost all the large and even in some of the small cities of the Empire, the retail-traders, barmen, innkeepers, owners of ferries and passenger boats, &c., issued their own money in the form of tokens and *jetons*. Great quantities of these *tesserae*, mostly of lead, have been found in the river Tiber at Rome, some in Aquileia, in Ostia, in Smyrna, and elsewhere. It is possible that in some parts even the cities made regular issues of such tokens, as the *metropoleis* in Egypt certainly did.[48]

The greatest owners of coined money were certainly the emperor and his *fiscus*. There is no doubt that they lent money at interest like private money-lenders and private banks. Their financial operations were certainly very numerous and the *fiscus* was probably the largest banker in the Empire. In times of crisis we hear of the emperors cancelling such private debts to the imperial treasury. In some cases, particularly in emergencies, the emperors acted in the same capacity as state-banks in modern times. An instance is furnished by the financial measure taken by the Emperor Tiberius on behalf of the landowners of Italy. The funds deposited by Augustus with the *aerarium militare* for the purpose of paying pensions to retired soldiers cannot have lain idle in the safe of this special treasury. The large foundations for the assistance of the free-born children of native parents (*alimenta*) created by Nerva and Trajan, and developed by their successors, required skilful management, and the financial operations of this department might be compared *mutatis mutandis* with those of modern state-banks which lend on landed security. We have very little information as to this side of imperial activity, but it is certain that these operations were never carried out methodically by the emperors nor on any system comparable to that practised by large modern state-banks.[49]

One of the most striking illustrations of the high development of economic life in the Empire in the first two centuries of our era is furnished by the Roman civil law of the period, as embodied both in the legislative acts of the emperors and of the Roman magistrates (to a certain extent, also, of the senate), and in the documents which record the various business transactions of the time. A third source of information is the juridical treatises, which are preserved in full or in fragments. Only a specialist is competent to deal fully with this subject. It is a misfortune that the scholar who was so well qualified to set forth the development of Roman civil law, from the juridical as well as the historical point of view, L. Mitteis, died before completing his standard work, of which only one volume was published.[50] To him we owe the fundamental discovery, based on the study of the Roman juridical sources and of the Greek papyri of Egypt, that along with the purely Roman civil law which regulated the business life of Roman citizens there existed in the provinces other systems of law regulating the life of the provincials, above all the system of Greco-Hellenistic law created by the Greek cities and the Hellenistic monarchs. How far this system of law was influenced in Egypt, Asia Minor, and Syria by the pre-existing systems of Egyptian, Hittite, and Babylonian law we do not know. The comparative study of law is still in its infancy, and we need a thorough study of the Oriental systems as revealed to us by Egyptian legal practice and by the codes of Babylonia, Assyria, and the Hittites. But the labours of Mitteis and his pupils leave no doubt that there was a fairly general system of Hellenistic civil law, known to us from the inscriptions of Asia Minor, from the parchments of Syria and the Syriac lawbook, and especially from the Greek papyri of Ptolemaic Egypt. We may presume, therefore, that in the other provinces of the Empire there existed less elaborate and less complete systems of law which formed the basis of their business life before the Roman conquest. We must bear in mind that Gaul, Spain, Carthage, and the Illyrian and Thracian lands had passed through centuries of civilized life before they came under Roman sway. All these local systems of law, and notably the Hellenistic system, were not eliminated by the Roman civil law or replaced by the so-called *ius gentium*. They continued to exist throughout the imperial period and formed the basis of legal practice in the various provinces. The extent to which their gradual development influenced the growth of Roman law, and was influenced by it, is still a matter of discussion. No less disputable is the origin of the system of late-Roman and Byzantine civil law represented by the great Byzantine Codices, the Codex Theodosianus, the Codex Justinianus, and the Digest.[51]

A careful historical study of these compilations, in the light of the thousands of Egyptian papyri and of some documents discovered in Italy and the Western provinces, would reveal the historical evolution both of Roman civil law and of the provincial systems; and such a history of the different systems of law which prevailed in the Empire would form the basis of a study of the economic conditions which underlay them. Until such a study has been made we must be very careful in our use of Byzantine compilations to reconstruct the economic conditions of any one period or any one portion of the Roman Empire.[52] Nevertheless some groups of documents and some legislative acts of the Roman emperors, if used with circumspection, may help us in our study of the social and economic conditions of the Empire. In this sense they have been used in the various chapters of this book. As a group, however, they testify to a marvellous development of business life both in the East and in the West. Specially instructive are the Greek papyri of Egypt. A glance at the Chrestomathy of papyri compiled by Mitteis and Wilcken, or at the fine collection of juridical papyri published by P. Meyer, suffices to show how complicated and elaborate business life was in the Roman provinces of Egypt. The different forms of contracts, the various devices for recording them and keeping them accessible, above all the activity of the Egyptian notaries public and of the record offices at Alexandria, and the marvellous institution of the βιβλιοθήκη ἐγκτήσεων—that combination of a land register and a record office for storing statistics about the fortunes of all residents in Egypt—all these convey the impression of a highly developed economic life, organized in a masterly fashion.[53] The information gathered in recent years concerning the juridical conditions obtaining in the Parthian Empire points in the same direction. The legal documents on parchment or papyrus discovered in the Parthian cities of Mesopotamia, though still only few in number, testify to a highly developed juridical system organized by the state, and of the same type as the Egyptian system.

The same impression is left by the study of the development of Roman civil law and by the study of the documents which illustrate this development—inscriptions, the wax-tablets of Pompeii and of Dacia, the rescripts, edicts, and letters of the emperors, in fact of all the material collected by Bruns–Gradenwitz and by Girard. It is worthy of note that in some spheres the imperial legislation took over the constructive achievements of the Hellenistic age: thus, for example, it accepted the so-called Rhodian sea-law and applied it to the regulation of maritime commerce.[54]

In the second chapter we have already dealt with the social and political divisions of the population of the Empire, as created by the civil wars and consolidated by Augustus. The social structure of the Empire did not greatly change in the second half of the first and in the second century A.D. The senatorial class remained the emperor's peers, men who had an inherited right to govern the state under his leadership. Instead of being an aristocracy of birth, as in the first century, it became an aristocracy of service. One of the qualifications of membership was still a certain amount of wealth. But this amount was easily acquired by public service in the various branches of the imperial administration, or it was supplied by the emperor to men whose services he appreciated. The aristocracy was composed not merely of servants but of faithful servants of the emperor. Its members were practically selected by him. The task of selection was made easy for the emperors, not only by the fact that they were always able to eliminate the undesirable but also by the fact that the senatorial families, even the new families, were very short-lived. With Augustus began the complaints against the unwillingness of the upper classes to rear children, and this reluctance was not overcome by the measures taken by him. If the class as such did not die out, the reason was that it was constantly recruited from the ranks of the imperial bureaucracy, the equestrian order.

This second class of the imperial aristocracy was far more numerous than the senatorial. It, too, was an aristocracy of service, wholly dependent on the emperor. A census was required, but not a high one. If we consider that it amounted only to 400,000 sesterces, and that the higher class of the imperial civil officers received 200,000 sesterces yearly, we can easily understand that the equestrian aristocracy was not a hereditary plutocracy but almost purely an aristocracy of bureaucratic officials. The members of this bureaucracy were recruited from the ranks of the wealthier residents in the cities who had served as officers in the army. They represented therefore, like the senatorial order, the intellectual, educated classes of the Empire. Most of them, too, like the senators, were not born in Rome or in Italy but belonged to the higher ranks of the city population of the West and of the East.[55]

Socially, therefore, the two classes of the imperial aristocracy belonged to the numerous urban aristocracy of Italy and the provinces. This large and powerful body has not been the subject of careful investigation from the social and economic point of view. Such an investigation would yield good results, if scholars studied the records of one city after another both in Italy and in the provinces. Meanwhile I give the impressions derived from a detailed study of some of the cities carried out by myself and some of my pupils. The government of the cities was in the hands of the upper section of the *bourgeoisie*, some members of which belonged to the senatorial and the equestrian classes, while the rest were at least Roman citizens. They formed an almost pure plutocracy: the municipal administration could be undertaken only by wealthy people, since office was elective— bestowed either by popular election, as most commonly happened in the West, or by the local senate, as appears to have been the custom in the East—and unpaid, and involved obligatory gifts to the city and a far-reaching financial responsibility towards the central government. The origin of this wealthy class was different in the various parts of the Empire. In Italy the municipal aristocracy was descended partly from the old stock of the times before the incorporation of the Italian cities in the Roman citizen body. During the civil wars this old stock had been partly replaced by veteran soldiers. Most of them were well-to-do landowners. In the industrial and commercial cities, side by side with this aristocracy of landowners, a new class was gradually springing up and taking the leading part in civic life, a class of rich merchants and shopkeepers, who were partly freeborn but mostly freedmen and their descendants. In the Celtic provinces of the West there was also an old stock of native aristocrats, almost all wealthy landowners. Alongside of them there appeared ever-growing numbers of emigrants from Italy. The original nucleus of this foreign population consisted of the veterans who were settled in the Roman colonies and the Italian merchants and money-lenders of the time of the conquest and of the first years after the conquest. The development of commerce and industry added an increasing number of new immigrants and of native merchants and shopkeepers, partly freedmen and their descendants. The same picture holds good for the cities of Spain, Africa, and the Danube provinces.

In the East a *bourgeoisie* of the Hellenistic type still survived in the old Greek cities. This class, consisting partly of Greeks, partly of hellenized natives, absorbed the Italian immigrants of the Republican period. Under the Empire the number of new settlers arriving from the West was relatively small. A few colonies of Roman veterans in Asia Minor formed for a time Italian islands in a Hellenistic sea, but they gradually yielded to Greek influences and became hellenized. The main stock of the wealthy *bourgeoisie*, therefore, remained native.

How stable this aristocratic element in the cities was, and how large its numbers, are questions beyond our power to answer. The constant growth of new cities throughout the Empire and the brilliant development of city life, which was based on the wealth of the *bourgeoisie*, show that in the first two centuries A.D. the *bourgeois* class rapidly increased in numbers. Their increase, however, as in the case of the senatorial and equestrian orders, seems to have been due not exclusively to the continuance of the old stock but to the rise of new men, especially natives and freedmen. The higher municipal classes appear to have been in many cases as sterile as the senatorial class at Rome. After one or two generations the aristocratic families in the cities very often disappeared or were maintained by adoption and recruited by the manumission of slaves. Only in this way can we explain the purely superficial romanization and hellenization which is characteristic of all strata of the city *bourgeoisie*, including the highest: it is enough to recollect the energy with which native elements appeared in the culture of the provinces, particularly those of the East, in the course of the second and third centuries. Note, for instance, the local fashions in dress, as represented on the funerary monuments of the provinces, and on religious monuments; and consider also the revival of local cults, which also occurred at this time. No less characteristic is the fact that Septimius Severus did not speak good Latin and that his sister did not speak it at all. The state of culture need not surprise us, since the process of romanization and hellenization had to begin over and over again with the new families of natives and with the freedmen who replaced the members of the old families.[56]

Description of Plate XXXI

1. The relief shows us on the right a bag of surgical instruments, on the left a doctor seated on a small bench, engaged in bleeding the leg of a patient. The doctor is seen in the process of binding up the calf of a man seated in front of him, who holds the leg in question in a basin. (G. Calza, *La Necropoli del Porto di Roma nell' Isola Sacra* (1940), p. 250, no. 39 and fig. 149.)

2. The relief, unique of its kind, represents a childbirth. The woman, seated on an obstetrical chair, is supported under the arms by a nurse, while the midwife, seated in front, seems to press the bottom of the uterus to deliver the child. (G. Calza, op. cit., p. 248, no. 38 and fig. 148.)

1. A SURGEON AT WORK

2. DELIVERY WITH OBSTETRICAL AID

XXXI. LIFE AND WORK AT OSTIA

1. BLACKSMITH'S FORGE

2. WATER-SELLER

XXXII. LIFE AND WORK AT OSTIA

Description of Plate XXXII

1. Representation of a blacksmith's forge. The blacksmith is represented in his workshop in which a remarkable variety of tools, surgical instruments, saws, hammers, anvils, hatchets, knives, &c., are hung up. The two figures are intent on manufacturing or touching up the instruments. (G. Calza, *La Necropoli del Porto di Roma nell' Isola Sacra* (1940), p. 251, no. 40 and fig. 150.)

2. As the inscription says, *Lucifer Aquatari(us)*, and as shown by the monument itself, this is a representation of the shop of a water-seller. A woman has come to buy some water, which is preserved in large pots. In the top panel amphorae of all sizes are exhibited. (G. Calza, op. cit., p. 255, nos. 45 and 46, and fig. 157.)

The importance of the upper class of the city *bourgeoisie* cannot be exaggerated. It was this class that gave the Empire its brilliant aspect, and it was this class that practically ruled it. From the point of view of the Roman emperors, it was, like the senatorial and the equestrian classes, an aristocracy of service, through which the emperors administered the cities and their territories. One step below on the social ladder stood the petty *bourgeoisie*, the shopowners, the retail-traders, the money-changers, the artisans, the representatives of liberal professions, such as teachers, doctors, and the like. Of them we know but little. We cannot say how large their numbers were as compared with the municipal aristocracy on the one hand and the city proletariate on the other. The ruins of the ancient cities of Italy and the provinces, with their hundreds of smaller and larger shops and hundreds of inscriptions, mentioning individual members of this class and their associations, lead us to believe that they formed the backbone of municipal life. But we shall never be able to say how many shops were owned by this petty *bourgeoisie* and how many were run by slaves and freedmen (*institores*) for the members of the municipal aristocracy. Moreover, we have no means of drawing a line between the higher and the lower *bourgeoisie*, as the former was certainly recruited from the latter. To the petty *bourgeoisie* belonged also the salaried clerks of the government and the minor municipal officers, a large and influential class, mostly slaves and freedmen of the emperor—that is, of the state —and of the cities (*servi publici*). As to the size of their salaries and the amount of the incomes of the petty bourgeois, our sources do not supply the slightest indication.

On a lower plane stood the city proletariate, the free wage-earners and the slaves employed in the shops and in the households. We have no means of defining their numerical strength or their material conditions. Our sources very rarely speak of them, and the ruins of the excavated cities do not yield statistics. But there is no doubt that the existence of slave labour kept the wages of the free workmen very low, hardly above the minimum required for bare subsistence. Yet some of them had money enough to pay their subscriptions to their associations, the so-called *collegia tenuiorum*, which secured to them a decent burial for themselves and the members of their families.[57]

How thorough the romanization and hellenization of the

middle and lower classes of the city population was, is beyond our knowledge. It seems as if most of them spoke and some even wrote Latin in the West, Greek in the East. The highly developed public life of the cities, the shows and performances in the theatres and amphitheatres, the daily meetings in the streets and in the markets, were powerful agents in spreading the two official languages of the ancient world. We should like to know for whom the public baths, the gymnasia, and palaestrae, the theatres and amphitheatres, were built and to whom they were accessible. It is difficult to suppose that they were not open to everybody. But good education on Greco-Roman lines was certainly a privilege of the higher classes only, and when the emperors of the second century decided to pay the salaries of the teachers in the public schools out of the *fiscus*, their intention was, not to educate the proletariate, but to help the city *bourgeoisie* in its effort to secure a fair education for the rising generation.

Such were the cities of the Roman Empire. The picture of their social conditions is not so attractive as the picture of their external appearance. The impression conveyed by our sources is that the splendour of the cities was created by, and existed for, a rather small minority of their population; that the welfare even of this small minority was based on comparatively weak foundations; that the large masses of the city population had either a very moderate income or lived in extreme poverty. In a word, we must not exaggerate the wealth of the cities: their external aspect is misleading.

VI

THE ROMAN EMPIRE UNDER THE FLAVIANS AND THE ANTONINES

The City and the Country in Italy and in the Western Provinces of Rome

WE have no statistics to show the comparative numbers of the city and the country population. But as every city had a large 'territory', that is to say, a large tract of land which together with the city itself formed a political, social, and economic unit, and as besides these city-territories there existed large regions which had no city life, it is fair to say in general that the population of the cities alike in Italy and in the provinces formed but a small minority as compared with the population of the country. Civilized life, of course, was concentrated in the cities; every man who had some intellectual interests and had therefore something to discuss with his fellow men lived in a city and could not imagine himself living elsewhere: for him the γεωργός or *paganus* was an inferior being, half-civilized or uncivilized. It is no wonder that for us the life of the ancient world is more or less identical with the life of the ancient cities. The cities have told us their story, the country always remained silent and reserved. What we know of the country we know mostly through the men of the cities, for whom the men of the country, the peasants, were sometimes the targets of jokes, as in the Greek and Roman *bourgeois*-comedy, sometimes a foil to set off the wickedness of city life, as in the works of the moral philosophers, the satirists, and the idyllic poets. Occasionally, though not very often, city people, like Pliny the Younger in his letters and Dio Chrysostom in some passages of his speeches, speak of the country in its practical aspect in relation to themselves, as a source of income. The voice of the country population itself is rarely heard. After Hesiod wrote his poem, the country remained silent for many centuries, breaking the silence from time to time with complaints about the hardships of its life and its ill treatment by the cities and by the government, which in its eyes represented them. These complaints are preserved in certain documents, most of them Egyptian papyri, some of them engraved on stone in other parts of the ancient world. Indirectly we hear of the country population and of its economic situation through official and private documents—laws, edicts and rescripts of emperors and imperial magistrates, orders of municipal authorities and decrees of municipal senates, acts of the representative bodies of the country population itself, decisions in lawsuits, and various business transactions. This information is, indeed, scanty and very difficult to use. Hence it is not surprising that in most modern works on the Roman Empire the country and the country population do not appear at all or appear only from time to time in connexion with certain events in the life of the state or the cities. Yet the question of the conditions of life in the country is as vital and as important as questions connected with the state and the cities. Without a careful investigation of this problem we can never understand the social and economic development of the ancient world.

Here even more than in other fields of historical research it is very dangerous to generalize and to speak about the country population as a unit. Country life differed in the various parts of the ancient world according to the economic and social conditions which prevailed in them; and even when these various parts lost their political independence and were incorporated in the Roman Empire it remained as multiform as it had been before. The upper classes in the Roman provinces and the city population in general were more or less romanized and hellenized; city life assumed common forms all over the Empire; intellectual interests and business life were more or less uniform in the various provinces; but country life, the life of the villages and the farms, remained almost wholly unaffected by this process of unification. While romanization and hellenization succeeded in the cities, the country was very slow to accept even the two official languages of the Empire. It used these languages in its dealings with the cities and the administration. But among themselves, in their homes and villages, the peasants still spoke their native tongues. This fact is well known and does not need proof. The Phrygian and Galatian peasants in Asia Minor spoke their own languages in the time of St. Paul and later, and so did the Berbers of Africa, the Celts of Britain and Gaul, the Iberians and Celt-Iberians of Spain, the Germans on the Rhine, the

Thracians and the Illyrians in the Balkan peninsula, the *fella-hîn* of Egypt and the hundreds of tribes, both Semitic and non-Semitic, in Asia Minor and Syria—the Aramaeans, the Phoenicians, the Jews, the Arabs, the Chaldeans on the one side, and the Lydians, the Phrygians, the Carians, the Paphlagonians, the Cappadocians, the Armenians, the Lycians, &c., on the other.[1] They kept jealously, too, their native religious beliefs. Their gods and goddesses might assume Greco-Roman forms and names. The names and forms were a product of Greco-Roman civilization and therefore were bound to be Greco-Roman, since the engravers of inscriptions, the sculptors, and the painters were educated in Greco-Roman schools and had at their disposal no written language and no generally intelligible forms except the Greco-Roman. But the gods worshipped under these official names and these irrelevant forms were still the old native gods of the peasants as they had conceived them centuries before.[2] And—what was not of least importance—the country population kept also the traditional forms of its economic and social life, the habits and customs which sometimes were stronger than even imperial legislation.

In this short sketch of the economic and social evolution of the Empire we can do no more than trace the general outlines of the problem as it presents itself nowadays. It is no easy task to trace even these general outlines: they involve the question of the development of agriculture in general and the evolution of the forms of land-ownership and land-tenure, and each part of the Empire must be treated separately.

We begin with Italy, on which we are better informed than on other parts of the Empire. It has been shown in the preceding chapters that Italy was still, at all events in the first century A.D. and the first half of the second, one of the best cultivated lands of the Empire. The goods imported from the provinces and from foreign lands were paid for, to a large extent at least, by the excellent wine which was still produced in large quantities all over the peninsula, especially in Campania and in the North. The production of wine was organized in a scientific way on capitalistic lines, mainly for sale and for export. The eruption of Vesuvius in A.D. 79 was, of course, a great catastrophe even from the economic point of view. The fact that the buried cities were not restored, despite the measures taken by the government and that no new city developed in this region, as would have been possible after the lapse of some decades, is typical of the decline of economic forces in Campania. But in truth we have no reason to suppose that the catastrophe of 79 seriously affected the general productivity of the district.[3] As, however, we have observed in the preceding chapters, vine-planting and the economy of Italy based on the export of wine suffered gravely from another development, which proved much more perilous for the country than occasional catastrophes like the eruption of Vesuvius, namely the economic emancipation of the provinces. The decay of industry and commerce in Italy meant a gradual impoverishment of the city *bourgeoisie*, which, as we have seen, was the main support of scientific and capitalistic agriculture. This explains in large measure the fact that the process of concentration of landed property in the hands of large capitalists did not cease in the second century A.D., but rather assumed larger proportions than ever, and went on at the expense not only of the peasants but also of the city *bourgeoisie*. We may follow this process of concentration even in such poor regions as the territories of Veleia and Beneventum. The history of these territories, as shown by the documents relating to the *alimenta*,* was in the main the history of a slow concentration of the *fundi* of these regions in the hands of a few landowners, most of them not natives of the territories of Veleia and Beneventum, and some of them apparently wealthy freedmen.[4] Our literary sources also (Juvenal, for instance) still use in the second century the familiar theme of first-century poets and moralists, the expulsion of small landowners from their paternal *fundi* by greedy large capitalists, and Pliny the Younger, one of the great landowners, speaks frankly of his investments in land and of his growing *latifundia*.[5]

It is easy to guess whence came the capital which was invested in Italian land. We have seen that the ancient aristocracy of Rome had disappeared. The land held by this aristocracy in the provinces became mostly the property of the emperors. We know very little of imperial estates in Italy; but it is not without significance that they are so seldom mentioned. This silence can only be explained by the assumption that the emperors were disinclined to keep these estates in their own hands: probably they conceded them in one form or another, especially to members

* See Chap. VIII.

Description of Plate XXXIII

1. PICTURE IN ONE OF THE LUNETTES OF THE MAIN ROOM OF THE EARLY CHRISTIAN GRAVE IN VIALE MANZONI. Viale Manzoni, Rome. G. Bendinelli in *Not. d. Scavi*, 1920, pl. IV, and *Mon. Ant.* 28, 1922, pl. XIII.

The upper part of the picture represents two farms or peasants' houses near a large fortified city. Between the two houses a large flock of animals (donkeys, cows, sheep, and goats) is grazing. On the meaning of the picture painted on the lower part of the lunette, see my paper, 'Une Tablette thraco-mithriaque du Louvre', *Mém. prés. à l'Acad.* 13, 1923, pp. 394 ff.

2. BAS-RELIEF OF A SARCOPHAGUS (?). Ince Blundell Hall, England. H. Blümner in *Arch. Zeit.* 1877, pp. 128 ff., pl. I; my article in *Röm. Mitt.* 26, 1911, p. 281, fig. 3; S. Reinach, *Rép. d. rel.* ii, p. 454, 1; B. Ashmole, *A Catalogue of the Ancient Marbles at Ince Blundell Hall* (1929), p. 108, no. 298, pl. 46.

The left part of the bas-relief shows a husband and wife shaking hands. They probably formed the central group of one of the long sides of a sarcophagus. On the right of them is depicted a large *cella vinaria*, which is at the same time a vineyard. Some slaves are busy filling amphorae from the *dolia* ('diffusio') and carrying them; some of them are resting. In the right-hand corner, under a shed, is a counter behind which a man is seated with a polyptych in his hands, engaged in discussion with a customer. On the counter lie some tablets. On his left sits an assistant, behind whom may be seen shelves with rolls (?) in them and a picture with the figure of a snake. In the right corner a young man, probably the son of the married couple. The scene, no doubt, represents a big wine cellar, which carries on an important wholesale business in wine. My view that the bas-relief is part of a sarcophagus is supported by the parallel of the well-known sarcophagus of Annius Octavius Valerianus in the Lateran (S. Reinach, *Rép. d. rel.* iii, p. 282, 2), figured below. The scenes shown on this are (1) ploughing and hoeing, (2) reaping the corn, (3) transporting it, (4) grinding it and baking bread. [Cf. pl. XXXIV for the other fragment of this sarcophagus.]

3. FRONT FACE OF A LARGE SARCOPHAGUS. For description see plate XXXIV, which reproduces the other fragment of the same face of the sarcophagus.

Sarcophagus of Annius Octavius Valerianus. Lateran, Rome

1. AN ITALIAN VILLAGE

2. A CELLA VINARIA

3. ON THE ROAD

XXXIII. LIFE AND WORK IN ITALY

of the new aristocracy of service. Of this aristocracy Pliny the Younger is a typical representative. He was a member of a well-to-do family, probably of large landowners, belonging to the municipal aristocracy of Comum. Both he and other members of his family increased their inherited fortune by taking an important part in the administration of the state: they started by becoming procurators of the emperor, like the elder Pliny, and finally, like the younger Pliny, after admission to the senate they served the state and the emperor as governors of provinces and managers of the various departments of the imperial administration, particularly in the city of Rome. Not that the younger Pliny and men of his type acquired their fortunes by robbing the provinces, though cases of such plundering were not infrequent both under the Flavians and under the Antonines. Even honest governors had not only large salaries but also various opportunities of enriching themselves without overstepping the limits of legality. Those imperial officials who were natives of Italy (as Pliny was) naturally looked for a safe investment for their money and, both from local patriotism and from considerations of efficient management, they preferred Italian land or mortgages on Italian land. Investment in land and, to a lesser extent, in mortgages was the best means of obtaining a safe, though moderate, interest on capital, and the ideal of the imperial *nobilitas* was still, as before, to enjoy a safe income, the ideal of those whom the French call *rentiers*. Nor must we underrate the numbers of the imperial officials who were natives of Italy: they still formed the majority of the imperial bureaucracy.

Many members, however, of this bureaucracy and of the senatorial aristocracy were natives of the provinces. They belonged to the wealthy municipal aristocracy of Spain, Gaul, and Africa in the West, Asia Minor and later Syria in the East. Their economic interests were naturally concentrated in the provinces; most, if not all, of them were rich provincial landowners. Many of them, however, on entering the imperial service became connected with the city of Rome, perhaps more intimately than with their native city. They took up residence in the capital and invested at least part of their money in Italian land, though their natural tendency was, of course, to return to their native province and to spend their old age there, surrounded by the esteem and admiration of their countrymen. This tendency might last for generations, but it might also disappear quickly, the second or the third generation being more attracted by life in the capital than by the prospect of a quiet existence in a little provincial *trou*. Moreover, as has already been said, the emperors desired that the senatorial families should have their domicile in Italy and insisted on their investing a part of their money in Italian land.

Besides the imperial aristocracy, there was the large body of wealthy wholesale merchants and shipowners, of thrifty imperial freedmen and slaves, of rich bankers and retail-traders in Rome and other Italian cities which remained wealthy and prosperous, like Aquileia and the cities of Northern Italy in general. We must remember that Rome constantly grew, and that she played in the life of Italy, if not in the life of the Empire, almost the same part as Paris plays nowadays in the life of France, and London in the life of England. Many of the rich men of Rome were born in Italy, most of them spent their life in Rome and had their homes there. It is not surprising that in looking for a safe investment for their money they thought first of Italian land, which was near at hand and easier to manage than land in the provinces.

Under the pressure of the large capitalists both the small holdings which were owned by the peasants, mostly in the hilly and mountainous parts of Italy, and the moderate-sized estates of the city *bourgeoisie* were bound to disappear and to be merged in the *latifundia* of the imperial aristocracy and of the Italian plutocracy. The statement of Pliny the Elder about the evil effects of the *latifundia* on the economic life of Italy was perfectly true. In speaking of the *latifundia* which *perdidere Italiam*, Pliny had in mind, of course, the disappearance not merely of peasant husbandry but also of the scientifically managed farms which were swallowed up by large estates run, as we shall see, on different principles. Pliny's statement was a commonplace not only for his own time, but for many generations to follow. The emperors were well acquainted with the facts so effectively summed up by him. They tried to save Italy in different ways. Claudius, Nero, and the Flavians, acting in the interests of the *fiscus* as well, endeavoured to restore to the state the public lands illegally occupied by private owners and to sell this land in small parcels to landless peasants.[6] Nero and Vespasian settled a considerable number of soldiers and marine troops in the declining cities of Southern Italy.[7] The measures of Domitian will be spoken of presently. Nerva bought large tracts of land to be divided among landless proletarians.[8] Trajan sought to come to the rescue of the city landowners, and perhaps of the peasants as well, by giving them cheap credit for the improvement of their lands and by helping them to educate, or rather to feed, their sons and, to a certain extent, their daughters. He also founded some colonies in Italy and forbade the dispatch of Italian colonists to the provinces.[9] Of the measures which were taken by Hadrian, Antoninus, and M. Aurelius we shall speak in the next chapter.

All these measures were fruitless. Economic evolution was stronger than the efforts of the government. The main cause— the emancipation of the provinces—could not be eliminated nor even rendered less dangerous for the economic prosperity of Italy. The gradual economic decline of Italy, due primarily to the decay of its industry and commerce, was aggravated by the crisis which befell the scientific and capitalistic rural economy of the country at the end of the first century, as a result of an over-production of wine, for which there were no buyers. The approach of this crisis has been alluded to in the third chapter. Wine was now, by a natural process of development, produced in most of the lands which had been the chief customers of South Italy—Spain, Gaul, and Africa. In the East, Italian wine had difficulty in competing with the wine of the Greek islands, Asia Minor, Syria, Palestine, and even Egypt. The only markets still remaining open to it were Germany and the Danube provinces. But these were chiefly markets for North Italy, as it was not easy to ship wine from the harbours of the Western coast of Italy to those of the Dalmatian and Istrian shores. The same fate was in store for the production of olive-oil. We have already shown that Spain became the chief producer of the fine brands of olive-oil and Africa of the cheaper ones. In the East, Italian oil was displaced by the oil of Asia Minor and the excellent product of the Syrian coast.

The developments briefly described above were more than a threat to the economic welfare of Italy and particularly of the Italian middle class. They were alarming for the state in general. The ancient world had never suffered from the over-production

Description of Plate XXXIV

FRONT FACE OF A LARGE SARCOPHAGUS. Porta Salaria, Rome, Museo delle Terme. Paribeni, *Not. d. Scavi*, 1926, pl. VIII.

Found in two pieces. The space reserved for the inscription is empty. On the fragment reproduced in this plate a peasant hut (resembling an African *mapale*) is shown; near by a peasant offers a basket of fruit to a bearded rustic god. Next come grazing sheep and a shepherd, and then the same god again. Finally, a woman with a child is sitting close to the peasant hut. The other fragment, reproduced on pl. XXXIII (3), represents a road on which are shown a milestone with the number V on it; a traveller on horseback, with a dog, and, in front of him, a courier; behind the traveller, a cart drawn by two oxen and laden with a gigantic wine-skin; and behind the cart, a house with three windows. Cf. a relief formerly in the Museo Borgia, in P. Tomassetti, *Campagna Romana*, i, p. 52, fig. 30, and the sarcophagus of Philippeville in S. Gsell, *Musée de Philippeville*, pl. II, 1.

XXXIV. PICTURE OF ITALIAN LIFE UNDER THE FLAVIANS AND ANTONINES

of foodstuffs, especially of corn. As has been frequently mentioned, Greece and Italy and even Asia Minor were dependent for grain on the countries which produced it in large quantities; Greece and Asia Minor were fed from South Russia, Italy from Sicily, Sardinia, Spain, Gaul, Africa, and Egypt. The spread of the culture of vines and olive trees, both in the West and in the East, not only meant economic ruin for Italy but might also result in a corn famine throughout the Empire. Rome, of course, was safe. Corn from Egypt and corn from the imperial and public lands in Sicily and Africa, to which Gaul and Spain also contributed, delivered as rent by the tenants, secured a sufficient supply for the proletarians of the capital and for the court. Besides, the emperors took certain preventive measures to guarantee sufficient grain for the population of Rome in general by giving her a prior claim upon the products of some of the corn-growing provinces, in other words, by prohibiting the export of corn from Egypt to other places than Rome save in exceptional cases.[10] But Rome was only one of the cities of the Empire which lived on imported grain. We have mentioned those of Greece and Asia Minor. These provinces were unable to live on the import from South Russia, as its production continued to decrease and much of the corn grown there was used by the imperial armies of the East. Thus, over-production of wine and olive-oil both in the East and in the West meant a permanent crisis in the East. The spectre of famine now hovered continually before the Greek cities: the reader may recollect the vivid picture in the Revelation of St. John, which is proved to refer to a widespread famine in Asia Minor by a Latin inscription of A.D. 93, discovered at Antioch of Pisidia.* The Roman government could not afford to let the Eastern provinces starve. Revolts like that of the proletariate of Prusa in the time of Vespasian, described by Dio of Prusa, were a serious danger. Hence measures were taken by the emperors to encourage the production of corn and to limit the production of wine and oil. Very little is known about them. We may infer from one accidental notice that Vespasian endeavoured indirectly to encourage corn-production in Asia. In an inscription of Cibyra of A.D. 73 a rich benefactor orders the money which he gave to the city to be invested in 'corn-bearing lands', and directs that the emperor and the senate shall

* *An. Ép.* 1925, 126; cf. Chap. V, note 9.

be informed of the fact. This inscription seems inexplicable except on the view that it testifies to a recommendation, at least, on the part of the senate and the emperor to the cities of Asia Minor to invest the funds of their foundations preferably in corn-bearing lands. Further, the emperors intervened forcibly to stop profiteering in times of famine. In the inscription of Antioch just mentioned a governor of Domitian takes strict and even violent measures (reminding us of the similar steps taken all over Europe during the first Great War) to put down such practices, and to secure for the city a supply of comparatively cheap grain.[11]

However this may have been, it is well known that a general order was issued by Domitian to promote the cultivation of corn in the provinces and to assist the wine producers of Italy. According to this order, no new vineyards were to be planted in Italy or in the provinces. Further, half of the existing vineyards were to be destroyed. We know that this measure was not carried out in full. A special embassy from Asia Minor, headed by the famous orator Scopelianus, saved the vineyards of his province and perhaps of the East in general. It is probable also that at least Southern Gaul and Southern Spain (the provinces of Narbonensis and Baetica) succeeded in keeping their vineyards. We know that wine was exported from these countries without interruption. But it is an exaggeration to speak of Domitian's measure as being entirely abortive. It was certainly enforced in Africa, to a certain extent in the Danube provinces, in Northern and Central Gaul, and in part of Spain. The fact is attested by the countermand of Probus (about two hundred years later) by which permission to cultivate vines was given to the Danube lands, Gaul, Spain, and even Britain, where such cultivation was unknown. Moreover, in Africa the well-known *lex Manciana* (of the time of Domitian or Trajan) allows the planting of new vineyards only to replace old ones, and another law of Hadrian's time does not mention vines in speaking of the utilization of virgin and waste land for various forms of cultivation.[12]

No measures of the same kind were taken to protect the production of olive-oil in Italy. On the contrary, a free hand was given to the Dalmatian coast, Spain, and Africa to increase their production of oil, and we know that these lands gradually became the main centres of the industry in the Empire. The importance of oil production in Africa and the solicitude of the emperors to transform the country into a land of olive-groves are shown by the laws of Hadrian on the virgin and waste soil, which were published in and for Africa, and by the fact that archaeological excavations have demonstrated that the South-western part of the country in the second and third centuries was an immense olive-grove extending for miles and miles both along the coast and inland.[13]

The protective measures of Domitian saved Italian viticulture, at least to a certain extent. But they did not succeed in saving progressive agriculture in Italy in general and those who carried it on, the middle-class landowners. In the crisis at the end of the first century the middle class was the first to suffer. The decay of industry and of commerce, which were not protected by the emperors, accelerated their ruin. Besides, labour, and especially slave labour, on which scientific agriculture was based, became more and more expensive. It is no wonder that the city *bourgeoisie* of Italy was unable to compete with the large capitalists of the city of Rome. The appearance of the latter class meant in fact the complete ruin of scientific agriculture.

It is needless to labour this point. Landowners like Pliny the Younger may have been good business men and good managers of their affairs in general, selling and buying land, lending money, and so forth. But agricultural prosperity cannot be based on men of such a type. They never lived on their estates, as they were busy in the city, and they never depended entirely on the income which they received from one estate, as was the case with many members of the city *bourgeoisie* of former times. Their attitude was, as we have said, that of *rentiers*. They wished to have as little trouble as possible, even at the expense of their income. The safest way to receive a good but moderate income from the land was, not to cultivate it in the scientific way by means of slaves, which involved a large amount of personal attention, but to let it. This system was already used by the great landlords in the first century B.C. It revived again after the ruin of the city *bourgeoisie*, which in the Augustan period took the place of the magnates of the first century, at least in Central and Northern Italy, and which included the veterans of the revolutionary armies. The system of letting meant, of course, giving up scientific management. Tenants, especially long-term tenants, are rarely good farmers, and in particular good wine-growers.

Besides, now that corn had become ever scarcer in Italy, corn-growing was at least as profitable as the production of wine, and it was less risky and required less personal attention alike from the landowners and from the tenants.

The chief difficulty was to find the tenants. The fact that the landowners did find the necessary number of them, as is shown by the experience of Pliny and by some incidental remarks of Martial,[14] has always been a puzzle to modern scholars. If the peasantry was already ruined in the time of the Gracchi, if it had completely disappeared in the first century B.C. and had been replaced by gangs of slaves, whence came the *coloni* of Pliny? If the reader has followed the exposition we have given above, he will have seen that we do not accept current views about the disappearance of the peasants in Italy. In South Italy, no doubt, after the 'Social' War the number of peasants decreased, especially in Apulia, Calabria, and Bruttium, and to a certain extent in Campania and in Samnium. But they still formed the majority of the population in Central Italy and in the valley of the Po. Some of them were no longer owners of their plots, but they still lived in their *vici* and *pagi* as tenants and as manual workers who found employment on the farms of the city *bourgeoisie*. In the vineyards, indeed, they were replaced by slaves, but the largest part of Italy consisted not of vineyards but of fields, and the fields were tilled by the peasants. It is possible that along with the old stock of peasants some slaves and freedmen were settled by the landowners as tenants on their estates, and that the numbers of the peasants were increased. However, the question of finding good and sufficient labour for the estates of the great landed proprietors remained most important and difficult to solve. There were peasants in Italy who were willing to rent the land of the large estates. But their numbers seem to have been too limited for the ever-growing demand, and they were rather lazy and inefficient workers. And yet, even under such conditions, the large landlords preferred the work of tenants to that of slaves. Pliny, for example, makes use of slaves in cases of emergency only, as a last resource. The main labour on his estates was that of tenants. Heitland indeed would not accept this statement. In his view the tenants were mostly overseers of a sort who supervised the labour of slaves, this labour being furnished by the landlord. But there seem to be no indications in our sources that the letting of parcels of land to tenants, with an inventory which included some slaves, was a common feature of the second century A.D. There is no doubt that Pliny regards his *coloni* not as middlemen but as tillers of the soil, as furnishing the main labour on the parcels which were rented to them. We do not deny that a prosperous *colonus* might purchase one or two slaves to help him in his work, and that some parcels were let with an inventory consisting of house, cattle, and rural implements, and of slaves. The modern *mercante di campagna* was a type well known to the ancient world. But the existence of this type in modern Italy does not mean that modern Italy has no peasants.[15]

Thus we must assume that in the second century there existed in Italy a large class of peasants, most of them tenants. They formed the population of the *pagi* and *vici* as opposed to the cities, they were the *vicani* and *pagani* as contrasted with the *intramurani*. The descriptions of Statius and of Martial and the characterization of Pliny show that this rural population of Italy formed a lower, humble class and that the attitude of that class in the second century did not differ from that of the *coloni* of a later period or from that of the serfs in the Middle Ages all over Europe. We may use the remarks of Martial, for instance, to illustrate the corresponding scenes on the Igel monument, near Trèves, of the third century A.D. and on some African mosaics of the fourth. I have no doubt that this attitude was not of a recent date. I am convinced that at least the *coloni* of Pompey behaved towards their *patronus* in the same way as did the *coloni* of the lawyer who was a friend of Martial.

From the economic point of view the most interesting feature of the second century in Italy is not the existence of a peasant population: there was no period in the development of Italy when a peasant population did not exist. The striking fact is that the peasants appear no longer as the free landowners which they had hitherto been, but as tenants of great landlords. As such they played a prominent part, or rather the leading part, in the agricultural life of Italy. The dominant type of husbandry now is not the middle-sized farm run on scientific lines, nor the large estate tilled by thousands of chained slaves, but once more the peasant plot which had prevailed in Italy in the period preceding the development of capitalism. The difference between that period and the second century A.D. was that the peasant plot was now the property of an absentee landlord, while the tiller of the soil was his tenant. Not that the medium-sized farms and the large estates tilled by slaves disappeared completely. Notoriously they did not. But these types of husbandry became more and more obsolete, they were mere survivals and did not represent the general condition of agricultural Italy, as they had done in the time of Varro and even of Columella, and as the free peasant system had done in the fourth and third centuries B.C.[16]

Clearly, then, there existed in Italy a large rural population. Socially and economically, it formed a lower class than that of the landlords, who usually resided in the city of Rome or in other Italian cities. Politically, of course, there was no distinction: all the residents of Italy were Roman citizens and all belonged to one or other of the groups of Roman citizens connected with one of the cities. With the exception of Northern Italy, where many of the Alpine tribes were, in Roman phrase, 'attributed' to Italian cities (Brixia, Bergomum, Comum, Tridentum, Tergeste, Aquileia), which meant that they did not share the franchise with the towns to which they were attached,[17] Italy had politically no gradation of citizens. As I have indicated above, even in Northern Italy, the tendency had been, from the earliest days of the Empire, to eliminate the *populi attributi* as such, and to incorporate them in the territories of the cities, granting them Roman or Latin citizenship. Practically, however, those who lived in the *vici* and *pagi* were regarded, like the urban proletariate, as far inferior to the landlords who resided in the cities. Thus the case of a 'pagan' becoming *decurio* of Sulmo, a city of the Paeligni, was regarded as an exception worthy of mention.* Socially there was not much difference between the *pagani* and *vicani* of the 'attributed' tribes in Northern Italy and the same classes in the other parts of the peninsula.[18]

Turning to the provinces, we find that the evidence about their social organization and, still more, about the forms of land tenure and exploitation is very unequally distributed. For some provinces (Egypt, Africa, and Asia) we have abundant information, for others almost none. Nevertheless it is necessary to give a survey of all the more important Roman provinces from the social and economic point of view. Such a survey has never been

* *CIL* ix. 3088 = Dessau, *ILS* 6531.

attempted for the whole of the Roman Empire and very seldom for single provinces, although the political aspect of their development, that is to say, their gradual urbanization, the transformation of tribes and clans, of *pagi* and *vici*, into territories with an urban centre administered by magistrates who resided in the city, has been frequently treated.

We begin with SICILY, SARDINIA, and CORSICA. In the preceding chapters it has been shown that Sicily in the time of the late Republic and the early Empire, except for a short interval during the last stages of the civil wars, was still one of the granaries from which large quantities of corn were exported to Rome. The testimony of Strabo and scattered notices of a later date furnish decisive evidence on this point. We have now to inquire what were the main features of the social and economic organization of the island during the early Empire as compared with the Republican period.[19] It is difficult to believe that Sicily, like Greece and Italy, was entirely subdivided into city-territories. Evidently the Phoenician part of the island and the extensive regions in the interior were not thus organized under Phoenician and Greek domination. The Romans never promoted a thorough urbanization of Sicily. Not a single new city was founded by them, nor did they make any attempt to revive the decayed Greek cities. In the Phoenician part they maintained even such a peculiar institution as the Asiatic temple of Venus at Eryx with its large number of sacred slaves and extensive territory. The picture which Cicero gives of the island shows that Rome divided the Greek cities into several classes according to their attitude towards her, and jealously kept the public lands which were not assigned to the territory of one or other of these cities, whether in the Phoenician or the Greek areas, as *ager publicus populi Romani* to be rented to Roman citizens and provincials by the Roman censors.

The land which belonged to the territories of the cities (with the exception of those few which were exempt from the land-tax) paid the tenth part of the produce to the Roman treasury. The collection of this tithe was regulated by a law of Hiero II, which was not changed by the new rulers. In these territories the land was in the hands of the city *bourgeoisie*, those whom Cicero calls the *possessores* or *aratores* (γεωργοί). The number of landowners, even including the men who rented arable land from the Roman state, was comparatively small (12,000 to 13,000). Large tracts of land outside the city-territories were in the hands of rich men, who kept on them great herds of cattle. These tracts do not appear to have been the private property of the Roman magnates. They probably leased them from the state. The labour employed for tilling the soil and herding the sheep was probably both slave and free labour (furnished by small tenants) for the fields, almost wholly slave labour for the pastures.

From the devastation caused by the slave-wars Sicily recovered quickly. The city *bourgeoisie* seems not to have been affected by them: in Cicero's time it was still numerous, influential, and prosperous. These conditions changed during the civil war. Sicily was the theatre of one of the most striking episodes of that war—the struggle between Sextus Pompey and Octavian, which lasted for years. Pompey derived his main support from slaves, and it is natural to suppose that he sacrificed to them the interests of the city *bourgeoisie*. However that may have been, it is an attested fact that after his victory Octavian was unable and unwilling to maintain the grant of Roman citizenship to the whole of Sicily, as projected by Caesar and carried out by Antony. The 'whole of Sicily' meant, of course, the citizens of the Greek cities, the class of landowners (*aratores*). In his reorganization Augustus set this grant aside, probably because it did not mean very much, the city *bourgeoisie* of Greek origin having been decimated and ruined by the civil war. Their ruin also accounts for the fact that he reinforced by Roman colonists the more important Sicilian cities—chiefly those which were the main export harbours for corn, wool, and sulphur—and that he granted to a few others, which probably contained large colonies of Italian immigrants, the rights of a Roman *municipium* or a Latin colony. But, in contrast to their policy in Spain, Gaul, the Danube lands, and Africa, neither Augustus nor his immediate successors attempted to revive city life and the city *bourgeoisie* in Sicily. The great majority of the *civitates* and *oppida* were subjected to a *stipendium*, to the payment of a land and perhaps a poll tax, and were thus placed in the lowest grade of the municipal scale. There were probably two reasons for the introduction into Sicily of the category of *civitates stipendiariae*, which was equivalent to dropping the system of tithes (*decumae*), as the *stipendium* was paid in money. The first was that the system of tithes which depended on the existence of a class of prosperous landowners did not pay any more, now that this class lay ruined and prostrate. The second was that in the territories of the *civitates* the leading part was now probably played by natives, not Greeks, and that some of these natives were not adapted for city life. Unfortunately our evidence on the *civitates stipendiariae* and *oppida* is very scanty: *civitas* does not necessarily imply an urban organization, it may denote a complex of villages or the territory of a tribe.[20]

Despite the ruin of the city *bourgeoisie*, Sicily remained a prosperous country. While some of the cities (like Messana and Tauromenium) developed a flourishing viticulture, yet, as has been said, the country in general remained a land of corn-fields and pastures. It looks as if this condition was intentionally maintained by the emperors. They would allow some cities to plant vines and fruit-trees, but they wished the largest part of Sicily to be a corn-growing land, while the mountains naturally remained the home of shepherds. This is probably why they abstained from pursuing in Sicily a policy of urbanization and kept the native population in its primitive condition. They needed the island as a granary of Italy and they did not greatly desire its general development. It was for the same reason that large tracts of land remained in the hands of the state. In the time of Domitian and Trajan there was in Sicily, as in Baetica, a special administration of the public lands which was called the administration 'of the public corn' (*frumentum mancipale*), that is, of the corn received from the tenants of public land.[21] To the same cause, too, was due the growth of large estates in the island and the corresponding increase of the imperial domains. We have dealt with the vast lands which Agrippa owned in Sicily. Many ancient geographical names recorded in the Itineraries are derived from Roman family names and show that Agrippa was not the only owner of wide tracts of country in the province. The outbreak of a revolt in the time of Gallienus, which was probably a revolt of peasants—such risings being a characteristic feature of the third century in general—shows that the growth of large estates did not cease during the first two centuries of our era.[22]

To sum up, Sicily in the first two centuries was a land

containing a few prosperous cities, inhabited to a large extent by Roman colonists, and scores of *civitates*, some of which still kept the external forms of city life, while some were mere aggregates of villages inhabited by the native population. Both the latter had certainly a purely rural aspect: they consisted of groups of peasants and shepherds. The estates of the Roman people and of the emperors were probably managed in the same manner as the great estates in other provinces. They were let out to farmers-general (contractors) and tilled by tenants. On the large estates of some rich landowners grazing was probably the main source of income and the herds were tended, as in the second century B.C., by large numbers of slaves. The Roman emperors succeeded, therefore, in keeping Sicily a granary of the Roman people, a land of fields and pastures with some oases of more progressive economic life.

The same picture applies to the province of SARDINIA. Sardinia had been the granary of Carthage, artificially kept in this condition by the ruling city, and it remained for ever the granary of Rome and Italy. Urban life developed but slowly under Roman administration alike in the Republican and in the Imperial period. The chief cities of the island were Caralis and Turris; both were large export harbours for the corn produced in the island and for the metals extracted from its mines, the former a *municipium*, the latter a colony of Roman settlers. Tribal organization prevailed in the interior even under the Empire, and the tribes did not advance towards city life. Some of them may have formed administrative units (*civitates*), some apparently lived on the territory of large estates—public, imperial, and private. They cultivated these estates as tenants, in a condition of half-serfdom, and attended to the herds of their masters. We have already mentioned the large estates of Acte, the mistress of Nero: they seem to have been typical of the economic structure of the land. In this way, by the colonization of a few cities and by the subjection of the natives, the island became, like Sicily, more or less romanized—thoroughly in the cities, very slightly in the country.

On CORSICA we have only very slight information. However, an inscription shows us that the island was chiefly inhabited by native tribes, which were organized in a definite form by Augustus. A great part of the soil—probably particularly the forests—

belonged to the emperor; another part had been allotted to a Marian colony. The rest belonged to the native population. One of the native tribes, that of the Vanacini, was sufficiently rich to buy land from Vespasian and to establish a semi-urban centre with a temple of Augustus (compare the centres of the provincial cult of the emperors in the Western provinces).[23]

SPAIN has always been considered the stronghold of Romanity, the most thoroughly romanized province in the West. Apart from the fact that the country still speaks a Romance language— less near, indeed, to Latin than is Romanian, the language of the latest and the most shortlived province of the Empire—the supporters of this view point out that Spain was (after Sicily, Sardinia, and Corsica) the most ancient province of Rome, and that she was completely urbanized by the Romans, all Spanish tribes and towns having received Latin rights from Vespasian. There is no doubt that one part of Spain was thoroughly romanized and urbanized. Baetica was a bit of Italy in Spain, as Narbonensis was in Gaul. The same (more or less) must be said of the coast of Tarraconensis and of the lowlands of Lusitania. This need not surprise us, for these parts of Spain had had a long cultural development before the Roman domination. We know how old Iberian civilization was, and how closely connected with the other civilizations of the Southern Mediterranean as early as the Minoan period. We know, also, that both Greeks (the Phocaeans) and Phoenicians (colonists first from Tyre, later from Carthage) settled down in Southern Spain and introduced city life in its Greco-Oriental form.[24] The Romans were the last to come. They took over what they found and did not at first add very much of their own. Gradually, however, Spain and especially Baetica became the Promised Land of Italian colonization. From the earliest times Roman colonies were sent out thither: but the colonization was essentially the work of Caesar and his adoptive son. It is probable that at this time, that is, during the civil wars, many Italians settled in the great commercial cities of Spain, both Greek and Phoenician. Of these cities the largest, most prosperous, and profoundly romanized was Gades, after which came Emporium. In this way the civilized and economically prosperous parts of the country became romanized, the old ruling classes in the cities and in the country being supplanted by Romans and Latin-speaking Italians. The rest of the city

Description of Plate XXXV

1. FRAGMENT OF A BAS-RELIEF. Found at Linares in Spain. A. Daubrée, *Rev. arch.* 43, 1882, pp. 193 ff., pl. v; H. Sandars, ibid., 4me sér., 1, 1903, pp. 201 ff., pl. IV; id. *Archaeologia* 59, 1905, pp. 311 ff. and pl. LXIX; S. Reinach, *Rép. d. rel.* ii, p. 192, 4; T. A. Rickard, 'The mining of the Romans in Spain', *JRS* 18, 1928, pp. 139 ff.

Nine miners in two files marching down a mining-gallery towards a pit. The last in the first line holds a miner's pick or hammer, the second from the end a lamp. The taller figure behind them is a foreman, who carries large double-looped tongs and a lantern (?; a bell, or an oil-can for the lantern, have also been suggested). All are dressed in the same manner: the upper part of the body and the legs are naked; round the waist is worn a short *tunica* (or trousers) and a belt or strap of leather. Linares (ancient Castulo) was one of the most important mining centres of Spain; its mines were very rich both in silver and in lead (Polyb. 10. 38; 11. 20; Strabo, 3. 2. 10; 147C); a paved road connected Castulo with the famous mines of Sisapo. See *CIL* ii, pp. 440 ff. and 949 ff. The town was rich and prosperous, as is shown by many Latin inscriptions found there and by a large number of coins (from the 1st cent. B.C. to the 4th cent. A.D.). Other finds are listed by Rickard, op. cit., pp. 141 ff.

2. SILVER CUP ADORNED WITH BAS-RELIEFS. Found at Castro Urdiales (Flaviobriga) in North Spain. In the collection of Antonio de Otañes at Castro Urdiales. E. Hübner in *Arch. Zeit.* 1873, p. 115, pl. XI; *Gaz. arch.* 1884, pp. 261 and 270; Daremberg–Saglio, *Dict. d. ant.*, fig. 6089; *CIL* ii. 2917; S. Reinach, *Rép. d. rel.* ii, p. 195, 3. Reproduced from a copy in metal in the Museo de Reproducciones Artísticas of Madrid.

The bas-reliefs which adorn the inside of the cup are surrounded by an inscription in letters inlaid with gold: *Salus Umeritana.* At the top is shown the personification of the Waters, the *Salus* of Umeri, reclining, half-naked, holding a reed in her right hand and leaning with her left on an urn, out of which a stream of water flows into a tank of big rough stones. On either side of her are old trees. The medicinal spring of Umeri (site unknown) probably made it one of the well-known health resorts in Spain. (On the Spanish health resorts see Pliny, *NH* 31. 2, cf. 23; and on the sojourn of Augustus at one of them in the Pyrenees, Krinagoras in *Anth. Pal.* 9. 419.) Near the spring a boy-servant is filling a large jar with water. Close to the spring a sick old man, seated in a wicker chair, takes a glass of water from the hands of a boy-servant. To the left the same man dressed in a toga (a patient who has recovered his health) is sacrificing at an altar. To the right a native traveller, or shepherd, places offerings on another altar. At the foot a third boy pours water from a jar into a barrel placed on a cart drawn by two mules. It is evident that Umeri was a flourishing health resort, one of many in the Pyrenees and other parts of the Roman Empire, and that it even exported its water to distant places. Cf. E. Hübner, *Römische Herrschaft in Westeuropa* (1890), pp. 288 ff., and p. 262. On health resorts in general, see Pauly–Wissowa, ii, cols. 294 ff.; L. Friedländer–G. Wissowa, *Sitteng. Roms*, 9th ed. i, p. 387; iii, p. 178.

1. SPANISH MINERS

2. A SPANISH HEALTH RESORT

XXXV. LIFE AND WORK

population—what remained of Greeks, Phoenicians, and Iberians—was absorbed by the new-comers and gradually adopted the language and the customs of the ruling class.[25]

The basis of the prosperity of Southern and Western Spain was the exploitation of the natural resources of the country. Agriculture, especially the cultivation of olives and flax, and mining (silver, copper, iron, tin, and lead) had been from ancient times the most important sources of wealth for the Spaniards. These natural resources led to the growth of a prosperous industry, particularly the fabrication of steel and the weaving of linen garments. This economic activity, and above all the mining industry, was developed by the Romans. For Spain was the richest mining district of the growing Empire, and the earliest to be exploited. Much attention was paid also to the excellent olive-oil of the country, which was better and cheaper than that of Italy.[26]

Rich and prosperous as it was, Southern Spain remained for long years a land of Italian colonization. Many a Roman capitalist, both of the senatorial and of the equestrian class, invested money in Spanish land. Together with the descendants of the old colonists and some representatives of the pre-Roman upper class, the new-comers constituted the city *bourgeoisie*. Among them were to be found business-managers of Italian capitalists and agents of the emperors, some of whom settled down in the attractive province. These continued to grow in numbers and in wealth. Their income was mainly derived from agriculture. We know that both in Baetica and in Lusitania the Roman colonists received unusually large holdings. This was the original source of their wealth, which steadily increased till it reached its climax in the second century A.D. The beautiful ruins of the cities of Baetica, Lusitania, and part of Tarraconensis—notably those of Italica, Tarraco, Emerita, and Clunia—attest a splendid growth of prosperity. It is reasonable to suppose that the foundation of this wealth was the exploitation of the land. Good examples of rich landowners are the families of the Emperors Trajan and Hadrian. Labour for such estates and for the mines was probably supplied by the natives, who remained what they had always been—tillers of the soil and miners.[27]

Southern Spain, however, contained large tracts of land which were not in the hands of private owners. From the first years of the conquest the Roman people possessed large estates and most of the mines. As in Africa and in Asia, the emperors of the Julio-Claudian dynasty rivalled the Roman people in the extent of their properties, which they steadily enlarged by confiscation and inheritance. The largest confiscations were carried out by Nero, and in the second century they were represented by huge tracts of patrimonial land. The same fate befell most of the mines. On the mode of cultivation of these patrimonial and public lands information fails, but we may fairly suppose that it did not differ from that which we find in Africa and Asia. The land was probably leased to large and small tenants, *conductores* and *coloni*. The former, who were farmers on a large scale, were townsmen; the latter lived on the estates and cultivated their farms with their own hands. We do not know what became in the end of the serfdom which had once existed here, as in Gaul. It is difficult to believe that the Romans abolished it everywhere, as they did in 189 B.C. at Hasta.* We are better informed regarding the exploitation of the mines: two inscriptions, as we shall see in the next chapter, give us the most detailed information about the organization of one of these mines, that of Vipasca.[28]

Far less romanized were the uplands of Lusitania and of the Hither Province, especially the districts of the Celt-Iberians, the Asturians, and the Callaecians. These districts did not attract colonists from Italy and so they retained their national aspect and the peculiarities of their social and economic system. Romanization and urbanization were superficial, and the division into clans and tribes (*gentes*) survived. The fact that Vespasian gave Latin rights to all the tribes of Central, Northern, and Western Spain does not imply that they were thoroughly romanized before the grant was made. It only meant that city life was not alien to the social system of Spain before the Roman domination and that, through service in the army, a part of the population of the tribal territories had become slightly romanized and could form a governing body on the Roman municipal model for the rest of the tribe and parts of other tribes. The reform of Vespasian was intended both to break up the national and tribal connexions and to secure for the Roman legions, which were no longer recruited in Italy, a supply of good soldiers who, being descendants of veteran auxiliaries and members of the urban aristocracy, were romanized to a certain extent and separated

* Dessau, *ILS* 15.

by their higher social standing from their kith and kin. While one group thus became members of a civic community, the rest remained in the same condition as before, living their wonted tribal life and sending soldiers to the auxiliary regiments of the Roman army. By this division of the population Vespasian probably met the criticism of those who reproached him with 'barbarizing' the army of the Empire.[29]

The meagre evidence which we possess as to the social and economic life of the uplands shows that even after the reform of Vespasian the land remained in a poor and primitive condition, just as it had been in the times of Polybius and Strabo.[30] The fact that, from the very moment when city life on the Roman pattern began, it was not easy to find a sufficient number of candidates for the municipal magistracies, proves that the formation of a city *bourgeoisie* was a somewhat slow process and that the population of the interior remained, even in the cities, largely composed of peasants and shepherds.[31] In these parts, as is shown by Schulten's excavations at Numantia, the cities never reached the state of prosperity which characterized those of the coast and the lowlands. They remained more or less what they had been before, native towns. Some of them, indeed, left the hills for the plains, but the complaints of the Saborenses show that this was not always a sign of prosperity. Naturally the capitals of large territories developed more rapidly than the rest.[32] Regarding the organization of the tribes and clans which lived in the territories of the new cities or, in some cases, in territories of their own, we have no evidence. The frequent mention in the city territories of *incolae* and of *contributi*, some of whom were even *intramurani*—that is to say, lived inside the cities— shows that those who held Latin rights and were more or less romanized formed a small minority of the population of Spain, while the status of the rest remained the same as it had been before the 'thorough urbanization' of the country.[33]

We are better informed about the social and economic life of GAUL. The masterly pictures which have been given by C. Jullian, F. Cumont, and F. Stähelin justify a very brief account.[34] Here again we must be very careful about generalizing. Gallia Narbonensis, like Baetica, was much more romanized than Aquitania and Gallia Lugudunensis (including Belgica). The Southern province was as thoroughly romanized as

Description of Plate XXXVI

MOSAIC. Found in 1890 at Saint Romain en Gal (ancient Colonia Julia Vienna) in southern France. Louvre Museum, Paris. G. Lafaye in *Rev. arch.*, 3ᵐᵉ sér. 19, 1892, pp. 322 ff., with drawings; *Inv. d. mos. de la Gaule*, i (1909), no. 246 and three photographic plates; Cagnat–Chapot, *Manuel*, &c. ii, p. 173; R. Billiard, *La Vigne dans l'antiquité* (1913), p. 425 and *passim*; S. Reinach, *Rép. d. peint.*, pp. 223 ff.

The mosaic formed the pavement of a large room in a private house at Vienne. Only one part of it is preserved. The whole consisted of forty squares surrounded by an ornamental frame (omitted in our plate). Of these, twenty-eight are preserved, but three have been badly damaged by fire. The four squares at each end of the mosaic were purely ornamental; the remaining thirty-two were filled with pictures referring to rustic life. The whole was intended to be a rustic pictorial calendar. The centre of the composition is occupied by four figures of *genii* mounted on four animals—a boar, a panther, a bull, and a lion. The *genii* certainly represent the four seasons: that on the boar is winter, that on the bull spring, that on the lion summer, and that on the panther autumn. The representation of seasons is quite common on ancient monuments, especially mosaics; see, e.g. our plates LVIII and LXXIX. The *genii* in the role of seasons are rather uncommon, but compare another mosaic of Vienne (*Inv. d. mos.*, no. 207). Seven pictures are grouped with the figure of each season; those which refer to the winter and autumn are complete; for the summer we have only three, and for the spring only two. The pictures show a close agreement with the descriptions of agricultural work both in the two rustic calendars which have come down to us (*Menologium rusticum Colotianum* and *Vallense*, *CIL* i², pp. 280 ff. (vi. 2305, cf. p. 3318) = Dessau, *ILS* 8745) and in our literary sources (the *Scriptores rei rusticae*, and Virgil). The number of the pictures cannot be brought into strict correspondence with the twelve months of the year (which is the order in the written rustic calendars). It seems that for the author of our calendar each season of ninety-one days was divided into sections of thirteen days each. A detailed description of the pictures cannot be given here, but they may be briefly enumerated in the natural order from above downwards. I. Winter. (1) Two persons seated near a stove inside a room. (2) A man bringing a bundle of reeds or osiers to a woman who is plaiting a basket (the calendar for January says: *salix, harundo caeditur*). (3) Two men are busy sowing something, probably beans (Cal. Dec.: *faba seritur*). (4) A man and a boy (slave?) performing a libation before the house on a portable altar (Cal. Jan.: *sacrificant dis penatibus*). (5) Grinding grain (Virg., *Georg.* i. 267). (6) Baking bread (?) in an oven. (7) Carrying manure to the vineyards (Cal. Dec.: *vineae stercorantur*). II. Autumn. (1) Much damaged. Perhaps the *arborum oblaqueatio* of Cal. Sept.? (2) Vintage (Cal. Oct.: *vindemiae*). (3) Pressing of the *marc du raisin*. (4) Picking apples or other fruit from the trees (Cal. Sept.: *poma leguntur*). (5) Treading grapes. (6) Pitching jars (Cal. Sept: *dolia picantur*). (7) Ploughing and sowing (Cal. Nov.: *sementes triticariae et hordiariae*). III. Summer. (1) Much damaged. Harvesting barley (Cal. Jul.: *messes hordiar[iae] et fabar[iae]*); it is too early for wheat, which is not reaped till August. (2) Perhaps a rustic festival-contest (throwing of javelins: Virg., *Georg.* ii. 529). (3) Sacrifice to Ceres. IV. Spring. (1) The arrival of the first stork. (2) Grafting trees.

It is noticeable that this rustic pictorial calendar (the designs of which were certainly taken from illustrated manuscripts) deals almost exclusively with viticulture and gardening. We must remember that Vienne was a great centre of agricultural life and that her speciality was her famous wine. Compare the large number of mosaics found at Vienne which refer to wine and vine-planting (*Inv. d. mos.*, nos. 169, 174, 187, 207, 220, 236, 243).

A RUSTIC PICTORIAL CALENDAR
(Mosaic of Vienne)

XXXVI. AGRICULTURE IN SOUTH GAUL

1. PROSPEROUS BOURGEOIS OF GAUL

2. A GALLIC BUSINESS MAN

4. REAPING CORN

3. SELLING TURNIPS OR PEARS.
HOEING AND DIGGING

5. A BUSINESS MAN AND HIS PEASANT
CUSTOMER

XXXVII. BUSINESS LIFE IN GAUL

Description of Plate XXXVII

1. FUNERAL STELE. Found at Sens (Agedincum). Museum of Sens. G. Julliot, *Musée gallo-romain de Sens* (1869–98), p. 73, pl. xiii; E. Espérandieu, *Rec. gén.* iv, no. 2803.

Husband and wife. The husband (on the right) is clad in the usual Gallo-Roman dress and holds in his left hand a large purse full of coins. The wife wears a similar dress and holds with both hands a small bottle, containing scent (?).

2. FRAGMENTS OF BAS-RELIEFS WHICH ADORNED A FUNERAL MONUMENT. Found at Sens (Agedincum). Museum of Sens. G. Julliot, *Musée de Sens*, p. 79, pl. xi; E. Espérandieu, *Rec. gén.* iv, no. 2806.

Men standing in niches. The best-preserved is dressed in the usual Gallo-Roman style. He is busy writing in his ledger, a thick polyptych.

3. TWO BAS-RELIEFS OF A FUNERAL *CIPPUS*. Found at Arlon (Orolaunum Vicus). Museum of Arlon. E. Espérandieu, *Rec. gén.* v, no. 4044 (with bibliography).

The front (not reproduced) is occupied by the figures of the deceased, the husband holding a purse and the wife a box, both standing in a niche (similar to no. 1 of this plate). On one of the sides (not reproduced) are figured a man driving in a two-wheeled car (*cisium*) and a woman selling fruit to a traveller. The other side is that reproduced in our figure. The upper panel depicts a shop where fruit or vegetables (turnips?) are exhibited for sale on a table, and are being sold by a man and a woman to a customer. Under the table are three baskets, and from the ceiling hang bunches of onions. In the lower panel two men are working in a field: one hoeing, the other digging. The couple portrayed on the *cippus* were probably landowners, who sold the products of their farm (or of their vegetable garden) in their own shop and on the road which passed near their farm.

4. FRAGMENT OF A BAS-RELIEF OF A FUNERAL MONUMENT. Found at Arlon (Orolaunum Vicus). Museum of Arlon. E. Espérandieu, *Rec. gén.* v, no. 4036.

A man and two animals (oxen?) in a cornfield. The operation represented is probably reaping by means of a machine drawn by a team of oxen.

5. PART OF A FUNERAL MONUMENT (?). Found at Arlon. Museum of Arlon. E. Espérandieu, *Rec. gén.* v, no. 4037.

A man in his office seated on a chair at a table, on which he pours out coins from a purse. Another bearded man stands in front of the table, his right hand lifted, in his left a cane. Perhaps a peasant in a bank making a payment or borrowing money?

the Northern part of Italy. Just as with Baetica, a predominant part in its life was played by the Roman colonies, to which large tracts of land were given. Some of these colonies (like Arelate and Narbo) became rich commercial and industrial cities, others (like Arausio, Vienne, &c.) were centres of large and well-cultivated rural districts. In the territories of the two most important tribes of the province, the Vocontii and the Allobroges, romanization followed a peculiar course, which is paralleled among the Helvetii in Gallia Comata. These territories remained for a very long time rural regions with few cities. The main development of life took place in the *pagi* and *vici*, the latter of which under the influence of growing prosperity naturally developed, to a certain extent, into regular cities. Their administration, however, remained non-urban in type, though it was separate from that of the rest of the land.[35]

As in Baetica, and perhaps more than in Baetica, landed property was concentrated in the hands of a few owners. We do not know how large the imperial share was, but it is not impossible that the beautiful villa of Chiragan near Toulouse was an imperial estate, and that the large mass of sherds from the province found on Monte Testaccio indicates the absorption of considerable areas of public land.[36] Moreover, Narbonensis has yielded inscriptions which speak of imperial agents of the *patrimonium*; and this is not surprising, for no doubt rich Roman senators of the Republican period possessed extensive properties there. The wealthiest landowners were certainly the residents of the large and prosperous cities, who were partly of Italian, partly of local origin. In the last chapter we have spoken of the important commerce which these members of the city *bourgeoisie* carried on, and we may be sure that the successful merchants invested much of their money in land. The beautiful buildings in the cities of Southern France and the gorgeous funeral shrines of the urban aristocracy testify to their great wealth and strong public spirit. How far moderate-sized and small estates developed alongside of the large domains of the Chiragan type cannot be even guessed. It may be seriously doubted whether the mention of *possessores* in Aquae Sextiae is to be taken as a proof of the existence of a group of small landowners in the territory of the city. It is more likely that by *possessores* are meant owners of houses, not of land.[37]

More definite is the picture which can be drawn of the life of
the other provinces of Gaul. There is no doubt that here the
cities developed slowly, and contained mostly a commercial,
industrial, and bureaucratic population. We can get a fairly
clear idea of some of these cities, which were advanced posts of
still homogeneous tribes, and whose specific names (for example,
Lutetia) were gradually replaced by those of their tribes, for
example, on the one hand, Avaricum (Bourges), Augustodunum
(Autun), Agedincum (Sens), and Rotomagus (Rouen), on the
other, Namnetes (Nantes), Mediolanum Santonum (Saintes),
and the Parisii. The remains of these cities, however, are in no
way comparable with those of Southern Gaul. The main source
of prosperity was, however, no longer the commerce and industry
of the cities, but the land. It is interesting to read the description
of the many innovations which were introduced into agriculture
by the Gauls before and after the Roman domination. The exploitation of land in Gaul was on the whole systematic. The representatives of this husbandry were the large landed proprietors,
the tribal aristocracy, which owned the land before and after the
Roman conquest, and the immigrants who acquired their wealth
by means of commerce, industry, and banking operations. There
is no doubt, too, that some of the native artisans and traders,
after building up their fortunes, invested their money in land.
These facts are proved not only by the descriptions of Gaul in
Polybius, Strabo, Caesar, &c., but also by the hundreds of ruins
of large and small villas which cover the soil of the Gallic lands.
The distribution of such villas all over the country is a well-known
fact, on which it is unnecessary to insist. Careful excavations
made in recent years both in France and Belgium and on the
Rhine (especially its left bank) have fully illustrated the different
types of these domains: on the one hand, the large villas of rich
landowners, the scattered farms of the cultivators, and the extensive *vici* of workmen attached (not by any law but by the economic conditions) to the villas, and on the other the more modest
villas, similar to those of Pompeii. It is worthy of note that many
of the modern names of cities and villages in these lands are
derived from the names of the owners of the villas.* They may,
indeed, be counted by thousands.[38] It is also a significant fact

---

* The estates (*fundi*) were designated by the owners' names formed into an adjective by
means of the suffix *-acus* or *-anus*.

Description of Plate XXXVIII

1 and 7. FUNERAL STELE. Sens (Agedincum, Senones). In the Museum. G. Julliot, *Musée gallo-romain de Sens*, p. 85 and pl. ix; E. Espérandieu, *Rec. gén.* iv, no. 2768.

Funeral monument of a fuller. The lower part (no. 7) shows the fuller treading the cloth in a basin, the upper (No. 1) the same fuller clipping a piece of cloth with a large pair of scissors.

2. FRAGMENT OF A FUNERAL STELE. Sens. In the Museum. G. Julliot, op. cit.; E. Espérandieu, op. cit., no. 2783.

A maker of wooden shoes (sabots) in his shop. In his right hand he holds a hammer, in his left a piece of wood (?). On the wall are shown his instruments.

3. FRAGMENT OF A FUNERAL STELE. Sens. In the Museum. G. Julliot, op. cit.; E. Espérandieu, op. cit., no. 2780.

Metal-ware shop. A customer is looking at two large pans hung on the wall, while the shopowner offers him a small one.

4. FRAGMENT OF A STELE. Sens. In the Museum. G. Julliot, op. cit., p. 93 and pl. ix; E. Espérandieu, op. cit., no. 2778.

A man near a counter, before which lie a basket and a bag.

5. FRAGMENT OF A STELE. Sens. In the Museum. G. Julliot, op. cit., p. 87 and pl. ix; E. Espérandieu, op. cit., no. 2784.

Business man or merchant behind his counter, holding a *stilus* in his right hand and tablets in his left. To the left a cloak with a hood hangs on the wall.

6. FRAGMENT OF A STELE. Sens. In the Museum. G. Julliot, op. cit., p. 86 and pls. ix and lii; E. Espérandieu, op. cit., no. 2781.

Funeral monument of a tailor. The tailor (whose hands only are preserved) is cutting a piece of cloth with a large pair of scissors. Two hoods are hung upon the wall. On the other side is a fragment of the funeral inscription (*CIL* xiii. 2953).

These fragments are grouped together on this plate because they all come from one place, a Gallic city of minor importance; cf. also E. Espérandieu, l.l., no. 2767 (wall painters); no. 2770 (a driver, *cisiarius*); no. 2775 (a dealer in birds); no. 2778 (masons?); no. 2782 (a merchant?), and many funeral stelae with portraits of the deceased which depict attributes of the man's profession to emphasize the fact that he was a business man; also pl. xxiv, 3, and pl. xxxvii, 1–2—all from the same place. The series conveys a good idea of the business life of a Gallic city of intermediate size.

1   2

3–5

6   7

XXXVIII. INDUSTRIAL LIFE IN GAUL

that many temples of the native gods of Central, Northern, and Western Gaul were not connected with the cities but formed centres of worship for the country people who lived in native Celtic villages. Some of these villages have been excavated, and we find that they do not differ very much from the Celtic villages of the pre-Roman period. Another interesting fact is the existence of many theatres scattered all over the land and associated mostly with the rural temples just mentioned. Originally, no doubt, they were used mostly for religious ceremonies connected with the native cults.[39]

We pass to GERMANY. It is well known that the two Roman provinces on the Rhine, Lower and Upper Germany (*Germania inferior* and *superior*), were of comparatively late origin (A.D. 82–90), and that the Rhine long formed the military frontier of the provinces of Gaul. We cannot here narrate once more the history of the military occupation of the Rhine by the Romans.[40] It will be enough to say that, after the failure of Augustus to form a province of Germany and to advance the frontier to the Elbe, the Rhine remained for about sixty years the frontier of the Empire. Military considerations on the one hand, and the over-population of Gaul on the other, combined with the necessity of finding good arable land for veteran soldiers, forced Vespasian and his sons to begin the conquest of Germany afresh, and with the same chief object of connecting the army of the Rhine with the army of the Danube by shorter and better roads. For this purpose it was necessary to annex the angle between the Rhine and the Danube—the fertile lands on the right bank of the middle and upper Rhine, on one section of the Main, and on the Neckar—and to surround the mountains of the Taunus and of the Schwarzwald (Black Forest) with a continuous chain of military posts. By the efforts of Vespasian, Titus, Domitian, and Trajan this task was gradually accomplished and a series of forti-fied posts with a continuous wall of earth and, farther to the South, of stone were built for the protection of the new territory and of the excellent system of roads which connected the Rhine with the Danube.

Though the literary evidence on this achievement of the emperors is very scanty, thorough archaeological investigation has revealed to us all the details of the military occupation. And more than that: it has enabled us to trace the broad lines of economic development in the Rhine lands and the salient features of the late Roman civilization which gradually grew up on both banks of the river in its middle and upper course. Our detailed knowledge of Roman Germany is one of the most notable triumphs of archaeology. Without the careful work of excavation done by German scholars, we should have known very little of the history of the Rhine lands under the early Empire and of the early history of Germany in general.[41]

After the districts on the East bank of the middle and upper Rhine had been incorporated in the Empire, the Rhine lands as a whole were treated by the Roman government no longer as the military frontier of Gaul but as two independent provinces, the province of the Lower and that of the Upper Rhine. The lower province was confined to the lands on the left bank of the river; the upper included large tracts on both sides, extending to the Main and the Moselle. The economic and social aspect of life in these two provinces demands a brief description.

From this point of view the division of the Rhine lands into a lower and an upper Germany appears purely artificial. In fact, the lands on the left bank of the river formed one unit, those on the right another. The former, especially in the South, did not differ greatly from the rest of Gaul, to which they originally belonged. It is true that the large cities on the left bank, with the exception of Augusta Treverorum, were all of military origin. Colonia Agrippinensis, Castra Vetera (Colonia Ulpia Trajana), Novaesium, Moguntiacum, Bonna, &c., all developed out of the settlements which arose round the great military fortresses, the so-called *canabae* which gradually took the form of one or many villages (*vici*). But these cities, half military and wholly Roman, lived a life of their own, distinct from that of the country surrounding them. Some of them, for example Colonia, developed enormously, since they played an important part both in the internal commerce of the province and in the commerce with other provinces—e.g. Britain—and in that which developed along the north coast with Germany. Gradually, though slowly, they received the usual constitution of a Roman community, while the country, as elsewhere in Gaul, was subdivided into large tribal territories (*civitates*), which practically coincided with the district inhabited by a single German or Celtic tribe, mostly German and Celtic mixed, like the Ubii with their capital at Cologne or the Treveri with their capital at Trèves.

At the time of the Roman occupation the left bank of the Rhine was not a No-Man's Land. It formed part of the Celtic commonwealth, with its own towns, villages, temples, and so forth, and with its own social and economic life, which has already been described. But the redistribution of population after the time of Caesar, the settlement of many German tribes in the region, and direct contact with the military frontier were new and important factors in the economic and social development of the whole land. From the economic point of view the country was a paradise for the capitalist, especially the districts of the Moselle and the Meuse. Rich and fertile, it was bound to become the granary of the Rhine armies and their main source of supply for wine, clothing, shoes, lumber, metals, pottery, and the like. From the outset the land attracted large numbers of immigrants who were chiefly engaged in the work of supplying the army with the things it needed most. These men were not sutlers, but merchants on a large scale and transport agents. Their main centres, apart from Lyons, which was the clearing-house for imports from Southern and Central Gaul and Italy, were Trèves on the Moselle, Cologne, and Neumagen (Noviomagus) on the middle and lower Rhine. Of these the most important was Trèves, the earliest Roman city on the Moselle. Trèves was not only a great centre of commerce; it became, as it was bound to become, the economic centre of the whole surrounding country.[42] The merchants of the city, who acquired great wealth by selling goods to the Rhine army, invested their money, as might be expected, in profitable undertakings in the vicinity, and their example was followed by the merchants of Cologne and the other commercial cities on the Rhine. The idea of producing corn, cattle, and wine on the spot instead of importing them, and of manufacturing wool, metals, leather wares and other goods in the neighbourhood, instead of shipping them from far distant places, was natural enough. The easiest way of realizing it was to promote agriculture, cattle-breeding, and viticulture on a large scale and on capitalistic lines. Gradually, therefore, the left bank of the Rhine, along with the valleys of the Moselle and the Meuse, became a great centre of capitalistic and mostly agricultural enterprise. It became, in Cumont's phrase, a land 'non de

Description of Plate XXXIX

1. ONE OF THE SCULPTURES OF A FUNERAL MONUMENT OF NEU-MAGEN (RESTORED). Found at Neumagen. Museum of Trèves. Hettner, *Führer,* &c., p. 14; E. Fölzer, 'Ein Neumagener Schiff neu ergänzt', *Bonn. Jahrb.* 120, 1911, p. 236; E. Espérandieu, *Rec. gén.* vi, no. 5193; *Germania Romana* (Atlas), pl. XLII, 2; S. Reinach, *Rép. d. rel.* ii, p. 90, 5, and iii, p. 528, 7.

A rowing barge loaded with four large wine-barrels, and manned by six oarsmen and two steersmen, one of whom is marking the time by clapping his hands. The barge, according to the restoration, had its prow and stern adorned with a ram's and a wolf's head.

2-3. FRAGMENTS OF BAS-RELIEFS ON THE FUNERAL MONUMENT OF A RICH MERCHANT OF MOGUNTIACUM. Found at Mainz. Central Museum of Mainz. *Mainzer Zeitschr.* 1, 1906, p. 31; E. Espérandieu, *Rec. gén.* vii, no. 5833; S. Reinach, *Rép. d. rel.* ii, p. 71, 3, 4; *Germania Romana* (Atlas), pl. XLII, 8 and 5. To the same monument belongs the bas-relief, pl. XXIV, 2.

Three workmen rolling barrels up a plank, which leads apparently to a ship. Four men unloading a ship: one has fallen down with his sack; two are ashore; the other is running down the plank. Are the ships laden with wine and corn, and was the owner of the monument a large dealer in these products?

4. ONE OF THE BAS-RELIEFS OF THE COLUMN OF IGEL. Igel near Trèves. E. Espérandieu, *Rec. gén.* vi, no. 5268, p. 454; F. Drexel in *Röm. Mitt.* 35, 1920, p. 92; H. Dragendorff-E. Krüger, *Das Grabmal von Igel*, pl. IX.

Transport of large bundles on horseback over hilly country. Two horses are crossing a hill. At each end of the road is a large building.

5. AS NO. 4. E. Espérandieu, *Rec. gén.* vi, p. 455; F. Drexel, loc. cit., p. 91, fig. 3; *Germania Romana* (Atlas), pl. XLII, 7; H. Dragendorff-E. Krüger, loc. cit., pl. XVI.

Two or more men (the relief is broken) are hauling a large and heavy ship loaded with two bales. A steersman is seated on the stern. Compare the bas-relief of Cabrières d'Aigues (Vaucluse), which represents the same scene with some new and very interesting details, F. Drexel, loc. cit., p. 109, fig. 10 (not in Espérandieu).

These five typical monuments, selected from scores which may be easily consulted in Espérandieu's *Recueil*, furnish good illustrations of the lively commercial life of the Rhine and its tributaries. Cf. Chap. V, note 27.

1. TRANSPORT OF WINE BY RIVER

2. LOADING WINE-BARRELS

3. UNLOADING A SHIP

4. CROSSING A HILL

5. HAULING A BARGE ALONG A RIVER

XXXIX. COMMERCE IN GAUL AND GERMANY

villes, mais de villas'. Its economic condition is depicted on the splendid funeral monuments which the wealthy merchants and landowners of the present Belgium, Luxembourg, and above all the neighbourhood of Trèves, built for themselves all over the country. The bas-reliefs which adorned these pillar-monuments have already been mentioned in connexion with the development of wholesale commerce in Gaul and on the Rhine. They are no less important as illuminating evidence of the rapid evolution of agriculture. Further testimony to the prosperity of the whole region is furnished by the fine ruins of large villas which are to be seen everywhere. Most of these villas were either luxurious residences of the city merchants or big agricultural and industrial concerns, combining a luxurious summer abode with a series of buildings of a purely business character.[43]

The funeral monuments and the ruins of villas tell us also of the social conditions of the land. Labour for the large industrial concerns was furnished by the native population, by the Ubii, Treveri, &c., who lived in villages and huts near the great villas. The bas-reliefs of the Igel monument near Trèves and the ruins of villages near some of the Belgian villas show that the native population gradually became clients, and in some cases tenants, of the rich city merchants. Though the bas-reliefs of Neumagen, which represent peasants making money payments to a city man, assisted by one or more clerks, do not necessarily depict the *coloni* of a great landowner paying their rent, yet the scene on the Igel monument, where peasants bring gifts in kind to their master, reminds us so strongly of the descriptions of Statius and Martial, which have been mentioned above, that we cannot help thinking that the peasants of the bas-reliefs are not only the clients and debtors but also, at any rate in some cases, *coloni* of the owners of the monuments.[44]

How the city capitalists became owners of the richest fields and the best pasture-lands in the region of the Rhine is a question difficult to answer. They certainly did not belong to the local tribal aristocracy. Such an aristocracy hardly existed among the Ubii and the Treveri, who were new German, or Celto-German, settlers on the left bank of the river. Certain bas-reliefs of the same series may suggest an explanation. Besides commercial and agricultural enterprises, the rich men of the Rhineland carried on money-lending on a large scale. They

were the bankers of the new society growing up under the influence of new economic conditions. I am inclined to explain
the so-called rent-pay scenes as illustrations of banking operations. The villas were not only large agricultural and industrial
concerns, they were also the local banks. It is easy to understand
how shrewd business men, by lending money to the villagers and
farmers of the neighbourhood, became the patrons and presently
the masters of their debtors, and gradually transformed into
tenants those who were formerly independent peasants and
landowners. The new system of Roman taxation helped them
to achieve their aim, and the new conditions of capitalistic life
which gradually developed on the left bank of the Rhine contributed to the same result.[45]

The very interesting discoveries recently made at Trèves and
Bonn are of interest not only for social, but also for religious history. I refer to the large complex of Celto-Germanic temples
at Trèves, which were excavated with remarkable energy and
competence from 1924 by Professor S. Loeschke, and to the finds
made in 1928 and 1929 by Professor H. Lehner under the church
of the monastery at Bonn. What we may call the Celto-Germanic
Olympia or Delphi at Trèves is particularly instructive. This
district was probably a cult-centre since prehistoric times. In
the first century A.D. it was covered with buildings by the inhabitants of Trèves, themselves neither Italians nor romanized,
nor Celts, nor Germans, with the help of Roman skill and Roman
art: the city of the gods was thus surrounded by a wall. It is difficult to say to what class the founders of these sanctuaries belonged. The social status of only one of them is known; he was
a soldier of the Rhine fleet, and perhaps at the same time a
retail-merchant of beer or of dyed stuffs for clothes (or perhaps
he belonged by birth to the corporation of dyers). The others do
not say who they are; but their names and the absence of any
title show that they were romanized natives, for the most part
of humble status: shopkeepers, artisans, labourers. Building
activity in the sacred city went on uninterruptedly: and after
two large fires the temples were restored. In the third century
A.D. the precinct contained not less than sixty temples, large and
small. A sacred theatre was attached to one of the larger ones; a
practice attested in other Celtic sanctuaries. On the seats the
names of the owners of the positions are inscribed in the same

way as in the temple of Atargatis at Dura. In these temples some of the idols and votive offerings are Roman, some of the names are those of Latin deities, and the inscriptions are always in Latin: all the rest is Celtic and in part Germanic. Characteristically the Persian god Mithras is associated with the Celtic and Germanic deities; this, however, was of later occurrence, and Mithras' cult was originally performed only in a private house. In about A.D. 337 this sacred city was totally destroyed by the Christians. None of its temples became a Christian church. The difference between what happened here and what happened in the Roman city is striking. It is clear that the real enemies of Christianity were precisely the Gods of this sacred city.[46]

The discoveries at Bonn are no less important. Was there here, also in the *canabae*, a Celtic city which provided the stones in the fourth century A.D. for the oldest church in Bonn? At all events, it appears that this sacred city and the individual Celtic sanctuaries of the *canabae* were held in great veneration in the time of Antoninus Pius and M. Aurelius even by the Roman population of the military camp and of the city. This is shown by the dedications to the Matres Aufaniae, to Mercurius Gehrinius (?) and to other deities, made by the 'bigwigs' of the camp, of the *canabae* and of the capital, Colonia, starting with the legate himself. The popularity of the native gods among individual Greeks and Romans in the second and third centuries A.D., and the attachment of the natives to their national religious faiths, are facts of the utmost importance not only for the history of religion, but also for the social history of the Roman Empire.[47]

On the right bank of the Rhine different conditions prevailed. The land annexed by the Romans was rich and fertile, but very thinly populated. For many years it had been a battle-field between Germans and Romans. The conditions were too unsettled to attract permanent settlers in large numbers. To this land the Romans brought peace for the first time. Forts were built, roads constructed, rivers opened to traffic. The forts, which were numerous, occupied the vantage-points on the rivers and the cross-roads. Villages arose around them. The native population began to till the soil more intensively. Settlers flocked to the new lands from Gaul. Veterans received parcels of land in the neighbourhood of the forts. The land near the forts formed their territory, which was exploited by the military authorities: they rented it to soldiers, who certainly sublet it to civilians, both natives and immigrants. But the territory assigned to the forts was never large. When the forts moved forward, the civil population remained and formed a village, a *vicus*. The whole land was state property and the greater part of it was managed as imperial estates (*saltus*) by the imperial administration. These estates were partly left in the hands of the natives, partly given to veteran soldiers, partly sold to immigrants or to richer soldiers and officers.

The more peaceful the conditions became, the more people were attracted to the new lands. New farms were created and new villages developed, some of which assumed the aspect of regular cities. The fact was recognized by the government. The land was subdivided on the pattern of Gaul into *civitates*, the most prosperous village in each becoming its capital and receiving in due time the organization of a city. Yet the region in general retained its rural aspect. Its distinctive feature, as revealed by systematic excavation, was not the villages but the isolated farms. Some of the farms lying near the *limes* were given, more especially in the third century, to active soldiers and became a nursery of recruits, but most of them were comparatively large capitalistic agricultural concerns, not of the same type as the Moselle estates, but rather resembling the Pompeian villas. The typical villa had a large and comfortable, though not luxurious, house, like the big farm of rural America today. The owners were certainly well-to-do men, though they were not wealthy absentee landlords from the cities. According to the nature of the land some of these farms produced corn, others were ranches, where cattle-breeding was extensively carried on. In the capitals of the districts, in the bathing and health resorts, and in the larger villages trade and industry also developed.[48]

In conformity with the economic trend the native population naturally became, for the most part, tenants and shepherds of the foreign farmers. Occasionally we hear of groups of *coloni*, who probably belonged to one or other of the larger estates. Thus on the right bank of the Rhine, as on the left, the population came to be divided into an upper class of well-to-do farmers and a lower class of peasants and tenants.[49]

BRITAIN was practically an annexe of Gaul. The subjugation of the lowlands, which were protected by the military occupation of the Western uplands on the one hand and on the other by the construction of the Roman *limes*, comparable to the German *limes*, against Scotland, amounted in fact to an extension of the provinces of Gaul and Germany northwards, with the shortest possible military frontier. In its social and economic development Roman Britain shows a great similarity to the Rhine lands, especially those on the right bank of the river. The brilliant sketch of the romanization of the province by F. Haverfield enables me to confine myself to a few brief remarks.[50]

Life on the military frontier was, of course, almost identical with that on the Rhine. Peculiar as it is and worth a closer study, it has but little bearing on our subject. City life in the lowlands developed in close connexion with the conquest and the military occupation of the island. The four colonies of Britain (Camulodunum, Glevum, Eburacum, and Lindum) were all of military origin and are comparable therefore to Colonia Agrippinensis, Castra Vetera (or Colonia Ulpia Trajana), Novaesium, Bonna, Moguntiacum, &c., in Germany. The richest commercial city was Londinium, which played in the life of Britain the same part as Trèves and Lyons in the life of Gaul and Germany. The health resort of Bath may be compared with the many watering-places on the Rhine. The other Roman cities of Britain, like most of the cities of Central and Northern Gaul and Upper Germany, were towns of the Celtic population which provided a market for farmers, *chefs-lieux* of tribal and rural districts, the centres of their administrative, religious, commercial, and industrial life. Two of them, Calleva Atrebatum and Venta Silurum, have been thoroughly excavated and they present the picture of a large village with some public buildings.[51]

Like Northern Gaul and Germany, Britain was a land not of cities but of farms and agricultural estates, a land of villas and squires, not of peasants and small proprietors. These landowners were partly Roman emigrants and veterans and their descendants, partly representatives of the native Celtic aristocracy. This character of the lowlands is proved by the widely distributed remains of villas. Although, in accordance with the smaller scale on which life developed in Britain, none of them was as large and as luxurious as the villas of Trèves, the courtyard type represents the houses of great landowners combined with a large farm run on capitalistic lines. The corridor and barn

1. ROMAN VILLA AT CHEDWORTH, GLOS. Reconstructed by A. Forestier (*Illustrated London News*, 1924, 12 July, p. 75). On the excavations, see G. E. Fox in *Arch. Journ.* 44, 1887, pp. 322 ff. and plate, and in *Archaeologia*, 59, 1905, pp. 210 ff., pl. LVII; J. Buckmann and R. W. Hall, *Notes on the Roman Villa at Chedworth, Gloucestershire*, Cirencester (1919).

The villa (see the appended plan) consists of (1) a large court with barns, storehouses, and quarters for the workmen on two sides, and an entrance gate in front, and (2) a smaller court and garden surrounded by three groups of buildings, of which one (the southern wing) housed the servants (?) and another, with a portico in front, formed the residence of the owner. The latter group contains a large dining-room and baths on the ground floor and living-rooms on the first. The dining-room was adorned with a fine mosaic showing figures of the four seasons (compare our pl. LVIII). The third, or northern, wing of the villa was occupied by a forge and by a large fullery (*fullonica*), too large to serve domestic purposes merely, see Chap. V, note 40. On the discovery of a temple near the villa, which is earlier than the villa itself, see R. G. Collingwood and M. V. Taylor, *JRS* 14, 1924, p. 231.

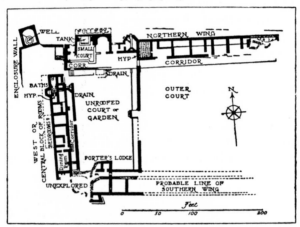

Plan of the villa at Chedworth

2. BRONZE STATUETTE OF A PLOUGHMAN. Found at Piercebridge, in County Durham. British Museum. *British Museum Guide to the Antiquities of Roman Britain* (1922), p. 90; E. Wooler, *The Roman Fort at Piercebridge* (London, 1917), facing p. 148.

The plough is drawn by a team of oxen. The ploughman wears the Celtic dress—a cloak with a hood. Models of a plough and of some agricultural implements have been found in a tumulus in Sussex; see *Guide to the Ant. of Rom. Brit.*, p. 42, fig. 39.

3. HANDLE OF A SILVER *PATERA*. Found in 1747 at Capheaton, Northumberland. British Museum. Bibliography in my article in *JRS* 13, 1923, p. 99, note 5.

The top of the handle is adorned with the bust of an empress, flanked on the left by a traveller carrying his pack and leaning on a stick, and on the right by a shepherd with his sheep; below (not reproduced here) is a temple with figures of Mercury and of Bacchus and Ariadne, and in the corners the personifications of a river and of a seaport. In the article quoted above I have endeavoured to show that this *patera* was probably made in Britain. The handle gives a general picture of the prosperity of the land under the enlightened government of Rome, with safe roads, a wealth of cattle, and communications by river and sea.

4. FUNERAL STELE IN THE FORM OF AN *AEDICULA*. Found at York (Eburacum). Museum of York. Gordon Home, *Roman York* (1924), facing p. 24.

A blacksmith hammering on an anvil a piece of metal which he holds with a pair of tongs.

1. VILLA AT CHEDWORTH (RESTORED BY A. FORESTIER)

2. A BRITISH PLOUGHMAN

3. BRITISH TRAVELLER AND SHEPHERD

4. A BRITISH BLACKSMITH

XL. LIFE AND WORK IN BRITAIN

examples are comparable, from the architectural as well as from the social and economic point of view, with the farms of Upper Germany on the right bank of the Rhine.[52]

It is natural to suppose that the economic and social development of Britain was very similar to that of Gaul and still more to that of the two Germanies. Life was created by the military occupation and lasted as long as the military occupation was real and its protection effective. The lowlands started their economic life under the shelter of the Roman peace, as the hinterland of the armies. The chief consumer of their products was the army: the country itself supplied a market later, but it never played a decisive part in the economic life of the island. Intensive cultivation of the land became profitable because a permanent market in the North and in the West was secured to the producers. The people of Britain soon realized their opportunities and used them. The Celtic landlords who kept their estates developed agriculture and cattle-breeding on the lines familiar to their kinsmen in Gaul. As in the valley of the Moselle, however, the owners of the large estates were mostly rich merchants, the business men of Londinium, who supplied the army with goods from the continent during the first years of the occupation. It was to them that the large courtyard villas belonged. Besides these, there were veterans who received and bought parcels of land, thrifty Celts who adopted the new fashion of intensive agriculture, and new settlers coming from the continent. These were the owners of the corridor and barn farm-houses.[53]

None of these landowners tilled the soil with his own hands or sent his sons and daughters to herd his sheep, pigs, and cows in the meadows and forests. Labour was supplied partly by slaves but mostly by the natives, who inhabited villages of the type of those which were excavated by General Pitt-Rivers near Salisbury and by Mr. D. Atkinson on Lowbury Hill (Berkshire). In the poorer parts of the lowlands the villagers may have possessed their own land and their own pastures, but in the more fertile regions they certainly became shepherds and tenants of the larger and smaller landowners. They learnt to use Roman pots and safety-pins. Those who lived in the cities learnt the Latin language and are probably those who have left the tags from Virgil which we find quoted in inscriptions, but in the mass they remained, like the *fellahîn* of Egypt, strangers to the very essence of Greco-Roman civilization—to city life and all that was connected with it. How large their numbers were as compared with the numbers of the soldiers, the city residents, and the country squires, we are unable to judge.[54]

On the ALPINE PROVINCES of Rome, of which Raetia and Noricum were the largest and most important, we cannot dwell at length. From the social and economic point of view, some parts of these mostly mountainous districts show almost the same features as the adjoining parts of Italy with the large cities of Augusta Taurinorum and Segusio, Augusta Praetoria and Eporedia, Comum, Bergomum, Brixia, Verona, Vicetia, Concordia, and Aquileia, all of which were originally Roman military colonies and became great agricultural centres with extensive territories and numerous Celtic and Raetian tribes attached to them. Other parts of the Alpine districts belong in fact to the mountainous regions of Southern Gaul. RAETIA, the second largest of the Alpine lands, was not very different in social and economic constitution from the adjoining parts of the country behind the *limes* of Upper Germany. At any rate the excavated cities of Raetia present no far-reaching peculiarities to mark them off sharply from those of Upper Germany.[55] In relation to the Upper Danube and its *limes* Augusta Vindelicorum (Augsburg, Augusta), the best known and the most important city of Raetia, probably played the same part as Trèves and Moguntiacum in relation to the Rhine *limes*. This is known, for instance, by the extent to which merchants, and especially merchants in clothes and pottery, figure in its life. Another interesting fact is that Castra Regina (Regensburg, Ratisbon), the largest military fort in Raetia, owned a large tract of land, on part of which the *canabae* of the fort gradually grew up. This military territory is called in an inscription of A.D. 178 *territorium contributum*. It is interesting to see that the chief magistrate of these *canabae* had the title of *aedilis*. We may assume that it was not devoid of inhabitants before it was attached to the fort; and it is probable that its pre-Roman occupants formed one of the numerous *gentes* of Raetia, and that, after the land became Roman, they continued to cultivate it as tenants of the fort.[56] A remarkable instance of a Gallo-Roman *civitas*, an urban centre of a Celtic *pagus*, is Cambodunum, the modern Kempten, the city of the Estiones. It flourished in the first century A.D., when it became an important centre of trade: in the second century its progress was halted, in the third it began to decay. The remains of the city, which have been carefully excavated, illustrate very clearly the rise and formation of a cantonal city, the urban development of which did not depend on military or administrative importance.

The largest of the Alpine provinces was the province, formerly the kingdom, of NORICUM, which had a Celtic population. It comprised the best and the most accessible lands in the Northeast of Italy, and stood for a long time under the influence of Aquileia. The penetration of Italian elements into the cities and valleys of Noricum was facilitated by the fact that the country had for long lived a peaceful life united under the sceptre of a native king. Almost without a struggle the kingdom was transformed by Augustus into a procuratorial province. United with Italy, its valleys soon reached a comparatively high degree of prosperity. Urban life developed, unhampered by wars and rebellions, in many old town centres of the various Celtic tribes, of which the largest were Virunum (the capital), Celeia, Teurnia, and Iuvavum. They all had vast territories, and consisted both of native and of Italian elements. The emperor Claudius organized these Celto-Roman *civitates* on Italian municipal models and gave to the more important centres of urban life the constitution of *municipia*. The inhabitants of the cities who were not Roman citizens received the Latin citizenship, while the country people, the peasants and shepherds, remained *peregrini* and retained their native habits and customs indefinitely, especially in the remote corners of the land, like Iuenna and the valley of Lavan.

The chief economic resources of Noricum were rich iron and lead mines, forests, excellent pasture land, and some good fields. These were mostly in the hands of the rich city *bourgeoisie*. The mines were owned chiefly by the state and were run, as in Dalmatia and Spain, through the medium of substantial 'entrepreneurs' (*conductores*). The forests, pasture lands, and fields belonged to the citizens of the cities. The less attractive parts of the territory were probably left in the hands of the native *peregrini*.[57]

We now turn to the lands inhabited by the two leading races of the Danube region—the ILLYRIANS and the THRACIANS. One section of the Illyrians, which had a strong admixture of Celtic

Description of Plate XLI

1–3. THE LARGE VILLA ON THE ISLAND OF BRIONI GRANDE NEAR POLA.

The villa was excavated by the Austrian Archaeological Institute. The director of the excavations, A. Gnirs, carried out the work with the greatest care and achieved splendid results. Fig. 3 (*Oest. Jahresh.* 10, 1907, Beibl., pp. 43–44, fig. 1) gives a general view of Val Catena, the charming bay around which the buildings of the villa were erected.

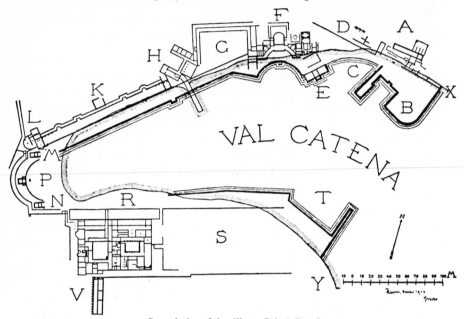

General plan of the villa on Brioni Grande

At the narrow end of the bay (see the above plan, reproduced from *Oest. Jahresh.* 18, 1915, Beibl., pp. 133–4, fig. 54) there was a fine quay, with three temples connected by a semicircular portico (fig. 1, from *Oest. Jahresh.* 7, 1904, Beibl., pp. 139–40, fig. 23). One of the temples (N on the plan) was probably dedicated to Neptune. Fig. 2 (*Oest. Jahresh.* 18, 1915, Beibl., pp. 127–8, fig. 52) gives the restoration of the main building of the villa, the so-called 'terrace-building'. The villa was built on a large *podium* rising above the quay. A long portico formed its front; the left (East) wing, built round a spacious court, was occupied by the business-rooms, the most notable being those used for making oil; the right (West) wing was a gorgeous dwelling-house. The other prominent buildings of the villa, as shown on the plan, are the harbour (B), the fish-tank (E), large bath-rooms, *thermae* (F), the long portico on the quay (K), a pavilion-like building (*diaeta*) at the end of the portico (L), another *diaeta* with a peristyle and an *atrium* (H), a garden (S), and a large water-tank (V). On the water-supply of the large villas in Histria generally, and on the cisterns of the villa on Brioni Grande, cf. A. Gnirs, *Strena Buličiana* (1924), pp. 138 ff.

1. THE THREE TEMPLES OF THE VILLA ON BRIONI GRANDE
(Restored by A. Gnirs)

2. THE MAIN BUILDING OF THE SAME VILLA
(Restored by A. Gnirs)

3. GENERAL VIEW OF VAL CATENA AND OF THE RUINS OF THE VILLA

XLI. A HISTRIAN VILLA

blood, namely Histria, became part of Italy at an early date; another which shared the land with Thracian and Celtic tribes was incorporated in the Roman Empire as the province of Illyricum, to be later subdivided into the mainly Illyrian provinces of Dalmatia and the two Pannonias, and the chiefly Thracian provinces of Moesia Superior and Moesia Inferior, the former being Thraco-Illyrian, the latter almost purely Thracian. The absence of any general work of recent date on the Illyrian and Thracian provinces, comparable to the volumes of C. Jullian, F. Haverfield, F. Cumont, K. Schumacher, and F. Stähelin on the Celtic and German parts of the Empire, necessitates a more detailed description of the social and economic conditions which prevailed in Histria, on the shores of the Adriatic sea, and on the Danube and its tributaries.[58]

In the early period of its life HISTRIA was not a land of barbarians. The excavations carried out in the native towns, the so-called *castellieri*, some of which were afterwards replaced by Roman cities, show that a high degree of civilization was reached as early as the late Mycenaean period. Histria was colonized by the Romans very early (chiefly in the first century B.C.) and became thoroughly romanized, so far at least as the large cities of the coast were concerned—Tergeste, though it did not belong to Histria from the administrative point of view, Parentium, and above all Pola with her beautiful harbour. The territories of these cities were to a large extent owned by the emperors and by the Italians resident in them, among whom there was but a slight admixture of native blood. (We leave aside the usual freedmen of many nations and a certain number of Greeks and Orientals.) One of the most prominent and most active Italian families was the family of the Laekanii in Pola, which may be compared in respect of its various economic activities with the family of the Barbii in Aquileia. Pola was full of members of this family, both descendants of the original Laekanii and freedmen and descendants of freedmen of the various members of it.[59]

These men introduced into the Histrian peninsula the scientific and capitalistic cultivation of land. Almost the whole of South Histria was transformed into an olive plantation, and so were the islands in the bay of Pola, especially the charming island Brioni Grande with its beautiful villa, a combination of a real palace and an enormous farm, which was thoroughly excavated

Description of Plate XLII

1. BAS-RELIEF ON COLUMN OF TRAJAN. Rome, Forum Traiani. C. Cichorius, *Die Reliefs der Traianssäule*, pl. xxv and text ii, pp. 155 ff.; S. Reinach, *Rép. d. rel.* i, p. 339, 27 and 28.

Departure of Trajan for his second expedition. Soldiers load expeditionary equipment on a river-vessel. Trajan himself, his staff, and a detachment of praetorians prepare to embark on another barge equipped with a cabin. The rowers are undoubtedly citizens and natives of the province. On the bank stands a large, well-built and fortified city, probably a city of the Danubian lands, perhaps Siscia on the Save; outside it is a stone amphitheatre. Close to the amphitheatre can be seen the *navalia*, the river-port of the city, with a large warehouse and two arches, one of which (that near the river) is crowned by a *biga*. Representations of sea- and river-ports are common on the reliefs of the column, but none can be identified with any certainty (cf. K. Lehmann-Hartleben, 'Die antiken Hafenanlagen des Mittelmeeres', *Klio*, Beiheft 14, 1923, pp. 228 ff.). Our relief shows how important the river-ports of the Danubian regions were. Certainly the *navalia* were not constructed for purely military purposes.

2. FUNERARY ALTAR FOUND AT SKELANI (Dalmatia). C. Patsch, 'Arch.-ep. Untersuchungen zur Gesch. d. röm. Prov. Dalmatien, VII', *Wiss. Mitt. aus Bosnien*, ii, 1890, p. 155, figs. 63–64.

Altar with a fragmentary and almost illegible inscription. On two sides of it the same man is represented; on one side he is shown standing in local dress, with a cane in his right hand and a bunch of ears of corn in his left; on the other side, he appears as a cobbler, with a shoe or a boot-tree in his right hand, and beside him the tools of his trade. The relief provides an excellent illustration of the acquisition of land by a native who had begun his career as a cobbler in a small city, or alternatively of the augmentation of the income of an owner or peasant from the profits of a cobbler's shop in the town.

1. RIVER-PORT AND CITY ON THE DANUBE

2. OWNER OF A PROPERTY AND COBBLER'S
SHOP IN DALMATIA

XLII. ECONOMIC LIFE IN THE DANUBIAN LANDS

by A. Gnirs and is the best example of a large villa of this type in the Roman world, whether in Italy or in the provinces. Remains of many other large and fine villas, which were centres of large estates, and the ruins of many scattered farm-houses, probably parts of these estates, have been found and partially excavated by local archaeologists and by the Austrian Archaeological Institute. They show a close similarity to the Pompeian and Stabian villas, except that production was concentrated not on wine (which was probably produced in no very large quantities) but on olive-oil. Another difference between the Pompeian and the Histrian villas is that the latter were the centres not of medium-sized estates but (at least in the best-known cases) of regular *latifundia* of a type similar to those of Gaul, Britain, Belgium, Germany, and Africa.[60]

Italians resident in the Histrian cities also owned large factories of tiles and jars, situated near Tergeste and Pola. These tiles and jars were used in Histria and Dalmatia and throughout the Danube lands. It is probable that the Italians who owned the large estates also bought up the wool produced by the native tribes in the mountains which lay behind the cities. Some flocks of sheep, no doubt, were owned by the city people and shepherded by their slaves. From this wool were made the famous Histrian woollen garments which competed with the slightly rougher and more primitive Gallic articles.[61]

Much less romanized was the interior of the peninsula and the land behind the territory of Tergeste. Tergeste itself was originally an Illyrian settlement and afterwards a village of the Celtic Carni. We have already quoted the inscription (Dessau, *ILS* 6680) which speaks of the Carni and Catali as being attached to Tergeste: their conditions of life were probably of the primitive rural type. Their 'chiefs' became Roman citizens, but the other members of these tribes probably never attained the Roman franchise. The same is true of the Illyrian tribes in Histria, as is shown by the Latin inscriptions they have left, for instance, those of the territory of Nesactium and Piquentum.[62]

The Illyrians of DALMATIA, PANNONIA, and of one part of MOESIA SUPERIOR were not a pure race. The earliest population of these lands was Thracian. Then came the Illyrians, who enslaved it. Later appeared the Celts, who mixed with the most important of the Illyrian tribes—the Liburnians, Dalmatians,

Iapudians, and Maezaeans in the Northern parts of the Adriatic area, and the Taulantians, the Encheleians, and the Ardiaeans in the Southern regions. The Illyrians when they first came into contact with the Romans (in the third century B.C.) had, like the Iberians in Spain, a long historical life behind them. In the late Bronze and in the early Iron Age they had been strongly influenced by the late Minoan civilization. Very early they had come into touch with the Greeks. Under these influences they developed a material civilization of their own, which was affected also by the civilization of their kinsmen on the Italian side of the Adriatic Sea. It shows many distinctive features of an interesting kind.

Socially, the various Illyrian tribes lived under rather primitive conditions. The distinctive features of their life were very similar to those of the Iberians. The tribes and clans had their centres in fortified towns on the tops of hills and mountains; grazing and agriculture were their main occupations; in some cases there existed a peculiar system of redistributing the land among the members of the tribe and the clans every eight years. Like the Iberians in Spain, the Illyrians formed from time to time larger political units under monarchical rule—the Encheleians near Apollonia and the Taulantians near Epidamnus, later the Ardiaeans, and finally the Dalmatians. But these states showed no real cohesion and were somewhat loose federations of tribes and clans rather than centralized monarchical states.[63]

The Romans dealt with the Illyrians and the Celto-Illyrians in the same way as they did with the Iberians and the Celt-Iberians. At a very early date they entered into diplomatic and commercial relations with the cities on the coast and protected the early Greek settlements and cities in the Illyrian lands. The more such Roman influence on Illyrian affairs asserted itself during the long period of renewed wars against the leading tribes, the closer did these relations become. In the second and first centuries B.C., when the military power of the Illyrians was broken for ever (although some tribes still maintained a nominal independence), large groups of Italian merchants and money-dealers settled in the more important maritime cities. It was they who, along with the earlier Greek emigrants and with the more or less hellenized natives, carried on the maritime trade, which since remotest times had been the life-blood of the cities.

They were assisted by the clever seamanship of the Illyrians, always famous as pirates. These now took service as sailors with the mercantile marine, and later provided a considerable part of the crews of the Imperial fleet of Ravenna (as the Egyptians did of the fleet of Misenum). When the Illyrian lands were finally annexed to the Roman Empire (in the time of Augustus from about 33 B.C. and under his first successors), the Romans transformed these cities into colonies: Senia, Iader, Salonae, Narona, and Epidaurum were the first to be colonized. Colonization meant the creation of almost purely Italian centres of urban life. To the colonies were assigned large tracts of the best arable land. Many of the colonists became prosperous landowners and probably used the native population as tenants and labourers. Some families resident in these cities were real pioneers in the new lands. They built villas in the lowlands of Dalmatia and introduced the capitalistic methods established in Italy and in Histria. Lumbering and grazing were their earliest forms of activity. Later came the production of corn, and still later the cultivation of vines and olive-trees.[64] Besides the cities, two legionary fortresses were established in the country, at Burnum and Delminium, as well as scores of smaller forts. In the time of Vespasian, however, the legions were removed from Dalmatia to Pannonia, though some of the smaller forts remained. These military establishments no doubt contributed largely to the romanization of the country. One of them—that at Burnum—owned large pasture lands in the neighbourhood.[65]

Meanwhile culture was gradually extending far into the interior of the Dalmatian country. Extensive recruiting among the Illyrian tribes gradually created a more or less romanized native aristocracy, consisting of the veterans who returned to their tribes and villages after completing their service in the auxiliary regiments. To these aristocratic elements Vespasian assigned the leading role in tribal life, and out of them and some Italian immigrants he formed the new *bourgeoisie* of the urbanized towns and fortified places of refuge in Dalmatia. His policy here was the same as that which he pursued in Spain and had the same end in view. The tribal organization afforded no guarantees of security. On the other hand Rome needed the tribes to provide recruits for the auxiliary troops. The only way out of the difficulty was to split up the tribes and to put control in the

Description of Plate XLIII

1. LOWER PART OF A PANNONIAN FUNERAL STELE. Found in Serbia. Museum of Belgrade. My article in *Röm. Mitt.* 26, 1911, p. 278, fig. 2; S. Reinach, *Rép. d. rel.* ii, p. 160, 2.

The office of a banker or a business man. The banker (in Roman dress) is seated on a chair near a folding wall-table. In his left hand he holds a triptych, his ledger (*codex accepti et expensi*), and on the table before him lies a large bag containing coins—the day's takings. In front of the table stands a slave reading his daily report from the *adversaria* or *ephemerides* (the daily record-book). On the book-keeping of the Romans, see R. Beigel, *Rechnungswesen und Buchführung der Römer* (1904) and cf. C. Bardt, *Woch. kl. Phil.* 1905, pp. 13 ff. On the development of civilization and art in Pannonia, A. Hekler, *Strena Buličiana* (1924), pp. 208 ff.

FIG. 4. *Agriculture in Moesia*

2. BAS-RELIEF OF A VOTIVE ALTAR (?). Unfinished. Found at St. Martin-am-Bacher (Pannonia) in the vicinity of stone quarries. Museum of Ptuj. V. Skrabar, *Strena Buličiana* (1924), p. 159, fig. 9.

A miner (or perhaps rather the god of the miners, Hercules or Silvanus Saxanus) in a gallery, half-naked, attacking the wall of the mine in front of him with a heavy mining pick or hammer. Near him are some quarried slabs of marble. The figure recalls Statius' well-known description of the Dalmatian gold-mines (*Silvae,* iv. 7. 13 ff.): 'quando te dulci Latio remittent | Dalmatae montes ubi Dite viso | pallidus fossor redit erutoque | concolor auro?' It is worthy of note that, for Statius, Dalmatia and Spain were the main gold-producing lands (*Silvae,* iii. 3. 89–90, cf. 1. 2. 153). Cf. our pl. xxxv, 1 (Spanish miners).

3. AKROTERION OF A SARCOPHAGUS. Found at Salona. Museum of Split. [K. Prijatelj, *Vjes. za arh. i hist. Dalm.* 53, 1950–1 (Split, 1952), p. 142, and pl. xii.] 4th cent. A.D.

Bust of a *femina stolata,* who certainly belonged to the local aristocracy. I owe the photograph to the kindness of Prof. M. Abramič.

4. FUNERAL *CIPPUS* FOUND AT ULMETUM IN MOESIA INFERIOR. Museum of Bucharest. *CIL* iii. 12491; V. Pârvan, *Inceputurile vieṭii Romane la gurile Dunarii* (1923), pp. 52 ff., figs. 31–33; see note 91 to p. 251. Fig. 4.

The *cippus* was erected on the tomb of a certain C. Iulius C. f. Quadratus, *princeps loci* and *quinquennalis* of the *territorium Capidavense.* The upper part shows the god Silvanus, the protector of agriculture and grazing; the lower, a man ploughing a field. On the other side a herd in a forest is visible.

1. A PANNONIAN BANKER

2. A PANNONIAN MINER

3. A DALMATIAN MATRON

XLIII. BUSINESS LIFE IN PANNONIA AND DALMATIA

XLIV. LIFE AND WORK IN DALMATIA:
A DALMATIAN BOATMAN

Description of Plate XLIV

FUNERARY STELE. Found in fragments in the Byzantine walls of Salona. Museum of Split. [M. Abramič, *Spomenici iz bedema stare Salonae, Vjes. za arh. i. pov. Dalm.* 50, 1928/9 (Split, 1929), pp. 56 ff.; K. Prijatelj, *Vjes. za arh. i hist. Dalm.,* 53, 1950–1 (Split, 1952), pp. 142 ff., and pl. VIII.] 1st cent. A.D.

The upper part of the stele was occupied by busts of the deceased. At the bottom a sailing-ship. The inscription says: *C. Utius Sp(uri) f(ilius) testament(o)* | *fieri iussit sibi et* | *P. Utio fratri suo et Clodia(e)* | *F[au]stae concubinae suae.* | *Mult[a per]agratus ego terraque marique* | *debit[um re]ddidi in patria, nunc situs hic iaceo.* | *Stat l[apis e]t nomen, vestigia nulla.* [=*L'An. Ep.* 1933, 74.] C. Utius was undoubtedly a merchant or a ship's captain, more probably the former, since he speaks of journeys by both land and sea in his metrical epitaph. His humble origin is to be noted. I owe the photograph to the kindness of Professor M. Abramič.

hands of the more or less romanized, or at least disciplined, members who had already served in the Roman army. On them was imposed also the obligation of furnishing recruits for the legions. As was natural—and here again we have an analogy to Spain—many of the new cities were transferred from the hill tops to the plain: cities situated in the plain were much safer for the Romans than eagle-nests on the tops of steep hills and mountains.[66]

The new *municipia* received in the usual way large and fertile tracts of land which were carved out of the tribal territories. Most of this land was divided among the newly created citizens, while the rest of the tribal territory remained in the hands of its previous owners, who formed the country population and were not inscribed on the roll of citizens but remained in the condition of *peregrini*. From the economic point of view, many of these *incolae* gradually became tenants of the well-to-do landowners, who lived in the city.[67] Alongside of agriculture a lively commerce grew up within the province and with other provinces, as well as local industries. On the funeral altar of a citizen of a municipality in the rich valley of the Drinus the deceased is represented twice: on one side of the stone as a landowner with ears of corn in his hand, and on the other side as a shoemaker.[68] Some of the members of the city aristocracy became very wealthy and owned large areas of arable and pasture land; as rich men they entered the imperial service, attained equestrian rank, and even occupied a seat in the Roman senate.[69]

A good example of one of these native cities is Doclea, formerly the fortified refuge of the tribe of the Docleates. It was excavated by a Russian archaeologist, and the results were admirably published by an Italian scholar of Trieste. Under Vespasian the town became a *municipium*. Its citizens consisted of native *principes* (leading men of the tribe), veterans, and immigrants from Salonae and Narona. The city soon became rich and prosperous: we find its wealthy landowners building a large forum with a handsome basilica, some temples, and a large bath. The same may be said of many inland cities of Dalmatia (for example, Asseria behind Iader).[70] It is worthy of note that none of these cities was granted the rank of a colony. The last colony was created by Claudius (Colonia Claudia Aequum); even under Hadrian, who established a new series of *municipia*, no Dalmatian city received the higher status.

The policy of the government was the same as we found in Spain, and in both countries it was evidently dictated by the same motives. The *municipia* were intended to break up the tribal life of Dalmatia. Their creation did not, however, mean that romanization was already achieved: it was a step towards that end, not a crown set on a work already accomplished. Moreover, a thorough romanization of city and country was not in the interest of the Roman government, as it deprived the state of excellent recruits both for the legions and the auxiliary troops. In these circumstances it is not surprising that the work of romanization was never completed in Dalmatia. Even in the cities the population was not at all thoroughly romanized, much less in their territories. Further, many of the tribes were never urbanized, but remained as they had been, and continued to live in the old fashion. The proof is given by scores of inscriptions on boundary-stones which describe the delimitation of territories between the various Dalmatian tribes. It is characteristic of the conditions prevailing in the country that a purely Roman 'centuriation', or delimitation, of the land was never carried out there, as it had been, at least to a certain extent, in Pannonia, Dacia, and Africa. Clearly, apart from some exceptions, the old-fashioned mode of cultivating the land remained, and a Roman division into *centuriae* was not required: all that was needed was a fair distribution of the land between the tribes and the newly created *municipia*.[71]

From the economic point of view, one of the greatest attractions of Dalmatia for the Romans was the rich iron mines which had been exploited by the natives from time immemorial. To the Romans the possession of them was extremely important for providing the Danube armies with arms and weapons; they were as important and as vital as the Gallic mines were for the Rhine army. Naturally, therefore, they were very soon taken under imperial administration and managed by special contractors under the direction of imperial procurators. The labour employed in them was supplied by the native tribes, whose members had been accustomed to this work for centuries. About the conditions under which they worked we have no knowledge, but we may suppose that they were similar to those which prevailed in the mines of Spain, where single pits were farmed out to individual miners.[72]

Similar was the social and economic development of the frontier provinces with a Celto-Illyrian or Thraco-Illyrian population—the two PANNONIAS and MOESIA SUPERIOR, which were the main centres of the military life of the Empire on the Danube frontier. We do not propose to describe the phases of the conquest and of the military occupation of these lands. That has been done in a masterly way by Mommsen and his collaborators in the *Corpus* of Latin Inscriptions, vol. iii, and the general outlines of the process were summarized by Mommsen in the fifth volume of his *Roman History*. New evidence has been supplied by the excavations carried out by the Austrians and their successors in some of the most important camps: Poetovio, Lauriacum, Carnuntum, and Aquincum.[73] For the purpose of this book it will be sufficient to say a few words about the main features of social and economic life in these provinces.

The progress of city life on the middle Danube, on the Save, and on the Drave, was determined by the great Roman military centres, which gradually moved from the Save to the Drave, and finally to the Danube. Siscia and Sirmium on the Save, Poetovio and Mursa on the Drave, Vindobona, Carnuntum, Brigetio, Aquincum, Singidunum, Viminacium, and Ratiaria on the Danube, and Scupi in the land of the unruly Dardanians, were all great fortresses of the legions and some of them remained so to the end of the Roman domination. Mursa was the chief station of the Danube fleet. The Roman troops, however, were not planted in a desert land. Celtic, Illyrian, and Thraco-Illyrian tribes occupied these regions, and they were not exterminated by the Romans. In fact most, if not all, of the fortresses were built in the immediate vicinity of large Celtic, Illyrian, and Thracian villages. Such a village certainly existed near Carnuntum; Siscia was an important Illyrian town, the capital of the tribe of the Colapiani; Scupi was a citadel of the Dardanians, and Ratiaria of the Moesians (Thracians). To meet the needs of the troops, large stretches of fertile land, meadows, woods, &c., were taken from the native tribes and assigned to the fortresses. The *prata legionum* are often mentioned in inscriptions. In the second and third centuries these lands were usually let out to soldiers for exploitation;[74] the larger part of a legion's territory, however, was not exploited directly by them, but was left in the hands of the inhabitants of the villages (*vici*), who probably were obliged to deliver part of the produce of their fields, meadows, forests, fisheries, and so forth to the fortress and to help the soldiers by personal labour. A good illustration of the use of native labour is furnished by the funeral *cippus* of a soldier belonging to the fortress at Carnuntum. In the pediment the deceased is represented, with a *virga* in his hand, leading a rustic cart dragged by two oxen and driven by an Illyrian peasant, who holds a whip and an axe. It is clear that the soldier was in charge of wood-cutting for the fortress, and employed for this purpose the services of one of the peasants of the neighbouring village (see pl. LXXIV, 2).[75]

Thus the territories of the legions and the native tribes which lived on them were under the management and control of the military authorities. The extent of these *prata legionum* is unknown to us. It is difficult to suppose that the lands of all the tribes which lived near the Danube were regarded, in the strict sense of the word, as territories of the different legions. But whatever the size of the *prata* may have been, the development of the fortresses was uniform all over the Danube provinces. Near them settlements of civilians, the so-called *canabae*, gradually grew up. On the other hand, the native villages assigned to the legions were gradually invaded by foreigners, mostly former soldiers of the fortress concerned, who settled down in them, organized a community of Roman citizens, and introduced Roman habits and customs and the use of the Latin language. We know, for instance, of a prosperous community of this type in the neighbourhood of Aquincum, called *vicus Vindonianus*, some of the members of which were even Roman knights.[76] Gradually these native *vici* coalesced with the *canabae* of the fort to form one settlement, which assumed the aspect of a real city. Fora and basilicae, baths, theatres, and amphitheatres were built, the streets were paved, the city style of house was adopted, and to this amalgamation of *canabae* and native *vici* were finally granted the rights of a *municipium* or a colony.[77]

Those parts of the Danubian provinces which were not, in the strict sense of the word, assigned to the forts but which maintained their tribal organization were ruled, at any rate in the first century A.D., as in Dalmatia, by military officers (*praefecti*) appointed by the emperor or by the governor of the province. Such a prefect of the tribe of the Colapiani was the well-known

Antonius Naso.[78] Gradually, however, urban life developed on those territories also, and some of the chief villages were transformed into *municipia*, while others were obliged to receive a colony of Roman veterans. In this way arose such cities as Savaria, Solva, and Scarbantia in Pannonia, and Ulpiana, Margum, and Naissus in Moesia Superior. Colonies of Roman veterans were sent out also to Poetovio in Pannonia and to Scupi in Moesia Superior, which had been in origin important military fortresses.[79] The transformation of such towns and villages into Roman cities meant, of course, at the outset a revision of the rights of property in the land. The best part was given to the colonists or to the citizens of the new city, the worst was left to the common members of the tribe. The land assigned to the colonists was usually centuriated in the Roman fashion.[80] In the territories of these colonies and *municipia* large tracts of land were gradually concentrated in the hands of a few landowners, partly natives and veterans, partly foreigners. In the territory of Ulpiana, for example, large estates were owned in the third century by a member of the senatorial class, a certain C. Furius Octavianus. Near Singidunum a native *princeps loci* built for himself and his family a beautiful tomb gorgeously painted and adorned with statues of the owner and of the members of his family. There is no doubt that labour for these large estates was furnished partly by a lively commerce in slaves from the other side of the Danube, partly by the native population.[81]

How much land was still owned by the native tribes and how many villages which were not assigned to one or other of the cities existed in Pannonia and Moesia Superior in the second and third centuries, we cannot say. Districts like Dardania no doubt retained their ancient tribal organization for a very long time, perhaps in perpetuity. But even in the regions assigned to cities and forts life retained its rustic character, and the land never became thoroughly urbanized and romanized. A glance at the Pannonian and Moesian funeral monuments shows to what an extent the natives retained their original habits and customs.[82]

Different was the aspect presented by the province of DACIA, the last acquisition of the Romans on the banks of the Danube. After the terrible war which was carried out in two campaigns by Trajan and after a systematic extermination of the best of the natives, Dacia became a land of intensive colonization, save in some districts which were left to the native tribes. The gold mines of the province were worked by Dalmatians, the Pirustae, who were brought thither from their native land. The arable land was measured out and distributed to colonists, most of whom came from the East (as, for instance, from Galatia). We must also remember the strong garrison of the new frontiers. In the many prosperous cities settled a motley crowd of ex-soldiers, Greek and Oriental merchants and artisans, and others. The land was rich and offered the most varied opportunities to the new settlers. We need not be surprised that an opulent *bourgeoisie* soon grew up in the cities. Thus we know of a family of Apulum which played, as traders and landowners, almost the same part in the life of the province as the family of the Barbii in Aquileia and in the provinces of Noricum and Pannonia.[83]

The original population of Dacia consisted mainly of THRA-CIANS, a large and powerful nation with a long and glorious history. Like the Illyrians, the Thracians belonged to the Indo-European stock and were closely connected in culture and religion with the population of Macedonia and Greece. The history of the Thracians is the history of a permanent struggle against enemies who threatened them from East, North, West, and South. Scythians, Illyrians, Celts, and Macedonians all tried to conquer the Thracian land and all failed. The Romans succeeded, but not without a long and bitter struggle in the Balkan and Transylvanian mountains and in the plains of Hungary and Romania.

Of the social and economic life of the Thracians we know very little. They have left but one written document, and this we are unable to understand. The archaeological evidence is as yet meagre and poor. The only ascertained fact about their social and economic life is that they were an agricultural people, a people whose life was concentrated in villages, not in cities. Some of their villages were fortified; one may have been the residence of the king, the capital of one or many tribes. But they were not real centres of urban life: we never hear of any large development of industry or commerce in them. The inhabitants of the villages were and remained peasants, tillers of the soil, hunters, fishermen, cattle-breeders. Their internal organization was tribal. The exchange of goods between the tribes took the form

Description of Plate XLV

1–2. THE LOWER PART OF THE COLUMN OF TRAJAN AT ROME. Rome, Forum of Trajan. C. Cichorius, *Die Reliefs der Traianssäule*, pls. IV–XX, text ii, pp. 17 ff.; K. Lehmann-Hartleben, *Die Trajanssäule*, 1926, pls. V–VI.

The first band of the decoration of the column is intended to give a glimpse of the lower course of the river Danube. The spectator is on the Dacian, or left, bank of the river; what is portrayed is the Roman, or right, bank. The first section (fig. 1, band 1) shows the system of fortifications on the lower Danube, along the flat bank of the river where it flows through modern Bulgaria and Romania. The Roman bank is protected by high wooden towers (*burgi*) surrounded by palisades. The ground floors of these towers were used as living-quarters by the garrison of auxiliary soldiers (cavalry and infantry), while the upper floor, furnished with a gallery, served as an observation-post from which the enemy could be watched and signals given by means of torches. Near the towers are seen piles of wood and straw, which may be interpreted as stocks of material for the repair of the buildings and of fodder for the horses, but more probably represent beacons laid ready for kindling (von Domaszewski, *Marcussäule*, p. 109, note). The next section (fig. 2, band 1, left part) shows more civilized conditions of life on the river. Soldiers are shipping supplies for the army up the river from the Greek cities at the mouth of the Danube and from South Russia, or down the river from North Italy and Aquileia; one barge is loaded with wine, another with the heavy baggage of the soldiers. On the bank of the river are two villages or Roman landing-places and depots—the nuclei of future cities—both fortified by palisades. Farther up the river begin the hills (fig. 2, band 1, right part). A city is built on the steep bank of the Danube and soldiers are bringing wine to it. Behind this city in the hills a strong fortress covers an important road into the interior of the country and another along the river. The bas-reliefs give an excellent summary of the military and civilizing work done by the Roman soldiers on the Danube. The cities and landing-places are types, and cannot be identified with any of the inhabited places on the Danube. Higher up (band 2) begins the story of Trajan's first campaign in the Dacian lands. The emperor has crossed the river and offers sacrifice to the gods in the presence of his soldiers before his camp, within which is seen his large tent (fig. 1, band 2). One of the next episodes is an address delivered by Trajan to his troops (fig. 2, band 2). The following pictures deal mostly with the work of fortifying the land occupied by the Romans, for the purpose of securing the rear of their army. Fig. 1, band 3, shows the construction of fortifications near a river on which a newly built bridge is seen; fig. 2, band 3, depicts the construction of a wooden bridge and of a stone fortress. As the Romans intended to remain in the land, all such constructions had more than a merely military purpose. Roman trade and civilization marched with the troops across the bridges, and concentrated in the new fortified centres of Roman life.

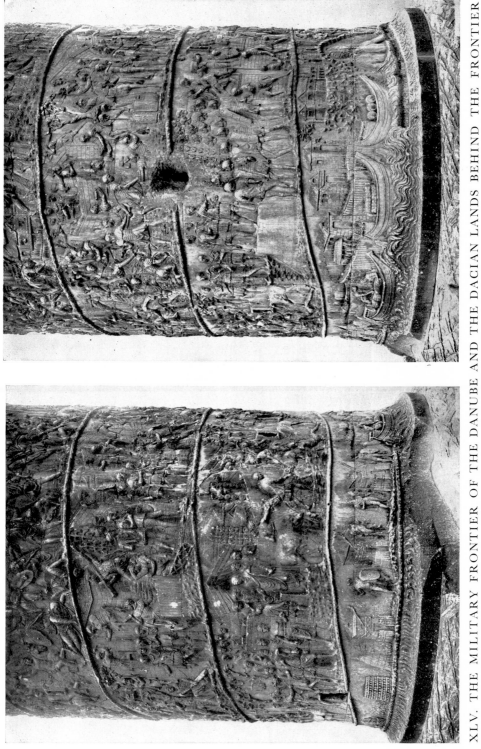

XLV. THE MILITARY FRONTIER OF THE DANUBE AND THE DACIAN LANDS BEHIND THE FRONTIER

(Column of Trajan)

of seasonal fairs, which are still the chief feature of the commercial life of many Slavonic peoples.[84]

The Thracians first came into contact with the Romans on the lower Danube in MOESIA INFERIOR, which was not organized as a procuratorial province till after the annexation of the Balkan Thracians by Claudius, and as a regular imperial province only after Trajan's Dacian Wars, but, had, in fact, been in vassalage to Rome since the time of Augustus and Tiberius.[85] The first to recognize Roman supremacy were the Greek cities on the Western shores of the Black Sea, formerly rich and powerful centres of Greek life—Histria, Tomi, Callatis, Dionysopolis, Odessos.[86] Their only chance of regaining something of their old prosperity was the establishment of a strong political force on the Danube and Black Sea. When the Roman government secured the lower Danube by a chain of fortresses (Oescus, Novae, Ratiaria, and from the time of Trajan, Durostorum and Troesmis), the Thracian tribes on the lower Danube and near the shores of the Black Sea became, by force of circumstances, the hinterland both of the Roman fortresses and of the old Greek cities. Without a reasonable economic and social organization in the rich land between the Danube and the Black Sea both fortresses and cities would be dependent on uncertain imports of foodstuffs from far distant regions. This was the reason why the Romans paid so much attention to the organization of the province of Lower Moesia and displayed so much interest in the affairs of the Greek cities on the Black Sea within and beyond the Roman frontier—at the mouth of the Dniester (Tyras) and the Dnieper (Olbia), and in the Crimea. So long as Dacia was independent, even the most intensive exploitation of the Dobrudja could not provide both the Roman army and the cities with sufficient quantities of foodstuffs. Import from South Russia was, therefore, welcome; and this meant that the Roman government must police the Black Sea and afford military protection to the Greek cities in South Russia.[87]

As in Dacia and Thrace, so also in Moesia Inferior, the foundations of the urbanization of the country were laid by Trajan after the conquest of Dacia. Trajan granted the status of Roman colonies to the stations which had grown up near the camps of Ratiaria and Oescus, after the legions had been transferred thence to Singidunum and Troesmis, and founded the new cities of Tropaeum Traiani, Nicopolis ad Istrum, and Marcianopolis. However the region was never wholly romanized; it remained a country of villages and large areas of open country.

The social and economic organization of the province involved first of all a revision of rights to ownership of landed property. The land was subdivided into territories belonging to the fortresses, to the Greek cities, and to the native inhabitants. A number of the latter had been transplanted thither by the Romans, who had forced them to migrate from the mountains of modern Bulgaria and from the lands beyond the Danube. As regards the military territories, the measures taken in Moesia Inferior did not differ from those adopted in Dalmatia, Pannonia, and Moesia Superior, and development followed the same lines.[88] In the ancient Greek cities the Romans endeavoured above all to revive their decaying economic life and to impart fresh vigour to it by attracting new settlers. It is quite clear that for this purpose they enlarged their territories and attached to them many native villages. To the new and old citizens they freely granted the Roman franchise. The inhabitants of the villages which became attached to the cities had, of course, no share in their government. From the Roman point of view they were and remained *peregrini*, from the point of view of the cities they were 'by-dwellers' (*incolae*, πάροικοι). On the other hand, when dwellers in the cities acquired land in the territories of the villages, they became members of the village communities. Being its richest members, they were recognized along with the native elders of the community as the 'senate' of the village, and as such they elected or nominated the 'chiefs', the *magistri* or *magistratus*. All the villages of a given territory appointed in turn one person to represent the territory. This man received the title of *quinquennalis* and probably had the duty of apportioning among the landowners of the villages the payments due to the state and to the city as well as personal services.[89]

The same type of organization developed in the territories of the native tribes. Here also the Roman citizens, who were mostly veterans and immigrants from the other Danube provinces, played an important part in the life of the village communities. These new settlers were, of course, the chief romanizing influences, but in fact they never succeeded in absorbing the native population and thoroughly romanizing it. With a few wealthier natives, who had assimilated Roman culture, they formed a small minority of well-to-do landowners amid the mass of peasants and tenants who worked the land for them.[90]

On the south of Moesia Inferior, in the hilly and mountainous land of the modern Bulgarians, the Thracians, who had been subjects of the Odrysian dynasty but from the time of Claudius were incorporated in the Roman province of THRACE, retained for about a century their ancient organization and their tribal and village life.[91] Hundreds of villages were scattered over the hills, mountains, valleys, and plains. Their inhabitants were hard-working peasants, tillers of the soil, shepherds, gardeners, hunters, just as they are today. To the Roman army they furnished sturdy and brave foot-soldiers and excellent horse. For the sake of an abundant supply of these soldiers to serve in the numerous cohorts of Thracians, the Roman government left the internal organization of the country as it had been under the kings. The main unit was the village; a certain number of villages formed a 'komarchy' (κωμαρχία); all the villages of a tribe or, in other words, an aggregate of 'komarchies' represented the administrative and territorial unit of a tribe (φυλή). Finally, one or more tribes formed a district (στρατηγία) under a military commander.[92]

The Roman peace and the good opportunities of selling their farm produce to the agents of the Roman military establishments and to the merchants of the Greek cities of the coast (Mesembria, Anchialus, Apollonia on the Black Sea, and Aenus, Maroneia, Abdera on the Aegean) brough wealth to the Thracian peasants. Their old tribal market-places, where the seasonal fairs (ἐμπόρια) were held, gradually developed into real towns. Some new market-places like the ἐμπόριον of Pizus, the nuclei of future cities, were created by the Roman government.[93] Roman citizens went to settle down in the richest regions. For a time the Roman government remained somewhat passive and did not make any strong effort to develop city life in Thrace; neither did it interfere with the life of the few old Greek cities of the interior (Philippopolis). One Roman colony was planted under Claudius (Apri), another (Deultum) under the Flavians. The first serious attempt to foster the growth of cities was made by Trajan in connexion with his military operations on the

Danube and in the East by the institution of the new province Dacia and by the reorganization of Moesia. To exercise more effective control over the life of the province he needed larger and better organized centres. New cities, almost all with Greek names and more or less Greek population and Greek customs (Augusta Traiana or Beroea, Plotinopolis, and Trajanopolis), were created, and municipal organization and municipal rights were granted to certain villages like Serdica (Sofia), Pautalia, Nicopolis ad Nestum, Topirus, and Anchialus, which became large and prosperous settlements. These new cities were organized in an individual manner. Not one of them was a Roman colony by origin. Some had the right to issue coinage, but on their coins the name of the provincial governor appeared beside that of the city. Here, as in Dacia and Moesia, the creation of these new cities probably attracted new inhabitants, particularly from the East. Hadrian continued his predecessor's policy. The well-known and beautiful city of Hadrianopolis still exists under its old name (Edirne).

Did this policy produce a real diffusion of city life? Did it result in the hellenization of the land? We say hellenization, for Greek influence in the Balkans was too strong to permit of romanization. I hardly think so. It resulted in the separation from the rest of the population of a city *bourgeoisie* consisting of immigrants and rich natives, in additional burdens for the villages, in the disappearance of some *strategiai*, which were replaced by city territories. But, even with her cities, Thrace remained a land of villages, of village communities, of small peasant landowners. For these peasants the cities were an evil, not a blessing, as can be clearly seen from the well-known inscription of Scaptopare, of which we shall speak in the eleventh chapter.[94] The peasants, too, jealously kept all the peculiarities of their life and their religion. A series of finds of the second and third centuries A.D. shows us that even in the Roman period some rich landowners in Thrace were buried, according to the old Scytho-Thracian (and also Celtic) ritual, in funerary chariots, in tumuli. In the Bulgarian mountains the ancient Thracian dress so often seen on funerary stelae of the Roman period may still be found today, and in the Christian churches may be seen the figure of the great unnamed God, of whom we have countless votive monuments of the Roman period, the hunter and fighter, galloping on his Thracian horse, revered by the peasants as the great Christian 'Herôs' St. George.[95]

The adjoining province of MACEDONIA (including Paeonia and the lands of the Adriatic shore with Dyrrhachium and Apollonia)[96] was never a land of intensive urbanization, apart from its Eastern coast. The strength of the Macedonian kingdom was based on the Macedonian peasantry, on the villages. During the Macedonian wars the country suffered heavy losses. Under the rule of the Roman Republic it experienced many disastrous invasions of barbarians. Then it became, with Thessaly, the main battle-field of the Roman generals during the civil wars. It was no wonder that this fertile land was less densely populated than it had been under its kings. The decline of population and the strategic importance of the land—through which passed the great road from Italy across the Balkan peninsula, by way of Egnatia, to the East—induced Augustus to attempt to romanize at least one portion of the province by sending out colonies, partly of veterans, partly of civilians, to many important places (Dyrrhachium, Philippi, Dium, Pella, Cassandrea, Byblis) and by granting to others the rights of a Roman *municipium*, as, for instance, to Beroea, the capital, to Thessalonica, the chief harbour, to Stobi in the land of the Paeonians. The numbers of the Romans were large enough to prevent their absorption by the more or less hellenized population of the Macedonian cities and to enable the emperors to recruit a considerable number of praetorians from among the Romans in the province. The new settlers, as usual, became mostly landowners and played an important part in the life not only of the cities but also of the villages. Many senatorial families possessed large estates in Macedonia. Nevertheless the impression one gains is that the economic backbone of the country continued to be the native tribes and the numerous villages, particularly the mountain villages, of peasants and shepherds.[97]

On the social and economic conditions which prevailed in GREECE (the province of Achaia) in the imperial period it is unnecessary to dwell at length. The general picture is familiar. It is a picture of poverty and gradual depopulation. The famous description of Euboea by Dio Chrysostom is, of course, a fiction. His general statement in the Tarsian speech is a rhetorical exaggeration. Yet the essential features of his description, the depopulation and the existence of large tracts of waste land, are certainly true.[98] A striking confirmation of Dio's picture is afforded by the economic situation of many of the great sanctuaries of Greece in the imperial period. The inscriptions of Delphi show that the income of that sanctuary was now derived mainly from the sacred land and the sacred herds.[99] An inscription discovered at Lycosura in Arcadia testifies to the extreme poverty both of the city and of the sanctuary, which were unable to pay the taxes due to the Romans without the aid of a rich citizen.[100] The explanation of these conditions is clear. The industry and the commerce of Greece were gone. As an agricultural country Greece is probably the poorest land in the Mediterranean area. It is not surprising that the Greeks, most of them clever and educated men, emigrated in masses to countries which offered better opportunities. But it is an exaggeration to speak of an almost complete devastation of the land. The cities still had a well-to-do *bourgeoisie* of landowners of the type of Plutarch of Chaeronea, and the richer lands in Greece still produced corn and oil, grapes and wine. Some of these products (the oil of Attica, the wine of some of the islands) were even exported to other provinces. As in the Hellenistic period, landed property was concentrated in the hands of a few families who lived in the various cities. The labour required for the lands of the city *bourgeoisie* was normally supplied, as might be expected, by slaves and tenants. The well-known general description of Plutarch must therefore be taken *cum grano salis*. What Plutarch had in mind was the Greece of the glorious times of Themistocles and Pericles. That Greece had gone for ever.[101]

VII

THE ROMAN EMPIRE UNDER THE FLAVIANS AND THE ANTONINES

The City and the Country in the Asiatic and the African Provinces of Rome

WHEN we cross the Aegean Sea or the straits from the West, we come to a different world, the world of an age-old Oriental civilization characterized by a peculiar social and economic organization. Islands of Hellenic culture set in an ocean of an Oriental population were unable thoroughly to transform the aspect of these lands, and in the time of the Empire we find here precisely the same contrast between Greek life in the cities and Oriental life in the country as had been so marked a feature of the Hellenistic period. The contrast was less pronounced in Africa where the development of city life was due not to the Greeks but to the Phoenicians, and after them to the Romans.

The Roman provinces of ASIA MINOR were rich and prosperous lands. Their economic and social conditions need not be treated at length, as they have already been discussed by the present writer in a special volume.[1] It will be enough briefly to recapitulate the conclusions reached in that book and to discuss the new evidence that has come to light in the last twenty years. In the provinces of Asia Minor there existed several types of land-tenure. The first was the system of small and large ownership which prevailed in the territories of the Greek cities, whether of ancient or of recent origin, and was recognized by the Romans. Land owned in this way was cultivated either by the owner himself or by his slaves or tenants. What proportion of the city territories was so cultivated we do not know. Some late documents show that in the cities near the sea this method of cultivation was widely spread.[2] Besides the land which was divided among the citizens (κλῆροι), many of the ancient Greek cities possessed extensive tracts which were cultivated and inhabited by natives. From the Roman point of view these villages were 'attached' or 'attributed' to the city; from the Greek point of view the villages were inhabited by 'by-dwellers' (πάροικοι or κάτοικοι) who never

Description of Plate XLVI

1. VOTIVE STELE TO THE GOD MĒN. Alleged to have been found in Attica but certainly brought from Asia Minor. British Museum. Th. Homolle, *BCH* 23, 1899, p. 389, pl. 1; A. Legrand in Daremberg–Saglio, *Dict. d. ant.* iii, p. 1395, fig. 4671; S. Reinach, *Rép. d. rel.* ii, p. 483, 1.

Inscription: *Μηνὶ Σωτῆρι καὶ Πλουτοδώτηι* (*sic*). The stele is a curious testimony to the popularity and rapid spread of the Solar pantheism of Asia Minor and Syria in the 2nd and 3rd cent. A.D. In Asia Minor these beliefs centre round the God Mēn. The cult of the gods of light was at the same time a cult of deities who had created civilization and prosperity. This idea is expressed alike in the inscription and in the bas-reliefs of our stele (cf. F. Cumont, *Les religions orientales*[4], (1929), p. 58, cf. 66). The upper part of the stele is occupied by a mask of Mēn-Sol, adorned with a solar crown, with the sun and the crescent in the centre, and resting on a large crescent. On right and left are three stars. The centre of the stele shows a curious composition. An object resembling a balance is formed by a scale-beam consisting of a snake with two heads, each crowned by a crescent, and scales composed of the attribute of Fortune (*cornucopiae*), with a lunar snake on it, and the attributes of Hercules (club and bow). The balance is supported by a large bull's head, a symbol of Mēn, with two crescents and two solar disks and a *cornucopiae* between the horns, while on its brow is a large eye surmounted by a crescent. Right and left of the head are shown the cult instruments of Mēn—the *harpe* and the syrinx and the two rudders of the goddess Fortune (all with crescents appended, like every object represented on the stele). Below them are the attributes of Vulcan (the tongs) and of Venus (the mirror). The *cornucopiae* of the balance rests on the two caps of the Dioscuri, and the club of Hercules on the wheel of Nemesis. The balance is flanked by two pairs of torches, one resting on a bull's head, the other on a goat's (symbols of Demeter and of the Eleusinian mysteries). The lower portion of the slab is filled with four signs of the Zodiac, symbolizing the four seasons—*Virgo* (Autumn) in the middle, supporting a plate with leaves and a cake stamped with a crescent, *Capricorn* (Winter) supporting Virgo, on the left *Aries* (late spring, May) with corn-ears and fruit behind it, and on the right the *Lion* (Summer) with a lunar snake behind it. Behind Aries is the *caduceus* of Mercury, beneath the capricorn the *omphalos* of Apollo, the crane, and the raven.

2. FUNERAL STELE. Found probably in Phrygia (Asia Minor), presumably at Dorylaeum or Cotiaeum. Istanbul Museum. [Mendel, iii. 1077.] P. Perdrizet, *BCH* 20, 1896, p. 64, pl. xvi; A. Legrand in Daremberg–Saglio, *Dict. d. ant.* iii, p. 1395, fig. 4670; S. Reinach, *Rép. d. rel.* ii, p. 174, 2; cf. W. H. Buckler, W. M. Calder, C. W. M. Cox, *JRS* 15, 1925, p. 158. no. (3).

Funeral stele of Apphion and her husband Gaius (the work of a local sculptor of Cotiaeum, *Τειμέας Μουρματεανός*) dedicated to, or put under the protection of, Hecate the Saviour. In the pediment stands the solar eagle of apotheosis. In the first panel is figured the triple Hecate, with the solar bust and the crescent above; on the left Mēn; on the right the solar and thunder god of Asia Minor, the god of the axe, and his sacred animal the dog. Above Mēn is the husband's ledger, the diptych; above the god of the axe are placed the symbols of the housewife—the basket and the dove, the mirror and the comb. The lowest panel contains the busts of Apphion and Gaius, the former holding a distaff. Underneath is a plough. A tombstone of a couple of honest, well-to-do, thrifty *bourgeois*, a landowner and his wife, who is a model housewife.

3. PART OF A SCULPTURED FRIEZE. Found at Ephesus. British Museum. J. T. Wood, *Discoveries at Ephesus* (1877), pp. 213 ff.; A. H. Smith, *Catalogue of Sculptures of the British Museum*, ii, no. 1285.

Two heavy carts, one drawn by a team of mules, the other by a team of oxen, and both loaded with big heavy sacks. Another part of the same frieze represents a gladiatorial combat. Wood suggests that the two friezes formed part of the decoration of the Magnesian gate of Ephesus. I am rather inclined to think of a funeral monument outside the gate. The sculptures recall a gladiatorial show given by the deceased (cf. similar monuments in Italy, e.g. the funeral monument of Umbricius Scaurus at Pompeii, see Mau, *Pompeji*, p. 438, fig. 258, and that of Rieti, S. Reinach, *Rép. d. rel.* iii, p. 334) and perhaps services which he rendered to the city by importing corn in time of famine or by taking the responsibility for the *prosecutio annonae* (*παραπομπή*), imposed on the city by the government; cf. Chaps. VIII and IX.

1. VOTIVE *STELE* TO THE GOD MĒN, THE
SAVIOUR AND GIVER OF WEALTH

2. FUNERAL *STELE* OF A PHRYGIAN
LANDOWNER AND HIS WIFE

3. TRANSPORT OF GOODS IN ASIA MINOR

XLVI. LIFE IN ASIA MINOR

had had and were never destined to have the full rights of municipal citizenship. How to deal with these large numbers of
peasants was as serious a question for the city aristocracy as was
the problem of the city proletariate. The villagers insisted on
their right to be admitted to the municipal citizenship; the
governing aristocracy endeavoured to postpone this solution of
the problem, as it probably involved certain financial consequences which were unpleasant for them.[3] In his well-known
speech on συνοικισμός Dio of Prusa gives us a glimpse into the
conditions created in the cities by this antagonism between the
city and the country. As a liberal and a philosopher, he insists
on a συνοικισμός which would unite city and country into one
social and economic body. The question was a vital one for
many cities of Asia Minor, for instance, the capital of Phrygia,
the prosperous Celaenae, which had numerous villages attached
to it.[4]

In spite, however, of the constantly growing number of cities
throughout the country there were many tracts of land which
never belonged to the territory of any city. Such tracts were
owned either by the emperor and members of his family—who
succeeded to the inheritance of the Hittite, Phrygian, Lydian,
and Persian kings, of the Populus Romanus, and of the rivals of
Caesar and of his adoptive son, to say nothing of other members
of the Roman aristocracy—or by members of rich senatorial
families, or by the ancient sanctuaries of the native gods and
goddesses which were scattered all over the peninsula.[5] Some of
these sanctuaries were either absorbed by the cities or attached
to them, but many of them, especially in Armenia, Cappadocia,
and Commagene, still formed special territories which were no
less independent of the cities than some of the imperial and senatorial estates.[6] Life on the lands which did not belong to any city
was of a rustic character. The peasants who cultivated the soil
as tenant-serfs of the emperors, as free tenants of the senators, or
as sacred slaves or serfs of the Anatolian gods, lived in villages far
remote from the cities and wholly alien from them in life and
civilization. Some of these villages increased in size and economic importance, and some of the villagers became rich and prosperous; and this development might be recognized by the grant
of a city constitution. But that was exceptional. The villages
of Asia Minor continued down to the days of the late Roman

Empire and of the Turkish conquest to be what they still are, mere agglomerations of peasants' cottages with a market-place, a shrine, an inn, and premises for local authorities and government officials.[7] Finally, in the wild mountains of Cilicia and Isauria, in the Taurus and Antitaurus, on the high plateaus of Cappadocia and Armenia, shepherd tribes lived their half-nomadic life, caring little to whom they had to pay their meagre annual tribute and robbing any one when opportunity offered.

It is difficult to say how much of Asia Minor was included in city territories and how much was exempt from city administration. The proportion varied in different parts of the country. On the coast the cities were certainly predominant: the valleys of the Hermus and the Maeander were almost wholly partitioned between city territories. But the farther we move from the sea and the large rivers, the rarer did they become. In parts of Cilicia, in Cappadocia, Armenia, and Commagene cities were quite exceptional. Cappadocia was still subdivided into *strategiai*, with a native sheikh or satrap as chief. But even in the territories of the cities life was mainly rustic. Outside the city itself it ran on the old Oriental lines and was diffused over hundreds of peasant hamlets. Despite the notable development of large and prosperous cities, Asia Minor remained a land of peasants and villages.[8]

From the time of Augustus the Greek cities and the semi-Greek state of Bosporus on the Northern and Eastern shores of the Black Sea and in the Crimea formed in fact part of the Roman Empire. With the political and cultural history of this region under the early Empire I have dealt in a separate book.[9] From the social and economic point of view the area in question may be subdivided into three sections: the territories of the Greek cities (especially Olbia and Chersonesus and the maritime cities of the Caucasian shore), the Bosporan kingdom, and the Thracian and Iranian tribes and states which were nominally vassals of the Bosporan kingdom. The territory of Chersonesus, as is shown by the archaeological remains, was probably subdivided into κλῆροι owned by the citizens and cultivated mostly as vineyards.[10] In Olbia and in the many half-Greek cities at the mouth of the Dnieper and Bug the conditions were different. We have no direct evidence about them, but we may suppose that the fertile land was cultivated by natives paying a tribute in kind to their armed lords, who left the cities in spring and summer to supervise the agricultural work.[11]

We have better information about the social and economic constitution of the Bosporan kingdom.[12] It comprised the so-called peninsula of Kerch and a part of the Taman peninsula—the territory of Panticapaeum, Theodosia, and some minor cities on the Crimean side of the straits of Kerch, and of Phanagoria and the other cities on the peninsula of Taman. This fertile, though not very large, territory was protected against the inroads of the half-nomadic population of the Crimea and the Taman peninsula by earthen walls with watch-towers and small *castella*. Inside these walls the land was owned partly by the king and the citizens of the Greek cities, partly by temples and their priests. The land was cultivated and the stock of the landowners (largely horses) was guarded by natives who lived in huts and caves and were practically serfs, if not slaves, of their masters.[13] In springtime the landowners with their families and their armed retinues left the cities in heavy four-wheeled carts and on horseback, settled in tents on their fields, and supervised the cultivation of the land and the tending of the flocks. Fully armed and accompanied by armed servants, they rode out in the morning and returned to their tents in the evening; if the approach of a robber host were notified by signals from the wall, all the landowners went forth with their retinues and a band of armed peasants to meet the enemy and, no doubt, to retaliate by raiding the fields and flocks of their neighbours. In the autumn they returned to their houses in the city and brought with them the reaped corn. The animals probably remained in the steppes under special protection.[14] The corn collected by the landowners was sold to merchants from Greece and from Asia Minor. A large proportion of it, partly paid as a tax by the landowners and partly garnered from the royal domains, belonged to the king, who, indeed, was the largest landowner and corn-merchant in the kingdom. Some of his corn was shipped to the Roman armies, especially those of Pontus, Cappadocia, and Armenia, and in payment he received an annual subsidy from the governor of Bithynia.[15]

On the steppes of the Crimea the Scythian king who had his residence in the half-Greek town of Neapolis, near the modern Simferópol, lived more or less the same life as the king of

Description of Plate XLVII

1. PART OF THE MURAL DECORATION OF A TOMB AT PANTICAPAEUM. Formerly at Kerch, now destroyed. *C.R. de la Comm. Arch. de Russie*, 1878, *Atlas*, pl. I, 1; N. Kondakoff, J. Tolstoi, and S. Reinach, *Ant. de la Russie Mér.* (1892), p. 203, fig. 187; M. Rostovtzeff, *Ancient Decorative Painting in S. Russia* (1913, in Russian), pl. LI; id. *Iranians and Greeks in S. Russia* (1922), pl. XXVIII, 1. The inscription reads Ἀνθεστήριος Ἡγησίππου ὁ καὶ Κτησαμενός [*IOSPE*, ii. 123.]

The scene represents the rural life of a large landowner of Panticapaeum. The dead man, armed and followed by a retainer, is riding towards his family residence, a tent of true nomadic type. His household (wife, children, and servants) is assembled in the tent and beside it, under the shade of a single tree; beside the tree is his long spear, while his quiver hangs from a branch. It is of course summer, and in the warmer weather the landowner, who lived as a rule in the city, went out to the steppes, armed and accompanied by armed servants. He supervises the work in the fields, and defends his labourers and harvesters from the attacks of neighbours, the Taurians from the mountains and the Scythians from the plains.

2. PART OF THE MURAL DECORATION OF A TOMB AT PANTICAPAEUM. Kerch. V. Stassoff in *C.R. de la Comm. Arch.* 1872, pl. X; Kondakoff, Tolstoi, and S. Reinach, l.l., p. 209, fig. 192; M. Rostovtzeff, *Anc. Decor. Paint.*, pl. LXXX, and *Iranians and Greeks*, pl. XXIX, 3; id. *JHS* 39, 1919, p. 152, pl. VIII; S. Reinach, *Rép. d. peint.*, 271. 2.

Fight between a Panticapaean landowner and a Scythian feudal chief from the lowlands of the Crimea. The Panticapaean is followed by his little army, composed of his friends, clients, and serfs. A band of shaggy-haired Scythians, bold archers and horsemen, is attacking him but is surrounded by the Panticapaeans, and one of the band lies slain, with his horse, on the prairie. Many Panticapaeans, as we learn from the inscriptions, met the same kind of death while defending their fields and herds.

3. AS NO. 2. Stassoff in *C.R. de la Comm. Arch.* 1872, pl. VI; Rostovtzeff, *Anc. Decor. Paint.*, pl. LXXVIII; id. *Iranians and Greeks*, pl. XXIX, 1; S. Reinach. *Rép. d. peint.*, 271. 4.

A Panticapaean knight attacking a Taurian foot-soldier.

1. A LANDOWNER ON HIS ESTATE

2. A LANDOWNER FIGHTING THE SCYTHIANS

3. A LANDOWNER FIGHTING A TAURIAN

XLVII. LIFE IN SOUTH RUSSIA

Bosporus. Here the landowners were the members of the dominant tribe. The corn was shipped from the harbour of Eupatoria
to Olbia and thence to Greece and to the armies of the Danube;
some of it was bought up by the merchants of Chersonesus.[16]
Not very different, in all probability, was the life of the Maeotian
and Sarmatian tribes in the peninsula of Taman, on the river
Kuban, on the shores of the Sea of Azov, and on the river Don.
The Sarmatians, for example, certainly enslaved the population
of the valley of the Kuban and forced it to work for them. The
produce was shipped down the Kuban to the Greek cities of the
Taman peninsula, and down the Don to Tanais and from there
to Panticapaeum. The same organization probably applied
mutatis mutandis to the fisheries at the mouths of the great Russian
rivers, in the Sea of Azov, and in the straits of Kerch. Merchants
from the Greek cities ultimately secured the produce and exported great quantities of salted and dried fish to the Greek and
Roman markets, including those of the Western provinces.[17]

Thus the population of the Greek cities was chiefly a population of landowners and merchants. In the kingdom of Bosporus
the king himself stood at their head, while under his leadership
the citizens formed a well-organized army, which co-operated
with the Roman garrisons in Chersonesus, Tyras, and Olbia.
The great merchants of Bosporus supplied the ships which formed
a part of the Roman navy cruising in Black Sea waters. Besides
the landowners and the large export merchants (most of the
latter being probably foreigners), there lived in the South Russian
cities some business men who manufactured articles which were
in demand in the Sarmatian and Scythian lands, some merchants who sent out their agents to trade with these lands, and
a large mass of proletarians, mostly slaves, who worked in the
docks, the harbours, and the workshops of the cities. There is no
doubt that the population of the cities formed only a small
minority even within their own territories, and that hellenism
and hellenization were not advancing but retreating on the
shores of the Black Sea, the Iranian elements gradually invading
and Iranizing even the city population.[18]

It is no easy task to form a correct idea of social and economic
life in the SYRIAN lands. To begin with, a warning must be
uttered against generalizing and speaking of the Syrian lands
as a single unit. We must sharply discriminate between the

Aramaean North-Syrian lands bordering on Asia Minor, the Phoenician coast-land, Palestine, and the lands bordering on the desert, including the great oases, particularly those of Damascus and Palmyra. The lands to the East of the river Jordan, the so-called Decapolis (the modern Hauran and the Ledjah) and Arabia Petraea, formed a unit by themselves. Modern archaeological investigation, especially in North Syria, the Hauran, and Arabia Petraea, has brought to light new and valuable material which helps us to form a conception of the social and economic aspect of these lands, where remains of ancient life, ruins of cities, villages, villas, and farms, exist in great abundance. But it is not only the ruins which reveal the differences between the modes of life in the various parts of Northern Syria: even today the conditions of life and types of settlement are as differentiated as they were many centuries ago. The modern traveller is struck by the contrast between the stone and brick houses of the Euphrates, and the tents of the Bedouin of the steppe. In the plain of Aleppo both houses and tents disappear, their place being taken by the white villages of peasants and shepherds, of an attractive appearance and a special type: they are larger or smaller groups of dwellings made of mud and shaped like beehives. The scene changes again on the stony hills between Aleppo and Antioch: the mud beehives give place to well-made stone houses, the form of which, on a smaller scale, is that of the beautiful houses of the late Roman Empire. The country is full of ruins of isolated villas, villages, and monasteries. Finally in the rich valley of the Orontes the native houses resemble Bedouin tents made of reeds. No doubt the ancient traveller, both in the Roman and pre-Roman age, saw the same or a similar picture.

We must bear in mind that the Roman period was only a short episode in the life of those regions, which extended over many centuries before and after the Roman domination. Rome had neither the time nor the strength radically to transform or even to modify the life of the country; she confined herself to some slight and inessential changes. A complete picture of the social and economic constitution of Roman Syria (in the large sense of the term) cannot be given without adequate information about pre-Roman conditions, which in fact is very scanty except for Palestine. The following sketch, therefore, is far from complete, but it may suffice for our present purpose.[19]

The North Syrian lands consisted mainly of the territories of four large cities, which were foundations of the Hellenistic period—Antiochia with her harbour Seleucia, Apamea, and Laodicea, sometimes together called the Syrian Tetrapolis. None of these cities has been excavated to any considerable extent (though excavations have been begun at Antioch by Americans and at Apamea by Belgians) and none has well-preserved ruins to show. Our epigraphical and archaeological evidence is, therefore, very meagre save for the district north of Antioch, which teems with beautiful ruins mostly of the late Roman period. On the other hand, our literary evidence is unusually good, at least for Antioch and especially for the fourth century A.D. Her citizens Libanius and St. John Chrysostom and, later, Malalas give us illuminating pictures of the life of this great city; the Emperor Julian also in his *Misopogon* and some other works furnishes excellent sketches.

Antioch, the capital of the Syrian kingdom of the Seleucids and afterwards of the Roman province of Syria, was one of the largest and most beautiful cities of the Empire. She possessed a vast territory. Julian speaks of her 10,000 κλῆροι, which were certainly leased to her citizens by the city council. In the fourth century the greater part of the municipal land was in the hands of a few rich owners,[20] to whom belonged the fine villas described by St. John Chrysostom. Their well-preserved ruins, investigated by H. C. Butler, show them to have been large and solidly built villas, with stables and rooms for cattle and slaves on the ground floor and luxurious apartments for the owners and managers above.[21] These wealthy proprietors represented, in the fourth century, about one-tenth of the population. Another tenth was formed by the proletariate, while the rest appear to have been moderately rich small landowners and shopkeepers. We have, therefore, in Antioch the same evolution as we find in Italy and the provinces in general, a gradual concentration of landed property in the hands of city landlords.[22] During that century the land was worked by small tenants and, as far as vineyards were concerned, by hired labourers. Their life is fully described in the brilliant picture given by St. John. We should expect to find *coloni* of the usual type attached to the soil, serfs and half-slaves of the landowners. Yet St. John gives no indication that such were the relations existing between the land-

Description of Plate XLVIII

1. BASALT STATUE OF THE GOD DUSARES. Found at Ghariyé-Shoubeih, south of Djebel ed Druz in the Auranitis. Museum of Aleppo. R. Dussaud, *C.R. Acad. Inscr.* 1923, p. 399, fig.; Ch. Virolleaud, *Syria*, 5, 1924, p. 51, pl. xx, 2.

The god Dusares is represented standing in a frontal position with a *kalathos* on his head, a *patera* in his right hand, and a *cornucopiae* full of grapes in his left. He is dressed in a *chiton* with short wide sleeves and a *chlamys*. Dusares was the great god of the Arabians in the Auranitis. In the Roman period he is the protector of vineyards and of agricultural life in general, being identified with Dionysos. He was worshipped under various names and is probably identical with the protecting deity of the new cities—the θεὸς Ἀδραηνῶν and the divine κτίστης of Soada; see Dussaud and Macler, *Voyage arch. au Safa*, pp. 182 ff.; id. *Mission dans les régions désertiques*, pp. 32, 270 ff., 309 ff., and Dussaud, *Notes de mythologie syrienne*, p. 168 (*Rev. num.*, 1904, p. 161). A bust of Dusares was found in the temple of Sei' near Soada, and is now in the British Museum (De Vogüé, *Syrie Centrale*, i, p. 34 and pl. III).

2. BRONZE STATUETTE OF A DONKEY. British Museum. H. B. Walters, *Catalogue of the Bronzes in the Br. Mus.* 1899, p. 280, no. 1790; *A Guide to the Exhib. illustr. Greek and Roman Life*, 2nd ed., 1920, p. 178 (3rd ed., 1929, p. 170); cf. S. Reinach, *Rép. d. stat.* ii, p. 745, 3.

Donkey with panniers, braying, with head raised and legs set stiff. A 'surtout de table' of the same sort is described by Petronius, *Cen.* 31: 'ceterum in promulsidari asellus erat Corinthius cum bisaccio positus, qui habebat olivas in altera parte albas, in altera nigras.'

3. TERRACOTTA STATUETTE OF A CAMEL. Found in Syria. British Museum. H. B. Walters, *Catalogue of the Terracottas of the Br. Mus.* 1903, p. 247, C. 544; *A Guide*, &c., p. 178 (3rd ed., 1929, p. 170).

Camel kneeling with panniers. In the pannier on the right side are two wine-amphorae in wicker baskets; that on the left side contains a boar's head and a cock in a large wicker basket (κόφινος); between the two the mouth of a jar is visible.

4. TERRACOTTA STATUETTE OF A CAMEL AND ITS DRIVER. Found in Asia Minor (Aphrodisias). Louvre, Paris. Unpublished (?). By permission of Mr. E. Pottier.

Camel kneeling, with its driver on its back. It load consists of a big wine-jar and a sheep (the head of the sheep, or kid, is broken off).

These statuettes illustrate the intercourse between the city and the country in Syria and in the East generally. Donkeys and camels were the chief draught-animals in those parts of the Empire; every day they brought the products of the country to the Syrian cities for sale in the market-places and bazaars. Hundreds of donkeys with panniers and sacks came daily with loads of corn, cheese, vegetables, &c., to cities like Antioch, where, as Libanius complains, they were requisitioned by the magistrates to carry away the city-refuse, see Libanius, Περὶ τῶν ἀγγαρειῶν (*Or.* L., ed. Foerster), 23 ff.

I. DUSARES, PROTECTOR OF VINEYARDS

2. DONKEY WITH PANNIERS

3. CAMEL WITH BASKETS

4. A CAMEL AND ITS DRIVER BRINGING COUNTRY PRODUCTS TO THE CITY

XLVIII. BUSINESS LIFE IN SYRIA

1. THE SHIP OF THE DESERT: THE CARAVAN-CAMEL

2. A MERCHANT SHIP OF SIDON

XLIX. COMMERCE OF SYRIA

Description of Plate XLIX

1. BRONZE STATUETTE OF A CAMEL. Found in Syria. Ashmolean Museum, Oxford. Unpublished. Reproduced by permission of the Visitors.

A loaded camel stopping on its march across the desert, with its legs set stiff. A typical feature of the Syrian desert.

2. BAS-RELIEF OF A SARCOPHAGUS. Found at Sidon. Museum of Beirout. G. Contenau, *Syria*, I, 1920, pp. 35 ff., pl. VI, and fig. 10 f.

The sarcophagus was found intact in one of the *hypogaea* of Sidon. The sides and one of the ends are adorned with garlands suspended from rings fastened in the mouths of lions' heads—a system of ornamentation, typical of Syrian sarcophagi, which reproduces in stone the bronze handles and the actual garlands of wooden coffins. The other end is covered with an elaborate design in very low relief showing a sailing merchant-ship floating on the waves of the sea, which is full of leaping dolphins and other fish.

The details of its construction are indicated in the appended drawing (reproduced from fig. 11 of Contenau's article, where illustrations of the details are given); on the Phoenician ships cf. A. Köster, *Das antike Seewesen* (1923), pp. 45 ff., and on merchant-ships in general, ibid., pp. 151 ff. The ship figured on this monument shows no important points of difference from the ordinary merchant-ships of the Roman Empire in general. It symbolizes, no doubt, the last voyage of the deceased.

owner and his workers. His picture implies rather that they were free tenants and hired labourers, exploited by their masters and living in extreme poverty, but not attached to the soil and enslaved.[23] However that may have been, the rustic peasant population is constantly represented by the writers of the fourth century as a poor and oppressed class, ground down by rich lords who were the landowners of the city and who prevented any improvement in their position.[24] At the first opportunity the peasants were ready to show their hatred of their oppressors.[25] It is highly improbable that these conditions were a development of the third and fourth centuries A.D. I am inclined to believe that they existed both in the Hellenistic and in the early Roman period.

It is probable that the tenants and the hired labourers on the large estates belonging to the citizens of Antioch were small landholders who lived in the villages scattered all over the territory of the city and attached to it. The inhabitants of these villages were, of course, the natives who lived there from time immemorial. There is not the slightest doubt that they had no share in the life of the city and could not even dream of ever becoming citizens. In this respect Syria was far behind even Asia Minor. While the city population sent hardly a single soldier to the Roman army, the villages were always the main source of the supply of reliable soldiers for the auxiliary regiments and the legions.[26]

It may safely be assumed that the same conditions prevailed in the territories of the other cities of North Syria. Besides the city territories, North Syria included some half-independent temple lands. One type is represented by the temple of Baitocaece, which owned a large village and was attached to the city of Apamea. A Greco-Latin inscription enables us to follow its destinies from the Hellenistic age to the time of Valerian. Throughout this long period the conditions remained almost unchanged. The temple enjoyed full immunity. It owned the land and collected the revenues. Its 'inmates', the κάτοχοι, supervised the annual fair which was connected with the temple and they represented the temple in its dealings with the city authorities. The latter in their turn forwarded the complaints of the temple to the higher authorities up to the emperor himself. Similar privileges, we may assume, were enjoyed by scores of other sanctuaries, such as the famous temple of Iupiter Dolichenus at Doliche, another village in North Syria, or that of Heliopolis (Baalbek). Some temple territories were still more independent. The Ituraeans in the districts of Abila and Chalcis in the Lebanon region formed vassal states as late as the reigns of Claudius and Trajan respectively. We may suppose that here the cities were no more than *chefs-lieux* of large agricultural territories, which continued to live their ancient rustic life.[27]

The territories of the great commercial cities such as Damascus, Epiphania (Hamath), Emesa, and Palmyra—to say nothing of those of cities like Edessa in Osrhoëne, which was never fully incorporated in the Roman Empire and retained for centuries its native dynasty—bore a greater resemblance to the Bosporan kingdom with Panticapaeum as its capital than to the lands of Roman provincial cities. We have already dealt with Palmyra. The rule of the city extended over a large region covered with villages as well as over some nomadic tribes. These villages, which were sometimes identical with the estates of the rich merchants of Palmyra, are mentioned in the well-known Palmyrene tariff. The villages and the tribes no doubt furnished the excellent archers and camel-riders (*dromedarii*) for the Palmyrene militia and the Roman army. Some places, like Dura, lying on the frontiers of the Palmyrene territory and commanding the military and trade routes leading into Parthia, developed into prosperous cities with strong Parthian garrisons, protected by fortifications—a surrounding wall and a strong citadel, both either of the Hellenistic or Parthian periods. From the time of Lucius Verus Dura became a frontier-fortress on the Roman *limes*, probably the most important Roman bastion on the middle Euphrates. Later still, in the third century, when Palmyra became, first partly and then wholly, independent, Dura probably shared its fortunes for a very short time.[28]

On the life of Dura we now have very detailed information. A Parthian fortress until A.D. 165, then a Roman fortress, the life of Dura changed little with change of masters. It remained a typical Hellenistic city of Mesopotamia, with an aristocracy consisting of the descendants of the Macedonian colonists and some rich merchants of Semitic origin; for the rest there were representatives of Iranian stock, and many Arabs of humble position. But Dura's days of prosperity were passed for ever. The era of

Description of Plate L

1–2. A SPHERICAL RED-GLAZED CLAY BOWL. Found near Teheran in Persia. Metropolitan Museum, New York. Gift of G. J. Demotte. M. Pézard, *La Céramique archaïque de l'Islam* (1920), p. 205, pl. vi, 6.

The realistic bas-reliefs of the bowl represent various scenes of rustic life. A couple of camels are resting: one is lying on the ground, the other is standing with one of its legs fettered. Behind is the man in charge, or the owner, in typical Iranian dress—a 'kaftan' and a 'bashlyk'—with a spherical bowl in his hands, praying. On the other side of the bowl is shown a long-bearded Persian dressed in a long 'kaftan', with a 'bashlyk' on his head, ploughing his field or herding oxen. Behind him comes another Persian with a stick in his left hand and a spherical bowl in his right. Our bowl seems to be a bowl for sacrifice, sacrifice performed for the safety of the men and the animals, and for the fertility of the fields.

Pézard appears to me to be right in thinking that this and similar bowls belong to the 3rd–4th cent. A.D. I am inclined to attribute them to the late Parthian art, as the style is very similar to the few extant Parthian sculptures and to some frescoes in the graves of Panticapaeum. Compare the bronze statuette in the British Museum, H. B. Walters, *Cat. of Bronzes*, p. 22, no. 222 and pl. iii (from Kameiros), a prototype of the Parthian art, and F. Sarre, *Die Kunst des alten Persien*, pp. 27 ff. and 59, pls. lxiv, lxv, and cxlvii. The bowl is an illustration of life in the Iranian part of the ancient world during the period of the Empire. In the neighbourhood of Palmyra life was probably not very different: see the documents of Avroman and Dura quoted in Chap. V, note 50. Other pots of the same series illustrate various sides of Parthian life, especially religion and cult. Compare M. Pézard, 'Pottery that reveals people', *International Studio*, 75, 1922, p. 225. (For this reference I am indebted to M. Dimand, Assistant Curator of the Metropolitan Museum.)

1. A TEAM OF CAMELS IN PARTHIA

2. PLOUGHING, OR HERDING OXEN, IN PARTHIA

L. LIFE IN PARTHIA

peace which reigned under Parthian rule did not return. Dura became more and more a military post, and was no longer a centre of caravan-trade. Roman soldiers now form the dominant class. An idea of the conditions in which a rich Semitic-Macedonian family lived at Dura in the third century A.D. can be gathered from the *graffiti* on the walls of the business premises of a rich citizen of Dura, Nabucbelus. These texts reflect not only the business-life of a small Semitic merchant (not that of an important merchant of the caravan-trade), but also his family-life, his religious interests, and his political preoccupations. The great fear in this period was of the advance of the Sasanid Persians.[29] The same picture probably applies *mutatis mutandis* to Damascus, whose territory bordered that of Sidon.[30] Emesa, as is well known, was ruled by its native aristocracy of priest-kings throughout the period of Roman rule. As in Palmyra and Damascus, this nobility entered for a short time the ranks of the imperial aristocracy and took an active part in the administration of the Empire, even before two members of it ascended the imperial throne. In the third century a scion of the old house of Sampsigeramus appears again as ruler of the Emesene land and, like the kings of Palmyra and the Abgari of Edessa, leads his subjects against the Persians.[31] The conditions which produced Oriental feudalism in Syria never disappeared completely, and the cities of Emesa, Damascus, Palmyra, and Edessa remained what they had been, the residences of priest-kings: they never became regular Greek cities, like Antioch. These states continued to be based, as of old, on the religious awe felt by Oriental peasants towards the representatives of god on earth, the prelate-princes.

Of the cities of Phoenicia in the imperial age we know very little save for the part they played in the commercial and industrial life of the Empire, of which we have spoken before. As regards Palestine, we must sharply distinguish from the rest of the land the old Greco-Philistine cities of the coast (Gaza, Anthedon, Askalon, Joppa, Ptolemais-Acê), the new foundations of Herod on the coast and inland, especially Caesarea on the sea, Tiberias, Sebaste (Samaria), and the later Roman city of Neapolis. It would be out of place here to trace the evolution of the 'heathen', that is to say, the hellenized cities of Palestine. There was probably no very great difference between them and the cities of Syria and Phoenicia. They all had a large territory peopled by natives and they lived to a large extent on their labour. But the largest part of Judaea, Galilee, and Samaria remained, as before, a land of villages and peasants. It is sufficient to read the Gospels from this point of view to realize the extent to which Palestine was an agricultural land and how rustic was the character of the life of the common people. The so-called cities of Judaea, including Jerusalem, were purely religious and administrative centres, *chefs-lieux* of rural districts which closely corresponded to similar districts both in Egypt and in Thrace and bore the Greek name of toparchies. The type of the rich man in Judaea is the wealthy owner of land or of large flocks of sheep and goats, or the tax-collector ($\tau\epsilon\lambda\acute{\omega}\nu\eta s$). The type of the common man is either the peasant toiling in his field or in his garden and vineyard, or the small village artisan, carpenter, blacksmith, cobbler, and the like.

The Gospel picture is corroborated by the evidence furnished by Josephus, particularly in his *Jewish War* and in his *Life*. Judaea, Samaria, and still more Galilee are studded with hundreds of villages, inhabited by peasants, above whom stands a native aristocracy of large landowners, who are patrons of the villages, men like Josephus himself and his rival John of Gischala, Philip son of Jakimus, and others. These men are not only rulers of the land and leaders in its religious life, but capitalists and merchants on a big scale, who sometimes add to their wealth by daring speculations (such as John of Gischala's sale of oil to the city of Caesarea) and keep their money in the national bank— the temple at Jerusalem. Still more opulent are the officials of the kings and tetrarchs, and the kings and tetrarchs themselves and their families. Lastly, we find estates of the Roman emperor himself and the imperial family, and even a Roman military colony established by Vespasian at Emmaus after the Jewish War. Such were the conditions of life in Palestine, and in later times there was clearly no change, except that landed proprietors of other than Jewish origin, like Libanius, increased in number.[32]

A peculiar picture was presented by the fertile land beyond the Jordan, the modern Transjordan, Hauran, and the adjacent strip of half-desert land inhabited by Arabian tribes. In the Hellenistic period it had been a field of colonization. Many Greek cities had been founded there, all of them semi-military, town-centres of large agricultural districts, with a population of landowners. Most of them took the place of what were formerly native villages. In the times when the Seleucid Empire was decaying they had either been captured and destroyed by the Jews or had gradually relapsed into the old manner of life, with native half-hellenized kings at the head of the communities. With the advent of Roman rule a new era opened in the life of these regions. As in many parts of Asia Minor, the Roman emperors entrusted the work of civilization to enlightened representatives of Greco-Roman life—the hellenized Idumaeans of Palestine, Herod the Great and his successors. Strabo and Josephus give a striking picture of the gradual hellenization of the fertile lands of Trachonitis as the result of repeated efforts to colonize them with a settled agricultural population and to subjugate and swamp the old stock of native (mostly Arabian) shepherds and robbers. When the Roman government, especially after the annexation of Arabia Petraea, established peace and security in the Hauran and in the adjacent stretches of cultivable land bordering on the desert, and when good Roman roads replaced the ancient caravan tracks and the most vital places on these roads, the water stations, were fortified and garrisoned by Roman soldiers, a new life blossomed in the Transjordanian region. The old cities became centres of a brisk trade, and grew rich and prosperous. The ruins of Bostra, Gerasa, Philadelphia, Canatha, and of many flourishing villages still testify to the splendour of the new buildings which vied with the best edifices in the Herodian cities of Palestine. Protected by the Roman troops, the inhabitants of the country turned definitely to a settled agricultural life, and many Arabian tribes transformed their tents into stone houses and their pastures into rich cornfields. Some, of course, adhered to their old nomadic life, but they gave up their habits of pillage and robbery. 'The stationary population,' says Dussaud, 'protected against surprises and relieved of the heavy tribute imposed by their nomadic neighbours, pushed back the limits of the desert by utilizing all the cultivable land. Numerous villages, now in ruins, sheltered a motley population of Syrians and Arabs, who developed a lively commerce with the nomads, cultivated the olive-tree, the vine, and cereals, and devoted themselves to the manufacture of woollen stuffs.'[33]

Hundreds of inscriptions and many imposing ruins of villages and farms attest this development. The fact that most of the inscriptions in the region of the Safaites are written in the Safaite language proves the persistence of the ancient tribes and the maintenance of their religion, habits, and customary occupations. Yet the general aspect of the land changed completely. Stone temples, with theatres adjoining, were built for the native gods in the larger villages; the water supply was secured by aqueducts, which replaced the old wells; inns and marketplaces built of solid stone became centres of a lively traffic; the tribal organization was hellenized and legalized under Greek terms. The ancient tribe became a φυλή, the ancient clan a κοινόν, the ancient sheikh a πρόεδρος or προνοητής, a στρατηγός or ἐθνάρχης. The larger villages (κῶμαι) became μητροκωμίαι, centres of a larger district, and a few of them (for instance, Philippopolis under Philip the Arab) were granted the title of cities. Every village had its land owned by the villagers, members of the modernized tribe.[34] The mainspring and the mainstay of the changed conditions were the veteran soldiers, native Arabs who returned to their native villages from service in distant places and brought with them new habits and customs of life. Many foreigners came with them and settled down in the Arabian villages of the new model.[35]

How many of the new villages were attached to the ancient cities we do not know. Most of them probably never became parts of a city territory but retained their tribal organization. One point, however, may be taken for granted. The new villages were inhabited, like the farms and villages of Germany, not by tenants and serfs but by small landowners, free members of a free village community. An aristocracy grew up here as elsewhere, but not a single inscription attests the growth in the borderlands of the desert of a system similar to the serfdom of Asia Minor.

Thus the period of Roman domination in the Syrian lands was a period of peace and security and, therefore, of prosperity. But it was not a period of radical change. The Syrian Orient remained under Roman rule what it had been before. Urbanization made no striking progress, nor did the land become hellenized. A few new half-Greek cities arose, and some elements of the rural population settled in the cities. But the mass lived on in the old fashion, devoted to their gods and to their temples, to their fields and to their flocks, and ready at the first opportunity to slaughter the men of the cities and to return to the life of peasants and shepherds under the rule of native priest-kings and sheikhs.[36]

With the social and economic conditions which prevailed in EGYPT in the first and second centuries A.D. it is impossible to deal at length. Our evidence is so abundant and so detailed, the number of problems raised by it is so large, and the problems are so complicated that it would require a special work, probably of several volumes, to treat adequately all the aspects of the social and economic evolution of Egypt even during the brief period of the first two centuries of our era. We must therefore content ourselves with a short summary of the main features, and refer the reader to the special works which deal with the various questions that arise in connexion with the life of Egypt in this age.

Egypt was the last Oriental land to be reached by the Romans. They found there a peculiar organization of social and economic life, the result of centuries of development. They perceived the hopelessness of attempting to remodel this life: they took its main features for granted, and they based on them and adjusted to them their own administrative system, which in truth did not differ much from that of their predecessors the Ptolemies. Both systems alike were based on the immemorial conditions of Egyptian religious, social, and economic life, conditions which could not be altered at the will of the new masters. In Egypt the Romans found the population divided into certain classes, to each of which was assigned a special function in the life of the country.[37] On the natives rested the whole fabric of the state. For the most part, they were peasants who tilled the soil; some toiled in the workshops of the villages, large and small, and manufactured various kinds of goods; others supplied labour for mines and quarries, fisheries, and hunting grounds; others again acted as drivers of the draught animals which were used for transportation and as sailors and oarsmen on the ships. In short, all the menial work was done by them, for slavery played a very restricted part in the economic life of the country. They lived in villages of varying size, some of which received in the Ptolemaic time the name of *metropolis*, just as some villages in Syria were called μητροκωμίαι. In sober fact these *metropoleis* remained

4735.1   T

throughout the Greek and Roman periods what they had been before, large and dirty Egyptian villages, with a more or less hellenized and civilized town-centre, of which we shall speak later.

In all these villages (variously named ἐποίκια, κῶμαι, μητρο-πόλεις) lived groups of natives following the same profession: peasants, artisans, factory workmen, fisherman, sailors, drivers, and so forth. The unity of these groups was based on the special service which they rendered to the state; and, not unnaturally, membership of one of them was compulsory for all, and migration from one group to another was under the strict control of the government. Under the direction of their elders, who were appointed by the state, and of a series of state officials these groups had to perform the task assigned to them by the state, be it the tilling of the soil, the manufacture of oil or clothes, or any other kind of work. In this way the members of any given group not only earned their living but also helped to maintain the state machinery. The notion of governing themselves or of taking any part in the affairs of the state (apart from their professional work) never occurred to the natives of Egypt.

For them the state, personified in the king, was an article of faith, a religious belief. The king was a descendant of the gods, he was a god himself, and he had to be worshipped and obeyed. He and the state, like the gods and religion in general, were above criticism and above control. They were paramount. The interests of the natives were concentrated on their domestic life and on the performance of their duties towards the gods and the state. As a matter of fact, both the state and the gods gave the natives very little and asked very much. When the demands became intolerable and made life a heavy burden for any group of natives, they resorted to passive resistance, to strikes. A strike was a resolve to submit the case to the judgement of the god, and was effected by leaving their usual place of residence and taking refuge in a temple. Here the strikers remained in idle resignation until the wrong was redressed or compulsion was used to make them resume their work. In Greek terminology these strikes were called 'secessions' (ἀναχωρήσεις). The fact that the state was represented in the Ptolemaic period by Macedonian foreigners, and later by another set of foreigners, the Roman emperors, did not mean very much to the natives, so long as the rulers showed reverence towards the Egyptian gods and so long as the gods, through the priests, recognized them as the legal rulers of Egypt. And the priests were too clever not to realize that a power which was supported by a good army of professional soldiers and disposed of large sums of money was worth recognition, even if they had little to expect from it, as they had from the Romans.

Some of the natives were rich, others were poor; some were clever, others were slow and stupid. The better elements naturally endeavoured to ascend the social ladder and to improve their condition of life. The only course open to them was to become either priests or state officials; but neither was easy. Though the priests did not form a close caste, they constituted nevertheless a somewhat select group of families which would not readily admit foreigners into their ranks. So it was under the Pharaohs, and so it remained in the Ptolemaic and in the Roman period. Since, however, under Roman rule the office of priest was treated as a 'liturgy' (λειτουργία) and so became less and less attractive, and readily accessible to anybody who had money, a native who had the necessary resources and education could, if he would, exchange the position of peasant or workman for that of priest, though the new position was no more pleasant than the old.

It was more difficult to become a member of the body of officials who assisted the king. In the times preceding the foreign domination it had been comparatively easy: any one who was well educated, who knew how to read and write, and was familiar with the language of the official documents and with the complicated system of state machinery, had the chance of becoming an official and of advancing to the highest posts.[38] But when the king ceased to be an Egyptian and the official language became Greek, the situation was much less simple. The Macedonian kings did not come to Egypt alone: they were surrounded by a strong foreign army consisting of Hellenic or hellenized soldiers, and by a host of Hellenic or hellenized fortune-hunters, intelligent and energetic men who regarded Egypt as a splendid field for the display of their ability and the acquisition of a fortune. To these Greeks the Ptolemies were bound by indissoluble ties. For the Egyptians—their mode of life, their religion, and their ideas—the Greeks had no understanding and no sympathy. To a Greek an Egyptian was a barbarian in the modern sense of

Description of Plate LI

1–2. TWO SECTIONS OF THE LOWER PART OF THE MOSAIC OF PALES-
TRINA. Found at Palestrina (Praeneste). Palace Barberini at Palestrina. S. Reinach,
Rép. d. peint., p. 374 (with bibliography), cf. my article in *Röm. Mitt.* 26, 1911, pp. 60
and 61 (the same two sections more complete).

The mosaic reproduces the most characteristic features of Ptolemaic and Roman
Egypt. The upper part of it is a sort of zoological atlas of the Egyptian Sudan, with all
the fabulous and real animals of this region and their names in Greek (cf. Philostr.,
Vit. Apoll. vi. 24). The lower part (figs. 1–2) gives the general aspect of Egypt, especially
the Delta, in time of flood. In the right-hand corner (fig. 1) a peasant's house is visible,
with a dove-cote near it. The owner of the house runs out of the door after his wife, who
stands in the garden looking at a boat with soldiers in it. In the other (left) corner of
the mosaic (not reproduced in fig. 2) are hippopotami and crocodiles. The centre of
the lower part is occupied by two buildings. One of them (fig. 1) is a fine pavilion with
a large curtain, behind which is seen a tower-villa with a large garden in an enclosure.
In the pavilion a group of Roman soldiers is ready to celebrate a festival: a big *crater*
and a number of drinking horns are set out for the party. At the head of the group a
laurel-crowned officer sounds the horn; he is greeted by a woman with a palm-branch,
who offers him a garland or a diadem; and apparently he gives a signal to a company
of soldiers approaching in a military rowing-boat (*liburnica*). Near the military pavilion
a party of civilians, including women, gathered under the shade of a pergola covered
with vines (fig. 2), is drinking to the strains of music: a woman sings a hymn, to the
accompaniment of the lyre, seemingly in honour of the victorious general. Behind these
buildings are two more bands of decoration. In the middle one is seen a small shrine
(fig. 1), with a religious procession moving through it: in front, two men carrying a
stretcher with a sacred symbol on it, and, behind, standard-bearers and a congregation
of worshippers. Near the temple is a statue of Anubis (the jackal) on a base. Behind the
pergola (fig. 2) we see a sacred enclosure and an osier-barn—a μοσχοτρόφιον, where
calves were reared for sacrifice (?). Before the entrance to the latter two men are talking,
one of them with a big fork in his hand, while a third man drives two oxen or calves
to the water; round the barn ibises are flying. The last band is filled with large temples.
The largest, behind the small shrine (fig. 1), has two pylons and colossal Egyptian
statues near the main entrance; in front of it is a man riding a donkey, followed by his
servant with his baggage. Behind the pergola and the barn (fig. 2) are three other
temples: the first is a shrine of ibises (ἰβιεῖον), the next a typical Egyptian shrine with
two towers, and the third a Greco-Egyptian temple. In the water are seen various
animals, flowers, canoes of the natives (one loaded with lotuses), and two large pleasure
and hunting boats with cabins (*dahabiahs*). The whole mosaic is the best and most
realistic of the extant pictures which serve to convey a vivid idea of the aspect of
Egypt in the Ptolemaic and Roman periods. In the light of the new discoveries in
Egypt it would be easy to give a detailed description of it, although this has never been
done. The original probably belongs to the early Ptolemaic period; the preserved copy
is late Hellenistic, according to the investigations of Marion Blake [cf. Rostovtzeff,
Soc. and Econ. Hist. Hell. World, pl. xxxviii, 1, text].

I

2

THE DELTA IN TIME OF FLOOD

LI. EGYPT

1. ALEXANDRIA

2. AN EGYPTIAN VILLAGE

LII. EGYPT

Description of Plate LII

1. A SILVER *PATERA* WITH AN *EMBLEMA*. Found in a villa near Boscoreale. Louvre, Paris. A. Héron de Villefosse, *Mon. Piot*, 5, 1899, pp. 39 ff. (description), pp. 177 ff. (analysis), and pl. i. Repeatedly reproduced since. Cf. S. Reinach, *Rép. d. rel.* i, p. 84, 1.

The *emblema* represents the bust of a beautiful stern-looking woman, her head covered with the spoils of an elephant. In her right hand she holds an *uraeus*, in her left a *cornucopiae* filled with grapes and fruit crowned by a crescent, which is attached to a cedar-cone, the well-known attribute of Attis. On the *cornucopiae* are figured the bust of Helios, the sun-eagle, and the two stars of the Dioscuri. In her lap the goddess holds various fruits (grapes, pomegranates, figs, cedar-cones, &c.). Among the fruit is a peacock, the bird of Hera, and, stepping over the fruit, a large figure of a she-panther. Corresponding to the *cornucopiae* dedicated to the gods of light, the right shoulder of the goddess is covered with the symbols of Heracles—the lion, the club, the bow, and the quiver. These symbols, which are as large as the *uraeus*, the panther, and the *cornucopiae*, are the primary attributes of the goddess. The others are much smaller. On the left is the *sistrum* of Isis, under the right hand a personification of the sea (waves and a dolphin), under the fruit the tongs of Hephaistos and the snake-sceptre of Asklepios. To the right of the *cornucopiae* is the lyre of Apollo. There is no doubt that the figure personifies not Africa, as Héron de Villefosse suggests, but Alexandria. This fact has been proved by P. Perdrizet, *Bronzes gr. d'Égypte de la coll. Fouquet* (1911), p. 39. The skin of the elephant's head is characteristic of certain portraits of Alexander, and was later used by some of the Ptolemies as a symbol of their power, inherited from Alexander (see, e.g. C. C. Edgar, *JHS* 26, 1906, p. 281, pl. xviii). The attributes of the goddess are extremely interesting. She is under the protection, first of all, of the Egyptian gods; she is the queen of Egypt: hence the *uraeus*, the symbol of the Egyptian royal power. Among her other protectors, the chief is Dionysos (the she-panther), the god of fertility and prosperity. Her prosperity is given by the gods of light—the Sun and the Moon (cf. pl. xlvi)—and by the great hero of civilization, the forefather of all Macedonian dynasties, Heracles. The other symbols emphasize the flourishing maritime commerce of Alexandria, her healthy conditions, her prosperous industry, and her prominence in art. The whole spirit of the figure is Hellenistic and Ptolemaic, though it may have been produced by Alexandrian or Campanian silversmiths in the 1st cent. of our era. Cf. M. Collignon, *Mon. Piot*, 22, 1918, pp. 163 ff., and *C.R. Acad. Inscr.* 1916, pp. 337 ff. (Egyptian statuette personifying Alexandria).

2. FRESCO FROM HERCULANEUM. Found at Herculaneum. *Pitt. di Ercolano*, i, pl. l, p. 257; W. Helbig, *Die Wandgem.*, &c., no. 1569; and my article in *Röm. Mitt.* 26, 1911, p. 56, fig. 31.

The fresco belongs to the class of so-called Egyptian landscapes which are frequently found throughout the Roman Empire, especially in the 1st cent. A.D. Although they were copied by men who probably had never seen Egypt, just as Japanese and Chinese landscapes are drawn in Europe in our own days, yet, as the originals were no doubt executed by men familiar with Egypt, the copies give a trustworthy general picture of the Egyptian land. Our fresco represents three farms on the banks of a canal. One (on the left) consists of two tower-like buildings, and is surrounded by a brick wall. The central one consists of a pylon, a high tower, and the main buildings—a farm-house and a tower, with trees behind. To the left are a 'shaduf' and a well (wells and shadufs —φρέατα and κηλώνεια or μηχαναί—are often mentioned in papyri of the Roman period; see *P.Flor.* 16. 10; *P.Ryl.* 99. 5; *P.Oxyr.* 2137. 27). Cf. M. Schnebel, *Die Landwirtschaft im hell. Aegypten* (1925), pp. 71 ff. The third farm, on the other bank of the canal, is similar though not identical. The garden behind the main house is surrounded by palisades. On towers as parts of ancient farms in Egypt, see F. Preisigke in *Hermes*, 54, 1919, p. 423, and cf. my article in *Anatolian Studies presented to Sir William Ramsay* (1923), p. 374, 1.

the word, a man who had no share in civilized life. As late as the third century A.D. an Egyptian Greek writing to his 'brethren' says: 'You may take me, brethren, for a barbarian or an inhuman Egyptian.'[39]

The Greeks in Egypt felt themselves masters and rulers, and they would never think of sharing with the despised natives the rights acquired by conquest and maintained by force. Any attempt by the kings to put such an idea into practice would have been regarded by the Greek population as a betrayal, as a crime, as an encroachment on their sacred rights in Egypt. These feelings were, of course, shared both by the Ptolemies and afterwards by the Roman emperors. The Ptolemies regarded Egypt as their personal property, acquired by conquest. For them Egypt was their 'house' ($oi\kappa o\varsigma$) or personal estate. The natives were a subject population whose task it was to support the 'house' of the kings by work and payments. On the other hand, the Greeks were the companions of the kings, men of the same stock and of the same civilization. It was natural therefore that the kings should assign to them the task of managing their 'house' and that they should never admit the Egyptians to the higher posts of administration. In the later period, indeed, after some revolts of the Egyptian population, caused by the weakness of the rulers, the Ptolemies tried to find in an Egyptian army and in the Egyptian priests a counterpoise to the political aspirations of the Greek army and the Greek population. But they never went so far as to identify themselves with the Egyptians and to appear as true Egyptian kings, as Pharaohs.

Thus access to the chief posts in the Ptolemaic administration was closed to the Egyptians unless they became completely hellenized and formed part of the Greek population, which, of course, was and continued to be exceptional. Accordingly the administration of Egypt, apart from the lower posts of scribes and policemen, was Greek. Greeks surrounded the king and formed his 'court'; Greeks governed the provinces, that is to say, the administrative divisions of the land, the $\chi\omega\rho\alpha$; Greeks were appointed chiefs of the police force, judges, chief engineers, inspectors of different kinds, managers of the state factories, supervisors of trade and industry, and so on. To the Greeks also was given the privilege of collecting the taxes, whether in the capacity of officials or of tax-farmers; and, supported and aided by the kings, they concentrated in their hands the growing foreign trade of Egypt.

The role assigned to the Greeks by the kings was an important privilege. Egypt was a rich land, and the management of this land for the king was a profitable and attractive occupation. We must remember that the economic activity of Egypt was highly centralized and nationalized, and that all branches of it were supervised, and some even monopolized, by the state. From the economic and legal point of view the king was the owner of the soil, and the tillers of the soil were his lessees. This involved for the peasants not only very high taxation but also careful supervision of their work and strict control over their resources. Without a system of dykes and canals Egypt could not exist. Her prosperity required minutely organized irrigation work before and after the Nile flood, equal distribution of water, drainage of swampy and marshy places, and so forth. Such work could only be accomplished by the joint efforts of the whole population; and these efforts, which took the form of compulsory labour (*corvée*), had to be regulated and organized. From time immemorial industry had been concentrated either in the temples or round the palaces of the rulers: the kings and the priests possessed the raw materials, and they knew the secrets of technique. And so it remained. The artisans in the various industries worked in the first instance, and sometimes exclusively, for the king. Here again organization and supervision were required. Trade and transportation were managed in the same way. All the traders and all the transporters, great and small, in the country (with the possible exception of Alexandria) were concessionaires of the state, and most of them were Greeks.

If we realize the vastness of the field thus opened to the activity of the Greeks in this land of centralization and nationalization (*étatisation*), and the numberless opportunities of enrichment, quite apart from regular salaries, we shall not be surprised that a well-to-do Greek *bourgeoisie* gradually grew up all over the country, a *bourgeoisie* of officials and tax-farmers. The humble occupation of retail-traders or artisans was, of course, left to the natives. In Alexandria another rich *bourgeoisie* was created by the steadily developing trade and industry of the capital of the Hellenistic world. Along with the members of the royal court and the king himself and his family, the merchants and exporters

Description of Plate LIII

1. TERRACOTTA STATUETTE. Found in Egypt. Collection Fouquet. P. Perdrizet, *Les Terres-cuites grecques de la collection Fouquet* (1921), ii, pl. cxxiii, 2, and i, p. 150, no. 411.

A cart (*carpentum*) drawn by two oxen or cows, and driven by a boy dressed in a thick cloak with a hood. The wheels of the cart are heavy and primitive. The cart is protected against the sun by a canopy.

2. AS NO. 1. P. Perdrizet, l.l. ii, pl. xcix, 2 and i, pp. 129 ff., no. 354. A replica in Alexandria Museum.

A peasant in the peculiar conical felt hat (cf. pl. li), gathering dates from the top of a palm tree, which he has climbed by means of a rope; the basket for the dates hangs from his shoulder. Compare another similar terracotta, Perdrizet, op. cit. ii, pl. xcix, 4 and i, pp. 129 ff., no. 355 (with a very instructive excursus on date-palms in Egypt).

3. AS NO. 1. P. Perdrizet, op. cit. ii, pl. cxxii, 2 and i, p. 148, no. 403.

A pack-camel carrying two baskets full of grapes. On its neck is a strap of the same sort as in No. 1, with a metal disc. Such discs may have been used to indicate the name of the owner and the class to which the camel was assigned for purposes of taxation (see my *Studien zur Gesch. des röm. Kolonates*, p. 128, note 1).

4. AS NO. 1. Found in Egypt. British Museum, Egyptian Room VI, case 277, 64 (37628). Unpublished (?). By the courtesy of the Trustees.

Camel with a heavy pack-saddle, to which are tied on each side three jars (*dolia*) with oil, wine, beer, or the like.

This set of terracottas vividly illustrates the evidence furnished by papyri about the organization of the transport-business and about agricultural life in Egypt. The camel was apparently unknown to the Egypt of the Pharoahs; it first appears, so far as our evidence goes, in early Ptolemaic times, and it becomes the most common draught animal in the Roman period. Cf. P. Perdrizet, op.cit. i, pp. 147 ff. (written before the publication of the Zenon papyri). The gathering of dates illustrates one of the most typical forms of productive activity in the southern provinces of Rome. Another peculiarity of Egypt—the *saqiyeh*—is probably reproduced in a terracotta published by C. C. Edgar in *Bull. Soc. arch. Alex.* 7, 1905, p. 44; cf. note 43 to this chapter.

5. SECTION OF A FRESCO OF THE CASA DELL' EFEBO AT POMPEII. Pompeii, *Casa dell' efebo*, Reg. 1, ins. vii, nos. 10–12. A. Maiuri, *Not. d. Scavi*, 1927, pp. 59 ff., no. ix, pl. ix, cf. L. Jacono, ibid., pp. 86 ff.

The fresco, of which a section is here reproduced, is part of the decoration which extended round the sides of a *triclinium* made of masonry, built in the garden of this house. All these frescoes are executed in the so-called Egyptianizing style and reproduce scenes of Egyptian life. Our fresco is a rural scene. Near a series of duck-ponds (νησσοτροφεῖα) is a pavilion, a rural hotel, with two visitors—a man and a woman—in an unmistakable attitude, a servant bringing wine, the woman hotel-keeper, and a flute-player (*scabillaria*). A poor *fellah* ensures a supply of water into the ponds, by the arduous method of keeping the *cochlea*, invented by Archimedes (κοχλίας in the papyri, M. Schnebel, *Die Landwirtschaft im hell. Ägypten*, p. 84), in motion with his feet. The fresco is well illustrated from a technical point of view by L. Jacono. Note that the *cochlea* is still used in Egypt today, not only in the Delta but also in Middle Egypt, and still has the same design and is managed in the same way as we see in this fresco. It is rarely mentioned in the papyri because, just as now, it was not used in the Fayyûm. Large numbers of machines exactly similar to the *cochlea* of the fresco have been found in Spain inside or beside mines. They were used to draw water from wells and galleries. See T. A. Rickard, 'The mining of the Romans in Spain', *JRS* 18, 1928, pp. 130 ff., and pl. xii.

I. CART WITH A CANOPY

2. GATHERING DATES

3. CAMEL LOADED WITH GRAPES

4. CAMEL CARRYING JARS

5. ARCHIMEDES MILL

LIII. LIFE IN EGYPT

of Alexandria formed the wealthiest class in Egypt. Without doubt most of the royal agents who stood nearest to the king were at the same time engaged in carrying on the foreign trade of Egypt: they owned ships and storehouses and were members of the powerful Alexandrian associations of ναύκληροι and ἐγδοχεῖς.

No less numerous than the class of officials and business men, and forming a reservoir for it, was the class of foreign soldiers, the officers and privates of the Ptolemaic mercenary army. We cannot here describe the organization of this force. Suffice it to say that after various experiments the Ptolemies chose a peculiar system of remunerating their soldiers during the period when they were not on active service but in the reserve. They settled them in the country and gave them parcels of land to work. Some of them received good arable ground in Upper, Middle, and Lower Egypt, but most of them were assigned lands in the Fayyûm and in the Delta, where the Ptolemies succeeded by skilful engineering work in reclaiming large tracts which were formerly marsh or desert. The assignation of these newly reclaimed lands had a double purpose. It did not encroach on the interests of the crown or diminish its revenues, as happened when cultivated and cultivable land was granted to the soldiers, for such grants meant that the actual tillers of the soil, the native peasants, paid part of their rent to the new holders instead of to the state. The plots of newly reclaimed ground had no cultivators and it rested with the soldiers to find them or to cultivate the land with their own hands. Besides, the soil in most cases was not very suitable for corn but was excellent for vineyards or olive groves. The soldiers, who were Greeks or natives of Asia Minor, were anyhow inclined to introduce these new and more profitable forms of cultivation, with which they were familiar in their old homes. Now the state invited them to do so, and opened to them the prospect of becoming not holders but owners of their plots, if they planted them with vines and trees. The same opportunity was offered to civilians, whether they were large capitalists of Alexandria, to whom large tracts of land were assigned as 'gifts' (δωρεαί), or well-to-do ex-officials or former tax-farmers, who purchased the land from the state.

In this way the Greek population of Egypt became more than a mere collection of soldiers, officials, and business men. Tied to the soil, the Greeks were no longer temporary residents but permanent settlers in the land. With this change a new era began in the economic life of the country. The notion of land-ownership was almost foreign to Egypt in the pre-Macedonian age. There may have been attempts to create private property in the Saitic period. But in fact there had been only two types of landed proprietors in Egypt—the king and the gods. Now a third type came into existence when Greek foreigners became not tillers of the soil (γεωργοί), but landowners (γεοῦχοι), like the king and the gods. The Ptolemies, however, did not carry out this reform to its logical conclusion. Property in land was confined to house and garden land, and even so with some restrictions which meant that the ownership was a temporary privilege which might be withdrawn by the government.

The gradual growth of the Greek population produced new phenomena in the life of Egypt. The Ptolemies certainly never intended to hellenize the country thoroughly. The Greeks were, and were intended to remain, a ruling minority in an Egyptian land. No Greek would toil and travail for the kings as the natives did. This was the reason why the influx of Greeks did not lead to the natural result of such a penetration, the urbanization of the land. No cities were built by the Ptolemies for the Greeks, with the exception of Ptolemais in Upper Egypt. It is probable that the original idea of Alexander and the first Ptolemies in creating Alexandria and in maintaining Naucratis and perhaps Paraetonium, and later in creating Ptolemais, was gradually to urbanize and hellenize the land, as was done in Asia Minor and Syria. But the attempt was shortlived: no other cities were founded by Ptolemy Soter and his successors. And even Alexandria and Ptolemais were not normal Greek cities. Alexandria was simply a Greek residence of Greek kings. If she had at the very outset a regular city organization, this was soon done away with and self-government was curtailed to such an extent that there was no difference between the capital and the other administrative centres of Egypt, except the beauty and splendour of the city. Ptolemais enjoyed a little more autonomy, but it never attained any importance in the life of Egypt.

In the rest of the country the Greeks could order their life as they chose, provided that they did not claim a city organization. As the ruling class, they had no desire to be absorbed by the natives and to be treated like them. They must have their own organization and maintain the peculiarities of their life. In these efforts they were supported by the government, except, of course, in the matter of municipal self-government. The form of organization which they finally achieved was singular enough. Not cities (πόλεις) but communes (πολιτεύματα) of fellow country-men were established throughout the country, a species of clubs or associations whose function it was to maintain the Greek nationality of their members and to secure a Greek education for the younger generation. As the richest men in Egypt, con-scious of their superiority over the Egyptians, the Greeks main-tained their nationality and their civilization with fair success. In the larger villages and in the capitals of the provinces they established Greek quarters with the usual Greek buildings, sur-rounded by an Egyptian village—Greek islands in an Egyptian sea.

The endeavours of the first Ptolemies to attract a thrifty Greek population to Egypt and to attach it to the land by economic ties were not unsuccessful. Large areas of land were reclaimed in the Fayyûm and in the Delta. Thousands of new Greek house-holds—based on gardening, on the culture of vine and olive, and on the scientific breeding of cattle and poultry—appeared as oases of individualistic capitalism in the desert of Egyptian nationalization, and some of them prospered and throve. Greek-speaking people became a common feature of Egyptian life everywhere. But the results were not so brilliant as they seemed to be. The new Greek settlers were landowners, not tillers of the soil: labour was supplied by the natives. It soon appeared that such a system was not sound or profitable in the long run. Moreover, the internal conditions of Egypt grew steadily worse. The first able kings were replaced by *epigonoi*, who had neither energy nor ability. The international prestige of Egypt sank. Wars swallowed up large sums of money. The administration became inefficient and corrupt. The natives were ground down. The position of the Greeks was no better. Revolts of the Greeks in Alexandria and of the natives in the country shattered the en-feebled state. The corporations of priests, speculating on the weak-ness of the kings and on their own influence over the population, became more and more arrogant and constantly demanded, mostly with success, new concessions, such as the right of asylum

Description of Plate LIV

STREET AND HOUSE-FRONT AT CARANIS. Notice the wooden pieces in the wall of a house, and the wooden frames of the doors and windows (cf. the description of pl. LV). Reproduced by kind permission of the Kelsey Museum of Archaeology, University of Michigan (U.S.A.).

LIV. CARANIS, VILLAGE OF THE FAYYUM

or grants of land. In these circumstances land which had been reclaimed by the first Ptolemies was lost. Wide tracts of it passed into the possession of temples or became waste, ownerless (ἀδέσποτα) and dry (χέρσος).⁴⁰

Such was the situation when Egypt passed under the rule of the first Roman emperor, after a long agony lasting through the first century B.C., during which she was exploited by her own kings, who in turn were robbed by the Roman politicians on whom they depended. Augustus found in the land a strong and rich foreign element—wealthy Alexandrians, an army of Greek officials, most of whom were men of substance, thousands of business men scattered all over the country and sometimes owning land like the Alexandrians and the officials, and a numerous country gentry, nominally soldiers but in fact landowners of different kinds (κάτοικοι and κληροῦχοι). He found also rich and influential temples with a numerous clergy and under them an enormous mass of natives, some of whom—those who had done military service under the Ptolemies (μάχιμοι)—were allowed to hold state land in the same way as the Greek soldiers. The economic situation was bad. The population groaned under the exactions of the tax-farmers and officials; the clergy were arrogant but unproductive, living as they did on the work of peasants and enslaved artisans; the rural population was half ruined, and many plots formerly cultivated lay abandoned and waste. In general the conditions were very similar to those which prevailed in Egypt before the Greek conquest.⁴¹

Was it a mere coincidence in the methods of two great statesmen or conscious policy on the part of Augustus, who was of course familiar with the history of Egypt and its organization in the early Ptolemaic times, that the measures he took to restore the economic prosperity of the land were almost exactly the same as those taken by Ptolemy Philadelphus? His efforts were not directed towards a thorough reorganization of Egypt; his main aim was to restore the paying capacity of the land, which was, as we know, his chief source of income as ruler of the Roman state. To secure this object three fundamental measures were necessary: the political and economic influence of the clergy had to be curtailed; the administrative system had to be reformed, and above all bribes and illicit gains abolished; and a new start had to be made in reclaiming cultivable land. The policy of

Augustus in regard to the temples has been set forth by the present writer in a special article, to which the reader must be referred. Its main feature was a thorough secularization of the landed property of the priests, a nationalization of the Church such as had been already attempted and almost carried out by Ptolemy Philadelphus, although dropped by the later Ptolemies. The result of Augustus' reorganization was that the temples and priests, while left unhampered in their religious activities, were entirely deprived of their economic grip over the population. Their lands and their revenue in general became one of the departments of the financial administration of Egypt, managed and controlled by the state like other departments. The money necessary for the maintenance of public worship and of the clergy was now in the last resort furnished by the state.[42]

In the sphere of administration no radical changes were introduced. The Ptolemaic system was kept almost intact. The only change was that the material responsibility of the agents of the government for the management of their job was emphasized, and this gradually led (as we shall see in the next chapter) to the transformation of officials and tax-farmers into agents of the state, responsible to it but not remunerated by it (λειτουργοί). In fact, however, the decisive steps towards this transformation were taken not by Augustus but by his successors at the end of the first century. The administration of Egypt remained Greek. Only the highest officials, the Prefect who represented the new ruler—the heir of the Ptolemies—his chief assistants, and the epistrategi of provinces were drawn from the ranks of Romans. All the other posts, from that of governor of the nome downwards, were filled by Greeks who lived in the country. The army —officers and legionaries alike—was also Roman, even though the latter were recruited mainly in the East, and without doubt spoke Greek. The auxiliary troops came from various parts of the Empire. The official language of Egypt also remained Greek, Latin being used only in dealing with the Roman elements of the population.[43]

But Augustus directed his efforts mainly towards the restoration of the economic strength of the country. Here again he had recourse to methods which almost coincided with those that were first introduced by Ptolemy Philadelphus. The system of taxation and the economic and financial organization remained as they were. The mainstay of the country continued to be the work done by the natives in agriculture, industry, and transportation. As before, they had no share in administration and were regarded simply as organized labour-units—peasants, artisans, drivers, sailors, and so forth. As before, they were not landowners but lessees of the state, who cultivated in that capacity the royal or public land (γῆ βασιλική or δημοσία). They still worked in their shops for the government, at the order and under the control of the state officials; and they still sold foodstuffs and manufactured goods with a special licence from the government, as concessionaires of the state.

A strong effort was made on new lines to restore the economic strength of the foreign elements of the population, Roman now as well as Greek. A new and decisive step was taken towards the creation of a prosperous rural *bourgeoisie*. The holdings of former soldiers of the Ptolemaic army were definitely recognized as the private property of the actual holders, the κληροῦχοι and κάτοικοι. The ranks of these landowners were reinforced by hundreds of Roman veterans, some of whom received plots of land immediately after the conquest of the country by Augustus, while some were given favourable opportunities of acquiring cultivable land for the nominal price of 20 drachmae for each *aroura*. This measure was intended to encourage reclamation of waste and abandoned land on the largest possible scale, and it was not confined to the veterans. Everybody was welcomed who had money and wished to invest it in land. Good cultivated and cultivable land was not, however, thrown on the market. It remained state property and was let out to the peasants. The purchase of a parcel of land from the state meant, therefore, the purchase of good but neglected land, for the cultivation of which money and energy were required. Good opportunities were provided also by the removal of unnecessary formalities which hampered free dealing in private land, and by the secularization of large tracts of temple land. The chances offered by Augustus were eagerly seized by those who looked for a profitable investment for their money, and there were plenty of them, both men and women. Peace and quiet stimulated business life in Alexandria. Rich Alexandrian merchants and industrialists were glad to invest their money in Egyptian land; many Roman capitalists, especially those who were acquainted with Egypt, were ready to try

1–8. TYPICAL OBJECTS IN DAILY USE FOUND IN THE RUINS OF PRIVATE HOUSES AT CARANIS.

1. Wooden chair.
2. Wooden painted box with portrait of the lady-owner on one side and a dove on the

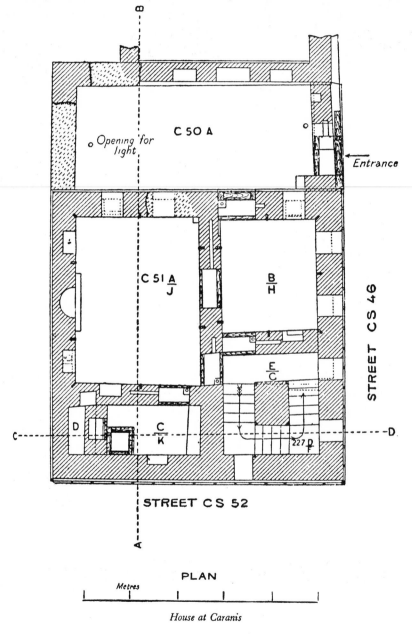

PLAN

Metres

House at Caranis

1. WOODEN CHAIR

2. WOODEN PAINTED
BOX

3. WOODEN COMB FOR
COMBING WOOL

4. BASKET

5. GLASS LANTERN

6. MALLET

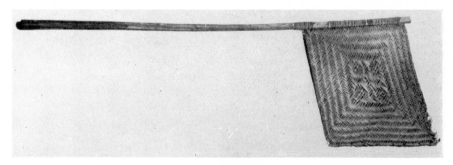

7. RAFFIA FAN

8. WRITING PEN

LV. CARANIS

other. Was it the wedding-box of a lady, containing jewels and other objects of value which formed her trousseau?

3. Wooden comb for carding wool.

4. Pretty little basket, probably for wool.

5. Glass lantern: it was supported by a wooden tripod.

6. Mallet.

7. Raffia fan.

8. Writing-pen.

Unpublished; reproduced here by the kind permission of the Kelsey Museum of Archaeology, University of Michigan.

The first scientific excavations of a Fayyûm village were undertaken in 1924 by the University of Michigan. The results have been surprising. Thanks to this complete investigation of the ruins of Caranis by the University of Michigan (under the direction of Mr. E. E. Petersen, with Professor A. E. R. Boak as scientific director), the everyday life of one of the characteristic villages of the Fayyûm is now illustrated in all its details.

On the earlier excavations of Caranis see Grenfell, Hunt, and Hogarth, *Fayum Towns and their Papyri* (1900), pp. 27 ff. and pl. II; cf. pls. XV–XVII. On the work of the University of Michigan expedition see A. E. R. Boak, *JEA* 13, 1927, pp. 171 ff.; cf. the bibliography given in *CAH* VII (1929), p. 894, 8, and the first report on the Caranis excavations published in 1932. [See A. E. R. Boak and E. E. Petersen, *Karanis, Topographical and Architectural Report of Excavations during the Seasons 1924–8*, Michigan (1931); A. E. R. Boak, *Karanis, The Temples, coin hoards, &c., Seasons 1924–31*, Michigan (1933).]

To illustrate the typical form of the houses of Caranis and the other villages of the Fayyûm, I reproduce the plan of one of the more completely excavated houses. The

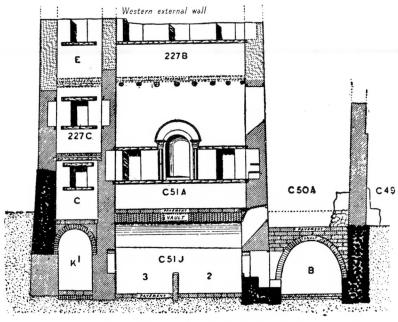

Section A–B from South to North. Seen from the East

plan (unpublished) is the work of Mr. Terentiev and is reproduced here by permission of the directors of the excavation.

At my request Professor A. E. R. Boak gives this description of the house (C. 51). 'We have here a characteristic house of the better type at Karanis, of the second or third ecntury A.D. It comprised a wine-cellar or ground-floor basement, with three, or perhaps four, floors above. The foundations and the lower parts of the walls above ground-level were made of local stone, without lime, the remainder of the walls of sun-baked brick. At some points the external walls were reinforced and covered with timber, and the frames of windows and doors were also of wood. The rooms of the cellar were domed and supported the main floor, which was also of brick, mixed with mud. The roofing of the steps was also covered with a dome, in such a way that the arch covering each flight supported the flight immediately above it. The interior walls were covered with plaster. The upper floors and the roof, made of reeds, matting, and packed mud, were supported on wooden beams. The rooms had niches and cupboards in the walls. The niches served in some instances as domestic chapels, while the cupboards often had wooden doors. The average height of the various floors was about 2·25 m., but in some instances, as in the room C. 51 A of the plan, it was as much as 4 m. Next to the house

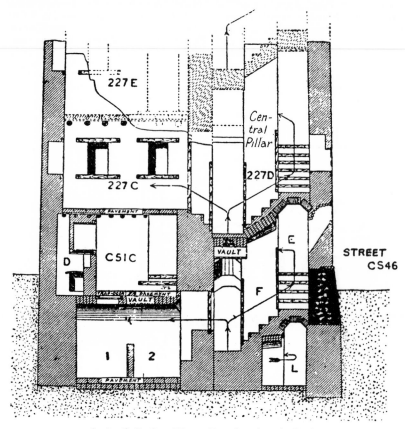

Section C–D, from West to East. Seen from the South

was a courtyard (C. 50) which opened on to the street. The plan of the house was a square of *ca.* 7·5 m. The greatest height of the walls, after the excavations, reached 6·25 m. at street level. They must originally have been about 8 m. high. The lower floor, with store-rooms, extended under the courtyard and under the house.' [The house is referred to in Boak–Petersen, op. cit., *passim*, and on p. 57 it is said that 'it will be described in detail in a later report'. This has not appeared. Photographs of parts of the house, ibid., pls. xxxvi, xxxviii, xxxix.]

their luck in this promising country; and, above all, thousands of the former officials and tax-farmers of the Ptolemies were eager to acquire landed property, when the conditions of life became settled and a vast market was opened up for Egyptian products.[44]

Thus the development of the landowning class, which had been arrested in the last years of the Ptolemaic régime, started afresh. The most characteristic and interesting new feature of this development was the rapid growth of large estates in the hands of Roman capitalists, which corresponds closely to the extension of δωρεαί under Ptolemy Philadelphus, and was encouraged by Augustus with the same purpose of attracting new capital and fresh energy to Egypt, and of introducing more modern methods of capitalistic economy into the stagnant agricultural life of the ancient land. The growth of new δωρεαί, or οὐσίαι as they were now called, is one of the striking features of Egyptian life in the first century A.D., and especially in the time of Augustus and Tiberius. The first to acquire large estates in Egypt were the members of the imperial family. It is probable that Drusus, the stepson of Augustus, was one of the earliest of the great Roman landowners there. His estate was inherited by his wife Antonia and by his sons Germanicus and the future Emperor Claudius. Another estate was owned jointly or successively by Livia, the wife of Augustus, and her grandson Germanicus, and still another, and a very large one, by Germanicus alone. The elder Agrippa, or his youngest son Agrippa Postumus, is also recorded as a proprietor, and the Emperor Gaius and his uncle Claudius are found as joint owners. Finally, Livia (the wife of Drusus, son of Tiberius) and her children, the children of Claudius by his first marriage and Antonia, the offspring of his second marriage, as well as Messalina and Agrippina (the first or the second?) occur in contemporary or later documents as owners of large estates. It is worthy of note that none of the reigning emperors appears in this list, except Gaius, who probably inherited his estate from his father. Occasionally we hear also of confiscated οὐσίαι owned by reigning emperors (Tiberius, Claudius, and especially Nero). I am inclined, however, to believe that the emperors before Vespasian did not retain these estates but gave them away to other holders of the type above described. Another interesting feature is the predominance of women and minors in the post-Augustan period. In the first case the explanation may be that Egypt was anyhow the property of the emperor as the successor of the kings, in the second that the emperors legitimately feared to permit members of the ruling family to obtain a hold on the land, the free disposal of which was one of the *arcana imperii* of the Julio-Claudian dynasty. Certainly both the appropriation of Egyptian lands by members of the imperial family and the spasmodic confiscations of their properties are clear proofs of the purely personal character of the rule of the Julii and Claudii.

Next to the emperors came the landed proprietors of the senatorial and equestrian classes. Some of their estates (for example, that of Falcidius) may have been formed in the time of Antony's rule, but the majority of them were certainly of Augustan origin. The most prominent owners were C. Maecenas and C. Petronius, the two friends of Augustus, both of the equestrian class. Along with them we meet many prominent senatorial families— the Aponii, the Atinii, the Gallii, the Lurii, the Norbani. To the same class belong a certain Severus and a Iucundus Grypianus. It is again to be noted that some of the owners were women (Gallia Polla and Norbana Clara), probably because it was difficult for men of the senatorial class to buy land in Egypt. The last of the series is the famous L. Annaeus Seneca, the philosopher and educator of the Emperor Nero.

Senators and knights were rivalled by the freedman favourites of the reigning emperors, of whom Narcissus, the well-known freedman of Claudius, and Doryphorus, the powerful secretary of petitions in Nero's reign, are recorded as landowners. To the class of imperial favourites belong also the members of the Jewish royal family C. Julius Alexander and Julia Berenice. And, finally, a group of rich members of the outstanding Alexandrian families —C. Julius Theon, Theon son of Theon, M. Julius Asclepiades, Asclepiades son of Ptolemaeus—may be identified with prominent Alexandrians who figure in our literary tradition. I am convinced that noble Alexandrians are also to be recognized in Lycarion and his daughter Thermutharion, in C. Julius Athenodorus, Ti. Calpurnius Tryphon, M. Tigellius Ialysus, Euander son of Ptolemaeus, Onesimus, Apion, Dionysodorus, Theoninus, Philodamus, and Anthus, who are all mentioned in documents, mostly of the first century, as owners of Egyptian οὐσίαι.[45]

Most of these estates were created by purchases of land which had formerly belonged to military settlers of the Ptolemaic period. Legally, therefore, they belonged to the category of γῆ κληρουχική or κατοικική. Some of them may have enjoyed freedom from taxation or a reduced rate of taxes (ἀτέλεια or κουφοτέλεια). The majority, however, were subject to the taxes usually paid by the category of land created by Augustus which bore the name of 'purchased' land, γῆ ἐωνημένη. As far as the evidence goes, a large part of this land was cultivated as vineyards, gardens, and olive-groves; there is abundant evidence showing that many new plantations were laid out by the new proprietors. The Alexandrians invested heavily in this 'purchased' land: it is sufficient to read the passages of the edict of Ti. Julius Alexander referring to it, and addressed to the Alexandrians, to realize how anxious they were to keep these properties when an attack on them was launched by the imperial administration, an attack which ended in their almost total disappearance.[46]

The efforts of Augustus and of his immediate successors met with fair success. Much land was reclaimed, and many new estates gave safe and good returns to their owners. But this is only the first chapter of the story. Under the reign of Nero, and still more in the time of the Flavians, the policy of the emperors abruptly changed. It was not that the emperors ceased to favour the formation of new private estates: as before, they gave every facility to the purchasers of abandoned or waste lands.[47] What they desired was that the buyers should be residents in the country, not influential men from Rome, not members of the imperial house nor of the senatorial or equestrian aristocracy, nor imperial favourites of the freedman class, nor even wealthy Alexandrians. They desired the purchasers to be the local Greek and Roman *bourgeoisie*, men whose whole life was connected with the land. The explanation of this change of policy is simple. It was not an easy task for the local administration of Egypt, or even for the prefects, to exact from the noble landowners and their agents a strict obedience to the laws in respect of the payment of taxes and the fulfilment of the obligations owed to the state by the workmen and lessees of the estates. For the state and for the administration the οὐσίαι were, therefore, a loss: they limited the amount of highly-taxed land without increasing the revenues of the crown. This situation caused great dissatisfaction in the second half of the first century A.D. The emperors of this period continually increased their demands for corn and money: governmental pressure made itself felt by all those whom it was able to reach, especially by the peasants and by the small landowners who served the state both as tax-contributors and as tax-collectors. The consequences of all this were disastrous. The distressed debtors took to flight, and towns and villages lost a substantial proportion of their population. The principle of collective responsibility invoked at this time did not help in avoiding the loss caused by the taxpayers, who were both discontented and unable to pay; nor was the obligation of cultivating the abandoned lands imposed on the larger and wealthier villages of any help.

The Flavians applied themselves to meeting the evil, not, however, by diminishing the burden of taxation, of compulsory levies and of liturgies, but by suppressing absentee ownership of large estates. They thus appropriated large tracts of fertile land, which could be let or sold to peasants or to anyone who wished to become a small local landowner. By this policy they aimed at increasing the number of landowners, and at assuring themselves good taxpayers and loyal tax-collectors who could not escape taxes and liturgies. In so acting the Flavians and after them the Antonines only applied to Egypt the policy followed by them elsewhere in the Empire. On the other hand, the new dynasty was afraid of pretenders, and it was the firm belief of the Flavian house, whose founder Vespasian owed his throne to the possession of Egypt, that the valley of the Nile was the most favourable base of operations for a rival claimant to supreme power. Thus the large estates were liquidated in one way or another, and no fresh ones were formed. Some rare exceptions only confirm the rule. The last of the emperors to own land personally in Egypt was Titus. A few descendants of ancient owners, who were harmless to the emperor and the administration, retained their inherited properties. Such was M. Antonius Pallas, a descendant of the famous Pallas. A very few new estates were formed. Such perhaps were the estate of Julia Berenice, the mistress of Titus, and those of Claudia Athenais—a member of the distinguished family of the Attici of Athens, the friends of the emperors of the second century and of Julia Polla. But these were exceptions.[48]

Yet the class of landowners did not cease to grow. Land was still bought and improved, new vineyards and olive-groves were planted. The purchasers were the local *bourgeoisie*, which consisted of the veterans of the Roman army, the officials of the imperial administration, the farmers of taxes, the owners of ships and of draught animals, and others. The dominant type of Egyptian landowner in the second century was the local squire, either a veteran or a Greek or half-Greek, who resided in one of the *metropoleis*. A striking picture of this type of proprietor is furnished by the correspondence of the veteran L. Bellenus Gemellus, a resident in the village of Euhemeria in the Fayyûm, an old man, but an excellent manager of his model estate. Another example is Apollonius, a *strategus* of the Heptakomia in the time of Hadrian, who devoted his life to the imperial service but whose interests were in his native city of Hermupolis Magna. Some very large fortunes were made by this Egyptian *bourgeoisie*. A very characteristic description of one of them may be quoted. It is given indeed by a bitter enemy, but it is probably trustworthy as regards the extent, if not as regards the source, of the fortune: 'You will find that he and his whole house owned originally no more than seven *arourae*. Now he owns himself 7,000, and 200 *arourae* of vines, and he has given a loan to Claudius Eutychides of 72 talents. All this has been made by thefts from the public storehouses and by cheating the treasury through the non-payment of taxes.'[49]

Another source of enrichment for the local gentry of the second century, at least for a short time, was the exploitation of the confiscated οὐσίαι of the first century, which now became state property and formed a special *ratio*, the department of the γῆ οὐσιακή, under the supervision of the high official who dealt with confiscated goods and fines in general, the ἴδιος λόγος. This land was usually leased to rich capitalists in large plots— the same system which we shall find at the same date elsewhere in Africa.[50]

Thus in Egypt, as in the other provinces of the Roman Empire, the second century A.D. was a prosperous time for the class which corresponded to that of the municipal *bourgeoisie* in the other provinces. It was indeed, in Egypt also, a municipal *bourgeoisie* in all but name. The second century witnessed a brilliant development of cities all over the land. They were not cities as

regards constitution, for the emperors of that century adhered
to the ancient practice of the Ptolemies and of Augustus and refrained from granting municipal rights to Egyptian towns. Even
Alexandria, despite renewed efforts, did not succeed in obtaining
a βουλή from the emperors. The 'cities' of Egypt remained legally
metropoleis, administrative *chefs-lieux*, but they were cities from
the social and economic point of view. The new landed gentry
did not live as a rule in the villages to which their properties were
attached. In fact their estates, like the οὐσίαι of the first century,
were scattered over one nome or even over many. Most of them
took up residence in a *metropolis*, whence it was easier for them
to supervise their scattered parcels of land. Thus the population
of a district town came to be more than a mere collection of
officials and tax-farmers, shopkeepers, artisans, and retail-
traders. The majority of its residents were landowners, γεοῦχοι.
They were Greeks, some of them being Roman citizens; a certain number were hellenized Romans, many were hellenized
Egyptians, the most thrifty and energetic of the natives, who
succeeded in accumulating a fortune and in entering the ranks
of the Egyptian Greeks by the purchase of land, by intermar-
riage, and so forth. The second century was the climax of the
process of hellenization in Egypt. We shall soon meet with its
decline. No doubt these rich Greeks desired to live, not the
miserable life of the Egyptian natives, but the comfortable life
of their fellow countrymen in Asia Minor, Syria, and Greece.
They needed a city life and they created it. The government did
not interfere; on the contrary, it promoted the movement from
the time of Augustus onwards, for reasons which will presently
appear. Thus the *metropoleis* assumed, so far at least as their
Greek quarters were concerned, the aspect of real Hellenistic
cities, and some of the larger villages did the same. Improvements of the type common all over the Greco-Roman world
were introduced: existing gymnasia were enlarged, baths were
built, streets were lighted at night. Hand in hand with this
material advance went the steady development of a sort of self-
government with magistrates half-elected, half-appointed, who
formed κοινά and held meetings, and even with some imitations
of a popular assembly. Even Antinoupolis itself, the creation of
Hadrian, which was reputed to be a new Greek city, differed
little from the Egyptian towns from the social and economic

points of view; as is well-known, its inhabitants were Egyptian Greeks.[51]

Such was the manner in which Egypt gradually emerged from her isolation and remodelled her life on the pattern of the other provinces. The change was, of course, one which touched the surface only, and it was of short duration. In Egypt more than in any other land the cities were a superstructure. Their growth and development were based on the toil and travail of the Egyptian masses. The life of these masses had not changed. In the next chapter we shall speak of the attempts of the Emperor Hadrian to stimulate the conversion of the peasants into a landed *bourgeoisie* and to amalgamate the Egyptians and the Greeks. The attempts proved futile and shortlived. In truth, the mass of the Egyptian peasants and artisans continued to live the very same life as had been their lot from the dawn of Egyptian history, and no one sought to bring changes into that life. For them the creation of a city *bourgeoisie* meant little, and it affected them not at all. As of old, they toiled and groaned over their primitive ploughs and developed looms, and, as before, their toil and pain were not for themselves but for what they were told was the Roman Empire, personified in the sacred and remote image of the Roman emperor. They lost even the consolation of refuge in a temple, for the right of asylum was gradually curtailed by the emperors. Attempts at revolt would have been madness in the presence of the Roman troops, with the whole Empire at their back, and there were few who would lead them in such attempts. The only resource left them was to flee and live the life of wild beasts and robbers in the swamps of the Delta, and that was not an alluring prospect.[52]

To the South, Egypt extended to the lands of Nubia, which in the Ptolemaic and Roman periods constituted the kingdom of Meroe. From the first to the fifth cataract this land on both sides of the Nile is doomed to poverty. The cataracts hinder any regular navigation of the river; agriculture and livestock-breeding are restricted to limited stretches of inundated land at the mouths of some of the torrents which debouch into the Nile. Conditions south of the fifth cataract are quite different. The triangle formed by the Nile, the Atbara, and the Blue Nile belongs already to the zone of tropical rains, and the conditions necessary for agriculture and ranching exist not only along the river courses, but also in a hinterland larger than Egypt itself. A part of this territory yields rich crops after the tropical rains, while other parts are admirably suited for rearing livestock on a large scale. In addition the country was rich in metals—iron, copper, gold—and precious stones.

The history of those lands is closely connected with that of Egypt. We can today reconstruct it from the prehistoric period down to the Arab conquest and beyond, thanks wholly to archaeology, to the systematic and scientific exploration of the ruins and necropoleis of southern Nubia and the Sudan. The excavations not only enable us to reconstruct the political history of the region, but offer us also a complete picture of the peculiar civilization which developed under Egyptian influence in the different periods of the history of the country. This is a new archaeological triumph, achieved mainly by English and American explorers, although German and Austrian scholars have also played their part.[53] Side by side with the accumulation of the material its historical study has been in progress. We owe valuable sketches of the early history of Nubia to Reisner and Griffith, and it was the same two students, along with Sayce and Garstang, the explorer of the city of Meroe, who laid the foundations for the reconstruction of later Nubian history, that contemporary with the Ptolemaic and Roman periods of Egypt: I refer here to the partial decipherment of the Meroitic inscriptions, both hieroglyphic and cursive, a remarkable achievement we owe to Griffith, and the reconstruction of a long chronological list of Meroitic kings—previously we knew only two or three—which has been possible as a result of the masterly exploration of the royal tombs (pyramids) of Napata and Meroe carried out by Reisner.[54]

I cannot deal here with all the periods of the secular history of the Nubian lands, nor can I venture into details regarding the kingdom of Meroe during the Ptolemaic and Roman periods. I feel, however, that the picture of the social and economic life of Roman Egypt would be incomplete if it were not accompanied by a short account of the same scope for the kingdom of Meroe, which politically, economically, and culturally was a mere appendix to Egypt.

As is well known, Egypt and Nubia had a long, though at times interrupted, period of trade relations in the pre-dynastic

Description of Plate LVI

1. INCISED BRONZE VASE. Found at Karanog in Lower Nubia in the large tomb G 187. Cairo Museum. C. L. Woolley and D. Randall-MacIver, *Karanog. The Romano-Nubian Cemetery* (Univ. of Pennsylvania, Egyptian Dept. of the University Museum, *Eckley B. Coxe Junior Expedition to Nubia*, iii, 1910), text, pp. 59 ff.; cf. pp. 37 ff. and pls. 26–27; G. Maspero, *Guide to the Cairo Museum*[4], p. 262. Probably 1st or 2nd cent. A.D.

Nubian queen on her estate

The incised design reproduces in the centre a small round hut made of branches driven into the earth and tied together at the top; above the solar disk. Behind the hut a mimosa-tree; before it sits a lady, clearly a queen, as can be seen from her attire and from the solar disk on top of the hut. The upper part of her body is naked, the lower part covered with a smooth dress. She is wearing a collar fitted tightly round her neck, and two necklaces, one of which has large pendants; on each arm she wears a bracelet and an armlet, while in her right hand she carries what is perhaps a dagger. Behind her stands a naked servant-girl. To the right is a steward who is issuing orders to an old shepherd, who presents the queen with a vessel, apparently a jug covered with wicker-work. At the feet of the shepherd five cups; perhaps the shepherd is pouring the milk from his jug into one of them. Behind him there is a double series of cows, five pairs. One of these suckles a calf, while another is being milked. Behind the fourth pair another shepherd with a jug. The last pair is facing in the other direction, namely towards the hut and another tree to which five calves are tethered. The same tomb yielded another cup of the same style, with similar figures (now in the University of Pennsylvania); many others of the same type have been discovered at Kerma (G. Reisner, *Harvard African Studies*, 5, 1923, 'Excavations at Kerma', pts. i–iii, p. 47, and ibid., 6, 1923, pts. iv–v, pp. 203 ff.). The art of the engraver displays a singular mixture of the neo-Egyptian and Hellenistic styles. The scene is well drawn and full of movement. The sort of life shown in these representations is typical of the kingdom of Meroe: the life of farmers and shepherds. Grazing provided the royal family with its best revenues. Compare the stele of Tanatamon in the temple of Ammon on the Gebel Barcal: 'he built another hall at the back for milking his many herds, in (their) ten thousands, thousands, hundreds, and tens. There was no counting the young calves with their cows' (G. Reisner, *Sudan Notes and Records*, 2, 1919, p. 54).

2. NUBIAN TERRACOTTA CUP, REPRESENTING A HUNTER. Found at Karanog outside tomb G 189. Cairo Museum. C. L. Woolley and D. Randall-MacIver, op. cit., p. 55 and pl. 43. Basic colour pale yellow with drawings in dark grey.

It represents a negro at the hunt, with two spears in his hand. In front of him is a dog with a studded collar. Further in front, a wood (indicated by a single tree) in which are two wild beasts.

1. NUBIAN QUEEN ON HER ESTATE

2. HUNTING IN NUBIA

LVI. SCENES OF LIFE IN THE KINGDOM OF MEROE

age, and under the first dynasties. These relations became regular in the period from the fourth to the sixth dynasties. Interrupted temporarily by anarchy in Egypt, they were renewed in the greatest and most productive period of Egyptian history, under the twelfth dynasty, in the form of half-military, half-commercial expeditions. Under the eighteenth dynasty southern Nubia was effectively annexed and the ways of life were almost entirely Egyptianized. Nubia was then simply one of the many provinces of Egypt. In fact she was more closely connected with Egypt than any of the other provinces and could be considered as a part of that country, and in this condition she remained in the time of the nineteenth and into the twentieth dynasty. Thus Egyptianized, Nubia reached the peak of her political power when a Libyo-Ethiopic dynasty of Napata reigned for a long time over the whole of Egypt, and led the Egyptians in their struggle against the Assyrians. Defeated by the latter, the Libyo-Ethiopic dynasty withdrew again to Napata and disappeared from history.

For the Pharaohs Nubia had no importance in itself. The country, as has been said, is poor and difficult to defend from the assaults of the desert tribes, the Blemmyes and Nobades. Nor was it worth while for them to hold the island of Meroe alone, for its products; a tribute of grain, livestock, dates, and metals would increase the wealth of Egypt but little, while the transport of such products would have involved considerable expense and trouble. If, in spite of this, the Pharaohs attempted persistently to control the country, if they built fortresses there, and dispatched colonists to it, they did so because the great caravan route from Central Africa, Abyssinia, and the eastern deserts between Nubia and the Red Sea to Egypt passed through it. Naturally, ivory, ebony, minerals, oil, hides—particularly leopard-skins—which were of great importance in the ceremonial dress of the Pharaohs, captured wild animals and negro slaves, all formed part of this trade, but the main item was the gold of the lands bordering on Abyssinia, which was transported to Egypt through the isle of Meroe. In fact the contribution from Nubia was the only gold on which the Pharaohs could reckon with safety; and it was Nubian gold which kept high the prestige of the new kingdom in Syria, in Asia Minor, and in the regions of the Euphrates. After the fall of Libyo-Ethiopic rule in Egypt, that dynasty, as we can see from the excavations carried out near Napata and in the great sanctuary of Ammon on the Gebel Barcal, reigned undisturbed at Napata for about 350 years. Some commercial contact with Egypt was maintained, but it was of relatively little importance. The second capital of the kingdom of Napata was Meroe, the importance of which grew continually from the seventh century B.C. In the same period Southern Nubia declined considerably. From this it may be inferred that the Ethiopian or Nubian kingdom lived at that time mainly on its agriculture and sheep-breeding, while trade played a very minor part.

The situation changed with the beginning of the Ptolemaic period. About 300 B.C. the centre of the Ethiopic kingdom was transferred to Meroe. In fact for a certain time there were two capitals and two kingdoms, that of Napata and that of Meroe (from 300 to about 220 B.C.). The two kingdoms were united by the famous Ergamenes mentioned by Diodorus, the contemporary of Philadelphus or of Philopator or of both, if it is true that his reign was so long. This state of affairs lasted until about 100 B.C. when, according to Reisner, a new dynasty arose, which reigned at Napata for about eighty years. Was this change due to diplomatic or military action by the Ptolemies? We must not forget that Philadelphus made an expedition into Nubia to appropriate the gold-mines of the country. Undoubtedly a partition of the Ethiopian kingdom was of use to whomever at that time ruled Egypt.

However that may be, it is certain that under the Ptolemies relations between Napata and Meroe on the one hand and Egypt on the other were very close. This is shown by the strong Hellenistic influence which is evident in the peculiar civilization of Napata and Meroe in the second half of the third and all the second century B.C. Under Ergamenes, Meroe, the capital, and in particular its citadel with its Hellenistic palaces, its Hellenistic bath, its Ethiopian-Hellenistic statues and decorative frescoes, became a little Nubian Alexandria. At the same time the Meroites began to use their own language in public and private documents, and in Ethiopia new and interesting styles in ceramics and metalwork, decorated by native craftsmen in a special Greco-Nubian style, began to develop. The men who carried into effect this work of hellenization and at the same time of nationalism, namely Ergamenes and Aza Khelaman, considered themselves strong enough and rich enough for a trial of strength with powerful Egypt. They succeeded in making themselves masters of the Egyptian part of Nubia (the Dodecaschoenus), and in provoking a rebellion in the Thebaid which detached that region from the Ptolemies for a space of twenty years (from the sixteenth year of Philopator to the nineteenth of Epiphanes, 206–186 B.C.). The struggle between the Ptolemies and Nubia ended under Philometor and Euergetes II. Ptolemaic authority was restored both in the Thebaid and—for most of the second century—in the Dodecaschoenus; this roughly coincided with the new division of the Ethiopic kingdom already referred to. A new revolt in the Thebaid in the years 87–84 B.C. failed and was easily suppressed in spite of the weakness of the Ptolemies.[55]

A further change occurred when Egypt passed under Roman rule. The rulers of Meroe, that is the Queen Mother—who bore the title of Candace—and her son, unquestionably ill-informed about the new rulers of Egypt, renewed the attempt to make themselves masters of the Thebaid. It is well known that Cornelius Gallus suppressed the insurrection in the Thebaid and that Petronius in two campaigns advanced into the territory of Napata, and destroyed Napata itself, the holy city of the Ethiopians. Whether, as Garstang suggested, he reached Meroe, we do not know: it seems unlikely. The Roman government was not prepared to occupy the Ethiopian lands, and it is clear that the victory was less complete than Strabo would have us believe. Augustus himself recognized this fact in his negotiations with the queen's envoys; he renounced the tribute imposed in theory by Petronius on the kings of Meroe and fixed the Egyptian frontier at Hiera Sykaminos (Maharraga), instead of at Primis (Kasr Ibrim), a little further south (about 70 miles). This settlement lasted for two centuries. The expedition through Meroe proposed by Nero was certainly aimed at discovering new commercial routes, not at preparing the annexation of the country.[56]

The second half of the first century and the second century A.D. were periods of greater material prosperity and of more progressive civilization at Meroe. Not only did it again become one large and splendid city—though perhaps not to the extent it had been under Ergamenes—but also numerous centres of civic and religious life arose in the rainy districts of the island

Description of Plate LVII

1. STATUETTE REPRESENTING THE BIRD-SOUL OF A NUBIAN KING. Found at Karanog in tomb G 187. Philadelphia, Museum of the University of Pennsylvania. C. L. Woolley and D. Randall-MacIver, *Karanog*, &c., p. 47, and pls. 1–2.

This statuette is the finest among 120 of the same type found at Caranog. It is of sandstone and was originally coloured. In accordance with Nubian custom, foreign to Egypt, it shows the soul (Ba) of the king, with human body and the wings of a bird. The king is represented in traditional dress; he wears a priestly robe with sleeves, beneath which a red tunic is visible. In the left hand he holds a stick, which probably had a round head at the top. The right hand is missing. The head shows negroid features.

2. SPHERICAL NUBIAN POT OR AMPHORA. Found at Karanog. Tomb G 566. Philadelphia, Museum of University of Pennsylvania. C. L. Woolley and D. Randall-MacIver, op. cit., pp. 56 and 262 and pl. 41. Black and white on red.

Giraffes stretching their necks towards the tops of some trees.

In the upper band a gigantic snake. On representations of the giraffe in ancient and modern art see B. Laufer, *The Giraffe in History and Art*, Field Museum of Natural History, Anthropology, Leaflet 27, Chicago, 1928 (the author has nothing to say of the Nubian pottery).

Both the figures on this plate are reproduced by courtesy of the University Museum of Pennsylvania.

1. STATUETTE REPRESENTING THE BIRD-SOUL OF A NUBIAN KING

2. NUBIAN GIRAFFES

LVII. THE KINGDOM OF MEROE

of Meroe and of Gezireh. Moreover, the tracts of fertile land in Southern Nubia near the Nile became wealthy and populous cities with temples, citadels, and royal palaces, and with rich necropoleis in which the characteristic royal pyramid tomb had pride of place. The ruins of Basa, Soda, Marabbaa, Gebel Geili, Mesauvarat, Naga, and Soba near Meroe, and those of Kerma, Karanog, and Faras in Lower Nubia evidence this unfamiliar prosperity in Ethiopia in striking contrast with the poverty in which the lower classes of Egypt lived at that time. We know almost nothing regarding the organization of the country at this time. It seems, however, certain that Meroe was the royal residence, and that the citadels, palaces, and pyramids of Lower Nubia belonged either to the king-governors (who bore the title of *peshate* or *psentes*) who ruled the country in the name of their sovereign at Meroe, or to feudal princes, chiefs of the various tribes, and vassals of the great king of Meroe.[57]

The prosperity of Ethiopia lasted as long as that of Egypt. The change began in the second half of the second century A.D.; at the end of the third century Ethiopia was again ruined. As long as the Romans were strong enough in Egypt to check the Blemmyes and the Nobades, the kingdom of Meroe was also safe; but when the anarchy of the third century weakened the Roman Empire, the Meroites were not able to defend themselves against the assaults of their different neighbours. As is well known, Diocletian ceded the Dodecaschoenus to the Nobades and undertook to pay the Blemmyes an annual amount as a subsidy. The situation of Meroe then became critical, but its dynasty, as Reisner has shown, lasted another sixty years, when the rise of the powerful civilization of the Axumites was able to save it from the Negro danger. Equally well known is the expedition of Aeizanas of Axum to Meroe to punish the black Nobades, who had expelled the 'red' Cushites or Ethiopians (Kasu) from their cities and lands on the island of Meroe.[58]

During the Hellenistic-Roman period social and economic life in the Ethiopian countries undoubtedly displayed contrasts even stronger than in Egypt. On the one hand we have the palaces and fortifications of the kings, on the other the grass and cane huts in which the peasants and shepherds, and probably also the miners and the employees of the mines and workshops, lived. The discoveries of various iron weapons and instruments in

Meroitic tombs, the hills of iron dross which surround the ruins of Meroe and of some Meroitic temples, and the remains of furnaces in which the iron was melted show that iron was abundant in the kingdom of Meroe.[59] We do not know whether iron and copper were exported to Egypt. For the rest, the lower classes usually led a pastoral life. The scenes on local pottery show that hunting was one of the chief occupations; cows and oxen also play an important part in the naturalistic decoration on clay and metal objects made at Meroe in the Hellenistic-Roman period. The two bronze vases of Karanog (see pl. LVI and description) are typical representatives of their class; they show that the local princes, the lords of the strongholds on the Nile, took pleasure in visiting their estates and receiving fresh milk from the hands of their shepherds and factors. So had things been from time immemorial. When the captains and kings of the middle and new kingdoms recount the victories won by them in the country of the Cush, they speak of thousands of head of livestock and of prisoners, and that is all. A large enclosure of the temple of Gebel Barcal was a grandiose cow-stall (see the description of pl. LVI).

Besides the rearing of cattle, sheep, and donkeys, a small amount of agriculture was carried on in the small tracts of fertile land in Nubia, along the rivers of the island of Meroe and in the rainy region of the interior. The ruins of vast reservoirs found in the island of Meroe show that the inhabitants fully understood how to secure themselves reserves of water. The importance attached to such works is shown by their sculptural decoration, consisting of lions on the surrounding walls and gigantic statues of frogs in the water.[60] It is, however, doubtful whether corn and cattle were reared for export. Certainly some corn was sold to the desert nomads, but little or none was sent to Central Africa, even less to Egypt, except perhaps in time of famine.

The prosperity of the kingdom of Meroe, the bloom of its peculiar civilization, did not depend only on agriculture and stock-breeding. In the Roman period, no less than before, it was commerce which enriched the princes and enabled the common people also to put remarkable pottery and metal tools in their graves beside the corpses. The existence of this commerce is explicitly attested by our literary sources, by papyri and ostraka, and by archaeological discoveries. It was still the same objects as in the past which reached Egypt by way of Nubia: ebony, ivory, metals, gold, wild beasts, slaves, and precious stones. Further, we know that in this period too, as before, the most important item was gold. Apart from the clear testimony of the literary evidence, it is sufficient proof of this that Garstang found two clay vases in the royal palace, full of nuggets and gold dust.[61]

However, the volume of this trade must not be exaggerated. The scarcity of imported goods in Nubian and Meroitic tombs tells a clear story: local industry sufficed for local needs. Still more important is the fact that, as some of our sources tell us, Meroitic commerce with Egypt was conducted in the primitive form of 'silent trade'. This is confirmed by the almost complete absence of both local and foreign coins in the tombs and ruins of the Nubian and Meroitic cities. In spite of the abundance of metal in the country, the Meroite kings did not coin money and the trade they carried on was mere barter, not what we understand by a regular commercial traffic. If there were commercial relations between the kingdom of Meroe and the Roman Empire, these observations show that they must have been very primitive and slight. At no time did the Egyptian merchants succeed in obtaining permanent access to the Meroite kingdom, but they founded commercial posts on the Nile above Hiera Sykaminos or Premis. It was therefore natural that the shrewd Axumites, more civilized and more hellenized, should succeed in attracting the main bulk of Central African commerce to Adulis, and that the Egyptian merchants preferred to sail along the coasts of the Red Sea as far as Adulis instead of undergoing the long, tiring, and unremunerative commercial expeditions upstream on the Nile. It is not impossible that the Meroite kings succeeded in monopolizing trade; they had no desire to attract the Romans to their country and thus to provoke military expeditions and finally the occupation of their country.[62]

The disasters of the third century A.D. deprived the Nile-trade of all its importance. The country was again reduced to poverty, and it is doubtful if the Nobades and the Blemmyes still had anything to export. Inevitably, Meroe became, as we said, a province of the growing kingdom of Axum which now came to monopolize the commerce between Central Africa and the Roman Empire.

We turn next to the province of CYRENE AND CRETE in the imperial period. We hear very little of its life. The fusion of these two lands into one province may be explained by the fact that both were for a long time subject to the Ptolemies and that in both the Greek cities played a leading part in the political, economic, and social life.

We have very little information on conditions in CRETE in the Roman period. The capital of imperial Crete, Gortyn, has been recently excavated by the Italian mission. The most conspicuous monument of the town is the large praetorium or basilica. Unfortunately it belongs to the fourth century A.D., and the numerous inscriptions found in it tell us nothing of the social and economic life of Crete in the early imperial period. The beauty of the ruins of imperial Gortyn conveys the impression that the island was neither poor nor decadent under the Roman Empire. The progress of excavation will probably provide more precise information.[63]

The material provided by the Italian excavations at CYRENE enables us to understand better today the scattered notices of our literary sources. Under Ptolemaic suzerainty the cities of Cyrenaica enjoyed great prosperity. When in 96 B.C. Ptolemy Apion, the last master of Cyrenaica, in accordance with the instructions of Euergetes II, bequeathed his land to the Romans as he died, the senate treated the Greek cities as free allies. The consequences were catastrophic: civil war, tyranny, and so on. In 86 B.C. Lucullus tried to restore peace and order, but without success. In 74 B.C. Cyrenaica was turned into a regular Roman province, which received its definitive statute in 67 B.C., after the annexation of Crete.

To judge from the information provided by the edicts of Augustus found at Cyrene, and from the well-known description of Strabo, the city was in fact not wealthy and flourishing. This is easily explained by the terrible conditions prevailing at the end of the Republic. The great Libyan war (*bellum Marmaricum*), which ended in A.D. 2, and which is mentioned in an inscription found at Cyrene,* may have contributed to this. This war was undoubtedly connected with the extensive movement of the African people in the early Empire.

It is, however, a serious mistake to attribute the economic

* *SEG* ix. 63.

decadence of Cyrene principally to the disappearance of *silphium* from the soil of Cyrenaica, as some ancient writers, followed by not a few modern ones, do. It is, in fact, certain that Cyrene produced no more silphium after the Hellenistic age. From antiquity onwards attempts have been made to explain this sudden disappearance. Strabo (835 c) attributed it to the nationalistic manœuvres of the Libyans, Pliny (*NH* xix. 15. 38 ff.) to the Roman *publicani* who used the land for grazing, although cattle destroyed silphium, Solinus (xxvii. 48) to the high customs-duties which some Roman governors imposed on the export of silphium. These factors may all be true, but the fundamental cause was the progressive reclamation of the soil of Cyrenaica. The reservation of large tracts of land for silphium was not a paying proposition. The competition of silphium from Asia may also have contributed. In any case its disappearance had little importance for the economic prosperity of the population as a whole. Undoubtedly the gathering and export of silphium was monopolized by the state; originally by the king, then by the city, then again by the king, and finally by the Roman government. Nor did the population derive any benefit from the cultivation of the plant, since it grew wild. The disappearance of silphium was therefore of little importance to the country as a whole.

But let us turn now to Augustan Cyrene. According to the above-mentioned edicts of Augustus, and to Strabo's description, the population of the city of Cyrene and probably also of all Cyrenaica consisted of a certain number of not very wealthy Roman citizens, partly immigrants, partly Cyrenaean Greeks who had obtained Roman citizenship, and of citizens of Cyrene and of the other cities of the Pentapolis. These latter,—along with the other inhabitants of the cities and villages who had had a Greek education and spoke Greek—were called Greeks, just as in the other Roman provinces, and enjoyed certain privileges not possessed by the 'non-Greeks'. The Jews, who undoubtedly possessed their own national organization, and the so-called γεωργοί, formed additional special groups. Who the γεωργοί were it is difficult to say. They were not citizens of Cyrene, nor yet foreigners; it may be conjectured that they were native Libyans. From the earliest times the Libyans had been treated by the Greeks of Cyrene in a very liberal way (for instance, one of the most characteristic local customs had always been the institution of mixed marriages between Greeks and Libyan women), and there is therefore no reason to suppose that the Libyan peasants were serfs. Strabo's γεωργοί were then free peasants who lived in the territory of Cyrene and the other cities and who had the same status in comparison with the citizens as the πάροικοι and κάτοικοι had in regard to the citizen-body of the Greek cities of Asia Minor. Some, it may be surmised, were owners of their plots, others rented them from the city, from private individuals, or from the king who was one of the largest landowners in Cyrenaica. We do not know their position under the Romans. It was probably the same as that of the *stipendiarii* in Africa and of the πάροικοι and κάτοικοι in Asia Minor. There may have been some descendants of mercenary soldiers settled by the Ptolemies, cleruchs and κάτοικοι, among these peasants. The edicts of Augustus show that in the early Empire Cyrene was not very prosperous and that its population was dissatisfied and restless.

The Roman people inherited the estates of the last Ptolemy (*agri regii*, χώρα βασιλική), which were subdivided into lots of 1,250 *iugera* each. In the obscure period following the Roman annexation, some parts of these estates, which had become *ager publicus*, were occupied by some Cyrenaeans, probably Greeks as well as Romans. Claudius, anxious to increase the revenues of the state, sent his own commissioner, Acilius Strabo, to Cyrenaica as *disceptator agrorum* with special instructions, without first consulting the senate. Strabo's activity aroused general indignation in the country, and in A.D. 59 a deputation was sent to Rome to lay complaints before the senate and the new ruler, Nero. The senate refused to take any responsibility and left the whole affair to the emperor. The happy opening *quinquennium* of his reign was not yet over, and Nero did not miss the opportunity of playing the part of the constitutional monarch and satisfying the provincials by annulling the measures which Claudius had taken. Vespasian, however, faithfully following the policy of Claudius, went to the root of the matter, as we know from literary and epigraphical sources.

The Italian excavations showed that under the peace established by Roman rule Cyrene began to flourish again. Not even the terrible devastation caused in the time of Trajan by the Jewish revolt, which had been preceded by a similar revolt under Vespasian, stopped Cyrene from becoming one of the most handsome and best-run provincial cities. It owed much to the care and attention of Hadrian. We do not know the extent to which the social character of the city was modified by the new colonists sent to Cyrene under Hadrian in order to fill up the vacancies in the decimated population. But the fact that a good proportion of the Romans in the list of Ephebes of Cyrene in A.D. 228—28 out of 60—lack the *gentilicium* of Aurelius probably means that Hadrian reinvigorated the old Roman stock of Cyrene with a certain number of Roman citizens from Italy and the provinces, in part veterans. The repopulation of Cyrene effected by Hadrian probably led to a new partition of land, since many of the old proprietors had perished in the Jewish revolt. There is no sign that Cyrene fell into rapid decay under Roman rule. Here, as in the other provinces, periods of progress and of retrogression alternated. In any case the Jewish war was not a mortal blow either for the city of Cyrene itself or for its rich territory; ruin began at Cyrene, as elsewhere, in the third century A.D.[64]

The evolution of the AFRICAN LANDS forming the four provinces established by Rome on the Northern shores of the continent— Africa Proconsularis, Numidia, and the two Mauretanias— shows peculiar features which do not recur in any other portion of the Roman world except Sardinia, Corsica, and certain parts of Sicily. We are comparatively well informed as to the social and economic development of these lands, which represented the former Carthaginian territory and the Numidian and Mauretanian kingdoms, and we owe our knowledge to their political fortunes. When, after the passing of Roman, Vandal, and Byzantine rule, Africa fell under the sway of the Arabs, it reverted, like the Syrian lands, to very primitive conditions of life similar to those that had prevailed before its colonization by the Carthaginians. Most of the cities, except a few on the coast, decayed and disappeared, leaving heaps of ruins behind. The population became once more nomadic and pastoral, and did very little harm to the ruins. When the French appeared on the scene, they found a vast field both for agricultural colonization and for archaeological work, and after some years of chaotic policy, during which the ruins suffered partial destruction, they organized the preservation and the scientific excavation of them in a model

Description of Plate LVIII

1. FLOOR MOSAIC. Found in the ruins of the *atrium* of a villa on the sea-shore between Sousse (Hadrumetum) and Sfax (Taparura) in Tunisia (Africa Proconsularis). Bardo Museum, Tunis. P. Gauckler, *Inv. d. mos.* ii. 1, Tunisie, no. 86 (and coloured plate); S. Reinach, *Rép. d. peint.*, p. 36, 2 (both with bibliography) [A. Merlin and L. Poinssot, *Guide du Musée Alaoui* (1950), pl. VIII].

An elegant mosaic in an exquisite geometric frame. The central medallion shows Neptune, the god of water, riding over the sea in his triumphal chariot drawn by four hippocampi. In his right hand he holds a dolphin, in his left the trident; his head is encircled by a halo. On left and right are a Triton and a Nereid. In the four corners are depicted the Geniuses of the four seasons. WINTER (an oldish woman), in a warm dark-blue dress and with a reed-crown on her head, carries two wild ducks suspended on a reed; she is set in a frame formed by two sprays of olive. On her right are reeds and her animal, the boar, on her left a man planting beans (or gathering olives?). SPRING, a naked young girl with a crown of flowers on her head, a gold necklace round her neck, and a pink *pallium* on her arms, holding in her right hand a rose and in her left a basket of roses, is enclosed within two sprays of roses. On her right is a dog, between roses, tied to a rose spray, on her left a blooming rose-garden and a boy carrying a basket full of roses. SUMMER, a completely naked woman with a crown of corn-ears on her head and a necklace round her neck, holding in her right hand a sickle, in her left a basket full of corn-ears and her violet *pallium*, is framed in stalks with ears of corn. On her right is a lion in a cornfield, on her left a man cutting corn-ears and placing them in a basket. AUTUMN is depicted as a half-naked woman, her legs covered by a greenish *pallium*, wearing the usual necklace and a wreath of vines, and holding in her right hand a *kantharos* from which she pours wine, in her left the *thyrsos*; she is surrounded by vines with grapes. On her right are vines and a panther, on her left a bearded man carrying two baskets with grapes. The idea of the mosaic is to glorify the creative forces of Nature —the beneficent water, so important for the dry land of Africa, and the various aspects of her productive powers exhibited in the four seasons, which correspond to the four ages of human life (cf. F. Boll, *Die Lebensalter* (1913)). This *motif* was very popular in Africa (see the indices to the three African volumes of the *Inv. d. mos.*). Scores of mosaics reproduce the four seasons; some connect them with the symbolical figures of the twelve months (see especially *Inv. d. mos.*, ii. 1, nos. 594, 666, and 752, to be compared with our pl. XXXVI), some with the signs of the Zodiac. The four seasons are often represented by the four winds. It is important to note that it is precisely in the agri-cultural provinces of the Roman Empire—Africa, Gaul, Spain, Britain—that such mosaics frequently occur and that they are closely connected with rural life and with the illustrations in the rustic calendars. There is no more eloquent testimony to the essentially rustic character of ancient life in general.

2. VOTIVE (?) STELE. Found in Tunisia, now in the Museum of Sousse (Hadrume-tum). Unpublished.

The sacred cone (*baetylos*) of the great Semitic and Berber goddess of Africa sur-rounded by ripe corn-ears, a striking symbol of the agricultural life of Africa.

3. CLAY LAMP. Found in the south of Tunisia. Museum of Sousse. Ch. Gouvet, *Bull. arch. du Com. des trav. hist.* 1905, pp. 115 ff.

A typical African villa with a long arched entrance-portico in front, a massive *atrium* behind it, and a pair of two-storeyed projecting wings, which give the plan of the villa the form of the Greek letter *Π*. On the road in front of the villa is a two-wheeled car (*cisium*), with a man seated in it, drawn by two mules, and preceded by a slave with his master's luggage. Behind the cart is an old tree. Compare similar lamps showing a harbour-city, H. B. Walters, *Catalogue of the Greek and Roman Lamps in the Brit. Mus.* (1914), no. 527, pl. XVI, and no. 758, pl. XXV, and my article in *Röm. Mitt.* 26, 1911, pp. 153 ff., fig. 66.

1. THE FERTILITY OF AFRICA

2. THE HOLY CORN

3. AN AFRICAN VILLA

LVIII. AFRICA

I. THRESHING FLOOR

2. DAIRY

3. AGRICULTURAL WORK

LIX. AFRICA: TRIPOLI

Description of Plate LIX

1. MOSAIC. Found in the ruins of an ancient villa on the sea-shore at Dar Buk Ammera (near Zliten in Tripoli). Museum of Tripoli. L. Mariani, *Rend. Acc. Lincei*, 1915, pp. 410 ff.; R. Bartoccini in *Aegyptus*, 3, 1922, p. 161, fig. 8; id. *Guida del Museo di Tripoli*, p. 20, no. 19; S. Aurigemma, 'I mosaici di Zliten', *Africa Italiana*, 2, 1926, pp. 93 ff., and p. 91, fig. 57. Our figures are reproduced from photographs kindly supplied by Professor Aurigemma.

The villa of Zliten was richly adorned with mosaics, some of which rank among the finest specimens of the 1st cent. A.D. They were partly floor-mosaics, partly wall-decorations. This example represents the threshing-floor (ἅλως) situated at some distance from the villa, which is seen in the background. It is covered with corn. One man (the *vilicus*) is supervising the work. Another drives with his stick a pair of oxen, which move slowly and reluctantly over the threshing-floor. At the other end two men are holding two kicking and prancing horses and driving them over the floor; the contrast between the phlegmatic oxen and the spirited horses is finely rendered. A fifth man is shaking the corn with a fork. Near the floor is a beautiful old olive-tree, under the shade of which a woman, probably the lady of the villa, gives orders to the men who are dealing with the horses.

2. AS NO. 1. R. Bartoccini, *Guida*, &c., no. 20; Aurigemma, op. cit., p. 92, and p. 88, fig. 54.

The dairy of the villa. Before the entrance to the pen, against which is a lean-to, with amphorae for milk on the roof, a shepherd sits milking a goat. In the middle distance goats and sheep are grazing, and in the background is the main dairy-building. Behind the milking shepherd stands a table on which are seen cylindrical baskets for making cheese. Compare the similar scene on the *lanx quadrata*, found in Derbyshire (England) in 1729, but of Gallic origin (Bayeux, Normandy), A. de Longpérier, *Gaz. arch.* 1883, pp. 78 ff.; A. Odobesco, *Le Trésor de Pétrossa* (1889–1900), i, p. 109, fig. 41. The mosaic found at Tivoli (?) in the Ince Blundell collection is very similar: B. Ashmole, *A Catalogue of Ancient Marbles at Ince Blundell Hall* (1929), p. 123, no. 412, pl. 51.

3. AS NO. 1. R. Bartoccini, *Guida*, &c., no. 21; Aurigemma, op. cit., pp. 85 ff. and p. 84, fig. 50.

In the background is the villa, in the right-hand corner the enclosure wall of a house and garden, with an entrance-gate—perhaps the dwelling of one of the tenants (*coloni*) of the villa. In the foreground children are playing on the grass. Behind them women are hoeing patches of ground under the supervision of an older woman (the *vilica?*).

The mosaics of Zliten are the earliest examples of a class peculiar to Africa, which are spoken of on p. 331 and in notes 94 and 100 to this chapter. They depict the various types of farms and villas which were scattered all over Africa, and seek to indicate the nature of the agricultural work which was done around the villa. The villa of Zliten was apparently the centre of a large estate devoted to corn-growing and dairy-farming on an extensive scale, which were carried on by the help of slaves and tenants. The other types will be described later in the present and the following chapters. We do not find a single picture of the same kind in other parts of the Roman Empire. The frescoes of the Pompeian houses and their Egyptianizing paintings and mosaics are different in purpose. They do not aim at giving the characteristic traits of a particular villa, that belonging to the man who ordered the picture. Cf. my article 'Die hellenistisch-römische Architekturlandschaft', *Röm. Mitt.* 26, 1911.

way. Africa now ranks with the Rhine lands as the best explored of the Roman provinces. Scores of sites, especially of Roman cities, have been thoroughly excavated and the well-preserved ruins are open to the study of all scholars; numerous museums have been established and almost everything that the spade has unearthed is stored in them; and the discoveries, whether written documents or the remains of artistic and industrial production, have been promptly and accurately published.[65]

Before the Romans set foot in Africa, an extensive and intensive work of colonization had been carried out by the Phoenicians under the leadership of the great city of Carthage. Carthage, Utica, Hadrumetum, and other towns were not only large centres of commerce, but each of them exploited in an efficient manner the large and fertile territory which it gradually occupied. Special attention was paid to the agricultural exploitation of such lands, particularly after the second Punic war, when the Phoenicians, unable to maintain their extensive and flourishing foreign commerce on the same scale as before, concentrated their efforts on the development of the natural resources of their own territory. This activity on the part of Carthage and the other Phoenician cities has been described in the first chapter, where we have emphasized the jealousy of the Roman landowners and suggested that the agricultural development of Africa was the chief reason why Cato and his partisans determined to destroy its flourishing communities. Olive-oil, fruit, and to a certain extent wine were the main products of the cities. The African coast in Phoenician times was a vast and beautiful garden. The fact is proved not only by many direct testimonies, but also by indirect evidence. We know that one of the most famous treatises on agriculture was that of the Carthaginian Mago. It is highly probable that his book was an adaptation to African conditions of the scientific Greek or Greco-Oriental treatises of the fourth and third centuries B.C. We know also that the Roman treatises on agriculture were partly derived from the work of Mago, partly from his Hellenistic sources. We may assume, therefore, that the main features of Mago's work were identical with those of the Greek and Roman treatises. In other words, Mago's theme was capitalistic and scientific agriculture concentrated mostly, not on corn-growing, but on vine and garden culture and still more on olive-growing. It is very probable that the labour employed by the Phoenician land-owners on their farms was mainly supplied by slaves.

It is usually held that the plantation system prevailed in the territory of Carthage, that large tracts of land were cultivated by gangs of slaves and serfs, and produced chiefly corn. I find no evidence in favour of this view. It derives no support from the fact that the territory of the Punic state included, besides the Phoenician cities of the coast, some hundreds of Berbero-Phoeni-cian cities (our sources speak of 300). It is much more likely that these Berbero-Phoenician cities, like the later Roman cities, were residences of landowners and merchants, partly Phoenicians and partly assimilated Berbers, who formed a well-to-do city aristo-cracy, chiefly of landed proprietors, as in the Phoenician mother-land. It may be assumed that, while their estates produced mostly corn, the labour employed on them was furnished by the natives, who were in the position of small tenants or serfs.

Under Punic influence, especially after the second Punic war, Numidia also, under the rule of her kings and petty princes, began to develop a flourishing agriculture and probably a thriv-ing city life. This is attested by her appearance in the second century B.C. as a seller of corn on the international market of Rhodes and Delos, as well as in Athens, and by the fact that the Numidian capital Cirta and other cities, particularly those on the coast (Hippo Regius, Rusicade, Chullu), gradually became centres of flourishing life. The same development took place later in the Mauretanian kingdom with its capital Iol, the Roman Caesarea.[66]

After the third Punic war, which ended with the conquest of Carthage, the Romans inherited the conditions created by cen-turies of Phoenician domination. Their first act was to destroy everything that had been done by Carthage. Carthage herself and many other prosperous cities were reduced to ruins, and it is a probable supposition that in the same ruthless way the con-querors annihilated the flourishing vineyards, olive-groves, and gardens of the Phoenician landowners except in the territories of a few cities of the coast, which had been their allies during the third Punic war (Utica, Hadrumetum, Lepcis Minor, Thapsus, Achulla, Uzalis, and the inland city of Theudalis). That is the reason (it may be mentioned in passing) why the earlier Roman remains and the best funeral monuments of the late Republican period are those of the maritime cities just mentioned, especially Hadrumetum, and why the land around Carthage is described by eye-witnesses as waste and desolate.[67]

Her new province Rome organized in the following way. The land was now owned by the Roman state, the *Senatus Populusque Romanus*. With the sole exception of the territories of the seven cities enumerated above and of some land given to the *perfugae* or deserters from the Carthaginian army, the African land became *ager publicus p. R.* Part of it was assigned to the former Punic and half-Punic cities, which lost their municipal rights and were regarded as agglomerations of tributaries (*stipendiarii*). Such were, for instance, the *stipendiarii* of the *pagi* or rural communities of the Muxsi, Gususi, and Zeugei, who erected a statue in honour of the quaestor Q. Numerius Rufus, a contemporary of Cicero, or again the *civitates* of the *pagus* Gurzensis. The tributaries, of course, retained their land *precario*, that is, without any guarantee to the holders and the tillers of the soil that it would not be taken away by the Roman state and given, sold, or leased to somebody else. The rest of the public land became *ager censorius*, that is, it was managed by the Roman censors to the greatest advantage of the ruling city. Most of it was leased to Roman citizens or to natives, according to circumstances.

A new epoch began for Africa with the brief supremacy of Gaius Gracchus in Rome. As is well known, he intended to re-build the city of Carthage and to settle the new city and her territory with Roman colonists. A general 'centuriation', or delimitation, of her former territory had been carried out immediately after its destruction. Out of this centuriated land lots ranging from 200 to 300 *iugera* were assigned to 6,000 Roman colonists. Gracchus' plan for the restoration of the city was not carried out, but the colonists (or at least part of them) went and settled down on the plots which they received from the state. The liquidation of the Gracchan reforms by the senate produced a general agrarian law of 111 B.C., by which the changed conditions of land-tenure both in Italy and in some of the provinces, particularly Africa, were legalized. Fragments of this law are still extant and give us valuable information on Roman agrarian policy in Africa. The most interesting chapters are those which deal with the *ager privatus vectigalisque*. This was land sold to big Roman capitalists under condition of paying regularly to the state a certain tax or rent (*vectigal*). It was probably thus that large areas passed into the hands of Roman capitalists, and that the foundation of the future *latifundia* of Africa was laid.[68]

Meanwhile Africa became a land of Roman colonization, carried out not by the state but by the Italians on their own account. Italians went to settle both among the *stipendiarii* of Africa and in the Punic cities, chiefly as merchants and money-lenders. Cirta, the capital of the Numidian kings, and Vaga became the favourite centres of Roman business men. They established themselves in hundreds and thousands in these flourishing cities, just as they did in Gaul, in Dalmatia, and in the East, and in smaller numbers in various cities of Numidia and Africa Proconsularis. They either invested their money in the fertile African land or acquired landed property in other ways, mostly in the new Roman province. Colonization proceeded apace during the civil wars. We hear incidentally that Marius settled his veterans in at least two African cities, and it is well known that both Caesar and the Pompeians were supported in Africa by large numbers of Roman citizens. The Caesarians were led by a shrewd and energetic adventurer, P. Sittius, who 'since the days of Catilina had been pursuing the career of a soldier of fortune in Africa at the head of a band of free-lances whom he had raised in Spain'. How he seized Cirta and handed it over to Caesar is a familiar story.[69]

With Caesar a new chapter opened in the history of Africa. After his campaign there the leading part was played by the two cities of Carthage and Cirta. The former was granted by Caesar the status of a Roman colony and also his scheme of rebuilding the city was carried out in 44 B.C., after his death; in the latter the partisans of Sittius were granted large plots of land and the rights of a Roman colony. Both received very large and fertile territories. Former African and Numidian cities and villages were attached to the two cities and were ruled by magistrates delegated by the Roman colonists. Each subdivision of their extensive territories had its fortified headquarters, since life was not yet safe in these parts. Some of them were called *castella* and appear to have been fortified refuges for the rural population; others resumed their old Punic quasi-municipal organization and took on again the aspect of regular cities, which they had borne under the rule of Carthage and in some cases, such as that of Thugga, during the period when they were ruled by the Numidian kings. How many of these municipal centres, if any, received from Caesar the rights of colonies, while remaining attached to Carthage or Cirta, it is very difficult to say. I suspect that, at any rate in the case of Carthage, these attached 'colonies' are an invention of modern scholars. Yet Carthage certainly played a very important part in the life of the renascent cities, as is attested by the fact that the cult of the city of Carthage persisted in many of the cities of the proconsular province even in much later times. It is probable also that, besides the colonists of Carthage and Cirta, many veterans of the Caesarian army received individual grants of land in Africa, and that many emigrants settled in the country on their own account.[70]

But it was under Augustus that the real urbanization of Africa began. At the beginning of his rule Africa, including Tripolis and Numidia, consisted according to Pliny of 516 *populi*, of which 51 were cities (six colonies, fifteen municipia, and thirty *oppida libera*) and 463 townless regions, mostly occupied by half-nomadic tribes (*gentes* or *nationes*). Pliny's statement (*NH.* v, 1–30) is based for the proconsular province on the well-known statistics of Agrippa, which he revised for Mauretania and Numidia (but not for Proconsularis) with the aid of new information dating from the Claudian and Flavian periods. His statement, at any rate for Africa and Numidia, is not fully supported by the epigraphical evidence. Inscriptions speak of at least ten colonies besides Carthage and Cirta; probably there were more—in all nineteen. We must therefore assume, if we do not accept the existence of nominal colonies of Julius Caesar attached to Carthage, that the work of urbanization proceeded after the completion of Agrippa's statistics and that new colonies and other centres of city life were established by Augustus. His chief motives were partly of a military character, as in the case of the foundation of at least eleven colonies in Mauretania which were real military fortresses, partly the desire to accommodate not only veterans of his army but also many residents in Italy who had lost their land through his own confiscations and purchases.[71]

This is not the place to examine in detail the discrepancies between the account of Pliny and the epigraphical data. It was not an easy task to fit the new Augustan creations into the recognized categories of Roman citizenship. They were of three kinds.

(1) Some were colonies where, along with the Roman settlers, there lived large numbers of natives organized as a *civitas* with their own magistrates. To this class belonged, for example, Carthage, Thuburbo Majus, and probably Hadrumetum and Hippo Diarrhytus.[72] (2) There were mixed communes where, along with the native *civitas*, the Roman settlers had their own territory and their own organization as a *pagus*. Such were Uchi Majus and Thibaris, where the settlers of the Caesarian and Augustan times met the former colonists of the times of Marius. Such also were Thugga, Numlulis, Civitas Avensensis, Masculula, Sua, Thignica, Tipasa, Sutunurca, Medeli, &c. In one place at least we know that the *pagus* did not consist exclusively of veterans. These *pagi* had sometimes very characteristic names like *pagus Fortunalis* and *pagus Mercurialis*: the new settlers had, of course, in mind the great goddess Fortuna Redux and the beneficent god Mercury who had come down from heaven in the person of Augustus. (3) Lastly, there were such large colonies as Sicca or 'the new Cirta', which received as large a territory, studded with villages and *castella*, as Carthage and the old Cirta.[73] In some places, as might be expected, we have no records of Romans: there the former Punic cities developed their own life, often on old Punic models, with magistrates who still bore the ancient Punic names. Such cities were numerous, and it would be useless to name them all: a very good example is the city of Gales in the proconsular province (*CIL* viii. 23833, 23834).

The demand for land seems to have been considerable in the reigns of Augustus and Tiberius. To meet it, both emperors undertook the difficult task of extending Roman rule to the South, which led to a long war with the native tribes and their chief Tacfarinas. In the train of the advancing Roman troops came land-measurers, *agrimensores*, to divide the newly acquired territories into Roman *centuriae*. The efforts of Augustus and Tiberius seem inexplicable except on the supposition that they were driven by the desire of accommodating many of those who took part in the 'great agricultural emigration' from Italy.[74]

Apart from the colonists from Italy who either received their land as a gift from Augustus or bought or rented it from the state in parcels of moderate size, there was undoubtedly a mass of great capitalists who were eager to invest their money in the rich virgin soil of Africa. The state was willing to meet their demand,

Description of Plate LX

1. THREE CLAY BOWLS WITH RED VARNISH. According to A. Merlin probably found at El-Auja, about 30 km. south of Cairuan. Paris, Louvre. Unpublished. Similar bowls (nearly identical), found in the same locality and in the possession of Bardo Museum, Tunis, have been published and studied by A. Merlin, *Bull. Arch. du Com. des trav. hist.* 1917, pp. ccxi ff., pl. xxxvi, cf. ibid., 1920, pp. 21 ff., and note 38 of our Chapter V. 2nd to 3rd cent. A.D.

All these bowls have the shape of a human head, and are undoubtedly intended to represent types of the native population of Roman Africa. Note the three different styles of coiffure; that of the woman closely resembles that of the late Ptolemaic period. The centre head is female, those on the left and right probably male. On the necks of the bowls are the names of the potters who made them, or of the owners of the respective factories: on one NABIG | PINGI, i.e. *Na(v)ig(ius)* | *pingi(t)* or *(f)in(x)i(t)* or *(f)in(x)i*; on the other EX OFICI | NAVIGI, i.e. *ex offici(na) Navigi*. These names show that the bowls are of local manufacture. El-Auia was an important centre of the production of red glaze pottery. The technique and decoration of these African pieces have been studied by A. Merlin, loc. cit.

2. TERRACOTTA. Found by General Goetschy at Sousse in the Roman necropolis. Paris, Louvre. Mentioned, but not reproduced, by Gen. Goetschy, *Bull. arch. du Com. des trav. hist.* 1903, 'Nouvelles fouilles dans les nécropoles de Sousse', p. 170, no. 4. (I owe this reference to A. Merlin.) Local work. 2nd or 3rd cent. A.D.

Young man in Roman dress on horseback. The physical characteristics and the style of costume show that this is a member of the African *bourgeoisie*, probably a landowner.

3. TERRACOTTA. Probably also found in the Roman necropolis at Sousse. Paris, Louvre. Unpublished. Local work. 2nd or 3rd century A.D.

Elderly peasant with tunic and thick cloak of Celtic style with *cucullus*; he moves towards the left. He probably holds something in his hands. Notable piece of realistic terracotta work.

1. THE NATIVE POPULATION

2. LANDOWNER

3. PEASANT

LX. AFRICAN TERRACOTTAS

because the investment of money in African land promised an increase of production which would keep the corn prices low, guarantee an abundant supply of grain for Italy, and increase the public revenue. To the large estates of the Republican aristocracy which had not been confiscated by Augustus there were thus added new *latifundia* belonging to the Roman plutocracy. Petronius' Trimalchio was true to type in dreaming of adding to his possessions in Italy and Sicily large tracts of land in Africa.

These considerations enable us to understand the annexation first of Numidia and then of Mauretania, which both required a considerable military effort and were not at all necessary from the political and military points of view. The African lands had to be opened to Roman colonization, and the first task of the government was to make them safe for this purpose. Under the successors of Augustus the work of colonization proceeded on the same lines. The lead seems to have been taken by capitalists. Large estates were created throughout the country. To Pliny the *latifundia* appear to be the outstanding feature of agricultural life in Africa. His statement that six landowners possessed half its area is, of course, a generalization which simplified the facts, but in essence it was probably true.[75]

The progress and the mode of colonization in Africa may best be understood by following the lines of development under Trajan and Hadrian, especially in Numidia and in the adjacent parts of Proconsularis. Trajan's chief problem was how to deal with the conquered tribes, which were not pure barbarians and some of which were accustomed to agricultural work and to life in fortified cities. They owned large territories in part already occupied in one way or another by foreigners. The time had come to put an end to this chaotic state of affairs. Three typical examples will serve to illustrate the method adopted. We take first the numerous and strong tribe of the Musulamii, one of a group of tribes of which Pliny says: 'most of them may justly be called not *civitates* but nations.'* Before their complete pacification the Musulamii, like other tribes, were governed by military officers called *praefecti gentium*. Their organization dates from Trajan. In the district occupied by them two military colonies, Ammaedara and Madaurus, were established with extensive territories; a large tract of their land was taken by the emperor,

---

* *NH* v. 30.

some portions were held by private landowners, the rest was given to the members of the tribe and was regarded as their domain. The land was measured out and boundary stones were set up. Probably at the same time part of the tribe was transferred to the district of Byzacena and furnished labour for many large estates.[76]

Near Madaurus and Ammaedara lived another large tribe, the Numidae. The tribe appears also in three other far distant places: in Cellae (Ain Zouarine), in Masculula (near Kef), and in Mauretania Caesariensis, in which province we find a district being assigned to the Numidae by the Emperor Hadrian. It is fairly clear that we have here a case of a powerful and numerous tribe being split up into several parts. This dispersion may have occurred at an earlier period, though it is only attested for the imperial period, in which there was urgent need of an agricultural population. The headquarters of the tribe, Thubursicu Numidarum, an old native town, became first a *civitas* and afterwards a *municipium*; the land assigned to the tribe formed the territory of the new city, but tribal representatives, native sheikhs styled *principes*, shared with the city magistrates in its local government.[77]

Our third example is the tribe of the Nybgenii in the southern part of Africa Proconsularis. One part of the territory of this tribe was assigned by Trajan to two Romano-Punic *civitates*, Capsa and Tacape, which subsequently became *municipia* and later *coloniae*; the rest was left to the tribe, whose town centre— Turris Tanalleni—afterwards received the status of a *municipium*. It seems as if the part of the tribe which was attached to Capsa retained its own *principes*, like the Numidae of Thubursicu. The same development may be traced in the case of many other tribes both in the Proconsular province and in Numidia and Mauretania, for instance, the Musunii Regiani (between Cillium and Thelepte), the Suburbures (near Cirta), the Nattabutes, the Nicivibus (the modern Ngaous), and the Zimizenses in Mauretania (between Chullu and Igilgili). Some tribes were, and continued to be, attached to larger cities, like the Saboides to Cirta and the Chinithi to Gigthis.[78]

There is no doubt, too, that the early history of such colonies of Roman veterans as Thamugadi (Timgad) and of the cities which grew up near the successive camps of the African legion

(Theveste and Lambaesis) was closely bound up with the fortunes of the African tribes, which lost their lands to the new settlers and were forced to work for them as hired labourers or tenants. If we had sufficient evidence about the history of scores of other African cities which developed into flourishing romanized communities, more particularly in the second century A.D., we should certainly be able to trace similar relations between them and the native tribes. The process was everywhere the same. The tribes were not exterminated or driven out of the country. Like the Arabs in Syria and in Arabia, they were first of all fixed in their original homes or transferred to other parts. A certain amount of land was assigned to them, and the rest was either given to a city inhabited by Roman immigrants (veterans and civilians) and by the native aristocracy, or transformed into estates, which were sold to wealthy members of the imperial aristocracy or reserved (under the title of *definitio* or *defensio*) for the emperor and members of the imperial family. As the amount of land assigned to the tribes was not large enough to support the growing population, numbers of the tribesmen were forced either to rent land from the foreign or native landowners or to work on their estates as hired labourers.[79]

A similar process of urbanization and differentiation developed in the wide territories of the three largest colonies of Augustus—Carthage, Cirta, and Sicca. In many cases the documents enable us to follow the development of *castella* into real cities. It will be sufficient to mention Thibilis (Announa) and Cuicul (Djemila), which have been recently excavated. Thibilis was a flourishing agricultural village of some size, attached to the territory of Cirta. This dependence continued even after Thibilis became a large and prosperous city.[80] Cuicul was also a dependency of Cirta. Nerva transformed it into a colony of veterans. Nevertheless the city maintained her close relations with her ancient metropolis.[81] Not very different was the position of the three original colonies attached to Cirta—Rusicade, Chullu, and Mileu. These three *coloniae contributae* were detached from the mother colony and became independent cities after the time of Alexander Severus.[82] Similar conditions existed in the territory of Sicca with its various *castella*, which were largely inhabited by Roman citizens. The general aspect of the territories of the large Caesarian-Augustan colonies presented much variety. There

Description of Plate LXI

THE FUNERAL MONUMENT OF GHIRZA AND ITS SCULPTURAL DECORATIONS. The monument was discovered and photographed by H. Méhier de Mathuisieulx, and described by him in *Nouv. Arch. d. miss. scient.*, 12, 1904, pp. 24 ff., pl. vi, 2; pl. viii; pl. ix, 2; pls. x and xi, 1. The first complete edition of the sculpture of the monuments of Ghirza is that of P. Romanelli, 'La vita agricola Tripolitana attraverso le rappresentazioni figurate', *Africa Italiana*, 3 (8), 1930, pp. 53 ff., 60 ff. This publication contains good photographs of the reliefs. [The photographs reproduced here, and provided by Mrs. O. L. Brogan, are published by permission of the Department of Antiquities, Tripolitania, Libya.]

The greater part of the rich sculptural adornment of the funeral temple lies scattered round the ruins of the building and is in a bad state of preservation. Most of the bas-reliefs depict scenes from the daily life of the landowning family to which the monument belonged. A long epitaph, giving many names (all native), is also preserved. The four fragments reproduced on this plate portray life on the fields of the estate. The reliefs show how unsafe life was on the borders of the desert; compare our pl. xlvii, illustrating life in the steppes of the Crimea. The first fragment [now in Tripoli Museum] represents the ploughing of the fields by means of camels and oxen; the second a combat with natives; the third a battle with wild beasts; the fourth the reaping of corn and the carrying of the grain in baskets. The monument cannot be earlier than the 4th cent. of our era.

AGRICULTURAL WORK AND RURAL LIFE ON THE VERGE OF THE DESERT

LXI. AFRICA

were the ruling city with a population of great landowners, merchants, government agents of different sorts, artisans, menial
workmen, and so forth; many large and .prosperous attached
cities, living their own life and possessing their own territory;
smaller *castella*, again, with their own territories and their population of landowners, in part Roman citizens; and, finally, tribes
living all over the city territory, some of them having their own
territories and their own tribal organization.

Another type of urbanization—if the term can be used in this
context—gradually carried out in some rural districts, is furnished
by the development of large estates, both imperial and private.
The residents on the estate, smaller and larger tenants, lived in
villages (*vici*). With the aid of the owners they formed a self-
governing body, a sort of religious association with elected presidents (*magistri*). In the villages seasonal fairs (*nundinae*) were
organized by the owners with the permission of the local authorities, sometimes even of the Roman senate. The villages grew in
importance. Some of the tenants became landowners, and the
vicus assumed the appearance of a city. Many of the *vici* possessed
the legal rights of a juristic person and received gifts, bequests,
&c. It is worthy of note that many of the residents in a *vicus* were
Roman citizens, for instance, the *vicani* of a *vicus* Annaeus near
Semta, the centre of a private estate, some of the inhabitants of
the *vicus* Haterianus in the district of Byzacena near the modern
Kairouan, of a *vicus* near Lambiridi, and of the *vicus* Verecun-
densis in the territory of Lambaesis. Like the cities, the *vici* had
two classes of residents, the regular *vicani* and the *incolae*. It is
uncertain whether these *vici* were ultimately recognized as cities;
no certain example survives.[83]

The development of city life and the diffusion of Roman
civilization in Africa made striking progress after the time of
Augustus. All the emperors promoted it—Claudius and the
Flavians in the first century and above all Trajan and Hadrian
in the second. The later emperors mostly legalized an already
accomplished process by conferring the titular rights of *municipia*
and *coloniae* on already existing and flourishing cities. To a large
extent the development of towns was due to natural causes. The
start was given by the large immigration from Italy during the
civil wars and immediately afterwards, and under the first emperors. The Italians naturally endeavoured to organize their life

on Italian patterns. Under subsequent emperors many colonies of veterans were founded. The growing class of well-to-do *bourgeois* did its best to improve the conditions of its life and introduce all the comforts associated with a city. The emperors sympathized with this movement and patronized it. They were interested in having new centres of civilized life, more nuclei of romanized residents. When Italy ceased to be able to furnish soldiers and officers for the army, the Empire urgently required more and more romanized communities to provide a constant supply of soldiers and officers, who should civilize and drill masses of native troops for the legions and the auxiliary regiments. In Africa we meet with the same phenomenon which we have observed in all the provinces of the Empire, the same encouragement of urbanization, especially in the period when Rome needed ever fresh supplies of recruits for her external wars. It is noteworthy that here, as on the Danube and the Rhine, this aim of the emperors was emphasized by the organization of the young citizens of the romanized cities in associations under the command of special prefects, the *praefecti iuvenum*. In many cities the organization was based on the general division of the citizen body into *curiae*. The *curiae iuniorum* were nurseries of future soldiers for the imperial army.[84]

And yet, in spite of the widespread extension of city life which impresses every one who visits the ruins of Northern Africa, the cities were only a superstructure based on a developed rural and agricultural life, and the city residents formed but a minority in comparison with the large numbers of actual tillers of the soil, the peasants, who were mostly natives, rarely descendants of immigrants. This statement is borne out by the following considerations. We find in Africa in the second century five forms of land-tenure: (1) land which was owned by the emperors and did not belong to the territory of any city, the imperial *saltus*, representing estates that had belonged to men of the senatorial class in the Republican period, and portions of tribal land reserved by and for the emperors; (2) land which was owned by senatorial families and was not attached to the territory of a city (the *saltus privati*)—large tracts of this land had been confiscated by the emperors in the time of Nero and the Flavians, but many such estates remained and some were formed later; (3) land which constituted the territory of a city, whether a colony, a *municipium*, or a plain *civitas* with quasi-municipal rights; (4) land which formed the territory of a tribe (*gens*) and was either measured out and organized by the imperial government, or still remained unmeasured and used mostly as pasture land by half-nomadic natives (especially in Mauretania); (5) some mining and forest districts, partly owned by the emperors and partly leased to companies of business men, like the *socii Talenses*, the 'company' of Tala, which was an important forest and mining district in the neighbourhood of Lambaesis.[85]

We are well informed concerning the manner in which certain of these lands, namely, the large estates in imperial and private possession, were farmed.[86] In our second-century sources there is no indication that they were cultivated by means of slave labour. We may suppose that this mode of exploitation existed in the Republican and in the early imperial period. But in the second century the prevailing method of cultivation was by means of tenants (*coloni*), who paid the owner part of the produce of the land and were also obliged to give him some days of their own and their cattle's labour. Some of these tenants were Roman citizens, but the majority were natives of the country. They lived in villages which lay within the estate near the big central farm or in the vicinity of the estate, but outside it. The rent which they paid was collected by the 'farmers-general' (*conductores*) of the estate, who at the same time leased from the owners such lands as were not let out to the *coloni*. For their cultivation they made use probably of slaves, certainly of hired labour and of the obligatory services (*operae*) of the tenants of the estate. The *conductores* were big men. They formed an influential class of the population of the cities which were situated near the large imperial estates, and they were probably at the same time landowners in the territory of their own and other cities. With a view to the promotion of their common interests they formed associations of the same type as the associations of merchants and shipowners, though these do not seem to have been recognized by the state.[87] Above them stood the imperial administration, numerous officials, high and low, of the patrimonial department—knights, freedmen, and slaves.[88]

In the city territories the land belonged mostly to the wealthier citizens, who were descendants of the original *coloni* sent out by the emperors, or of the original Roman settlers, or even of the

Description of Plate LXII

1. FLOOR MOSAIC. Found at Dougga. Bardo Museum, Tunis. A. Merlin in *Bull. arch. du Com. des trav. hist.* 1919, pl. 1; S. Reinach, *Rép. d. peint.*, p. 256, 1; [A. Merlin and L. Poinssot, *Guide du Musée Alaoui*, i (1950), pl. xx, 3].

Two slaves are carrying large jars of wine on their shoulders. They wear the typical slave-dress and a long necklace, with an amulet against the evil eye, round their necks. On one of the jars is written *ΠΙΕ* (i.e. *πίε*), 'Drink', on the other *ZHCHC* (ζήσῃς), 'Live long', words which are quite commonly inscribed on drinking-cups and wine-jars. One of the jars is adorned with charms against the evil eye, which frequently occur on the buildings and on the utensils of Roman and modern Africa, though they have never been collected and investigated. The slave to the left holds in his right hand a green branch, that to the right a smaller water-bottle. Behind the former is a slave boy carrying water and towels, behind the latter another boy with a green bough in one hand and a basket of flowers in the other. Both slaves pour out wine from their jars for two men, one of whom is dressed like a charioteer of the circus. The fresco represents preparations for a banquet in a private house or a wine-shop. Similar scenes were often painted in the dining-rooms of rich palaces and in modest wine-shops. S. Reinach, *Rép. d. peint.*, p. 249, 8, and p. 250, 4–9; cf. 1–3 and 10, and the scenes on the walls of wine-shops at Pompeii, Reinach, op. cit., p. 254, 5–6. A new explanation of the Pompeian frescoes has been given by M. Della Corte, *Case ed abitanti di Pompei* (1929, 2nd ed. 1954), passim.

2. MOSAIC OF A THRESHOLD. Found at Sousse (Hadrumetum) in a funeral *hypogaeum*. Bardo Museum, Tunis. P. Gauckler, *Inv. d. mos.* ii. 1 (Tunisie), no. 189 and plate; S. Reinach, *Rép. d. peint.*, p. 273, 3; [Merlin and Poinssot, op. cit. pl. xx, 2].

A merchant ship landing a cargo, probably of metal bars, in a shallow harbour. Two workmen are wading through the shallow water, each carrying one ingot. On the shore two other men are weighing the ingots in a large pair of scales. The mosaic furnishes a good illustration of the conditions of navigation in the shallow Syrtes.

3. FRAGMENT OF A MOSAIC. Found at Sousse (Hadrumetum) in the ruins of a house. Museum of Sousse. P. Gauckler, *Inv. d. mos.* ii. 1 (Tunisie), no. 166.

Two fast ships with a cabin at the stern, an elaborate system of sails, and nine pairs of oars each. They were probably messenger and police boats of the African fleet (*naves tesserariae*).

1. SERVING WINE TO GUESTS

2. UNLOADING A SHIP

FAST SEA-GOING SHIPS

LXII. AFRICA

1. LIFE ON AN AFRICAN ESTATE

2. THE STABLE AND OTHER FARM BUILDINGS OF AN AFRICAN ESTATE

LXIII. AFRICA

Description of Plate LXIII

1. MOSAIC. Found in the ruins of a large villa in the neighbourhood of Uthina (Oudna) in Tunisia (Africa Proconsularis). It adorned the floor of one of the *atria* of this luxurious house, which belonged probably to the family of the Laberii. P. Gauckler, *Mon. Piot*, 3, 1897, pp. 185 ff. The mosaic is described on p. 200, no. 21, and reproduced on pl. xxii of this article; compare the plan of the building, pl. xx; id. *Inv. d. mos.* ii. 1 (Tunisie), no. 362 and plate (with bibliography); S. Reinach, *Rép. d. peint.*, p. 390, 1. It belongs to the early 2nd cent. of our era. [A. Merlin and L. Poinssot, *Guide du Musée Alaoui*, i (1950), pl. xi].

In the centre of the picture we see a peasant's house or a barn, in the doorway of which stands a man, probably a shepherd, leaning on a long staff and looking at an approaching herd. In the side-wall of the house are three windows and a low door; against it rests a plough. Towards the building moves a flock of goats, sheep, and cows, while two dogs run in the opposite direction across the fields. Above the flock, a man ploughs a field with a team of oxen. Near the house are a tent ('gourbi') and a primitive well, from which a man has just filled up a semicircular trough to water a horse. Another horse is tethered to a stake between the well and the house. Towards the right a man dressed in a heavy cloak drives a donkey. This central portion of the mosaic certainly represents part of a large estate—in all probability the cattle-shed and barn of the villa, hardly the house of one of the *coloni*. The central picture is surrounded on three sides by scenes portraying the various occupations of the owners of the estate and their workmen. On the left three men elegantly dressed and mounted on beautiful horses attack and kill a lioness. At the foot are depicted other hunting scenes. In a rocky landscape a man, disguised as a goat, is moving slowly on hands and knees, driving four partridges before him into a net. Another man, naked except for a cloak which flutters from his shoulders, attacks a wild boar among rocks on marshy ground, while his companion tries to hold in a big mastiff which leaps at the boar. On the right of the central picture we have scenes of rustic life. A shepherd in the fields playing his pipe under an olive tree; near him his flock of goats, one of which is milked by another shepherd; while on the right a negro slave gathers olives from a tall tree.

2. MOSAICS. Found in the ruins of a *trifolium* (probably a large dining-room), which formed part of a large and luxurious villa near Tabarka (Thabraca). P. Gauckler, *Inv. d. mos.* ii. 1 (Tunisie), no. 940 and two plates, one coloured (with bibliography); my article in *JDAI* 19, 1904, p. 125, fig.; S. Reinach, *Rép. d. peint.*, p. 392, 3, 4. 3rd or 4th cent. A.D.

Of the four mosaics which formed the decoration of the *trifolium* two are reproduced here. The central one (of which only fragments are preserved) represented hunting scenes in the African prairies. The mosaic of the central 'leaf' portrays the residential part of the villa surrounded by a luxurious park and flower-garden (παράδεισος) full of various birds, wild and domestic (S. Reinach, op. cit., p. 391, 5; my article, p. 125). The lateral mosaics, here reproduced, give pictures of the farm buildings. That on the left represents a large and stately stable set amid olive trees and vines; in the background are hills with partridges, in the foreground a shepherdess seated under a poplar, spinning and guarding sheep which graze among trees; near the stable prances a fine horse. The mosaic on the right represents a large barn and storehouses, with rooms probably for the olive and wine presses, surrounded by olive trees and vines; in front of it is a poultry-yard with some trees and two buildings, probably the poultry-houses, near a pond for fish, ducks, geese, &c. The mosaics of Thabraca give an instructive picture of a large estate devoted to the production of wine and olive-oil, to horse and cattle breeding, and to poultry-farming—an important agricultural concern run on scientific lines. Cf. the mosaic of Julius, pl. lxxix, and Chap. XII. These late monuments are reproduced here as in all probability the type of the African villa did not change very much in the interval between the 2nd and the 3rd–4th cent. of our era.

group of more influential men who formed the aristocracy of the Berbero-Punic communities. The military and civil colonists of the earlier times received as a rule large plots of land, larger than could be cultivated by a single colonist and his family. The early and the later immigrants from Italy, who formed the ruling class in the African cities, were, of course, not peasants (who were people in a small way, living in the country as tenants of the large estates), but landowners on a more or less extensive scale. The natives, too, who lived in the cities certainly did not belong to the class of dwellers in the *mapalia*, but to the well-to-do Berber and Punic aristocracy. The owners of estates within the municipal territories, therefore, were members of the municipal *bourgeoisie* and resided in the cities. They managed their estates either personally or through special agents, but they never worked the land with their own hands. The labour was furnished by the natives, either as hired workmen or as tenants. Small landowners of the independent peasant type may have existed on the municipal territories, in the native *civitates*, and in the territories of the tribe, but the general tendency was towards a concentration of the land in the hands of a few rich proprietors.

In many cases we can trace the growth of municipal families from very modest beginnings to a dominating position in the city. Many members of these families entered the state service and reached equestrian rank or a seat in the Roman senate. We meet with such families in almost every city of the African provinces which has been thoroughly excavated. A few examples may be given. The first consul of African origin, Q. Aurelius Pactumeius Fronto (A.D. 80), was a citizen of Cirta. The family of the Antistii from Thibilis finally became connected with the imperial house.[89] The family of the Attii of Thuburbo Majus and Uchi Majus furnished two *praefecti praetorio* to the Empire.[90] The city of Gigthis had at least five senatorial families in her citizen body.[91] A notable instance is L. Memmius L. f. Quir. Pacatus. No one, probably, would doubt that this rich man, who was knighted by Hadrian, was a Roman of Italian origin, and yet the tribe of the Chinithi proudly says of him: 'L. Memmio L. f. Quir. Pacato flam(ini) perpetuo divi Traiani, *Chinithio*, in quinque decurias a divo Hadriano adlecto, Chinithi ob merita eius et singularem pietatem qua *nationi suae* praestat sua pecunia posuerunt.'[92] Other examples might be quoted.

It is a striking fact that, in every case where we can trace the origin of the large fortunes of wealthy municipal nobles, we find them to have been derived from the ownership of land. In their funeral inscriptions many of them boast of having acquired their fortune by careful management of their estates. We have already quoted the case of L. Aelius Timminus from Madaurus.[93] Another notable instance is Q. Vetidius Juvenalis from Thubursicu Numidarum, who says of himself in his funeral inscription: 'omnibus honorib(us) functus, pater III equitum Romanorum, in foro iuris peritus, agricola bonus.'[94] Another such 'agricola bonus' was the famous landowner of Mactar. He was born in a poor home of humble parents. From his childhood he lived on the land and for the land, granting no rest either to it or to himself. In harvest time he served as foreman of gangs of corn-reapers (*turmae messorum*). In this way he acquired a large fortune and was honoured with a seat in the local senate: 'elected by the senators', he says with pride, 'I sat in the shrine of the senate, and from a peasant I became a censor.'[95] The same conclusion may be drawn from the numerous mosaics which adorned the city and country houses of the African aristocracy. From the first century onwards the owners of these houses liked to have their life depicted in minutest detail on the floors of their dining and sitting rooms. Unlike the tombs of the Rhine, none of these floor mosaics represents the owner as a merchant or a factory owner. All display before us scenes of rural life: threshing of corn in Oea, gathering of olives, ploughing and so forth in Uthina, sheep and poultry breeding, vine-growing, &c., in Thabraca, horse-breeding near Hadrumetum, cornfields, poultry, sheep, vines and olives in Carthage. Everywhere the master is shown, not particularly busy in managing his estate but mostly hunting hares, deer, and cranes in his forests and prairies. The land is cultivated either by tenants, who lived in houses like that represented on an African sarcophagus and some of whom were certainly natives (like the threshers on the mosaic of Oea), or by negro slaves (as on a mosaic of Uthina). The modest peasants appear also on the mosaic of Carthage.[96]

There can be no doubt, therefore, that the leading type of husbandry in Africa was cultivation of the land by peasants who were either owners of small plots, or tenants and hired workmen on the big estates of the emperors and of the imperial and

Description of Plate LXIV

HARBOUR OF LEPCIS MAGNA. TEMPLE OF JUPPITER DOLICHENUS. Along the quays on the south-west the high podium and flight of steps leading to a large Roman temple have been discovered. Two altars in front of the temple bear in relief the symbols of the cult of Juppiter Dolichenus, and one of them also has a dedication which begins with the words I. O. M. DOLICHENO. It is possible that the apex of the pediment of the temple served as a bearing for ships entering the harbour.

LXIV. HARBOUR OF LEPCIS MAGNA. TEMPLE OF JUPPITER DOLICHENUS

1. THE ROMAN MARKET OF LEPCIS MAGNA

2. COLUMN WITH CAPITAL OF ORIENTAL STYLE

LXV. AFRICA: LEPCIS MAGNA

Description of Plate LXV

1. THE ROMAN MARKET OF LEPCIS MAGNA. Has undergone numerous transformations and reconstructions. In its final shape it was a rectangle with colonnades supported by columns of black granite. In the middle are two octagonal buildings, one of stone, the other with columns and marble revetments. The *mensae* were arranged under the porticoes of the rectangle, and in the intercolumniations of the octagonal building. [N. Degrassi, *Quaderni di archeologia della Libia*, 2, 1951, pp. 27 ff. 'Il mercato Romano di Leptis Magna'.]

2. COLUMN WITH CAPITAL OF ORIENTAL STYLE. This is the only architectural fragment of Phoenician or Carthaginian style which has so far been found in the excavations of Lepcis Magna. It probably belonged to the market of the early *emporium*, and was preserved in the various reconstructions of the Roman period as a record of the original building.

municipal aristocracy. The peasants, who were mostly natives, formed the vast majority of the population, and were the economic backbone of the country. The cities were inhabited by landowners who formed the ruling aristocracy. The landowners, whether they were veterans or other immigrants or natives, were the only legally recognized citizens of the cities. The rest—the petty merchants, artisans, and workmen—were *incolae*, not citizens. To the same category belonged the peasants of the city territory, and it is to be noted that they were *incolae* of an inferior rank, even as compared with the *incolae intramurani*, who lived in the city. It is not open to doubt that this mass of peasants was very slightly romanized, and that no great improvement took place in the conditions of their life. The civilization of the city did not reach them: they still worshipped their native gods, still lived in their *mapalia*, and still spoke their native tongues.[97]

Special conditions, in some respects different from those of the other African provinces, existed in that part of Africa Proconsularis which we call TRIPOLITANIA. Before the Italian occupation of this region, very little was known of the three cities of the African Tripolis, namely Lepcis (or Leptis) Magna, Oea, Sabratha. The Italians have done admirable archaeological work in these territories. At Oea (the modern Tripoli) the arch (tetrapylon) of Marcus Aurelius has been freed from the modern buildings which surrounded it, and restored; a splendid archaeological museum has been formed in the picturesque fortress of the town. Systematic excavations are in progress at Sabratha and a part of the town has been cleared and some buildings restored. Finally, at Lepcis, every year throws new light on the life and beauty of this city, which was 'the dream of an Emperor'. Furthermore, the network of Roman roads which joined the three cities with each other and with the outer world has been discovered and traced, while the desert-*limes* has been explored, and some military posts excavated.[98]

Thanks to this outstanding work we know enough now regarding the development of Tripolitania to be able to devote some pages of this book to its history. The country occupied by the territory of the three cities mentioned above formed a sort of fertile coastal oasis, rising from the sea in three terraces to the high desert belt of the Sahara, attracting to itself a very considerable rainfall. Elsewhere in the desert region of which

Tripolitania forms part rainfall is very slight. The fertile terraces of Tripolitania are completely different from the great plateau of Cyrenaica, and resemble much more the adjacent region of the ancient Carthaginian territory which later became the Roman province of Africa Proconsularis.

While the history of Cyrenaica was always linked with that of Egypt, the cities of Tripolitania depended completely on Carthage, and shared its fortunes. For some time the Tripolis was a Carthaginian province, with Lepcis as its capital; later it was joined to the kingdom of Numidia, and later still the cities became free allies of the Roman Republic, and were eventually annexed to the province of Africa Proconsularis. From the earliest Imperial period they were granted the title and the privileges of Roman colonies.

The existence of the three cities was due to two causes. In the first place they were all natural harbours for the trade which reached the Mediterranean by way of the Sahara desert, from the Sudan and Central Africa (the Congo region). The three cities of Tripolitania, like Gightis and Tapace (Gabes), lay on the shore of the deep gulf made by the sea in the desert, shortening the distance from the Mediterranean to Central Africa. On the other hand, the fertility of the soil and the rainfall enabled the Phoenicians, and later the Romans, to transform the vast territories of the three cities into fine orchards and, more particularly, olive groves, by diligent care and arduous work. It was just this commerce with Central Africa across the desert, and the production of large quantities of olive-oil, which gave the cities of Tripolitania their wealth and prosperity, and enabled them to pay heavy tribute in cash to Carthage, to give Caesar an enormous contribution of olive-oil (3,000,000 *librae*), and later to make a voluntary gift of oil to Septimius Severus, by which he was enabled to make a free distribution to the people of Rome.

The trade across the Sahara was as old as the cities themselves. The centre of this in the desert was the large, prosperous oasis of the Garamantes (the modern Fezzan), which was connected with the cities of Tripolitania by several roads. This trade developed under difficult conditions, but was very remunerative. The main product of Central Africa which reached the coast was elephant-tusks. This state of affairs, of long standing, continued unchanged in the Roman period. The coat-of-arms of Lepcis and Sabratha

Description of Plate LXVI

1. BUST-PORTRAIT. Five bust-portraits of persons who represent the type of roman-ized native have been found in the Roman market of Lepcis Magna. In antiquity the busts rested on brackets, one of which is preserved: it carries a bilingual inscription in neo-Punic and Latin, which records that the bust is a portrait of a local magistrate, named Boncart, and is dedicated to *Liber Pater*. [*Inscr. Trip.* 294].

2. BASE OF AN HONORIFIC MONUMENT IN THE MARKET OF LEPCIS MAGNA. It supported a *biga*, granted by the 'splendidissimus ordo' of the decurions in honour of a certain Porfyrius, *amator patriae et civium suorum*, who was found worthy of honour because he had presented *civibus suis quattuor feras dentatas vivas* [*Inscr. Trip.* 603]. The *ferae dentatae* are probably elephants. Porfyrius was certainly an exporter of beasts from central Africa; this is clear from his gifts and the ships carved as emblems on the pilasters of the little honorific monument.

1. PROSPEROUS CITIZEN OF LEPCIS MAGNA,
OF LIBYO-ROMAN TYPE

2. BASE OF STATUE OF A PROSPEROUS CITIZEN OF LEPCIS
MAGNA, WITHOUT DOUBT A RICH EXPORTER

LXVI. AFRICA: LEPCIS MAGNA

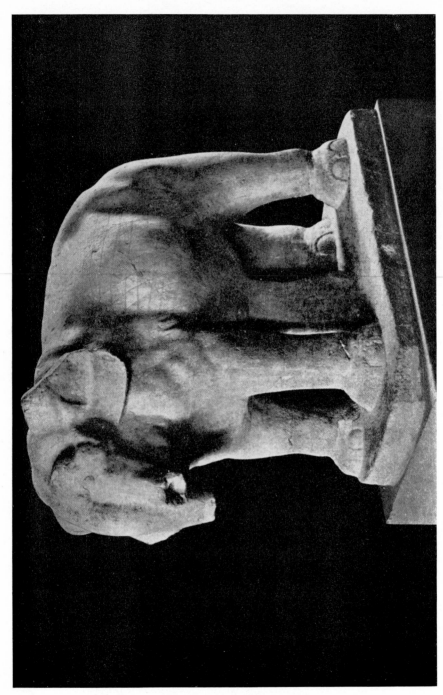

LXVII. THE ELEPHANT FROM THE MAIN STREET OF LEPCIS MAGNA

Description of Plate LXVII

ELEPHANT. Marble elephant discovered in the *decumanus* of Lepcis Magna. The import of elephants from central Africa and the ivory-trade were sources of wealth for the traders of the *emporia* of Tripolitania. The emblem of the *statio Sabratensium*, preserved in a mosaic-pavement of the 'square of the Corporations' at Ostia, is an elephant [*Not. d. Scav.* 1912, p. 435 = *L'an. Ép.* 1913, 203]. A *cippus* in Tripoli Museum, discovered in the nearby Oasis, supported in antiquity two elephant tusks dedicated to the God Liber. [*Inscr. Trip.* 231.]

alike was the elephant; in the main street of Lepcis a marble statue of an elephant came to light (pl. LXVII); the mosaic which adorns the entrance of the Sabratha *annona*-office (*statio Sabratensium*) at Ostia has an elephant on it; and the rich citizens of the cities of Tripolitania usually offered elephant-tusks to their gods.

In addition, ostrich feathers, the skins of wild animals, and perhaps some gold and precious woods reached the coast. If we add, for the Roman period, the rare African beasts which were used in the games throughout the Empire, we have a rough list of what reached the ports of Tripolitania from the Fezzan, and thence to Italy and the provinces of the Empire. The merchants of Tripolitania were, on the one hand, like the merchants of Palmyra and Petra, organizers of the caravans which went from the coast to the Fezzan, and, on the other, shipowners (*navicularii*) who exported the merchandise brought by the caravans to the rest of the Roman world (see pl. LXVI, 2, the base of an honorific statue of a shipowner who may have exported wild beasts).

Trade across the desert flourished so long as the power which protected Tripolitania was powerful and able to safeguard the caravan-routes of the Fezzan. Carthage, in her prime, and later the Numidian kings had been able to effect this. Then there followed a long period of relative decadence. First came the Roman civil war, with all its attendant suffering; then, not unconnected with that and with the colonization of Africa Proconsularis, a grave conflict among the tribes bordering on Roman Africa and on Tripolitania and Cyrene. We have record of an expedition sent against the Garamantes in 20 B.C., with which the *bellum Gaetulicum* mentioned in an inscription* of Lepcis may be connected. This war perhaps raged in Tripolitania at about the same time as the Marmarides and Garamantes invaded Cyrenaica and were defeated by the famous Quirinius (Flor. ii, 31, and a metrical inscription of Cyrene†). The last phase of the same disturbance was that linked with the name of Tacfarinas. In one of the mosaics of Zliten one can see prisoners taken in this war being cruelly killed in the amphitheatre.

Conditions in Tripolitania did not return to normal until the second half of the first century A.D. From this time onwards until the second half of the third century the country enjoyed profound

* *Inscr. Trip.* 301. † *SEG.* ix. 63.

peace and complete security. Moreover, just at this period the demand for the products of Tripolitanian trade became greatest, especially for wild animals. At the same time the camel made its first appearance in Tripolitania. This animal was ideal for desert-trade, making it safe and regular, and was put into use on a large scale both in trade and in agriculture (pl. LXI, 1).

It is natural that from this moment the cities of Tripolitania suddenly began to develop. New public buildings (temples, basilicas, baths, and so on) were constructed, harbours were improved, roads built. Splendid villas, the owners of which made use of improved methods of agriculture, sprang up in the country-side. Like the rest of Africa, Tripolitania was a land of large estates. First came those of the emperors: Augustus owned vast tracts of land near Sabratha, and under Septimius Severus and Caracalla there was a special *regio Tripolitana* of the *res privata*. Next came the estates of the Roman aristocracy and the local magnates. Villas like those of Zliten, decorated with fine mosaics (pl. LIX), are eloquent witnesses to the prosperity enjoyed by the large estates in the second half of the first century A.D.

A curious episode in the life of one of these three cities—Lepcis Magna—was its rapid development under Septimius Severus. The emperor, who was a native of the city, wished to make it the first city of Africa. And Lepcis became the city of his dreams. He visited it after his accession in A.D. 204, and on this occasion the interesting tetrapylon decorated with reliefs* was erected in his honour. Undoubtedly he inspected on that occasion the large works of reconstruction, as a result of which a new Severan town was to all intents and purposes created, conceived by the emperor himself. He intended to endow Lepcis with a magnificent harbour, equal to that of Trajan at Rome (pl. LXIV), and connected by a fine main street to his own Forum Novum Severianum, where the emperor and empress were enthroned as Juppiter and Juno. The port and forum have now been excavated. Our sources mention a palace, which has not yet been found.

This, though interesting, was no more than an episode. The harbour was too big for the city and its maintenance constituted too heavy a burden for it. However, as long as the city remained prosperous, the donations of Septimius Severus were not disastrous. The decay began later here than in the rest of the Empire. This

* [R. Bartoccini, *Afr. Ital.* 4, 1931, pp. 32–152.]

is not the place to recount the history of the decline: it was in part the general decline of the vital forces of the Roman Empire.[99]

The survey of the provinces which we have given in the preceding pages would not be complete without a sketch of the conditions prevailing in the extensive areas occupied by mines and quarries, forests and fisheries, which have already been mentioned incidentally. These districts were clearly of enormous importance for the Roman Empire. The imperial government certainly did not neglect this side of public economy. It is not an exaggeration to say that most, if not all, of the mines and quarries which are worked nowadays in those parts of Europe, Asia, and Africa which were included in the Empire—with the exception of the coal-mines and workings for certain other minerals unknown to, or little used in, the ancient world—were exploited by the Romans, who inherited them from their previous owners. How many new mineral sources were discovered in the imperial age we do not know. It seems as if in this matter the Romans relied upon the work of past generations and did not add to it very much.

Our information on the exploitation of the natural resources of the Empire, apart from agriculture, is very scanty indeed. What we do know relates chiefly to mines and quarries. The exploitation of forests and the industries connected with it, and the method of extraction of salt remains almost a blank in our knowledge. A few remarks of Pliny and some scattered inscriptions do not allow us even to attempt a general characterization of those departments of public economy. As regards mines and quarries, we know that most of the workings were situated in the provinces. Italy was rather poor in mineral resources, and no efforts were made by the state to exploit in an intensive way such as did exist. A striking example is the marble industry of Luna. The rich quarries producing the beautiful white marble of Carrara were never worked on a very large scale, and not before the end of the Republican period. The Romans preferred to import different kinds of marble from far distant places, Greece, Asia Minor, Egypt, Numidia. The explanation of this curious fact probably lies in the peculiar conditions of the economic and social life of Italy in general. In the later days of the Republic the state endeavoured to stop the development of mining in Italy by reducing the number of workmen allowed by law in mines. The reason appears to have been the fear that large numbers of slaves concentrated in the mines might become dangerous hotbeds of revolt, while the employment of free men would diminish the sum total of peasants and agricultural workmen so urgently needed on the estates both of the Roman aristocracy and of the city *bourgeoisie*, especially after the servile wars in Sicily and Italy. Besides, there was no need to work the mines and quarries of Italy intensively, since the state possessed the rich mines of Spain, Macedonia, and Asia Minor, and gradually added to them those of Dalmatia, Noricum, and Gaul.[100] There was no state monopoly of mines either under the Republic or under the Empire. The state was, indeed, the largest owner of mines, being heir of the former proprietors alike in the Hellenistic kingdoms and in the Western provinces, where they had been state property. But in Gaul Rome apparently did not concentrate all mines in her own hands, nor did she object to the discovery and exploitation of new ones on the large estates of the Gallic nobility. In Republican times most of the mines owned by the state were leased to private capitalists, who formed powerful associations or companies. Such was the case at least in Spain and Sardinia, and we may suppose that the same system was applied to the mines in the East, both in Asia Minor and in Macedonia. The labour employed by such companies in Spain and Sardinia was mostly, if not wholly, that of slaves, who were brought in masses to work in the mines and in the quarries. In Macedonia, on the contrary, the work was done mostly by free men who rented single pits either directly from the state or from the mining companies.

When large mining districts in the new provinces (Gaul, Britain, Noricum, Dalmatia, Pannonia, and Dacia in the West, and the new Asiatic provinces and Egypt in the East) passed into the possession of the state and the emperors, the system of exploitation became more diversified through adaptation to the special conditions of each district. We cannot enter into details here, but in general it may be said that our scanty evidence attests all the possible types of exploitation in the various mines of the Empire: leasing to large capitalists (as in Noricum, Dalmatia, Gaul); leasing of single pits to small *entrepreneurs*, whose rent was collected either by tax-farmers or by state officials; exploitation of quarries by contractors (*redemptores*), who received fees proportionate to the amount of material extracted, the work being done under the supervision of civil or military officers; extraction of minerals and stone by convicts (*damnati in metallum*) or slaves under the supervision of soldiers; the use of compulsory labour, especially in Egypt. Side by side with these different systems employed in the public and imperial mines and quarries, there existed all over the Empire mines and quarries owned by private people who paid a certain amount of the produce to the state. How large this amount was, and how the collection of the payments was organized, we cannot say.

The general trend of imperial policy in regard to mines and quarries was gradually to eliminate the great capitalists and to concentrate the exploitation of them in the hands of state officials. Preference was given to the letting of single pits to small contractors, especially in the time of Hadrian and his successors. Such was the system used, for instance, in Spain in the mining district of Vipasca, as attested by the fragmentary inscriptions found there, the content of which is derived from a special law which regulated the exploitation of the mines. The part of the intermediaries was confined in practice to the exaction of the rents and of the other taxes due from these small concessionaires. The rules of Vipasca are based on the theory that half the yield of each gallery belongs to the state and half to the individual who is prepared to expend his capital in the extraction of the mineral. It is a matter of dispute, with which we are not concerned here, whether this principle derives from the rules governing the discovery of treasure hidden in the earth, or from the very ancient system of exploitation of domanial land by means of *coloni partiarii*. It is, however, important to emphasize that the emperors adopted the same system in the exploitation of mining districts as in public and Imperial lands, aiming at encouraging the initiative of small contractors. Later, this system seems to have given place to the direct exploitation of the mines by means of convicts and by the use of compulsory labour.[101]

We can observe an interesting fact in the development of the most important mining districts, and particularly with reference to the extraction of metals. The final introduction of monetary economy throughout the Empire, even in those regions which had not previously used money as a means of exchange, increased the demand for precious metals, particularly silver. Hence came the efforts of the Roman government to annex to the Empire one mining district after the other, and to organize them in a more efficient manner. The further increase in demand, particularly of silver, and the gradual exhaustion of some silver mines, for example those of Spain, caused the government grave, though not insuperable, difficulty. Efforts were made to attract miners to the silver-mines by the grant of certain privileges and to adapt the value of the coinage to changed conditions. The difficulty, however, must not be exaggerated; there was no question of the complete exhaustion of silver-yielding mines. If in the third century A.D. the silver crisis became acute, this was the result not of the exhaustion of the mines, but of the chaotic conditions of the period. The great problem, in the mining industry no less than in agriculture, was not the lack of material, but the lack of workers; not shortage of *metalla*, but of *metallarii*. When in the fourth century the Empire had surmounted the crisis, the main preoccupation was not to find fresh mines, but fresh labour with which to exploit the old ones.[102]

The survey which we have given will enable the reader to grasp and appreciate many salient features of the economic and social life of the provinces of the Roman Empire. One of the most striking is the capital importance of the part played by agriculture. It is no exaggeration to say that most of the provinces were almost exclusively agricultural countries. In some of them we have, of course, extensive mining activity, as in Spain, Britain, Gaul, Dalmatia, Noricum, Dacia, and Asia Minor. Some were famous for their quarries, especially of different kinds of marble—Asia Minor, Egypt, Africa, and the mainland and islands of Greece. But the mines and quarries formed merely small islands in a sea of fields and meadows. Though statistics are lacking, we may safely affirm that the largest part of the population of the Empire was engaged in agriculture, either actually tilling the soil or living on an income drawn from the land.

A second important feature is the extension of agriculture, viticulture, and gardening over countries which previously either lived exclusively on grazing and hunting or followed a very primitive method of tilling the land. Where agriculture was introduced for the first time, it was introduced in its highly developed forms, chiefly in the form of a capitalistic and more or less scientific tillage of the soil. Notable examples are the Decumates Agri in South Germany, the fields of Britain and Belgium, the valleys of Noricum and Dalmatia, the dry steppes of the Dobrudja, and in the East such regions as the Syrian half-desert and the plateau of Trachonitis. No less important was the development of Africa, where steppes and plateaus were converted by scientific irrigation into rich cornfields and later into olive-groves, extending for mile after mile over regions where in our own days a few sheep and camels live a half-starved life in the dry prairie. The victorious advance of the culture of vine and olive in almost all Roman provinces has already been described.[103]

The third point which emerges from our survey is the general tendency throughout the Empire towards the concentration of land in the hands of a few proprietors who lived in the cities or belonged to the highest ranks of the imperial aristocracy, with the emperor himself at the head. What had formerly been a characteristic feature of Italy and Greece only, is now found in every province: the land was owned by men who were not themselves experts in agriculture but were townsmen for whom land was a form of investment. On the other hand, by the force of circumstances, land became more and more the property of the state, withdrawn from the market and concentrated in the hands of the emperors, a development which gradually brought about a reversion to the forms of landownership which had prevailed in some monarchical states of the Hellenistic period and in the Oriental monarchies.

Parallel to this concentration of land in the hands of the city *bourgeoisie*, the imperial aristocracy, and the state, we observe the gradual disappearance all over the Roman Empire of small independent landowners living a free life in their tribal, rural, or city communities. In Italy and Greece former proprietors were degraded to tenants and formed a socially inferior class. In Italy they were Roman citizens, but economically and socially they occupied a very modest position. In Gaul those who had been clients of the wealthy aristocracy were regarded and treated as a lower class, which had no right to take any part in the public life of the community; in the cities as in the villages this right was reserved for the wealthier landowners. The same is true of the Danube lands, though here we have considerable groups of flourishing village communities, where the peasants tilled land owned by themselves and not rented from a rich landowner of the city. In Asia Minor the vast majority of the tillers of the soil were either second-class citizens of the Greek cities, who mostly held tenancies from proprietors resident in the cities or from the cities themselves (which had their public land), or they were half-serfs of the imperial estates and temple domains. Some mountain tribes, as well as the inhabitants of most of the Syrian and Palestinian villages, were in a better position. In Egypt, despite a notable development of private property in land, which was, however, confined almost exclusively to the Greek and Roman section of the population, the *fellahîn* remained what they had been under the Ptolemies, half serfs and half tenants, the latter status prevailing. Finally, in Africa the majority of the population did not live on their own lands, but tilled and toiled for the emperor and his farmers-general or for the members of the city *bourgeoisie*.

The increase in the number of absentee landlords and the transformation of small landowners into tenants did not in any way improve agricultural technique or even maintain it on the high level which it had reached on the capitalistic estates of the Hellenistic and early Roman period, which were cultivated by slave labour. In Italy scientific agriculture gradually decayed as soon as the land slipped from the hands of the local city *bourgeoisie*, and was incorporated in the *latifundia* of the imperial aristocracy. In the provinces, however—in Egypt, Africa, Syria, and the Celtic and Thraco-Illyrian lands—the type of the thrifty agriculturist, the 'agricola bonus', still prevailed, or rather came into existence, particularly in the Danube lands, in Egypt, and in Africa. There the leading type of proprietor was for a time that represented by the owners of the Pompeian *villae rusticae* of the first century A.D., of whom many examples have been cited. But the growth of imperial estates and the formation all over the Empire of a wealthy city *bourgeoisie*, of landed magnates who had higher ambitions than to be 'agricolae boni', caused an extension to the provinces of that decay of scientific agriculture which was characteristic of Italy.

Lastly, our survey reveals the enormous importance which the rural population had for the Empire in general. The tenants and farmers formed its backbone. Together with the slaves and artisans of the cities they constituted the working-class of the Roman Empire, the class which, under the direction of the city *bourgeoisie*, produced the goods required by the cities and by the imperial army, which were the chief consumers. Numerically they certainly far exceeded the numbers of the city population, including both *bourgeoisie* and workmen. We have no statistics, but a glance at the map of the Roman Empire and a simple calculation of the number of hands which were necessary to feed both the country population and the cities, and even to export some foodstuffs to foreign lands, will convince everyone that the country people who tilled the soil formed an enormous majority of the population of the Empire. The Roman Empire was, it is true, urbanized to a very high degree. Indeed, if we take into consideration the forms of its economic life and the purchasing power of the population, we may say that it was urbanized to excess. Nevertheless the rural population was in no way absorbed by the cities, not even from the point of view of the diffusion of their civilization. Civilized life was reserved for the cities. The rural communities lived in very primitive conditions. They had no schools, no gymnasia, no palaestrae, no libraries of their own, and those of the cities were too far away. All they had was one or more modest shrines of local gods, and sometimes a bath or an amphitheatre. They learned, of course, to speak, and perhaps to read and write, a little Latin or Greek. What sort of Latin or Greek, we may judge by reading a few of the inscriptions in which is immortalized the rural population of the Danube provinces or of Asia Minor. But their progress was slow, exceedingly slow. The state paid no attention to the needs of the villages; the cities were occupied in making their own life as comfortable as possible and had no money to spare for the villages; the villagers themselves were too poor to improve their conditions of life and most of them were very badly organized. That is the reason why the country still spoke the Iberian, Celtic, Illyrian, Thracian, Phrygian, Lydian, Syrian, Egyptian, Phoenician, or Berber tongues, while the cities spoke and wrote almost exclusively Greek and Latin.

From the political point of view, the rural population was in no respect equal to the burgesses of the cities, whatever their legal condition, whether they were Roman colonies, *municipia*, or *civitates stipendiariae*. The last-named category, it should be noted, gradually disappeared from view. In all the *civitates stipen-diariae* the ruling aristocracy at least had either the Latin or the Roman franchise. The country people in the provinces belonged to the class of *peregrini*, with the rare exceptions of some Roman citizens who happened to live in the villages and formed the village aristocracy and of some unlucky persons who sank to the position of tenants. We know very little of the legal status of this class. It looks as if it included several categories. This is a notorious fact in the case of Egypt, where the Alexandrians formed the highest class of *peregrini*, the Greeks in the country the second, and the *fellahîn*, the native peasants, the lowest. Was this distinction peculiar to Egypt, or did it also exist in the other parts of the Roman Empire, especially in the East? This problem cannot be discussed here. As is well known, it is the subject of lively controversy, connected with the restoration and inter-pretation of an edict of Caracalla, fragments of which have been found in Egypt (*P.Giss.* 40). The question is far from having re-ceived a satisfactory solution. The reference in this document to *dediticii*, undoubtedly in some connexion or other with the famous edict of Caracalla by which Roman citizenship was bestowed on all the inhabitants of the Roman Empire, remains unexplained. The most recent investigations still do not put out of court the hypothesis that the *dediticii* of *P. Giss.* 40 may be the rural popula-tion of Egypt. However that may have been, there is no doubt that in the first and second centuries the different classes of *pere-grini* far outnumbered the Latin and Roman citizens, that the majority of them lived not in the cities but in the country, and that they constituted, at any rate in the East, the lowest class of aliens.[104]

The last question that arises about the country population concerns the material welfare of the villagers. To this question we can hardly give an adequate general answer. The only pro-vince for which we have considerable details relating to the daily life of the rustic population is Egypt. The impression conveyed by the study of the ruins of some of the Egyptian villages, and of the thousands of documents found in them, is that we can scarcely speak of any improvement in the economic condition of the Egyptian *fellahîn* during the Roman domination. There was a brief revival of prosperity in Egypt in the first decades of Roman rule, but it was short-lived. For the new Egyptian landed *bourgeoisie* this revival lasted longer than for the peasants of the crown-estates and the tenants of the landowners. The situation of the latter grew steadily worse. The conditions under which the masses of the Egyptian population lived were far from normal. Taxation was oppressive, the mode of collection was brutal and unfair, compulsory work bore heavily upon the peasants, the honesty of the state officers was a pious hope, very seldom a fact. It is not surprising that discontent grew and that the prosperity of the land declined. As early as the beginning of the second century, and even in the first, we hear repeatedly of villagers refusing to pay taxes or to perform compulsory work and resorting to the ancient Egyptian practice of striking, that is to say, leaving the villages and taking refuge in the swamps of the Delta. Little wonder that, when an opportunity offered, the fugitives were ready to raise the banner of revolt, and that they found many sympathizers among the population which remained in the villages. We know very little of the revolt of the Jews in Egypt and in Cyrenaica in the reign of Trajan. The official version was that the Egyptians fought the rebels on the side of the government. I rather suspect that the government was aided by the *bourgeoisie*, the Greeks and hellenized natives, while the Jews were supported by the robbers of the marshes and some of the *fellahîn*. This view is confirmed by the fact that, very soon after the Jewish revolt, both Hadrian and Antoninus Pius had to face new rebellions in Egypt, and this time not of Jews. These were small affairs for a powerful Empire, but they were very typical of the mood of the Egyptian *fellahîn*. A more serious revolt, as is well known, broke out in the time of M. Aurelius, and this rising of the cowherds (Βουκόλοι) was not so easy to quell.[105]

Was Egypt an exception? Was the situation of the working-classes in the other rural parts of the Roman Empire better than it was in Egypt? It is impossible to give an adequate answer to this question. The speeches of Dio Chrysostom, and the evidence quoted above on the antagonism of the rural πάροικοι of some cities of Asia Minor towards the landowners of the cities; the pictures given in the Gospels and other contemporary sources of the life of the peasants in Palestine, which are far from rosy and show the prevalence of bitter poverty and oppression; the revolt of peasants under Mariccus in Gaul in the first century; a similar revolt of native peasants in Dacia and Dalmatia at the time of the campaigns of M. Aurelius—all these show that, alike in the countries where the peasant population lived in a condition of half-serfdom and in those where free peasants predominated, the situation was not much better than in Egypt.[106] Such indications, however, are exceptional. The impression given by the few inscriptions of the villages testifies rather to a growing prosperity or at any rate to a quiet mood on the part of the peasants. As a rule the village remains silent in the first and second centuries. If it speaks, it speaks to glorify the Empire. But we must not forget that those who spoke were the village aristocracy, not the mass of the peasants.

After this survey of the Roman provinces we may return to the much-vexed question of the relative weakness of Roman industry as compared with commerce and agriculture. Why did ancient industry not reach the heights of development attained in the modern world? Why did the industrialization of the ancient world stop, and why did the Roman Empire fail to evolve the capitalistic forms of industry peculiar to our own times?

The answer given to this question by leading modern economists like K. Bücher, G. Salvioli, and M. Weber[107] is that industry could not develop because the ancient world never emerged from the forms of primitive house-economy (*Oikenwirtschaft*): it never reached the higher stages of economic development achieved in modern times—the stages of city-economy and state-economy. Assuming the correctness of Bücher's phases of economic evolution (namely, house-economy, city-economy, state-economy, and world-economy), though it is more than questionable, I maintain that the economists' diagnosis as applied to the ancient world is wrong. It is true that that world, and particularly the Roman Empire, shows more survivals of house-economy than some modern states of the nineteenth and twentieth centuries, both in the management of the large estates of absentee landlords and in the husbandry of the peasants. But it is evident that these features of house-economy were mere survivals. Home production alike in Italy and in the provinces was limited to a certain amount of spinning and weaving. For everything else recourse was had to the market; agricultural and domestic implements, pottery, lamps, toilet articles, jewellery, clothes, and the like, were not produced at home even in the villages. The excavations of poor rural cemeteries prove this up to the hilt. Thus there was no such thing as the prevalence of house-economy throughout the ancient world in all the stages of its evolution. Pure house-economy did not exist even in the earlier times of the Oriental monarchies, and with the advance of Oriental and Greco-Roman civilization it gradually disappeared from large areas of Europe, Asia, and Africa. The question is why the survivals of house-economy still persisted even after the powerful economic development which took place under the Roman Empire, and why capitalistic industry did not hold the field which it began to conquer, first in the East, later in Greece, and finally in the Roman Empire, the gradual extension of the field keeping pace with the advance of Greco-Oriental civilization? Why had not industry the power to eliminate these survivals, and why did they gradually become the prominent economic feature of the ancient world? Some modern scholars have found the cause of the weakness of ancient industry in the existence of slave labour.[108] They explain that the cheapness of slave labour, the docile character of the slaves, and the unlimited supply, which permitted a constant increase of the numbers of workmen, prevented the invention of labour-saving machinery and thus made it impossible to build up factories. Against this theory I would point out that ancient industry reached its highest level in the Hellenistic period when it was based wholly on slave labour. It began to decay under the Roman Empire when slaves were gradually replaced, even in the field of industry, by ever-increasing numbers of free workmen. On the other hand, the arguments about an unlimited supply of labour and about its character are grossly exaggerated. Slave labour was notoriously not at all cheap, the slaves were by no means docile (as the slave revolts showed), and the prices paid for them were generally very high. If strikes were infrequent, that was due to the low standard of industry and not to the docile mood of the workmen and to the employment of slaves. Why then should the employment of slaves prevent an energetic shop-owner from using new technical devices, which would have been a good way of making his products cheaper and better? It is a striking fact that industry began to decay just at the moment when technique ceased to advance, simultaneously with an arrest in the advance of pure scientific research, and this fact cannot be explained by the employment of slaves. We have therefore to seek for other explanations of the decay of industry in the Roman Empire.

To my mind the explanation should be sought in the general social and political conditions of the Empire. The weak point in the development of industry in the imperial period seems to have been the lack of real competition, and this lack depended entirely on the character, number, and buying capacity of the customers. The advance made in the Greek and Hellenistic periods in the sphere of industry, both in the matter of technique and division of labour and in mass production for an indefinite market, was due to a constant increase in the demand for manufactured goods. Besides the requirements of the Greek cities themselves, the few centres of industrial production in Greece during the fifth and fourth centuries B.C. met the demands of a steadily expanding Greek and non-Greek market in Italy, Gaul, Spain, on the shores of the Black Sea, and in other regions. The buyers, apart from the Greek colonies, were the countless half-barbarian inhabitants of these countries, who gradually became more and more hellenized in their tastes and habits: the graves of the natives of Italy and South Russia are full of the products of Athenian and Hellenistic industry. In the Hellenistic period the number both of industrial centres and of consumers rapidly increased. The East was opened to Greek industry and commerce, and through Carthage Greek industrial centres came into contact with Africa, Spain, Britain, and the Northern lands in general. The Greek manufacturers knew how to adapt themselves to the requirements of their new customers and how to attract buyers. A keen competition arose between the different centres of industry. The number of customers of good purchasing power was growing apace when Rome came into contact with the Hellenistic world. The destructive work done by the Romans in the East was not of serious moment, though temporarily it had very injurious effects by steadily reducing the buying capacity of large numbers of the prosperous population. Much more important was the fact that Rome succeeded in transforming the whole of the ancient world into one Empire, incorporating in a single state almost all the flourishing and more or less advanced peoples of the Mediterranean basin. After the transitory period of conquest and civil wars, which ·was more destructive than constructive, the victory of Augustus restored peace and normal conditions. An economic revival followed. The industrial centres awoke to new life, and the number of consumers increased. But the question is, To what extent and for how long?

The market for Greco-Roman industry was now confined almost entirely to the population of the Empire. In the fifth chapter emphasis was laid on the fact that the volume of Rome's foreign commerce must not be underestimated. But the character of this commerce must be taken into consideration. The barbarians and the poor population of Northern Europe could not absorb large amounts of industrial products, and the political conditions were such that trade could never become regular but remained more or less speculative. The Far East was, of course, safer, but it had a highly developed industry of its own, and its demand for the industrial products of the Roman Empire continued to be limited to certain articles, and was maintained only so long as it did not learn to produce imitations of them. The only clientele left was the population of the Empire. While the expansion of Roman civilization was in progress, industry throve and developed. We have spoken of the gradual industrialization of the provinces. But with Hadrian the expansion ceased. No new lands were acquired. The romanization, or partial urbanization, of the provinces reached its climax in Hadrian's time. The market for industry was now limited to the cities and the country districts of the Empire. The future of ancient industry depended on their purchasing power, and while the buying capacity of the city *bourgeoisie* was large, their numbers were limited, and the city proletariate grew steadily poorer. We have seen that the material welfare of the country population improved very slowly, if at all. The fabric of Roman industry rested therefore on very weak foundations, and on such foundations no expensive capitalistic industry could be built up.

VIII

THE ECONOMIC AND SOCIAL POLICY OF THE FLAVIANS AND ANTONINES

AFTER Augustus had concluded his great wars on the Rhine and the Danube and completed the pacification of Spain and Africa, the Roman Empire was not disturbed by foreign wars of importance for about a century. Claudius' annexations of Britain, Mauretania, and Thrace, the ambitious projects of Nero in the East, and the Jewish war in the time of Vespasian were local 'colonial' wars which did not affect the Empire as a whole. Her dangerous neighbours and rivals, the Germans and the Sarmatians in the North and North-east and the Parthians in the South-east, remained more or less quiet. The only serious shock was the civil war of A.D. 69, in Italy, followed by some complications on the Rhine frontier. Little wonder that under such circumstances the fabric of the Roman Empire appeared solid and everlasting, and that economic life steadily progressed despite the personal extravagances and the follies of some of the emperors. We must bear in mind that the colonial wars just mentioned, resulting as they did in the annexation of comparatively rich and civilized lands, added to the prosperity of the Empire by opening fresh markets for Roman commerce and industry and providing new and excellent recruiting areas.

Meanwhile, however, the conditions gradually changed. The Germans who lived in close contact with the Empire learnt to improve their military equipment and technique, they discovered that the Roman *limes* was not an insurmountable barrier, and they grasped the need of a better organization of their internal life. Besides, those who were Rome's nearest neighbours saw before them the wealth and prosperity of the provincial cities and were eager to participate in the civilized life of the Empire. The constantly increasing numbers of the German tribes provided another stimulus to push forward and endeavour to acquire new lands. Some of the German tribes were, indeed, diverted by the Roman barrier towards the South-east, into the region of the Dnieper; but this outlet was not large enough or safe enough to satisfy them, in view of the strength of the Sarmatian peoples who were masters of the Russian steppes. A similar migratory movement westwards was also a marked tendency of the Sarmatian tribes. Well armed and well organized, living at constant feud with their neighbours who pressed on them from behind—Germans on the North and other Sarmatian tribes on the East—the Sarmatians of the West, the Iazyges and the Roxalani, were eager to settle down on the Danube in the immediate vicinity of the Roman *limes*. The Iazyges in fact succeeded in setting foot in the region North of the Danube which lay West of the kingdom of Dacia. The Roxalani, who arrived later, failed in this since they were held back by the Roman armies, but they remained for long a permanent danger to the countries South of the Danube. The Parthians, finally, never gave up their claims to the Syrian lands and to Armenia, and had never suffered a blow crushing enough to have reduced them to lasting impotence. On the contrary, they were well aware that the Syrian legions of Rome were not an obstacle which could prevent them from attempting again the invasion of the ancient dominions of the Persian Empire.

It would be out of place to deal here with the foreign policy of the Roman Empire. It must suffice to say that in the time of Domitian and Trajan the far-seeing politicians and generals of Rome, who were acquainted with the conditions on the frontiers, felt the necessity of renewing the policy of Augustus, of starting another victorious advance into the lands of their enemies, unless Rome were to be confronted with the task of defending her Empire from serious attacks in the North, the East, and the South. The necessity was fully realized by Domitian, though his expeditions were not very successful and led to some grave disasters. His efforts were renewed by Trajan with more consistency and with better success. It is well known that in two expeditions Trajan annexed the last half-civilized and well-organized state on the Danube, a buffer state between the Roman Empire and the German and Iranian tribes—the Dacian, that is, the Thracian, kingdom of Decebalus. The Roman Empire now faced directly the two waves of invaders, the Germans coming from the North and the Iranians coming from the East. Our knowledge of the conditions which existed on the lower Danube and of the relations between the Dacian state and Rome is too slight to permit us to judge whether the attack of Trajan was justified by the policy of Decebalus, and whether it was really easier to deal with the Germans and the Sarmatians direct. But it is clear that the annexation of Dacia required a more intensive military occupation of the Danube lands, the Roman frontier being now much more complicated. Furthermore, the Empire had to furnish the conquered land with a new population, whose special task was to carry out the work of urbanizing Dacia. The same policy of urbanization and colonization became necessary for the hinterland of Dacia, that is for Moesia Inferior and Thracia. The policy of annexation was adopted by Trajan in the South and the South-east, in Parthia, Arabia, and Africa. Africa and Syria gained enormously. A fresh start was given to the colonization of fertile lands and to the establishment of city life in vast areas that were formerly waste. How far the annexation of Mesopotamia, which provoked a strong and dangerous outburst of national feeling among the peoples of the East, was a real gain from the military and political point of view is still a matter of discussion.[1]

The successes of Trajan were won at the cost of a severe strain on the whole Empire. The military operations required levy after levy and the burden of them fell almost wholly on the Roman and romanized areas, including the cities of Italy, which furnished the praetorian guard and the officers. The men who went to the new lands in the East and South rarely returned to their homes: many were killed, and large numbers were utilized to colonize and urbanize the newly acquired provinces. We have already mentioned Trajan's strenuous effort to develop town life in the Danube lands and so to create another Gaul in the rear of the Danube *limes*. We know, too, that he founded many colonies in Africa and that under his rule the urbanization of some districts in Syria was rapid and effective. All this was done at the expense of the older and more romanized (or hellenized) Roman provinces—Spain, Gaul, Dalmatia, and Asia Minor. It is not surprising that the cities of Spain became alarmed and protested against the ever-recurring levies.[2]

The time was past when Roman wars paid for themselves and when victories enriched the conquerors. The war booty of Dacia and of the Mesopotamian lands was not enough to cover the

Description of Plate LXVIII

1. ONE OF THE BAS-RELIEFS OF THE ARCH OF TRAJAN AT BENEVEN-
TUM. Benevento. The bibliography of the arch is quoted in full in note 7 to this
chapter; here reference need be made only to S. Reinach, *Rép. d. rel.* i (our relief is on
p. 65, 1). In note 7 I have given the general explanation of the bas-reliefs of the arch.

Two veterans are introduced to the emperor and his staff (all in civil dress) by a group
of deities. The chief of these is Virtus, who holds in her hand a *vexillum* with five *aquilae*,
symbols of five legions. Virtus is accompanied by Diana and Silvanus Domesticus,
deities of the forests and fields and protectors of settled domestic life in the country. It
is easy to interpret the bas-relief as celebrating a grant of land by Trajan to soldiers of
five legions, probably not in the provinces but in Italy, as is shown by the place occupied
by the relief, on the Roman side of the arch, and by the evidence of the *Liber Coloniarum*.
Cf. note 7 to this chapter.

2. AS NO. 1. S. Reinach, op. cit., p. 65, 2.

The emperor in civil dress greets, and is greeted by, three Roman citizens in civil
dress. These three men represent a place which is under the protection of three gods:
one is Apollo (on the left), the second is Hercules, and the third has been recognized as
Portunus; the city which the three gods protect is, therefore, a harbour city. As the
divine protectors of the *navale* of the city of Rome were precisely Portunus, Hercules,
and Apollo, we may accept the explanation of von Domaszewski, who suggests that the
emperor is greeted by the business men of Rome—the merchants of the Forum Boarium,
the most important business centre of the capital.

3. AS NO. 1. S. Reinach, op. cit., p. 66, 4.

Solemn reception of the emperor by a group of four women and two men. The
women are symbolical figures; they are wearing turreted crowns and personify, no
doubt, four cities of Italy; one of them holds a baby in her arms. The two men are
Roman citizens; each carries a young boy on his shoulders, and has another older boy
by his side. In the right-hand corner are trees. As the bas-relief adorns the inner archway, and as the other bas-relief of this archway refers to the city of Beneventum, it is
natural to explain our scene as symbolizing the gratitude of four cities of South Italy,
of which Beneventum was one, to Trajan for the institution of the *alimenta*. Italy is producing more men, and she is doing it with the help of the *alimenta*. This is the leading
idea of the relief.

4. AS NO. 1. S. Reinach, op. cit., p. 61, 2.

A majestic woman wearing a turreted crown and leaning on a plough (the attribute
in the right hand is missing) faces the Emperor Trajan, who introduces to her two children—a little boy and an older girl—who worship her. The woman is protected by the
god Mars. Behind the emperor stand two stately women wearing diadems, one with the
cornucopiae. The scene was explained by Petersen as *Italia agricola* (agricultural Italy),
worshipped by the children educated by Trajan. It symbolizes, he thinks, the agricultural renascence of Italy under the protection of Trajan's victorious arms (Mars), the
prosperity of Italy, and her repopulation as the result of the institution of the *alimenta*.
As the bas-relief faces, not Italy and Rome, but the provinces, and as the institution of
the *alimenta* has been already glorified in no. 3, von Domaszewski explains the scene as
symbolizing the spread of Roman citizens over the provinces by means of new Roman
colonies organized by Trajan. I prefer to recognize in it a symbol of the Roman Empire
growing rich and populous again as the result of a reasonable military policy. Mars,
the god of war, in protecting the Roman Empire, restores its fertility, stops depopulation, and creates Abundance everywhere. The second diademed figure standing beside
Abundance may be Justitia or Clementia, symbolizing the fair, just, and clement
administration of the provinces by Trajan and Hadrian, or rather by Hadrian as
Trajan's heir.

1. TRAJAN AND THE VETERANS

2. TRAJAN AND THE BUSINESS MEN

3. *ALIMENTA* FOR THE CITIES OF ITALY

4. TRAJAN AND THE PROVINCES

LXVIII. TRAJAN AND HADRIAN

heavy expense of military operations systematically carried on year after year by huge armies in far distant fields. The constant movement of troops towards the theatres of war, which are so artistically depicted on the column of Trajan, required the repair of old, and the construction of new, roads, the construction of expensive bridges—one thinks of the famous bridges on the Danube—the building of new ships, the mobilization of masses of draught animals and drivers, quarters in the cities for soldiers on the march, the concentration of vast quantities of foodstuffs at special points (which also called for good roads and abundant means of transport), the provision of a regular supply of countless arms and weapons, of clothing and shoes. Only those who know from experience the difficulties presented by these problems in modern times, despite the existence of railroads, motorcars, and large factories, can realize what it meant for the Roman Empire to carry on, not a 'colonial', but a real, war for years on end. Moreover, after the Dacian war Trajan expended large sums to give *congiaria* to the people and *donativa* to the soldiers, to organize games and other spectacles. Still heavier was the expenditure needed to meet his lavish building activity in Rome, Italy, and the provinces. We must not forget that after Augustus and Nero Trajan was the emperor most active in regard to building. At the same time, however, he carefully avoided increasing taxes and straining the contributive capacity of Roman citizens.[3]

We have very little evidence how the needs of the army were met. But there is enough to indicate that the method used was primarily that of requisitions, implying compulsory work both in Italy and in the provinces. Even the scanty information we have shows how heavily the construction and repair of roads and the feeding and quartering of the troops bore on the Danubian provinces and on Thrace, Macedonia, and Bithynia, through which passed the main roads leading from Italy to the Danube and from the Danube to the Parthian theatre of war. Some striking facts are revealed by inscriptions. We find Trajan insisting upon the repair of a road in the territory of Heraclea Lynkestis, for which the city and the attached tribes were responsible; rich citizens of Beroea in Macedonia come to the rescue of their town and help it to carry its heavy burden; the payment of taxes and the provision of sufficient corn to feed the population has become a difficult task for the Macedonian cities, and this in a province which was comparatively rich in corn-lands. It is no wonder that the position became specially acute at the beginning of the reign of Hadrian, when the resources of the province were already exhausted.[4] We meet with the same situation in Bithynia. It was no accident that in A.D. 111, a few years before the Parthian war, Trajan sent thither one of his best men, Pliny the younger, to put in order the financial affairs of the Bithynian cities and to supervise the general administration of the province and its relations with the vassal kingdom of Bosporus, one of the most important sources of supply for the armies of the East. Nor was it an accident that the cities on the main road to the East (Byzantium and Juliopolis) complained bitterly of the constant strain put on their resources by the movement of troops.[5] As in Macedonia, wealthy men came to the aid of their provinces: members of the former royal house of Galatia and the Lycian millionaire Opramoas both mention the part which they took in providing for Trajan and Hadrian and their troops just before Trajan's death and after it.[6] One need only read Pliny's well-known description of what an imperial journey meant for the provinces, in order to realize how heavy the burden was even under the enlightened rule of Trajan, particularly in time of war when urgent needs forced the emperor to have recourse, oftener than he would have liked, to emergency measures. On this point our information is more detailed for the later period (see below, pp. 423 ff.), but there is no doubt that the devices then adopted were not new.

It is, however, somewhat surprising to find how thoroughly disastrous Trajan's wars were for the Roman Empire in general. Trajan himself was too busy and too much occupied with his military enterprises to realize fully that his expeditions were destroying the vital forces of the Empire. He perceived, indeed, the rapid decay of Italy and sought to remedy it, following the lines which had already been traced by the Flavians and Nerva. The dread symptom of this decay was the depopulation of the peninsula and the concurrent decline of Italian agriculture. We have seen how Domitian tried to save Italy by prohibiting the planting of vines in the provinces. Nerva endeavoured to repopulate the country by reviving the plan of distributing land to poorer citizens; and he was also the first to think of achieving his end by the introduction of *alimenta*. Trajan forbade emigration from Italy and settled Roman veterans in the immediate vicinity of

Rome; he forced senators to acquire land in the mother country; and he helped Italian landowners in general, both large and small, to improve their situation by supplying them with cheap credit. It is evident that the last measure was closely connected with the first three and was another method of achieving the same object as Nerva had in view. It was not enough to stop emigration from Italy and so to create artificially a large mass of workless proletarians. Work and homes had to be provided for them. Nerva's endeavour to give them land as their private property was too expensive and could not be carried out on a large scale. Trajan tried another plan. He attracted capital to Italy, both by compelling senators to invest their money in Italian land and by giving cheap loans to existing landowners. In this way land which was gradually running to waste was reclaimed. Since the slave economy of the first century was no longer profitable (as has been shown in the sixth chapter) and the system of husbandry now prevailing was the cultivation of the land by tenants, the reclaiming of land meant a permanent increase in the demand for free tenants and increased opportunities for the landless proletarians to acquire a home, farming implements, cattle, and a smallholding on the estates of landowners. By investing his money in Italian land and letting this land to tenants, Pliny was acting in accordance with Trajan's ideas and helping him to carry out the task of repopulating Italy. Another aspect of the same policy was the manumissions in mass of this period, which were facilitated by imperial legislation. Still another was the employment, for the education of the children of the Italian proletariate, of the interest on the money which was lent by the state to Italian landowners—the institution of the *alimenta*, which, again, was imitated by wealthy proprietors of the type of Pliny and gradually extended to the provinces.

Thus in his economic and social policy Trajan's aim, like the aim of his predecessors on the throne, was to save Italy's leading position and restore her to her former economic supremacy in the Empire. To assist him in this work he created special officials of the senatorial class, whose function it was to direct the efforts of the Italian cities towards the common goal. His endeavours were not crowned with complete success. The decay of Italy was perhaps arrested for a brief space, but it could not be stopped.

Description of Plate LXIX

1. ONE OF THE BAS-RELIEFS OF THE COLUMN OF TRAJAN. Rome, Forum Trajani. C. Cichorius, *Die Reliefs der Trajanssäule*, iii, p. 203, pl. LXXXI.

In the background is the Roman camp, separated from the scene on the first plane by a range of mountains (the left part of the picture belongs to the preceding scene, where the soldiers are shown entering a recently built camp). The first plane is occupied by a rich cornfield; the wheat is ripe and the crop excellent; the Roman soldiers have crossed the mountains to reap the enemy's fields and transport the corn on mule-back to the camp. Without a doubt they would treat their own provinces in the same way, if necessary, especially in time of civil war.

2. ONE OF THE BAS-RELIEFS OF THE COLUMN OF M. AURELIUS. Rome, Piazza Colonna. E. Petersen, A. von Domaszewski, G. Calderini, *Die Marcussäule*, pls. CI and CII, no. xciii; S. Reinach, *Rép. d. rel.* i, p. 323, no. 115.

The train of M. Aurelius' army. Heavy carts drawn by oxen and horses, and loaded with the *impedimenta* of the army, are moving slowly under an escort of soldiers. The enormous number of draught animals required for the transport of the soldiers' baggage, war material, and foodstuffs may be easily imagined. Most of these animals were certainly requisitioned in the Roman provinces, the enemy's land contributing only a small proportion.

3. AS NO. 2. E. Petersen, &c., op. cit., pl. LXXXII, no. lxxiii; S. Reinach, op. cit., p. 317, no. 91.

Roman soldiers convoying the war booty, consisting of herds of cows and goats and of women captives. The scene is typical and is frequently repeated on the column; compare, e.g. op. cit., pl. XXXIII, nos. xxv and xxvi; pl. CXIX *a*, nos. cx–cxi, &c. Men do not appear among the captives; the booty consists wholly of cattle, women, and children.

The reliefs of the columns of Trajan and M. Aurelius form a contrast to those of the arch of Beneventum, which express the programme of the Antonines; they give a realistic picture of life and effectively illustrate the heavy burden imposed on the Roman Empire by the difficult wars which it had to wage in order to guarantee the safety of Italy and the provinces.

1. TRAJAN'S ARMY FORAGING IN THE ENEMY'S LAND

2. THE BAGGAGE-TRAIN OF
M. AURELIUS' ARMY

3. THE BOOTY AND THE
CAPTIVES OF WAR

LXIX. THE BURDEN OF WAR

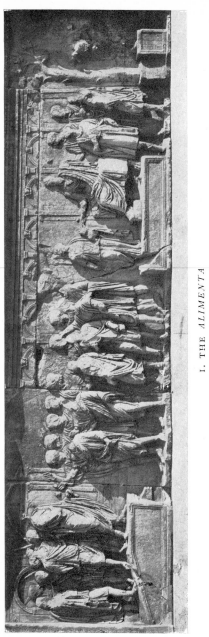

1. THE *ALIMENTA*

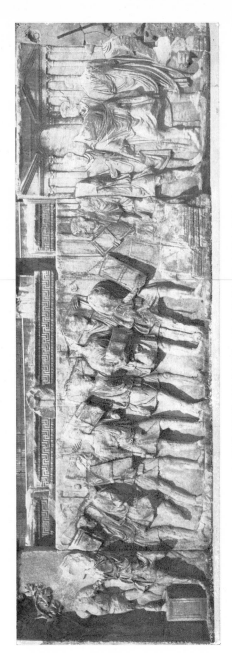

2. BURNING RECORDS OF DEBTS TO THE STATE

LXX. TRAJAN AND HADRIAN

Description of Plate LXX

1. BAS-RELIEF OF ONE OF THE TWO BALUSTRADES OF THE FORUM. Found in the Forum at Rome, and at present in the Curia. Mrs. A. Strong, *Roman Sculpture*, pp. 150 ff., pl. XLV (cf. *La Scultura romana*, pp. 138 ff.); S. Reinach, *Rép. d. rel.* i, p. 278 (all with bibliography). Often reproduced elsewhere.

The emperor, probably Trajan, standing on the *Rostra* of the Roman Forum (the buildings of which are shown in the background, with the symbol of Rome—the statue of Marsyas and the sacred fig-tree—in the right-hand corner), announces some good news to the Roman citizens. The announcement is received with applause and satisfaction. Its nature is explained by the next scene. The emperor is seated on a tribunal, surrounded by Roman citizens. A symbolical figure, probably Italy, presents a child to him. In Petersen's view the figures of the emperor and of Italy represent a statuary group. It is evident that the relief was intended to glorify the institution of the *alimenta*, which was expected to arrest the depopulation of Italy.

2. BAS-RELIEF OF THE SECOND BALUSTRADE OF THE FORUM. Found in the Forum at Rome, and at present in the Curia. Mrs. A. Strong, op. cit.; S. Reinach, op. cit., p. 279.

The emperor (Trajan or Hadrian?), seated on the *Rostra*, gives an order to a higher magistrate, probably the prefect of the city or of the praetorians, which is instantly carried out. Praetorians in half-military dress (tunic and sword-belt) bring documents and pile them up before the emperor. Behind the figures are seen the buildings of the Forum and, at the other end, the statue of Marsyas and the sacred fig-tree. The scene is usually explained as representing the burning by Trajan of the records of the arrears of taxes owing by the provincials. It may also represent Hadrian's cancellation of debts due to the *fiscus* from individuals in Rome and Italy. Cf. Chap. V, note 49. Like so many monuments on which Trajan appears (e.g. the arch of Beneventum), the balustrades may have been executed by Hadrian to glorify both his predecessor's and his own achievements. These two reliefs illustrate once more the main preoccupations of the Antonines—the depopulation of Italy and the heavy burden of payments to the state which ruined the Empire. Cf. W. Seston, 'Les "Anaglypha Traiani" du Forum Romanum et la politique d'Hadrien en 118', *Mél. de l'Éc. fr. de Rome*, 44, 1927, pp. 154–83.

Pliny's experience with his tenants was typical of the conditions of the country. Italy was not, and could not be, any longer the economic centre of the Empire.[7]

Meanwhile the condition of the provinces grew steadily worse. It is not fair to say that Trajan paid no attention to their needs. Reference has been repeatedly made to his systematic activity, as far-reaching as that of Vespasian, in promoting the development of city life in some of the provinces. He endeavoured to stop the too prevalent misgovernment by dishonest governors: witness the many prosecutions in which Pliny took such an active part. He tried to set in order the financial affairs of the provincial cities by appointing special curators to help them to manage their property more efficiently and to reduce the expense of making city life easier and more comfortable. The ruin of the cities meant the ruin of the state, as they were responsible for the payment of the taxes due from their residents and from the inhabitants of the territories attached to them.[8] Such half-measures, however, did not save the situation. When Trajan died on his way back from Mesopotamia to Rome, the position of the Empire was extremely critical. His victories had failed to stop the attacks of her most dangerous neighbours; the Iazyges on the Theiss and the Roxalani on the lower Danube resumed their threatening movements against the provinces, which had been arrested for a time by the conquest of Dacia. Another war broke out in Britain, still another in Mauretania. The Jews in Mesopotamia, Palestine, Egypt, and Cyrenaica began dangerous and bloody revolts, the last of which terribly devastated Cyrenaica. The cities of Italy and the provinces were not in a position to bear the cost of the fresh series of wars which seemed inevitable.[9]

The perilous situation of the Empire explains the policy of Trajan's successor, Hadrian. It is idle to say that Hadrian displayed a lack of understanding and of energy in abandoning his predecessor's conquests in Mesopotamia and in making, after some successful military operations, certain concessions to the Sarmatians. Hadrian was a man of great energy and great intellect. His acts showed both. There was no emperor so popular with the soldiers as he, though he maintained the strictest military discipline. No emperor, as we shall see, had such a thorough appreciation of the needs of the Empire. If he desisted from the aggressive policy of Trajan, it was because he realized that such a policy could not be carried out, that the resources of the Roman Empire were not ample enough to support a policy of further conquests. The first task of a prudent ruler of the Empire was to establish strong and true foundations before proceeding to embark on far-reaching military conquests, and that was Hadrian's policy. He did not shrink from reducing the Sarmatians to submission, which was a plain necessity, but he abstained from annexing new territory and he was satisfied with their willingness to protect the frontiers of the Roman Empire in return for an annual subsidy, therein following the policy which Trajan had adopted in his relations with the Bosporan kingdom. He quelled the revolt of the Jews in the East and repopulated Cyrenaica by sending out colonies. He was successful both in Mauretania and in Britain, and in both countries he carried out some important improvements in the military defences. In Mesopotamia he created certain buffer states to serve as bulwarks against the attacks of Parthia, and he retained and organized Arabia Petraea and the adjacent lands. By gradually introducing the system of local recruiting, he infused new strength into the military corps, which were now familiar with the needs of the provinces in which they were stationed. His reinforcement of the fortifications of the Roman *limes*, far from transforming the Empire into another China relying on her walls alone, facilitated the task of defending the provinces. Their main defence was still the spirit and discipline of the Roman soldiers, and these qualities never reached so high a standard as in the time of Hadrian.[10]

Hadrian's main task, however, was to consolidate the foundations of the Roman Empire. The facts that he began by remitting the usual accession tax (*aurum coronarium*, στέφανος) to Italy and by reducing it for the provinces, that this first measure of relief was followed by a general cancellation of debts to the *fiscus* in Italy and a partial cancellation of the arrears of the provincial cities, and (not least important) that generous help was given to the cities of the Empire, show that the general situation was highly critical and required immediate alleviation. To a certain extent the trouble was due to the lawlessness and corruption of the imperial officials, which were promoted by the almost permanent state of war in Trajan's time. We have seen that Trajan was aware of this evil and fought it. Hadrian's remedy for it was to regulate and improve the bureaucratic machinery of the state

Description of Plate LXXI

BUST OF HADRIAN with the head half turned towards the left shoulder. British Museum. A. H. Smith, *A Catalogue of Sculpture*, &c., iii (1904), p. 158, no. 1897.

a. AUREUS OF TRAJAN. Obv. IMP. TRAIANO AVG. GER. DAC. P. M. TR. P. Bust of Trajan to r. with laurel crown. Rev. ALIM(enta) ITAL(iae). COS. V. P. P. S. P. Q. R. OPTIMO PRINCIPI. Trajan standing to l. in civil dress distributing money to two children. *Ca.* A.D. 107. Cf. Cohen, ii, p. 19, no. 15.

b. DENARIUS OF HADRIAN. Obv. IMP. CAES. TRAIANVS HADRIANVS AVG. Bust of Hadrian to r. with laurel crown. Rev. LIB(ertas) PVB(lica). P. M. TR. P. COS. III. The goddess Libertas seated to l. *Ca.* A.D. 120. Cf. Cohen, ii, p. 184, no. 948.

c. AUREUS OF HADRIAN. Obv. IMP. CAESAR TRAIAN. HADRIANVS AVG. Bust of Hadrian to r. with laurel crown. Rev. SAEC(ulum) AVR(eum) P. M. TR. P. COS. III. Personification of the Golden Age in an oval mandorla (aureola) holding in her right hand a globe, on which is perched the Phoenix. *Ca.* A.D. 120. Cohen, ii, p. 216, no. 1321.

d. DENARIUS OF HADRIAN. Obv. HADRIANVS AVGVSTVS. Head of Hadrian to r. with laurel crown. Rev. COS. III. Abundance, with *cornucopiae* and *patera*, seated to l. before a *modius*; at her side, a globe. *Ca.* A.D. 127. Cohen, ii, p. 138, no. 379.

e. DITTO. Obv. HADRIANVS AVGVSTVS. Bust of Hadrian to r. with laurel crown. Rev. CLEMENTIA AVG. P. P. COS. III. The goddess standing to l., with *patera* and sceptre. *Ca.* A.D. 133. Cohen, ii, p. 122, no. 233.

f. DITTO. Obv. HADRIANVS AVGVSTVS. Head of Hadrian to l. Rev. INDVLGENTIA AVG. P. P. COS. III. The goddess seated to l., with sceptre. *Ca.* A.D. 133. Cohen, ii, p. 177, no. 857.

g. DITTO (reverse only). IVSTITIA AVG. P. P. COS. III. Justice seated to l., with *patera* and sceptre. *Ca.* A.D. 133. Cf. Cohen, ii, p. 180, nos. 884 ff.

h. DITTO (reverse only). SECVR(itas) PVB(lica) COS. III. P. P. The goddess seated to l. *Ca.* A.D. 133. Cohen, ii, p. 222, nos. 1399 f.

i. DITTO. Obv. HADRIANVS AVGVSTVS. Bust of Hadrian to r. Rev. TRANQVILLITAS AVG. COS. III. P. P. The goddess standing to l. *Ca.* A.D. 133. Cf. Cohen, ii, p. 225, no. 1440.

j. DITTO. Obv. HADRIANVS AVG. COS. III. P. P. Head of Hadrian to r. with laurel crown. Rev. ANNONA AVG. *Modius* with four ears of corn and two poppies. *Ca.* A.D. 135. Cohen, ii, p. 118, no. 170.

k. DITTO. Obv. HADRIANVS AVG. COS. III. Head of Hadrian to l. Rev. FIDES PVBLICA. The goddess standing to l., head to r., with corn-ears and fruit basket. *Ca.* A.D. 136. Cohen, ii, p. 168, no. 218.

l. AUREUS OF HADRIAN. Obv. HADRIANVS AVG. COS. III. P. P. Head of Hadrian to r. Rev. SECVRITAS AVG. The goddess seated to r. *Ca.* A.D. 136. Cohen, ii, p. 222, no. 1402.

m. DENARIUS OF HADRIAN. Obv. HADRIANVS AVG. COS. III. P. P. Head of Hadrian to r. Rev. TELLVS STABIL(ita). The goddess standing to l., with a plough; to the right, two corn-ears. *Ca.* A.D. 135. Cohen, ii, p. 224, no. 1425.

All these coins are in the British Museum. The selection of them, the casts, and the dates I owe to the courtesy of Mr. H. Mattingly.

HADRIAN

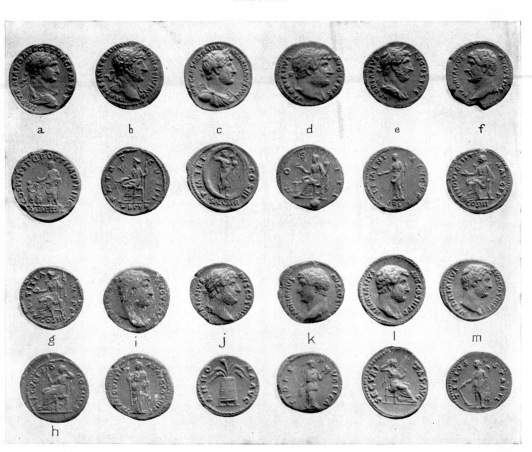

COINS OF HADRIAN

LXXI. HADRIAN

and to utilize for this purpose the services of the ablest and most intelligent class in the Empire, the knights. The collection of taxes, so far as it was not done by the cities, was almost entirely concentrated in the hands of the equestrian class, partly as direct agents of the state, partly as its concessionaires (*conductores*), closely watched and controlled by imperial officials. The institution of city curators was maintained and developed. The emperor's wide experience showed him that there was no other means of keeping the finances of the cities in equilibrium. All these reforms, it is true, increased the burden of the taxpayers. But Hadrian believed, and was perfectly right in believing, that it was a lesser evil than never-ending war.[11]

Yet Hadrian was the first to realize that all such measures were palliatives which could not by themselves save the Empire. Its weakest feature was not bad administration nor the squandering of money by the cities; it was not even the necessity of defending the frontiers by aggressive wars; it was the frailty of the foundations, especially the economic foundation, on which the whole fabric of the Empire rested. The Empire was not civilized enough, that is to say, its economic life was not progressive enough, to bear the heavy burden of maintaining itself as a single political unit. That was the reason why Hadrian, while helping and protecting Italy, finally gave up the idea of restoring her supremacy over the rest of the Empire and devoted his life to the provinces. It was not mere curiosity that prompted him to pay repeated visits to the remotest corners of the Empire. His intellectual interests helped him to endure and even to enjoy the life of a constant traveller, but it was not his passion for sightseeing that guided him in his travels. He desired to know the Empire which he governed and to know it personally in complete detail. He fully realized, too, that he was the ruler of a Greco-Roman Empire and that it was idle to try to give a preference to one part over another. That accounts for his phil-Hellenic policy, which was in turn promoted by his intellectual and artistic interests.

There was one way and only one, at least from the standpoint of ancient thinkers, to improve provincial life and raise it to a higher standard, and that was by further urbanization, by the constant creation of fresh nuclei of civilized and progressive life. This belief and the desire to base the army on those civilized elements induced Hadrian to pursue a consistent policy of fostering town-life in all the provinces of the Empire. How many cities he created during his travels it is impossible to say. Our evidence is very meagre. But it is safe to assert that after Augustus, Claudius, Vespasian, and Trajan he was the emperor who did most to urbanize the Empire. His activity was devoted chiefly to the lands which by their position were destined to be the bases on which the most important military frontiers rested. The Rhine frontier, of course, was secure, based as it was on Gaul and Spain. But there was no Gaul and no Spain to cover the rear of the Danube, Euphrates, and African *limites*. Despite the efforts of Claudius, the Flavians, and Trajan, urban life was still in its infancy in most of the Danube provinces, and particularly in the Thracian regions; large districts of Asia Minor and Syria still lived their ancient primitive rustic life; and the same was true of large areas in Africa. In the last two chapters we have described Hadrian's activities in these provinces. *Municipia Aelia* are common in the Danube lands, and cities with the name of Hadrianopolis or similar designations are frequent in the Greek-speaking parts of the Balkan peninsula and in Asia Minor. Besides the well-known foundation of Antinoupolis in Egypt, notable instances of Hadrian's efforts are Hadrianuthera and Stratonicea in Asia Minor, both previously villages; and many places in Africa were first converted by him into cities. To village communities which were not yet ripe for town life, Hadrian granted valuable privileges which made life in them very similar to life in real cities.[12]

There were, however, large areas which were not affected by city life. Such were the fields of Egypt and the great imperial domains in Africa and Asia. Hadrian knew thoroughly the conditions of life on these estates. He knew that the Empire depended to a large extent on the income derived from them, and that it was dangerous to transform them into city territories and so divert a good deal of their produce to the maintenance of a city. Nor is there any doubt that he was well aware that the economic conditions which prevailed on these imperial estates were far from normal. The peasants in Egypt, especially after the Jewish war, complained bitterly of high taxation; in the African domains the farmers-general (*conductores*) preferred pasture lands to fields and gardens, and allowed cornfields and vineyards to decay and run to waste, thus diminishing the territory which might support families of agriculturists. Hadrian's ideal, as far as we may judge from some remains of his legislation, was to have on his estates a robust stock of thriving landowners, who would introduce higher forms of cultivation, contribute sturdy soldiers to the army, and pay their taxes to the state regularly. He did not desire to have humble tenants lazily working on their plots and complaining about the misdeeds of the farmers-general and the imperial officials, and about the heavy burden of their rent and their compulsory work. He wanted good gardeners and vine-dressers, holders (_possessores_) of land in place of tenants, and he acted in accordance with his ideal.

Certain documents found in Egypt show that Hadrian transformed some of the royal land into holdings similar to those which were held as private property. The name for this new class of land was βασιλικὴ γῆ ἰδιωτικῷ δικαίῳ ἐπικρατουμένη or βασιλικὴ γῆ ἐν τάξει ἰδιοκτήτου ἀναγραφομένη. The change, which was effected as early as A.D. 117, was prompted by the serious decay of agriculture in some parts of Egypt, due in part to the Jewish war; and the intention was, by lowering the rent and by guaranteeing to the holders a long tenure similar to that of private property, to stimulate the energy of the royal tenants and induce them to bring greater skill to bear on their agricultural work. There is no evidence as to the scale on which Hadrian's reform was carried out. The fact that petitions for a reduction of taxation, which probably meant the transformation of some parcels of depreciated royal land into the new category of royal private land, are confined to his reign, and that the new class of land rarely appears in the land-surveys of the later period, indicates that in this country of ancient traditions Hadrian's reform was shortlived and had no lasting effects.[13] It is worth while mentioning in this connexion another document which shows Hadrian's interest in the needs of Egyptian landholders and illustrates his relief methods in Egypt. In two papyri, both containing copies of the same document, we have an edict of a much later date (A.D. 135–6) than his first attempt to better the agricultural situation of Egypt. He had grown old and probably more conservative. He went to Egypt in 130 and became thoroughly acquainted with the peculiarities of Egyptian life. He was no longer ready to embark on radical reforms. A series of bad years had induced the Egyptian peasants (γεωργοί) to ask for a reduction of their payments. Encouraged by a good year which followed the bad ones, Hadrian answers the petition in his peculiar pious and sarcastic way. He flatly declines a general reduction: the divine Nile and the laws of nature shall help the tillers. However, he makes a concession and allows the arrears of the money payments to be distributed over five or four or three years according to the situation of the land. The mention of money payments and the unusual expression προσοδικά, employed to describe the payments in general, lead me to think that the tillers of the soil who asked for reduction were not peasants but landowners, perhaps the group of half-tenants, half-owners created by Hadrian's early measure.[14]

Still more characteristic of the policy of Hadrian are some African documents which refer to the management of imperial lands. In reorganizing the imperial *saltus* after the great confiscations of Nero, the Flavians and Trajan had endeavoured to secure reliable long-term tenants bound to the soil by strong ties of economic interest in it. For this purpose one Mancia, probably a special envoy of one of the Flavians, not a rich landowner of senatorial rank, published a regulation, called later *Lex Manciana*, by which a free hand was given to those who wished to sow or to plant virgin soil in the imperial and public domains. So long as the occupants tilled the soil, they remained holders of it: they had the *ius colendi*, without any special contract, on the conditions defined by the law. If they had planted the land with fruit trees (or olive trees), they had even the right to mortgage it and to bequeath it to their heirs. If they ceased to cultivate it for a certain period of time, the land reverted to the owner and was supposed to be cultivated by the farmer-general, or contractor, of the estate. They were obliged also to take up their domicile on the estate and so to become permanent settlers on it, differing in this respect both from the inhabitants of the native villages who rented a portion of the estate and from the tenants who lived in the houses built for them by the owner and cultivated the land, probably on a short-time contract.

While maintaining the main provisions of the *Lex Manciana* Hadrian went further in the one or two laws which dealt with the virgin soil and the waste land of the imperial estates in Africa. He wanted more permanent tenants to settle on the imperial lands, and he wanted them to introduce higher forms of cultivation and by planting olive and fig trees to become real farmers closely connected with the holdings which their own efforts had transformed into gardens and olive groves. Thus he permits the occupants to sow and plant not only the virgin soil but also land which had not been cultivated by the contractors for ten years, and he allows them also to plant the waste land with olive and fruit trees. Moreover, he grants to the occupants the right of *possessores*, that is, of quasi-owners of the land. They now receive not only the *ius colendi* but also the *usus proprius* of both the arable and the garden land, with the right to transmit it to their heirs, provided that they cultivate it and fulfil their obligations towards the owner and the contractor of the estate. There is no doubt that Hadrian's leading idea was to create a class of free landowners on the imperial estates and thus to improve the cultivation of the soil. In all probability the efforts of Hadrian and the other emperors of the second century were crowned with fair success. I feel convinced that the rapid spread of olive-growing all over Africa was due to a large extent to the privileges granted by Hadrian to the prospective olive planters.[15]

The same policy was pursued by the emperor in the other provinces, especially in Greece and Asia Minor. In the sixth chapter mention has been made of the great work of delimitation which he carried out in the province of Macedonia. It is highly probable that in this way Hadrian endeavoured to organize on stable foundations the primitive agricultural life of the province.[16] In Attica the land which formerly belonged to the well-known Hipparchus, a victim of Domitian, was sold to small tenants. In Asia Minor Hadrian furthered the interests of small landholders on the former estate of the temple of Zeus at Aezani. And a still unpublished inscription testifies to his work in reclaiming the land near Lake Kopais in Boeotia.[17] Moreover, as has been pointed out in the last chapter, it was Hadrian who promoted in the imperial and public mines the system of letting single pits to small employers or occupants instead of working them by slaves or convicts. Here again he pursued the policy of creating a strong group of hard-working men who might form the nucleus of a future community, first a village and later a city.[18]

There was nothing new in these efforts. We have seen that the restoration of small landowners was one of the chief items of the programme of the enlightened monarchy, advocated in the most eloquent way by Dio Chrysostom in his Εὐβοικός. But no one will deny the strenuousness of the effort made by Hadrian and the liberality of mind which he displayed in pursuing the same policy throughout the Empire without giving any special preference to Italy.[19]

In other spheres of economic life Hadrian acted with equal consistency. He was the real foster-father of the policy which was inaugurated by Nerva and Trajan and adopted by all the emperors of the second century and even, or perhaps especially, of the third—the policy of defending the weak against the strong, the poor against the rich, the *humiliores* against the *honestiores*. This policy is reflected in many legislative measures of the second and third centuries, measures affecting freedmen and slaves, protecting the *collegia tenuiorum*, introducing innovations in the courts, to support the *tenuiores* against the *potentiores*, and modifications in the sphere of obligations which show the same tendency.[20] The active part taken by Hadrian in this movement is illustrated by documents found in the Eastern part of the Empire, which deal with details of a petty character but are none the less symptomatic of the general trend of his economic ideas. Like Solon, Hadrian himself regulated the question of the oil trade in the city of Athens, forbidding by a strict ordinance the unlimited export of oil and insisting on its being sold in Athens. Another rescript of the same kind, influenced again by reminiscences of old times, fulminates against the retail-traders who make the prices of fish prohibitive for poor people: 'The whole amount of the fish must be sold either by the fishermen themselves or by those who first buy the fish from them. The purchase of the same wares by third parties for re-sale increases the price.' In the same spirit he or his governor intervenes in the contest between the bankers and retail-traders of Pergamon, protecting the interests of the weaker party.[21]

We cannot here deal at length with the rule of Hadrian and its importance for the history of the Roman Empire. The subject is worth treating in a separate volume. It is clear that Hadrian did his best to enlarge and consolidate the foundations of the Empire. He grasped the main problems and worked hard to solve them in a satisfactory way. To him the Empire was indebted for the brief period of quiet and prosperity which followed the difficult years of Trajan. We must, however, bear in mind that peace was secured not only by Hadrian's diplomatic successes but, first and foremost, by the splendid victories of Trajan, which made the diplomatic activity of his successor possible and enabled him to rely on the fidelity and the discipline of the Roman army.

The quiet reign of Antoninus Pius, which developed the seeds sown by Hadrian, shows some interesting features. It seems as if Hadrian's endeavours to restore the prosperity of the Empire had not been altogether successful. The provinces recovered slowly: their recovery was retarded by the many journeys of the emperor, by his further development of bureaucracy, and by his building activity throughout the Empire, all of which required large sums of money. Antoninus endeavoured to reduce even such expenditure as much as possible. Hadrian had been a great builder in Rome as well as in the provinces. Antoninus showed the greatest economy in this respect. He deliberately refrained from imposing on the budget of the provincial cities the heavy burden which imperial visits to the provinces involved. He did not increase the number of government officials: in accordance with the wish of the senate he rather reduced them by restoring Italy to the care of that body. He also went so far as to sell superfluous property belonging to the imperial household, and some of its estates. All this proves that we must not exaggerate the wealth of the Empire: there were factors which undermined it even in times of complete peace.[22]

With the reign of Marcus Aurelius began another critical period for the Empire. The facts need not be repeated here. The tension between the Parthians and Rome became so acute that, despite the peaceful disposition of the great emperor, the interests of the Empire required an expedition against the Eastern power on the scale of Trajan's. As soon as it was over, plague began to rage among the soldiers of the Eastern army, and it spread to Italy and to some other parts of the Empire. The Germans and the Sarmatians took advantage of the absence of the best troops from the Danube frontier to invade the Danubian provinces and advanced as far as Aquileia. The war which ensued was interrupted by the abortive attempt of the victor of the Parthian war, Avidius Cassius, to seize the imperial power, but it was resumed as soon as the revolt was crushed. It became clear both to Marcus himself and to all the leading men of his time that another

Description of Plate LXXII

a. SESTERTIUS OF NERO. H. Mattingly, *Coins of the Roman Empire*, i, p. 220, nos. 127–130, pl. XLI, 6 (*ca.* A.D. 65).

ANNONA AVGVSTI CERES S. C. Annona standing to r., holding a *cornucopiae* in her left hand; facing her, Ceres seated to l., holding corn-ears in her right hand and a torch in her left; between them, an altar on which stands a *modius* with corn-ears; in the background, the stern of a ship.

b. SESTERTIUS OF NERVA. Cohen, ii, p. 13, no. 143 (A.D. 97).

VEHICVLATIONE ITALIAE REMISSA S. C. Two horses unyoked, grazing. The type emphasizes the heaviness of the burden of furnishing horses for the post-service.

c. SESTERTIUS OF HADRIAN. Cohen, ii, p. 185, no. 950 (*ca.* A.D. 120).

LOCVPLETATORI ORBIS TERRARVM S. C. The Emperor seated on a tribune; near him, Abundance with *cornucopiae*, and two citizens receiving the Emperor's gifts.

d. DITTO. Cohen, ii, p. 209, no. 1213 (*ca.* A.D. 120).

RELIQVA VETERA HS NOVIES MILL. ABOLITA S. C. Lictor burning the records of arrears in the presence of a group of Roman citizens. Cf. pl. LXX, 2.

e. DITTO. Cohen, ii, pp. 213 f., no. 1285 (*ca.* A.D. 120).

RESTITVTORI ORBIS TERRARVM S. C. The Emperor raising a kneeling figure symbolizing the *Orbis Terrarum*. A similar type was used for various provinces (*h*) and cities of the Roman Empire.

f. DITTO. Cohen, ii, p. 162, no. 657 (*ca.* A.D. 133).

FELICITATI AVG. COS. III. P. P. S. C. The happiness of the times is illustrated by the figure of a galley carrying the Emperor across the sea to the provinces.

g. DITTO. Cohen, ii, p. 175, no. 823 (*ca.* A.D. 135).

HISPANIA S. C. Personification of the province of Spain leaning on a rock, with an olive-branch in her hand and a rabbit beside her. Similar coins mentioning other provinces of the Empire commemorate the visits paid them by the Emperor.

h. DITTO. Cohen, ii, p. 209, no. 1216 (*ca.* A.D. 135).

RESTITVTORI ACHAIAE S. C. The province of Achaia raised from the ground by the Emperor. Before her, a jug with a palm-branch (symbol of the famous *agones* of Greece). Cf. *e* and *g*.

i. DITTO. Cohen, ii, p. 217, no. 1340 (*ca.* A.D. 138).

SALVS AVG. S. C. The personification of the welfare of the Roman Empire sacrificing at an altar, round which winds a snake, and supporting with her left hand a rudder which rests on a globe.

j. DITTO. Cohen, ii, p. 225, no. 1433 (*ca.* A.D. 135).

TELLVS STABIL(ita) S. C. Mother Earth reclining on the ground, her right hand resting on a globe, a vine in her left, her arm leaning on a basket full of fruit. The prosperity of the earth firmly established by the efforts of the Emperor.

k. DITTO. (Posthumous.) Cohen, ii, p. 175, no. 817 (*ca.* A.D. 138–9).

HILARITAS P. R. COS. III. S. C. *Hilaritas* with the *cornucopiae* and a palm-branch which she receives from a naked boy; behind her stands a girl. Cheerfulness is the result of the repopulation of the Empire.

All these coins are in the British Museum.

The coins reproduced on this plate and on pl. LXXI represent a small selection of the types by which the Roman emperors sought to emphasize the reforms which they planned and achieved. The series of Hadrian is the most explicit of all. The various types speak for themselves. Cf. note 7 to this chapter and pls. LXVIII and LXX. For the selection of coins, the casts, and the dates, I am indebted to the courtesy of Mr. H. Mattingly of the British Museum.

LXXII. COINS ILLUSTRATING THE REFORMS OF NERO, NERVA, AND HADRIAN

strenuous military effort was needed to secure a fresh period of peace for the Empire, an effort which would show to Rome's neighbours that she was still the same power that had celebrated so many triumphs over rivals and enemies. The Empire bore very well the military test of the dangerous and bloody wars of this reign. The soldiers displayed the same splendid training and discipline as under Trajan and Hadrian; there was no lack of good generals and, in spite of the pest and the revolt, Marcus would have ended the war by the annexation of a large part of Germany but for his premature death.[23]

But if the army stood the test, not so the finances of the Empire. The treasury was empty. Marcus objected to the introduction of any new taxes: he preferred to dispose of his valuables by a public sale, which lasted for two months. And yet he could not avoid the imposition of new taxes. We hear casually that, under the strain of a maritime invasion by some German and Celtic tribes, he was forced to collect a special tax in Asia Minor modelled on the precedents of the Hellenistic period.[24] The Empire which he had inherited from his adoptive father was evidently not in such a flourishing state as one would have expected. Otherwise Marcus would not at the very outset of his rule have renewed Hadrian's measure by abolishing debts (including probably arrears) to the _fiscus_ and to the _aerarium_, and he would not have been faced all through his reign with ever-renewed requests from the cities for gifts or remission of taxes.[25] When the soldiers applied to him for an increase of pay after the great successes in the Marcomanic war, he gave them the bitter but resolute reply: 'Anything that you receive over and above your regular pay must be exacted from the blood of your parents and relatives. Concerning the imperial power God alone can decide.' It seems as if the refusal might even have imperilled the position of the courageous emperor, a ruler supremely devoted to his duties and to the welfare of the Empire which was entrusted to him by God. Such an answer could not have been given by a man who did not fully realize the critical position of the taxpayers all over the Empire.[26]

Hand in hand with the steadily increasing demands of the state for men and for money, discontent was growing and assuming very dangerous forms throughout the provinces. Spain again refused to send soldiers to the army, and the emperor had to yield.[27] Gaul and Spain were full of deserters, who pillaged and robbed and became so numerous that under Commodus a certain Maternus was able to start a regular war against the government.[28] The numbers of those who fled from the villages of Egypt to the swamps of the Delta to escape the burden of levies, compulsory work, and taxes became so large that the fugitives (who were called Βουκόλοι), under the leadership of a priest, could challenge the imperial government.[29] We need not be surprised that under the pressure of these circumstances Commodus, the son of M. Aurelius, who inherited his father's power but not his energy, resolution, sense of duty, and influence over the soldiers, decided in spite of the silent protest and the hot indignation of the senate, which realized the fatal results of the step, to abandon the military operations against the Germans and end the war by a treaty which was branded by the senatorial opposition with the epithet 'ignominious'. The answer of Commodus was a new Terror, and the developments of Domitian's reign were repeated. Of these we shall speak in the next chapter.

Despite the pressure of war, plague, poverty, and rebellion, the rule of M. Aurelius showed the same features which had characterized the government of his predecessors. He was forced to resort to hard measures in times of emergency, and these measures aroused an ever-growing discontent, but he did his best to mitigate their effects and to come to the rescue of the oppressed. One of the most interesting features of his rule is the attention he paid to the position of slaves and freedmen and the measures he took to make their life easier and more human. For these the reader must be referred to the special treatises on the subject.[30]

The survey we have given of the economic and social policy of the emperors and of the economic situation of the Empire in the second century shows how weak and unstable were the foundations on which the apparent prosperity of the state rested; and the fact that every serious war brought the whole fabric of the Empire to the verge of ruin proves that the measures taken by the emperors to strengthen its foundations were fruitless or were at any rate powerless to neutralize other factors which continuously undermined it. Certain modern scholars have suggested that there was one fundamental cause of the gradual economic decay of the Empire which was stronger than any efforts of man.

Otto Seeck considered it to be the gradual depopulation of the Empire, J. Liebig and his followers the gradual exhaustion of the soil.[31] I see no reason whatever to accept these explanations.

As regards the first view, Seeck adduced some strong arguments to prove that depopulation gradually increased both in Greece and in Italy. It is true that the population of both countries gradually dwindled; but are we justified in generalizing and affirming that the same was true of the other parts of the Empire? We have of course no direct evidence on the point, no statistics showing that the population of the provinces was not in fact decreasing. But there are some facts which make Seeck's theory highly improbable. The case of Greece was exceptional. Greece was one of the poorest parts of the whole ancient world, and as soon as she ceased to be the purveyor of oil, wine, and manufactured goods for the rest of the world she was bound to decay. In Italy conditions were more or less similar. As every Roman citizen had much better opportunities of earning a living in the provinces, Italy was constantly being drained of her best men, and the gaps were filled by slaves. When an abundant supply of slaves ceased to be available, Italy began to decay in her turn, for the process of emigration never stopped, as one land after another was opened up for settlement.

In the other parts of the Empire the situation was different. All through the first and the second century new lands in East and West were won for Greco-Roman civilization; lands which formerly had been prairies and woods, swamps and pastures, were transformed into fields and gardens; and one new city after another arose and enjoyed prosperity for a while. In view of these facts we cannot seriously believe in the theory of depopulation so far as concerns Egypt, Asia Minor, and Syria in the South and South-east, Africa, Spain, Britain, Germany, and Gaul in the South and West, and the Danube lands in the North-east. The growth of a city like Thamugadi (Timgad) in Africa which, as we can infer from the study of its ruins, rapidly developed from a small military colony, consisting of a few blocks and of no more than 2,000 inhabitants, into a comparatively large city with a population at least three times that size, was clearly due to a general increase of the population of the district. Without this assumption it is impossible to explain who were served by the shops and bazaars of the town, and for whom the numerous baths and the large theatre were built. Recent excavations have un-covered the industrial quarters, all of them of a comparatively late date. They contain large shops, some of which are real fac-tories on a small scale. They lay around the original city and belong to a time when the population both of the city and of the adjacent country was steadily growing. As Thamugadi was founded by Trajan, this increase was going on all through the second and the third century and even later. Many other cities in Africa and the other provinces had a similar history. The caravan-cities of Syria, Transjordan, and Arabia, such as Petra, Gerasa, Philadelphia (Amman), and Palmyra, are good ex-amples. All these cities prospered in the post-Trajanic era, and continued to grow until late in the third century A.D.

Equally unconvincing is the theory of the exhaustion of the soil. Here again the statement may be true for some parts of Greece and Italy. The impoverishment of some districts in Italy was due to foolish deforestation and to the neglect of the drainage work which had been carried out in many parts of the country at a time when they had a dense population confined to a very restricted area. Those districts were Latium, parts of Etruria, and some of the territories of the Greek cities in South Italy. In all these areas the land is not fertile and requires intensive labour and attention to yield good harvests. It was natural that they should be the first to be deserted when new and better lands were opened up: little wonder if the Roman Campagna was soon abandoned to pasture and villas and became infested with malaria. Yet in the better parts of Etruria the land was still rich and attractive enough to be purchased at a high price by the landlords of Rome. It is striking that, while Pliny often complains of bad crops, he never speaks of the exhaustion of the soil as a general condition. When Nerva proposed to give land to landless proletarians, he was obliged to buy it, a fact which shows—and the inference is confirmed by the alimentary tables—that at the beginning of the second century there was no waste, and there-fore no exhausted, land in Italy apart from some areas in the regions mentioned above. There can be no question at all in regard to such lands as Campania or the valley of the Po. One has only to read Herodian's description of the territory of Aqui-leia and to compare it with the actual conditions to realize that 'the exhaustion of the soil' in Italy in the second and third centuries is a generalization that cannot be accepted.

Still less possible is it to speak of exhaustion of the soil in the provinces. The only proof (apart from some evidence of a later date) which is adduced in support of the theory as applied to Africa, is the fact that in Hadrian's laws some parts of the imperial estates are mentioned as being left uncultivated by the contracting farmers. It must be remembered, however, that the prime object of the emperors in Africa was to break up new lands, to reduce the area of pasturage, and to increase that of fields and gardens. The land which was not cultivated by the contractors was of subsidiary importance. It is probable that they preferred to have it as pasture land and hunting-grounds and that this preference met with imperial disapproval. In any case there is not the slightest indication here of a general exhaustion of the soil. We find no complaint of such exhaustion in Africa; what troubles the emperors is the existence of too much virgin land and the shortage of labour and of rain, which last necessitated large irrigation works. As late as the fourth century the cultivated area of Africa Proconsularis was exceedingly large, as is shown by official statistics.[32]

If we exclude depopulation and exhaustion of the soil, what were the causes of the economic instability of this huge and civilized Empire, which possessed so many and so varied natural resources and so large a population? I think that the gradual decay of the vital forces of the Empire may be explained by two sets of phenomena, both of them connected with one prominent feature in the life of the ancient state in general—the supremacy of the interests of the state over those of the population, an age-old idea and practice, which had to a large extent undermined the prosperity of the Oriental monarchies and of the Greek city-states and which was the chief cause of the weakness of the Hellenistic monarchies, the immediate predecessors of the Roman Empire. As soon as this supremacy became decided and succeeded in subordinating the interests of individuals and of social groups, it was bound to act as a depressing influence on the masses and to cause them to lose all interest in their work. But the pressure of the state on the people was never so heavily felt as under the Roman Empire. The acute consciousness of it had become the most marked feature of social and economic life as early as the second century A.D., and it steadily increased there-after.[33] In the Oriental monarchies the supremacy of the state was based on religion, and was taken for granted and regarded as sacred. In the Greek city-states it was never fully developed and always met with strong opposition from the most influential groups of the population. In the Hellenistic monarchies it was less felt because it bore mainly on the lower classes, which were used to it from time immemorial and regarded it as a matter of necessity, as one of the fundamental conditions of their life. Under the Roman Empire fateful developments took place. Let us trace them in outline.

As has been said, two sets of phenomena resulted from and reflected the growth of the supremacy of the state. The first is closely connected with the gradual urbanization of the Empire. In the first chapter, and again in dealing with the provinces of the East, we have shown how in Syria and in Asia Minor during the Hellenistic period the Greek city-state assumed the shape of a superstructure resting on a basis formed by the masses who tilled the soil in the country and toiled as workmen, both bond and free, in the towns. The Greek cities, or rather the upper class in them, which consisted of Greeks and hellenized Orientals, became by degrees the rulers and masters of a half-enslaved population of natives. The same phenomenon *mutatis mutandis* recurred in Egypt. The Greek and hellenized residents in the land, though not organized in city-states, nevertheless became masters of the rest of the population. The natural development of this process was arrested for a time by the Roman conquest. In the earlier period of their domination the Romans did not promote the further urbanization of Asia Minor and Syria, but acquiesced in conditions as they were. When, however, during the period of the civil wars and under Augustus and his succes-sors, the Roman league of Italian cities, owning certain domains outside Italy, coalesced in course of time into a single state, both the leaders in the civil wars and the Roman emperors involun-tarily reverted to the Hellenistic practice of urbanization, creat-ing all over the Empire two types of men—those who were civi-lized and therefore rulers, and those who were barbarians and therefore subjects. For a time the ruling class was the Roman citizens; the rest were subjects, *peregrini*. But in fact this distinc-tion remained always purely theoretical, especially in the East.

The inhabitants of the Greek cities may legally only have been Greek and hellenized *peregrini*, but these *peregrini* remained socially and economically the ruling class in the Eastern provinces.

As time went on, it was realized that the basis formed by the Roman citizens of Italy and of the few Roman and Latin colonies in the provinces was too weak to support the political fabric of the Empire, and in particular the imperial power; and the emperors embarked on a policy of developing city life, which they pursued in both East and West with ever-increasing energy. From the social and economic point of view, this policy meant the gradual creation of new centres of privileged residents, consisting of the richest and the most civilized men—of those who were landowners and shopowners and for whom the rest of the population had to work. The new class was not only a source of fresh support for the imperial power, but provided a supply of good administrative officials for the Empire. Every new citizen of a new city was an unpaid official of the state.

The process of urbanization has been described in the preceding chapters, where we have shown that it produced a division of the population of the Empire into two great classes—the rulers and the ruled, the privileged *bourgeoisie* and the working classes, the landowners and the peasants, the shopowners and the slaves. The larger the number of cities created, the deeper became the gulf between the two classes. Every increase in the numbers of the privileged class meant heavier work for the unprivileged. One section of the city residents, the business men, was certainly not idle; by its energy and skill it contributed to the prosperity of the Empire. But the main type of city resident came more and more to be the man who lived on his income, which was derived from landed property or from shops. The driving force in economic life was now the middlemen, mostly slaves and freedmen, who stood between the owners and the labourers.

This division of the population into two classes, which in time crystallized into something very like two castes, was not felt as a serious evil so long as the Empire was undergoing expansion and there were constant accessions of territory in which urban life could be developed and the position of rulers granted to the most energetic elements of the population. In course of time, however, the process of expansion came to an end: Hadrian was the last who profited by the strenuous military activity of his predecessor. Cities continued to be founded, but after Hadrian very slowly. The result was that those who were privileged remained privileged, and those who were not had very little hope of mounting higher on the social ladder. The existence of two castes, one ever more oppressed, the other ever more idle and indulging in the easy life of men of means, lay like an incubus on the Empire and arrested economic progress. All the efforts of the emperors to raise the lower classes into a working and active middle class were futile. The imperial power rested on the privileged classes, and the privileged classes were bound in a very short time to sink into sloth. The creation of new cities meant in truth the creation of new hives of drones.[34] Yet the vital problems of the life of a huge Empire had to be faced. As soon as the Roman state refrained from aggression and ceased to expand, it was attacked and obliged either to resume an aggressive policy or to concentrate its efforts on efficient defence. The administration of the vast Empire required more and more attention, and the only method of countering the selfish policy of the ruling classes was by the constant development of imperial bureaucracy, which swallowed up a large part of the state's resources over and above those which were absorbed by the ruling classes in the cities. In times of emergency, when the regular taxation did not cover the necessary expenditure, the state had no alternative but to resort to the theory of its supremacy over the individual and to translate that theory into practical forms. These had been already worked out in the previous history of the ancient state. Every member of an ancient community, whether a monarchy or a city-state, was expected to sacrifice his private interests to the interests of the community: hence arose the system of 'liturgies' or public burdens (λειτουργίαι), which involved compulsory work and threw on the privileged and wealthier classes responsibility for the poor.

The liturgical system of the ancient world was as old as the state. The obligation of every subject to assist the state with his labour and his means, and the responsibility of the agents of the government for the proper fulfilment of their duties were the fundamental principles of the Oriental monarchical system, and as such they were inherited by the Hellenistic states. The responsibility of government-agents was not only personal, the official being subject to punishment, but also material, the official paying from his pocket for losses caused to the state by dishonesty or inefficiency. The Romans took over these principles not only in Egypt, where they existed in their purest form, but also in the other Oriental provinces. In Egypt they did not abolish a single obligation customarily lying on the people. Compulsory work remained the chief moving force of the economic system, and the government never renounced its right to demand from the population in cases of emergency, especially in war time, foodstuffs and fodder for its soldiers and officers, in addition to normal taxes. A very good and well-attested example is the so-called *angareiae*. The term is of Persian or Aramaean origin, and means the compulsory supply, by the population, of animals and drivers as well as of ships for the transport of men and goods which were being moved on behalf of the state. This institution was never abolished by the Romans. They tried to regulate and to systematize it, but without success, for, so long as the practice existed it was bound to produce evil effects. Edict after edict was issued by the prefects, who honestly endeavoured to stop the arbitrariness and the oppression inherent in the system, and it is noteworthy that one of the first measures of Germanicus in Egypt was the publication of an ordinance dealing with the matter. But the institution remained oppressive. The same must be said of the supplementary deliveries of foodstuffs and other things needed by the state, which were simple requisitions. They might take the form of compulsory purchase, they might be controlled by the higher officers, yet their nature made them an intolerable burden.[35]

Nor did the principle of the material responsibility of officials disappear in Egypt under Roman rule. The officials of the Ptolemies were mostly their personal, salaried agents. In case of dishonesty they might be prosecuted and their fortune confiscated, but their service was in principle a personal service for pay. Yet the idea of the obligation of every one to serve the state, if required, even without remuneration never died out in Egypt, and it is possible that the minor officials taken from the ranks of the natives never received a salary even in the Ptolemaic period. However that may have been, the Romans, who at first maintained the practice of the Ptolemies, gradually found it cheaper and more convenient to reduce the number of salaried officials and to increase the number of those who were required to give their services to the state without remuneration, thus introducing a sort of compulsory work for the higher and richer classes, who were free from the menial forced labour of the lower classes. How rapidly this system developed, concurrently with the growth of the middle class in Egypt (of which we have spoken in the preceding chapter), is shown by Oertel's careful investigation. In the first half of the second century A.D. the system was already fully developed, and almost all official posts in Egypt were 'liturgies', that is to say, their holders were not only not remunerated but were responsible for the efficiency of their service. In the financial administration this meant responsibility for loss suffered by the state. If a tax was not paid and the payment could not be exacted from the taxpayer, the official was forced to pay. If he was unable to do so, his property was confiscated and sold. It is probable that this system was connected with the development of tax-farming, the tax-farmers having been gradually replaced by state officials, who inherited their liability for the full amount of the taxes payable by the people.

At the same time, contributions to the state, of whatever nature, were exacted with greater harshness; taxes, requisitions, compulsory buying and selling, forced labour. The procedure by which debts, both public and private, were recovered had always been hard and merciless in antiquity. The debtor answered not only with his estate, but also with his person, his body ($\pi\rho\hat{a}\xi\iota\varsigma$ $\dot{\epsilon}\kappa$ $\tau\hat{\omega}\nu$ $\sigma\omega\mu\acute{a}\tau\omega\nu$), and this responsibility often extended also to relatives. Throughout the ancient world, both in the ancient monarchies and in the city-states of the Greeks, imprisonment, corporal punishment, and torture were means commonly employed to overcome the bad will of the debtor. The means to which the government resorted to recover its own debts were even more drastic than those used in the case of private debts. The state was considered as the supreme power, and on this theory the defaulter was treated as a criminal. In Egypt, already under the Ptolemies, the practice of recovering debts towards the state $\dot{\epsilon}\kappa$ $\tau\hat{\omega}\nu$ $\sigma\omega\mu\acute{a}\tau\omega\nu$ was very frequent; but it reached its peak in the Roman period, when the recovery of taxes and other payments due to the state was included in the system of liturgies. The greater the demands of the government, and the worse the economic condition of the taxpayers became, the more ruthless became the agents charged by the state with the recovery. In the second half of the second century A.D. the system was already, as we have seen, in full swing. Not only was the practice of extorting payments from the 'bodies' of taxpayers general, but a system of group-responsibility was also introduced, in which members of the family, neighbours, community and corporation were included. This was only the logical development of the idea of the supremacy of the interests of the state. Augustus tried to improve matters by granting the insolvent debtor the right of ceding his patrimony to the creditor, thereby avoiding distraint by his body (*cessio bonorum*); this privilege, restricted at first to Roman citizens, was gradually extended to provincials also. But the measure achieved nothing. The ancient πρᾶξις ἐκ τῶν σωμάτων was so deeply rooted in the traditions of the ancient world that it was never abandoned even for a moment. We shall see how rapidly it was extended in the difficult times of the late second and third centuries.

Whether this system derived from Egypt, or whether, as appears to be more probable, it was applied at the same time in the other parts of the Empire also, it is certain that it came to be used on an increasingly large scale along with the diffusion of the system of liturgies throughout the Empire. Documentary evidence on the point is slight, but it seems to permit the inference that conditions identical with those in Egypt existed in the other provinces also; in fact πρᾶξις ἐκ τῶν σωμάτων may have had even deeper roots in the juridical concepts and the institutions of the city-state than in the oriental monarchies. The effects of the system were disastrous. The recovery of debts owed to the state was entrusted to privileged classes; and the brutal harshness with which they carried out their task—whether in the interests of the rights of the individual community or of the state—widened still further the gap between the *honestiores* and the *humiliores*. Of course, the system had no limit; logically, the same *honestiores* were liable to the same treatment, when they did not meet their obligations, and no *cessio bonorum* could save them from imprisonment and torture.[36] As regards compulsory work, the Romans took over the practice from their predecessors all over the East and never dreamt of abolishing it. On the contrary, they even transferred the system to Greek lands and to the West. The Oriental practice is illustrated, for instance, by the well-

known Gospel story of how Simon the Cyrenaean was pressed
into service to carry the cross of Christ on his way to Golgotha.
The word used by the Gospels for the act of coercion is ἀγγαρεύειν:
Simon was subjected to an ἀγγαρεία. When we find the word
ἀγγαρεία used in juridical sources throughout the later Roman
Empire to denote the compulsory provision of cattle and drivers
for the transportation of state goods, it is perfectly clear that not
only the word but the institution it describes was an inheritance
and not an invention of the Romans.[37]

Thus there is no doubt that throughout Asia Minor and Syria
the institution of compulsory work for the state was in vogue
long before the Romans. In the early period of their rule, apart
from the time of the civil wars, we do not hear very much of its
application. It is quite certain, however, that the system persisted, especially in the matter of transport, and was resorted to
every time the Roman government had to move large masses of
men and goods over Italy and the provinces. It is no accident
that one of the edicts of Claudius* deals with the heavy burden
of transportation imposed on Italy and the provinces, and endeavours, in the same way as the similar edicts of Egyptian
governors, to regulate it and to mitigate its evil influence on the
prosperity of the Empire. The edict shows that the Oriental institution was transplanted, probably as early as the times of the
civil wars, both to Greece and to the Western parts of the Empire, including Italy. Pliny's description of the travels of Domitian
affords a good illustration of what the system meant for the
peaceful population of the Empire; and the scattered notices
which have been quoted in this chapter in connexion with the
wars and travels of Trajan and Hadrian show that even these
emperors had recourse to the same system in cases of emergency.
Other occasional allusions testify to the use of compulsion and
requisition for feeding the army and for providing soldiers and
officers with quarters and supplies.

In Asia Minor and Syria as well as in Greece and the West,
when most of these lands had been urbanized by the emperors,
the burden of compulsory work and of requisitions was imposed
not, as in Egypt, on individuals or groups of individuals like the
professional guilds, but on the administrative units of the Empire, the cities. The municipal magistrates and the city councils

* Quoted in Chap. III, note 2.

were the responsible authorities and had to distribute the burdens among the population of the city territory. That meant
that the actual bearers of them were not the ruling classes but
the tillers of the soil in the country parts and the workmen in the
cities, particularly the former: the *sordida munera* were never performed by the landowners and the shopowners. As in Russia
under the old régime, which presents the best modern parallel
to this side of ancient life, the privileged classes knew how to
escape such burdens and shift them on to the shoulders of the
peasants, even when, as in the case of road construction, they fell
not on individuals as such but on their landed property. Generous people, of course, would sometimes undertake the expense
themselves, but such cases were exceptional and, being rare, are
occasionally mentioned in inscriptions. What these additional
burdens meant for the population is easy to understand. The
taxes, heavy as they might be, were regular demands which could
be anticipated and reckoned with. But people never knew when
a Roman magistrate or a city official would come and demand
men and animals from the villages or take up his quarters in
their houses; and the movements of large armies, or the journeys
of the emperors with their big staffs, were real calamities. The
cattle which were the main resource of the peasants and in which
were invested almost all their savings, the fruit of long years of
labour, were taken away, maltreated, underfed, and returned
with their drivers, if returned at all, at a time when they might
be needed no more by the owner.

Naturally, the problem of regulating transport was the most
vital which the government had to solve. We must not forget the
essential point recently brought out by Lefebvre des Noettes. If
we take as our criterion the maximum load which an animal
can carry, we must admit that the ancient style of cart-building,
the method by which yoke animals, horses and mules no less
than donkeys and oxen, were harnessed, and the system of road-
construction were all very defective in comparison with modern
methods. The *Codex Theodosianus*,* in passages dealing with the
cursus publicus, establishes the maximum load of light carts at
from 200 to 600 librae, and for heavy carts at from 1,000 to
1,500 librae—that is, at the most a fifth of the average weight

* *Cod. Theod.* viii. 5. 8 (A.D. 357); 17 (A.D. 364); 28 (A.D. 368 (?), 370 (?), 373 (?)); 30 (A.D.
368); 47 (A.D. 385).

which carts carry today in western Europe. This shows how much labour was wasted, how slow transport was, and what an immense number of beasts and drivers were needed for heavy transports. In such circumstances the state could not organize its own transport-system, and had to apply the disastrous oriental system of requisitions and forced labour, which was bound to become the cancer of the economic life of the Empire. Certainly, the methods introduced in the Persian, Hellenistic, and Roman periods were a great advance over the transport systems in the oriental monarchies and in Greece, especially in regard to road-building. The principal purpose of the latter, however, was not the furtherance of commerce and private traffic, but, exclusively, to meet military needs. That is why improvements of transport and the possibility of sparing men and beasts were not seriously investigated.[38]

It is not surprising, therefore, in these conditions, that the Roman emperors never seriously thought of abolishing the oriental system of providing for transport by forced labour and requisitions, even though they were conscious of the harmful consequences of the system. The edict of Claudius and the corresponding documents of Egypt have already been quoted. For sea-transport they had recourse to the existing commercial fleet, and they treated the matter in business-like fashion. The associations of merchants and shipowners, or the individual members of these associations, worked for the state on the same basis as they would have worked for any other customer, according to special contracts. But, when the services of the shipowners were required in larger measure, as in time of war, the system of requisition and of compulsory service was applied with the same ruthlessness as in the matter of land transport. The fact that the emperors from the time of Hadrian repeatedly granted important privileges to the associations of merchants and shipowners shows that such privileges were intended as a compensation for the compulsory work which the associations were forced to perform for the state.[39] No associations of the same kind existed, however, for land transport. In Egypt, it is true, special guilds of owners of draught-animals were supposed to work on behalf both of the state and of other customers. Organizations of the same kind existed in some cities of the Roman Empire. But these institutions never developed into anything comparable even to the associations of sea merchants and shipowners, not to speak of modern transport companies. Thus, in Egypt as well as in the other provinces, land-transport was always based on compulsory service. One part of the problem—the forwarding of state messages and the conveyance of state officials, the *cursus publicus*—was tackled by Nerva and Hadrian and later by Antoninus Pius and Septimius Severus. The idea was to take over the institution and to organize it as a state service. Something may have been achieved in the way of a further development of this branch of administration on bureaucratic lines. But it seems very doubtful whether a real state service, with masses of men and animals solely and entirely employed for the purpose, was ever organized. The basis of the system remained, as it did for centuries in Russia, the compulsory service of the population which lived near the roads; and, even if the *cursus publicus* was managed by the state, the transmission of goods and the provision of means of transport for the armies were certainly based wholly on requisitions and compulsory work.[40]

This, however, is only one part of the picture. The idea of liturgy was not alien to the organization of the city-state. Its citizens, as is well known, were expected to assist the state in critical times both with their material resources and with their labour. Yet compulsory labour always remained exceptional in the life of a city community, being resorted to only in cases of emergency. More firmly established was the custom of requiring from the richer citizens supplementary contributions, under the name of liturgies, to meet vital needs of the community—contributions towards the feeding of the population in time of famine, compulsory loans for the payment of war debts and the like, money for building ships or for training the choruses for the games, and so on. In Hellenistic and Roman times there was a great development of municipal life, and the more the leading role in civic life became the privilege of the propertied classes, the more they were expected to contribute out of their own pockets towards the needs of the cities. Gradually the difference between ἀρχαί and λειτουργίαι, corresponding to that between *honores* and *munera* in the West, disappeared, and every magistrate of a city was expected to pay for the honour conferred upon him, quite apart from undertaking real liturgies, which by degrees assumed the form of regular offices. The burden was heavy, but, so long as it was not excessive, it was borne by the richer classes willingly and with a wonderful display of public spirit. As early, however, as the end of the first century, even in the rich provinces of the East, it became increasingly difficult to find men ready to serve the city without remuneration and at the cost of material sacrifices. In the West, for instance in Spain, from the very moment when municipal life was being established in the poorer parts of the country, measures were taken to provide the necessary numbers of magistrates and members of city councils by compulsion, if necessary.[41]

The situation was aggravated by the part which the cities had to play in the financial organization of the Empire. The Republican system of farming out the direct taxes—the land and poll tax—to companies of tax-farmers (*publicani*) was very soon dropped by the emperors. The first to deal a heavy blow to the system was Julius Caesar. Augustus and Tiberius followed on the same path. Gradually the great companies of tax-farmers in the provinces disappeared, as far as the direct taxes were concerned. Their place was taken by the magistrates and the senates of the cities. The cities were glad to get rid of the exactions of the *publicani*. They had had their full measure of suffering in dealing with those sharks, and they were therefore willing to help the state in collecting the taxes of their districts. Whether from the very beginning their co-operation implied responsibility for the full amount of the taxes to be paid to the Treasury is unknown, but it is highly probable, since the state must have had some guarantee for its income and used to have such security in the companies of tax-farmers. As the direct taxes were reasonable, the responsibility for their collection did not bear heavily on the city *bourgeoisie*. On the contrary, they may have derived some small profit from it. The general assessment of the taxes was always the function of the central government, but it could not have been carried out without the help of the cities, and here the big men may have had opportunities of getting some reduction in the assessment of their property.[42]

Gradually, however, the responsibility of the municipal capitalists was extended to other fields. The collection of indirect taxes remained for a while in the hands of companies of tax-farmers. But the emperors kept a watchful eye on them. The imperial procurators were there to protect the interests both of the

Treasury and of the taxpayers. Their rights in this respect, including even a certain amount of jurisdiction, were steadily
increased, especially under Claudius. Nevertheless the collection
of indirect taxes remained a weak point in the financial administration of the Empire. The constant complaints of the public
seem to have been the reason why Nero, in a characteristic fit of
benevolence, contemplated the abolition of the indirect taxes; but
they were retained and the system of farming them out as well.
The only change—it was inaugurated probably by Vespasian,
whose father had himself been a tax-farmer, and then fully
developed by Hadrian—was to eliminate the companies, which
in any case were dying out, and to replace them by rich men
holding a sort of intermediate position between tax-farmers and
procurators. The most important feature of the position of these
new tax-farmers, the *conductores*, was their responsibility for the
full collection of a given tax. As the office in itself was not very
remunerative and the responsibility was very heavy, the state
had more and more difficulty in obtaining men to fill it, and
it gradually began to resort to compulsion and to regard tax-
collection as a burden, a liturgy, a *munus*. The practice was not
entirely new, as it had been already adopted by the Ptolemies,
but it was never before applied so consistently. I am inclined to
think that it was at the same time—that is, after Vespasian and
especially under Hadrian—that the system of leasing the large
imperial estates to farmers-general (*conductores*) took firm root,
inasmuch as these farmers were regarded chiefly as agents who
collected the rent (including the land tax) of the small tenants
on behalf of the emperor.[43]

The responsibility of individuals for the collection of taxes and,
as in the case of the contractors of the imperial estates, for the
performance of compulsory work by the small tenants was a new
feature in the relations between the state and the *bourgeoisie*. Its
introduction may have been suggested by the experience of the
emperors in Egypt, where the principle of the personal responsibility of the well-to-do for those who were economically weak
had prevailed from the most ancient times, and had been
applied to a certain extent by the emperors from the outset of
their domination there. By degrees the practice was extended to
the relations between the state and the cities. About the development of this new type of relations very little is known. In the

third century and later the new principle is dominant. It is no longer the magistrates and the council of the city who are collectively responsible for the collection of the taxes, for the supplementary payments, and for the performance of compulsory work by the population. Individual wealthy, or supposedly wealthy, men now bear the responsibility, and are liable for the payment of arrears on pain of losing their property, which might either be confiscated by the state or voluntarily made over in part or in whole.[44] In the cities of the West it is apparently a group of senators, the 'first ten', *decemprimi*, who are primarily responsible for the collection of the regular taxes, while the responsibility for the supplementary taxation (*annona*) and for the compulsory work falls upon men specially appointed to bear it.[45] All over the East abundant evidence is supplied alike by the juridical sources and by many inscriptions to prove that the responsibility for the collection of the regular taxes rested on a special group of the wealthiest citizens, the 'first ten' or δεκάπρωτοι, who in some places were replaced by the 'first twenty', εἰκοσάπρωτοι. They and the curators of the cities or λογισταί, as they were styled in the East, whose office gradually became one of the regular municipal burdens, were the outstanding men and the greatest sufferers in all the Eastern communities, including the newly municipalized Egypt.[46] (See Chap. IX.)

The origin of this institution is wrapped in obscurity. The early evidence, which is scanty, shows that in some places, both in West and in East, it was customary to give the title of the 'first ten' to the most prominent members of the city council or of the citizen body in general. We know nothing of the development of the institution in the West. In the East, especially in Asia Minor, the title of δεκάπρωτος begins to appear in inscriptions of the early second century A.D., and it is used at first as a term denoting a liturgy of a modest character, often coupled with the mention of κυριακαὶ ὑπηρεσίαι, an expression which means, not state services, but imperial services performed within the city by a city magistrate or λειτουργός, perhaps in connexion with the office of δεκάπρωτος. In some inscriptions the liturgy appears not as an annual but as a quinquennial duty. In one, belonging to the time of M. Aurelius, the duty is specified as that of collecting a special tax imposed by the emperor in connexion with the inroad of the Bastarnae into Asia Minor. It looks as if the 'first ten' were municipal *leitourgoi* who were obliged to deal with requirements of the government, and originally to undertake the supervision of, and responsibility for, certain extraordinary burdens imposed on the city. It appears probable, too, that the establishment of the institution was contemporary with that of the city curators and was connected with the difficult times during and after the wars of Trajan. Later it gained in importance, and spread to other parts of the East, the bearers of the title becoming the chief *leitourgoi* of the city, with the duty and responsibility of collecting the regular taxes on behalf of the government.[47]

It would appear, then, that the transition from the principle of collective responsibility to that of individual liability was effected in the second century and was connected with the general change of imperial policy towards the cities, which was manifested, for example, in the creation of special inspectors (*curatores*) of the cities and of special supervisors of their invested capital (*curatores kalendarii*). We have noted that in the critical times of Trajan, and again under M. Aurelius, the cities were unable to fulfil their duties to the state. They asked repeatedly for the cancellation of arrears and for a reduction of taxes. In granting the remissions and reductions, both Hadrian and M. Aurelius tried to effect a permanent improvement in the position of the cities. The method which they adopted took the form of a sharp control of the management of financial affairs and a gradual introduction of the principle of personal liability. In the third century these innovations were legally established and became the financial foundation of the economic policy of the Empire.

The method of improving the financial management of the Empire which its rulers adopted proved fatal. With one hand they endeavoured to create a healthy middle class and establish new centres of civilized life, and with the other they destroyed their own work by retaining the baneful system of compulsory labour, of requisitions, and of supplementary levies, and by giving to the principle of the liability of the rich for the poor a practical application which undermined both the spirit and the material welfare of the most energetic elements in the Italian and provincial cities. As the regular income of the state was not adequate to meet emergency needs, the emperors, instead of prudently increasing the taxes, which they disliked doing, resorted to far worse expedients by attacking not income, as before, but capital. The result was disastrous. As early as the time of Trajan there were in Bithynia very few men willing to bear the heavy burden of municipal service, and the same was true of Italy. The senate of Aquileia was delighted when Trajan granted them permission to include the *incolae* of the city in the system of liturgies. The explanation might be sought in the special part played both by Italy, particularly Aquileia, and by Bithynia in the wars of Trajan. A little later, however, in the time of Antoninus, the city of Tergeste, suffering under the burden of liturgies, implored the emperor to extend the *ius honorum* to the members of the attached tribes of the Carni and Catali, and humbly thanked him for granting the request. It was precisely in the second century, too, that some general measures seem to have been introduced with the object of making the public service more attractive, for example, the institution of the *Latium maius*. In the time of M. Aurelius the disease is so deeply rooted that a minor relief granted by the emperors to the Western municipalities in respect of gladiatorial shows provokes an almost hysterical expression of thanks by a Roman senator of provincial origin: 'I move, therefore,' he says in his speech in the senate, 'that our special thanks be expressed to the two emperors, who by salutary remedies, disregarding the interests of the *fiscus*, have restored the shattered state of the cities and the fortunes of the leading men, which trembled on the verge of utter ruin.'[48]

What the feelings of the lower classes were, we cannot tell. I recall here what I have said above (pp. 380 ff.) concerning the system of tax-collection, by which it was not only the *patrimonium* of the debtor which suffered, but also his own body, and concerning the responsibility of whole groups for the taxes of the individual. Methods like this were bound to make the daily life of the humble intolerable. No wonder, then, that discontent grew; witness the observations made above about the revolts which broke out under M. Aurelius. Later, when in the peculiar atmosphere of the third century the petitioners became confident that they would obtain a hearing directly from the emperors themselves, without the mediation of city and state officials, they began to send to Rome a shower of complaints about the unparalleled maltreatment to which they were subjected. Of these complaints we shall speak in the following chapters.

IX

THE MILITARY MONARCHY

THE enlightened rule of the Antonines was based, as we have seen, on the support of the educated upper classes throughout the Roman world, and its aim was to widen this basis as much as possible by reinforcing these classes, by raising the standards of life of the lower classes, and by spreading city civilization all over the provinces. The results were of far-reaching importance. The senate of Rome, which by its constitution represented the cream of the educated classes of the Empire, gained enormously in power. Not in political power: administrative and legislative functions were concentrated in the hands of the emperors, and they never thought of sharing it with the senate. But its moral power, the prestige which it had in the eyes of the educated classes everywhere, constantly grew; it rested on the fact that the senate was the true representative of their aspirations and that its conduct was in harmony with those aspirations. Any one who reads the correspondence of Pliny will realize how high was the standard of requirements to which the senators had to conform in order to maintain the authority of the body. Nor can we deny that a large portion of the senate satisfied these requirements, and that it was in the main a body conscious both of its dignity and of its duty towards the Empire.

When, after the death of M. Aurelius, Commodus assumed the imperial power, the mood of the senate was far from favourable to the new emperor. In making his son his partner in power and in leaving him as his successor, Marcus broke a tradition which now, after nearly a century of observance, was firmly rooted. Every one knew that Commodus became the successor of Marcus, not because he was the best fitted among the members of the senatorial class, but because he was the son of Marcus. This explains the haste of Avidius Cassius to seize the throne as soon as he heard the rumour of Marcus' death, which turned out to be false. As long, however, as Marcus lived, his personal authority was too high to permit of any opposition to him. Commodus had not his father's authority, and his first acts aroused the indignation of the senate. The hasty conclusion of peace—

against the opinion of the best generals of the day and the definite plans of his father, in the midst of military operations which had not achieved lasting results—his readiness to purchase an ignominious peace if necessary, his splendid triumph after such a peace, his lavish gifts to the soldiers when the finances of the Empire were in a critical state, his life of pleasure and amusement before, during, and after the triumph, were not calculated to establish good relations between the emperor and the senate.[1]

We refrain from relating once more all the events of Commodus' reign. The fact was that he had not the slightest desire to find a *modus vivendi* with the senate. At once he became violent, and instituted a régime of favourites. The reply of the senate was a conspiracy against his life. Its failure opened the period of terror which marked the following years of his rule. Like Domitian, Commodus began a resolute war against the senate. In doing so, he was bound to look for support elsewhere, and he naturally turned to the soldiers of the praetorian guard and the provincial armies. The struggle for the support of the praetorians is best illustrated by the repeated executions and dismissals of their commanding officers, which gradually took the form of a veritable *danse macabre*—Paternus, Perennis, a long series of prefects between Perennis and Cleander, Cleander himself, Julianus, Regillus, Laetus, of whom all but the last fell victims to the emperor's suspicious mood. To secure the allegiance of the praetorians and of the provincial armies, he repeatedly gave *congiaria* and raised the pay of the soldiers at the end of his reign without any apparent necessity.[2] The natural result of the terror was a series of conspiracies, which further aggravated the situation. How far the grave disturbances in Spain, Gaul, and Africa may be ascribed to political propaganda, is uncertain. It is more probable that they were due to the general exhaustion of the provinces, to the pressure of taxation and of conscription, and to the slackening of discipline among the soldiers and the imperial officers alike.[3] There is some reason to suppose that the disturbances in Africa were connected with abnormal conditions in Egypt, which resulted in the danger of Rome's being deprived of regular corn-supplies and in a correspondingly heavier pressure on Africa to make up the deficit; the story of Cleander and the *praefectus annonae* Papirius Dionysius is a good illustration of the uncertainty of supplies. It should be noted that at the end of his reign Commodus organized the African corn-fleet on the model of the Alexandrian, which involved a considerable amount of state control.⁴

A strong propaganda, however, certainly developed against the emperor not merely in the capital but also in the larger cities of the provinces. The watchwords were the same as in the time of the Flavians. The 'tyranny' of Commodus was contrasted with the 'kingship' of his father, and Commodus was branded as the typical tyrant, the degenerate offspring of great ancestors. There are some indications that the philosophers once more took a lively part in this propaganda; after the death of Commodus one of them was brutally killed by the praetorians. In Alexandria the opponents of Commodus resorted again to the political pamphlets of which we spoke in a previous chapter.* Some disturbances may have occurred in Alexandria, and some Alexandrian nobles were again tried in Rome before the emperor. It is possible that the disturbances were connected with the terror which raged alike in the capital and in the provinces, and perhaps with the extermination of the descendants of Avidius Cassius. The alleged account of this trial is fuller of the usual Cynic themes than any other. The dominant note is 'Commodus the tyrant' and 'Marcus the philosopher and king'. The senate appears as the legitimate judge in criminal affairs, and its justice is contrasted with the arbitrariness of Commodus.⁵

In his fight against the opposition Commodus, as has been said, relied on the soldiers and particularly on the praetorians. On the other hand, he endeavoured to emphasize the sacred character of his power. The god of his predilection was Hercules, the great exemplar of toil and pain undergone for the sake of mankind, the great fighter and the great sufferer of the Stoics and Cynics. The connexion of the cult of Hercules with the enlightened monarchy was not new: all the Antonines paid the god special reverence. There is no question that Commodus chose Hercules as his guardian deity, not because of his predilection for the profession of a gladiator, but because of the connexion of the god with his predecessors, and because Hercules was the divine embodiment of the chief ideas of the enlightened monarchy. So long as the bitter fight against his enemies did not obscure the emperor's mind, Hercules was prominent and

* See Chap. IV, note 33.

Description of Plate LXXIII

1. HEAD OF A BRONZE STATUE OF SEPTIMIUS SEVERUS. Found in Cyprus. Nicosia, Cyprus Museum of Antiquities. Published by permission of the Director.

The statue closely resembles another bronze statue of the same emperor in the Musée du Cinquantenaire, Brussels. I do not believe that our piece is a local Cypriot product. The statue was probably made in Rome and transported to Cyprus.

2. Portraits of the emperors of the dynasty of the Severi, and of the ladies of their court.

a. AUREUS OF SEPTIMIUS SEVERUS. Obv. SEVERVS PIVS AVG(ustus). Bust of Severus to r. with laurel crown. Rev. RESTITVTOR VRBIS. Goddess Roma to l. Cohen, iv, p. 63, no. 605.

b. DOUBLE *AUREUS* OF CARACALLA. Obv. ANTONINVS PIVS AVG. GERM. Bust of Caracalla to r. with radiate crown. Rev. P. M. TR. P. XVIIII COS. IIII P. P. Jupiter seated to l. with sceptre, Victory, and eagle. Cohen, iv, p. 180, no. 341.

c. AUREUS OF ELAGABALUS. Obv. IMP. ANTONINVS PIVS AVG. Bust of Elagabal to r. with laurel crown. Rev. P. M. TR. P. V. COS. IIII P. P. Elagabal in a *quadriga* to l. Cohen, iv, p. 344, no. 217.

d. AUREUS OF ALEXANDER SEVERUS. Obv. IMP. C(aesar) M(arcus) AVR(elius) SEV(erus) ALEXAND(er) AVG(ustus). Bust of Alexander Severus to r. with laurel crown. Rev. P. M. TR. P. VI COS. II P. P. Mars to r. helmeted, with trophy and spear. Cf. Cohen, iv, p. 434, no. 331.

e. AUREUS OF JULIA DOMNA. Obv. IVLIA AVGVSTA. Bust of Julia Domna, draped, to r. Rev. HILARITAS. The goddess with *cornucopiae* and long palm-branch to l. Cf. Cohen, iv, p. 112, no. 71.

f. AUREUS OF JULIA MAESA. Obv. IVLIA MAESA AVG. Bust of Julia Maesa, draped, to r. Rev. IVNO. Juno with sceptre and *patera* to l. Cf. Cohen, iv, p. 393, no. 15.

g. AUREUS OF JULIA MAMMAEA. Obv. IVLIA MAMAEA AVG. Bust of Julia Mammaea with a diadem, draped, to r. Rev. VESTA. Goddess Vesta to l., with *palladium* and sceptre. Cf. Cohen, iv, p. 497, no. 80.

All these coins are in the British Museum. For the selection of the coins and for the casts I am indebted to the courtesy of Mr. H. Mattingly of the British Museum.

1. HEAD FROM BRONZE STATUE
OF SEPTIMIUS SEVERUS

2. COINS OF THE SEVERI

LXXIII. THE SEVERI

became gradually the chief object of his devotion, his protector, companion, and guide. As soon, however, as he lost his balance, he insisted that he himself was an incarnation of the god and that, therefore, any opposition to him was sacrilege. It is needless to repeat all the familiar facts about this attitude, but one point must be emphasized—that they all belong to his very last years and that his identification of himself with Hercules was, in the main, an expression of the same tendency to consecrate the imperial power as had been shown by Caligula, Nero, and Domitian. It is also worthy of note that the cult of Hercules was made prominent in the religion of the Roman army, and that there it was coupled with the cult of the native gods of the province concerned, a concession which was probably first made to the provincial armies by Commodus. We must remember that the provincial armies now consisted almost entirely of men raised in the provinces where the armies were stationed, men belonging mostly to the class of the peasants, who always adhered to their local religion.[6]

Apart from the struggle with the senate and the well-marked tendency to find support among the soldiers in this struggle, we know very little of Commodus' policy. For the provinces peace, though disturbed by local revolts, was naturally a blessing; but how much he did for the provinces is unknown. It is noteworthy that in his attitude towards the lower classes he followed the policy of Hadrian, and that these classes looked upon him as their protector and benefactor. At any rate, the peasants of the imperial estates of Africa, overburdened with compulsory work and waging a long and persistent campaign against the farmers-general, were of that opinion when in their struggle they addressed bitter complaints to the emperor personally. One of these complaints is largely preserved, of another we have only a fragment. In the former the story of the struggle was told from the very beginning. The earliest attempt of the tenants of the *saltus Burunitanus* to get a hearing from the emperor miscarried; their first letter to him, full of bitter denunciations, was sent perhaps in the time of M. Aurelius. This first attempt was probably followed by a strike, which provoked ruthless reprisals in the shape of a punitive expedition; the danger latent in such a strike was not to be taken lightly. A dozen such local strikes would have constituted a real revolt, and they would take real fighting to suppress. I imagine that the rebellion of Maternus in Gaul and Spain was of a similar nature, and I am inclined to think also that the *seditiones* repressed by Pertinax in Africa were connected with outbursts of discontent such as that to which the inscriptions of the *saltus Burunitanus* bear witness. The second attempt was more fortunate. The success of the tenants was due probably to the personality of the man whom they chose as their plenipotentiary, Lurius Lucullus. His name shows that he was a Roman citizen; his interest in the tenants of the *saltus* indicates that he was himself one of them. The fact that Lucullus received an imperial rescript in answer to his petition attests his personal influence with the emperor. I am fairly confident that Lurius Lucullus was a soldier, probably one of the soldiers stationed in Rome, not a praetorian (as he was of provincial origin) but an *eques singularis* or perhaps a *frumentarius*. We know how important and influential the *frumentarii*, the military secret police, were under Commodus.[7] The tone of the petition is significant of the mood of the lower classes. They have confidence in the emperor, but they are full of hatred against their oppressors, the farmers-general and the procurators. They say: 'Help us; we are rustic folk, poor people who scarcely earn our living by heavy manual work, and so before your procurators we cannot cope with the farmer-general, who enjoys great favour with them, thanks to large bribes, and is well known to them by long years of tenure and by the conditions of his position; take pity on us, therefore, and deign to order by your sacred rescript,' &c. They appeal to the protection of the *Lex Hadriana*, they insist upon their rights. It is probable that those rights were violated under the pressure of government exactions. No less interesting is the attitude of Commodus. He gives a direct reply to the petition. He does not ask for supplementary evidence, he does not refer the case to the local authorities. He decides the little affair himself, and decides it in favour of the plaintiffs. The fighting temper is a striking feature in the above-mentioned fragment, which is what remains of another series of documents. The tenants threaten a strike, a real Egyptian ἀναχώρησις. They say: 'We will flee to some place where we may live as free men.'[8]

The fall of Commodus was not an accident. The repeated conspiracies show that the leading classes had definitely decided to get rid of him. In this endeavour they were supported by the provincial armies. Commodus committed the same mistake as Nero had made. He relied too much on the praetorian guard and the police corps of the capital, and neglected personal relations with the provincial armies, which were left in the hands of their commanders, most of them good generals who successfully fought the enemies of the Empire, the Sarmatians, the Britons, and the Moors. The repeated doles and other favours bestowed on the garrison of the capital offended the provincial armies and aroused their jealousy; as in the time of Nero, they were ready to listen to their actual commanders and to absorb the propaganda against Commodus. The first military revolt, of which very little is known, occurred in Britain. It was not easy for the emperor to quell it. Commodus was aware of the danger which threatened him, but whether because of his love for the dissipated life of the capital or because he was afraid of leaving Rome to itself, he made no effort to restore his authority by personal visits to the armies at the front. He preferred to grant some privileges to the soldiers, and even resorted in the last instance to a general increase of their pay. It was all in vain. The rumours about his dissipated life, his ignominious behaviour, and his liking for charioteers and gladiators, which were spread by the efforts of the officers, made it possible for the commanders of the most important armies, those of Britain, Pannonia, and Syria, to prepare the troops to take part in a military pronunciamento. We do not know whether there existed a real conspiracy of the military leaders in conjunction with their respective supporters at Rome and with their officers and colleagues, but it is certain that the army was ready for a military revolution. Its outbreak was hastened by events in Rome. By mere chance one of the many court conspiracies, in which the soldiery of the capital took no part, proved successful and the conspirators succeeded in killing the emperor. To satisfy the praetorians, the successor of Commodus was appointed not in the provinces but in Rome, in the person of the stern general and influential member of the senate, P. Helvius Pertinax. His reign was short. He was not the candidate of the praetorians and they got rid of him as soon as possible. As they had no candidate of their own, they took the next best, the man who made the highest bid for their support, Didius Julianus. The shameful auction aroused a storm of indignation in the provincial armies, and one after another they proclaimed their leaders emperors: L. Septimius Severus in Pannonia, C. Pescennius Niger in Syria, D. Clodius Albinus in Britain.

It would be out of place here to tell the full story of the contest for the imperial power which followed the murder of Pertinax and the accession of Didius Julianus, but we may emphasize the fact that it was a longer and more bitter struggle than that which followed the death of Nero. It had a political complexion, each army endeavouring to advance its leader to the imperial throne. No separatist tendencies are noticeable. But in fact the three armies recruited in the three main portions of the Empire, the Celto-Roman army of Albinus, the Illyrian and Thracian army of Severus, and the Asiatic (Syrian and Arabian) and Egyptian army of Niger had each of them its special character and its special aspirations, and the bitterness of the struggle reflected this diversity and foreshadowed the later division of the Empire into its Celto-German, Slavonic, and Oriental parts. Another important feature of the wars of succession was the hopeless weakness of Italy. The praetorians who fought so valiantly for Otho were no longer able or willing to fight for their own candidate, whoever he might be. They yielded to the provincial soldiers and asked for mercy. Furthermore, a noteworthy peculiarity of the wars after Commodus' death is the fact that they affected not only Italy but the whole Empire and ruined its most prosperous areas, Gaul and Asia Minor, economically the most flourishing and the most progressive provinces. And, finally, it was no accident that the victors were the free peasants of Germany, Thrace, and Illyria, the inhabitants of the most recent Roman provinces. They proved themselves stronger and better supporters of their general than the tenants of Gaul or the serfs and peasants of Asia and Egypt.[9]

The rule of Septimius Severus, of his Oriental wife, and of his half-Oriental children is of high importance in the history of the Roman Empire. About its character and historical significance two divergent views are held. The most eminent scholars affirm that Septimius Severus was the first to break with the traditions and the policy of the Antonines and to start on the path of thoroughly barbarizing the Roman Empire. Others are inclined to think that Septimius Severus was 'a patriotic but broad-minded ruler, intent on extending the culture and material

advantages of Italy and the older 'provinces to those on the frontiers of the Empire'. There appears to be an element of truth in
both views. The rule of Septimius Severus and of his immediate
successors was at once the last link in the chain of development
begun by the Antonines and the first in that of the new development which ended, after the terrible experiences of the second
half of the third century, in a complete remodelling of the Roman
state on Oriental patterns. Let us consider the facts.[10]

. Septimius Severus was a military usurper. He received his
power from the soldiers and retained it as long as the soldiers
were willing to support him. He forced himself upon the senate,
and the recognition and legalization of his power was voted by
the senate under military pressure. In this respect his position
was much more precarious than that of Commodus, the son and
legitimate heir of M. Aurelius. Hence his endeavours to purchase the allegiance of the senate and—after he became conscious that he was much less popular with it than his rivals
Pescennius and Albinus, and succeeded in crushing them one
after the other—the savage régime of terrorism which followed
his victories and ended in the extermination of the most prominent senators. From the very outset he was well aware that his
dynastic policy, his firm decision to transmit his power to his
children, could not fail to arouse protests and opposition in the
senate, since it was an open break with the traditions of the
Antonines, a break of the same kind as had made that body fight
Commodus, the last Antonine, with all the means at its disposal.
So long as Septimius pretended an intention to maintain the
system of adoption, that is to say, so long as he recognized
Albinus as his associate, the senate did not show its hand. But as
soon as, after the defeat of Pescennius, Septimius broke off his
relations with Albinus and declared his son Caracalla co-regent,
open war with the senate began and was carried on until senatorial opposition had been definitely crushed. The well-known
fact that the terrorism of the victor was not confined to Rome
and Italy but was extended on a large scale to the provinces,
especially those of the East and Gaul, where the provincial
aristocracy had supported his rivals, cannot be explained merely
by his financial difficulties. He knew that the provincial aristocracy, which dwelt in the largest and richest cities of the Empire,
shared in the devotion to the Antonine dynasty and would not

accept without protest a new rule based on the negation of the principles that guided the policy of the enlightened monarchy, and he endeavoured to silence this opposition as he had silenced it in Rome and in Italy.[11]

With the senate and a large part of the provincial aristocracy against him, Septimius was forced to make one concession after another to the army. I am not alluding to his gifts and bribes to the soldiers of the provincial armies during the struggle against his rivals, nor to the disbandment of the praetorian guard, the introduction of a new system of recruiting that guard, and the quartering of a legion in the neighbourhood of Rome. These were measures of safety dictated, not by military considerations —not by the desire to have an army ready to hand to lead against enemies on the borders of the Empire—but by the necessity of having more than one corps of reliable troops in Italy to support his power and even to fight each other if necessary. The Ἀλβάνιοι were there to check the praetorians; the *frumentarii*, the *equites singulares*, and the urban cohorts were so many strong military units unconnected with each other, which might be useful in case the praetorian guard or the Alban legion should attempt again to impose their will on the emperor or to depose him. The important concessions made by Septimius to the army were the more lasting military reforms which he introduced. It is an exaggeration to speak of his having thoroughly barbarized the corps of officers: the officers still belonged as a rule to the ranks of the senatorial and municipal aristocracy of the Empire. But it is clear that the ranks of this aristocracy were filled more and more with the *élite* of the common soldiers, the non-commissioned officers, all of whom (as well as their descendants) were now members of the equestrian class. By giving the privilege of the gold ring to private soldiers Septimius emphasized the fact that every soldier, if brave and loyal to the emperor, might by pro-motion to the centurionate become a member of the privileged classes. The militarization of the upper classes did not, indeed, mean their immediate barbarization. The centurions were more or less romanized as the result of their service in the army, although if we take into account the composition of the army at the end of the second century (of which we spoke in the fourth chapter), we may safely say that the romanization of most of them was very slight. Another measure of the same character was the militarization of the administration by widening the sphere of office open to knights and enlarging the activities of equestrian officials. Such facts as the appointment of a knight as governor of Mesopotamia, the appointment of knights as commanders of the Parthian legions at Albano and in Mesopotamia, the increased importance of the prefect of the praetorians, the practice of temporarily replacing proconsuls in senatorial provinces by procurators, and the role which the knights now played among the *comites Augusti*, all show that Septimius intended gradually to open to the common soldiers the highest posts in the imperial administration.

On the other hand, the increase of the soldiers' pay, the privileges given to the veterans (exemption from municipal liturgies), the protection of club life in the fortresses, and (not least important) the legal recognition of marriages contracted by soldiers, which resulted in a gradual migration of the married soldiers from the barracks to the *canabae*, were serious concessions which were bound to undermine the military spirit and to create an influential military caste within the Empire. It is evident that such concessions were granted under the pressure of necessity. We have only to bear in mind the many military revolts, especially at the very beginning of his reign, to appreciate how difficult it was for Septimius to consolidate his influence with the soldiers. Facts like the pitiful failure of all the attempts to capture Hatra in the second Parthian expedition, which was due to the lack of discipline among the soldiers of the European legions, prove that the policy of Septimius did actually undermine discipline and was adopted not from choice but from necessity. His last words addressed to his sons, 'Be united, enrich the soldiers, and scorn the rest,' if not genuine—though there seems to be no reason why they should not be—were in full conformity with his general policy. Beyond doubt Septimius was the first to base his power firmly and permanently on the army. Though many of his predecessors in the first century, and particularly Domitian, did the same, nevertheless, after the rule of the Antonines and after the practical elimination of any influence of the senate on the administration of the Empire, the militaristic policy of Septimius was a new phenomenon. What he aimed at was not a military tyranny but a hereditary military monarchy.[12]

Yet it is idle to speak of Septimius as establishing an Oriental military despotism. His military monarchy was not Oriental, it was Roman in its very essence. The principate of Augustus was completely militarized by Septimius, emphasis was laid on the title *imperator*, chief of the Roman army, but the emperor remained the chief magistrate of the Roman Empire, and the army remained an army of Roman citizens. If the Empire now comprised all the Roman provinces and if the supremacy of the Italian stock, still maintained by Trajan and not openly repudiated even by Hadrian, was gone for ever, there was nothing radically new in that. It was a normal development, inaugurated by the civil wars and gradually worked out by one Roman emperor after another. Septimius took decisive steps in provincializing the army and in giving a larger number of provincials access to administrative posts, but in principle he pursued a policy which had long ago been established by the rulers of the Empire. There was nothing revolutionary in this policy. Its baneful aspect was, not that he made the army democratic, but that he militarized the principate; and that was in fact a necessary consequence of his usurpation of power and of his establishment of a hereditary monarchy.

Septimius was, therefore, perfectly consistent in emphasizing his respect for the enlightened monarchy of the Antonines. He wished to be recognized as the legitimate heir of Commodus and he very soon ceased to pose as the avenger of the senate's nominee, Pertinax. When he proclaimed himself the brother of Commodus, when he consecrated his memory, when he forged an adoption of himself by M. Aurelius, he was perfectly well aware that these gross absurdities could not deceive anybody. His object was to lay stress on his allegiance to the last great emperor and on his willingness to carry out his policy. Another reason was, of course, the pressing need for a legitimization of his usurped position. Legal sanction was extorted from the senate, but the imperial power did not depend merely on a *senatus consultum*; it rested primarily on the imperial cult, and now, after a century of peaceful evolution, that cult was closely connected with the name and the traditions of the Antonines. It is not surprising that Septimius wished to appear as the son of the sainted Marcus and with that object introduced his own image into the municipal shrines and the legionary chapels, nor that he allowed his sons to assume the name of Antoninus in order that they should become the heirs not only of the name but also of the reverence paid to the name. Never before, except in the times of Caligula and of Domitian, was the imperial cult more personal and more dynastic. It was symptomatic that on the crowns of the municipal *flamines* the busts of the Capitoline triad were replaced by the busts of Septimius and his two sons, the new Antonines.[13]

It must be recognized that in some respects the policy of Septimius was in fact a genuine continuation of that of Hadrian and of the Antonines. It is notorious that the legislation of the Empire was never more humane than in the age of the Severi. The great jurists of this time, Papinian, Ulpian, and Paulus, were given a free hand to develop their favourite humanitarian ideas of equal law for everybody and of the duty of protecting human life in general and the weak and poor in particular. On the eve of the great social revolution for which the militarization of the Empire was preparing the way, Roman law displayed for the last time its noblest and most brilliant aspect. It is needless to dwell on this familiar theme.[14] It is manifest, however, that the liberal social policy of Septimius was designed first and foremost to consolidate his own power and that of his dynasty. Like Commodus, he determined to base his power on the classes from which his soldiers were drawn: hence his liberal legislation and his measures for the protection of the peasants and the city proletariate against the ruling classes and the imperial administration. It is to be noted that he restored the *alimenta* which Commodus had abolished. In Africa he continued the policy of the Flavians, of Trajan, and of Hadrian. It is no freak of chance that the copy of the *Lex Manciana* which we possess probably dates from the time of Septimius Severus, and that the *ara legis Hadrianae* belongs to the same period. Septimius apparently wished to increase the numbers of free landowners on his estates, and he insisted on the strict adherence of the contractors and the procurators to the provisions of his predecessors. After the persecutions of the partisans of Pescennius in Egypt, which shattered the economic prosperity of the land and led to an increase in the number of those who fled from their villages, he published, in connexion with the usual census, a special proclamation calling upon the peasants to return to their fields and villages. On this proclamation was based the edict of the governor Subatianus Aquila. To these documents appeal is made, for instance, by the peasants of the village of Soknopaiou Nesos in the Fayyûm, when they say in their petition directed against certain rich men who took advantage of their absence to occupy the land which they used to cultivate: 'Our lords, the most sacred and invincible emperors Severus and Antoninus, during their stay in their own land of Egypt, among many other benefactions, desired those who did not reside in their own abodes to return to their homes, eradicating compulsion and lawlessness.'[15]

The same spirit of confidence in the emperor and the same allegiance to him personally, as contrasted with the hostility shown to his agents and officials, was shown by the peasants of the imperial estates in Asia Minor. We possess three or four petitions dating from the time of Septimius, all recently found in Lydia. After making complaints to the high officials, and suffering disillusionment, the peasants appealed directly to the emperor, using the most devoted and loyal language. In one of the petitions their representative says: 'We beg of you, greatest and most sacred of all emperors, that having regard to your laws and those of your ancestors, and to your peace-making justice to all, and hating those whom you and all your ancestors on the throne have always hated, you will order &c.' In another petition another group of peasants emphasize their hereditary allegiance to their imperial masters, saying: 'We shall be forced . . . to become fugitives from the imperial estates where we were born and bred and where, remaining from the times of our ancestors tillers of the soil, we keep our pledges to the imperial *fiscus*.' Like the tenants of the *saltus Burunitanus*, the peasants of Mendechora presented their petition to the emperor through their representative. It is a pity that we do not know his name, but the fact that in later times such petitions were regularly forwarded to the emperor by soldiers makes it possible that the peasants of Mendechora acted through one of their number who happened to be a soldier or an officer of the imperial army.[16]

Thus the policy of Septimius towards the humble was a policy of protection and concessions. Towards the cities his attitude was different. It is true that Septimius was not hostile to the cities as such. For those which staunchly supported him he showed both sympathy and understanding of their needs, especially for those of his own native land of Africa, for those of Syria, his wife's home, and for those of the Danube provinces, whence his soldiers were drawn. In his reign the cities of all these countries flourished and prospered. Many were promoted to a higher municipal dignity, a large number were honoured by gifts and new buildings, some received a colony of Roman veterans (Tyre in Phoenicia and Samaria in Palestine). Naturally they glorified the beneficent régime of the emperor and erected to him, to his wife, and to his sons statues and triumphal arches one after another. But it would not be just to generalize and say that in regard to the cities Septimius fully maintained the policy of his predecessors. We cannot forget the fate of Lyons in Gaul and of Byzantium. The former never recovered from the ruthless punishment meted out to it. Severe chastisement was also inflicted on Antioch. Scores of cities were obliged to pay enormous contributions, because they had been forced to furnish money to Pescennius Niger and, apparently, during the Parthian war all the cities of the Empire were invited to send considerable gifts in money to the emperor. Of the confiscation of the property of many members of the provincial aristocracy we have already spoken.[17]

More important than these temporary measures of repression was the general policy of Septimius towards the upper classes of the city population. In speaking of liturgies in the preceding chapter, I laid stress on the fact that Septimius was the first emperor who insisted upon the personal responsibility of the municipal magistrates. He was also the first who, with the help of his jurists, developed the oppressive system of liturgies into a permanent institution legalized, regularized, and enforced by the state. The jurists who did most to elaborate the system and the theory of the *munera* were Papinian and Callistratus, the contemporaries of Septimius, and Ulpian, the adviser of Alexander Severus.[18] The development is especially clear in the case of the *decaprotia* and *eikosaprotia*. The references to this burden in the Digest begin in the third century. Herennius Modestinus and Ulpian and later Arcadius Charisius and Hermogenian are the first to record its transformation into one of the most important municipal *munera*, and it is not till Caracalla's reign that the inscriptions of Asia Minor reflect the change. Some time, too, in the third century the decaproty was introduced into the new municipal life of Egypt; about the middle of the century it had become one of the most important institutions in the financial life of the country.[19]

It is certain also that more systematic pressure was exercised by Septimius and his successors on the associations and corporations which served the state. The fact that Callistratus, in speaking of the organization of the *munera* in municipal life, devotes so much attention to the corporations, shows that Septimius, following the lead of his predecessors, particularly Hadrian, M. Aurelius, and Commodus, minutely regulated the relations between the corporations and the cities. Specially important were the *navicularii* and the merchants, and to them is devoted the largest part of the excerpt from Callistratus which is preserved in the Digest. It is significant of the position of these corporations that Callistratus emphasizes the *assistance* of the merchants and the *service* of the shipowners, and that he insists upon the point that both are performing a *munus publicum*. That explains his collection of all the earlier rules which had regulated the activity of these corporations and his further development of them.[20] In the preceding chapter it has been pointed out that the special care of Septimius for the corporations of merchants and shipowners was probably dictated by the constant complaints of these corporations, provoked by the regular use which he made of them during the civil and the Eastern wars. The *navicularii* of Arelate, who probably transported men and supplies from Gaul to the East during the second Parthian expedition and during the stay of Septimius and Caracalla in the East, bitterly complained in a petition of A.D. 201, a copy of which was found at Berytus (Dessau, *ILS* 6987), of the vexations and exactions to which they were subjected in performing their service to the state. It is likely that their insistent complaints, which were coupled with threats of a strike, induced Septimius to revise and complete, and even to extend, some of the privileges which were granted to them. One of the most important was exemption from municipal burdens.[21]

Similar special privileges, and in particular that of exemption from the municipal liturgies, were granted to other groups of men who belonged to the urban population of the Empire. The most important was the group of men who farmed the taxes and of men who farmed the imperial and public estates, the latter of whom were treated by the imperial legislation on the same lines as the former. There was no great difference, from the point of view of the state, between these two sections of the group, as both of them performed practically the same public service by collecting in the name of the state payments which were due to it. We have described in the preceding chapter the important part which the tax-farmers played in provincial life in the second and the early third century. The farmers of the customs in the Danube provinces and in Africa were prominent and influential men.[22] Still more influential were the farmers of the imperial estates, particularly in such provinces as Africa and Asia and especially in the reign of Septimius, who confiscated enormous tracts of land from his supposed enemies. These *conductores* have been spoken of in the seventh chapter. The earliest references to their corporate organization date from the time of the Flavians and of Trajan. Hadrian protected them and M. Aurelius extended to them the privilege of freedom from the municipal liturgies. All these privileges were maintained by Septimius Severus, as is clear from their careful registration by Callistratus.[23]

But, while helping in this way some members of the privileged classes whose service was needed by the state, or rather while endeavouring to ease somewhat the increasing pressure of the burden which lay on their shoulders, Septimius never forgot the interests of the humbler and poorer classes. It is probable that it was he who extended the privilege of exemption from the municipal liturgies to the tenants of the imperial estates. Very likely he was moved to do so by their repeated complaints about the arbitrary way in which, though not resident in the cities, they were forced by the municipal magistrates and the imperial officers to share the municipal burdens. In the petition of Aga Bey in Lydia the peasants lay great stress on this point and threaten the emperor with a mass strike in the form of an ἀναχώρησις. In accordance with his general policy, Septimius yielded to these demands and freed the tenants from the burden of municipal liturgies, while maintaining the claim of the state to demand compulsory work and the discharge of other *munera* which concerned it.[24]

Another important group of the municipal population which was exempted from municipal burdens, on the same plea of serving the state in another capacity, consisted of the corporations which 'performed manual work indispensable for public-utility services'.* Such in particular were the corporation of the

---

* *Dig.* 50. 6. 6, § 12.

fabri and *centonarii*, who performed the duties of firemen in the cities. It is now clear that the views expressed about these *collegia* by Callistratus in a well-known passage reflected the ideas of Septimius, as a rescript of Septimius and Caracalla which was found at Solva in Pannonia contains the same regulations in almost the same words. The main principle of Septimius' policy in regard to the *centonarii* and *fabri* is identical with that which guided him in dealing with the merchants and shipowners. He grants to the members of these corporations exemption from municipal burdens, but he is anxious that none should enjoy the privilege who do not actually perform the duties connected with membership. The latter are the richer members. For them there is no exemption, but the privilege is maintained in full for the humbler, the *tenuiores*, who really help to extinguish fires, and no limit is fixed to the number of such members.[25]

It is evident that all these exemptions, while making the burden a little easier for some and to a certain extent assisting the poorer classes, added to the burden of those who were now left to bear the municipal liturgies unaided. Some of the richest men being thus exempt, the owners of land and shops, belonging chiefly to the middle class, remained the sole bearers of the liturgies. It was no wonder that they tried by various ingenious devices to escape these burdens, which undermined their economic prosperity. From this point of view also the introduction of municipal life into Egypt must be regarded. We know that in A.D. 199 a municipal council was granted to Alexandria and it is reasonable to suppose that the grant was gradually extended to the *metropoleis* of the country. This meant that Egypt, the original home of the system, was subjected to the same set of liturgies as the rest of the Empire. For Egypt the change involved no privilege, perhaps not even a new burden: the *bourgeoisie* of Egypt was anyhow accustomed to bear responsibility for the rest of the population. But it meant rearrangement and systematization. Liturgies which heretofore had been imposed on the *bourgeoisie* were now gradually classified, not without some modifications, and piled as a whole on the shoulders of the unhappy members of the new municipal councils.[26] The same motives explain the endeavours of Septimius to equalize the burden upon the rural and the city population, the full and the second-class citizens, in some cities of Asia Minor, such as Prusias. The country population had henceforth to bear its share not only of compulsory work, of taxes, and of extraordinary payments, but also of the responsibility which previously had rested on the full citizens only.[27]

The radical and ruthless measures of Septimius may be attributed to the desperate state of the imperial finances caused by the extravagances of Commodus and by the civil war at the beginning of his reign, which was followed by serious and expensive external wars. The reign of Septimius was not a time of peace: out of eighteen years not more than six were free from war. Certainly by his relentless measures he accumulated in his own hands an enormous fortune, especially landed property, which was organized as a new department of administration, the *ratio privata,* and filled up the empty treasury of the Roman state. But it is clear that this was done chiefly to promote his own interests and to satisfy his personal ambition. Money, acquired by confiscations and contributions, was spent lavishly in bribing the soldiers and the Roman mob. The finances of the state were restored, but at the expense of the people. There is not the slightest ground for affirming that the Empire was happy and prosperous under Septimius. The provinces—apart from Africa, which was not affected by the civil war to such an extent as the rest of the Empire, the Danube provinces, whence he drew his chief support, and Syria, which was under the special protection of Julia Domna—as well as Italy were far from flourishing. During and after the civil war the Empire was full of homeless people who were tracked and persecuted by the emperor's police agents, his *frumentarii* and *stationarii.* Wandering about in desperation, they formed bands of robbers and devastated the land. We hear that an army of bandits under Bulla was the terror of Italy for years, and that a military force was necessary to suppress him and his partisans, while some other scattered notices seem to attest similar conditions in Germany and Gaul and certain other provinces.[28]

The causes of the growth of robbery, particularly in those provinces which had been affected by the civil war and lay near to the theatres of external wars, are not far to seek. Confiscations of landed property *en masse* convulsed economic life to an extent which must not be underestimated. Private capital and private initiative were thus removed from large and flourishing concerns and were replaced by a new system of management, bureaucratic and lifeless in the extreme. Political persecutions on a large scale scared thousands of people, both guilty and innocent, and forced them to flee from their homes. The chief evil, however, was the enormous number of government agents, mostly soldiers performing the duties of policemen—the *frumentarii, stationarii*, and *colletiones*—who in their pursuit of political 'criminals' penetrated into all the cities and villages and searched private houses, and who were, of course, accessible to bribes. Still more serious were the exactions of these same agents in connexion with the frequent military expeditions of the emperor. In time of civil war no one cared a straw for the people. New recruits were levied in masses and compulsorily; means of transport and men were requisitioned for armies on the march; foodstuffs and war material also had to be supplied by the people, and quarters provided in their homes for soldiers and officers. The inscriptions mention many prominent men who were in charge of the war chest, that is to say, whose function it was to levy money-contributions and war-supplies from cities and individuals. These men naturally could not perform their duties without the aid of a mass of minor officials and soldiers, who swooped down like a swarm of locusts on the cities and villages, devouring their substance and scaring and exasperating all classes of the population.[29]

Another remarkable feature of the period was the large number of military deserters. We have noted the same phenomenon in the time of Commodus, when Septimius Severus was sent to Gaul to suppress bands of such runaways. Evidently the situation did not improve during the civil war. That is clear from the collection of regulations on the subject contained in the Digest. Most of these were collected and illustrated by the jurists of the time of the Severi, especially by Arrius Menander, a member of the council of Septimius and Caracalla—a fact which attests the wide extension of the evil, which was a serious trouble to the Empire from the end of the second century till the close of the third. It is clear (as has been pointed out in the fourth chapter) that recruiting, particularly in time of war, was now almost wholly compulsory, and this compulsory recruiting under the conditions of civil war was regarded as a heavy burden by the inhabitants both of the cities and of the villages. A Lydian inscription, which is the earliest document attesting a compulsory levy, should be dated in all probability to the time of one of the Severi—it may be Caracalla or Elagabalus or Alexander.[30]

The relations of Septimius to the lower classes of the Empire have been illustrated above by some petitions addressed by Lydian peasants to the emperor personally. These men believed in the emperor's goodwill and sympathy, but they were full of hatred towards the minor agents of the imperial power, the *colletiones, frumentarii,* and *stationarii.* The burden and the tone of the complaints are the same in all four documents. '[These men],' they say in one petition, '[appear in the villages] . . . doing no good but squeezing the village by unbearable requisitions of goods and by fines, so that, exhausted by the immense expenditure for these visitors and for the multitude of *colletiones,* it has been forced to give up even its public bath and has been deprived of the necessary means of subsistence.' The other petitions deal with the lawlessness and brutality of the same agents in arresting, imprisoning, and even killing prominent men of the village who were unable or unwilling to bribe them. If we take into consideration the severities of execution on the person as prescribed by the law and widely applied, especially when the *humiliores,* or unpropertied people, were concerned, we may understand the sufferings and the feelings of the peasants. In the best preserved of these petitions the peasants of the village (the modern Aga Bey) say: 'As suppliants of your divine and sublime royalty, most sacred of all emperors, inasmuch as we are hindered from attending to our agricultural toil by the threats of the *colletiones* and their representatives to put us, who still remain unhampered, in peril of our lives, and inasmuch as we are unable, owing to the obstruction of our agricultural work, to do our duty in the matter of imperial payments and other obligations in the future, we beg you', &c.[31]

The deterioration in the currency was a disquieting symptom of the serious financial situation of the Empire. From the time of Nero onward, silver, the metal of which the most used coinage, namely the denarius and its fractions, was made, had suffered a slow but increasing addition of copper. This was due to various causes: export of silver coinage as a result of foreign trade—one recalls the discoveries made in India, Germany, and South Russia—the gradual exhaustion of a series of silver mines without the discovery of new ones, the lavish expenditure of money by some emperors, which was not covered by the regular revenues of the state. However, as long as the state enjoyed credit and business flourished, this was far from dangerous. But already under Septimius Severus the denarius, with a half-silver content, was not the coin it once had been. The reason for the depreciation is clear: the difficult wars of Marcus Aurelius and the civil wars of the first years of Severus, and the ensuing economic instability. Gold and silver were hidden, and disappeared from circulation —a fact which explains the discovery of coin-hoards of the late second century. The production of the mines was not enough to make good the deficiency. Hence arose the pressure exerted upon the population to make payments in kind. This in its turn arose from the rise in prices and other similar factors.[32]

We cannot, then, speak of the time of Septimius as a time of peace and prosperity. There was no peace and consequently no prosperity. The situation improved somewhat in the last six years of the reign, and the improvement was not impeded by the colonial war in Britain. The ageing emperor lost his ferocious energy and found a *modus vivendi* with the senate, which had been terrified by the savage executions of his earlier years. The economic conditions became slightly better and the population was glad to have some rest at last. This feeling and the sympathy which Septimius showed towards the soldiers and the lower orders made him and his sons popular with the masses, exhausted as they were by long years of civil and external war. But the leading classes, the city aristocracy of Italy and the provinces, were not reconciled to the new militaristic and autocratic régime, and in the few years of peace which were granted to them their opposition grew steadily stronger. Everybody felt that the strife between the military monarchy and the enlightened rule of the Antonines was not yet ended. The city *bourgeoisie* was too powerful to resign its position and its influence without a further effort. Caracalla, the eldest son of Septimius, who grew up as the companion and associate of his father, who was educated by him and by his mother to share their views and aspirations, and who from childhood spent his time among the members of the highest aristocracy of Rome, thoroughly realized how unpopular his father's ideas and plans were with the cultured classes of the Empire. From the very beginning of his rule he showed that he was fully determined to pursue his father's policy and to make no concessions to the higher classes. The strife between him and his brother Geta, which filled the first months of their joint rule, afforded a good test of the loyalty of the senate and its supporters. Though the senate knew very well that Geta was of the same brand as his brother, most of the leading men sided with him in the quarrel and displayed undisguised hostility to Caracalla. The result was the treacherous murder of Geta and the policy of terror alike in Rome and in the provinces which revived the worst times of Septimius.[33]

We have sufficient materials to form a fair judgement on Caracalla's general policy. It is true that the detailed pictures which have been given by Cassius Dio, a contemporary and an influential member of the senatorial class, by Herodian, another contemporary, who belonged to the group of intellectuals of Greek origin and was probably an imperial official, and by a historian of Roman origin who was the chief source of the biography contained in the collection of Latin lives by the so-called *Scriptores Historiae Augustae*, are not unbiased and represent in the main the point of view of the higher and cultured classes of the Empire, who were thoroughly hostile to the emperor and regarded him as the worst tyrant in the history of Rome.[34] There is no doubt, however, that neither Dio, nor Herodian, nor the unknown Roman senator has invented the facts, and that they have well expressed the current opinion which prevailed among the best informed and the most intelligent inhabitants of the Empire. The hostility of these men towards Caracalla is in itself a significant fact, which must not be underestimated. The causes of this hostility are fully explained by our sources.

In his policy Caracalla declared openly and frankly, more frankly than his father, that he was determined to base his power not on the higher classes—the city *bourgeoisie* and the Italian aristocracy—but on the lower classes and their representatives, the soldiers. It is notorious that he favoured the soldiers and endeavoured to appear as one of them, to say nothing of his increase of their pay and pensions and his lavish donatives. This might be explained as a means of buying their fidelity and support after the murder of Geta. On the other hand, he openly showed his contempt of, and hostility towards, the propertied and intellectual classes. Dio is positive on this point, and his

Description of Plate LXXIV

1. FRAGMENTARY FUNERAL STELE. Found at Kostolatz (Moesia Superior). Museum of Belgrade. Inscription: 'D(is) M(anibus) L. Blassius Nigellio specul(ator) leg(ionis) VII Cl(audiae) .vixit ann(os) XXXV'—*CIL* iii. 1650, cf. p. 1021 = Dessau, *ILS* 2378. Bas-relief: my article in *Röm. Mitt.* 26, 1911, pp. 268 ff. Only the upper part of the stele is reproduced here.

The sculptured face of the stele represents a two-storeyed *aedicula*. The pediment, adorned with a Medusa-head and two *Genii* with torches, is supported by two columns which form the upper storey of the *aedicula* and are separated from a lower storey, which contains the inscription, by a frieze depicting two dogs hunting a hare and a bear. Inside the *aedicula* is seen a four-wheeled car drawn by three horses, with a driver on the box, a traveller seated on a bench, holding in his right hand a short staff or a roll, and behind him a servant seated on the baggage, carrying a long spear with a peculiar head—the *insigne* of the *speculator*. There is no doubt that the deceased is represented travelling in his official capacity, and using a carriage and horses requisitioned by the government for its postal service (*cursus publicus*). On the *speculatores* and their *insignia*, see Chap. XI, note 17; on the type of funeral reliefs with scenes of travel, pl. xxxiii, 3.

2. A FUNERAL STELE. Found at Carnuntum. Museum of Deutsch Altenburg. Inscribed 'C. Attius C. f. Voturia Exoratus miles leg(ionis) XV Apo(llinaris) anno(rum) XXXXIV stipend(iorum) XXIIII h(ic) s(itus) e(st). M. Minicius et Sucesus l(iberti) posierunt'. E. Bormann in *Oesterr. Limes*, xii, pp. 318 ff., figs. 37, 38; A. Schober, *Die römischen Grabsteine von Noricum und Pannonia* (1923), p. 50, no. 105, fig. 45. Cf. above, p. 245, with note 75.

A soldier in military dress but without arms, holding a short staff in his right hand, leads a rustic cart dragged by a team of oxen and driven by a peasant who holds an axe. A dog follows behind. As indicated in the text, the scene represents an *angareia* performed by a peasant with his cart, probably for the purpose of cutting wood in the forest. On the *angareiae*, see Chap. VIII, notes 35–37, and especially the text of Epictetus quoted in note 37. Cf. the bas-relief of a *beneficiarius* of Intercisa in *Arch. Értesitö*, 1905, p. 230, no. 11.

3. FRAGMENT OF A FUNERAL STELE. Found at Strasbourg (Argentorate). Museum of Strasbourg. R. Henning, *Denkmäler der elsässischen Altertumssammlung*, pl. L, 3, p. 53; *Germania Romana* (Atlas), 1st ed., pl. xxxiv, 6; E. Espérandieu, *Rec. gén.* vii, no. 5499. The fragmentary inscription is given in *CIL* xiii. 11630.

On a road planted with trees a soldier, with his sword under his arm, is driving a four-wheeled cart drawn by two mules. The cart is loaded apparently with foodstuffs. The relief represents the provisioning of a fort from the neighbouring country by a soldier.

1. A SPECULATOR ON AN OFFICIAL TOUR OF
INSPECTION

2. SOLDIER AND PEASANT

3. SOLDIER DRIVING A CART LOADED
WITH FOOD

LXXIV. LIFE IN THE PROVINCES

statement suits very well Caracalla's notorious tendency to identify himself with the humblest soldiers. Nor can we disbelieve in the genuineness of one of his most favourite sayings, also recorded by Dio: 'No one but myself ought to have money, and that in order to give it to the soldiers.' His conduct and his policy, too, are in full accord with the attitude which this saying expressed.[35]

To corrupt the soldiers, Caracalla needed enormous sums. The stock of money accumulated by Septimius was soon depleted. To fill his treasury, he was therefore obliged to resort to extraordinary measures. The sources of his income are fully enumerated by Dio. It was mostly derived from a systematic draining of the wealth of the propertied classes. The land-tax and the poll-tax—the chief taxes paid by the working classes—were not increased, but the crown-tax (*aurum coronarium*), an extraordinary supplementary income-tax, which mainly affected the richer classes, was repeatedly demanded. The contributions in kind were a heavy burden. Though everybody had to make such contributions, which were used for the maintenance of the soldiers, the chief payers were the large landowners who always had great quantities of foodstuffs in store, while the peasants had practically no surplus. Dio emphasizes the fact that for these contributions no money was paid, and that the rich classes often bought the foodstuffs which they were obliged to deliver. Finally, an abundant source of income was the compulsory gifts extorted both from rich individuals and from the cities, a heavy and arbitrary capital levy very like pure robbery. The only regular taxes which were increased (by being doubled) were the tax on inheritances and the tax on manumissions, which were always closely connected. It is evident that these taxes were paid chiefly by the well-to-do classes.[36]

The mutual hostility between Caracalla and the upper classes in the cities is best shown by the terrible, though mysterious, story of the murders perpetrated in Alexandria before the emperor's Parthian expedition. Without any pretext Caracalla treacherously and secretly killed off the young generation of Alexandrian citizens, and completed his work of extermination by mass murders in the houses where his soldiers and officers were quartered. Our sources give no explanation of this violent act. One cannot, of course, believe that he committed it because he was offended by gibes hurled at him by the Alexandrians who were certainly discontented because of the growing burden of forced levies on property and municipal liturgies. I cannot help thinking that the military preparations for his Parthian expedition were carried out mostly at the expense of Egypt. Towards the city of Antioch, for instance, Caracalla acted as a protector and benefactor, not as an executioner. Syria, the native land of his mother, was spared and the whole burden was imposed on Egypt. It is no wonder that Egypt, and especially Alexandria, bitterly resented such treatment. It is very likely, therefore, that Alexandria was far from friendly to Caracalla; it was probably at this time that the so-called 'Acts of Heathen Martyrs' were collected into one pamphlet, which was circulated all over Egypt. Caracalla was aware of the situation and became alarmed. He was afraid that during his absence in Parthia the country might revolt and cut off his supplies; he may have believed in the existence of a conspiracy in Alexandria; and he acted accordingly, displaying all his cowardice and vileness. Be that as it may, the episode clearly reveals the real attitude of Caracalla towards the city *bourgeoisie* and the readiness of the army to support him in any cruel measure which he might take against the cities.[37]

I am convinced that it was the same spirit of hostility towards the upper classes that produced the famous *constitutio Antoniniana* of A.D. 212, by which Roman citizenship was granted to all *peregrini*. The ordinance of Caracalla remains a puzzle even after the discovery of some fragments of it in Egypt, and it is very difficult to determine what its real intention was. The original text of the measure—if such it is—as discovered in Egypt, apparently excludes the *dediticii* from the grant. How many of the *peregrini* were styled *dediticii* in the time of Caracalla? Were the free peasants of the villages (for example, in Thrace and Syria) included in this class? What about the rural population of the city territories? were all the tenants of the emperors *dediticii* or not? So long as we are reduced to mere guesswork on all these vital points, we are practically helpless to decide what the historical importance of the *constitutio* is, and what purpose Caracalla endeavoured to effect by publishing it at the very beginning of his reign. If it really excluded from the grant all the rural elements and concerned the cities only, if in the cities it affected the full citizens (the *honestiores*) but not the lower classes (the *humiliores*), it cannot be regarded as a great step towards political equalization, towards levelling up the masses of the population throughout the Empire. It becomes a partial measure which enlarged the numbers of Roman citizens in the cities, and especially in the cities of the East.

Moreover, even if the grant was not limited to such small numbers, but had a wider application, the fact that it was individual and did not affect the legal standing of the city as such, so that a 'peregrine' city remained what it had been although all its citizens were now *cives Romani*, reduces the importance of the measure to very small proportions. It leads us to believe that, apart from its effect on taxation, which Dio emphasizes, the act of Caracalla had two special objects. By giving the Roman citizenship to the municipal class and to the upper stratum of the village population (thereby effecting the 'συνοικισμός' of the rural and the city population), as well as to some members of the lower classes, Caracalla enlarged the numbers of those who were liable to the city liturgies. Having now equal political rights, the new Roman citizens had no ground of escape from this heavy burden. Furthermore, by the grant of Roman citizenship to these former outcasts Caracalla intended to flatter them and to win their allegiance. But his main aim was not so much to raise the lower classes, as to degrade the upper, not only in Rome and Italy but in the provinces, and thus to reduce the pride and self-confidence of the ruling class in the cities, the imperial and municipal aristocracy. Roman citizenship was now such a common thing, such a cheap honour, that it had lost all value and might be extended even to the *dediticii* without any prejudice to anybody. In fact Caracalla's grant did not help any one and had no real social or political importance. The burden of taxation and of liturgies remained the same; the gulf between the city residents and the peasants, as well as between the city proletariate and the city middle class, was not bridged; the new Roman citizens became subject to the Roman law, which in this period of the development of an all-imperial law did not mean very much; and that was all.

However small the practical importance of Caracalla's measure may have been, from the historical point of view the *constitutio* marks the end of one period and the beginning of another.

It symbolizes the death of the Roman state as founded on the *Senatus Populusque Romanus,* which was still the ideal of the enlightened monarchy. Everybody was now a Roman citizen, and this meant in plain fact that nobody was such any more. As soon as the Roman citizenship became a mere word and a mere title, it lost every shred of importance. To be a Roman citizen meant a good deal as late as the times of Trajan and Hadrian. The Roman citizens, even if no longer the masters and rulers of the world, still formed the higher class of the urban population, an important and influential group socially, if not legally and politically. For Aristides the Roman citizens were still the highest and the best. Bestowed on all and sundry, Roman citizenship was a mere name: it only meant that the bearer of the title lived in one of the cities of the Empire. Later it became synonymous with an inhabitant of the Roman Empire in general, that is, a subject of the Roman emperor, who was now the embodiment of the state. With the rise of the imperial power Roman citizenship had lost its political value. Now it lost its social importance as well. It is difficult to tell whether Caracalla realized this when he promulgated his measure.[38]

The principal facts concerning the political and military events of the short reign of Caracalla need not be retold here. After some military successes in Germany and a short stay on the Danube frontier, he started a great expedition against the Parthians. It was evident that the Parthian question had not been settled by Septimius, and that the agony of the Parthian dynasty afforded Caracalla a good opportunity of achieving lasting results. We are ill informed about the expedition. Before anything of importance was achieved, the emperor was killed by one of his officers at the instigation of the prefect of the guard M. Opellius Macrinus. A short civil war followed the proclamation of Macrinus as emperor. Indulged by Caracalla and full of confidence in the benevolence of the family of the Severi, the army was not very willing to recognize an outsider as emperor of Rome and to keep its allegiance to him. As soon as a rival appeared in the person of a nephew of Caracalla, the young Bassianus, surnamed Elagabal (or Heliogabalus), chief priest of the god of Emesa, the soldiers preferred him to the unknown Macrinus, whose first steps and whose dealings with the senate had not been welcome to the soldiers.[39] Elagabal's rule was brief and full of incident. His religious experiments are well known. His attempt to achieve by them the creation of a world-religion acceptable to everybody and a consecration of the power of the emperor, as the representative of God on earth, was abortive. But he nevertheless succeeded in arousing the indignation of all honest Romans throughout the Empire and of some soldiers. The result was that two of the three clever Syrian women who had arranged his accession and ruled in his name, Julia Maesa and Julia Mammaea, replaced him against the will of his mother Julia Soaemias by another Bassianus, his cousin, who received the name of Severus Alexander.[40]

We need not dwell on the political aspect of the rule of Alexander. Dio and, to a certain extent, Herodian, praised it as an almost complete return to the principles of the enlightened monarchy. There may be some truth in this view so far as the intentions of the emperor were concerned. But he was not free. Behind him stood the army, the compact mass of soldiers who had been spoilt by the Severi and accustomed to methods of policy which excluded any real return to the principles of the Antonines. The soldiers would not allow a genuine recovery of power by men of the senatorial and of the old equestrian classes. They would not suffer a strong and resolute man to be the adviser of the young emperor. They were sharply opposed to any reduction of their pay and to the restoration of discipline. Under such conditions a revival of the principles of the Antonines was a dream. The emperor was a tool and a slave in the hands of the soldiers, and had to bow to bitter necessity.[41] As an instrument of protection for the Empire, the army became more and more unfit. The war against the new rulers of the East, the Persians, was an almost total failure and, if it did not end in disaster, it was because the Persians had their own affairs to settle. Grave troubles on the German frontier led to an attempt on the part of the emperor to purchase peace, and this resulted in his treacherous murder by his own soldiers.[42]

The foundations of the new structure of the state laid by Septimius and consolidated by Caracalla were destined to abide. Externally there was no change. As before, the emperor ruled as the highest magistrate of the Roman people; as before, the supreme power in the state lay with the senate, which handed it over to the emperor; as before, the senatorial and equestrian classes furnished the officers required to command the army and to administer the Empire; as before, the cities were ruled by the city aristocracy; and the army continued to be an army of Roman citizens. But in fact there was nothing left of the ancient state save the names, and any attempt to change the conditions was bound to miscarry. The soldiers were determined to remain the rulers and the masters of the Empire and not to permit the upper classes, still strong and numerous, to rise again to power. The Roman Empire faced one of the greatest crises in its history.

The reigns of Caracalla, Elagabal, and Alexander were times of great misery for the Empire. There were indeed no long and bloody civil wars, with the sole exception of the war between Macrinus and Elagabal, which was local in character and did not affect the Empire as a whole. But the organism of the Empire was exhausted to such an extent that it was unable to stand the strain of the serious external wars which threatened it. The extravagances of an Elagabal, to which the ruin of the imperial finances is ascribed by our sources, had but a minor importance. The main problem was how to meet the expense of the great campaigns which had to be undertaken unless the Roman Empire were to become the prey of continual invasions by the Iranians in the East and by the Iranians and the Germans in the North-east. A great effort was needed, and needed at once. This was generally understood throughout the Empire: it was realized by Septimius Severus, by Caracalla, and by Alexander Severus, who in this matter were all the exponents of public opinion. Caracalla's dream of becoming a new Alexander the Great and of carrying out the great Macedonian's purpose of amalgamating into one nation and one state the two warlike and cultured races of the world, the Iranians and the Romans, in order to stem the tide of barbarism which threatened to engulf both the Roman Empire and the Parthian kingdom, was no quixotic ideal, though it shows the romantic aspirations of those difficult times. It would be childish, however, to regard this romantic dream as a great political idea which the crime of Macrinus prevented from being realized. But the dream, which was in such striking contrast with the bitter reality, is characteristic of the conditions of the decaying Empire. The fact that the second Bassianus assumed the name of Alexander indicates that the Utopian idea originated in the boundless fantasy of the

Syrian empresses and was inherited from them by the two Bassiani.

The experiments of Caracalla and Alexander failed, not only because of the degenerate condition and the steadily decaying discipline of the army, but first and foremost because the Roman Empire was too poor to bear the enormous cost of such a colossal enterprise. To carry out their abortive schemes, Caracalla and Alexander alike plundered the Empire. It appeared very quickly that the confiscations of Commodus and Septimius Severus and the enormous increase of the financial resources of the state at the expense of private fortunes had resulted not in the enrichment, but in the impoverishment, of the Empire. Pertinax, who was himself an *agrarius mergus*, a land-grabber, was obliged, in order to stop the increase of waste land, to have recourse to a general measure which was to a certain extent a repetition on a larger scale of the measures of Hadrian. He launched an appeal to the population of the Empire to occupy the waste land and so become landowners instead of tenants. So far as we know, the appeal was fruitless.[43] Alexander was forced to resort to the method, which had been introduced by M. Aurelius, of ensuring the cultivation of waste land by settling on it captives brought from beyond the frontier. We hear incidentally, too, that in his time there was an acute shortage of cattle in Italy and that the meat-markets of Rome remained empty.[44]

It is thus plain that there was in the organism of the Roman state a deep-rooted trouble which could not be cured by palliative measures. The state was constantly draining the capital which was the life-blood of the Empire: all the measures designed to restore the public finances were ·merely repeated attempts to extract more money, whether they were of a violent nature, like the confiscations of Septimius, or whether they were more systematic but not less harmful. The wars of Septimius Severus and those of Caracalla and Alexander were based, like the wars of Trajan and M. Aurelius, though to a much greater extent, on the system of liturgies, on the compulsory work of the *humiliores* and the compulsory responsibility of the *honestiores*. The great Roman Empire was on the brink of returning to natural economy, because it could not acquire the requisite quantity of good and stable currency. The attempt made by Caracalla to revitalize the currency by the introduction of his famous

Antoninianus—a modern term for the coin he introduced, worth two or one and a half denarii—failed. Prices rose, good money was hidden, currency deteriorated still more. Whatever explanation of this be preferred, it is certain that it destroyed the faith of the population in the imperial currency.* The state itself recognized this fact and relied more and more on exactions in kind. In the documents of this period we constantly meet with mentions of such exactions. In Egypt the system of compulsory deliveries seems to reach an unparalleled regularity both in the time of Caracalla and in that of Alexander. Even earlier, in the reign of Septimius, the liturgies became so onerous that one benevolent citizen of Oxyrhynchus asked for permission to establish a special foundation to make the burden more tolerable for the population of some villages of the nome. The system of requisitions was rampant: corn, hides, wood for spears, and draught animals had to be delivered, and payment for them was irregular and indeed problematic.[45]

The same conditions prevailed in Asia Minor and Syria. Many inscriptions testify to the heavy burden of the παραπομπή or *prosecutio*, that is, the responsibility for a methodical transportation both of troops and of supplies (*annona*) for the army. The greatest sufferers were the members of the municipal aristocracy. Another plague was the exactions of the imperial and municipal officials, who on their journeys requisitioned quarters and food from the inhabitants of the cities and of the villages alike. The quartering of soldiers was a real disaster: the population of Syria regarded an occupation by the Parthians as a relief in comparison with a prolonged stay of Roman troops. The time was past when rich men of the province would voluntarily undertake such burdens. If provincials still occasionally mention the performance of liturgies in inscriptions, they do it to show that they discharged their duties and that the duties were not light. The type of the rich benefactor of a city is disappearing, and in his place we find members of the city *bourgeoisie* overburdened with liturgies but still able to bear them.[46]

Towards the lower, as towards the upper classes, the policy of Caracalla and of Alexander was the same as that of Septimius. They were favoured by imperial legislation: one of the most striking instances is the legislation about the schools, which has

* See the bibliography in note 32.

been spoken of in the fourth chapter.* The third century represents the climax in the spread of primary education all over the
Empire. To the schools in the small villages of Egypt, which were
probably connected with the temples, we owe most of the recently
discovered literary papyri, which served as text-books for the
pupils; and it is in the third century, in the time of Alexander
Severus, that we first hear of village elementary schoolmasters
as a class. In the third book of his *Opiniones* Ulpian speaks of these
schoolmasters and emphasizes the fact that they were to be
found both in the cities and in the villages.[47]

Still more important are the facts concerning the relations
between the emperor and the rural population, especially the
tenants of the imperial estates. There is no question that after
the time of M. Aurelius and Commodus the army definitely
became an army of peasants, drawn from the villages in the city
territories and on the imperial estates. These villages now became
the main support of the imperial power, the cities being hostile
to the military monarchy established by Septimius and his successors. The emperors realized this and acted accordingly. We
have already emphasized the confidence in, and allegiance to,
Septimius and his house—the legal successors of the divine
Antonines—which were displayed by the rural population in
general and by the tenants of the imperial estates in particular;
and we have shown that these feelings were based on the sincere
efforts of Septimius to improve the position of this class as a
whole, and especially that of the imperial tenants, by raising
them to the status of landowners on the largest possible scale, in
full accord with the policy of Hadrian.

Another aspect of the same policy is revealed by some inscriptions found in the region of Sitifis and brilliantly elucidated
by J. Carcopino in two special articles.[48] The region of Sitifis
was, or became under Septimius, one vast imperial estate, cultivated by tenants who were partly romanized people, partly
natives. When in the time of Septimius (A.D. 202) this region was
deprived of its garrison of Roman troops, probably under the
pressure of urgent military necessities, there began a process of
concentrating the agricultural population in fortified *castella*, a
process certainly started and encouraged by the emperors. This
concentration meant a considerable urbanization of the life of

* See especially note 33.

the peasants, and it involved also a certain, probably a large, amount of self-government in the shape of a half-municipal organization with a strong military flavour, which was natural, since the concentration had a purely military purpose. The tenants of these fortified villages certainly received many privileges besides the quasi-municipal organization. They became, like the free villages of Thrace and Syria, the main foundation of the army of the Severi, and consequently they were probably treated, from the economic point of view, as landowners and not as tenants. Without doubt their numbers were increased by the establishment from time to time of new settlers who received land in the imperial *defensiones* and *definitiones** and who, though in name tenants (*coloni*), were practically small militarized landowners.[49] The policy of Septimius was carried on both by Caracalla and by Alexander. The numbers of the *castella* constantly increased, their earth-walls were replaced by stone fortifications, public buildings were constructed, and so on. Numerous inscriptions attest this policy of the Severi in the borderlands of Africa. As has been said, it implied a special protection of this section of the population, the last warlike elements which survived in the Empire. The phenomenon was too conspicuous to be passed over even by our literary sources, and the Latin biography of Alexander expressly mentions his efforts in this connexion.[50] Familiar with the bravery of the peasants of the Danube and of the Syrian lands, and greatly admiring their military abilities and their physical strength, the Severi endeavoured to create a similar class in Africa. Thus, in the period of the Severi the borderlands became the most prosperous part of the African provinces, and they showed their gratitude to the emperors by according them most enthusiastic praise in inscriptions.

The movement was not confined to Africa. A similar policy of urbanizing and militarizing peasants, whether landowners or tenants, may be traced in the Thracian lands. The activity of Septimius in this direction is attested by a document discovered there, the charter of a newly founded ἐμπόριον called Pizus, to which is appended as a supplement a list of new settlers and a letter from the governor of the province. Pizus was only one of many similar foundations of Septimius: the fact is explicitly stated by the governor in his letter. Such ἐμπόρια were

* See above, p. 323.

neither cities nor villages. In speaking of them the governor calls them also σταθμοί, *stationes*, which emphasizes their military character. They were not, however, settlements of soldiers or veterans. The settlers were drawn from neighbouring villages. I am convinced therefore that the ἐμπόρια of Thrace corresponded to the *castella* of Africa and had the same purpose: they were fortified market-places for the population of an agricultural district, and militarized agricultural colonies. It is to be noted that they had no real self-government, though they bore the external aspect of a city. Their presidents were τόπαρχοι βουλευταί, *praefecti*, appointed by the governor, and granted by him a certain amount of jurisdiction. The best parallel to these prefects is thus afforded by the *praefecti* of the early Roman colonies and the *municipia* of Italy.[51]

In the provinces of Upper Germany a like policy was pursued by Septimius and by his successors. Here, however, it was not a matter of turning peasants into soldiers but rather of turning soldiers into tillers of the soil. It is well known that in Germany in the time of Septimius the new *castella*, which protected the frontier, were manned either by Roman soldiers or by native *numeri*. To these *castella* a piece of land was assigned, which was cultivated by the soldiers of the garrison, each of them receiving a plot and paying for it out of his income to a special farmer-general, who also was a soldier. We may compare such *castella* with the *burgi* of the Danube frontier. Furthermore, behind the line of these fortified *castella*, with their population of peasant-soldiers, some *vici* and some *canabae* of former forts were developed into towns, and were regarded and treated as seminaries of soldiers for the army of occupation in Germany.[52]

Finally, we may mention in this connexion the so-called κολωνίαι of Roman veterans in Egypt. These settlements, which are found in various parts of Egypt, especially in the Fayyûm, date from at least the early second century A.D. They consisted of ex-soldiers who acquired parcels of land from the government at a nominal price, and formed in the territory of a given village a body of Roman citizens with a certain measure of self-government (on the pattern of the old πολιτεύματα of the Ptolemaic period). Under Septimius many new κολωνίαι of the same type were founded. The settlers received their plots of ground as a grant from the emperor, and enjoyed probably a larger amount of self-government. The institution was shortlived, being probably merged in the development of municipal life in Egypt which followed the grant of Roman citizenship to all the privileged classes of the population in A.D. 212. It cannot be denied, however, that Septimius, while reviving the policy of the early emperors by repeatedly sending out colonies of Roman veterans to various existing cities (like Tyre and Samaria in Phoenicia and Palestine, Uchi Majus and Vaga in Africa), endeavoured by the foundation of new κολωνίαι in Egypt to achieve the same result as in Africa, Thrace, and Germany. In these groups of new settlers distributed all over Egypt he endeavoured to create so many seminaries for his army and so many nuclei of staunch supporters of his régime, the régime of a dynastic military absolutism.[53]

I think it very likely that the Severi followed the same policy in Syria also. Since the Flavians and Trajan this region had acquired great importance as a centre of recruitment for the Roman army, which it provided with valuable *cohortes*, *alae*, and *numeri* of mounted archers, which were used on a large scale throughout the Empire, including Syria itself. Part of them came from the ranks of the veterans stationed in Syria and possessing Roman citizenship. Probably in the age of the Severi a new step was taken. The emperors, not satisfied with the regions comprised within the province of Syria, were anxious to make greater use, for military purposes, of the half-independent territories bordering on Syria. The most important and the most civilized of these was the territory of Palmyra. Perhaps from the time of Trajan onwards, and certainly from that of Hadrian, Palmyra, though autonomous, none the less had been occupied by a Roman garrison. In return she furnished the Roman army with troops, armed and dressed in the national style, the Palmyrene *numeri*, who were stationed outside the territory of Palmyra and outside Syria. Under the Severi regular units of the Roman army, the 'Palmyrene' *cohortes*, undoubtedly recruited on Palmyrene territory, appear side by side with these *numeri*. In the time of Alexander Severus one of these cohorts, the twentieth, provided the garrison for Dura. The Palmyrene cohorts were certainly part of the Roman army, and were commanded by Roman officers. At the same time the emperors granted Palmyra and the cities of the Euphrates, for example, Dura, and of the new province of Mesopotamia, all of which were important military centres, the title of Roman colonies. These facts can be explained thus. The Severi by giving Palmyra the title of *colonia* and by recruiting at Palmyra cohorts instead of *numeri*, without destroying the autonomy of the city intended to convey to the city that from now on it was part of the Roman Empire. The Severi were completely confident that she would adapt herself to her new role. They permitted the cohorts levied at Palmyra to be employed in the neighbourhood of the city, almost in its own territory, and continually increased the number of these cohorts, which thus became a real Palmyrene army, although they officially belonged to the Roman army in Syria. By these means the Severi thought that they could create a bulwark of the Roman Empire on the Parthian, later the Sassanid, frontier; could effect, in fact, what they had effected in Africa, on the Rhine and on the Danube, but by using different means. It was a dangerous gamble, and the confidence placed by the Severi in the loyalty of the Palmyrenes was exaggerated. Some decades later Palmyra, as is well known, detached itself from the Roman Empire. It is likely that the nucleus of the army of Odenathus and Zenobia was formed by the Palmyrene cohorts which were stationed near Palmyra. Unfortunately we know nothing for certain about the composition of the armies of Odenathus and Zenobia.[54]

In the sixth chapter we have pointed out how closely the creation of *castella* and the urbanization of villages and *canabae* throughout the Empire was connected with the spread in these half-cities, half-villages, of the associations of young men, the *collegia iuvenum*, which in fact were special associations for training and educating future soldiers and officers in the proper spirit. Is it not striking to see these associations, created by Augustus and intended as a foundation of the military structure of the Empire and of the new form of government, dying out in Italy and in the urbanized provinces and migrating to the borderlands of the Empire? This migration is the characteristic feature of the time. The only classes on which the Empire may now rely are the half-civilized dwellers in the lands which stood in direct contact with the countries of Rome's enemies.[55] Caracalla, with his predilection for the blond Germans and the warlike Persians, instinctively felt the bitter truth that the Roman Empire had

now to trust to these elements. There was no other salvation.[56]
It is likely that in the new African *castella* similar associations of
young men were developing.[57] These facts fall into line with the
practice, which has been mentioned above, of settling barbarians
within the Roman Empire.

The policy of the Severi, as I have tried to describe it in the
preceding pages, for the various parts of the Empire, had the
most serious consequences. It led to the at least partial transformation of the Roman army into a body of sedentary peasants,
and this proved just as unsatisfactory as it had been in Ptolemaic
Egypt. In undertaking this reform the Severi may have been
prompted principally by two considerations: in the first place by
faith in the military, political, and social capabilities of a peasant
army. A belief of this kind would not be very surprising: it is to
be found, for example, also in Alexander I and in Nicholas I of
Russia, who were led by it to try the same experiment. The
second consideration was that of the state of finances; serious
monetary difficulties may have suggested to the Severi the idea
of paying troops at least in part in real values, by giving them
land to cultivate. This latter consideration may in its turn have
been the cause of the legal recognition granted to soldiers' marriages. It cannot, however, be determined whether or not these
financial motives were decisive, since we do not know whether
or not the soldiers thus tied to the soil received less pay than the
others.[58]

Despite repeated efforts to improve the position of the lower
classes, both they and the upper classes, with a few exceptions,
were very badly off, especially from the economic point of view.
The heavier the pressure of the state on the upper classes, the
more intolerable became the condition of the lower. Law and
administration were helpless to improve the situation. Alexander
Severus, or rather the members of his cabinet, the great jurists of
this period, saw the critical state of the Empire and tried to save
it. Some taxes, such as the heavy tax of crown gold (*aurum
coronarium*), which had been ruthlessly exacted by Elagabal, were
partially abolished. Some remissions and privileges were granted
to the upper classes and to the cities. But such measures did not
produce the desired result.[59] Alexander had recourse again and
again to the system of compulsory work and liturgies. In this
sense must be interpreted certain new devices which he intro-

duced in connexion with the associations of merchants and of industrialists. To attract the merchants especially to the capital, he abolished the tax which was paid by them and replaced it by a new tax levied on the artisan producers, and at the same time he himself imported from Egypt masses of industrial products, which were paid to him as a tax in kind by the peasants and the artisans of that country (*anabolicum*). The measure shows how low the productivity of the local industries in Rome was, and how seriously sea commerce and trade in general were overburdened by taxes and compulsory service. On the other hand, he increased the number of those associations which were supposed to be useful to the state and from which compulsory service was demanded. We have seen that the corporations of shipowners and of merchants had been subjected to a large measure of state control as early as the beginning of the second century. We have mentioned the privileges which they received from various emperors as compensation for their compulsory service, and have emphasized the importance of the steps taken by Commodus to organize the African commercial fleet on the model of that of Alexandria. Certain other corporations, probably of the city of Rome, were now organized on the same principle. They were not only recognized as legal associations but as corporations in the service of the state. Our sources mention the dealers in wine and in lupines, and the shoemakers, but they give these names *exempli gratia* and indicate that Alexander's measure had a more general character, and affected almost all the corporations. In any case the tendency of the reform is evident: without compulsion and, in the last resort, without state control the government was helpless. The army devoured the resources of the state, and the population, even of Rome, was more and more deprived of the necessary supplies. In this terrible plight the state resorted to compulsion.[60] As has already been pointed out, the increasing deterioration of the currency was a symptom of the bankruptcy of the state. This may have been inevitable, but it destroyed the credit of the state and contributed in part to the uncertainty in economic life and the convulsive fluctuation in prices.*

The result of the situation of the Empire and of the policy pursued by the emperors was what might have been expected.

* See note 32.

The slight improvement which had been felt in the last years of Septimius vanished. During the reign of Alexander robbers again infested both land and sea. Extraordinary measures were taken, especially against the pirates. The Roman Empire seems to have reverted to the deplorable condition of the first century B.C., when piracy made commerce practically impossible. No wonder that writers like Cyprian, describing the conditions of the Empire at the end of this period, are full of pessimism, and speak of the complete exhaustion of the forces alike of nature and of mankind. We may say that Cyprian was a Christian, and that he was making the colours of his picture darker than the reality, but we can hardly believe that he could speak in this tone, unless the picture which he painted was perfectly familiar to his audience.[61]

X

THE MILITARY ANARCHY

THE period between the death of Alexander Severus and the accession of Diocletian is one of the darkest in the history of the Roman Empire. So long as we have the work of Herodian and the fragments of Cassius Dio, which enable us to check the statements of the Latin biographies of the emperors, and so long as these biographies are based on a more or less reliable and well-informed source, we are able not only to trace the general lines of the political development of the Empire, but also, with the help of the juridical sources and the documentary material, to recognize the main features of its social and economic evolution. With Alexander Severus the history of Cassius Dio ends, and his continuator, known to us by some fragments, is not so well informed as the great senator of the time of the Severi. Herodian narrates the history down to Maximinus and the Gordians, giving in his seventh book a splendid picture of these troubled years, and stops there. For the following period we have nothing similar to these substantial and well-composed accounts.

The only literary sources for the second half of the third century, the period of the great social revolution and the thorough reconstruction of the Empire, are on the one hand the Latin biographies of the emperors, the second part of the so-called *Scriptores Historiae Augustae* (with a gap from 244 to 253, covering the reigns of the Philippi, the Decii, Hostilianus, Gallus, Volusianus, Aemilianus, and the beginning of the rule of the Valeriani), and on the other hand the short and meagre Breviaries and Chronicles, both Latin and Greek. The Latin compendious histories are those of Eutropius, Aurelius Victor, and the author of the so-called *Epitome de Caesaribus*, wrongly ascribed to Aurelius Victor. All of these date from the second half of the fourth century. With the exception of the fragments of the well-known sophist Eunapios, which belong to the second half of the fourth century, the Greek chronicles of Zosimos, Zonaras, Kedrenos, Synkellos, and others, date from the Byzantine period. The information transmitted by the Latin short histories and by the Greek chronicles is exceedingly meagre, and contains nothing about social and economic conditions. It is not history but the barest skeleton of history. The only source, therefore, which has the external appearance of real history is the collection of Latin biographies of the emperors.[1]

Thus, the question of the value of this source becomes much more important for the period which we are now considering than for that which precedes, and at the same time the means of estimating its value are much more limited than before. It is not surprising to find that there is a wide divergence of opinion, not so much about the value of this source, as about the origin of the biographies, and the time when the collection was put together. Thanks to the careful investigations of Enmann and Dessau, and of many other scholars, we now know that the chief source both of the Latin biographies and of the Latin epitomists was a general history of the Roman emperors in the form probably of short biographies, in the style of Suetonius, compiled about the time of Diocletian. A similar source, but written in Greek, was used by the Greek chroniclers, and probably this source was occasionally consulted by the author, or the authors, of the Latin lives of the emperors of the third century. Thus far there is a fair measure of agreement among modern scholars. Much more difficult is the question of the character of the supposed biographical history of the Emperors. Was this source as dry and jejune as Eutropius, Aurelius Victor, and the *Epitome*? Did it contain only a skeleton, though a reliable skeleton, of the history of the third century, or was it more like the work of Suetonius, giving some account of the personal history of the emperors and some facts besides their internecine wars and episodes of their foreign wars? In other words, did the author, or the authors, of the Latin biographies draw all his, or their, trustworthy information from a source which was very similar in form to the Latin epitomists, while the rest is fabrication, or did he, or they, take more material from this source than the epitomists and from time to time fill up gaps by consulting other works, partly Greek, partly Latin, including perhaps some documents?

If we are to believe what is said on the matter by the author, or the authors, of the Latin biographies, we must assume that the second alternative is correct; and the assumption might find support in the fact that the writer of the biographies of the

Maximins, of Pupienus and Balbinus, and of the Gordians, used as his main source the work of Herodian. But a careful analysis of the documents inserted in the biographies has shown with complete certainty that all of them—letters, *senatus consulta*, speeches of the emperors and of other persons, and so forth—are forgeries. Furthermore, almost all the authors whom the biographies quote are, with very few exceptions, completely unknown, and there is therefore a presumption in favour of regarding these quotations as mere fictions. All this shatters our confidence in the trustworthiness of the information given by the biographies, where it does not coincide with the statements of the Latin epitomists and of the Greek chroniclers. These are of course suspicions, but they are suspicions based on a careful verification of the few data which can be verified and on general probability. The Latin biographies, therefore, cannot be used for the reconstruction of more than an outline of the history of the Empire after the time of the Gordians. We may accept their meagre information about social and economic life only when it is supported by some trustworthy testimony found either in the epitomists or in the juridical sources or in documents such as papyri and inscriptions, or on coins. As a matter of fact, such coincidences very rarely occur, not only because of the character of our source but also because of the nature of the supplementary material: apart from coins, which supply very scanty evidence, our documentary material is not abundant, as is natural in a period of troubles and endless wars and revolutions, and what we do possess very rarely refers to facts and events that interested the ancient historians and find a place in their narrative.

There is another question concerning the *Scriptores Historiae Augustae* not less important than the question of the sources of the biographies. It is the problem of the time when the biographies were compiled and published, and of the personality of their authors or author. According to the narratives themselves, the cross-references, and the titles, they were compiled by six authors, three of them—Aelius Capitolinus, Trebellius Pollio, and Flavius Vopiscus Syracusius—being responsible for the lives of the emperors after Alexander. According to their own statements, and to the dedications of the biographies to the emperors, they all lived in the time of Diocletian and Constantine. If this were so and if the authors were really contemporaries of the events of the third century, poorly informed as they were, we might expect to find in their accounts, especially in those relating to the end of the century, some reliable information not taken from literary sources and, what is more important, in reading them we might expect to breathe the atmosphere of the period. In that case we might disbelieve in the authenticity of the documents and speeches, we might find the narratives excessively rhetorical (and conventionally rhetorical too), we might brand the sayings and utterances of the emperors as fabrications, but we should have to assume that in reading these third-century biographies we are listening to men who were born and bred in the turmoil of the civil wars and that, indifferent writers as they were, they have expressed the feelings and the mood of the age.

Until quite recent times, nobody questioned the fact that the six authors in question were contemporaries of Diocletian and Constantine. The last of them, Vopiscus, for instance, gives a detailed account of some episodes in his own life and of some men whom he knew, an account which agrees with perfectly trustworthy documents. It was this observation and others of a similar kind that led even quite modern and eminent scholars of the critical school who carefully investigated the problem, like H. Peter, Ch. Lecrivain, G. de Sanctis, G. Tropea, Th. Mommsen, and Diehl—not to speak of many younger English and American scholars—still to believe in the joint authorship of the six men, in their reality, and in the exactness of their statements about the time to which they belonged, and this in spite of many strong arguments adduced by a group of scholars who regard the whole set of names and alleged dates as mere fiction. It was H. Dessau who first pointed out, in two articles, that the biographies could not have been written in the time of Diocletian and Constantine, that they breathe the atmosphere of the later and very different age of Theodosius, and that therefore all the names of the authors and all the information about their lives are an impudent forgery, the real author being a contemporary of Theodosius and a member of the circle of the Symmachi and the Nicomachi. Dessau's attack made a powerful impression. O. Seeck at once supported his theory by many new arguments, fixing, however, the date of the forgery still later (fifth century), and A. von Domaszewski took up the question himself and induced numbers of his pupils to devote their efforts to a thorough investigation of the problem, with the main object of proving the general correctness of Dessau's hypothesis. This Domaszewski has supported, though he differs from Dessau in regard to the date of the forgery, which he would assign to the time of Gregory of Tours (end of the sixth century). The views of Dessau have been accepted by other distinguished historians like O. Hirschfeld and E. Kornemann, and propagated by their pupils.

The arguments produced by Dessau and his followers, though not conclusive, were beyond doubt exceedingly strong and convincing, and they induced many eminent scholars of the opposite school to compromise. Thus, Mommsen was ready to recognize that the stock of imperial biographies of the time of Diocletian and Constantine was taken over and revised by a contemporary of Theodosius, who was responsible for most of the fabrications and for the flavour of the Theodosian epoch which the biographies have. Mommsen's compromise, though accepted by some scholars, has been rejected by the majority of German historians, who still insist on the full acceptance of Dessau's main thesis. The crucial question of the reasons which induced the forger to compile his work has lately been answered by Geffcken and Hohl, who suggest that his purpose was to present to the readers of the time the history of the Roman emperors from the point of view of the last pagans, such as Symmachus, advocating tolerance towards the pagans and introducing some veiled attacks on Christianity. Another aim may have been to glorify the senate and give a survey of imperial history from the senatorial point of view. Certainly this point of view is very strongly expressed in the biographies, where a sharp line is drawn between the good emperors, those who favoured the senate, and the bad ones, the enlightened monarchs and the military tyrants, who promoted the principle of adoption and that of hereditary succession. Taking this standpoint, the circle of Symmachus did not dare to speak in its own name, but pretended to publish a work written by authors of a comparatively remote past, of the time preceding the victory of Christianity and the final establishment of Oriental despotism. The prevalent ignorance of that period was so profound that nobody would think of verifying the forger's statements and proving that the series of imperial biographies was a mere fraud.

A modification of this last theory regarding the aims of the author or authors has been proposed by Norman H. Baynes, who relates the biographies to the age of Julian and to the leading ideas of his government, thereby placing the book nearer to the end of the civil wars than do Dessau and his followers. Although it must be admitted that the biographies are at one and the same time both popular and tendentious works, yet neither Baynes nor Dessau and his followers succeeded in adducing cogent proof for the dates proposed by them. The problem concerning the date of composition of the biographies is thus still unsolved.

Such, in its main outlines, is the theory held by the supporters of Dessau. There are still many points which need elucidation, and the task of showing the thoroughness of the work of the forger, or forgers, in piling up a heap of inventions on a bare historical sketch is far from accomplished. However, if the kernel of the theory is sound—and it is very difficult to prove that it is not—the *Scriptores Historiae Augustae* must be almost completely eliminated from the series of trustworthy sources for the life of the third century. They represent the point of view of the late fourth century, and this point of view was in many respects different from that of men who lived in the third. An age of stagnation and of resignation cannot thoroughly understand the mood of a revolutionary period, and can hardly give a true picture of it, especially if the writer's purpose is to establish particular ideas cherished by leading men of his own time. We must, therefore, exercise great caution in using the material supplied by the *Historia Augusta*. If a statement is not corroborated by other and better sources, the right course is to disregard it and to refrain from building any conclusion upon it at all.[2]

Thus, in dealing with the time after Alexander Severus, we are justified in making full use of Herodian, who is specially well informed on the conditions of the time of the Maximins and the Gordians; we may use (as will be shown later) the contemporary speech 'To the emperor' of a rhetor or sophist of the third century; we must restore the historical outlines with the aid of the epitomists and chroniclers and the documentary material furnished by coins, inscriptions, and papyri. As all these sources, except the inscriptions and the papyri, give very little information on the social and economic evolution, our reconstruction must rest as far as possible on the documents. Though our material is scanty and fragmentary, the task in itself is in no way hopeless. Some parts of the Roman Empire have recently yielded abundant and valuable information, which has never been used to restore the main outlines of the picture as a whole.

Before endeavouring to recover the main features of the social and economic development of the Empire after the death of Alexander, and prior to the accession of Diocletian, it will be well to give a short sketch of the political events of this troubled period, a survey of the internal and external wars which ravaged the Empire.[3] After the treacherous murder of Alexander (A.D. 235) the soldiers proclaimed as emperor one of their leaders, a man of low origin, a Thracian peasant who was an officer of no very high rank, but a brave, able, and strong soldier, who knew the army and the mood and aspirations of the common soldiers, C. Julius Verus Maximinus.

His brief rule was an unbroken period of external war and civil strife. Maximinus probably never asked to be recognized by the senate, and he never appeared in Rome. He was a real soldiers' emperor. A good general and a man whom the army obeyed, he gained some important successes on the Rhine and Danube frontiers (A.D. 236), but he succumbed to a strong resistance, offered chiefly in Italy but also in Africa, to the principles on which his rule was based (A.D. 238). Of these we shall speak later. In Africa an old senator, at the time governor of the province of Africa Proconsularis, M. Antonius Gordianus, was proclaimed emperor and was supported by the upper classes of the population. He and his son perished in the struggle against the regular army of Africa, which was led by Capelianus, the legate of Numidia. After their death the senate, which had recognized Gordian as the rightful ruler, elected in his place two senators, M. Clodius Pupienus Maximus and D. Caelius Calvinus Balbinus, who with the help of a special committee of twenty senators organized the defence of Italy against Maximinus. Maximinus, contrary to his own expectation and that of everybody else, was unable to obtain access to Italy, and perished under the walls of Aquileia, which barred his way to Rome.

About a month after his death the praetorian guard got rid of the two senatorial emperors by a *coup de main*, and recognized as sole emperor the grandson of the elder Gordian, the young boy

Description of Plate LXXV

1. MARBLE BUST OF MAXIMINUS. Capitoline Museum, Rome. Helbig–Amelung, *Führer*, i, p. 454, no. 62; A. Hekler, *Die Bildnisskunst der Griechen und Römer*, pl. CCXCVI, *a*; H. Stuart Jones, *A Catalogue of the Ancient Sculptures*, &c. *The Sculptures of the Museo Capitolino* (1912), p. 207, no. 62, pl. XLIX.

2, *a*. SILVER *ANTONINIANUS* OF PUPIENUS. Cohen, v, p. 14, no. 3.
Obv. IMP. CAES. PVPIENVS MAXIMVS AVG. Bust of Pupienus to r. with radiate crown. Rev. CARITAS MVTVA AVGG. Two clasped hands.

b. SILVER *ANTONINIANUS* OF BALBINUS. Cohen, v, p. 11, no. 17.
Obv. IMP. CAES. D. CAEL. BALBINVS AVG. Bust of Balbinus to r. with radiate crown. Rev. FIDES MVTVA AVGG. Two clasped hands.

c. *AUREUS* OF GORDIAN III. Cohen, v, pp. 47 f., no. 265 (A.D. 242).
Obv. IMP. GORDIANVS PIVS FEL. AVG. Bust of Gordian to r. with laurel crown. Rev. P. M. TR. P. V COS. II P. P. Gordian in military dress standing to r. with a spear and a globe.

d. *AUREUS* OF PHILIP I. Cohen, v, p. 111, no. 164.
Obv. IMP. PHILIPPVS AVG. Bust of Philip I to r. with laurel crown. Rev. ROMAE AETERNAE. Roma seated to l. holding Victory and spear, with her shield beside her.

e. *AUREUS* OF DECIUS. Cohen, v, p. 190, no. 48.
Obv. IMP. C. M. Q. TRAIANVS DECIVS AVG. Bust of Decius to r. with laurel crown. Rev. GENIVS EXERC(itus) ILLVRICIANI. Genius of the Illyrian army, wearing mural crown, naked, standing to l., with a *patera* and a *cornucopiae*. To the r. a military standard.

These coins (all in the British Museum) show the features of the various emperors of the period of military anarchy, which differ strikingly from the aristocratic heads of the Antonines, and (on the reverse) some of the chief emblems of their short reigns. Pupienus and Balbinus emphasize their mutual affection and loyalty, Gordian his military exploits, Philip the eternity of Rome, which had just celebrated her millenary, Decius his relations with the Illyrian army. The selection of coins and the casts for this plate and pl. LXXVI I owe to the kindness of Mr. H. Mattingly of the British Museum.

MAXIMINUS

a. PUPIENUS   *b.* BALBINUS
c. GORDIAN III   *e.* DECIUS   *d.* PHILIP I

LXXV. THE EMPERORS OF THE EARLY THIRD CENTURY

GALLIENUS

a. CLAUDIUS GOTHICUS   b. AURELIANUS
c. TACITUS   d. PROBUS
e. CARUS   f. CARINUS

LXXVI. THE EMPERORS OF THE LATE THIRD CENTURY

Description of Plate LXXVI

1. MARBLE BUST OF GALLIENUS. Museo delle Terme, Rome. Helbig–Amelung, *Führer*, ii, p. 178, no. 1414; A. Hekler, *Die Bildnisskunst der Griechen und Römer*, pl. CCXCVIII; R. Delbrück, *Antike Porträts*, pl. LIII.

2, *a*. *AUREUS* OF CLAUDIUS GOTHICUS. Variant of Cohen, vi, p. 145, no. 161.
Obv. IMP. C. CLAVDIVS AVG. Bust of Claudius to r. with laurel crown. Rev. MARTI PACIF(ero). Mars the peace-bringer running to l., with a laurel-branch and a spear.

b. *AUREUS* OF AURELIAN. Cohen, vi, p. 175, no. 1.
Obv. IMP. CL. DOM. AVRELIANVS P. F. AVG. Bust of Aurelian to r. with cuirass and radiate crown. Rev. ADVENTVS AVG(usti). Aurelian in military dress on horseback to l., with a spear in his left hand, makes the gesture of greeting with his right.

c. *AUREUS* OF TACITUS. Cohen, vi, p. 233, no. 122.
Obv. IMP. C. M. CL. TACITVS AVG. Bust of Tacitus to r. with laurel crown. Rev. ROMAE AETERNAE. Roma seated to l. with spear, globe, and shield.

d. *AUREUS* OF PROBUS. Unpublished.
Obv. IMP. C. M. AVR. PROBVS AVG. Bust of Probus to r. with laurel crown. Rev. P. M. TR. P. V COS. IIII P. P. ANT(iochiae). Probus riding to l. in a triumphal chariot, with palm-branch and sceptre.

e. *AUREUS* OF CARUS. Cohen, vi, p. 360, no. 86.
Obv. DEO ET DOMINO CARO AVG. Bust of Carus to r. with laurel crown. Rev. VICTORIA AVG. Victory standing to l. on a globe, with wreath and palm-branch.

f. *AUREUS* OF CARINUS. Cohen, vi, p. 397, no. 131.
Obv. IMP. CARINVS P. F. AVG. Bust of Carinus to r. with laurel crown and cuirass. Rev. VENERI VICTRICI. Venus standing to l., holding a Victory and a globe.

All these coins are in the British Museum.

This series of coins serves the same purpose as that on pl. LXXV. Note that the type of Philip is repeated by Tacitus: both of them endeavoured to revive the constitutional monarchy of the Antonines. Note also the military character of the coins of Claudius, Aurelian, Probus, Carus, and Carinus. Claudius emphasizes the fact that his ultimate aim was an enduring peace.

Gordian III, whom Pupienus and Balbinus were forced to associate with themselves in the Empire before the final catastrophe (A.D. 238). The reign of Gordian III was as disturbed as those of his predecessors. The situation both in the North-east and in the East became extremely grave. In the North-east the Goths, who in the second half of the second century had formed a strong state in the prairies of South Russia, invaded the Danube provinces, in alliance with some Iranian tribes and the Thracian Carpi; in the East the first kings of Persia, Ardashir and Shapur I, took possession of the Syrian dominions of Rome. The peril was averted on the Danube by the strong hand of Tullius Menophilus, the defender of Aquileia; in the East by the emperor himself, who under the guidance of his father-in-law, C. Furius Sabinius Aquila Timesitheus, defeated the Persians and liberated Syria. When the army was ready to enter the enemy's land, Timesitheus died, and Gordian III was killed by the soldiers in a bread-riot, caused by lack of supplies, probably at the instigation of Timesitheus' successor in the command of the imperial guard, the son of an Arabian sheikh of the Hauran, M. Julius Philippus (A.D. 244).[4]

Philip hastened to put an end to the Persian war by making large concessions to the Persians and evacuating Mesopotamia, and hurried to Rome. On his way thither he defeated some German tribes and almost annihilated the Thracian Carpi on the Danube. While in Rome, he celebrated the thousandth anniversary of the foundation of the city (A.D. 248); but meanwhile the legions of the Danube revolted, after a disastrous invasion of Moesia by a handful of Goths, and proclaimed one of their noncommissioned officers, Ti. Claudius Marinus Pacatianus, emperor. Another usurper, Iotapianus, arose in the East. Philip dispatched against Pacatianus his best general, C. Messius Quintus Trajanus Decius, a native of Pannonia; Marinus and Iotapianus were killed by their own troops but Decius was forced by his soldiers, who threatened to kill him in case of refusal, to become emperor and to march against Philip, whom he defeated near Verona (A.D. 249).[5] Installed as sole ruler, Decius conferred great benefits on the empire by repairing the roads in all the provinces, improving the administration, and restoring discipline in the army. But times were difficult. Beside the work of restoration, Decius' first duty was to defend the Danube provinces. At the end of A.D. 250

or beginning of 251 he hastened to the Danube to beat off a new and formidable invasion of the Goths. They passed through Moesia and overran Thrace, besieged Philippopolis, the capital of Thrace, and defeated the emperor, who went to the rescue of the rich and prosperous city. Through the treason of Priscus, the commander of the garrison of Philippopolis, who aspired to ascend the throne with the help of the foe, Philippopolis was taken and plundered by the Goths. On their way back, they were intercepted by Decius with a new army, but he was defeated again and fell in the battle together with his son (A.D. 251).[6] The Goths returned safely to their own land, laden with booty. The Roman troops proclaimed C. Vibius Trebonianus Gallus emperor. Under the pressure of a disastrous plague, which broke out in the Danube provinces, Gallus bought peace from the barbarians and left for Rome. After his departure the governor of Lower Moesia, M. Aemilius Aemilianus, a native of Mauretania, succeeded in defeating the Goths and was proclaimed emperor by his troops (A.D. 253). In the struggle between the two emperors, Gallus and Aemilianus, the former was killed in a battle near Interamna in Italy, and the latter was murdered by his own soldiers at Spoletium. P. Licinius Valerianus, the governor of Raetia, who marched from the Rhine to Italy to aid Gallus, was proclaimed emperor and was recognized by the senate.

As soon as Valerian reached Rome he associated with himself in the imperial power his son P. Licinius Egnatius Gallienus.[7] The situation of the Empire on the Rhine, the Danube, and the Persian frontier was almost desperate. The Franks and the Alemanni broke through the Rhine frontier and invaded Gaul. Though the Goths were stopped on the Danube frontier by some able generals of the Danubian armies, they and the Borani used the resources of the rich kingdom of Bosporus, which became their vassal, to assemble a fleet of Greek ships, crossed the Black Sea to the shores of the Caucasus and to Trapezus (Trebizond), and afterwards coasted along to the rich province of Bithynia. No Roman navy worth mention existed at the time and piracy reigned on the seas, so that the Goths had every opportunity to carry out their daring raid successfully. Still worse was the situation in the East. The Persians invaded Syria and threatened Asia Minor, where they intended to effect a junction with the Goths. Valerian moved against them, recaptured Antioch and prevented the conjunction with the Goths, and, although his army suffered from the plague, entered Mesopotamia. Near Edessa he was utterly defeated and captured by the enemy (A.D. 259). Asia Minor and Syria were rescued, the former by Callistus, a Roman general, who drove the Persians out, and the latter by the praetorian prefect Macrianus and by Ballista, one of his generals. The sheikh of Palmyra, Odenathus, who was recognized as a Roman general by Valerian, again defeated the invaders when they tried to cross the Euphrates on their way back to Persia.

At this critical moment the Roman Empire was saved by the energy and persistency of Gallienus. He was forced to evacuate a part of Gaul, but he succeeded with his German and British soldiers in saving Italy from a German invasion, and in defeating on the Danube two usurpers, Ingenuus and Regalianus, who had been proclaimed emperors one after the other (A.D. 258). On the other hand, the provinces seem to have realized the great danger which threatened them and took their salvation into their own hands. In Gaul the troops and the people of the province proclaimed as their emperor M. Cassianius Latinius Postumus, the *restitutor Galliarum* and the founder of the *imperium Galliarum*, and succeeded in driving the Germans out of the province (A.D. 259). On the Euphrates similar success was achieved by Odenathus of Palmyra against the Persians and two Roman pretenders. In fact, after the capture of Valerianus, his praetorian prefect Macrianus had assumed the purple with his two sons Macrianus and Quietus (A.D. 260). The two Macriani marched towards Europe, while Quietus remained in Syria. The first two were defeated and put to death by Aureolus, the general of Gallienus, and Odenathus put an end to the rule of Quietus and his adjutant Ballista. Odenathus was recognized by Gallienus, and ruled over Syria and part of Asia Minor until he was killed in A.D. 266/7, when he was succeeded by his son Vaballathus, in whose name the government was carried on by his mother, Queen Zenobia.[8]

Gallienus meanwhile was still engaged in fighting the pretenders and the barbarians, and in endeavouring to defend Africa (against the Moorish king Faraxen), Gaul, Italy, and the Danube lands. Despite some successes against Postumus, he was finally forced to recognize him as *de facto* ruler of the Gallic provinces, being handicapped by a great inroad of the Goths by land and sea and by repeated attempts of pretenders to seize the throne. Plague also raged in the Empire, and a severe earthquake destroyed many flourishing cities of Asia Minor (A.D. 262). Further, insubordination of the troops caused grave damage: Byzantium, for example, was plundered by her own garrison. A renewed invasion of the Goths laid waste the Balkan lands and Greece a second time, and when these devastations were at their worst, one of Gallienus' best generals, Aureolus, to whom he had entrusted the command of a strong force of cavalry regiments destined to fight Postumus, turned his arms against his master. Gallienus rushed from the Danube to Italy, defeated and besieged Aureolus in Milan, but was killed by his own soldiers, who proclaimed as emperor M. Aurelius Claudius, an officer of the Danubian army and an Illyrian by birth (A.D. 268). With Claudius begins a series of Roman emperors, mostly brave generals of the Roman army, Danubians by origin, who endeavoured to restore the unity of the Empire and to prevent it from being entirely flooded by its Northern and Eastern neighbours. They had, of course, like their predecessors, to face the insubordination and the treacherous attitude of the army. Like their predecessors, too, almost all of them fell victims to military plots, and, during the reign of each, usurpers sprang up in different parts of the Empire. But, while such behaviour seemed to have become a kind of tradition or firmly rooted habit of the army, we find signs of a sound reaction against the dismemberment of the Empire and the licentious conduct of the soldiers. From the purely military point of view the troops, and not the troops of the Danube regions only, appear to be better trained and show a better fighting spirit. As a whole, they were true to their allegiance to the emperors: the latter, indeed, were mostly the victims of treacherous conspiracies, but these conspiracies were the work of small groups in which the mass of the soldiers took no active part.

We must content ourselves with a very brief sketch of the complicated and dramatic history of the last thirty years of the third century. The rule of Claudius[9] was distinguished by exploits in Germany and on the Danube, where he finally crushed the forces of the Goths and stopped their advance towards Italy for more than a century. He fully deserves the surname of

Gothicus under which he is known to history. He had, however, no time to reunite with the Roman Empire the independent Gallic Empire, though it was in a state of internal dissolution, one emperor succeeding another in rapid succession after the death of Postumus (Ulpius Cornelius Laelianus, M. Aurelius Marius, M. Piavonius Victorinus). More prosperous and better consolidated was the eastern Empire of Palmyra under the rule of Zenobia and her young son Vaballathus who had added Egypt to their Empire. Gradually Zenobia formed the idea of creating an independent Eastern Roman Empire with an independent Augustus as its ruler.

In 270 Claudius perished on the Danube, a victim of the plague which again ravaged the ranks both of Romans and of barbarians. His brother M. Aurelius Claudius Quintillus was proclaimed emperor in the West and was recognized by the senate, but he was unable to maintain himself against L. Domitius Aurelianus, the ablest of the generals of Claudius, a Danubian peasant like Maximinus, and a soldier who had made a brilliant career for himself by personal merit.[10] The short reign of Aurelian was a time of extreme peril for the Roman Empire but also of brilliant triumphs for the Roman arms, comparable to those of Trajan and M. Aurelius. His first task was to defend Italy from a formidable invasion of German tribes, the Juthungi and the Alemanni. After some successes against the Juthungi in Raetia and against the Vandals in Pannonia, Aurelian had to face an overwhelming invasion of Italy by the joint forces of the Juthungi and Alemanni. Defeated by them near Milan, faced with a rebellion in Rome and in some of the provinces, threatened by a new invasion of the Goths, and confronted with a definite breach of allegiance by the Palmyrene Empire, Aurelian fortified the cities of Italy, including Rome, called the youth of Italy to arms, and finally succeeded in driving the barbarians from Italy and in re-establishing his authority both in Rome and in the provinces. After defeating the Goths, he marched against Queen Zenobia, and in a difficult campaign restored the supremacy of Rome in the East, reconquered Egypt, and captured both the city of Palmyra and the rulers of the Palmyrene Empire, in spite of the help sent them by the Persians. Returning to Europe, where he had to fight the Carpi on the lower Danube, he was suddenly recalled to the East by the outbreak of revolts in Palmyra and Alexandria, the latter headed by a wealthy Alexandrian merchant and industrial magnate named Firmus. Both rebellions were swiftly crushed, and it remained for Aurelian to complete the restoration of imperial unity by reducing the Gallic Empire to obedience. The task proved a comparatively easy one, as the last Gallic emperor, C. Pius Esuvius Tetricus, a Roman senator, betrayed his own army and at the critical moment passed over to the side of Aurelian. After a splendid triumph in Rome (A.D. 274) Aurelian left again for the provinces, to restore peace in Gaul and to prepare an expedition against the Persians. During these preparations he was killed by a band of conspirators near Perinthus in Thrace (A.D. 275).

The conspirators had no candidate of their own, and the troops referred the election of a new emperor to the senate. Apparently, even the army, accustomed as it was to create and depose emperors, was still convinced that the legitimacy of an emperor depended in the last instance on the senate. The senate elected its *princeps*, the first on the list of senators, M. Claudius Tacitus, the last ruler who endeavoured to restore the co-operation of emperor and senate on equal terms. Called by an invasion of the Goths to Asia Minor, Tacitus took the field against them and routed them, but in the hour of victory fell by the hand of conspirators.[11] The Eastern army elected M. Aurelius Probus in his stead; the West recognized as its emperor the brother of Tacitus, M. Annius Florianus. A new civil war broke out. Near Tarsus the rivals met, but Florianus was slain by his own troops before a battle took place. The rule of Probus shows the same features which marked all the reigns of the last half of the third century. Not only had he the heavy task of fighting the barbarians both in Syria and in Gaul, which was overrun in 276 by the Germans, who pitilessly destroyed the flourishing cities and the fertile fields of the province. He had also to combat rivals or usurpers, Bonosus and Proculus in Gaul, Saturninus in Syria. While preparing for an expedition against the Persians, he was killed in A.D. 282 by his own soldiers at Sirmium, his birthplace.[12] His successor was M. Aurelius Carus, another Danubian,[13] whose main exploit was a successful expedition against the Persians while his son Carinus ruled the West. During the Persian expedition Carus died, and his second son Numerianus was assassinated in Asia Minor on his return journey from the East by his father-in-law Arrius Aper, who hoped to succeed to the throne. Aper, however, was not elected emperor. The officers of the army proclaimed C. Aurelius Valerius Diocletianus, and he was at once recognized by the East. In the civil war which followed between Carinus and Diocletianus, Carinus was defeated and slain, and Diocletianus remained sole emperor.[14] Contrary to all expectations, Diocletian was able to maintain his position as emperor unopposed and unchallenged for the whole of his reign. He was no worse and no better than his predecessors, and if he succeeded in the task in which they had failed, it was because the time was ripe and the measure of suffering was full. The Roman Empire bitterly needed peace and was ready to accept it from the emperor at any price.

Before attacking the difficult task of analysing and explaining the great social and political revolution which we have outlined, a revolution which took more than fifty years to exhaust itself, we must examine the policy which was followed by the Roman emperors during this crisis. Even a superficial reader of the sources which refer to this troubled period may easily recognize in all the measures taken by the emperors, and particularly in the daily practice of their administration, the leading principles which had been once and for all laid down by the Severi and which were partly based on precedents set in the period of the enlightened monarchy. Most of the emperors after Alexander were faithful disciples of Septimius, no less faithful than the members of his own house. From time to time we notice a strong reaction against that policy, desperate attempts to get back to the glorious and blessed times of the Antonines, but in fact these attempts caused additional bloodshed and resulted in a still more devoted allegiance on the part of succeeding emperors to the main principles of the policy of Septimius.

Of these we have already spoken, and we have explained their origin, but it may be helpful to summarize them briefly. From the political point of view, Septimius began a systematic militarization of the government, which had been completely bureaucratized by his predecessors. A militarized bureaucracy was the watchword, and at the head of this bureaucracy a monarch with autocratic power, hereditary in his family, his power being based on the allegiance of the army and the state officials and on the personal worship of the emperor. To militarize the bureaucracy was equivalent to barbarizing it, as the army now consisted almost wholly of peasants from the less civilized parts of the Empire and of the children of settled soldiers and veterans. To attain these objects—the militarization of the government and the security of the imperial power—the old upper classes were gradually eliminated from the commanding posts in the army and from the administrative posts in the provinces. They were replaced by a new military aristocracy. Like the emperors themselves, this aristocracy sprang from the ranks of the Roman army and, like the emperors, it was subject to perpetual change: new men constantly rose from the rank and file of the army to replace those who were advanced to equestrian offices and to a seat in the senate.

The system of administration conducted by this militarized bureaucracy was mainly dictated from above, and its character was a natural consequence of the utter instability of the imperial power. It might be defined as a system of permanent terrorism which from time to time assumed acute forms. The most important part in the administration was played by countless thousands of policemen of different denominations, all of them personal military agents of the emperor. Their duty was to watch the people closely both in the cities and in the country, and to arrest those who were considered dangerous to the emperor. They were probably employed also to quell any troubles and strikes that might arise from the heavy pressure of the government on the population in the matter of taxation and compulsory work, and to use physical compulsion against those who failed to pay their taxes or to discharge the public burdens to which they were liable.

A salient feature of this system of organized terrorism was the further development of the principle of compulsion in all dealings of the government with the population, particularly in the sphere of taxation and forced labour. Along with taxation, but much more oppressive than it, and no less methodically applied, went the system of requisitioning foodstuffs, raw material, manufactured goods, money, ships, draught cattle and men for transport purposes, and so forth. A complement to the system of requisitions was the demand made on the people for personal work. On it was based, for instance, the method of recruiting and the arrangements for all emergency work required by the government. The same system of compulsion also reigned supreme in the organization of the economic activities of the state. The richer members of the community were made responsible for the cultivation of the land which belonged to the state, for the collection of taxes and of requisitioned goods and money, and for the transport of goods and men moved on behalf of the state. As the success of the system depended on its power easily to reach and keep within call everybody who was subject to compulsion, there was a natural tendency to bind every individual alike to his place of residence and to the particular group to which he belonged by birth and by profession. A tiller of the soil ought to remain in his domicile, and he ought to carry on his work without regard to his desires and inclinations. A soldier should remain in camp, and his children should take up military service as soon as they reached a certain age. A member of the municipal aristocracy should be at hand in his own city to carry out the obligations connected with his position. A shipowner was called upon to remain a member of his corporation as long as he was able to conduct his business. And so on.

There was nothing new in the system as such. But under the conditions of a permanent revolution it assumed unparalleled proportions and, being used not as a subsidiary, but as the main, resource of the government, it became a real plague which undermined and destroyed both the prosperity of the Empire and the spirit of its inhabitants. It no longer amounted to a series of emergency measures carried out in difficult times and dropped as soon as normal conditions were re-established, as had been the case under the Antonines and even under the Severi. When abnormal conditions ceased to be the exception and became the rule, measures which had been regarded as temporary emergency measures became the regular system of administration, the foundation of the whole fabric of government.

It is no easy task to sketch the development of this system in the troubled times of the military anarchy. Our information is scanty and little to be trusted. There is, however, one moment at the very beginning of this age when we have ample and good information, on which we can thoroughly rely—the period following the murder of Alexander and extending over the short reign of Maximinus and the reaction after his death, but not including the rule of Gordian III and the six years of Philip, on which we have almost no evidence. For the reign of Maximinus we have the substantial and dramatic report of a contemporary, Herodian, which is repeated by the Latin biographies of the emperors of the time, with some additions taken from another Greek historian of the third century, perhaps Dexippus. For the rule of Philip we have the speech entitled 'To the Emperor' (*Εἰς βασιλέα*), written by a contemporary, a man of good education and of comparatively high standing, who was well acquainted with the conditions of his time, especially in the East.[15] There may be many exaggerations in his characterization of Philip; there is undoubtedly a certain idealization of his character; but even this part of the speech is interesting and important, as it shows not so much the ideas and ideals of Philip as those of the educated classes of the time. In that respect the speech is comparable with those of Dio and with some of the orations of Aristides. On the other hand, its negative portion, which was intended to present a contrast to the endeavours of Philip and to the aspirations of the educated classes, gives a true and perfectly trustworthy picture of the conditions which prevailed in the Empire before Philip's accession. This picture agrees in all its details with that given by Herodian and Dexippus.

The question whether Maximinus, after the murder of Alexander, endeavoured to obtain confirmation of his power by the senate is not of great moment.[16] His activity after his accession and after his first victories over the Germans, when he was in urgent need of money and full of hatred towards the better classes of the population, is much more important as an indication of his real attitude and aspirations. His rule began and ended with a régime of terror. 'What was the use', says Herodian, 'of barbarians being annihilated'—an allusion to the military successes of Maximinus in Germany—'when greater slaughter took place in Rome itself and in the provinces?' We may believe or disbelieve in the statement that he ruthlessly exterminated all the higher officials of Alexander Severus, yet there is not a shadow of doubt that his reign opened with a relentless extermination of his enemies, which never ceased.[17] The fact is not only stated by Herodian and the Latin biographer but is also expressly affirmed in the speech *Εἰς βασιλέα*. In speaking of the accession of Philip, the author says: 'Those others began their rule'—he is alluding, of course, specially to Maximinus—'with wars and many murders, destroying numbers of the officials and bringing on a multitude of others irremediable calamities, so that many provincial cities were desolated, much land was laid waste, and many human beings perished.'[18] When the revolt against Maximinus in Africa was suppressed by his legate Capelianus with the help of the African army, wholesale murder raged all over the country. For evidence we have not only the assertions of Herodian and the Latin biographer but also a touching inscription found in Africa: 'Sacred to the memory of L. Aemilius Severinus called also Phillyrio, who lived for about sixty-six years and died for his love of the Romans, being captured by this (fellow) Capelianus. Victorinus, called also Verota (erected the monument), in memory of friendship and mindful of piety.'[19] The reader will note the opposition of the Romans to the barbarians led by Maximinus and Capelianus. We shall revert to this feature later.

Such a method of terrorism was not new: we have seen that the same method of propping up the imperial power was inherited by the military tyrants of the first century A.D. from the leaders in the civil wars of the first century B.C., and that it was revived by Domitian, and consistently carried out by Septimius and his house. The novelty was the unprecedented cruelty of the Thracian soldier and the fact that, once started, the system was pursued by the successors of Maximinus for more than fifty years. Another novel feature was that the victims of the terrorism were not only, as under Septimius, the higher classes of the imperial aristocracy and a section of the municipal aristocracy but the whole of the intellectual and *bourgeois* class. A corollary to this campaign of murder was, as in the time of Septimius, the replacing of the victims by men who, like the emperor himself, belonged to the lower classes, mostly common soldiers who had quite recently become members of the new equestrian class. Once more our sources are very explicit on the point.[20]

If Maximinus' terrorism was not confined to the imperial nobility, the chief reason was his pressing need of money, which led him to attack the *bourgeoisie* of the Empire in general, and especially that of the cities, and to rob them as if they belonged to a conquered foreign state instead of being Roman citizens, who mostly owed their citizenship to Caracalla's grant of a few years before. We may quote again the bitter but perfectly justified words of Herodian, himself a member of the persecuted class: 'Every day one could see the wealthiest men of yesterday beggars today. Such was the greed of the tyranny which used the pretext that it needed a constant supply of money to pay the soldiers.'

But [he proceeds] as long as these things were done to individuals and the calamity was confined to the classes nearest to the court, the people of the cities and of the provinces did not pay much attention to them. The misfortunes of the rich, or those whom they think to be well off, are not only disregarded by the masses, but sometimes even delight ill-disposed persons of the baser sort, because they are jealous of their betters who are favoured by fortune. But when Maximinus, after reducing most of the distinguished houses to penury, found that the spoils were few and paltry and by no means sufficient for his purposes, he attacked public property. All the money belonging to the cities that was collected for the victualling of the populace or for distribution among them, or was devoted to theatres or to religious festivals, he diverted to his own use; and the votive offerings set up in temples, the statues of the gods, the tributes to heroes, all the adornments of the public buildings, everything that served to beautify the cities, even the metal out of which money could be coined, all were melted down. This conduct greatly grieved the people of the cities. . . . Even the soldiers were displeased at what was done, for their relatives and kinsfolk reproached them, bearing them a grudge, since it was on their account that Maximinus did these things.[21]

It is impossible to say how far Herodian is right in generalizing about the conduct of Maximinus and speaking of a wholesale pillage of the cities throughout the Empire. The fact that after his reign we have very few of those inscriptions, so frequent in the second century and in the first years of the third, which mention large donations to the cities by rich citizens, and foundations established by them for the very purposes enumerated by Herodian, shows that the well-to-do class was alarmed by the confiscations of Maximinus, and that his methods were probably taken over by his successors. One cannot believe that the wealth accumulated by generations in the cities could disappear at once, but the ruthless procedure of Maximinus and of those who followed his example evidently dealt a mortal blow at the civic spirit of the higher classes, and induced them to conceal their wealth and appear as poor as possible. The system of liturgies, moreover, diverted everything that had formerly been spent by the cities, or by rich citizens on their behalf, into the treasury of the state and into the pockets of the financial agents of the government. Thus the accumulated capital of the Empire, which (as we have seen) was not very large, was severely assailed and never recovered from the deadly blows administered to it by Septimius Severus and by the emperors of the period of military anarchy.[22]

As in the time of Septimius, the system of terrorism was carried out by an army of spies and military police. In the speech Εἰς βασιλέα the orator says of Philip:

> About his justice let what I have said suffice. What benevolence can be greater and more conspicuous than this? All the provinces lay cowering and enslaved by fear, since many spies went round all the cities listening to what people were saying. It was impossible to think or speak freely, when all temperate and just liberty of speech was destroyed and every one trembled at his own shadow. From this fear he released the souls of all and set them free, restoring to them their liberty full and complete.

If we compare this statement with the inscriptions of the time of Septimius which have been quoted in the preceding chapter, we shall realize that there is no exaggeration in the orator's words and that the system of Maximinus was only the logical outcome of the practice first systematized by Hadrian, and afterwards developed in a masterly fashion by Septimius. We may be confident that in the period subsequent to Maximinus there was no change in this respect, except perhaps for the worse.[23]

But all the measures taken by the emperors to safeguard their power and to fill up their treasury were in vain. The same author emphasizes this point by insisting on the heavy burden of taxation and on the emptiness of the treasury.[24] The documents corroborate his statement and reveal to our eyes the working of the system and all its consequences. We shall speak of it later, in describing the economic situation of the Empire in the third century. Everybody saw, of course, that the root of the evil was the army, those bands of greedy and licentious soldiers who were the real masters of the emperors and who did not love work or fighting but enjoyed robbing and pillaging their own fellow citizens. The fact is definitely stated by the author of the speech

'To the Emperor', and both Herodian and the Latin biographer support him. He says once more of Philip:

> Many [of the previous emperors] were brave in face of the foe, but they were ruled or mastered by their own soldiers. He, however, easily mastered them and so reduced them to order that, although they received many vast sums and might have been troublesome and formidable if they did not receive as much or even more, their covetous desires were not whetted.[25]

Under the pressure of the system of terrorism, which had never before been carried out so systematically or so pitilessly as under Maximinus, tension became so high and the population, especially the population of the cities,[26] so exasperated that, despite the terror, revolts broke out one after another, first in Africa, and then in Italy. The events in Africa are generally misrepresented by modern scholars, who persist in speaking of a peasant revolt, in face of the clear statement of Herodian, our best source, who was misunderstood and mistranslated by the Latin biographer of Maximinus. What really happened was as follows. After the accession of Maximinus the procurator of Africa received a commission to extort money there for the emperor. That he was appointed governor of the province in place of the aged proconsul M. Antonius Gordianus, who retired to the city of Thysdrus, is a very attractive hypothesis of von Domaszewski.[27] The procurator, reluctantly helped by the quaestor and his assistants, proceeded in the usual ruthless manner and attacked particularly the rich landowners of the province, who formed, as we know, the most influential portion of the population of the African cities. Some of these men, described by Herodian as 'well-born and rich', being threatened with the prospect of losing their 'paternal and ancestral estates', organized a plot. To ensure its complete success, they ordered some of their οἰκέται (slaves or tenants, probably the former) to come from their estates to the city armed with axes and sticks. Such a crowd would not look suspicious to the procurator, who was accustomed to receive from the peasants complaints against their landlords. These men killed the procurator, and thereupon the leaders of the plot, a group of African landowners, whose numbers were increased by other men of the same class, proclaimed Gordian emperor.[28] Gordian, however, did not succeed in receiving any support from the African army. His forces were a motley crowd

Description of Plate LXXVII

1. MOSAIC. Found in the ruins of a rich house near El Djem. Museum of Bardo, Tunis. *Inv. d. mos.* ii. 1 (Tunisie), no. 64 (and a coloured plate); S. Reinach, *Rép. d. peint.*, p. 298, 1; [A. Merlin and L. Poinssot, *Guide du Musée Alaoui*, i (1950), pl. XVI].

The picture is arranged in three bands. The upper shows two young men, who have probably just left the villa, riding slowly in an olive grove; between them walks a servant on foot carrying a sort of fork (to act as a beater). In the second band another servant is seen, holding on a leash two tall hounds ('slouguis'), which he is ready to launch against a hare found by two dogs in a bush. In the third the hare is being pursued by the two horsemen and the hounds. Hunting scenes are as popular in Africa as agricultural scenes. See our pl. LXIII, 1, cf. *Inv. d. mos.* ii. 1 (Tunisie), no. 375 (Oudna); no. 601 (Carthage); ii. 2 (Algérie), no. 260 (Oued Atmenia), &c. Cf. our plates LXXIX, 1, and LXXX.

2. MOSAIC. Found in the ruins of the fine house of a certain Sorothus near Sousse (Hadrumetum). Museum of the 4th regiment of the Tirailleurs at Sousse. *Inv. d. mos.* ii. 1 (Tunisie), no. 126; S. Reinach, *Rép. d. peint.*, p. 360, 3. Cf. the companion mosaic in *Inv. d. mos.* ii. 1, no. 124.

The four corners of the mosaic are occupied by four medallions, in each of which are represented two race-horses near a palm tree, with their names written above and below them—Amor, Dominator, Adorandus, Crinitus, Ferox . . ., Pegasus. . . . The lunettes between the medallions are filled with the figure of a hare hiding in the bushes. The centre of the mosaic depicts a meadow at the foot of a range of mountains, from which a river flows. Watch-towers are seen in the mountains, trees and grazing goats on the slopes of the hills, and a herd of mares with colts grazing in the meadow. The horses are beautifully drawn. Cf. our pl. LXIII, 2.

1. AN AFRICAN HUNTING SCENE

2. HORSE-BREEDING IN AFRICA

LXXVII. AFRICA IN THE THIRD AND FOURTH CENTURIES

consisting of a few soldiers (perhaps the *cohors urbana* of Carthage) and a militia composed of men who dwelt in the cities, probably the members of the *curiae iuniorum*. They were attracted by Gordian's promise to banish all the spies and to restore the confiscated estates. These troops were badly equipped and badly organized. They had no weapons and used such as were to be found in the houses of the African *bourgeoisie*—swords, axes, and hunting javelins (the equipment of hunters may be seen on numerous African mosaics).[29] It is hardly probable that many peasants and tenants joined his standard. No wonder that his army was easily vanquished by the regular troops of Africa, led by the Numidian *legatus* Capelianus, his personal enemy. The victory was followed by an orgy of murder and confiscation. Capelianus first executed all the aristocracy of Carthage and confiscated both their private fortunes and the money belonging to the city and the temples. He then proceeded to do the same in the other cities, 'killing the prominent men, exiling the common citizens, and ordering the soldiers to burn and pillage the estates and the villages'.[30]

Meanwhile Gordian had been recognized at Rome, and the Romans, even after his death, persisted in their revolt against Maximinus. The revolt spread quickly all over Italy and assumed the same form as the revolt of Africa: it was a desperate fight of the city *bourgeoisie* against the soldiers and their leader, the soldier-emperor. The task of the senate was to organize and lead this *bourgeoisie*. Pupienus formed an army, which consisted of recruits collected in Rome and Italy and which was supplied and supported by the city population throughout the peninsula. That the emperors elected by the senate had the full support of the cities is proved by the behaviour of the people of Emona, who thoroughly devastated their own territory in order to deprive Maximinus of supplies, and by the valiant and heroic resistance of the city of Aquileia, which decided the fate of Maximinus. The victory of Pupienus and Balbinus was thus a temporary victory of the *bourgeoisie*.[31]

In fighting Maximinus, the cities fought against the new system of administration introduced by Septimius. Their enemy was the military monarchy, and their ideal was the enlightened monarchy of the Antonines based on the city *bourgeoisie*. This is shown by the fact that after the death of Maximinus no attempt was made to restore the Republican form of government. The election of Pupienus and Balbinus emphasized the senate's point of view that the emperor should be the best representative of the senatorial class, and not a nominee of the soldiers. The same view that the best man should be emperor permeates the speech in honour of Philip, of which we have frequently spoken. In its main ideas the speech reproduces the ideal picture of an emperor given in the speeches of Dio, and it is not an accident that the ἐγκώμιον of Philip bears the title Εἰς βασιλέα. By βασιλεύς the author meant, of course, the Stoic holder of supreme power. Another remarkable coincidence may be noted between this speech and the edict of Alexander Severus on the *aurum coronarium*, referred to in the preceding chapter, which contains a summary of the programme of the new ruler. In this edict Alexander Severus, or rather his advisers, laid stress on the point that the emperor intended to follow the examples of Trajan and Marcus and that his rule was to be based on σωφροσύνη, φιλανθρωπία, εὐεργεσία, κοσμιότης, and ἐγκράτεια, all the Stoic virtues.[32] Still more explicit is the speech Εἰς βασιλέα. It is addressed to the φιλάνθρωπος βασιλεύς. First and foremost, the 'King' is praised as a man who has received the imperial power, not like the others by opposing force to justice and not 'as though to save the regular sequence and succession in one family', but by the voice of public opinion, by the general consent of the population of the Roman Empire. The orator proceeds to set forth the main features of Philip's rule and praises the emperor as ὅσιος and εὐσεβής, as πρᾷος and ἄοκνος, and above all as σώφρων, δίκαιος, ἐγκρατής, and φιλάνθρωπος. In every field of activity his policy is the direct opposite of that of the military monarchy: he puts no trust in spies and informers, he does not rob his subjects, he is a good general, but, more than all, he is a successful politician and diplomat, and he is not the slave but the master of his soldiers. Is not this precisely the Stoic ideal of the just and wise king which was applied to Trajan by Dio? It does not matter that the picture hardly corresponded to the reality, that Philip was not a Trajan. The orator describes the emperor as he ought to be—the reader will note the attack on hereditary succession, despite the fact that Philip made his son an associate in power—and tries to bring into his ideal picture the actual traits of the emperor, so far as they were in keeping with it.

The reaction against the military monarchy was shortlived, and the endeavours of the city *bourgeoisie* to restore the enlightened monarchy of the Antonines were not crowned with success. About the rule of Gordian III very little is known, but it seems that the methods of his father-in-law Timesitheus were not different from those of the military monarchy.[33] Philip, and after him Decius, were ready to follow the path of Marcus. Philip, for instance, made some attempts to restore order and justice, to reorganize the army, to bring a certain relief to the cities, and to re-establish the authority of the senate. These feeble attempts were probably the cause of his unpopularity with the soldiers and of his downfall at their hands. The bitter reality was that the army was master of the situation, and that it was futile to dream of the restoration of a rule based on the peaceful elements of the population as represented by the city *bourgeoisie*. Philip's successors, and in some respects even Philip himself, understood the position and suited their action to it.[34]

The policy of the military monarchy thus triumphed over the last attempt of the city *bourgeoisie* to restore the supremacy of the intellectual and propertied classes in the Roman Empire. But the victory of the army was won at the expense of the safety and the prosperity of the Empire. The victors indulged in a real orgy and reduced the Empire to such a condition that its very existence was for a while imperilled. We have spoken of the formidable attacks of the barbarians and of the gradual disintegration of the Empire under their pressure. The chief cause of these repeated attacks was, of course, the internal strife which never ceased within the Empire. The victory of the army was the triumph of the militaristic and autocratic form of government. The truth was realized by those emperors who now, under the most difficult conditions, undertook the task of saving the state and restoring its unity at any cost. Little wonder if these emperors definitely gave up the dream of restoring the system of the Antonines and began to build up and to systematize the militaristic state, which was supported by the only real force in the Empire, the army. After the experiences of the reigns of Maximinus and his immediate successors, it became evident that the *bourgeoisie* was too weak and too ill organized to lend effective support to the central power.

The first to recognize this painful fact fully was the Emperor

Gallienus, himself a member of the senatorial aristocracy, a man with intellectual interests and of good education. He therefore began to build up the fabric of a militaristic state based on the army. Evidently this could not be done all at once: Gallienus and his successors were bound to make minor concessions to the opposite camp and introduce the new system gradually. But the day of compromise, when attempts might be made to maintain the chief institutions of the Antonine period, as had been done under the Severi, was past and gone. From this time onwards these institutions become more and more survivals, and the leading part is played by the militaristic methods initiated by Septimius. Even our scanty information permits us to see that Gallienus was the first to deduce the consequences involved in the policy of thoroughly militarizing the Roman bureaucracy. It was he who excluded the senatorial class definitively from the posts of command in the army and who took the decisive step of regularly appointing as governors of the provinces members of the equestrian class, that is to say, former soldiers. Himself of senatorial origin, Gallienus was forced to deal the death-blow to the aspirations of the upper classes and to build up the new military aristocracy of the Empire. After his time no member of the senatorial class had access to the post of commander of a legion or of a special detachment for military purposes (*vexillatio*). On the other hand, Gallienus avoided offending the senatorial class. Some imperial provinces still had senatorial governors, but it is doubtful if their authority extended over the equestrian commanders of the legions; and there is no doubt that elsewhere the military men reigned supreme, alike in the provinces and at the imperial court where the officers and the civil servants were considered more and more as a personal following of the emperor. The equestrian career was now in fact a purely military career, the civil posts playing but an insignificant part in the militarized administration of the Empire. Nor must we forget the close relations between the emperor and the common soldiers.[35]

The rule of Aurelian, short as it was, seems to have been another stage in the same process. The Empire presents to us the appearance of a beleaguered country, where a state of siege reigns and where all the cities are merely so many fortresses ready to repulse the attacks of the enemy. The same is true of

many villages and of the great villas, the centres of large private
estates. It is unfortunate that our evidence on the important
reign of Aurelian is so meagre and that the few data which we
have very often refer to subsidiary matters and to local measures
of very little importance. It is generally assumed that Aurelian
took the last and decisive step in transforming the imperial
power into a pure military autocracy, based on religious sanction. On this view the emperor is now king 'by the grace of God',
and God is the almighty Sun, the supreme god of the Illyrian
troops. There is no doubt that Sol was the god of Aurelian's
predilection, and that in his time the cult played a part in the
city of Rome similar to that played by the cult of the Syrian
Elagabal during the rule of his chief priest. It is certain also that
a kind of solar monotheism was supreme among the Danubian
troops before and after Aurelian.[36] How far, however, we may
rely upon the testimony of the continuator of Cassius Dio (Petrus
Patricius), who affirms that during a revolt of his troops Aurelian
laid emphasis on the fact that it was God, and not the troops,
that had given him the purple, is not at all clear. It is worth
noting that the same saying was attributed by Cassius Dio,
almost in the same circumstances, to M. Aurelius.[37] On the
other hand, apart from his devotion to Sol and to Hercules,[38] the
chief god of the Antonines, there is very little evidence about
Aurelian's theocratic tendencies. As a matter of fact, he was as
much an autocrat as many of his predecessors. A strong personality, conscious of what he thought to be his duty, he ruled
the reunited Empire with a firm hand, and ruled it alone. But
the same is true of many of his predecessors. As regards his attitude towards the senate and the city *bourgeoisie*, he adopted at
the beginning of his reign the policy of terrorism, which was
somewhat relaxed when after his victories over Zenobia he was
able temporarily to fill his treasury with the spoil of a part of the
Empire.

How far Aurelian developed the militarization of the imperial
administration, it is impossible to say. He was known as a good
administrator, as a man who maintained discipline both among
his military and civil officers and among his soldiers, but we can
hardly rely upon the details furnished in this connexion by his
Latin biographer. There are practically only two measures
wholly attributable to Aurelian which were real attempts to

concentrate the life of the state in the hands of the emperor and so constituted a further development of the policy pursued by his militaristic and autocratic predecessors. The first of these was the energetic action taken to regulate the utterly disorganized currency of the Empire, to unify it, and to eliminate almost all the local autonomous mints, including the senatorial mint at Rome. It was one of the last blows aimed at the autonomy of the cities of the Empire and at the prerogatives of the senate.

The second measure affected the associations which were in the service of the state. We have followed the consecutive stages of the evolution of these associations. The government steadily assumed increased control of the most important of them, especially those formed by the shipowners and by the wholesale merchants dealing in foodstuffs. Side by side with this *étatisation* went the nationalization of the associations of workmen engaged in special work connected with trade and transport in the large cities, and of such corporations as were connected with the security of life in the Italian and provincial cities, especially the local fire-brigades, known under the names of *collegia dendrophororum et centonariorum*. The men occupied in the imperial mints were also brought under full state control and quasi-military discipline. In each case there was involved not only strict control of the corporations by agents of the state, but also the attachment of individuals both to their profession and to their place of residence, and the tendency to transform the individual's obligation into a hereditary *munus*. We have seen how Alexander Severus extended government control to those associations which were important for ensuring a regular food-supply for the capital. Aurelian seems to have taken a decisive step in this connexion. The allusion is not to his temporary militarization of all the associations of Rome for the purpose of building the walls of the city. Similar measures may have been taken in other cities of the Empire which were transformed into fortified castles. I cannot think that this measure, which consisted in a careful registration of all the members of the building corporations and in giving to these corporations the title of *Aureliani* (with which may be compared the corresponding measures of Commodus in respect of the *navicularii*), was perpetuated, and that it should be considered as the beginning of a new era for all the corporations of the capital. On the other hand, it is highly probable that, in connexion with the reorganization of the system of victualling the city of Rome, Aurelian reorganized the associations which were connected with the food trade and the transport of foodstuffs and made them real agents of the state, departments of the administration, subject to stern discipline under the strict control of officers of the Roman garrison. For the corporations this meant that their members were now definitely bound to them, and that they themselves might be reinforced by the compulsory enrolment of new members. If such a measure was taken by Aurelian for the capital, which indeed is no more than an hypothesis, it was doubtless extended at least to the cities of Alexandria and Carthage; and in all probability the same system was gradually imposed by individual rescripts on local corporations all over the Empire.[39]

The strong and consistent rule of Aurelian—the great restorer of the Roman Empire, who once again, and more efficiently than before, centralized the government of the Empire in the city of Rome and appeared as the head of a thoroughly militarized bureaucracy, whose work was based on the compulsory participation of all groups of the population of the Empire in the work of administration and also in furnishing the Empire with the means of existence and with a supply of labour—ended quite surprisingly in what seemed to be a temporary restoration of senatorial rule over the Empire. Nor was this the result of a counter-revolution, as in the period after Maximinus, of a bitter struggle between the cities and the army; it was the consequence of a decision taken by the army. Instead of Aurelian, the senate elected as sole emperor Tacitus, the *princeps senatus*. It is evident that such a possibility implies the disappearance of the sharp antagonism, which had existed under Maximinus, between the senate, as representative of the city *bourgeoisie*, and the army. I can see only one explanation of this amazing event in the history of Rome, and that is that the senate no longer represented the city *bourgeoisie* of the Empire, and that, in regard to the vital questions of state life, there was now a perfect accord between the senate and the emperor, the commander-in-chief of the army. The senate felt as strongly as the emperors, what indeed was beginning to be felt in the ranks of the army, the urgent necessity of restoring order if the Empire and Roman civilization were to be saved; and consequently it gave up, so far at least as the majority of its members were concerned, the golden dream of restoring the conditions of the Antonine period. The old words and formulae were still used, for example, to glorify the new era which had dawned for the Empire with the rule of the first senator Tacitus, but they were mere words and did not imply any acts or change of policy.

The fact is that after the terrible years of Maximinus, and still more after the reforms of Gallienus, the senate no longer represented the same classes of the population as before. The members of the senate were now mostly former generals of the army, who had risen from the lowest grades of military service, and former military officers and officials of the imperial administration. Taken all together, it was a new aristocracy. It was also an aristocracy of great landowners. We shall see in the next chapter how on the ruins of the old landed aristocracy, imperial and municipal, there grew up a new class of landowners, mostly ex-soldiers and ex-officers. Alongside of them stood some of the ancient landowners, who had succeeded not only in emerging safe from the storms of the revolutionary period but even in increasing their estates by grabbing new land. The senate now represented these new men and no longer the enslaved and half-ruined city *bourgeoisie*. Such an aristocracy was, of course, vitally interested in the restoration of order. It was indifferent to the past glory of the cities, and was ready to support the emperor and the army in their endeavours to restore the Empire. It was willing to see the new social order which arose out of the convulsions of the revolutionary age stabilized and consolidated.[40]

The city *bourgeoisie* never recovered its position as the leading class of the Roman Empire. Its forces were broken by the savage executions and confiscations of Maximinus, and still more by the system of liturgies which completed the ruin begun by the acute spasms of terrorism. Whether, after Septimius and Maximinus, it was subjected to new attacks of the same kind we cannot say. There is no direct evidence that it was; but to complete its ruin no new attacks were needed. The general economic conditions of the Empire which will be described in the next chapter, the ruin of commerce and industry, the terrible barbarian invasions of the provinces—especially Gaul, the Danube provinces, Greece and Asia Minor, and to a certain extent Africa and even Egypt (by the Blemmyes)—which wiped out the flourishing centres of _bourgeois_ life, the constant draining of the wealth of this class by the various exactions of the government and by the liturgical system, all these factors are sufficient to explain the gradual decay of the cities and of their _bourgeoisie_. I do not assert that the class disappeared: that would be notoriously untrue. It is not so easy, even by violent means, to reduce to naught resources accumulated by centuries. The middle class survived, and there were still some rich citizens in the provincial and Italian cities. But it was a new _bourgeoisie_, of a mean and servile type, which practised subterfuges and various tricks to evade the obligations imposed by the state, a _bourgeoisie_ which based its prosperity on exploitation and speculation, but which nevertheless steadily went down. In the main it lived on the past and did not add very much to the resources accumulated by the past. We shall come back to this problem in the next chapter.

To sum up what has been said. In the period after Alexander Severus we see the emperors under the constant pressure of the army completing the process begun by Septimius. The real diarchy of the age of the enlightened monarchy, the diarchy of the central government and the self-government of the cities, came to an end. The senatorial and the ancient equestrian classes, which represented the municipal _bourgeoisie_, gradually lost their social and political privileges and disappeared. The municipal aristocracy was still employed by the government and kept some of its social privileges, but was enslaved: it no longer enjoyed initiative and freedom. Its members acted on behalf of the state in the capacity of servants, who closely resembled slaves. The new system of government was based on the emperor and on a new militarized bureaucracy, supported by the army. This was the last phase of the development and the main result of the long years of military anarchy.

Was this development the ideal of the emperors of the third century? We have tried to show that the policy was forced upon Septimius by his usurpation of power. His real ideal was the enlightened monarchy of the Antonines. As often as the emperors were allowed by circumstances to show their true colours, they appeared as supporters of the ancient ideology. With the exception of Maximinus, who cordially hated the old régime, they all proceeded reluctantly and without enthusiasm on the path which led through the development of a militarized bureaucracy to the destruction of the ancient foundations of the Roman Empire. It is evident that they did so because they were forced, and because they saw that the ideals of the second century became more and more a sorrowful anachronism. The master of the state was the army, and the emperors had to adjust themselves and the structure of the state to this bitter reality. The army showed with perfect clearness that it was not prepared to tolerate any preponderance of the old privileged classes, and the emperors had no alternative but to comply with its demand. By complying gradually and, as far as possible, without excesses, they showed a real understanding of the situation and a real patriotism. Their chief aim was, not the destruction of the ancient social structure and the establishment of a dictatorship of the army, but such an adjustment of the constitution and the administration of the Empire as would enable them, in the chaotic conditions which resulted from the reigning anarchy, to keep the fabric of the Roman state solid and intact, to protect it against dismemberment and against conquest by enemies on its borders.

Gradually there came to be one vital question, that of military defence. To solve this question, all available forces were concentrated on the one task of maintaining a strong army able to fight the enemy. This task required a subordination of the interests of the people to those of the state. The chaotic manner in which it was gradually accomplished was due to the military anarchy, which in the last resort was the result of the expiring efforts. of the city *bourgeoisie* to restore its vanishing supremacy. As soon as this struggle was over and the *bourgeoisie* was finally crushed, the emperors devoted themselves wholly to the task of restoring the unity and the strength of the state. The main obstacle in their path was no longer civil war between the *bourgeoisie* and the army but the army itself, which had little efficiency and was utterly licentious. The efforts of the emperors from Gallienus onwards were consequently devoted to the task of reforming the army so as to make it an efficient military instrument and, so far as possible, neutral as regards politics. It was the same task as had been accomplished by Augustus after the civil wars.

About the military reforms carried out by Gallienus and his successors we have scanty information, and what we have is little to be trusted. It is evident, however, that from the military point of view the main task was to create a strong mobile army, always ready to be moved to any threatened frontier and therefore concentrated as near as possible to the emperor's place of residence. This was the reason for the formation of a powerful army of cavalry under the direct command of the emperor or of the most trusted of his generals. It was also the reason for the decay of the provincial armies, which gradually became units of local militia. Hence, too, the creation of a special military aristocracy of *protectores*, bound to the person of the emperor by ties of purely personal allegiance. But this was only one part of the problem. The inefficiency of the army was due not only to its provincial character—to its decentralization—but also to its constitution: it had become an army of mobilized peasants, levied compulsorily and not drawn from the best elements of the Roman population. That constitution, as will be shown in the next chapter, accounted also for its rebellious spirit. To do away with this army of peasant proletarians was, therefore, another heavy task for the emperors of the third century, as it had been the main task of Augustus and of Vespasian. The solution was gradually found in the replacement of conscripts by mercenary soldiers. The masses of the population ceased to serve in the army. For actual service was substituted payment, the so-called *aurum tironicum*, and the money was used to hire good mercenaries. The successive stages of this cardinal process cannot be traced. We have seen that the working of the new system began as early as the Severi. Its final consequences were probably drawn by Gallienus and the great military leaders of the last half of the third century. The mercenary soldiers were carefully selected partly from among the least civilized tribes of the Empire—Illyrians, Thracians, Arabs, Moors, Britons—partly from among the Germans and the Sarmatians. The last were attracted by the prospect of good pay, or they were captives of war, who were enrolled in the Roman army individually or in groups. Conscription was as far as possible limited to the sons of the settled soldiers, many of whom were originally barbarian captives, and to the more warlike tribes of the Empire; and this material was used to man the frontier forts and to fill up the ranks of the provincial armies. Thus the emperors could rely upon the kernel of their troops, who felt that they stood and fell with them, being entirely foreign to the population; and they were free to use these troops even against the provincial armies in case of necessity.

The consolidation of the army was achieved by a radical and, indeed, desperate measure. The new Roman army was no longer a Roman army. It was an army of the Roman emperor or of the Roman state, but not an army of the Roman people, even in the broadest sense of the term. It was not a part of the Roman population and did not represent the interests of that population. It was a special caste, maintained at the expense of the population to fight foreign enemies. This caste now furnished the administrative personnel of the Empire, the greater portion of the ruling class, and the emperors themselves. Such an army could not be completely romanized and absorbed by the population. Its romanized elements, of course, merged in the mass of the population, but it was constantly being recruited by new elements coming from foreign lands, and so it remained a foreign military caste. Its upper layers now formed the ruling aristocracy of the Roman Empire. They in turn, as soon as they became romanized, were replaced by new-comers, the strongest and the ablest among the soldiers of the foreign military caste.[41]

XI

THE ROMAN EMPIRE DURING THE PERIOD OF MILITARY ANARCHY

WE possess no general description of the Roman Empire in the third century comparable to that of Aelius Aristides, but the misery of the times is frequently expressed by contemporaries and is reflected in all the documents of the period. Any one who reads attentively the speech Εἰς βασιλέα, which has been repeatedly quoted in the preceding chapter, and compares it with the speeches of Dio and Pliny on the one hand and of Aristides on the other, will realize the enormous difference not only in the actual conditions but also in the mood of the population as a whole and of the highest classes in particular. No less impressive is the tone of the Latin biographies of the third-century emperors, as contrasted with those of the second century. We may believe that these biographies were written in the fourth century and that they reflect the interests and the attitude of the upper classes of Theodosius' time, but we cannot deny that even the writer (or the writers) of the fourth century, with contemporary sources before them, would unconsciously reflect not only their own feelings but also those which they found in their sources.

One of the most striking utterances of a general character finds expression in the well-known dream of the Emperor Probus. I cannot help thinking that the rhetorical exclamations of the author of his biography were called forth by a genuine saying of the emperor, familiar to his contemporaries and famous in his time; and I am convinced that even the almost hysterical expressions used by the biographer himself adequately represent the general desires and aspirations of the third century, which did not differ greatly from those of the fourth, when conditions were somewhat more stable, but still uncertain and far from satisfactory. I therefore quote the relative passages from the life of Probus. Some sentences are trivial rhetoric, but some phrases (especially those which are here printed in italics) would be impossible in a picture of the golden age drawn, let us say, in the first or the second century A.D. 'Very soon, he [Probus] said, we shall not find soldiers necessary,' writes the biographer, and adds:

Is not this the same as to say: there shall be no Roman soldiers any more? The Roman state shall rule everywhere, shall possess all things, in full *security*. The world shall forge no arms, it shall not be compelled to supply the *annona*. Oxen shall be used for the plough, the horse shall be born in peace. There shall be no wars, no prisoners, everywhere shall be peace, everywhere the laws of Rome, everywhere our judges.

Summarized briefly, the desires of the biographer are for *securitas, pax, abundantia*, and *iustitia*. He becomes still more specific when he enlarges on the same theme.

The provincial shall not have to deliver the *annona*, no pay shall be disbursed to soldiers out of *compulsory gifts*, the Roman state shall possess *inexhaustible stores*, nothing shall be spent by the emperor, nothing shall be paid by the owner. It was indeed a golden age that he promised. There shall be no fortresses, nowhere shall be heard the military trumpet, there shall be no need to manufacture arms. That host of soldiers, *which now oppresses the state with civil wars*, shall cultivate the land, shall spend its time in studying, in practising the arts, in sailing the seas. Nor shall any one be slain in battle. Ye good gods, what sin did the Roman state commit against you so great that ye took away such an emperor?[1]

It is far from easy to give a picture of the general situation of the Empire in the third century, especially in the period after Alexander Severus, but some outstanding facts, which are sufficiently attested, illustrate its rapid economic ruin and the corresponding decline of civilization all over the Mediterranean world. One of the most striking phenomena in economic life was the rapid depreciation of the currency and a still more rapid increase in prices. The turning-point in the gradual depreciation of the silver currency and in the disappearance of gold coins from the market was the reign of Caracalla, who replaced the *denarius* by the *Antoninianus*. From his time onwards the purchasing power of the imperial coins steadily diminished. The *denarius*, which corresponded in the first century to about eightpence halfpenny, and fell just a little in the second, became towards the middle of the third century worth rather less than a farthing. This decline was not checked even by the reforms of Claudius II and Aurelian (who introduced the new currency, καινὸν νόμισμα, as it was called in Egypt), though these reformers definitely broke with the ancient practice of issuing real money, with a real commercial value corresponding to the quantity and purity of the metal, and introduced a new system of fiduciary money, which had almost no real value at all and was only accepted and circulated because of its recognition by the state.[2]

The depreciation of money was closely connected with the rise in the prices of products of prime necessity. No statistics are available, but the investigation of thousands of papyri shows clearly, at least for Egypt, how ruinous was the rise in prices in the third century and how unstable they were all through the century, and especially during the second half of it, as compared with the relatively stable prices of the second century. It is sufficient to refer the reader to the facts produced by F. Oertel, and to the valuable, though incomplete, lists of A. Segré. But one or two examples may be given here. The price of wheat in Egypt was surprisingly steady in the first and second centuries, especially in the second: it amounted to 7 or 8 drachmae for one *artaba*. In the difficult times at the end of the second century it was 17 to 18 drachmae, almost a famine price, and in the first half of the third it varied between 12 and 20 drachmae. The depreciation of money and the rise in prices continued, with the result that in the time of Diocletian one *artaba* cost 20 talents or 120,000 drachmae. Of course the coins were now fiduciary currency, but the leap is amazing. Unfortunately we have no data for the period between Gallienus and Diocletian. A similar variation occurred in the rate of wages. An adult male unskilled workman received in the first two centuries A.D. wages amounting to 4–6 obols a day, a sum which corresponded to 2–3 *artabae* of grain a month and was hardly sufficient to keep a family alive. We must bear in mind, however, that we can hardly presume the existence of a specific wage-earning class of labourers in Egypt. The majority of wage-earners worked occasionally and had another permanent occupation (most of them being peasants); moreover, women and children worked along with the men. The position of labour in industry is almost unknown. In the first half of the third century wages rose to about 2, 3, and 5 drachmae; but, as the price of grain almost doubled and steadily increased, the conditions of the workmen remained as bad as before. When fiduciary money came into vogue, wages became utterly unstable, and the whole question of labour conditions underwent a radical change.[3]

It is not surprising that under such conditions speculation of the wildest kind was one of the marked features of econonic life, especially speculation connected with exchange. There are two typical documents referring to the grave consequences of such speculation. In the time of Septimius Severus, about A.D. 209–11, the city of Mylasa in Caria decided to protect the bankers, who were its own concessionaires, against the clandestine exchange which was going on in the city and which caused serious loss not only to the bankers, who enjoyed a monopoly of exchange, but to the city as a whole. The concluding portion of the document shows that it was not only the loss of income to the city that induced the city council to take such strong measures. 'In very truth,' it says, 'the security of the city is shaken by the malice and villainy of a few people, who assail it and rob the community. Through them speculation in exchange has entered our market-place and prevents the city from securing a supply of the necessities of life, so that many of the citizens, and indeed the community as a whole, suffer from scarcity. And on this account also the regular payment of the taxes to the emperors is delayed.' The trouble, as we see, was not confined to the breaking of the monopoly. A wild speculation was going on, which probably consisted in the hoarding of good silver by profiteers, who secured it by paying a handsome rate of exchange. This is indicated in the *succlamatio* of the members of the council which is appended to the decree.[4] About half a century later (in A.D. 260) in Oxyrhynchus, during the short rule of Macrianus and Quietus, the tremendous depreciation of the currency led to a formal strike of the managers of the banks of exchange (κολλυβιστικαὶ τράπεζαι). They closed their doors and refused to accept and to exchange the imperial currency (τὸ θεῖον τῶν Σεβαστῶν νόμισμα). The administration resorted to compulsion and threats. The *strategus* issued an order to the bankers and to other money-changers 'to open their banks and to accept and exchange all coin except the absolutely spurious and counterfeit'. The trouble was not new, for the *strategus* refers to 'penalties already ordained for them in the past by his Highness the Prefect'. It is worthy of note that in several contracts of the same time the money specified is not the current imperial issues of billon but the old

Ptolemaic silver, masses of which probably lay hidden all over Egypt.[5]

The general insecurity of business life led to a fluctuation in the rate of interest, which in the second century had been as stable as prices. Our evidence on this point is, of course, scanty and does not permit wide conclusions of a general character. But if Billeter is right in thinking that the rate of interest showed an extensive decline in the period between Caracalla and Alexander Severus, the fact may be explained by the general uneasiness of business life and the stagnation caused by the prevailing insecurity. People refrained from borrowing money, and on the market there was more supply than demand.[6] What happened later we do not know. Our evidence for the second century and the first decades of the third is mostly confined to documents dealing with investments connected with donations and foundations, and we have seen that after the Severi a prodigious decline in the number of donations may safely be inferred even from our scanty information.[7] A phenomenon of the same type, due largely in all probability to the depreciation of currency and to the decay of initiative on the part of business men, was the almost complete cessation of commercial relations between India and the Roman Empire, especially Egypt. Practically no coins of the third century have been found in India. Business relations were not resumed till order and a stable gold currency had been re-established in the Byzantine period.[8]

This tremendous depression in business activity was due in large measure to the constant danger to which the most progressive and richest provinces were exposed. We have spoken of the repeated invasions of Gaul by the Germans and in particular of the catastrophe of A.D. 276, when the richest parts of Gaul were pillaged and devastated and most of the cities lost all power of recovery. The Danube lands repeatedly suffered similar devastation. We have mentioned the capture of the largest and richest cities by Goths and Sarmatians: the fate of Philippopolis was typical. The rich and flourishing province of Dacia was finally given up by Gallienus or Aurelian, and the population had to emigrate to the other Danubian provinces. Even in those cities which had not been pillaged and destroyed by the Goths we observe a rapid and disastrous decay. A good example is Panticapaeum in the Crimea, which was in vassalage to the Goths from the middle of the third century. The city was not destroyed, like Olbia, but the conditions of life, as revealed by excavation and by its coinage, changed quite suddenly: poverty and oppression now reigned supreme.[9] In Asia Minor and Syria things were no better. While the advance of the Persians was arrested by the dynasts of Palmyra, the cities of Asia Minor frequently suffered from Gothic invasions by sea, while native tribes, like the Isaurians, resumed their old habits of pillage and devastation: Probus indeed was forced to carry on a regular war against them.[10] In Syria the energy of the Palmyrenes helped the country only for a short time: the brilliant victories of Aurelian over Zenobia, which restored the unity of the Empire, undermined the vital forces of this flourishing city, which never recovered from his blows. Egypt was quieter but suffered also from repeated invasions of the Blemmyes, especially under Probus.[11] And, finally, the prosperous land of Africa experienced serious attacks at the hands of Libyan and Moorish tribes. The insurrection of 253, the invasion of the Bavares and of the Quinquegentanei with the help of Faraxen in 258–60, and the war with the Baquates and their king Nuffusis followed each on the heels of the other. Although it is not mentioned by our literary sources, the last was important enough to engage the attention of the Emperor Probus, who probably made important concessions to Nuffusis.[12] There is no doubt that the condition of Spain was equally bad. The only exception seems to have been Britain, where the third century appears to have been a time of peace and prosperity.[13]

Still more disastrous were the constant wars between the rival emperors. The real evil was not the loss of some thousands of lives in battle, a loss which could readily be made good, but the utter impossibility of establishing under such conditions any semblance of an orderly and legal administration. Every pretender, every emperor, needed first and foremost money, food, clothes, arms, and so forth for his army, and no one had either the time or the desire to act in a legal manner and confine himself to the regular income of the state. The policy of all the emperors, with a very few shortlived exceptions, was therefore more or less similar to that of Maximinus—compulsory levies of soldiers, compulsory contributions of money and foodstuffs, and compulsory labour. And not the least of evils was the utterly lawless behaviour of soldiers, officers, and officials, natural as it was in the circumstances. To the excesses of the soldiers even the poor and meagre literary sources which we possess make frequent allusion. The speech Εἰς βασιλέα and the reflections of the biographer of Probus, which have been quoted, will recur to the reader. In the biography of Aurelian there are other statements of the same type. The alleged punishment of the soldier who violated the wife of his host is frequently quoted. In a forged letter Aurelian enumerates the common crimes of the soldiery:

> If you want to be a tribune [he says], nay, if you want to remain alive, restrain the violence of the soldiers. Let none of them steal a chicken, nor take a sheep. Let no one carry off grapes, nor thresh the crops, nor exact olive-oil, salt, and wood. Let every one be content with his *annona*. Let them live on the spoil taken from the foe, and not on the tears of the provincials.

Such an utterance would have been impossible even for a writer of the fourth century, had he not found in his sources countless references to the licentious conduct of the troops, which in fact was as bad in the time of Theodosius as in that of Gallienus.[14] When we come to describe life in some of the provinces in the third century, we shall quote certain specific facts which show that the biographer of Aurelian was perfectly correct in his statements about the violence of the soldiers. Here we may lay stress on the fact that, though our information is limited to certain provinces, we are justified in extending it to other provinces. We have to remember that there was not a single portion of the Roman Empire, save Britain and Spain, that had not set up one or many pretenders and emperors who obtained recognition. That was by no means a privilege of the Danube lands: Syria, Asia Minor, Greece, Egypt, Gaul, and Africa all took an active part in creating Roman emperors.

Under the conditions of the 'state of siege', which was the permanent state of the Empire, the militarized bureaucracy, whether government or municipal officials, acted in the same way as the soldiers. The former were responsible with their lives to the emperor, the latter were threatened with degradation, ruin, and execution if they failed to carry out the orders of the imperial bureaucrats. Thus all classes of the population suffered heavily under the pressure of both foreign and internal wars. The robberies of the soldiers were not entirely due to greed. The impoverishment of the provinces and the bad organization of the supply and transport service often forced the soldiers to acts of violence merely to safeguard their own lives. The upper classes of the cities, who were responsible for the population of the city territories, did their best to save the remnant of their fortunes and oppressed the lower orders. The lower orders, indeed, were oppressed and robbed by everybody. Added to all were the frequent plagues, which were largely due to the disorganization of life in general, to poverty, to underfeeding, to unsanitary conditions in the cities, and the like. It is very probable that, influenced by the dreadful conditions of life, race-suicide became typical of the age. This was favoured by Roman legislation concerning the exposure of infants, and abortion.[15]

Small wonder if in such circumstances the salient social and economic feature of the period was depopulation. Plagues, invasions, civil and foreign wars decimated the peoples. Still more serious were the general insecurity of life and the constant oppression of its subjects by the state. Under the pressure of these conditions, which seemed to be permanent, people fled from their places of residence and preferred to the intolerable life of the cities and villages a life of adventure and robbery in woods and swamps.[16] The utter disorganization of the naval forces caused a revival of piracy, and the seas again became as unsafe as they had been in the first century B.C. In some places, such as Sicily (under Gallienus) and Gaul (the scene of the so-called Bagaudae revolts), the lower classes of the population organized formal rebellions, which were suppressed *manu militari*.[17] And finally we have every reason to believe that very few families either of the upper or of the lower classes cared to rear children. Depopulation, which in the early imperial period was confined to a few areas, like Greece and to a certain extent Italy, and was caused mostly by emigration to other parts of the Roman world, became now the outstanding feature of the life of the Empire.[18]

As a result of these conditions, the general productivity of the Empire constantly decreased. Larger and larger tracts of land ran to waste. Irrigation and drainage works were neglected, and this led not only to a constant reduction in the amount of land under cultivation, but perhaps also to the spread of malaria, which gradually became one of the most terrible scourges of mankind.[19] The exchange of goods became more and more

irregular, and the various parts of the Empire came increasingly
to depend on what they themselves produced. Hence the frequent occurrence of famines; hence, too, the decay of industry,
which worked more and more for a small local group of
consumers, whose demand was confined to the cheapest and
plainest products.[20] Naturally every home, large and small, endeavoured to become as self-supporting as possible, and home-
production flourished as it had never done before. No partial
measures could counter this progressive decay. Groups of war
captives were planted on the depopulated lands. Measures were
taken to make the cities responsible for waste land. Flight from
one's place of residence was regarded as a crime. It was all in
vain. The process of decline could not be arrested by such devices: the productivity of the Empire steadily fell, and the
government found itself forced to resort with increasing energy
to violence and compulsion.[21]

Such in broad outline was the general situation of the Empire.
If we proceed to seek for specific evidence about individual provinces, we find that it is exceedingly scanty. Nevertheless it is
possible to draw a more detailed picture at least of Asia Minor
and Egypt. In Asia Minor, as well as in Syria, one of the leading
features of life was the gradual reversion to the feudal system.
We have already described how the local dynasts of Palmyra
became for a while rulers of the Eastern part of the Empire, and
we have spoken of the revival of the dynasty of the Sampsigerami
in Emesa.[22] The so-called revolt of the Isaurians in Asia Minor
is another symptom of the same tendency towards the formation
of almost independent states within the Empire.[23] Still more
characteristic of the conditions of the third century is an inscription of Termessus in Lycia belonging to the time of Valerian
(A.D. 253). Here a man with a good Roman name, Valerius
Statilius Castus, appears with the strange title κράτιστος σύμμα-
χος τῶν Σεβαστῶν, that is, *egregius socius Augustorum*. He is commander of the local detachments of soldiers, no doubt a local
militia, and he is praised for having established peace on land
and sea. He took an active part in the life of the city, though he
did not reside in it, and showed his respect and loyalty to the
emperors. It is evident that we have here, as at Palmyra and
Emesa, an instance of the self-defence of a Roman province
against marauding bands of Persians and against pirates, who

were natives as well as Goths. Here, too, it takes the form of the establishment of an almost independent vassal state under the leadership of a strong man, who was probably a descendant of a local romanized noble family of former dynasts of the land.[24] A good parallel to these Lycians and Syrians is furnished by the usurper Proculus, a man of Ligurian origin and one of the chiefs of the tribe of Ingauni (modern Albenga near Genoa), who specialized in robbery, became rich and influential, formed a little army of 2,000 men, and with its help aspired to the throne of the Roman Empire.[25]

Another side of life in Asia Minor is illustrated by a well-known document recording a petition made by a certain Aurelius Eclectus in the name of a group of imperial tenants, and presented to the Emperor Philip through an intermediary named Didymus, who was a member of the military police (*frumentarius*) of high rank (*centenarius*). The peasants' complaint is as follows:

> While in the most happy times of your rule, most pious and most blessed of all kings that ever have been, all other men live a peaceful and undisturbed life, since wickedness and exactions have wholly ceased, we alone are suffering misfortunes out of keeping with your most happy times. We, therefore, forward to you the following petition. We are your estate, most holy emperors, a whole community, and as such we appeal and make supplication to your majesty. We are most atrociously oppressed and squeezed by those whose duty it is to protect the people. . . . These men—officers, soldiers, city notables holding authority (magistrates), and your subordinate agents— . . . come to our village and take us away from our work and requisition our plough-oxen, exacting from us what is not due to them, so that we are suffering no ordinary injustice and extortion.[26]

We see that conditions, far from improving since the time of Septimius, have become much worse. The peasants of Araguê may praise the happy time of Philip's reign, but their own situation is no better than it was. As a matter of fact, the chief offenders are the same as under Septimius, and so are the methods of oppression. A contemporary and almost identical petition to Gordian III (A.D. 238), presented to the emperor by a soldier named Pyrrhus and supplemented by a statement of a lawyer (?), Diogenes of Tyre (*defensor* of the village?), depicts almost the same conditions as prevailing in Skaptopare, a Thracian village in the territory of Pautalia. The petitioners are not tenants of the emperor, but owners of land and houses (οἰκοδέ-σποται). Their grievance is, again, the exactions and extortions of soldiers, minor agents of the emperors, and other people. The village had the misfortune to be situated near a health resort and near an important market-place with a great seasonal fair. Under normal conditions that would have been a blessing, and so it had been for a long time, but in the third century it became a real plague for the villagers. The numerous visitors to the health resort and the fair, and other travellers, used the village as a suitable resting-place on their journey and as a source of supplies. They demanded quarters and food without payment, and gradually reduced the place to such poverty and misery that the number of its inhabitants steadily decreased. The villagers beg for help, failing which they threaten to flee from their ancestral homes, thus depriving the imperial treasury of their payments and other services.[27]

We pass to Egypt. Papyri of the time after Alexander Severus are not very frequent, compared with those of the second century and the first thirty years of the third. Yet they give a very good, though incomplete, picture of conditions in the third century. An excellent bird's-eye view of the chief preoccupations of average residents of different classes in Egypt is furnished by a list of questions addressed to an oracle. They were probably typical of the questions which were commonly asked, and so they were catalogued by some one who either wanted to ask some of them or more likely had to answer them. Some of them are of a neutral character, like the questions commonly asked in the second century, 'Shall I marry?' or 'Is the prospect of doing business good?' But of the twenty-one questions preserved in the papyrus eight at least are peculiar to this particular time (the end of the third century), and reflect its special interests. 'Shall I be sold up?' is an inquiry which clearly refers to confiscation of property. The same question is put in a different form, 'Is my property to be sold by auction?' Other typical questions are: 'Am I to become a beggar?', 'Shall I take to flight?', 'Shall I become an envoy?', 'Am I to become a member of the municipal council?', 'Shall my flight come to an end?', 'Shall I receive my salary?', and so on.[28] One sees what were the great perils that threatened a man's career. They arose from the interference of the state with the life of the individual. It was an everyday occurrence for a man to have his property sold up, to become a beggar, to flee from his place of residence, or, what was worse, to become a member of the council or, as such, to be sent as an envoy to the capital on behalf of his city, which of course involved him in great expense. Another glimpse into the state of affairs in a large house, belonging probably to one of the great men of Hermupolis, is furnished by a letter from an agent to his master, enumerating his expenditure for a certain time.[29] Most of the items are connected with requisitions and bribes or regular payments to the soldiers, for example 'price of Knidian wine to the soldier in the house of Demetrius the *tarsicarius*' (l. 12); 'Plution the *beneficiarius* of the prefect demanding *annona*, two spadia of wine' (l. 15); 'to his servant lest he should inform the soldier that the *praepositus* is here' (l. 18); 'price of wood for heating for the *praepositus* of the legion' (l. 27), &c. The tone of the postscript to the letter is one of sheer despair: the manager asks for a speedy reply and for directions.

The predominant features of Egyptian life in the third century were the gradual depopulation of the land, the decay of the irrigation system, and the increase of waste and unproductive land. The papyrus of Theadelphia, for instance, which contains the correspondence of a certain Sakaon dating between the years A.D. 280–342, shows that in the territory of this once flourishing village the land was in a very poor state. At the beginning of the fourth century the amount of cultivable, and therefore taxable, land was no more than 500 *arourae*, of which only 200 were cultivated.[30] Conditions were no better in Philadelphia, another large and flourishing village. Three rich landowners, who owned numerous parcels of land in its territory, complained to the *decaprotoi* that the πραγματικός (the accountant) of the village had overestimated the size and the quality of the parcels owned by them. This over-estimate was probably due to the fact that in the books the parcels were listed as larger and more fertile than they really were. The difference on a total of $80\frac{5}{12}$ *arourae* of taxed land was $33\frac{21}{32}$ *arourae*, which were probably wholly unproductive. Besides, some land which is recognized by the owners as forming part of their property is specified as practically unproductive or as requiring hard work. It consisted partly of uninundated land, but chiefly of areas planted with trees, which were either waste or on which the trees were partially or totally cut.[31]

This state of things was not confined to the Fayyûm. In a document of the time of Gallienus (A.D. 265–6) a commission reports to the council of Hermupolis Magna on the conditions of some estates assigned to the Sarapieion of the city, and leased to two of the important municipal officials. The report states that 22 *arourae* of vineyards contain 'very few vines still bearing fruit, and they are in a state of terrible neglect and overgrown with rushes, while the estate is surrounded by much uncultivated land and rushes'; the wine-presses and the basins are in very poor condition; and most of the other parcels are in just the same plight. It is evident that the land investigated by the commission had been confiscated from the former owners, who had become debtors to the state in their capacity of city or state officials, and that the decay of the land was due to the disappearance of private initiative and careful private management.[32] Waste land and state land became gradually synonymous. The state might assign the land to the communities or to rich landowners, or burden them with it (the well-known system of ἐπιβολή), or it might sell it for a nominal price to persons willing to try their luck, yet in most cases the result was deplorable. Once flourishing vineyards and olive groves ran wild and could not easily be restored to their former fertility. It was, of course, mostly land which had formerly been private that suffered this fate, uninundated land which in the good old times had been brought under cultivation by the efforts of private landowners and by means of artificial irrigation. The crown land accessible to the floods was still fertile and always found plenty of cultivators. The deterioration of the land was due entirely to the pernicious system of liturgies, which ruined the medium-sized and small properties of the well-to-do *bourgeoisie*. The peasants and, as we shall see later, the large landowners survived.

The immediate cause of the land going to waste was, of course, the neglect and the consequent deterioration of the system of dykes and canals all over the country. This deterioration was injurious not only to the private landowners but also to the state-peasants. It was due to the repeated wars and revolutions, to bad management of the distribution of work among the population, and to the illicit gains and bribes to which the state officials were so open. The government tried to restore the irrigation system as far as it could, but it followed its usual method of violence and compulsion. The greatest effort was made by the Emperor Probus, and it was so famous as to be mentioned even by his Latin biographer.[33] A papyrus of A.D. 278 shows in what way and by what means the restoration was carried out. All the landholders were mobilized. No excuses were accepted and no permission was granted to substitute payment for personal work. Special curators were appointed from the ranks of the municipal magistrates and of private landowners under the supervision of the *dioiketes*, the *strategoi*, and the *decaprotoi*. The sanction was very strict: 'If any one dares to attempt anything of the kind [that is, to accept money instead of work] or neglects these orders, let him be assured that he will be staking not only his money but his life for injury done to measures intended for the salvation of the whole of Egypt.'[34] Another document, about twenty years later (A.D. 298), shows that the strict measures of Probus did not improve the morals of the Egyptian officials who dealt with the dykes and canals, nor force them to honesty. In this petition the representatives of a village complained about the oppression and tricks of the officials. The expressions they used are striking: 'We should find it difficult, my lord,' the peasants say, 'even when justice is shown to us in commands concerning us, to accomplish our duties in full, so much so that, if any advantage is taken of us, our weakness will make it hopelessly impossible for us to discharge them.' It was, indeed, a minor affair—the unjust assignment of a work of 150 cubic measures done by one group to the credit of another group—but it shows the rottenness of the system and its ruinous effect on the population.[35]

The decline of economic prosperity in Egypt, as we have already pointed out repeatedly, was due principally to the baneful system of liturgies, which destroyed the work of the early emperors in spreading the system of private ownership of land all over the country and thereby restoring large parts of it to their former prosperity. It has been explained in the ninth chapter that no change was effected in the system of liturgies by Caracalla's grant of citizenship, which was preceded by the introduction of municipal life into Egypt. Municipal institutions were in fact introduced into Egypt at a time when they had everywhere lost their original meaning. Their establishment was no longer a means of extending self-government to parts of the ancient world which had never shared in it; it was now in reality a means of binding the population to the state by ties of personal service and material responsibility. By creating new masses of citizens, the intention of the government was to create new masses of burden-bearers, new λειτουργοί or *munerarii*, organized in groups to facilitate control. From time immemorial the peasants and artisans of Egypt had formed professional groups bound to their profession and to their domicile. Hitherto the propertied classes had escaped the obligation to perform special work for the state, and were left free to develop their economic life as they chose. Now they were organized according to their place of residence into groups of state servants under the glorious name of Roman citizens and of free citizens of Greek communities. The special work assigned to them was to bear the responsibility for the payment of the various taxes which were due to the state and to help the state to collect them. Another aspect of the same work was the responsibility for the discharge of compulsory work by the population and for the income derived from the state property, and above all for waste and abandoned land. What in the second century was still an individual responsibility falling on certain members of the privileged classes became now a responsibility resting on the individual members of definite organized groups of them, one member replacing another in case of default. These groups were called city councils, and to them parts of the Egyptian land with the peasants and artisans belonging to them were assigned.

The burdens which lay on the population and for which responsibility fell on the cities, represented by their dignitaries and the members of the city council, had never been so heavy as in the third century. The severest burdens were not the normal ones to which the population was accustomed time out of mind, the taxes and the regular compulsory work, but the emergency burdens—extraordinary payments, extraordinary deliveries (*annona*), and transportation. We need not wonder that in the minutes of the meetings of the city councils in the second half of the century, of which we possess some fragments (from the cities of Oxyrhynchus and Hermupolis), the members of the councils and the officials speak exclusively of liturgies—how they are to be distributed among the richer men of the cities and who is to be chosen as the next victim destined to be ruined and to take to flight. About A.D. 270–5, in the reign of Aurelian, the senate of Oxyrhynchus had a warm debate about the money to be spent for the crowns which were to be offered to the emperor in memory of his recent victory.[36] As the second half of the third century was crowded with wars and movements of troops, one of the greatest worries of the city councils was the collection and delivery of food supplies for the soldiers (*annona*). In A.D. 265 measures were taken by the president (*prytanis*) for the collection of the supply of corn for the legions.[37] In the same year foodstuffs were delivered to the soldiers who accompanied the prefect Claudius Firmus.[38] In 281 bread was furnished to 'the soldiers and sailors on the march' (τοῖς χωρήσασι στρατιώταις καὶ ναύταις).[39] In 299 chaff was given 'for delivery to the most noble soldiers marching through the city'.[40] To the reign of Diocletian and Maximianus belongs a long account of the delivery of εἴδη εὐθηνιακά (*species annonariae*), which were destined for the soldiers.[41] Whereas in the second century the *annona* was an emergency addition to the taxes collected, and the supplies delivered were probably supposed to be paid for by the government, in the third century it was a pure requisition, an additional tax levied from landowners and lessees of the public and imperial land. The city councils were responsible for its delivery, and individuals were specially appointed by them to supervise the collection of foodstuffs and forage, their transportation to the harbours or to the city, and their delivery to the representatives of the troops.[42] What terror the *annona* inspired both in the collectors and in the taxpayers is shown by a private letter of the end of the third century. The writer explains that his letter is an appeal for help sent at the request of a γνωστήρ, a person whose duty it was to suggest names of people who should be appointed to bear liturgies, and who found himself in difficulties. He proceeds:

He [the γνωστήρ] says, 'I gave him great help in the matter of the *annona*'. He says also that the *annona* is now being claimed. If then you can again get him off yourself, good luck to you; but if not, give instructions as to what preparations you wish to be made. Do not neglect this, for they [the collectors of the *annona*?] have not yet gone away. If you are strong enough to get him off, it will be a great achievement, since we have no cattle or pigs.[43]

Another difficult problem which faced the city councils was

the transportation of the *annona* and of the taxes in kind to the landing-places on the Nile and to Alexandria. The transport by land was carried out, under the supervision of special agents appointed by the council (καταπομποί or παραπομποί, *prosecutores*), by guilds of owners of draught cattle, for whom either the municipal *decaprotoi* or the great landowners and the farmers-general of the imperial land were responsible. The river transport was in the hands of special associations of shipowners or lessees of ships which belonged to the government.[44] And again special agents of the councils had the duty of watching over the shipments, and were responsible for the safety of the transported goods. These men were supposed to accompany a caravan of river vessels and to be present at the delivery of the freight in Alexandria. The liturgy of the *prosecutio annonae* was one of the heaviest and the most dangerous. It was no wonder that in the time of Diocletian two sons of municipal senators, who had been appointed 'to forward down the river' wine and barley, both took to flight and disappeared. The members of the council were busy finding substitutes for the fugitives. At a meeting of the council 'the members of the council said, "Don't press the matter, lest they [the substitutes] run away" '. Meanwhile the sureties of the fugitives were seized.[45] The hardships which a *prosecutor annonae* had to endure are described in a papyrus of the fourth century, and there is no doubt that experiences were similar in the third century. It seems (though the matter is not quite clear) that the wretched *prosecutor* or καταπομπός was driven out of the ship on which he sailed, and was cheated, beaten, and injured by a certain Aurelius Claudianus and by the commander of the fleet, the stolarch.[46]

The system of requisitions and the responsibility laid upon the city magistrates, the members of the city councils, and rich citizens in general, affected the organization of industry and brought back the conditions which had prevailed during the Ptolemaic period. Industry, which had become to a certain extent emancipated in the second century, was again subjected to state control, which was exercised in the manner peculiar to Ptolemaic times. In the cloth industry the reason for its re-establishment was the heavy demand of the state for soldiers' clothing. A glimpse into the organization of this branch of industry is afforded by a papyrus which records the proceedings of a meeting of the

council of Oxyrhynchus in A.D. 270–5. The question debated was
the delivery of linen vestments for the temple. It appears from
the debate that both manufacture and delivery were organized
on Ptolemaic models. Yarn was collected by the city from the
peasants and given to the weavers; if there was a deficiency of
material, it was bought by the city on the market. The weavers
were obliged to work for the city at a fixed price and to deliver
as many clothes as it ordered. The surplus was probably sold to
dealers and private customers.[47]

The same return to the Ptolemaic system is noticeable in the
organization of some branches of industry and retail trade which
were vital for the supply of the cities, for example, the manufacture and sale of oil. We meet with concessionaires who were
granted a monopoly of the retail trade, and who appear as
lessees of oil factories connected with the temples. It is worthy
of note that the same development is to be found in the organization of supplies for the city of Rome carried out by Alexander
Severus and Aurelian, which we have already described.[48]

The municipal *bourgeoisie* of Egypt, organized for the first time
by Septimius, was therefore as badly off as the *bourgeoisie* of other
parts of the Roman world. Every day they were threatened not
only with ruin by losing their property but also with degradation,
which meant that they would cease to belong to the class of
honestiores and would be ranked with the *humiliores*. This involved
liability to imprisonment and to corporal punishment at the hands
of the state officials, which was a common feature of life in the
fourth century, as we know from Libanius. At the beginning of
the third century, indeed, according to the imperial ordinances
—of which the earliest was issued by Augustus—those who renounced their property were exempted from corporal punishment in accordance with imperial orders. This is explicitly stated
in a rescript of Severus: 'Your citizenship, however, will in no
way be prejudiced thereby, nor will you be subjected to corporal
punishment.' These rescripts were in force as late as A.D. 250. In
a document of this period a certain Hermophilus quotes them
in renouncing his property. Practice, however, was different.
Otherwise Aurelius Hermias would not, in giving up his property, humbly beg the procurator to abstain from corporal
punishment. 'Perforce,' he says, 'I throw myself at your feet . . .
and beg that my person be not harshly treated and outraged, so

that I may by your humanity remain undisturbed in my native land.'[49] Evidently corporal punishment very often followed financial ruin, and the only way to escape it was to flee from one's domicile. Such flights were an everyday occurrence in Egypt in the third century. The reader will recollect the questions to the oracle quoted at the beginning of this chapter. A striking private letter from Oxyrhynchus may also be quoted. Charmus writes to his brother Sopatrus: 'The prefect has sent an amnesty here, and there is no longer any fear at all; so, if you will, come boldly; for we are no longer able to stay indoors. For Annoë is much worn out with her journey, and we await your presence, that we may not withdraw without reason; for she considers herself to be keeping house here alone.' The enigmatic sentences, comprehensible to the addressee, remind me of many letters which I receive from Soviet Russia. The system of terrorism gives rise to the same phenomena everywhere and at all times.[50]

The instruments of oppression and exaction were soldiers, in accordance with the regular administrative practice of the third century. They were a real terror to the population and were much used for the most various purposes. Some time after A.D. 242 a *stationarius* was ordered by a centurion to find, arrest, and send to the centurion the heirs of an unfortunate *decaprotos* who had been responsible for the payments of an imperial estate and whose default was threatening the success of the ἐμβολή, that is, the shipment of corn to Alexandria (and Rome) or to the troops of occupation in Egypt.[51] Orders addressed to soldiers to arrest decurions and to send them to higher military officials are quite common in Egypt in the third and fourth centuries.[52] In the correspondence of Heroninus, of which we shall speak presently, the soldiers play a not unimportant part. When one of the magnates, in whose service Heroninus was, is at the end of his wits to know how to enforce his orders on a recalcitrant φροντιστής (manager) or some other subordinate, he always resorts to the threat of sending soldiers: 'Do it at once,' says Alypius, 'lest you should be forced to do it by a soldier'; 'do not be negligent about it lest a soldier should be sent against them [those who did not pay the arrears]'; and he adds 'a soldier was about to be sent against them. It was I that stopped him.' One sees what the sending of a soldier meant to the population of a village. In fact, the soldiery was now master of the situation in Egypt. Even in disputes among themselves, the peasants and the landowners resorted, not to the regular administration, but to the omnipotent centurion.[53]

Under conditions like these we are not surprised to find that life was far from safe in Egypt and that the land was infested by robbers. Those who took to flight, 'anachorets' as they were called, were bound to take to robbery to avoid starvation. Hence mention is often made in the third century of men specially appointed by the villages to catch robbers, the so-called λῃστοπια-σταί. As might be expected, this service was a liturgy, and it was not very efficient. It is no mere accident that all the documents referring to robber-hunting which Wilcken collects in his *Chrestomathy* belong to the third or fourth century. It is typical, too, of the conditions of this time that the regular policemen were not equal to the task of suppressing robbery and had to be supplemented by such auxiliaries. One of the documents is particularly striking. The *strategos* writes: 'Notice has been given to the robber-hunters (λῃστοπιασταί) listed below to join the village police and find the malefactors who are being sought for. If they neglect to do so, let them be sent in fetters to his Excellency the Prefect.' The five men on the list are natives, who certainly had never been trained for the job of finding and catching robbers. How large were the numbers of homeless people who were searched for by the administration is shown by a document of Gordian's time, where a regular chief of village-police (ἀρχέφοδος) swears to the two municipal chief constables for the nome of Hermupolis (εἰρηνάρχαι)—a new liturgical office introduced into Egypt from Asia Minor with the municipal system in general—that four men of another village whom the administration was looking for were not hiding in his village.[54]

Naturally the main sufferers from the system of requisitions and of compulsory responsibility were those who belonged to the class of well-to-do, but not very rich, men and those who were comparatively honest. Such men lost their property, were degraded, and took to flight, living in hiding all over the country.[55] Better off were the rich and unscrupulous men who had the means and the cunning to bribe the officials and to found their prosperity on the misfortune of their poorer and more honest colleagues. In these circumstances it is not surprising that large estates flourished again and that new οὐσίαι came into being.

The amount of confiscated property increased daily. The cities were overburdened with such land, for which they bore collective responsibility. Confiscated land was mostly uninundated, and required special care.[56] The same was true of the parcels of land belonging to the category of γῆ οὐσιακή (that is, imperial land), for which the state tried hard to find suitable lessees. Both the state and the cities resorted to various measures to save waste land from complete neglect. The ancient practice of selling it to soldiers and veterans for a nominal price was revived. Some veterans tried their luck, for instance, a *beneficiarius* of the prefect in A.D. 246, and the three Philadelphian farmers of the Wisconsin papyrus quoted above. It seems that Philip was specially energetic in trying the method of nominal purchase to restore the prosperity of Egypt, and that his prefect and καθολικός (*rationalis*) issued a special order with this purpose. The experience of the Philadelphian farmers was, however, not very encouraging. By means of ἐπιβολή, that is, by adding unproductive land to the productive, or by means of false and exaggerated measurements, the administration tried to force the new landowners to pay for more land than they intended to, and the result was probably in most cases the ruin of the new landowners.[57] It is not a mere coincidence that in the same year, A.D. 246, the *prytanis* of Oxyrhynchus was going on an embassy to Alexandria to appeal against an ἐπιβολὴ τοῦ ἱεροῦ ἀποτάκτου, that is, an increase of the rent of state-land which had been imposed on the nome and for which, of course, the landowners of the nome had to pay.[58]

Another way of securing the cultivation of the imperial land and the land for which the cities were responsible was to find rich lessees and let the land to them on attractive conditions. The best method was to find somebody who was willing to do the work, but it seems that from time to time, especially in the case of the cities, compulsion was used in one form or another. Such managers of large tracts of land, rich men and women, appear frequently in the third century. They are at the same time owners of parcels of land, which they probably bought from the state, and lessees of imperial land. The best known is Alypius, whose correspondence with Heroninus, his manager (φροντιστής) in the village of Thraso, has been brought to light through the discovery of portions of the archives of the latter in the ruins of the village of Theadelphia. Among the other correspondents of Heroninus were similar rich and influential holders of extensive estates, especially Appian, a former *exegetes* at Alexandria. It is evident that all these men were lessees of large blocks of imperial land. They organized their enterprise on a very great scale and probably invested considerable sums of money in their properties. Unfortunately we know very little of their relations to the state. We are even ignorant of the actual functions of a φροντιστής. It looks as if he were not a private employee of the great landholder but a nominee of the state, subordinate to the magnate who was responsible to the imperial administration for the land assigned to him. How long these landholders and half-officials held their land or their office we do not know. It is possible that their tenure was a kind of *emphyteusis*, of lease without any fixed term (*locatio perpetua*), and that gradually they became practical owners of the large οὐσίαι which are so frequently mentioned in Egypt in the fourth century.[59]

In point of fact Alypius and Appian were both exceedingly influential persons in close relations with the administration of the nome and also of the province: we have seen that they had military force at their disposal. On the other hand, the tone of the letters written to their subordinates plainly indicates that they were accustomed to give orders and to be obeyed. It is to be noted that most of the land which they cultivated was of the type held by private owners: it consisted to a very large extent of vineyards formerly in the possession of private people. Almost the whole economy of the great landlords was based on wine, and it is highly characteristic of the time that wine was the chief currency on the estate of Alypius, money being very little used. Such an economically progressive land as Egypt was gradually reverting to the conditions of natural economy. The other large estates of the third century were apparently run on the same lines, as is shown, for example, by the numerous papyri of Oxyrhynchus which deal with the separate portions of the extensive estate of a certain Aurelius Serenus, *alias* Sarapion, who seems to have flourished about A.D. 270–80. Whether he was a lessee of γῆ οὐσιακή we do not know. He certainly increased his property by purchases of land from the state at a nominal price;[60] and his chief interest seems to lie in vineyards and orchards. Many rich women also were land-holders of the same type, such as Claudia

Isidora ἡ ἀξιολογωτάτη, *alias* Apia (about A.D. 222), and Aurelia
Thermutharion, *alias* Herais (about A.D. 261).[61] Clearly, then, in
Egypt the third century was an opportune time for the display
of certain qualities which helped a few men not only to keep but
also to increase their fortunes, while others suffered the greatest
hardships. Along with some Alexandrian magnates we frequently
find members of the militarized bureaucracy using their opportunities to acquire and increase their holdings and so to obtain
a prominent place among the provincial aristocracy. Many such
ex-soldiers have already been mentioned: we may add to the
list a certain Publius Vibius, a former soldier and *officialis* of the
prefect of Egypt, later a decurion of Alexandria and a large
landowner, whose affairs were managed after his death by a
πραγματευτής or *actor* on behalf of his heirs (A.D. 268/9).[62]

Incomplete as it is, the picture which we have drawn shows
very clearly the chaos and misery that reigned throughout the
Roman Empire in the third century and especially in the second
half of it. We have endeavoured to show how the Empire gradually reached this pitiful state. It was due to a combination of constant civil war and fierce attacks by external foes. The situation
was aggravated by the policy of terror and compulsion which the
government adopted towards the population, using the army
as its instrument. The key to the situation lies, therefore, in the
civil strife which provoked and made possible the onslaughts of
neighbouring enemies, weakened the Empire's powers of resistance, and forced the emperors, in dealing with the population,
to have constant recourse to methods of terror and compulsion,
which gradually developed into a more or less logically organized system of administration. In the policy of the emperors we
failed to discover any systematic plan. It was a gradual yielding
to the aspirations of the army and to the necessity of maintaining
the existence of the Empire and preserving its unity. Most of the
emperors of this troubled period were not ambitious men who
were ready to sacrifice the interests of the community to their
personal aspirations: they did not seek power for the sake of
power. The best of them were forced to assume power, and they
did it partly from a natural sense of self-preservation, partly as a
conscious sacrifice of their own lives to the noble task of maintaining and safeguarding the Empire. If the state was transformed by the emperors on the lines described above, on the

lines of a general levelling, by destroying the part played in the
life of the Empire by the privileged and educated classes, by sub-
jecting the people to a cruel and foolish system of administration
based on terror and compulsion, and by creating a new aristocracy which sprang up from the rank and file of the army, and
if this policy gradually produced a slave state with a small ruling
minority headed by an autocratic monarch, who was commander
of an army of mercenaries and of a militia compulsorily levied,
it was not because such was the ideal of the emperors but because it was the easiest way of keeping the state going and
preventing a final breakdown. But this goal could be achieved
only if the army provided the necessary support: and the emperors clearly believed they could get its help by the policy they
pursued.

If it was not the ambition of the emperors that drew the state
ever deeper into the gulf of ruin, and threatened to destroy the
very foundations of the Empire, what was the immanent cause
which induced the army constantly to change the emperors, to
slay those whom they had just proclaimed, and to fight their
brothers with a fury that hardly finds a parallel in the history of
mankind? Was it a 'mass psychosis' that seized the soldiers and
drove them forward on the path of destruction? Would it not be
strange that such a mental disease should last for at least half a
century? The usual explanation given by modern scholars suggests that the violent convulsions of the third century were the
accompaniment of the natural and necessary transformation of
the Roman state into an absolute monarchy. The crisis (it is said)
was a political one; it was created by the endeavour of the emperors to eliminate the senate politically and to transform the
Augustan diarchy into a pure monarchy; in striving towards this
goal the emperors leaned on the army, corrupted it, and provoked
the state of anarchy, which formed a transitional phase that led
to the establishment of the Oriental despotism of the fourth century. We have endeavoured to show that such an explanation
does not stand the test of facts. The senate, as such, had no
political importance whatsoever in the time of the enlightened
monarchy. Its social prestige was high, for it represented the
educated and propertied classes of the Empire, but its direct
political participation in state affairs was very small. In order to
establish the autocratic system of government there was not the

slightest necessity to pass through a period of destruction and anarchy. Monarchy was established in actual fact by the Antonines without shedding a drop of blood. The real fight was not between the emperor and the senate.

The theory that a bloody struggle developed in the third century between the emperors and the senate must therefore be rejected as not fitting the facts. Certainly, the transformation of the principate into a military monarchy did not agree with the wishes of the senate, but that body had no political force to oppose to the emperors. Recognizing this fact, some leading modern scholars have attempted to explain the crisis in another way, but still in terms of political causes; on the assumption that the crisis of the third century arose not so much from the active opposition of the senate as from the relations between the emperors and the army. The new army of the second part of the third century was no longer the army of Roman citizens recruited from Italy and the romanized provinces; the elements of which it was composed were provinces of little or no romanization and warlike tribes recruited beyond its frontiers. No sooner had this army recognized its own power at the end of the Antonine age, than it was corrupted by the emperors with gifts and flattery, and familiarized with bribery; it felt itself master of the state and gave orders to the emperors. The conditions imposed by it were partly of a material, and partly, up to a certain point, of a political, nature: for example, that the privileges enjoyed by the ruling classes should be extended to the army. As the emperors had not succeeded in giving their power a juridical or religious basis which was sufficiently clear to convince the masses and the army without delay, it became increasingly clear that they governed only by the grace of the soldiers; each body of troops chose its own emperor and regarded him as the instrument for the satisfaction of its wishes.[63]

This theory, which I hope I have summarized exactly, is undoubtedly nearer the truth and coincides in the main with the views set forth in this book. I have shown how the Roman emperors tried hard to find a legal basis for their power. Emperors like Vespasian and, even more, Domitian saw clearly that the dynastic principle of hereditary succession, founded upon the oriental conception of the divine nature of imperial power, and therefore upon the apotheosis of the living emperor, was much more intelligible to the masses than the subtle and complex theory of the principate as formulated by Augustus and applied by the majority of his successors, particularly the Antonines. Yet the simplification proposed by Domitian could not be accepted by the leading classes of the Roman Empire, since it implied the complete negation of the idea of liberty, which they cherished so dearly. These classes fought against the transformation of the principate into an unconcealed monarchy, and in their tenacious struggle they had, if not as an ally, at least not as an enemy, the army composed of citizens who held to a great extent the same opinions as themselves. The result was a compromise between the imperial power on one side, and the educated classes and the senate which represented them, on the other. This compromise was effected by the Antonines. When, at the end of the second century A.D., the barbarization of the army was complete, that body was no longer able to understand the delicate theory of the principate. It was instead prepared to accept the hereditary monarchy established by Septimius Severus, and the emperor, with the army's help, was able to suppress without difficulty the opposition aroused by his action. So far I am in the fullest agreement with the theory described above.

But at this point difficulties begin. Why did the dynasty of the Severi not last, after it had been established, and accepted willingly by the army and unwillingly by the educated classes? How are we to explain the fact that the soldiers murdered Severus Alexander, and later even killed and betrayed the emperors they had themselves elected, thereby creating that political chaos which exposed the Empire to the greatest dangers? The continuous upheavals must have had a deeper cause than the struggle for the hereditary monarchy of divine right. This goal had been reached from the first moment; why did the struggle continue for another fifty years?

Perhaps the wisest course would be to be satisfied with this partial explanation, in the company of the majority of scholars. Our evidence is scanty, and the most comfortable way is always that of *non liquet* and *ignoramus*. In the first edition of this work I dared to offer a theory which is to some extent supported by our inadequate evidence, and which, if it proved acceptable, would enable us to understand the nature of the crisis of the

Roman Empire. The five pages devoted to this explanation attracted the attention of the majority of my critics, and much has been written against my 'theory', though without a single fact being adduced against it. The chief argument invoked against my 'theory' is that the trend of my thoughts was influenced by events in modern Russia. Without entering upon an argument on this topic, I see no reason to abandon my previous explanation simply because I may, or may not, have been led to it by the study of similar events in later history. It still satisfies me and agrees with the facts in so far as I know them.

In my opinion, when the political struggle which had been fought around the hereditary monarchy between the emperors, supported by the army, and the upper classes, came to an end, the same struggle was repeated in a different form. Now, no political aim was at stake: the issue between the army and the educated classes was the leadership of the state. The emperors were not always on the side of the army; many of them tried to preserve the system of government which the enlightened monarchy had based upon the upper classes. These efforts were, however, fruitless, since all concessions made by the emperors, any act which might mean a return to the conditions of the Antonine age, met the half-unconscious resistance of the army. In addition, the *bourgeoisie* was no longer able to give the emperors effective aid.

Such was the real meaning of the civil war of the third century. The army fought the privileged classes, and did not cease fighting until these classes had lost all their social prestige and lay powerless and prostrate under the feet of the half-barbarian soldiery. Can we, however, say that the soldiery fought out this fight for its own sake, with the definite plan of creating a sort of tyranny or dictatorship of the army over the rest of the population? There is not the slightest evidence in support of such a view. An elemental upheaval was taking place and developing. Its final goal may be comprehensible to us, but was not understood even by contemporaries and still less by the actors in the terrible tragedy. The driving forces were envy and hatred, and those who sought to destroy the rule of the bourgeois class had no positive programme. The constructive work was gradually done by the emperors, who built on the ruins of a destroyed social order as well, or as badly, as it could be done and not in the least in the spirit of destroyers. The old privileged class was replaced by another, and the masses, far from being better off than they had been before, became much poorer and much more miserable. The only difference was that the ranks of the sufferers were swelled, and that the ancient civilized condition of the Empire had vanished for ever.

If the army acted as the destroyer of the existing social order, it was not because as an army it hated that order. The position of the army was not bad even from the social point of view, since it was the natural source of recruits for the municipal *bourgeoisie*. It acted as a powerful destructive and levelling agent because it represented, at the end of the second century and during the third, those large masses of the population that had little share in the brilliant civilized life of the Empire. We have shown that the army of M. Aurelius and of Commodus was almost wholly an army of peasants, a class excluded from the advantages of urban civilization, and that this rural class formed the majority of the population of the Empire. Some of these peasants were small landowners, some were tenants or serfs of the great land-lords or of the state; as a mass they were the subjects, while the members of the city aristocracy were the rulers; they formed the class of *humiliores* as contrasted with the *honestiores* of the towns, the class of *dediticii* as compared with the burgesses of the cities. In short, they were a special caste separated by a deep gulf from the privileged classes, a caste whose duty it was to support the high civilization of the cities by their toil and work, by their taxes and rents. The endeavours of the enlightened monarchy and of the Severi to raise this class, to elevate it into a village *bourgeoisie*, to assimilate as large a portion of it as possible to the privileged classes, and to treat the rest as well as possible, awakened in the minds of the *humiliores* the consciousness of their humble position and strengthened their allegiance to the emperors, but they failed to achieve their main aim. In truth, the power of the enlightened monarchy was based on the city *bourgeoisie*, and it was not the aim of the *bourgeoisie* to enlarge their ranks indefinitely and to share their privileges with large numbers of new-comers.

The result was that the dull submissiveness which had for centuries been the typical mood of the *humiliores* was gradually transformed into a sharp feeling of hatred and envy towards the privileged classes. These feelings were naturally reflected in the rank and file of the army, which now consisted exclusively of peasants. When, after the usurpation of Septimius, the army became gradually aware of its power and influence with the emperors, and when the emperors of his dynasty repeatedly emphasized their allegiance to it and their sympathy with the peasants, and treated the city *bourgeoisie* harshly, it gradually yielded to its feelings and began to exert a half-conscious pressure on the emperors, reacting violently against the concessions made by some of them to the hated class. The *bourgeoisie* attempted to assert its influence and to save its privileges, and the result was open war from time to time and a ruthless extermination of the privileged class. Violent outbreaks took place after the reign of Alexander, whose ideals were those of the enlightened monarchy, and more especially after the short period of restoration which followed the reaction of Maximinus. It was this restoration that was ultimately responsible for the dreadful experiences of the reign of Gallienus; and the policy consequently adopted by that emperor and most of his successors finally set aside the plan of restoring the rule of the cities, and met the wishes of the peasant army. This policy, although it was a policy of despair, at least saved the fabric of the Empire. The victory of the peasants over the city *bourgeoisie* was thus complete, and the period of the domination of city over country seemed to have ended. A new state based on a new foundation was built up by the successors of Gallienus, with only occasional reversions to the ideals of the enlightened monarchy.

It is, of course, not easy to prove our thesis that the antagonism between the city and the country was the main driving force of the social revolution of the third century.[64] But the reader will recollect the picture we have drawn of Maximinus' policy, of his extermination of the city *bourgeoisie*, of the support given him by the African army of peasants against the city landowners; and he will bear in mind the violent outbreaks of military anarchy after the reign of Pupienus and Balbinus, of Gordian III, and of Philip. Many other facts testify to the same antagonism between country and city. It is remarkable how easily the soldiers could be induced to pillage and murder in the cities of the Roman Empire. We have already spoken of the destruction of Lyons by the soldiery after the victory of Septimius over Albinus, of the

Alexandrian massacre of Caracalla, of the demand of the soldiers of Elagabal to loot the city of Antioch. We have alluded to the repeated outbreaks of civil war between the population of Rome and the soldiers. The fate of Byzantium, pillaged by its own garrison in the time of Gallienus, is typical. Still more characteristic of the mood both of the peasants and of the soldiers is the destruction of Augustodunum (Autun) in the time of Tetricus and Claudius in A.D. 269. When the city recognized Claudius, Tetricus sent a detachment of his army against the 'rebels'. It was joined by gangs of robbers and peasants. They cut off the water-supply and finally took the flourishing city and destroyed it so utterly that it never revived. The two greatest creations of the period of urbanization in Gaul—Lyons and Autun—were thus laid in ruins by enraged soldiers and peasants.[65] One of the richest cities of Asia Minor, Tyana, was in danger of suffering the same fate in the time of Aurelian. It was saved by the emperor, and the words he used to persuade the soldiers not to destroy it are interesting: 'We are carrying on war to free these cities; if we are to pillage them, they will trust us no more. Let us seek the spoil of the barbarians and spare these men as our own people.' It was evidently not easy to convince the soldiers that the cities of the Empire were not their chief enemies.[66] The attitude of the soldiers towards them was like that of the plundering Goths, as described by Petrus Patricius. His words certainly expressed the feelings of many Roman soldiers. 'The Scythians jeered at those who were shut up in the cities, saying, They live a life not of men but of birds sitting in their nests aloft; they leave the earth which nourishes them and choose barren cities; they put their trust in lifeless things rather than in themselves.'[67]

We have frequently noted also the close relations existing between the peasants and the soldiers. It was through soldiers that the peasants forwarded their petitions to the emperor in the time of Commodus and Septimius as well as in that of Philip and Gordian. In fact, most of the soldiers had no knowledge or understanding of the cities, but they kept up their relations with their native villages, and the villagers regarded their soldiers as their natural patrons and protectors, and looked on the emperor as their emperor and not as the emperor of the cities. In the sixth and seventh chapters we described the important part played during the third century by soldiers and ex-soldiers in the life of the villages of the Balkan peninsula and Syria, the lands of free peasant *possessores*, as contrasted with the lands of tenants or *coloni*, and we pointed out that they formed the real aristocracy of the villages and served as intermediaries between the village and the administrative authorities. We showed how large was the infiltration of former soldiers into the country parts of Africa in the same century; and in describing the conditions of Egypt during that period we repeatedly drew attention to the large part played in the economic life of the land by active and retired soldiers. All this serves to show that the ties between the villages and the army were never broken, and that it was natural that the army should share the aspirations of the villages and regard the dwellers in the cities as aliens and enemies.

Despite the changed conditions at the end of the fourth century, the relations between the army and the villages remained exactly as they had been in the third. The cities still existed, and the municipal aristocracy was still used by the government to collect the taxes and exact compulsory work from the inhabitants of the villages. It was no wonder that, even after the cities almost completely lost their political and social influence, the feelings of the peasants towards them did not change. For the villages the cities were still the oppressors and exploiters. Occasionally such feelings are expressed by writers of the fourth century, both Western (chiefly African) and Eastern, especially the latter. Our information is unusually good for Syria, and particularly for the neighbourhood of Antioch, thanks to Libanius and John Chrysostom. One of the leading themes which we find in both writers is the antagonism between city and country. In this constant strife the government had no definite policy, but the soldiers sided with the peasants against the great men from the cities. The sympathies of the soldiers are sufficiently shown by the famous passage in Libanius' speech *De patrociniis*, where he describes the support which they gave to certain large villages inhabited by free peasants, the excesses in which the villagers indulged, and the miserable situation of the city aristocracy, which was unable to collect any taxes from the peasants and was maltreated both by them and by the soldiers. Libanius, being himself a civilian and a large landowner, experienced all the discomfort of this *entente cordiale* between soldiery and peasants. The tenants on one of his own estates, perhaps in Judaea, who for four generations had not shown any sign of insubordination, became restless and tried, with the help of a higher officer, who was their patron, to dictate their own conditions of work to the landowner. Naturally Libanius is full of resentment and bitterness towards the soldiers and the officers. On the other hand, the support given by the troops to the villagers cannot be explained merely by greed. The soldiers in the provinces were still themselves peasants, and their officers were of the same origin. They were therefore in real sympathy with the peasants and were ready to help them against the despised inhabitants of the cities.[68]

Some scattered evidence on the sharp antagonism between the peasants and the landowners of the cities may be found also in Egypt. In a typical document of the year A.D. 320 a magnate of the city of Hermupolis, a gymnasiarch and a member of the municipal council, Aurelius Adelphius, makes a complaint to the strategus of the nome. He was a hereditary lessee (ἐμφυτευτής)* of γῆ οὐσιακή, a man who had inherited his estate from his father and had cultivated it all his life long. He had invested money in the land and improved its cultivation. When harvest-time arrived, the peasants of the village to the territory of which the estate belonged, 'with the usual insolence of villagers' (κωμητικῇ αὐθαδίᾳ χρησάμενοι), tried to prevent him from gathering in the crop. The expression quoted shows how deep was the antagonism between city and country. It is not improbable that the 'insolence' of the peasants is to be explained by their hopes of some support from outside. They may have been justified: the proprietor may have been a land-grabber who had deprived them of plots of land which they used to cultivate; but the point is the deep-rooted mutual hostility between the peasants and the landowners which the story reveals.[69]

I feel no doubt, therefore, that the crisis of the third century was not political but definitely social in character. The city *bourgeoisie* had gradually replaced the aristocracy of Roman citizens, and the senatorial and the equestrian class was mostly recruited from its ranks. It was now attacked in turn by the masses of the peasants. In both cases the process was carried out by the army under the leadership of the emperors. The first act ended with the short but bloody revolution of A.D. 69–70, but

* Compare pp. 490, 530.

it did not affect the foundations of the prosperity of the Empire, since the change was not a radical one. The second act, which had a much wider bearing, started the prolonged and calamitous crisis of the third century. Did this crisis end in a complete victory of the peasants over the city *bourgeoisie* and in the creation of a brand-new state? There is no question that the city *bourgeoisie*, as such, was crushed and lost the indirect influence on state affairs which it had exerted through the senate in the second century. Yet it did not disappear. The new ruling bureaucracy very soon established close social relations with the surviving remnant of this class, and the strongest and richest section of it still formed an important element of the imperial aristocracy. The class which was disappearing was the middle class, the active and thrifty citizens of the thousands of cities in the Empire, who formed the link between the lower and the upper classes. Of this class we hear very little after the catastrophe of the third century, save for the part which it played, as *curiales* of the cities, in the collection of taxes by the imperial government. It became more and more oppressed and steadily reduced in numbers.

While the *bourgeoisie* underwent the change we have described, can it be said that the situation of the peasants improved in consequence of their temporary victory? There is no shadow of doubt that in the end there were no victors in the terrible class war of this century. If the *bourgeoisie* suffered heavily, the peasants gained nothing. Any one who reads the complaints of the peasants of Asia Minor and Thrace which have been quoted above, or the speeches of Libanus and the sermons of John Chrysostom and Salvian, or even the 'constitutions' of the Codices of Theodosius and Justinian, will realize that in the fourth century the peasants were much worse off than they had been in the second. A movement which was started by envy and hatred, and carried on by murder and destruction, ended in such depression of spirit that any stable conditions seemed to the people preferable to unending anarchy. They therefore willingly accepted the stabilization brought about by Diocletian, regardless of the fact that it meant no improvement in the condition of the mass of the population of the Roman Empire.

XII

THE ORIENTAL DESPOTISM AND
THE PROBLEM OF THE DECAY OF
ANCIENT CIVILIZATION

AT the end of the third century, after a bloody and cruel civil
and social war which had lasted for scores of years, the general
situation was very similar to what it had been at the end of the
civil war of the first century B.C. The people, including a large
part of the soldiers, were wearied and disgusted and craved for
peace and order; the fighting temper of large groups of the
population had passed away and everyone was ready to accept,
or to submit to, any conditions that should guarantee the security
of life and the possibility of resuming daily work without the
daily apprehension of a new convulsion, a new wave of war and
destruction. But the Roman Empire of the third century A.D.
was very different from the Roman Empire of the first century
B.C. The civil war of the first century was ultimately a fight
against the domination of a small group of families, and an
attempt to remodel the structure of the state in accordance with
the changed conditions of its life, to adapt the constitution of the
city-state of Rome to the needs of the Roman Empire. After a
period of transition, inaugurated by the reforms of Augustus—
a period when the struggle against the old senatorial class, representing the ancient ruling families of Rome, was brought to a
close and the new structure of the state was gradually consolidated and accepted by the population (as was shown in the
crisis of 69)—the constitutional Empire of Rome, based on the
cities and on the city *bourgeoisie*, enjoyed a period of calm and of
peaceful development. The civil war and its sequel, the military
tyranny, did not affect the most vital forces of the Empire and
of the ancient world in general. It left intact the most important
institution of the ancient world, with which ancient civilization
stood and fell—the city-state. It seemed as if, after long efforts, a
constitutional arrangement had been found by which the city-
state was made the basis of a world-empire. That arrangement
was the enlightened constitutional monarchy, assisted by an

influential and well-trained body of experts, the Roman senate and the Roman knights, and by thousands of similar bodies all over the Empire, the municipal councils.

So long as the Empire was not faced by grave external dangers, so long as the awe which Roman arms, Roman organization, and ancient civilization inspired in the neighbours of the Empire endured, the fabric of the new Roman state remained firm. When, however, the feeling of awe gradually vanished and Rome's neighbours renewed their attacks, the structure of the state began to show dangerous signs of yielding. It became clear that the Empire, based on the propertied classes alone, could not stand the strain of foreign wars, and that an enlargement of the basis was necessary to keep the structure erect and firm. The city *bourgeoisie*, whose economic life had for centuries rested on the work and toil of the lower classes, and especially of the class that tilled the soil, appeared unwilling and unable to shoulder the burden of defending the Empire against foreign enemies. The attempts to revive the *bourgeoisie*, to increase its numbers, and to restore its military spirit, which were made over and over again by all the emperors of the dynasty of the Antonines and of the Severi, proved futile. For the defence of the state the emperors were forced to resort to the tillers of the soil, on whom the economic prosperity of the Empire rested and whose toil and travail never brought them any share either in the civilized life of the cities or in the management of local affairs. The Roman army gradually became an army of peasants, led and commanded by members of the ruling classes, and indeed an army of the poorer peasants, of peasant-proletarians, since they were the only men who would volunteer or would be sent by a village community when a compulsory levy was ordered. As regards its social (though not its racial and political) composition, the army of the second half of the second century was thus no different from the armies of Marius and Sulla, Pompey and Caesar, Antony and Octavian.

It was natural, then, that this army should in the end seek to realize the ambitions of the lower classes of the Empire, just as the armies of the first century B.C. had expressed the desires of the poorer Roman citizens of Italy. The instruments through which it tried to realize them were, of course, its leaders, the emperors, whom it appointed and supported. As its aspirations were never clearly formulated and its programme—if the vague desires of the soldiers can be so described—was more negative than positive, the process assumed very chaotic forms. Moreover, the *bourgeoisie* gradually became aware of the danger which threatened it and strove repeatedly through the same military leaders, the emperors, to save its privileged position and to prevent the overthrow of the structure of the state as it was in the second century. Hence the renewed outbreaks of civil war which raged all over the Empire and brought it to the verge of utter destruction. What the army wanted was an equal share in the management of the Empire, a thorough levelling. As far as this negative side of its programme was concerned, the struggle was crowned with success. The *bourgeoisie* was terrified and decimated; the cities were brought to the verge of ruin; the new rulers, both emperors and officials, sprang mostly from the peasant class.

Gradually, however, as in the first century B.C., it became evident that the civil war was disastrous to the state as a whole, and that its main result was the political and economic ruin of the Empire. On the other hand, as we have said, the masses of the people became weary of the strife and longed for peace at any price. It became evident, too, that the chief task of the moment was the restoration of the fabric of the state, the preservation of the Empire. As soon as this task was achieved by the strenuous efforts of the army itself and of its great leaders, a reorganization of the state in accordance with the changed conditions, stabilizing and systematizing them, became imperative and did not brook delay. It was the same situation as in the time of Augustus. Here again the main lines of reconstruction were dictated by the social and economic conditions, and were laid down by the practice of the leaders in the civil war and the partial reforms which they carried out. To the activity of Marius, Sulla, Pompey, and Caesar corresponded that of Septimius, Gallienus, and Aurelian; and the great work of Augustus, Vespasian, and the Antonines was paralleled by the reorganization of the state effected by Diocletian and Constantine and their successors. The chief reform needed was one which would, above all, stabilize the state and organize it in a manner that would accord with the changed conditions, economic, social, political, and psychological. Levelling and equalization were dictated as the basis of the reform by the imperative desire of the people, and it was evident that in the new state there was no place for the leading role which the cities and the city *bourgeoisie* had played in the state of Augustus and of the Antonines. The state had now to be based on the country and the peasants. On the other hand, a simplification of its structure was a necessary consequence of the changed economic and cultural conditions.

Thus arose the state of Diocletian and Constantine. In organizing it the emperors did not have a free hand. They took over a heavy heritage from the third century, to which they had to conform. In this heritage there was almost nothing positive except the fact of the existence of the Empire with all its natural resources. The men who inhabited it had utterly lost their balance. Hatred and envy reigned everywhere: the peasants hated the landowners and the officials, the city proletariate hated the city *bourgeoisie*, the army was hated by everybody, even by the peasants. The Christians were abhorred and persecuted by the heathens, who regarded them as a gang of criminals bent on undermining the state. Work was disorganized and productivity was declining; commerce was ruined by the insecurity of the sea and the roads; industry could not prosper, since the market for industrial products was steadily contracting and the purchasing power of the population diminishing; agriculture passed through a terrible crisis, for the decay of commerce and industry deprived it of the capital which it needed, and the heavy demands of the state robbed it of labour and of the largest part of its products. Prices constantly rose, and the value of the currency depreciated at an unprecedented rate. The ancient system of taxation had been shattered and no new system was devised. The relations between the state and the taxpayer were based on more or less organized robbery: forced work, forced deliveries, forced loans or gifts were the order of the day. The administration was corrupt and demoralized. A chaotic mass of new government officials was growing up, superimposed on and superseding the former administrative personnel. The old officials still existed but, foreseeing their doom, strove to avail themselves to the full of their last opportunities. The city *bourgeoisie* was tracked out and persecuted, cheated, and maltreated. The municipal aristocracy was decimated by systematic persecution and ruined by repeated confiscations and by the responsibility imposed on it of ensuring the success of the organized raids of the government on the people. The most terrible chaos thus reigned throughout the ruined Empire. In such circumstances the task of any reformer would be to reduce the chaos to some sort of stable order, and the simpler and more primitive the methods, the better. The more refined system of the past was utterly destroyed and beyond restoration. What existed was the brutal practice of the third century, rude and violent as it was. That practice was to a certain extent created by the situation, and the simplest way out of the chaos was to fix and stabilize it, reducing it to a system and making the system as simple and as primitive as possible. The reform of Diocletian and Constantine was the legitimate offspring of the social revolution of the third century, and was bound to follow in the main the same lines. In their task those emperors had as little freedom as Augustus. For both of them the goal was the restoration of the state. By his genius Augustus succeeded in restoring not only the state but also the prosperity of the people. Diocletian and Constantine sacrificed, certainly against their will, the interests of the people to the preservation and the salvation of the state.

The chief object of this volume has been to investigate the social and economic conditions of the early Roman Empire, to trace the evolution which gradually resulted in the suppression of the leading part played by the cities in the history of the ancient world. The new state based on the peasants and the country was a new phenomenon in history, and its progressive development requires as careful an examination as we have endeavoured to make of the history of its genesis. The reader will, therefore, not expect a detailed analysis of its growth in this book. Another volume of the same size, and written from the same point of view, would be necessary for a study of the social and economic conditions of the late Roman Empire. No such book has yet been written. Nevertheless a short sketch of the main lines which the reforms of Diocletian and Constantine followed, as well as a general picture of the social and economic conditions, may be desirable here to convey some idea of the new régime and its relation to the world of the early Roman Empire.[1]

The problems which Diocletian and his successors had to face were manifold. One of the most important was that relating to the central power, the *power of the emperor*. There was no question of eliminating that power. If there was one thing that held together the fabric of the Empire and guaranteed its existence, if there was any institution popular among the masses, it was the imperial power and the personality of the reigning emperor. Everything else was discredited. Despite the convulsions through which the Empire had passed, the idea of the imperial power stood intact. If there was any salvation for the Roman Empire— such was the general belief of the people—it must come from above. There was a deeply rooted feeling among all its inhabitants that without an emperor Rome could not and would not exist. And the bitter facts of the third century showed the truth of this belief. The only question was how to stabilize and organize the supreme power so that the emperor would no longer be a puppet in the hands of the soldiery. The conception of the imperial power formed in the first two centuries was too subtle, too complicated and refined, to be understood by the masses of the peasants on whom it was based. It was a creation of the high culture of the privileged classes. These classes were decimated and demoralized, and even their standard had become degraded and simplified. The idea of the ruler as first magistrate of the Roman citizens, whose authority was based on the conception of duty and on consecration by the great Divine Power ruling the universe, was one which did not reach, and was not comprehensible to, the mass of semi-barbarians and barbarians who now formed the staff of officials, the army, and the class which supplied both—the peasant population of the Empire. A simpler conception was urgently needed, a broader and plainer idea which would be intelligible to every one. Diocletian himself still adhered to the old idea of the ruler as the supreme magistrate, of the imperial power as vested in the best man or the best men, the *princeps* or *principes*. He emphasized, however, the supernatural and sacred character of his power, which was expressed in the identification of the emperor with God and in the Oriental ceremonial introduced at court. The cult of the emperor, which had been impersonal in the second century, became attached to the person of the emperor. The doctrine thus introduced was not new. Many attempts had been made to establish it—by Caligula and Nero, by Domitian and Commodus, by Elagabal and Aurelian. They had failed because the doctrine had adhered too

Description of Plate LXXVIII

1, *a.* GOLD MEDALLION OF DIOCLETIAN. Bibliothèque Nationale, Paris. Cohen, vi, p. 441, no. 264; F. Gnecchi, *I medaglioni romani*, i, p. 11, no. 5, pl. IV, no. 12.

Obv. IMP. C. C. VAL. DIOCLETIANVS P. F. AVG. Head of Diocletian, bare, to r. Rev. IOVI CONSERVATORI ALE. (Alexandria). Jupiter seated to l., with thunderbolt and sceptre. Near him, the eagle.

b. GOLD MEDALLION OF DIOCLETIAN. Bibliothèque Nationale, Paris. Cohen, vi, p. 421, no. 50; F. Gnecchi, l.l., p. 11, no. 2, pl. IV, no. 9 (A.D. 296).

Obv. Same inscription. Bust of Diocletian, draped, to r. with laurel crown. Rev. CONSVL VI P. P. PROCOS. S. M. A. (Antioch). Diocletian to l. in consular dress, with a globe and the short consular sceptre.

c. GOLD MEDALLION OF DIOCLETIAN. British Museum. *Num. Chr.* 1900, p. 32; F. Gnecchi, l.l., p. 11, no. 7, pl. IV, no. 14.

Obv. Same inscription. Head of Diocletian to r. with solar crown. Rev. PERPETVA FELICITAS AVGG. P. R. (Rome). Jupiter standing to l., with thunderbolt and sceptre, trampling on a conquered barbarian. Before him Victory to r., offering him a globe.

2, *a.* GOLD MEDALLION OF CONSTANTINE. Bibliothèque Nationale, Paris. Cohen, vii, p. 288, no. 502; J. Maurice, *Numismatique Constantinienne*, 1911, ii, p. 468; xix, pl. XIV, no. 14 (A.D. 326).

Obv. D. N. CONSTANTINVS MAX. AVG. Bust of Constantine to r. with laurel crown, dressed in the rich and heavy Oriental imperial cloak, holding a sceptre with an eagle and a globe. Rev. SENATVS S. M. T. S. (Thessalonica). The emperor standing to l. in consular dress, with a globe and the short consular sceptre.

b. AUREUS OF MAXIMIANUS. British Museum. Cohen, vi, p. 519, no. 271.

Obv. MAXIMIANUS P. F. AVG. Bust of Maximianus to r. with laurel crown. Rev. HERCVLI PACIFERO P. R. (Rome). Hercules naked, holding in his right hand a laurel branch, in his left the club and the lion's skin.

c. AUREUS OF GALERIUS. British Museum. Cf. Cohen, vii, p. 113, no. 121.

Obv. Same inscription. Head of Galerius to r. with laurel crown. Rev. IOVI CONSERVAT(ori) AVGG. ET CAESS. P. R. (Rome). Jupiter seated to l., with thunderbolt and sceptre.

d. AUREUS OF LICINIUS. British Museum. Cohen, vii, p. 205, no. 167.

Obv. LICINIVS P. F. AVG. Bust of Licinius to r. with laurel crown. Rev. VBIQUE VICTORES P. T. R. (Trèves). Licinius in military dress to r., with a spear and a globe, standing between two conquered barbarians.

Note the reverence paid by Diocletian and his co-rulers to the gods Hercules and Jupiter, the great deities of the German soldiers in a Roman disguise; the military character of this group of emperors, the last emperors of the period of the great civil war; and the Oriental aspect of the figure of Constantine in his heavy Persian mantle. The selection of coins and the casts I owe to the courtesy of M. Jean Babelon (Bibliothèque Nationale, Paris) and Mr. H. Mattingly (British Museum).

1. *a–c.* DIOCLETIAN

2. *a.* CONSTANTINE   *b.* MAXIMIANUS   *c.* GALERIUS   *d.* LICINIUS

LXXVIII. DIOCLETIAN AND CONSTANTINE

much to the special religions of particular sections of the population. Apollo and Hercules were vague conceptions which made no general appeal; the Syrian Sol, Mithra, the amalgamation of Jupiter and Donar, appealed to a minority but did not satisfy the masses. The prominent feature of the spiritual life of the Empire was the increase of religiosity. Religion was gradually becoming paramount for almost everybody. The more religious society grew, the sharper became the divisions between the various groups. A believer in Mithra would not accept an emperor who was the incarnation of the German Donar, an adherent of the Egyptian cults would not devote his soul to the incarnation of such a vague deity as the Stoic Hercules, and so forth. Moreover, the Christians would resolutely reject them all and refuse to accept a living incarnation of God in a mortal man. It was futile to persecute them: every persecution made their cohesion closer and the organization of the church more solid. In the third century the Christian church acquired enormous strength. As a state within the state, its organization steadily improved in proportion as that of the state deteriorated. Oppression, compulsion, persecution were the mottoes of the state; love, compassion, consolation were the maxims of the church. The church, unique in this respect among the other religious communities, not only administered spiritual relief but promised and gave practical help in the miseries of actual life, while the state oppressed and persecuted the helper.

But the Christians, increasing in numbers and in strength, grew tired of being outcasts and of fighting the state. The time was ripe for a reconciliation of state and church, each of which needed the other. In the opinion of some scholars it was a stroke of genius in Constantine to realize this and act upon it. Others believe this was a major error, to which he was led by his superstitious tendencies. For my own part, I believe that both factors combined, and that the final impulse came from reasons of state. In any case, he offered peace to the church, provided that she would recognize the state and support the imperial power. The church—to her detriment, as many scholars believe—accepted the offer. For the first time the imperial power became firmly established on a solid basis, but it lost almost completely, save for some irrelevant formulae, the last remnants of its constitutional character as the supreme magistrature of the people of the

Empire. It now resembled the Persian monarchy of the Sassani-
dae and its predecessors in the East, the monarchies of Babylonia,
Assyria, Egypt, and the rest. It was based at once on force and
compulsion and on religion. Individual emperors might fall victims to military conspiracies and court-plots. The imperial power
was eternal like the church, which supported it, and it was a
world-power as the church was a world-church. The work of
simplification was thus accomplished and the new supreme
power was acceptable at least to that part of the population
which was prepared resolutely to reject any other solution.
Gradually the Christian minority became, with the help of the
state, a strong majority and imposed itself on those who never
were able nor prepared to fight and to make sacrifices for their
religious creed. Even to them Christianity brought in the main
a satisfactory solution of their religious aspirations.[2]

Second in importance to the question of the imperial power,
and intimately connected with it, was the problem of the reorganization of the *imperial army*. Our last chapter showed how
critical this problem was for the Empire. In view of the grave
foreign wars and the repeated inroads of the tribes bordering on
the Empire, the army had to be increased in numbers and its
discipline and technique maintained at the level reached under
Trajan, Hadrian, and M. Aurelius. On the other hand, an army
levied, as the existing army was, by conscription from the ranks
of the peasants—a militia composed of the poorer peasants with
a long term of service—was an instrument both inefficient and
dangerous. The only way out of this difficulty was to return to
the more primitive and simpler military system of the Hellenistic
and the Oriental monarchies.

The first steps towards a reorganization of the army were
taken by Diocletian. Realizing, as no emperor before him had
done, the necessity of permanent reserves for the frontier armies
of the provinces, he increased the military forces on a large scale;
but, while augmenting the number of effectives, he introduced
no new methods of recruiting nor did he change the military
system. These reforms were reserved for Constantine. The main
military force of the Empire, as Constantine saw, could only be
an enlarged praetorian guard, a strong army of horse and foot,
stationed near the residence of the emperor, or the residences of
the co-emperors, and always ready to march against the enemy.

This field army, like the armies of the Hellenistic kings (with the exception of the Antigonids of Macedonia), had to be a mercenary one, consisting mostly of barbarians, recruited among the allied and vassal German and Sarmatian tribes and among those of the same stock who lived within the Empire. It was composed of different corps, some of them strictly belonging to the emperor's bodyguard, but the most important were the *comitatenses*, one part of which was called the *palatini*, and which formed a ready well-trained and well-organized field army. The armies which garrisoned the provinces, and whose duty it was to suppress revolts within their borders and to meet the first onslaughts of external foes, were organized on the pattern of the reserves of the Hellenistic kings. The soldiers of the provincial armies were conscribed from among the men who were settled on the frontiers with the obligation of hereditary military service. These military settlers were largely barbarians, Germans and Sarmatians, while some were descendants of the active soldiers and veterans who had received land from the emperors of the third century in the border districts. If more troops were needed, they were obtained by the enrolment of volunteers and by compulsory enlistment among the population of the Empire, mostly the rural population of the more warlike provinces, Thrace, Syria, Britain, and the two Mauretanias. The emphasis was laid on the *auxilia*, the barbarian units, while the legions, the regiments of Roman citizens, played but a subsidiary part. The leading idea of the Roman Republic and of the early Empire, obligatory military service for all the inhabitants of the Empire, was not dropped. But in practice the obligation of service was transformed into a tax, the *aurum tironicum*, levied from the landowners and expended in meeting part of the cost of the mercenary army and in finding sufficient recruits among men who were not attached to a special profession or to a plot of land within the Empire (*vagi*). In no case was the staff of officers for these types of troops drawn from any special class. The senatorial class was barred from military service, the equestrian class disappeared. Every one who showed military capacity could hope to rise gradually from the position of non-commissioned officer to that of an officer (*tribunus*), commanding a detachment or a legion or an auxiliary regiment, and then to the post of commander of an army (*dux*) or even commander-in-chief of the cavalry or infantry (*magister equitum* or *peditum*). Such at least was the theory and sometimes the practice. Naturally the families of higher officers became in course of time the main source of supply of officers in general, and thus a new military aristocracy was formed, which, however, never became a closed caste.[3]

In remodelling the *administration* of the Empire, the policy of the emperors of the fourth and fifth centuries was to increase the number of officials, to simplify and standardize their duties, and to a certain extent to give the hierarchy a quasi-military character. While the governing bodies of the cities, the municipal councils, lost one after another almost all their rights of self-government, and were reduced to the position of unpaid agents of the state, responsible for the repartition and the collection of taxes, as well as for the apportionment of compulsory work and other burdens lying on the population of the city and the territory attached to the city, the staff of state officials, alike in the capital and in the provinces, grew in numbers and importance. In the early Empire the bureaucratic system was slowly replacing the system of city government in the capital, but was more or less adjusted to, and co-ordinated with, the principle of local self-government in the provinces and in Italy. Now it was systematically developed and extended to every field of administration. We cannot trace here the gradual growth of the organization of the all-powerful bureaucracy of the late Roman Empire, and its successive modifications. It was a sphere in which almost all the emperors endeavoured to introduce some changes and some improvements—a feature which is common to all bureaucratic governments, reforms being here both easy and in appearance efficient. Suffice it to say that from the time of Diocletian and Constantine the aim of the central government was to build up a well-organized bureaucratic machinery which, under central direction, would be equal to the task of managing all the affairs of an immense state. Compared with the delicate and complicated system of the early Empire, in which stress was laid on the self-government of the cities, while the bureaucracy was a subsidiary organ and an organ of control, the system of the late Empire, despite its apparent complexity, was much simpler, much more primitive, and infinitely more brutal. Being supreme and omnipotent, and not subject to any control exercised in one way or another by those who were the life-blood of the state, the bureaucracy gradually became utterly corrupt and dishonest and at the same time comparatively inefficient, in spite of the high professional training of its members. Bribes and illicit gains were the order of the day, and it was idle to seek to put an end to them by means of a vast system of espionage and of mutual control exercised by officials over each other. Every addition to the army of officials, every addition to the host of supervisors, served to increase the number of those who lived on bribery and corruption. The worst were the thousands of secret police agents, the *agentes in rebus*, who were the successors of the *frumentarii* and whose duty it was to keep an eye on the population and on the host of imperial officials. Corruption and inefficiency is the fate of all bureaucracies which are not checked by wide powers of self-government vested in the people, whether they are created in the name of autocracy or of communism. Manifestly a highly elaborate system of bureaucratic government was incompatible with the fusion of military and civil government in the hands of the higher officials; and the two departments, which there had always been a tendency to manage separately, were now sharply divided and highly specialized. Manifestly, also, the host of officials must be recruited not from a special class but from the ranks of those who seemed to be the most suitable. Yet, in view of the privileges attaching to the position of a government officer, official posts naturally tended to become the hereditary privilege of a special caste. The higher posts were distributed among the candidates by the emperors personally, and many new men obtained them in this way. But by force of circumstances a new aristocracy of higher bureaucrats arose, and this aristocracy had practically a monopoly of all the higher offices of the Empire.

It is easy to understand why the emperors replaced the old system of administration by the new. The social revolution of the third century had been directed against the cities and the self-government of the cities, which had practically been concentrated in the hands of the city *bourgeoisie*. It was much easier and much safer for the central government, instead of remodelling municipal self-government on new and more democratic lines —which required a great deal of creative initiative—to accept existing conditions and to kill the whole idea of self-government by making all the members of the city community responsible to the state, and by piling up duties on them without any corresponding rights. The self-government of the cities being thus destroyed, the functions of control had to be performed by somebody else, and supervisors had to be appointed to watch and coerce the municipal councils; the natural candidates for this office were the officials of the central government, who had hitherto played a modest part in the life of the provinces. It is futile to maintain that this reform was gradually and systematically built up by the early Empire because of the bankruptcy of the cities, which had demonstrated their utter incapacity to manage properly municipal affairs. The bureaucracy of the early Empire was different in principle from that of the late Empire. It managed, as was natural, the affairs of the state and interfered very little with the affairs of the cities. If it did interfere, it was to help the cities to develop a more efficient management of their own affairs. The change was brought about by the revolution of the third century. The self-government of the cities was destroyed by the long period of anarchy. Instead of restoring it on new lines, the late Empire left things as they were, and put the cities, not under the control, but under the command, of the agents of the central government, made them the servants and the slaves of the state, and reduced their role to that which they had played in the Oriental monarchies, save for their responsibility for the payment of taxes. The reform was carried out not for the sake of the people but for the sake of simplifying the government's task. The interests of the people were sacrificed to what seemed to be the interests of the state. The germs of self-government, which had developed in the village communities in the second century and even in the third, were involved in the common ruin and disappeared.[4]

Closely connected with the reform of the administration was the momentous and pernicious reform of *taxation*. We have often insisted on the fact that the taxation of the early Empire, highly differentiated as it was and based on the traditions prevailing in the various parts of the Empire, was not very oppressive. The stress was laid on the indirect taxes and on the income derived by the state and the emperor from the land and other real estate owned by them. The direct taxes—the land-tax and the poll-tax —were paid in the various provinces in accordance with their traditions. Of their amount we have no knowledge except for the province of Egypt. But we know that many parts of the Empire were partly or completely (as in the case of Italy) exempt from these taxes, and that this exemption was rather extended than limited. If the provinces complained of their burdens, it was not because of the taxes. What bore heavily on them was the extraordinary payments, the provisioning of the armies and of the officials by means of compulsory deliveries, the war requisitions, the spasmodic confiscations, and the forced work. The responsibility for the assessment and the collection of the taxes was not resented as a very heavy burden by the municipal aristocracy. What they complained of was the responsibility for the extraordinary burdens imposed on the population, and compulsory payments like the crown gold. It was the chaotic manner in which the extraordinary payments were exacted that ruined the city *bourgeoisie* and the working classes alike. In the troubled times of the third century these extraordinary payments became the main revenue of the state. The state was living not on its normal income but on a system of more or less organized robbery.

The Roman state had never had a regular budget, and when it was faced with financial difficulties, it had no fixed and stable reserve to draw upon. From time to time thrifty emperors had accumulated some money, but it was easily squandered by spendthrifts who happened to occupy the throne, and it never represented capital well managed and invested in good securities. In case of emergency, therefore, the emperors had no reserve to resort to, nor did they ever seek to increase the regular income by a gradual increase in taxation; the usual way of getting the money, according to the principles of the city-state, was to demand it from the population either by means of extraordinary taxation or by means of requisitions and confiscations. It is not surprising that in the difficult times of the third century the ordinary taxes were rather neglected, and that greater store was set by the extraordinary taxes (especially the crown gold) and by extraordinary deliveries of foodstuffs, raw material, and manufactured goods. This and the general insecurity of the times led to the disorganization of trade and industry, and therefore to an enormous decrease in the yield of indirect taxes. The foolish policy of the emperors in systematically depreciating the currency, and the general economic conditions, as well as the system of organized pillage (the liturgies), produced violent and spasmodic fluctuations of prices which did not keep pace with the steady depreciation of the currency. Such were the conditions inherited by the emperors of the fourth century from their predecessors. So long as they lasted, there was no hope of restoring economic stability and of placing the currency on a sound basis. All attempts in this direction failed. The most notorious failure was that of Diocletian, both in respect of the currency and in regard to stabilization of prices. His well-known edict of 301, by which fixed prices were established for the various products, was no novelty. The same expedient had often been tried before him and was often tried after him. As a temporary measure in a critical time, it might be of some use. As a general measure intended to last, it was certain to do great harm and to cause terrible bloodshed, without bringing any relief. Diocletian shared the pernicious belief of the ancient world in the omnipotence of the state, a belief which many modern theorists continue to share with him and with it.

After the civil war had quieted down a little, it became evident to every one that the time had come to settle the mode of taxation. Two courses were open to Diocletian. He might go back to the traditions of the Antonines, cancel the emergency measures which had accumulated like a deposit over the system of the early Empire, and, in doing so, take account of the peculiarities of economic life in the various provinces. This, of course, was the more difficult and the more painful path. To restore the prosperity of the Empire years of quiet development were required—as many years of peace and of orderly government as were granted to the Roman Empire by Augustus, who had faced almost the same difficulties after the end of the civil wars. Diocletian was unwilling, and probably unable, to wait. Circumstances were not such as to allow him patiently to lead the Empire back to normal conditions. On the frontiers enemies were ready to attack, the internal situation was far from quiet, and the increased and reorganized army absorbed enormous sums of money. Thus, Diocletian and his successors never thought of restoring the ancient complicated and individual system of taxation. They followed the other course which was open to them: to take for granted the practice of the third century, to transform the emergency measures into a system, and to simplify and generalize that system as far as possible by applying it to all the provinces without taking into consideration the peculiarities of their economic life and social structure. As the currency was debased and unstable, the system of taxation could not be a monetary one. In place of money-taxes the emperors of the third century had invented or revived the primitive system of taxes in kind, under the form of repeated emergency collections of food-stuffs for the use of the army, the city of Rome, and the agents of the state; in addition thereto, raw material and manufactured goods were collected in the same way. This was the famous *annona*. What was easier than to transform these emergency deliveries into a regular tax? The needs of the army, the capitals, the court, and the officials would be covered, and the other expenditure of the state might be met as before from the old taxes, which were not abolished, and from the systematized extraordinary payments of the third century. It was not, however, easy to foresee what the needs of the state would be in the future: they might increase or decrease according to circumstances. That was the reason why the *annona* retained its aspect of an emergency delivery. Every year the emperor fixed the amount of payments required for the current year. The *annona* was thus stabilized, but stabilized in the worst possible form. In the third century men still hoped that the day might dawn when taxation would become regular and fixed. By the organization of Diocletian that hope was turned into a dream. Nobody could know in advance what he would have to pay in the next year; no calculations were possible until the state had announced the amount of its demands for that year.

Yet by the establishment of the *annona* as a permanent institution the problem of taxation was far from settled. The most important question was that of a fair and just assessment. In the third century this question had been settled differently for the different provinces. In Egypt it was based on the elaborate register of cultivated land, in the urbanized provinces on the data of the census and on the paying capacity of the various cities and other large units of taxation (the imperial and senatorial estates, and the land belonging to the temples and to vassal princes). This system was too complicated and elaborate for Diocletian. It depended in most of the provinces on the activity of the cities, and it was not easy to grasp at once in all its details. It was much simpler to leave aside the work of centuries and to introduce the most rough and primitive system of assessment which had ever existed. Every soldier could understand it, although any fool could see that in this case what was simple was not fair and just. The cultivated land, whether arable or planted, was divided into *iuga* or teams of oxen. The size of the *iugum* varied according as the land was situated in a plain or on a mountain slope, and according as it produced grain or wine or olive-oil. No further differentiation was attempted. No local conditions were taken into account. It may be that our idea of the reform of Diocletian, incompletely known as it is, exaggerates its simplicity. Perhaps the system was less rigid than it appears, and varied in different places. However, its main lines are beyond doubt and they show a tendency to simplify the problem of taxation, even if it be to the detriment of the taxpayer. It may be also that the intention was to establish a system adapted to the intelligence of the peasants, on which it depended, and to distribute the burdens equally on the population. The emperors of the period of the military monarchy were anxious to appear just and benevolent to the *humiliores*; this policy was never abandoned, at least in theory, and Diocletian often emphasized it. The *iugum* may have been familiar to Diocletian from his own experience, and may have been used as a unit of taxation among the Illyrians and Thracians who still lived under the conditions of tribal economy.

The division into *iuga*—the *iugatio*—was, however, only one side of Diocletian's system. A plot of land without labour is a lifeless thing: a *iugum* presupposes a *caput*—a head, a man who cultivates it. The question of labour had grown acute in the third century. The population of the Empire became more and more shifting. Oppressed in one place, the tillers of the soil would try another. We have quoted many documents in which the final argument of the peasants is a firm threat to take to flight and seek another home if their desires are not granted. The ancient world grew up in the fixed belief that a man belonged to a particular place, his *origo* or ἰδία. But only the serfs of the old Oriental monarchies were bound to their place of residence. Ever since the Roman Empire had united the civilized world, all others had been free to move as they liked. Such freedom was prejudicial to the success of the primitive *iugatio* of Diocletian. A piece of land might be cultivated one year and left waste the next: the peasant might migrate and settle somewhere else, or he might drop his profession altogether and become a proletarian in one of the cities. The yield of the large estates was proportionate not only to the number of *iuga* which it contained but, above all, to the number of *capita*. The gradual depopulation of the Empire, and especially the decrease in the number of peasant cultivators, made the unit of taxation not so much the *iugum* as the *caput*. Hence the taxable unit after Diocletian was a combination of both. Every one who cultivated a piece of land was supposed to make a declaration of the land which he cultivated and of the number of *capita* employed on it, including the animals. This declaration made the man responsible for his land and his *capita*: wherever he was, he was bound to pay the tax assessed upon it. As he formed with the land a single unit, he lost his liberty of movement, he became bound to his land and to his work, exactly like his predecessors the 'royal peasants' of the Oriental and Hellenistic kings. There was nothing new in this system for Egypt and some parts of Asia Minor, nor perhaps for some Celtic lands; the novelty lay in the revival and general application of a system which in the time of Hadrian seemed to have been doomed to disappear for ever.

The same primitive system of assessment was applied to other taxes, none of which was new. While in respect of foodstuffs and certain raw materials the needs of the state were met by the landowners, the money and manufactured goods required had to be found chiefly by the cities and their inhabitants. The artisans and the shopowners were expected to pay a uniform tax. How it was assessed, we do not know. They were also expected to deliver a certain amount of manufactured goods to the state or to the city at a special price. The large landed proprietors, the senators, paid a special tax in money for their estates (*collatio glebalis*). Finally, the artisans, the cities, and the senators had to pay the traditional crown gold (under different names) once every five years, and additional money when a new emperor came to the throne. The reorganization of taxation brought no improvement in the matter of compulsory exactions in cases of emergency. In time of war, requisitions and robbery reigned as before, and in the long list of the obligations of the people there still figured compulsory work and deliveries of draught cattle for transport (ἀγγαρεῖαι). How heavy the latter burden was, is shown by the 'constitutions' of the Codex Theodosianus and by the speech of Libanius Περὶ τῶν ἀγγαρειῶν. Everywhere, then, we meet with the same policy of simplification coupled with a policy of brutal compulsion, to which the ancient world had become accustomed in the dark days of the third century.

The mode of collecting the taxes has already been spoken of. The system of the city-state, which used the services of tax-farmers, was to a large extent gradually superseded under the early Empire, and in those branches of taxation where it was retained (the customs and the collection of the payments in kind and money-taxes assessed on the imperial estates) it was very effectively improved. A highly specialized army of state-officials was created to check the attempts of the tax-farmers to cheat both the treasury and the taxpayers. Most of the taxes, however, apart from a few which were managed directly by the state (the inheritance tax, the taxes on manumission and auctions, and the customs-duties), were collected by the cities and paid by their representatives into the treasury of a given province. How they were collected inside the city was a matter of indifference to the state. The co-operation of the agents of the state—the governors of the provinces and their staffs and the imperial procurators— with the city magistrates was limited to a joint settlement of the amount of the taxes to be paid by the city, which was based on the municipal census and on a similar census carried out for the whole province by the central government. In giving a free hand to the cities, the emperors insisted upon two main points, that the assessment must be fair and just, and that the taxes must be paid in full without arrears. For this the municipal administration was responsible. In actual fact arrears accumulated in difficult times, and the emperors very often cancelled them completely or partially. To make the collection of the taxes more methodical and to guarantee themselves against arrears, the emperors appointed (in addition to the governors and the procurators) special agents of high standing to assist the cities in managing their financial affairs. From the time of Hadrian they tried to check the accumulation of arrears by making the richest members of the community responsible for them, especially for those connected with the departments of emergency-deliveries and supplementary taxation. In the third century, when the burdens of collecting the taxes, securing transport for the state, and provisioning the armies became excessively heavy, imperial pressure on the municipal _bourgeoisie_ steadily increased and its responsibility to the state was more and more minutely regulated. Compulsion was freely used as the _bourgeoisie_ became more impoverished and reduced in numbers, and as the paying capacity of the taxpayers decreased. Some of the essential rights of free men and citizens of Rome, as the municipal _bourgeois_ were from the legal point of view, were curtailed. The government became harsh and sometimes violent. And yet the _bourgeoisie_ remained the privileged class of the provincial population and still enjoyed some of its old privileges.

Diocletian made no effort to change the conditions which he inherited from the military anarchy of the third century. He never thought either of reducing the city _bourgeoisie_ to the level of the rest of the population of the city territory by making every member of it a mere taxable unit, or of restoring the past glory of the cities. He took over the legislation of his predecessors, which tended to transform the _bourgeoisie_ into a group of unpaid hereditary servants of the state, and developed it in the same spirit. The _curiales_ (those who were eligible for the municipal council and the magistracies) formed a group of richer citizens responsible to the state through the magistrates and the council both for the welfare, peace, and order of the city and for the fulfilment by the population of all its obligations towards the state. Like the tillers of the soil, each of the _curiales_ personally formed a single unit for purposes of taxation, and the whole of the _curiales_ formed one large unit, representing the amount of tax and of compulsory work demanded from the population of the city. It was natural that every _curialis_ and the group as a whole should be treated in the same way as the individual tillers of the soil. Their responsibility was not only material but personal. Thus they had strictly to observe the rule of _origo_, to remain in their city and not seek to escape to another place of residence, and in dying they had to substitute for themselves another taxable and responsible unit in the person of their children. An army of officials was on the spot to keep close watch on them, and to use compulsion and violence if any of them tried to break away from the iron circle in which he was included. Have we not here the plainest proof of Diocletian's utter incapacity to invent anything new or so to adapt existing institutions to the conditions of his time as to safeguard as far as possible the rights and the prosperity of the people? Like the rest of his reforms, his reorganization of municipal life appears to me to be a striking *testimonium paupertatis*, typical of an age devoid of all creative power and helplessly submitting to current practice, which owed its origin to a period of revolution and anarchy. Augustus had faced the same difficulties, for the time of the civil wars had been a time of oppression and of legalized robbery; but he never dreamt of legalizing robbery and oppression in his turn and making them permanent. In the mind of Diocletian the state meant compulsion, and organization meant organized violence. We cannot say that his hand was forced by the will of the army. Diocletian never thought of eliminating the antagonism between city and country by transferring the responsibility for taxation and compulsory work from the city councils to state officials. He kept the antagonism alive, with the result that in the fourth and fifth centuries the country hated the city as cordially as it had done in the third: witness Salvian and his attacks on the tyrants from the cities. We cannot say, then, that Diocletian had no other course open to him. Many were open to him, but he took the old beaten track which led directly to ruin and slavery.[5]

The return of stable conditions and the restoration of a certain peace and order could not fail to have some effect. The terrors of the second civil war were not followed by an Augustan Golden Age; but it cannot be denied that some improvement in economic conditions occurred after the reforms of Diocletian and Constantine. For example, Egypt enjoyed a certain revival in the fourth century, and the same is true also of various cities of the Roman Empire. It is no less significant that Constantine succeeded in a field where Diocletian had failed: namely in stabilizing the currency and in restoring, to some extent, the prestige of money in public and private life. But this restoration was of brief duration, not because of the external conditions or of the incompetence of the successors of Diocletian and Constantine, but mainly because of the system, which had been responsible for the decay and contained in itself the seeds of a further decline. Oppressive and unjust taxation based on the enslavement alike of the tillers of the soil and of the city-artisans; the immobilization of economic life, which was hampered in its free development by the chains which bound every individual; the cruel annihilation, consciously pursued and gradually effected, of the most active and the most educated class of the Roman Empire, the city *bourgeoisie*; the steady growth of dishonesty and of violence among the members of the imperial administration, both high and low; the impotence of the emperors, despite the best intentions, to check lawlessness and corruption, and their boundless conservatism as regards the fundamental principles of the reforms of Diocletian and Constantine—all these factors did not fail to produce their natural effect. The spirit of the population remained as crushed as it had been in the times of the civil war. The only difference was that a wave of resignation spread over the Roman Empire. It was useless to fight, better to submit and bear silently the burden of life with the hope of finding a better life—after death. The feeling was natural, for the best efforts of honest men were bound to fail, and the more one produced, the more would be taken by the state. If a peasant succeeded in improving his land and adding to it, he knew that his fate was to be promoted to the position of a *curialis*, which meant slavery, oppression, and, in the last resort, ruin. Better to produce enough to support his family and not make useless efforts to better his position. A soldier knew very well that, so long as he was a soldier and so long as he condemned his children to the same life, he might be comparatively prosperous. As soon as he tried to break the spell, he knew that his fate, too, or at least the fate of his children, would be to join the *curia* and exchange bad for worse. The tenant of a large landowner was content to perform his duties and to enjoy the protection, and the oppression, of his master. The fate of his neighbour, the free peasant, was not attractive enough to induce him to strive to become one. The same was true of the artisans of the cities and the unfortunate *curiales*. In moments of despair the individual might try by desperate means to ameliorate his lot: the *colonus* and the peasant might seek to enter the army or to turn to robbery, the soldier to desert the army, the *curialis* to become anything—an official, a soldier, a *colonus*, or a peasant. It was all in vain. If they succeeded, their situation was every whit as bad. Thus the reigning mood was resignation, and resignation never leads to prosperity.

The salient trait of the economic life of the late Roman Empire was gradual impoverishment. The poorer the people became, the more primitive grew the economic life of the Empire. Commerce decayed, not only because of piracy and barbarian inroads, but mainly because customers disappeared. The best clients, the city *bourgeoisie*, decreased constantly in numbers and in purchasing power. The peasants lived in extreme poverty and reverted to an almost pure 'house economy', each home producing for itself what it needed. The only customers left were the members of the privileged classes, the officials, the soldiers, and the large landed proprietors, and they were provided for, as far as the necessities of life were concerned, either by the state (their salary being paid in kind) or by the produce of their own estates. Thus the first branch of commerce to suffer decay was the most important one, commerce in articles of prime necessity within a province and between provinces. Local retail-trade still lingered on, and trade in luxuries even prospered. This accounts, for instance, for the revival of the commerce with the East. The commercial class as such, however, remained unprogressive and despised. There was no chance to develop any large commercial enterprise. As soon as a man tried to do so, as soon as he bought ships or established commercial relations, he was made a member of one of the corporations, the *navicularii* or *mercatores*, and was forced to work for the state, to transport goods on its behalf, and for a miserable remuneration, or to give the state the first offer of what he had to sell. Thus the situation of the merchants and shipowners was as bad as that of the *curiales*, and compulsion was employed to keep the members of these groups bound to their profession and to keep the number of the groups complete by enrolment of fresh members. Like the ownership of land, commerce and transportation became a hereditary burden from which there was no escape. The same held good of industry. Customers were few, the market became more and more restricted, and the state more and more oppressive. Apart from the production of some standardized articles for the masses and some luxuries for the few rich, industry lived on the orders of the state. But the state was a selfish and a brutal customer: it fixed the prices and, if we take into consideration the profits of the officials, fixed them ruinously low for the artisans. Naturally the large industrial concerns gradually disappeared. As the state needed them, especially for the army, for the court, and for the officials, many industrial establishments were transformed into state factories, which were managed on Egyptian and Oriental patterns, with a staff of workmen bound to their profession and bearing a hereditary burden.

In the preceding chapters we have endeavoured to show that the social crisis of the third century had been, to a large extent, brought about by a revolutionary movement of the masses of the population which aimed at a general levelling. Was this aim achieved by the reforms of Diocletian and Constantine? Can we say that the late Roman Empire was more democratic than the Empire of the Julio-Claudians, the Flavians, and the Antonines? It is true that one privileged class of the past, the equestrian, disappeared. It is true that for a time advancement in the army and in the civil service was open to everybody, especially in the third century. But in actual fact the late Roman Empire, though it was a democracy of slaves, was less democratic than the early Empire. There were no castes in the early Empire. An active and clever man could easily, by increasing his fortune, rise from the position of peasant to that of landowner, and as such he could join the ranks of the municipal aristocracy, receive the Roman citizenship, become a knight, and finally a member of the senatorial aristocracy. We have seen that such an advance was easily accomplished in two or three generations. Even in the army promotion from the rank of private to the high post of first centurion was normal, although the advance of a common soldier to the equestrian or senatorial posts in the army was rare and exceptional. So it was in the civil service. Even slaves were no exception to the general rule. Emancipated slaves had brilliant opportunities of becoming procurators of high standing, and there was nothing to prevent them or their children from entering the ranks of the municipal aristocracy.

The situation was different after the reforms of Diocletian and Constantine. There was no legal way of advancing from the position of a *colonus* even to that of a free peasant or a city proletarian, not to speak of other classes. A *colonus* might exceptionally become a soldier, but it was a very rare exception. The reform of taxation by Diocletian and the edicts of later emperors made the *colonus* a serf, so that, already in fact bound by heredity to his plot of earth, he became bound to his domicile and to his master; he became a member of a close hereditary caste. The same was true of the free small landowner, who was a member of a village community: he was tied to his land, to his village, to his profession. The only possible advance was to the position of a *curialis*, which in fact was a move downwards. Some might serve in the army, particularly if they happened to live in military provinces; but, as the legislation against deserters shows, this was not regarded as an enviable privilege. The municipal landowners, the *curiales*, were in the same position. They were less free than even the small landowners, and they formed a close and very select class, select because everybody dreaded the very idea of entering it. The rest of the city population—the shipowners, the merchants, the artisans, the workmen—were all gradually bound to their profession and to their place of residence. One privileged class was that of the workless proletarians and beggars in the city and in the country, for whom the Christian church was supposed to care. They at least were free—to starve and to riot. Another free and privileged class was the robbers, who steadily increased in numbers on sea and land. The class of officials was not indeed hereditary, at any rate not legally. It was a privilege to be an official, and the emperor was free to recruit his officials from the best men in the country. But his freedom was limited. A *curialis* could not become an official, and if one of them succeeded in evading the rule, he might expect every moment to be sent back to his *curia*. Nor were merchants and shipowners eligible. The peasants and the city proletariate do not come into consideration. The military career was sharply separated from the civil, and a soldier was not eligible for a civil office. Thus by force of circumstances officials were recruited from the families of officials, and the official class became practically, though not legally, a close caste. The same description applies to the new senatorial aristocracy. It was an aristocracy of service, admission to which was granted by the emperors to the higher civil and military officers, and membership was hereditary. Gradually it became also an aristocracy of birth and education, for the intellectual traditions of the class were jealously guarded.

From the social point of view, then, there was no levelling and no equalization. In the late Roman Empire society was subdivided not into classes, but into real castes, each as close as possible, in some cases because of the privileges connected with the caste, in others because of the burdens and hardships, which prevented anybody from desiring to be admitted, and made membership hereditary and compulsory. Nor was there even equality in the common slavery to the state. There was indeed equality of a negative kind, for no political freedom was tolerated, no remnant of self-government was left, no freedom of speech, thought, or conscience was permitted, especially after the victory of Christianity; but even this equality of slavery was superficial and relative. The great landed proprietors were slaves of the emperor but masters of the tenant-serfs who lived on their estates. The *curiales* were slaves of the administration and were treated by it as such, but they were masters not only of the tenants of their estates, but also of the population of the city and the city territory, inasmuch as they apportioned and collected the taxes and supervised the compulsory work; and by these they were regarded and hated as masters who were themselves unfree and could not protect but only cheat their own slaves. Little wonder if these slaves appealed for protection to senators, officials, and soldiers, and were ready to pay any price for it and to deprive themselves of the little money and the little liberty which they still had. The working class of the cities stood in the same relation to the members of the various corporations, the owners of ships, shops, and factories. The last were in truth much more like minor supervisors of their own concerns on behalf of the state than their owners; they were themselves in bondage to the officials of the various departments and of the commanders of the various military units. Lastly, the officials and the soldiers of various ranks, though wielding an enormous power over thousands of men, were subjected to an iron discipline of a servile type and were practically slaves of each other and of the agents of the secret police. General servitude was, indeed, the distinctive feature of the age, but while there were different grades and shades of bondage, there was no equality. Slavery and equality are incompatible, a fact which should not be forgotten by the many modern defenders of the principle of equality.[6]

Above all, there was no equality whatsoever in the distribution of property. The senators, the knights, the municipal aristocracy, the petty *bourgeoisie* of the early Empire were, of course, ruined and degraded. Their patient and creative work, by which they had accumulated their fortunes and built up the civilized life of the cities, had disappeared for ever. But the old propertied classes were replaced by new ones, which even from the economic

Description of Plate LXXIX

1. MOSAIC. Found at Carthage. Museum of Bardo, Tunis. A. Merlin in *Bull. arch. du Com. des trav. hist.* 1921, pp. 95 ff.; cf. above, Chap. VII, note 100. Reproduced from a photograph kindly supplied by Mr. A. Merlin; [A. Merlin and L. Poinssot, *Guide du Musée Alaoui*, i (1950), pl. xxii].

The general composition of the mosaic is quite original. It endeavours to combine two motifs which are usually treated separately—the four seasons (see, e.g. our pl. LVIII, 1) and life on a large estate (see, e.g. our pl. LXIII). In the centre of the picture is shown a large villa, a combination of a residential house and a fortress. Its dominant features are two high towers at the corners, a massive ground floor with an arched entrance, giving access to the household apartments and probably to a large court behind, and a handsome loggia on the first floor where the living-rooms are concentrated. Behind the main part of the building are seen two separate buildings—the stable (?) or the *atrium*, and a large bath with domed roofs. The villa is surrounded by a park. On the two sides of the villa is depicted a hunting éxpedition of the master. Two servants lead the way, a beater and a man in charge of the hounds; in the field is the object of the hunt, a hare; while behind comes the master, riding a beautiful horse and followed by a third servant who carries a bag of provisions. In the upper and lower bands of the picture are scenes of life on the estate. Each season occupies one corner. In the upper left-hand corner it is WINTER time. A man carries two live ducks; two boys gather olives; a woman carries a basket full of black olives. They represent the family of a *colonus* portrayed in their relation to the master: they bring the fruits of the season to the lady of the villa, who is seated on a bench, with a fan in her hand, in that part of the park which formed the chicken pen: on her right a cock is displaying its beauty, and in front of her is a chicken-house with chickens before it. The right corner of the same band, depicting SUMMER, shows the family of another *colonus*: in the background is their modest house, a 'gourbi' (*mapale*), or round hut, made of reeds (cf. the same type of hut on the sarcophagus of Philippeville, figuring in a similar scene of rustic life, S. Reinach, *Rép. d. rel.* ii, p. 3, no. 5); in the foreground is seen the *colonus* himself, herding his flock of sheep and goats with the aid of his dog, and holding a shepherd's horn in his left hand. His wife or daughter brings a kid to his mistress (the figure of the lady serves for both scenes). In the left corner of the lower band is pictured SPRING. The lady of the villa stands in front of her chair, elegantly dressed, amid flowers, with her pet dog in the background; before her stands a servant-maid holding a necklace and a toilet box, while a boy deposits three fish at her feet; behind her a boy-servant, or a *colonus*, brings a basket full of flowers. The remaining corner represents AUTUMN. The master of the house is seated under the trees of his orchard, which are laden with ripe fruit; behind him lies his vineyard. A *colonus* runs through the orchard carrying two cranes and a roll inscribed *Ju(lio) dom(ino)*, probably a complimentary address or a petition. From the vineyard comes another *colonus*, carrying a basket of grapes and a live hare, which he has probably just caught among the vines. The mosaic gives prominence to the part played by the *coloni* in the economy of the estate: the whole life of the villa is based on their toil and their contributions. Cf. Chap. XII, note 6.

2. BAS-RELIEF OF A FUNERAL MONUMENT. Part of the sculptural decoration of the Igel column. Igel near Trèves. E. Espérandieu, *Rec. gén.* vi, p. 442; Dragendorff and Krüger, *Das Grabmal von Igel* (1924), Taf. 9.

Six *coloni* in procession bring various contributions in kind to their master's house. They have just entered the court of the house through an arched gate, and they are received before the entrance to the *atrium* (half-closed by a curtain) by the master himself or his steward. The gifts, or contributions, consist of a hare, two fish, a kid, an eel (?), a cock, and a basket of fruit. Practically the same scene is represented on a funeral monument of Arlon (Orolaunum vicus) which is now lost (E. Espérandieu, *Rec. gén.* v, p. 271, no. 4102). There the master receives his *coloni* seated on a chair behind a table; the contributions are a cock, fish, a basket of fruit, and a sucking-pig.

1. THE ESTATE OF JULIUS
(Mosaic of Carthage)

2. *COLONI* BRINGING GIFTS
(Monument of Igel)

LXXIX. AFRICA AND GERMANY IN THE THIRD AND FOURTH
CENTURIES

I. A ROMAN OF THE LATER EMPIRE ON A HUNTING EXPEDITION

2. A VILLA AND ITS OWNER IN AFRICA DURING THE VANDALIC OR
BYZANTINE PERIOD

LXXX. ITALY AND AFRICA IN THE TIME OF THE LATE ROMAN
EMPIRE

Description of Plate LXXX

1. FRAGMENT OF A MOSAIC. Found at Rome near the church of St. Bibbiana. Antiquarium Comunale, Rome. *Bull. Com.* 32, 1904, p. 375; Helbig–Amelung, *Führer*, i, p. 603, nos. 1072–1074.

One of three fragments of a large mosaic, showing a man on horseback hunting a wild boar in a forest with the help of a large and fierce Molossian dog. The man is bearded and dressed in the late-Roman fashion; his saddle and horse-trappings are richly adorned. The other two fragments portray other hunting scenes—netting antelopes and capturing bears with a wooden trap. Stylistically, our mosaic must be compared with the mosaics of the palace of Theodoric at Ravenna, and it certainly belongs to the same time; see G. Ghirardini in *Mon. dei Lincei*, 24, 1918, pl. v (an almost identical hunting scene). The noble Roman of our fragment is undoubtedly a Gotho-Roman.

2. PART OF A MOSAIC. Found at Carthage at the foot of the hill Bordj-Djedid. British Museum. *Inv. d. mos.* ii. 1 (Tunisie), no. 763, cf. no. 886, citing A. W. Franks in *Archaeologia*, 38, 1860, p. 225, no. 5; N. Davis, *Carthage and her Remains* (1861), pp. 531 ff.; Morgan, *Romano-British Pavements*, pp. 272 ff., quoting *The Builder*, 42, 1882, pp. 757 ff.; *British Museum Guide to the Graeco-Roman Sculptures*, ii (1876), Part II, pp. 80 ff. Our fragment has not, so far as I know, been reproduced before. The building which is depicted on it has been described and reproduced (as a part of the walls of Carthage!) by A. Graham, *Roman Africa* (1902), p. 24, and plate.

The mosaic is one of the latest replicas of the typical African examples with hunting scenes (cf. pls. LXIII and LXXVII, 1). On the portion figured here the owner of an estate is seen riding in the hilly country around his villa, which he has just left. With his right hand he makes a gesture of greeting. His dress, the style of his horse-trappings, and his facial type suggest a Vandal or a Roman African of the Vandal or Byzantine period. The mark on the horse's haunch, consisting of three reeds and a crescent forming a cross, is a charm to avert evil. Our fragment is part of the first band of the mosaic. In the second band the same man (on the same horse) is seen hunting two gazelles (*Inv. d. mos.*, no. 763), while another man is catching a stag by means of a lasso (ibid., no. 886). Other fragments show a boar and a dog, a hare, &c. The mosaic had at least two, perhaps three, bands.

On hunting scenes in late-Roman art, especially on sarcophagi, see G. Rodenwaldt in *Röm. Mitt.* 36/37, 1921/2, pp. 58 ff.

point of view were much worse than their predecessors. The fortunes of the early Empire were the result of the growing prosperity of the Empire in general. They were derived from commerce and industry, and the capital acquired was invested in land, improving its cultivation and the types of crop produced. The wars of the second century undermined these fortunes and retarded or even arrested economic development. Yet they did not work ruin, and a recovery under more normal conditions was possible. The catastrophe of the third century dealt a severe blow to the prosperity of the Empire and weakened the creative energies of the better part of the population. The reforms of Diocletian and Constantine, by giving permanence to the policy of organized robbery on the part of the state, made all productive economic activity impossible. But it did not stop the formation of large fortunes, rather it contributed to their formation, while altering their character. The foundation of the new fortunes was no longer the creative energy of men, nor the discovery and exploitation of new sources of wealth, nor the improvement and development of commercial, industrial, and agricultural enterprises; it was in the main the skilful use of a privileged position in the state to cheat and exploit the state and the people alike. Public officials, both high and low, grew rich on bribery and corruption. The senatorial class, being free from municipal burdens, invested their spoil in land and used their influence, the influence of their caste—which in this respect was more powerful than the emperors and nullified all their good intentions—to divert the burdens of taxation on to the other classes, to cheat the treasury directly, and to enslave ever larger numbers of workmen. We cannot here discuss how and under what title they grabbed large tracts of fertile land, both private and crown property.[7] We have seen them at work in Egypt in the third century. In the fourth they proceeded farther on the same path. Purchase, lease, patronage, lease without term, hereditary lease with the obligation to cultivate (*emphyteusis*) were all used to make the senatorial class the class of large landed proprietors *par excellence*, and to form vast estates scattered all over the provinces and resembling small principalities. Few of the members of the senatorial class lived in the capital or in the cities. The majority of them built large and beautiful fortified villas in the country and dwelt there, surrounded by their family, their slaves, a real retinue of armed clients, and thousands of rural serfs and dependants. We are well acquainted with their mode of life from the descriptions of Ausonius, Paulinus of Pella, Sidonius Apollinaris, and Salvian, from the numerous ruins of their villas, and from some mosaics which portrayed on their floors the beauty of their châteaux in town and country. The class was large and influential. Every successful 'new' man tried hard to become a member of it, and many succeeded. They were good patriots, they possessed a genuine love of Rome and the Empire, they were faithful servants of the emperors, and they appreciated civilization and culture very highly. Their political outlook was narrow, their servility was unbounded. But their external appearance was majestic, and their grand air impressed even the barbarians who gradually became masters of the Empire. For the other classes they had sympathy and understanding in theory only, expressing their commiseration in literature, without practical results. They regarded them as far inferior beings, in this respect resembling the aristocracy of Rome in the first century B.C. and the first century A.D. The senators of the second century were not nearly so exclusive or so self-confident. There were, of course, exceptions, but they were few. Thus, more than ever before, society was divided into two classes: those who became steadily poorer and more destitute, and those who built up their prosperity on the spoils of the ruined Empire—real drones, who never made any contribution to economic life but lived on the toil and travail of other classes.

The social revolution of the third century, which destroyed the foundations of the economic, social, and intellectual life of the ancient world, could not produce any positive achievement. On the ruins of a prosperous and well-organized state, based on the age-old classical civilization and on the self-government of the cities, it built up a state which was based on general ignorance, on compulsion and violence, on slavery and servility, on bribery and dishonesty. Have we the right to accuse the emperors of the fourth century of having deliberately and of their own choice built up such a state, while they might have taken another path and have constructed, not the slave-state of the late Roman Empire, but one free from the mistakes of the early Empire and yet not enshrining the brutal practice of the revolutionary period? It is idle to ask such a question. The emperors of the fourth

century, and above all Diocletian, grew up in the atmosphere
of violence and compulsion. They never saw anything else, they
never came across any other method. Their education was
moderate, and their training exclusively military. They took
their duties seriously, and they were animated by the sincerest
love of their country. Their aim was to save the Roman Empire,
and they achieved it. To this end they used, with the best intentions, the means which were familiar to them, violence and compulsion. They never asked whether it was worth while to save
the Roman Empire in order to make it a vast prison for scores of
millions of men.

Every reader of a volume devoted to the Roman Empire will
expect the author to express his opinion on what is generally,
since Gibbon, called the decline and fall of the Roman Empire,
or rather of ancient civilization in general. I shall therefore
briefly state my own view on this problem, after defining what
I take the problem to be. The decline and fall of the Roman
Empire, that is to say, of ancient civilization as a whole, has two
aspects: the political, social, and economic on the one hand, and
the intellectual and spiritual on the other. In the sphere of politics we witness a gradual barbarization of the Empire from
within, especially in the West. The foreign, German, elements
play the leading part both in the government and in the army,
and settling in masses displace the Roman population, which
disappears from the fields. A related phenomenon, which indeed
was a necessary consequence of this barbarization from within,
was the gradual disintegration of the Western Roman Empire;
the ruling classes in the former Roman provinces were replaced
first by Germans and Sarmatians, and later by Germans alone,
either through peaceful penetration or by conquest. In the East
we observe a gradual orientalization of the Byzantine Empire,
which leads ultimately to the establishment, on the ruins of the
Roman Empire, of strong half-oriental and purely oriental
states, the Caliphate of Arabia, and the Persian and Turkish
empires. From the social and economic point of view, we mean
by decline the gradual relapse of the ancient world to very primitive forms of economic life, into an almost pure 'house-economy'.
The cities, which had created and sustained the higher forms of
economic life, gradually decayed, and the majority of them practically disappeared from the face of the earth. A few, especially

those that had been great centres of commerce and industry, still lingered on. The complicated and refined social system of the ancient Empire follows the same downward path and becomes reduced to its primitive elements: the king, his court and retinue, the big feudal landowners, the clergy, the mass of rural serfs, and small groups of artisans and merchants. Such is the political, social, and economic aspect of the problem. However, we must not generalize too much. The Byzantine Empire cannot be put on a level with the states of Western Europe or with the new Slavonic formations. But one thing is certain: on the ruins of the uniform economic life of the cities there began everywhere a special, locally differentiated, evolution.

From the intellectual and spiritual point of view the main phenomenon is the decline of ancient civilization, of the city civilization of the Greco-Roman world. The Oriental civilizations were more stable: blended with some elements of the Greek city civilization, they persisted and even witnessed a brilliant revival in the Caliphate of Arabia and in Persia, not to speak of India and China. Here again there are two aspects of the evolution. The first is the exhaustion of the creative forces of Greek civilization in the domains where its great triumphs had been achieved, in the exact sciences, in technique, in literature and art. The decline began as early as the second century B.C. There followed a temporary revival of creative forces in the cities of Italy, and later in those of the Eastern and Western provinces of the Empire. The progressive movement stopped almost completely in the second century A.D. and, after a period of stagnation, a steady and rapid decline set in again. Parallel to it, we notice a progressive weakening of the assimilative forces of Greco-Roman civilization. The cities no longer absorb—that is to say, no longer hellenize or romanize—the masses of the country population. The reverse is the case. The barbarism of the country begins to engulf the city population. Only small islands of civilized life are left, the senatorial aristocracy of the late Empire and the clergy; but both, save for a section of the clergy, are gradually swallowed up by the advancing tide of barbarism.

Another aspect of the same phenomenon is the development of a new mentality among the masses of the population. It was the mentality of the lower classes, based exclusively on religion and not only indifferent but hostile to the intellectual achievements of the higher classes. This new attitude of mind gradually dominated the upper classes, or at least the larger part of them. It is revealed by the spread among them of the various mystic religions, partly Oriental, partly Greek. The climax was reached in the triumph of Christianity. In this field the creative power of the ancient world was still alive, as is shown by such momentous achievements as the creation of the Christian church, the adaptation of Christian theology to the mental level of the higher classes, the creation of a powerful Christian literature and of a new Christian art. The new intellectual efforts aimed chiefly at influencing the mass of the population and therefore represented a lowering of the high standards of city-civilization, at least from the point of view of literary forms.[8]

We may say, then, that there is one prominent feature in the development of the ancient world during the imperial age, alike in the political, social, and economic and in the intellectual field. It is a gradual absorption of the higher classes by the lower, accompanied by a gradual levelling down of standards. This levelling was accomplished in many ways. There was a slow penetration of the lower classes into the higher, which were unable to assimilate the new elements. There were violent outbreaks of civil strife: the lead was taken by the Greek cities, and there followed the civil war of the first century B.C. which involved the whole civilized world. In these struggles the upper classes and the city-civilization remained victorious on the whole. Two centuries later, a new outbreak of civil war ended in the victory of the lower classes and dealt a mortal blow to the Greco-Roman civilization of the cities. Finally, that civilization was completely engulfed by the inflow of barbarous elements from outside, partly by penetration, partly by conquest, and in its dying condition it was unable to assimilate even a small part of them.

The main problem, therefore, which we have to solve is this. Why was the city civilization of Greece and Italy unable to assimilate the masses, why did it remain a civilization of the *élite*, why was it incapable of creating conditions which should secure for the ancient world a continuous, uninterrupted movement along the same path of urban civilization? In other words: why had modern civilization to be built up laboriously as something new on the ruins of the old, instead of being a direct continuation of it? Various explanations have been suggested, and each of them claims to have finally solved the problem. Let us then review the most important of them. They may be divided into four classes.[9]

(1) The political solution is advocated by many distinguished scholars. For Beloch[10] the decay of ancient civilization was caused by the absorption of the Greek city-states by the Roman Empire, by the formation of a world-state which prevented the creative forces of Greece from developing and consolidating the great achievements of civilized life. There is some truth in this view. It is evident that the creation of the Roman Empire was a step forward in the process of levelling, and that it facilitated the final absorption of the higher classes. We must, however, take into consideration that class war was a common feature of Greek life, and that we have not the least justification for supposing that the Greek city-community would have found a solution of the social and economic problems which produced civil war in the various communities. Further, this view suggests that there was only one creative race in the ancient world, which is notoriously false. Another explanation, tending in the same direction, has been put forward by Kornemann.[11] He regards as the main cause of the decay of the Roman Empire the fact that Augustus reduced the armed forces of the Empire, and that this reduction was maintained by his successors. The suggestion lays the whole emphasis on the military side of the problem, and is therefore a return to the antiquated idea that ancient civilization was destroyed by the barbarian invasions, an idea which should not be resuscitated. Besides, the maintenance of a comparatively small army was imperatively imposed by the economic weakness of the Empire, a fact which was understood by all the emperors. Still less convincing is the idea of Ferrero,[12] that the collapse of the Empire was due to a disastrous event, to an accident which had the gravest consequences. He holds that by transmitting his power to his son Commodus instead of to a man chosen by the senate, M. Aurelius undermined the senate's authority on which the whole fabric of the Roman state rested; that the murder of Commodus led to the usurpation of Septimius and to the civil war of the third century; and that the usurpation and the war destroyed the authority of the senate and deprived the imperial

power of its only legitimacy in the eyes of the population which was its main support. Ferrero forgets that legally the power of the emperors in the third century was still derived from the senate and people of Rome, that it was so even in the time of Diocletian, and that the same idea still survived under Constantine and his successors. He also forgets that the subtle formula of Augustus, Vespasian, and the Antonines was incomprehensible to the mass of the people of the Empire, and was a creation of the upper classes, completely outside the range of popular conceptions. Finally, he fails to understand the true character of the crisis of the third century. The struggle was not between the senate and the emperor, but between the cities and the army— that is to say, the masses of peasants—as is shown by the fact that the lead in the fight was taken not by Rome but by the cities of the province of Africa. A deeper explanation is offered by Heitland.[13] He suggests that the ancient world decayed because it was unable to give the masses a share in the government, and even gradually restricted the numbers of those who participated in the life of the state, ultimately reducing them to the emperor himself, his court, and the imperial bureaucracy. I regard this point as only one aspect of the great phenomenon which I have described above. Have we the right to suppose that the emperors would not have tried the plan of representative government if they had known of it and believed in it? They tried many other plans and failed. If the idea of representative government was foreign to the ancient world (and as a matter of fact it was not), why did the ancient world not evolve the idea, which is not a very difficult one? Moreover, the question arises, Can we be sure that representative government is the cause of the brilliant development of our civilization and not one of its aspects, just as was the Greek city-state? Have we the slightest reason to believe that modern democracy is a guarantee of continuous and uninterrupted progress, and is capable of preventing civil war from breaking out under the fostering influence of hatred and envy? Let us not forget that the most modern political and social theories suggest that democracy is an antiquated institution, that it is rotten and corrupt, being the offspring of capitalism, and that the only just form of government is the dictatorship of the proletariate, which means a complete destruction of civil liberty and imposes on one and all the single ideal of material welfare, and of equalitarianism founded on material welfare.

(2) The economic explanation of the decay of the ancient world must be rejected completely. In speaking of the development of industry in the ancient world,[14] I have dealt with the theory of K. Bücher, accepted with modifications by M. Weber and G. Salvioli. If the theory fails to explain even this minor point, much less will it serve to explain the general phenomenon. Those who defend this theory forget that the ancient world went through many cycles of evolution, and that in these cycles there occur long periods of progress and other long periods of return to more primitive conditions, to the phase of economic life which is generally described as 'house-economy'. It is true that the ancient world never reached the economic stage in which we live. But in the history of the ancient world we have many epochs of high economic development: certain periods in the history of many Oriental monarchies, particularly Egypt, Babylonia, and Persia; the age of the highest development of the city-states, especially the fourth century B.C.; the period of the Hellenistic monarchies, where the climax was reached in the third century B.C.; the period of the late Roman Republic and of the early Roman Empire. All these periods show different aspects of economic life and different aspects of capitalism. In none of them did the forms of house-economy prevail. We may compare the economic aspect of life during these periods to that of many European countries in the time of the Renaissance and later, although in no case would the comparison be perfect, as there is no identity between the economic development of the modern and that of the ancient world. According to the different economic conditions of these several periods in the history of the ancient world, the relations between house-economy and capitalistic economy varied, and they frequently varied not only in the different periods but also in different parts of the ancient world during the same period. The ancient world was in this respect not unlike the modern world. In the industrial countries of Europe, such as England and some parts of Germany and France, economic life nowadays is by no means the same as it is in the agricultural countries, like Russia and the Balkan peninsula and large parts of the Near East. The economic life of the United States of America is not in the least identical with the

economic life of Europe or of the various parts of South America, not to speak of China, Japan, and India. So it was in the ancient world. While Egypt and Babylonia had a complex economic life, with a highly developed industry and wide commercial relations, other parts of the Near East lived a quite different and much more primitive life. While Athens, Corinth, Rhodes, Syracuse, Tyre, and Sidon in the fourth century B.C. were centres of a developed commercial capitalism, other Greek cities lived an almost purely agricultural life. In the Hellenistic and Roman periods it was just the same. The main fact which has to be explained is why capitalistic development, which started at many times and in many places, and prevailed in large portions of the ancient world for comparatively long periods, yielded ultimately to more primitive forms of economic life. Even in our own times it has not completely ousted those forms. It is evident that the problem cannot be solved by affirming that the ancient world lived throughout under the forms of primitive house-economy. The statement is manifestly wrong. We might say exactly the same of large areas of the modern world, and we are not at all sure that a violent catastrophe might not bring the modern capitalistic world back to the primitive phase of house-economy.

To sum up what I have said, the economic simplification of ancient life was not the cause of what we call the decline of the ancient world, but one of the aspects of the more general phenomenon which the theories mentioned above try to explain. Here, just as in the other spheres of human life, the political, social, intellectual, and religious, the more primitive forms of life among the masses were not absorbed by the higher forms but triumphed over them in the end. We may select one of these phenomena and declare it to be the ultimate cause; but it would be an arbitrary assumption which would not convince any one. The problem remains. Why was the victorious advance of capitalism stopped? Why was machinery not invented? Why were the business systems not perfected? Why were the primal forces of primitive economy not overcome? They were gradually disappearing; why did they not disappear completely? To say that they were quantitatively stronger than in our own times does not help us to explain the main phenomenon. That is why many economists, who are aware that the usual explanation only touches the surface and does not probe the problem to the bottom, endeavour to save the economic explanation, and the materialistic conception of historical evolution in general, by producing some potent physical factor as the cause of the weakness of the higher forms of economic life in the ancient world. Such a factor has been found by some scholars in the general exhaustion of the soil all over the ancient world, which reached its climax in the late Roman Empire and ruined the ancient world. I have dealt with this theory above.* There are no facts to support it. All the facts about the economic development of the ancient world speak against it. Agriculture decayed in the ancient world just in the same way and from the same causes as the other branches of economic life. As soon as the political and social conditions improved in the various parts of the Empire, the fields and gardens began to yield the same harvests as before. Witness the flourishing state of Gaul in the time of Ausonius and of Sidonius Apollinaris; witness the fact that in Egypt, where the soil is inexhaustible and those parts of it which are not flooded are very easily improved by the most primitive methods, agriculture decayed in the third and fourth centuries, just as in the other provinces. It is plain that the economic explanation does not help us, and that the investigations of the economists reveal, not the cause of the decline of the ancient world, but merely one of its aspects.

(3) The rapid progress of medicine and of biological science has had its influence on the problem of the decay of ancient civilization. A biological solution has been often suggested, and the theories of degeneration and race-suicide have been applied to the ancient world. The biological theory supplies us with an apparently exhaustive explanation of the decline of the assimilative forces of the civilized upper classes. They gradually degenerated and had not the power to assimilate the lower classes but were absorbed by them. According to Seeck,[15] the cause of their degeneration and of their numerical decline was the 'extermination of the best' by foreign and civil wars. Others, like Tenney Frank,[16] think of the contamination of higher races by an admixture of the blood of inferior races. Others, again, regard degeneration as a natural process common to all civilized communities: the best are neither exterminated nor contaminated, but they commit systematic suicide by not reproducing and by

* See p. 376.

letting the inferior type of mankind breed freely.[17] I am not competent to sit in judgement on the problem of degeneration from the biological and physiological point of view. From the historical point of view, I venture to remark against Seeck that in wars and revolutions it is not only the best that are exterminated. On the other hand, revolutions do not always prevent the succeeding period from being a period of great bloom. Against Franck I may suggest that I see no criterion for distinguishing between inferior and superior races. Why are the Greek and Latin races considered the only superior races in the Roman Empire? Some of the races which 'contaminated' the ruling races, for instance, the pre-Indo-European and pre-Semitic race or races of the Mediterranean, had created great civilizations in the past (the Egyptian, the Minoan, the Iberian, the Etruscan, the civilizations of Asia Minor), and the same is true of the Semitic and of the Iranian civilizations. Why did the admixture of the blood of these races contaminate and deteriorate the blood of the Greeks and the Romans? On the other hand, the Celts and the Germans belonged to the same stock as the Greeks and the Romans. The Celts had a high material civilization of their own. The Germans were destined to develop a high civilized life in the future. Why did the admixture of their blood corrupt and not regenerate their fellow Aryans, the Greeks and the Romans? The theory of a natural decay of civilization by race-suicide states the same general phenomenon of which we have been speaking, the gradual absorption of the upper classes by the lower and the lack of assimilative power shown by the upper. It states the fact, but gives no explanation. The problem this theory has to solve is, Why do the best not reproduce their kind? It may be solved in different ways: we may suggest an economic, or a physiological, or a psychological explanation. But none of these explanations is convincing.

(4) Christianity is very often made responsible for the decay of ancient civilization. This is, of course, a very narrow point of view. Christianity is but one side of the general change in the mentality of the ancient world. Can we say that this change is the ultimate cause of the decay of ancient civilization? It is not easy to discriminate between causes and symptoms, and one of the urgent tasks in the field of ancient history is a further investigation of this change of mentality. The change, no doubt, was

one of the most potent factors in the gradual decay of the civilization of the city-state and in the rise of a new conception of the world and of a new civilization. But how are we to explain the change? Is it a problem of individual and mass psychology?[18]

None of the existing theories fully explains the problem of the decay of ancient civilization, if we can apply the word 'decay' to the complex phenomenon which I have endeavoured to describe. Each of them, however, has contributed much to the clearing of the ground, and has helped us to perceive that the main phenomenon which underlies the process of decline is the gradual absorption of the educated classes by the masses and the consequent simplification of all the functions of political, social, economic, and intellectual life, which we call the barbarization of the ancient world.

The evolution of the ancient world has a lesson and a warning for us. Our civilization will not last unless it be a civilization not of one class, but of the masses. The Oriental civilizations were more stable and lasting than the Greco-Roman, because, being chiefly based on religion, they were nearer to the masses. Another lesson is that violent attempts at levelling have never helped to uplift the masses. They have destroyed the upper classes, and resulted in accelerating the process of barbarization. But the ultimate problem remains like a ghost, ever present and unlaid: Is it possible to extend a higher civilization to the lower classes without debasing its standard and diluting its quality to the vanishing point? Is not every civilization bound to decay as soon as it begins to penetrate the masses?

PRINTED IN GREAT BRITAIN
AT THE UNIVERSITY PRESS, OXFORD
BY VIVIAN RIDLER
PRINTER TO THE UNIVERSITY

Date Due

McK DUE	NOV 1 0 2004	

IF YOUR BOOK IS RECALLED YOUR DUE
DATE WILL BE SHORTENED. YOU WILL BE
NOTIFIED BY MAIL.